A COMPANION TO GREEK

BLACKWELL COMPANIONS TO THE ANCIENT WORLD

This series provides sophisticated and authoritative overviews of periods of ancient history, genres of classical literature, and the most important themes in ancient culture. Each volume comprises approximately twenty-five and forty concise essays written by individual scholars within their area of specialization. The essays are written in a clear, provocative, and lively manner, designed for an international audience of scholars, students, and general readers.

ANCIENT HISTORY

Published

A Companion to the Roman Army
Edited by Paul Erdkamp

A Companion to the Roman Republic
Edited by Nathan Rosenstein and Robert Morstein-Marx

A Companion to the Roman Empire
Edited by David S. Potter

A Companion to the Classical Greek World
Edited by Konrad H. Kinzl

A Companion to the Ancient Near East
Edited by Daniel C. Snell

A Companion to the Hellenistic World
Edited by Andrew Erskine

A Companion to Late Antiquity
Edited by Philip Rousseau

A Companion to Ancient History
Edited by Andrew Erskine

A Companion to Archaic Greece
Edited by Kurt A. Raaflaub and Hans van Wees

A Companion to Julius Caesar
Edited by Miriam Griffin

A Companion to Byzantium
Edited by Liz James

A Companion to Ancient Egypt
Edited by Alan B. Lloyd

A Companion to Ancient Macedonia
Edited by Joseph Roisman and Ian Worthington

A Companion to the Punic Wars
Edited by Dexter Hoyos

A Companion to Augustine
Edited by Mark Vessey

A Companion to Marcus Aurelius
Edited by Marcel van Ackeren

A Companion to Ancient Greek Government
Edited by Hans Beck

A Companion to the Neronian Age
Edited by Emma Buckley and Martin T. Dinter

LITERATURE AND CULTURE

Published

A Companion to Classical Receptions
Edited by Lorna Hardwick and Christopher Stray

A Companion to Greek and Roman Historiography
Edited by John Marincola

A Companion to Catullus
Edited by Marilyn B. Skinner

A Companion to Roman Religion
Edited by Jörg Rüpke

A Companion to Greek Religion
Edited by Daniel Ogden

A Companion to the Classical Tradition
Edited by Craig W. Kallendorf

A Companion to Roman Rhetoric
Edited by William Dominik and Jon Hall

A Companion to Greek Rhetoric
Edited by Ian Worthington

A Companion to Ancient Epic
Edited by John Miles Foley

A Companion to Greek Tragedy
Edited by Justina Gregory

A Companion to Latin Literature
Edited by Stephen Harrison

A Companion to Greek and Roman Political Thought
Edited by Ryan K. Balot

A Companion to Ovid
Edited by Peter E. Knox

A Companion to the Ancient Greek Language
Edited by Egbert Bakker

A Companion to Hellenistic Literature
Edited by Martine Cuypers and James J. Clauss

A Companion to Vergil's *Aeneid* and its Tradition
Edited by Joseph Farrell and Michael C. J. Putnam

A Companion to Horace
Edited by Gregson Davis

A Companion to Families in the Greek and Roman Worlds
Edited by Beryl Rawson

A Companion to Greek Mythology
Edited by Ken Dowden and Niall Livingstone

A Companion to the Latin Language
Edited by James Clackson

A Companion to Tacitus
Edited by Victoria Emma Pagán

A Companion to Women in the Ancient World
Edited by Sharon L. James and Sheila Dillon

A Companion to Sophocles
Edited by Kirk Ormand

A Companion to the Archaeology of the Ancient Near East
Edited by Daniel Potts

A Companion to Roman Love Elegy
Edited by Barbara K. Gold

A Companion to Greek Art
Edited by Tyler Jo Smith and Dimitris Plantzos

A Companion to Persius and Juvenal
Edited by Susanna Braund and Josiah Osgood

A Companion to the Archaeology of the Roman Republic
Edited by Jane DeRose Evans

A Companion to Terence
Edited by Antony Augoustakis and Ariana Traill

A Companion to Roman Architecture
Edited by Roger B. Ulrich and Caroline K. Quenemoen

A Companion to Sport and Spectacle in Greek and Roman Antiquity
Edited by Paul Christesen and Donald G. Kyle

A Companion to the Ancient Novel
Edited by Edmund P. Cueva and Shannon N. Byrne

A COMPANION TO GREEK MYTHOLOGY

Edited by

Ken Dowden and Niall Livingstone

WILEY Blackwell

This paperback edition first published 2014
© 2014 John Wiley & Sons, Ltd

Edition history: Blackwell Publishing Ltd (hardback, 2011)

Registered Office
John Wiley & Sons, Ltd, The Atrium, Southern Gate, Chichester, West Sussex, PO19 8SQ, UK

Editorial Offices
350 Main Street, Malden, MA 02148-5020, USA
9600 Garsington Road, Oxford, OX4 2DQ, UK
The Atrium, Southern Gate, Chichester, West Sussex, PO19 8SQ, UK

For details of our global editorial offices, for customer services, and for information about how
to apply for permission to reuse the copyright material in this book please see our website at
www.wiley.com/wiley-blackwell.

Library of Congress Cataloging-in-Publication Data

A companion to Greek mythology/edited by Ken Dowden and Niall Livingstone.
    p.   cm. – (Blackwell companions to the ancient world)
    Includes bibliographical references and index.
    ISBN 978-1-4051-1178-2 (hardcover : alk. paper) ISBN 978-1-118-78516-4 (pbk. : alk. paper)
1. Mythology, Greek. 2. Greece–Religion.
    I. Dowden, Ken, 1950–   II. Livingstone, Niall.
    BL783.C66 2011
    398.20938–dc22

                                                2010041346

A catalogue record for this book is available from the British Library.

Cover image: Mainad, from the House of the Ship, Pompeii, 1st century bc– ad 79 (fresco)
Museo Archeologico Nazionale, Naples/Lauros/Giraudon/The Bridgeman Art Library
Cover design by Workhaus

Set in 11/13.5pt Galliard by SPi Publisher Services, Pondicherry, India
Printed in Malaysia by Ho Printing (M) Sdn Bhd

1   2014

Contents

Illustrations

Maps

Tables

Notes on Contributors

JEAN ALAUX (alaux.j@wanadoo.fr) is Professor of Greek Language and Literature at the Université Rennes II. His work focuses in particular on Homeric epic, tragedy, and Greek representations of identity and kinship. His publications include *Le Liège et le filet: filiation et lien familial dans la tragédie athénienne* (Paris 1995), *Lectures tragiques d'Homère* (Paris 2007), *Origine et horizon tragiques* (Paris 2007). He has also edited a collection of essays on Euripides' *Phoenician Women* (*Les Phéniciennes: la famille d'Oedipe entre mythe et politique*, Paris 2007).

NICHOLAS J. ALLEN (nick.allen@anthro.ox.ac.uk) studied first classics, then medicine, before qualifying in social anthropology at Oxford; his DPhil was based on ethnographic fieldwork in Nepal. From 1976–2001 he lectured at Oxford, where he became Reader in the Social Anthropology of South Asia. He has published on the Himalayas, kinship theory, the Durkheimian School, and Indo-European Cultural Comparativism – see, for instance, his *Categories and Classifications* (New York, Oxford 2000). Since retirement he has concentrated on the last three topics.

RICHARD H. ARMSTRONG (richard.armstrong@mail.uk.edu) is Associate Professor of Classical Studies at the University of Houston. He is author of *A Compulsion for Antiquity: Freud and the Ancient World* (Ithaca 2005). Recent publications include: 'Freud and the Drama of Oedipal Truth', in K. Ormand (ed.) *A Companion to Sophocles* (forthcoming); 'Marooned Mandarins: Freud, Classical Education, and the Jews of Vienna', in S. A. Stephens and P. Vasunia (eds) *Classics and National Cultures* (Oxford 2010); and 'Being Mr. Somebody: Freud and Classical Education', in A. D. Richards (ed.) *The Jewish World of Sigmund Freud* (Jefferson, NC 2010).

JAN N. BREMMER (j.n.bremmer@rug.nl) is Emeritus Professor of Religious Studies at the University of Groningen. Amongst his publications are *Greek Religion* (Oxford 1994), *The Rise and Fall of the Afterlife* (London 2002), *Greek Religion and Culture, the Bible and the Ancient Near East* (Leiden 2008), and *The Rise of Christianity through the Eyes of Gibbon, Harnack and Rodney Stark* (Groningen 2010). His research interests include Greek, Roman, Early Christian, and contemporary religion.

CLAUDE CALAME (claude.calame@unil. ch) is Director of Studies at the Ecole des Hautes Etudes en Sciences Sociales in Paris. Most of his books have been translated into English, for instance, *Choruses of Young Women in Ancient Greece* (Lanham MD, London 1997), *The Poetics of Eros in Ancient Greece* (Princeton, Chichester 1999), *Poetic and Performative Memory in Ancient Greece* (Cambridge MA 2009), and most recently, *Greek Mythology. Poetics, Pragmatics and Fiction* (Cambridge 2009). He is currently working on a book on Greek tragedy seen in the perspective of choral song.

KEN DOWDEN (k.dowden@bham.ac. uk) is Professor of Classics and Director of the Institute of Archaeology and Antiquity at the University of Birmingham. He writes on Greek mythology (*Uses of Greek Mythology* (London, New York 1992)), religion (*European Paganism* (London, New York 2000); *Zeus* (London, New York 2006)), on historians – usually of Greek mythic times – for the *Brill New Jacoby*, and on many aspects of the Latin and Greek novels, particularly Apuleius and Heliodoros, often in the pages of *Ancient Narrative*.

RADCLIFFE G. EDMONDS III (red monds@brynmawr.edu) is Associate Professor of Greek, Latin, and Classical Studies at Bryn Mawr College. His current research interests include mythology, religion, and Platonic philosophy, especially the marginal categories of magic and Orphism within Greek religion. He has published *Myths of the Underworld Journey: Plato, Aristophanes, and the 'Orphic' Gold Tablets* (Cambridge 2004) and edited a volume of essays entitled *The 'Orphic' Gold Tablets and Greek Religion: Further Along the Path* (Cambridge 2010).

MATTHEW FOX (m.fox@classics.arts. gla.ac.uk) studied in Oxford and Berlin, and from 1992 to 2007 lectured in Classics at the University of Birmingham. He is now Professor of Classics at the University of Glasgow. He has written two books, *Roman Historical Myths* (Oxford 1996), and *Cicero's Philosophy of History* (Oxford 2007). He has also published on ancient rhetorical theory, on gender, and on the state of Classical studies in the eighteenth century.

FRITZ GRAF (graf65@humanities. osu.edu) is Distinguished University Professor of Greek and Latin at the Ohio State University. He has worked on Greek and Roman religion, myth and magic, often with an eye on the epigraphical record. In recent years, he has also become interested in early Christianity and its interactions with the polytheistic cults of Greece and Rome. His books include *Greek*

Mythology (Baltimore 1993), *Magic in the Ancient World* (Cambridge MA 1999), *Apollo* (London, New York 2008), and, with Sarah Iles Johnston, *Ritual Texts for the Afterlife* (London, New York 2007).

ALAN GRIFFITHS (a.griffiths@ucl.ac.uk) is a Senior Honorary Research Fellow at University College London, where he taught in the Department of Greek and Latin for nearly forty years. He now lives in Derbyshire, attempting to manage five computers (running Linux) and two cats (running wild). His interests cover all forms of ancient narrative with a special focus on Herodotos, on whose third book he is writing a commentary; also Greek poetry, myth, and art.

BIRGIT HASKAMP (birgit_haskamp@yahoo.co.uk) studied Near Eastern Archaeology and Assyriology at Heidelberg University and is currently Honorary Research Fellow at the University of Birmingham. Her interests range from the history and archaeology of Mesopotamia to the languages, culture, and history of the Hittite Empire. Together with Alasdair Livingstone she is currently working on a cultural history of the Neo-Assyrian Empire.

DIETER HERTEL (dieter_hertel@web.de) is Professor of Classical Archaeology at the University of Cologne. He received his PhD at the University of Bonn. His research interests include the Roman portrait art of the Julio-Claudian dynasty, the archaeology and history of Troy and of the whole Aiolis. He is presently conducting a project of the *Deutsche Forschungsgemeinschaft* on the so-called Aiolian Colonization including a new publication – documents and finds – of the old British excavations at Antissa, Lesbos (W. Lamb).

FRANÇOISE LÉTOUBLON (fletoublon@wanadoo.fr) is Professor of Greek Literature and Linguistics at the Université Stendhal, Grenoble. She is the author of *Il allait, pareil à la nuit. Les Verbes de mouvement en grec: suppletisme et aspect verbal* (Paris 1985) and of *Les Lieux communs du roman* (Leiden 1993). She has edited *La Langue et les textes en grec ancien*. Colloque Pierre Chantraine (Amsterdam 1993), *Impressions d'îles* (Toulouse 1996), *Hommage à Milman Parry: le style formulaire de l'épopée homérique et la théorie de l'oralité poétique* (Amsterdam 1997), *Homère en France après la Querelle* (Paris 1999). She is currently working on Homeric poetry, oral poetry, mythology, and their reception, from antiquity (Greek novels) to modern times (for instance in Angelopoulos' films).

SIAN LEWIS (sl50@st-andrews.ac.uk) is Senior Lecturer in Ancient History at the University of St Andrews. Her research interests lie in Greek social and political history; she is the author of *The Athenian Woman: An Iconographic Handbook* (London 2002) and co-editor of *The World of Greek Vases* (Rome 2009), and has recently published a survey, *Greek Tyranny* (Bristol 2009).

ALASDAIR LIVINGSTONE (a.livingstone@ bham.ac.uk) is Reader in Assyriology at the University of Birmingham and specializes in the cultural history and languages of the ancient Near East. He has worked extensively on Mesopotamian mythology and is the author of *Mystical and Mythological Explanatory Works of Assyrian and Babylonian Scholars* (Oxford 1986) and the *Court Poetry and Literary Miscellanea* volume in the State Archives of Assyria series (Helsinki 1989). He is currently preparing an edition of Assyrian and Babylonian hemerologies and menologies.

NIALL LIVINGSTONE (n.r.livingstone@ bham.ac.uk) studied at Christ Church, Oxford where he also gained his DPhil. He taught at Oxford and St Andrews before joining the University of Birmingham in 1999, where he is now Senior Lecturer in Classics. His research is mainly on the history of literature and thought in the Greek world from the Archaic to the Hellenistic period, with a focus on the performance culture of democratic Athens. His publications include *Pedagogy and Power* (co-edited with Y. L. Too, Cambridge 1998), *A Commentary on Isocrates' Busiris* (Leiden 2001), and a Greece & Rome New Survey of *Epigram* (co-authored with G. Nisbet, Cambridge 2010).

NANNO MARINATOS (nannom@uic. edu) has a double specialism in Minoan and Early Greek religion, with a great interest in Egyptology. She is the author of six books: *Thucydides and Religion* (Königstein 1981), *Art and Religion in Thera* (Athens 1984), *Minoan Sacrificial Ritual* (Stockhold 1986), *Minoan Religion* (Columbia SC 1993), *The Goddess and the Warrior* (London, New York 2000), *Minoan Kingship and the Solar Goddess* (Urbana 2009). Since 2000 she has been Professor at the University of Illinois at Chicago.

ANATOLE MORI (moria@missouri.edu) received her PhD from the University of Chicago and is an associate professor of Classical Studies at the University of Missouri, Columbia. Her research addresses the historical context of Greek poetry, particularly the political aspects of early Hellenistic literary culture. Recent publications include *The Politics of Apollonius Rhodius' Argonautica* (Cambridge 2008), as well as contributions to I. Worthington (ed.) *A Companion to Greek Rhetoric* (Malden, MA, Oxford 2007), P. McKechnie and P. Guillaume (eds), *Ptolemy II Philadelphus and his World* (Leiden 2008), and *Brill's New Jacoby*.

PENELOPE MURRAY (penelope.a.murray @googlemail.com) read Classics at Newnham College, Cambridge, where she also took her PhD, and was a founder member of the department of Classics at the University of Warwick. She works on Greek poetry and poetics, especially the views of Plato, on ancient literary criticism and on the Muses. Her books include

Plato on Poetry (Cambridge 1996), *Classical Literary Criticism* (new Penguin edn 2000, reprinted 2004), and *Music and the Muses: The Culture of Mousike in the Classical Athenian City* (ed. with P. Wilson, Oxford 2004). She is currently working on the *Blackwell Companion to Ancient Aesthetics* (with Pierre Destrée).

ZAHRA NEWBY (z.l.newby@warwick.ac.uk) Reader in Classics and Ancient History at the University of Warwick. Her research focuses on ancient art within its broader cultural contexts. In addition to publishing a number of articles, she is author of *Greek Athletics in the Roman World. Victory and Virtue* and co-editor (with Ruth Leader-Newby) of *Art and Inscriptions in the Ancient World*. She is currently working on a book on the uses of Greek myth in Roman art.

IAN RUTHERFORD (i.c.rutherford@reading.ac.uk) is professor of Greek at the University of Reading. His major interests are in early Greek poetry and religion, ancient Anatolia, and Greco-Egyptian literature. He is the author of *Pindar's Paeans* (Oxford 2001) and co-editor of *Seeing the Gods: Pilgrimage in Graeco-Roman and Early Christian Antiquity* (with J. Elsner, Oxford 2005), of *Anatolian Interfaces* (with B. J. Collins and

M. Bachvarova, Oxford 2008) and of *Wandering Poets in Ancient Greek Literature* (with R. Hunter, Cambridge 2009).

SUSAN WOODFORD (drswoodford@blueyonder.co.uk) taught Greek and Roman art at the University of London and does research in the Greek and Roman Department of the British Museum. She writes scholarly articles and books for students and the general public such as *The Parthenon* (Cambridge 1981), *The Art of Greece and Rome* (Cambridge 2004^2), *An Introduction to Greek Art* (London 1986), *The Trojan War in Ancient Art* (London 1993), and *Images of Myths in Classical Antiquity* (Cambridge 2003; winner of the Criticos Prize 2003).

NICOLAS WYATT (niqmad3@gmail.com), received his PhD from Glasgow in 1977 and DLitt from Edinburgh in 2008, and is Emeritus Professor of Ancient Near Eastern Religions in the University of Edinburgh. He has written numerous articles in Ugaritic and Old Testament studies. Amongst his books are *Myths of Power* (Münster 1996), *Space and Time in the Religious Life of the (ancient) Near East* (Sheffield 2001), *Religious Texts from Ugarit* (Sheffield 1998 [2002^2]), *The Mythic Mind* (Sheffield 2005), and *The Archaeology of Myth* (Sheffield 2010).

To the Reader

Organization of this book

Mythology is multidimensional, but books are linear. We have structured this book to give an illusion of advancing chronology and of increasing complexity. We thought it mattered to give our view of the subject and its significance from antiquity to the present day at the outset (CH. 1), and to show, in the process, how our chapters fit into that story. Part I (Establishing the Canon) then deals approximately with archaic Greece, though with some extensions into the classical period, and approximately with the laying down of that which would later count as Greek mythology, though not without the recognition that deviance was there from early times. Part II presents the heyday of the mythology, the Classical Age, and the variety of media and occasion where myth acted on society and society acted through myth. Myth does not of course stop there, and the function of the Part III is to provide a window onto the kaleidoscope of new societies and peoples to whom Greek mythology came to matter: those who lived in a much expanded Greek world following the conquests of Alexander the Great; those strange barbarians, the Romans, whose generous adoption of Greek culture (*paideia*) ensured that myth spoke to the West (even in death) and eventually to Europe; those who worried for their souls and salvation but found that myth allowed their abstract religious thought to find accessible expression; and finally the Christians, whose unlikely job it would be to preserve classical culture from ancient into modern times.

With that we move, in Part IV, from history to how Greek myth came about and to its larger contexts. Like most things, Greek myth, where not freshly invented, was either inherited or borrowed. Inheritance logically takes us back to the Indo-Europeans; borrowing most visibly takes us to the world of the Near East and other urban civilizations very much more ancient than the Greek. We then, like Yudhiṣṭhira reaching Sanskrit heaven in *Mahābhārata* 18, arrive at Part V, whose job is *explanation* – how people of our times have attempted the explanation of myth (assuming, CH. 21, they know which myth they are really dealing with), and how we ourselves might account for what it does, relative to our ever-evolving world of ideas. With that, it only remains to close the collection and the single-chapter Part VI looks over the whole history of the study of Greek myth.

Any principle of organization will make some part, or some aspect, of the mythology hard to find, or scatter it. We have taken particular care to present readers with useful indexes that will empower them to defy the structure of the book and enable them to exercise their own priorities.

Companions

A certain amount of ink has been spilt on what 'companions' should be and whether they are a necessity or a plague. Our answer to this is simple and unrepentant: like a human companion, they should be friendly, interested in you (rather than themselves), and helpful. To try to bring this about we have adopted the same approach to our contributors, who, we feel, have all in their varied ways sought to help readers to understand the fascination of their area and provide them with the tools to look at it for themselves. But these ways are varied and not only different authors but also different areas demand different lengths of chapter, different scales of endnotes, and impose different demands on the reader. Semiotics is never going to be easy (you haven't understood it if you think it is), and a pioneering statement of the nature of Near Eastern mythologies is not going to be arrived at in a few thousand words. Critics may demand a different balance, but this is the balance that can be delivered that will actually benefit the reader across a pretty large vista.

Details

It remains to deal with little things, which nevertheless can niggle:

- *Spelling of Greek names.* No system works. We ourselves like to make Greek look like Greek rather than like Latin (except of course when talking about Romans, as in CH. 14). Names are spelt with *k* not *c*, with *ai* not *ae*, with *oi* not *oe*, with *ou* not *u*, with *-os* not *-us*: Herakles not Hercules, Athenaios not Athenaeus, and Dioskouroi not Dioscuri. But we cannot bring ourselves to be so consistent as to write Aischylos, Ploutarchos, Thoukydides, Oidipous, and Korinthos for Aeschylus, Plutarch, Thucydides, Oedipus, and Corinth. Those who are not classicists need to understand that this is a cross we bear and that you need to exercise a little ingenuity in consulting the index of names (e.g., it's under K not C).

- *References to this book.* We have tried to be helpful by including a number of cross references to other parts of the book. These are distinguished in the case of chapters by small capitals – e.g., 'see CH. 14'.
- *Dates.* We retain the traditional BC/AD terminology (rather than BCE/CE) because it is clearer and we mean nothing religious by it, any more than we worship Woden on Wednesdays.
- *Subheadings.* These represent one area of relative uniformity that we have imposed on the whole book, in order to orient the reader.
- *Bibliographic conventions.* We began with the Harvard system but have adapted it to meet our needs and to maximize simplicity and minimize punctuation. We include states and countries only to disambiguate bibliographic entries. We all know where Princeton is. We may perhaps be forgiven the Eurocentrism of taking Cambridge, London, Paris, and so forth as being in Europe unless otherwise specified.

We have taken much pleasure in this book as it has come together. We hope you will share our experience.

Acknowledgements

It is right that our debts should be registered at this point. Our Blackwell companions, Al Bertrand, Haze Humbert, and Galen Smith, have shown what very great virtues patience and friendship are. All our contributors, without exception, have made our job seem possible when we hit those black moments, but we would like to single out Susan Woodford and Nick Allen, who have endured most, for their unfailing and sympathetic support over an unreasonably vast span of time.

Megan Lewis, as an undergraduate student, formed a one-woman focus group, read absolutely everything, and delivered advice that excelled in good sense and perceptiveness. All editors should have a Megan. And finally we owe debts of gratitude for our sanity to Liz on the one hand, and Sophie on the other. But they know that.

KEN DOWDEN & NIALL LIVINGSTONE
INSTITUTE OF ARCHAEOLOGY & ANTIQUITY
UNIVERSITY OF BIRMINGHAM
1 AUGUST 2010

Glossary

And finally a little help on terms which can be difficult for those new to study of this area:

Aetiology
An explanation of how things came to be the way they are. Some myths are therefore *aetiological*.

Charter myth
A myth which provides a justification ('charter') for a political situation or social institution.

Chthonic
Belonging to the earth and what is in or beneath it (Greek *chthōn*, earth), as opposed to the heavens above.

Colophon
Something to mark the end of a text – a few words ('this is the end of Book 4 of ...'), or an emblem or both.

Corpus
A body (*corpus*) of literature, of texts, of evidence – like the corpus of Mesopotamian mythological writings (CH 19). Plural, *corpora*.

Diachronic
'Through time', referring to studies which trace the development of phenomena from one period of time to another. Opposite of *synchronic*.

Enunciative
Considered as actually 'being uttered', being enunciated, being spoken live. For example, 'the enunciative character of these ... lines' (p. 512), namely their significance when you think of them as performed in a particular environment, for instance in a ceremony.

Eponym
Person after whom someone or something is, or is said to be, named. Adjective *eponymous*. So Aiolos is the eponym of the Aiolian Greeks; Medea is the eponymous heroine of Euripides' *Medea*.

Eschatology
Originally, in Christian theology, the study of the 'four last things': Death, Judgement, Heaven, and Hell. Hence used more generally of accounts of the fate of the human soul after death, especially when a judgement is involved. Adjective: *eschatological*.

Function	'Role' (French *fonction*). This apparently innocent word is used oddly, for the English-speaker, by two authors. Vladimir Propp (cf. CH. 27) analysed narratives (primarily folktales) as consisting of thirty-one 'functions', namely invariable narrative motifs which, if present, must follow each other in a certain order and play a certain role. Georges Dumézil (cf. CH. 18) analysed Indo-European ideology as focusing on three roles in society: effectively that of rulers, the military, and the economic/productive. This, in his opinion, drove Indo-European mythologies. Because he proposed three functions, his theory is *trifunctional.*
Incipit	'It begins.' The first few words, or opening line, of a text. Sometimes used as a title, like *When the Storm God Thunders Frightfully* (p. 374). The opposite is *explicit* ('it ends').
Koine	A shared language (Greek *koinē dialektos* 'common speech'), especially the widespread standard form of Greek that developed in the Hellenistic period; hence, by extension, any idiom shared between people and cultures. Thus CH. 20 charts an East Mediterranean *koine* of beliefs about the Beyond.
Motifeme	In comparative narratology, a motif which is a basic significant unit of narrative.
Mytheme	A fundamental unit in the narrative structure of a myth. Cf. mythologem, but mytheme (modelled on the linguistic term phoneme) is a narrower technical term in structuralist analysis of myth.
Mythologem	An individual unit or element of a mythic narrative (Greek *mythologēma*, a piece of mythic narrative).
Narratology	The 'science' through which we can analyse narratives such as novels and myths. Adjective, *narratological.*
Parabasis	In Aristophanic comedy, a portion of the play in which the chorus or chorus leader addresses the audience directly, sometimes appearing to speak in the playwright's own voice.
Paradigm	An 'example' of how something should be. Also, in Greek, mythological *paradeigma* (CHS. 2, 6) – the use of myths to steer you towards (or away from) a particular sort of behaviour. The Latin for *paradeigma* is *exemplum.*
Pragmatics	The study of speech and text as deriving its significance from *performance* in a particular context or type of context.
Redaction	Producing a new, definitive, version of a text, sometimes organizing it more or abridging it somewhat.
Semiotics	The study of 'signs', of how meanings are indicated, of communication and the tools of communication, for example, myths.

Structuralism The study of the nature of, for example, a myth, or mythic cycle, by reference to its structure, and of how that structure reflects our thought processes and reveals a deep level of meaning.

Synchronic 'At the same time', referring to studies which trace the structures and relationships of phenomena at a given moment in time. Opposite of *diachronic*.

Abbreviations

Abbreviations of the titles of journals/periodicals (e.g., *JHS* for *Journal of Hellenic Studies*) follow *L'Année philologique* (Paris 1928 –date), whose list may be found at http://www.annee-philologique.com/aph/files/sigles_fr.pdf. Other abbreviations are as follows:

ad loc.   *ad locum*, referring to a writer commentating 'on that passage'.

ANET   J. B. Pritchard (ed.) (1969) *Ancient Near Eastern Texts Relating to the Old Testament*[3] with supplement, Princeton.

BNJ   I. Worthington (ed.), *Brill's New Jacoby*. A new version of *FGrH* (below), with English translation and English commentary. Currently only available online, by subscription. Many academic libraries subscribe. www.brillonline.nl.

BNP   H. Cancik and H. Schneider (eds) (2002) – *Brill's New Pauly: Encyclopaedia of the Ancient World*, 22 vols, Leiden. Also available online, by subscription. Many academic libraries subscribe. www.brillonline.nl.

CS   *Context of Scripture*: see Hallo (2003a,b,c).

DK   H. Diels and W. Kranz (eds) (1951–2) *Die Fragmente der Vorsokratiker*[6], Zurich.

F   Fragment. A part of a lost work that has survived, for example, on papyrus or by being quoted or referred to or used by a later author. 'F 4 Pfeiffer', for instance, means 'fragment 4 in Pfeiffer's collection of the fragments'.

FGrH   F. Jacoby, *Die Fragmente der griechischen Historiker* (Berlin 1923–30; Leiden 1940–58). A collection, in the original language, of all references to lost Greek historians and lost Greek historical works; also a commentary on much of the collection, mainly in German.

Gantz   T. Gantz (1993) *Early Greek Myth: A Guide to Literary and Artistic Sources*, Baltimore, London.

IG XII.5   *Inscriptiones Graecae* XII,5. *Inscriptiones Cycladum*, ed. F. Hiller von Gaertringen, 2 vols, Berlin (1903–9).

IGSK   H. Engelmann (1976) *Die Inschriften von Kyme* [*Inschriften griechischer Städte aus Kleinasien* 5], Bonn.

KRS   G. S. Kirk, J. E. Raven, and M. Schofield (1983) *The Presocratic Philosophers: A Critical History with a Selection of Texts*², Cambridge.

KTU   Collection of Ugaritic cuneiform texts: M. Dietrich, O. Loretz, and J. Sanmartin (eds) (1976) *Die keilalphabetische Texte aus Ugarit, einschließlich der keilalphabetischen Texte außerhalb Ugarits.* Alter Orient und Altes Testament 24, Neukirchen-Vluyn.

LIMC   *Lexicon Iconographicum Mythologiae Classicae*, 8 vols, Zurich (1981–97). A thorough catalogue and set of photographs for all ancient mythological characters from A to Z (see CH. 8, 'Further Reading').

Most   G. W. Most (2006–7) *Hesiod* [Loeb Classical Library], 2 vols, Cambridge MA. Fragments are in Vol. 2 (with English translation).

MW   R. Merkelbach and M. L. West (1967) *Fragmenta Hesiodea*, Oxford, significantly updated by R. Merkelbach, M. L. West, and F. Solmsen (eds) (1990) *Hesiodi Theogonia, Opera et Dies, Scutum, Fragmenta Selecta*³, Oxford Classical Texts, Oxford. (Both in the original Greek.)

OA   Orphic *Argonautika* (Vian 1987).

OF   Orphic fragments, whose number ends with either B (Bernabé 2004, 2005, 2007) or K (Kern 1922).

OGIS   W. Dittenberger (1903) *Orientis Graeci Inscriptiones Selectae I–II*, Leipzig.

OH   Orphic *Hymns* (Morand 2001).

OT   Orphic *Testimonia* (Kern 1922).

PCG   R. Kassel and C. Austin (1983–98) *Poetae Comici Graeci*, Berlin, New York.

PEG   A. Bernabé (ed.) *Poetae Epici Graeci*. Part 1, Leipzig (1987); Part 2.1, Leipzig and Munich (2004); Part 2.2, Munich (2005); Part 2.3, Berlin (2007).

PMG   D. L. Page (ed.) (1962) *Poetae Melici Graeci*, Oxford.

PT   Pyramid Texts: see J. P. Allen (2005).

SIG³   *Sylloge Inscriptionum Graecarum*³, 4 vols. Vols 1–3, ed. W. Dittenberger, Leipzig 1915–20; Vol. 4, index, by F. Hiller von Gaertringen, Leipzig 1924.

SH   H. Lloyd-Jones, P. Parsons (eds) 1983 *Supplementum Hellenisticum*, Berlin.

T   Testimonium. Used by Jacoby to present evidence (*testimony*) of lost works.

TGF   S. Radt (1985) *Tragicorum graecorum fragmenta* III *Aeschylus*, Göttingen; (1977) *Tragicorum graecorum fragmenta* IV *Sophocles*, Göttingen; R. Kannicht (2004) *Tragicorum graecorum fragmenta* V *Euripides*, Göttingen.

TLG   *Thesaurus Linguae Graecae*: an enormous database of digitized ancient Greek texts, available by subscription online at www.tlg.uci.edu.

APPROACHING MYTH

CHAPTER ONE

Thinking through Myth, Thinking Myth Through

Ken Dowden and Niall Livingstone

Mythology as System

Everyone knows the Greeks had myths. But the use of the word 'myth' in modern times only goes back to its use in 1783 by arguably the first modern theorist of mythology, Christian Gottlob Heyne (Bremmer, CH. 28). Myth is therefore as much a product of the modern history of ideas from the end of the Enlightenment onwards as it is an objective product of ancient Greece. It is more than mere stories, but in describing that 'more' and conducting the *interpretation* of myth we play out the intellectual history of our own times – the romantic and anthropological revolutions of the nineteenth century, and the crises, grand theories, interdisciplinary certainties, and doubt triumphant of the twentieth century And on top of all this there lurks behind mythology its failure to be scripture, to provide the holy books the Greeks surely ought to have had – in order to be an intelligible nation to us and to our nineteenth-century forebears.

It is vital to realize that there is no one thing called 'myth', and for that reason there is no definition that will satisfy all significant uses of the word. 'Myth' (which derives from the Greek word *mythos*, not always 'myth' in our sense) refers to a network of Greek stories to which it is conventional to apply the term 'myth'. This is a matter of empirical fact, not philosophy or circular definition. We know a Greek myth when we see one and have need of no definitions, guidance, or codes of practice to identify it as such. It is, however, not a random network but has a strong core of a system that was on occasion told as a system. Thus, Apollodoros' *Library* (first century AD) may serve to

A Companion to Greek Mythology, First Edition. Edited by Ken Dowden and Niall Livingstone.
© 2014 John Wiley & Sons Ltd. Published 2014 by John Wiley & Sons Ltd.

define that system for us, as his lost predecessor, 'Hesiod' had in the *Catalogue of Women* (see Dowden, CH. 3). Anything that forms part of this is myth. Anything that looks like this is myth. Homer, himself, knew an astonishing repertoire of myths (see Létoublon, CH. 2) and then, like a tragedian, but one much more wayward and self-confident, bent the mythology he had inherited to develop his own economical but panoramic epics.

This system of myth exists not only on paper or papyrus: it is internalized by all Greek poets, all their historians and thinkers, and by the whole Greek nation. And it was externalized in the sculptures, paintings, and decorative arts for which we still celebrate Greece (Woodford, CH. 8 – and the key moment captured at the beginning of that chapter). Thus Greek mythology defines what it is to be Greek (Graf, CH.11), and Greeks by their common agreement to *remember* these myths forge a powerful tool of social identity that has been explored by Halbwachs ('Collective Memory') and more recently by Jan Assmann ('Cultural Memory'). Myths are not, however, remembered in isolation: they are interactive, with each other and on countless occasions with every aspect of Greek life and thought. They are a continual point of reference, or system of references, and they constitute what since the late 1980s has been recognized in literature under the term 'intertext' (see Dowden 1992: 7–8). Anything that can be thought can be thought better with myth, or against its backcloth, or against it altogether (as in the case of Plato – Murray, CH. 9).

Mythology as History

As a condition of its being woven into a system, Greek mythology must gain internal links and sequences between its component myths. Thus, genealogy connects one myth with another and gives the illusion of narration in time. The action occurs, too, for the most part in real Greek landscapes. Indeed, geography is a key principle of the organization of the mythological system (see CHS 3, 11). Myth may exist across a gulf, across the 'floating gap'[1] in another time system altogether – *in illo tempore*, as Eliade used to say (e.g., 1969: ch. 2) – but there remains a sense that the genealogies that reach down from gods to heroes and from heroes to other heroes might in the end cross that gulf and link aristocrats of today to heroes of the past (Graf 1993a: 128–9). With this the illusion of history is complete and the mythology has now become the history that Greece did not have, neither the history of transmitted written record nor that of archaeology.

So if myth has wrapped up oral traditions and masquerades as the history of the world from the beginnings of the gods to the Trojan War and its aftermath, what credence did the Greeks give it? *Did the Greeks Believe in their*

Myths? – the title of a classic book of Paul Veyne (1988). Almost any answer can be given to this question – yes, no, or it depends what you mean by 'believe'. There are wonderful insights in Veyne's discussion:

> The truth is the child of the imagination. The authenticity of our beliefs is not measured according to the truth of their object … As long as we speak of the truth, we will understand nothing of culture …
>
> The Greeks … were never able to say, 'Myth is completely false, since it rests on nothing.' … The imaginary itself is never challenged. (1988: 113)

But Thucydides (1.11) certainly thought it was worth accounting for the length of time it had taken the Greeks to capture Troy and the historians themselves can disconcert us by their acceptance of, or subscription to, myth (see Alan Griffiths' discussion in CH. 10).

This particular difficulty extends to our own reading of Greek myth. Can we really say that there is *nothing* preserved of the lost Greek history in Greek mythology? Some have come close to this extreme position (Dowden 1992: ch. 4). Yet even they will acknowledge that some genuine movements of Greek peoples are reflected in the mythology: the colonization of Rhodes by peoples of the Argolid may be reflected in the mythology (Dowden 1989: 150) and Troy may reflect the takeover of the Asia Minor seaboard by the colonizing Greeks (Dowden 1992: 68). But Troy is the key case where we need to set aside naive views, stemming from Schliemann, which dignify material finds through association with mythic culture as though it were simply history. Hertel tests the case of Troy in CH. 22 and demonstrates, with due caution, what sort of moves may be involved in trying to cut myth down to a possible historical core. A different approach has been that of Margalit Finkelberg (2005) who has looked at how succession to kingdoms works in Greek myth and found in it a system so intelligible in the light of systems that are known elsewhere in the world that she considers the mythology to preserve *actual* successions. It is a powerful case and perhaps we do not yet have the measure of how to detect history in myth.

Local Mythology, National Mythology, Inherited Mythology

There can be no doubt that myth grew out of local traditions. This lesson, first understood clearly by Karl Otfried Müller (1825), is repeatedly forgotten in the history of the study of mythology and is forcefully restated in this volume by Graf (CH. 11). Many myths remained local; for instance, accounting for landscapes and customs (Dowden 1992: ch. 8.1; Buxton 1994: e.g., ch. 6). Such a mythology might seem much more like the mythologies we learn about in simpler societies. It was their incorporation into a system, and above all their historicization in the trans-local epic as a tale about manhood at war, the society of heroes, that led to what we know as Greek mythology. This was not, however, some one-off spontaneous generation of mythology as we know it. The collection of the mythology in the Dark Ages was only the latest unification in a dialectic between the national and the local. We sometimes think of nations as a modern structure, as indeed in some senses they are. But a consciousness of one tribal people as belonging to a larger grouping suffices:

> I resume, Gentlemen: man is a slave neither of his race nor his language nor his religion nor of the course of rivers nor that of mountain chains. A great gathering of men, sound in spirit and warm in heart, creates a moral awareness that is called a nation. (Renan 1992 (1882): 56)

The history of religion is full of tribal groupings marking their affiliation through ceremonies held at multi-year time intervals (see Dowden 2000: ch. 14). It is likely that a unificatory mythology is maintained in such groupings, as the memory of mythology is necessary for the maintenance of identity. It is therefore no surprise that other 'nations' related to the Greeks should display some elements of parallel mythology (see Puhvel 1987), notably the Sanskrit tradition in India that finds expression in the huge epic *Mahābhārata*. The nations related to the Greeks are the Indo-European peoples – such as the English whose kings descended from Woden – and it is there, in the hypothetical reconstructed Indo-European grouping of peoples, that the story of Greek mythology, in one sense, must start (Allen, CH. 18). Here we confront the extraordinarily doctrinaire approach of Georges Dumézil (1898–1986), who claimed to identify the underlying ideology of the Indo-Europeans and the ways in which it found expression in myth. Many classical scholars have simply rejected Dumézil, and his sympathy for some forms of fascism scarcely helped, but there are more intelligent ways forward than this and his system has been thoughtfully and temptingly extended by others, such as, notably, Nick Allen himself (CH. 18) and Pierre Sauzeau.[2]

Borrowed Mythology

However, ancestry is not all. Peoples do not move from one quarantined area to another. The tale of migration is also a tale of merger and of communication with new neighbours creating new mutual influences. Very few indeed of the names of Greek gods stand any chance of going back to Indo-European

(Dowden 2007: 48). Zeus does, perhaps Poseidon, perhaps even Dionysos (< *Diwos-sunos, 'son of Zeus'?). Helen and the Dioskouroi probably belong there too. But not Athānā (as Athene originally was) and not Artemis or Aphrodite either: Athene and Artemis go back to the Bronze Age, appearing as they do on the Linear B tablets, and must belong with the populations of Greece before the Greek-speakers or with the populations that preceded or influenced them. Aphrodite stands a fair chance of being a form of the Phoenician Ashtart (Greek Astarte). Not only the names of gods, but the mythology that gives them substance can follow these paths. It is clear that the societies of the Near East above all possessed highly developed mythologies and were in seamless contact with each other, and in every period – Mycenaean, Archaic, Classical, and Hellenistic – with the Greek world.

Several scholars worked on the influence of Near Eastern cultures on Greek and in particular on Hesiod. After the pioneering studies of the Hittitologist Güterbock (1946, 1948), this subject increasingly interested classicists until two key publications of 1966 by Peter Walcot and Martin West dealt squarely in their own ways with the issue of Hesiod and his relation to Near-Eastern material. Meanwhile Astour (1967) produced a study of Near-Eastern influence on Greek religion and culture in Mycenaean times, not well received. Then later Burkert (1992 [1984]) produced a brilliant, idiosyncratic, study of the archaic and orientalizing period; and a decade later again West (1997) produced a characteristically massively informed study of influence on archaic and classical literature.[3] We did not want to repeat this work in the present volume, but decided in the end that it was time to give the experts on the Near East their voice (which they had not had in this discourse since Güterbock, with the partial exception of Astour), so that the character of this mythology might shine out on the basis of the latest and most accurate information, particularly given that primary material is constantly being read for the first time in this discipline, a very different situation from the world of Greece and Rome where there is a huge bedrock of established texts and authors. This is what Livingstone and Haskamp provide in CH. 19, in a substantial contribution which authoritatively marks new ground in the presentation of Near-Eastern mythology to students of mythology.

However, in the travelling conditions of Greek times, the Phoenicians were the Greeks' immediate port of call in the Near East, though we know little about Phoenician mythology. That changed, at least for their prehistory, when we discovered the archives of Ugarit. Here was a rich seam of religious and mythological material, and one which bears interesting relation to Old Testament material. This is to be expected as the Canaanites are in effect the Phoenicians looked at through an Old Testament window. A treatment by Wyatt of the Ugaritic (and some Hebrew) material on the afterlife and the Beyond and by Marinatos of Egyptian material and the influence which it appears to have had on conceptions of the Underworld, or rather the Beyond, in the *Odyssey* are, unusually, brought together in CH. 20. These are the sorts of contexts in which the choices of Homer, and the mythology he represents, are made.

The Implementation of Mythology

By this stage we can see how huge and complex a job it is to define Greek mythology and situate it within its diachronic and synchronic historical contexts. The next task is to understand the implementation of mythology in Greek culture. This is a question partly of generic horizons, partly of audiences and their expectations, and partly of the ingenuity of the individual writer.

What Homer does with myth is to use it as a backdrop for conspicuously modern plots in a genre that had previously, maybe, served more to bring traditional episodes to life.[4] Though his work amplifies and extends what later generations will accept as myth, he presents a starkly realistic portrait of very mortal heroes against what they perceive as a mythology: Achilles is found singing the *famous deeds of men* (*klea andrōn*, *Iliad* 9.189), that is, traditional mythology but also the deeds he is thwarted from undertaking by his industrial action; and Helen weaves a web of what for us is mythology of the Trojan War (3.125–8) but for her is a regretful photograph of reality. As Létoublon observes (p. 27) Homer is far from a recitation of myths. But, equally, his world depends on a multidimensional adoption of mythology as a framework of reference and meaning. From the cosmogony to the endgame of Troy, the mythic section of the 'Homeric Encyclopedia' flows over with ambience (pp. 38–40).

We do not know as much as we would like about early performances of epic poetry, though Homer gives us imagined glimpses both of the professional singer at work, in the shape of the bards Demodokos and Phemios of the *Odyssey*, and of the more amateur performance of Achilles mentioned above.[5] Epics were clearly performed competitively at festivals; Hesiod mentions travelling to Euboia for such an occasion (*Works & Days* 651–9), and a later legend arose of a rather peculiar song-competition which pitted Hesiod against Homer himself. This was only a small part, however, of a much wider song culture, in which almost every significant occasion was marked by its appropriate form of song, often accompanied by dance and other forms of performance, and often presenting myth. (The particular way in which such performances make myth present, connecting the ancient and traditional with the here and now, is described in more detail by Calame, pp. 517–20.)

Our most important representative of this song culture is Pindar (late sixth–mid-fifth century BC), a poet who comes late in this tradition and at its pinnacle of sophistication, but who is also in some respects quite conservative.[6]

Pindar's use of myth is analysed by Rutherford in CH. 5. Where Homer uses myth as a foundation for his own highly individual plots and as a backdrop lending depth to the epic landscape, for Pindar, it is a system within which he works, and a world which he and his aristocratic patrons inhabit. For Pindar (as for Homer) the function of myth is not primarily to be *told* in any straight-forward way. These are family stories; we may remind each other of them, take pride in them, derive solidarity from them, occasionally debate which is the authentic version, but we do not need to be told them. Where the *Iliad* and *Odyssey* mark a seam or caesura between the heroic then and the everyday now, in Pindar's songs there is no such seam: the world of myth is superim-posed on the world of the victorious athletes and other great figures whose achievements he celebrates.

To say that the world of myth is familiar is not, of course, to say that it is ordinary: it has a magical glamour akin to that of the golden Sparta of Menelaos and Helen in the *Odyssey*. In Pindar's victory odes in particular, myth is used to demonstrate how the victor's extraordinary achievement in winning a Panhellenic contest places him on a par with the heroes of legend, close to the gods. Here as often, the telling of myth places often local or familial traditions in the context of a wider Panhellenic system of stories, a dynamic which is obvi-ously appropriate when celebrating local potentates for whom victory at the Olympic, Pythian, Isthmian, or Corinthian games represents a moment of Panhellenic stardom (a moment which the poems themselves, of course, serve to perpetuate). Pindar's poems are good examples of two functions of myth of lasting importance. First is the use of myth as an allusive poetic shorthand, making it possible to communicate and evoke a great deal in very few words; this role of myth is increasingly important as the classical literary tradition trav-els and mutates from Greece to Rome and beyond. Second is the role of myth as a rhetorically powerful virtual world, like and yet unlike reality, and highly charged (with authority, glamour, beauty, and emotive force), in such a way that intense effects may be achieving by linking the two. Here Pindar stands near the head of the very important tradition of praise and (to a lesser extent) blame in ancient oratory, in which myth (and later, mythologized history, though as Alan Griffith makes very clear in CH. 10 this is never an easy line to draw) plays an important role as kings and princes are likened to heroes of old. Myth can also be used to deliver warnings – especially, not to aim beyond the pinnacle of human achievement by aspiring to equal the gods. (Such warnings also, of course, function as praise by implying the person's success is so great that he might actually be in danger of starting to feel like a god.)

From the performance of mythic song emerges drama, above all, though not exclusively, in Athens in the fifth century BC.[7] The question of why a city with a burgeoning democratic system should wish to devote a significant part of some of its most important festivals to rehearsing, in tragedy, the household traumas of Bronze Age princes and princesses has been much discussed. The importance of this question has in turn itself been called into question.[8] Almost all tragedies, as well as their less well-known relatives the satyr plays, tell stories drawn from myth, and from epic in particular.[9] Comedy is generally set, at least partly, in a world closer to the reality of contemporary Athens, but it too makes extensive use of myth, sometimes in parodies of tragedy or epic. (It is also clear that if more comedies had survived, especially from the early fourth-century BC period of the genre's history conventionally known as Middle Comedy, we would have many more examples of extended mythic plots.)

Drama obviously represents a new development in the 'making present' of mythic events which we have already encountered in the performance of lyric, and here, once again, powerful effects result from the superimposition of different worlds. Myth helps drama to tackle the extremes of emotion, the horrors of war, the pain of familial conflict and bereavement, the deepest personal dilemmas, while also retaining a measure of reflective distance. Through using myth, the plays can confront darkest the most terrifying aspects of human experience while also providing the audience with enjoyment and – according to prevailing ancient Athenian assumptions, at any rate – edification from the experience. Christiane Sourvinou-Inwood provided the helpful metaphor of 'zooming' and 'distancing' devices by which the tragedians make us aware at one moment of the heroic remoteness of their characters, at another of the closeness of their concerns and experiences to our own (whether 'we' are modern readers or members of an Athenian audience, though, of course, somewhat differently in each case).[10] This is one instance of the wider phenomenon of myth functioning as a lens through which things are seen in a new light, the familiar made unfamiliar or vice versa.[11]

One Athenian comic dramatist teased the tragedians for having such an easy life: not only are their plots ready-made for them, coming as they do from myth, but the audience knows them already![12] As Jean Alaux demonstrates in CH. 7, however, the tragedians were very far from adopting any passive approach to their mythic material. Myths are not simple hand-me-downs; nor are they a straitjacket. The availability of different versions enables playwrights to make highly significant choices and changes of emphasis, and to engage in constant dialogue with the tradition (including previous plays, as well as epic and other poetry) and with their audience-members' expectations, a point once made exceptionally strongly by Peter Walcot.[13] The experience of myth is also transformed by its presentation in the theatre in front of a mass audience as the citizens of Athens together watch the affairs of mythical cities brought to life and, often, their leading figures brought to ruin, before their eyes.[14] This, then, becomes a matter of 'pragmatics' (cf. Calame, CH. 27), the vital significance of the occasion for the meaning. But it is a much harder question whether myth in itself necessarily conveys the messages that the tragedians found in it. It is a remarkable fact about myth that it constantly serves new purposes and one of those purposes, a powerful one, has been to reflect the new interest in women's studies that began in the 1960s. But perhaps we have rushed too readily to the conclusion that myth is a 'source' for attitudes to women and should pause to consider the provocative paradox which Lewis drives home in CH. 23: 'the centrality of mythology in gender scholarship has never been matched by a strong interest in gender amongst those who study mythology.' And at root, as she demonstrates, lies the *polysemy* of myth – its capacity to bear meanings, many meanings. Myth is Protean, but the myth of Proteus might direct our thought to many other things instead.

So myth provides virtual worlds which are, in a variety of ways, good to think with. A particular case of this is what we may call, if we are forgiven for invoking a contemporary cliché, virtual learning environments. The fashionable teachers known as sophists of the fifth century BC and onwards use myth to add appeal and authority to their classes in ethics, politics, and persuasive speech: Prodikos instructs the young with a tale of Herakles choosing between personified Vice and Virtue, while Hippias has a Spartan audience spellbound with advice supposedly given by Nestor to the young Neoptolemos. N. Livingstone dips into this tradition in CH. 6. Like so much else, it goes back to Homer, in whose poems examples from myth, *paradeigmata*, are already powerful if far from straightforward instructive tools, and whom the sophists themselves are predictably keen to hail as their model and ancestor.

The greatest 'thinker with myth' of them all, however, and the most fascinating and influential, is the sophists' leading critic: Plato, whose myths are Murray's subject in CH. 9. Where the sophists borrow mythological settings such as the Trojan War or the Labours of Herakles for didactic performances, Plato does something much more radical, creating philosophical myths which use traditional material and 'feel' old, but are in fact (probably: the case of Atlantis, for instance, has been much discussed) essentially new. It seems strange that he should choose to present us with such fictions, in view of Socrates' relentless insistence in his dialogues on the absolute importance of Truth and Reality and on dialectical reasoning as the means of attaining it. Murray demonstrates that, in spite of this paradox, myth is no add-on, but central to Plato's philosophy. Platonic myth is a way of exploring the inadequacy of our understanding of what Truth really is, of pushing at the limits of our understanding and ability to understand, and of groping our way towards understanding of things which, within the limitations of the written dialogue and until such time as the light of philosophical enlightenment dawns, we are unable to talk about any other way. This insight is not restricted to philosophy, as Griffiths makes clear in CH. 10. His examples from the ancient and modern worlds alike demonstrate just how hard it is to eliminate myth from storytelling, and especially from the telling of stories about the past.

So far this discussion may have given the impression that myth in the ancient world was primarily a verbal phenomenon. This is far from being the case: visual images of myths were almost as pervasive in ancient cities as brand and advertising images are in the modern developed world.[15] Scenes from myth were in private homes on more-or-less everyday pottery, a good deal of which survives, and on deluxe precious-metal ware, most of which is lost; they were in public buildings such as temples and porticos in the form of wall paintings – of which, again, sadly little survives – and sculpture. Woodford vividly reminds us of the importance of this visual world of myth by opening CH. 8 with a remarkable first scene in one of Euripides' tragedies. Here, a group of women find a sense of being 'at home' on a visit to an unfamiliar city because they recognize the stories the temple sculptures tell. The women excitedly report to each other what they see: for the benefit of the audience, of course,[16] but at a naturalistic level this is also a reminder that, for ancient Greeks as for us, visual representations of stories provoke an impulse to tell the stories verbally. The old saw that 'a picture is worth a thousand words' cuts both ways. How we, like the women in Euripides' chorus, can know what we are seeing, Woodford explains in CH. 8. Having thus assisted and emboldened us, she sounds a note of caution later in the volume, in CH. 21, where she warns us of a number of ways in which this enterprise of 'telling what's in the picture' can go wrong.

The long reign of Philip II of Macedon (lived c. 382–36 BC, ruled 356–36 BC) and the short, brilliant career of his son Alexander III (the Great, 356–323 BC, ruled 336–323 BC) transformed the Greek world. Philip progressively brought the cities of mainland Greece under Macedonian control and established Macedon as a dominating power. Alexander's conquest of the Persian empire expanded Greek horizons unimaginably – though in fact this was precisely what the Athenian political writer and teacher Isocrates (438–336 BC) *had* imagined, and had lobbied Philip, amongst others, to do.[17] Not surprisingly, Alexander became mythologized in his own lifetime, fulfilling, as Mori explains in CH. 12, a childhood ambition to rival Achilles; the gods Dionysos and Herakles were also role models.[18]

In the 'Hellenistic' world shaped by Alexander's successors, the collective Hellenic identity which (alongside local identities) myth had played such an important part in constructing in the Archaic and Classical periods became a kind of reality. This was facilitated by the spread of the 'common speech', or *koinē*, as the basic language of literacy and, above all, by the prestige of Greek literary culture, *paideia*, which became a route to prominence for mixed Greco-Macedonian and non-Greek elites in cities across a huge swathe of the Near and Middle East. Isocrates' favourite fantasy had been that Athens would lead the Greeks in war against the barbarians, and he would have bitterly regretted the loss of the city's freedom (one story has it that it was news of the defeat of Athens and her allies by the Macedonians at the battle of Chaironeia that finally led to the old man's death at the age of ninety-eight). He would have been gratified, however, by the hegemonic role of Athens, culturally though not politically, in the emerging Hellenistic identity. The *koinē* was a modified version of Attic, the dialect of Athens, and Athenian texts – the plays, histories, speeches, and philosophic writings – formed, together with Homer and others, the bedrock of *paideia*.[19] Mori demonstrates the importance of this identity, and of myth in particular as its vehicle, to Alexandrian Greeks making themselves at home on the threshold of North Africa, a 'kindred other'.[20] She shows how the flexibility of myth enabled Hellenistic Greeks to maintain an equilibrium between assimilation of non-Greek ideas and practices and assertion of the primacy of old Hellenic traditions.

The Hellenistic age was an age of collecting, not least collecting information. The information is now in the books (*ta biblia*), the books are in the library, and, if we are in Alexandria (home to the most famous, but not the only, great library of the period), the catalogue 'tables' (the *Pinakes*) of the great scholar-poet Callimachos are there to help you find it. Myths are sorted and organized, for example into aetiologies, explanations for the way things are, as in Callimachos' hugely influential (but now sadly fragmentary) poem the *Aitia*; unusual and obscure versions are competitively sought out, evaluated, and put to poetic use.[21]

The Problem of Rome

The Hellenistic collation (gathering and sorting) of Greek culture, including myth, left it conveniently packaged for its next great cultural step: appropriation by Rome.[22] It is hard here to avoid quoting the brilliant poetic soundbite of the first-century BC Roman poet Horace: *Graecia capta ferum victorem cepit*, 'captive Greece captured its savage conqueror' (*Epistles* 2.1.156); an instance of the principle, which has applied throughout human history, that colonization can also happen in reverse. We might draw an alternative metaphor from myth itself: the story in which Zeus' first wife Metis – Cunning Intelligence personified – is pregnant with the wise goddess Athene, and Zeus is warned that his next offspring will be a son destined to overthrow his father. Zeus pre-empts this by swallowing Metis. Metis becomes the Intelligence of Zeus, and Zeus himself gives birth to Athene (Hesiod, *Theogony* 886–900; F 343 MW, F 294 Most). In the case of Rome and Greece, though, what is swallowed is not so much intelligence as memory. The consequence is that Greek myth in Roman literature and culture has an added dimension, another level of potential mythic remoteness to be exploited, becoming a kind of 'myth squared'. The virtual world of myth is mediated by the additional virtual world of its Greek landscape and cultural contexts.

Of course, the analogy with Zeus and Metis is a slightly strained one (as mythic analogies often are). For one thing, Roman 'consumption' of Greek myth certainly did not happen in one big gulp; it had begun long before Rome came to dominate the Mediterranean world including Greece, itself a process which took some time.[23] For this reason, as Fox shows in CH. 12, the history of Roman myth is inextricably bound up with Greek myth. At one level this might just seem like a further extension of the Panhellenic umbrella, with another set of local traditions to be found a place and incorporated. And sometimes it does seem to work that way. Where were the Romans in the Trojan War, say? Their ancestor, it turns out, was the Trojan Aineias/Aeneas. On the wrong side, then, but it could be worse: Aeneas gets quite a good press in the myths, and after all the Trojans of the *Iliad* are not so alien as all that. They seem to have no problem communicating in Greek, for one thing, unlike the 'babble-voiced Karians' of *Iliad* 2. 867, and, as Dieter Hertel points out in CH. 22, their champion Hektor, the defender of his city, is a representative of quintessentially Greek *polis* values.[24] So we have Vergil's *Aeneid*: a foundation epic for Rome which is also, at one level, just another *Nostos* or hero's 'return' from Troy in the Greek epic tradition – with the difference that Aeneas' old home was Troy itself, and he can never reach his ultimate destined new home because it lies in the future. Such naturalizing approaches found favour in particular with Romanized or Roman-friendly Greeks. Thus the historian and literary critic Dionysios of Halikarnassos (first century BC) held that the Romans *were* really Greeks and that the Latin language was a dialect of Greek.[25] We may compare this with other integrative ventures like Plutarch's *Parallel Lives* (first–second centuries AD) of prominent Greeks and Romans both legendary and historical, setting up a kind of shared myth-history.[26]

Fox emphasizes, however, that the reality is by no means that simple. It is possible to integrate Roman myth with Greek myth and to Romanize Greek myth, but the fact remains that Roman myth is not the same kind of thing as Greek myth. This is because Roman myth is inseparable from traditions which lay claim to historical veracity, such as the biographies of the early kings of Rome. Of course, it is true that in Greece, too, the line between myth and history is often hard to draw, as we see CH. 10 and elsewhere. The difference here is that the question of the veracity of these Roman traditions is important to Roman writers in a way we do not see in the Greek world. The Romans, by contrast with what Veyne says of the Greeks above, *did* challenge 'the imaginary itself'. (This is not the same phenomenon as Greek philosophers' scrutiny of myth from a moral perspective, although, when we come to look at the close relationship between myth and religion, similarities do emerge.) Roman authors' interest in the authenticity of their myths has also, as Fox demonstrated, affected the way modern readers have responded to them from the eighteenth century AD onwards, and has often led to them being regarded as somehow 'inauthentic', whether relative to Greek myths or relative to some more 'original' version of Roman myth which we might somehow uncover.

The visual presence of myth was no less strong in the cities of the Roman world than in Greece, as Newby makes clear in our second Roman chapter, CH. 14. Interestingly, we are not much concerned here with the specifically Roman myths examined in CH. 13. Scenes such as the infancy of Romulus and Remus do appear occasionally, but for the most part we find the stories already familiar from Greek art and literature. Public art in Rome used myth to convey political and ideological messages, to glorify those who put works of art on display and demonstrate their connoisseurship (many of these artworks were plundered or otherwise acquired from Greece), and simply to entertain the public. In the decoration of lavish dining rooms, art could be used to transport guests into the virtual world of myth, an effect intensified when visual representations were complemented by dramatic re-enactments by actors. Slave attendants in costume and character as figures from myth could also be intermingled with statuary in order to blur the gap between myth and reality, life and art still further. Such entertainments had a grisly counterpart in the staging of executions as gruesome mythical death scenes, presenting an audience with, for example, Orpheus (in a slightly unusual version of his story) not charming wild animals with his singing but being savaged to death by them instead. On a happier note, the highly elaborate mythical decoration of some dining rooms seems designed to set the tone for appropriately erudite and witty conversation: as in Euripides' play above, pictures are an excellent talking-point. Another kind of mythic 'virtual world' is the *trompe l'oeil* wall-painting, designed to make a room seem to open into an imaginary mythic landscape extending beyond the wall. Myth may be organized thematically around a room or rooms; in collections of pictures, just as in collections of poems, juxtaposition and arrangement can be used to create a whole which is much more than the sum of its parts.

Religious Change

This, then, is myth as décor, myth as culture, myth as providing the coordinates for your identity – personal or national. But myth also continued to belong in the world of religion and religious thought. Myth may not be scripture, as we have argued above, and it is certainly not Bible or Koran. However, once we have understood that much and freed ourselves from the danger of anachronism and misconception, we can look at the points at which myth and scripture do in fact resemble each other and at how evolving religious demands on mythology created a new sense of myth that eventually interacted with Judaeo-Christian scripture and was able to welcome it into the textual imagination of the Greek and Roman worlds.

Myth was tradition, and tradition was authority. It was commonplace in Plato's Athens to appeal to Homer as an authority (N. Livingstone, CH. 6), and tragedians in confronting the deepest ethical, religious, and political issues spoke through the vehicle of myth, perceived as enshrined above all in the works of Homer (Alaux, CH. 7). Did not Aeschylus himself pronounce his work 'slices from the great banquets of Homer'?[27] If Homer's mythology had not had this authority, the philosophers would not have been so concerned to attack it or defend it. Tragedy was not a medieval European Christian Mystery play, but it did employ traditional stories and did teach lessons. Thus it became increasingly possible for those that wanted to teach lessons or reveal truths (or indeed advertise truths by concealing them) to employ a mythology for the purpose. Such were the creators of literature by Orpheus, Mousaios, and such hallowed gurus, whose purposes were so distant from their contemporaries as well as from those of modern scholars that Edmonds in CH. 4 provides us with a radical revision and reconceptualization of this 'new-wave' activity. But such too was our revered Plato when he composed (better, of course) myths of his own (Murray, CH. 9). And such were those who allegorized myth or exploited its capacity to depict the soul and its salvation (Dowden, CH. 15). It is ironic in the light of later European history that Philo must draw out the authority of Old Testament scripture by turning it into Homer, and deploying the tools which non-scriptural Greeks had developed for ratcheting up the religious and philosophical significance of Homer's epics, in order to match his authority. Thus the models for the authority of Judaeo-Christian scripture amongst thinking people in the ancient world were in fact, on the one hand, the increasingly doctrinaire pronouncements of philosophers and, on the other, the literary mythology – such that it barely mattered whether you were talking about Odysseus, Abraham, Pythagoras, Jesus, or Apollonios of Tyana – or indeed Aeneas in Vergil's *Aeneid* (see CH. 15).

Somewhere, then, in the mid-ground for more general consumption, at least amongst the wealthy, lies the stone sarcophagus. Replete with mythological images, sometimes almost baroque in their profusion, but surprisingly limited in their range, the myths serve to suggest a discourse about death and the Beyond. And somewhere between the Pythagoreanism of Franz Cumont (1942) and the later twentieth-century AD suspicion of the grand view lies a judicious understanding of the hints and proprieties of this rich medium, as shown by Newby (CH. 16).

In the end the triumph of the Christians would be more or less complete. But it did not mean that all those who became Christian lost their literary, cultural, and mythographic heritage. They might have adopted the cultural memory of a different tradition, a remarkable shift in identity, but their individual lives should not, as Graf shows (CH. 17), be fictionalized into a pagan phase and a post-conversion phase just because they wrote works that rested on Greco-Roman culture. The ever-flexible tools of allegory and *exemplum* take myth well into the sixth century AD and set us up for the Middle Ages (CH. 17).

subsidio	with the help
Fortune labilis	of slippery Fortune
cur prelio	why in battle
Troia tunc	does Troy once
nobilis	notable
nunc flebilis	now weepable
ruit incendio?	blaze in ruin?

Carmina Burana 14.4 (twelfth–thirteenth century AD, the work, maybe, of a bishop)

Myth and the Moderns

The history of myth in modern times is even more voluminous and even more complex than its history in ancient times. Four-fifths of Bremmer's chapter (CH. 28) rightly deals with the period from the Renaissance to the present day, when in some ways the notion of myth was invented.

Myth is a much huger subject than we imagine when we first encounter it, perhaps at an early age – occupying the same mental space as fairy stories – now Jack and the Beanstalk, now Theseus and the Minotaur. But myth is more than merely imaginative Greek stories that happen through a quirk of history and an accident of education to have become a common inheritance of European and to some extent global culture. Yes, it has provided rich material to art[28] since the Renaissance sought other material than the Judaeo-Christian repertoire (itself a mythology), and it has provided plots for numerous operas.[29] Even there it would not have done so unless it had provided a space for meaning, for ideas, for argument that was applicable far beyond the narrow limits of an ancestral Greece. Greek myth, in fact, is universal, and it is in the nature of myth altogether to be universal.

It is exceptionally hard to describe the relation between a myth and its 'meaning' as it is applied to some new circumstance. There is something indirect about it, the recognition that the apparent meaning of the story (once upon a time …) must be transmuted into a rich new source of reflection and realization in a second level of meaning. This, according to Roland Barthes,[30] was how myth worked. To study myth is, in this sense, to study meaning itself, to study systems of signification, namely *semiotics*. Barthes was run over by a laundry van in Paris in 1980, on his way home from lunch, notably, with President Mittérand – a myth in itself. His work had aroused the interest of advertisers as they sought to tap the wellsprings of human motivation. It was with remarkable power that he had evoked the mythic quality of steak and chips, or of the Citroën DS, that glorious emblem of modernity, at the 1955 Paris motor show. This was the same car that the obscurantist neo-psychoanalyst Jacques Lacan bought, and in which the Lacans and the Lévi-Strausses used to go for outings,[31] a surreal icon for the reader of this book. These Barthian explorations spill over into another area that we would have wished to include in this volume, that of *mythocritique* – the 'myth-criticism' of literature, analysing its power as deriving from the myths it tells, not maybe myths in our Greek sense but in a much deeper one. This was the area ploughed, largely in ignorance of each other, by Northrop Frye in the USA,[32] still revered, and by Gilbert Durand (e.g., 1992) in Grenoble, less so. Particularly in the hands of Durand, this approach to mythology swung very close indeed to the psychoanalysis of Carl Jung.[33] That, in turn, had coincided, to the extent of some partnership in writing books,[34] with the work of Carl Kerényi, whose oeuvre, particularly the series 'Archetypal Images in Greek Religion',[35] largely puzzles and frustrates readers today if they have not approached it with an understanding of his effectively psychoanalytic convictions.

No book can rise to the total challenge of myth and our readers will look in vain for some of the above (classical tradition, Barthes, *mythocritique*). But we are delighted to be able to take the story up to the opening of the Christian Middle Ages (Graf, CH. 17), and to open up, in a profound and challenging way, modern developments in semiotics – from the structuralism of Lévi-Strauss to pragmatics (Calame, CH. 27). These chapters are both characterized by a sense of the huge variety of thinkers and writers whose variety and interrelationships need to be made intelligible. That is also the challenge posed by trying to master 'psychoanalysis' as though it was one thing. The story of psychoanalysis unfolded by Armstrong (CH. 25) is itself riven by factions and complicated by variants: was Oedipus too negative an example? should we have turned improvingly instead to Odysseus' very healthy relationship with Telemachos?

Theories that look different do merge into each other, as we have seen with *mythocritique* and psychoanalysis. And structuralism itself supposes that we think, in groups or universally, in particular ways, which again is the general presupposition of psychoanalysis. It is no coincidence that one formative moment in the life of Lévi-Strauss was when his girlfriend's father turned out to be the man who introduced the thought of Freud to Paris. In a way, his whole system of thought was designed to make better sense than psychoanalysis had, but on rather similar suppositions. At the same time, the theory of initiation (Dowden, CH. 26) may appear at first to be a classic and distinctive individual theory, tracing mythology back to particular customs and rituals which are known from anthropology. However, it eventually becomes clear that this type of behaviour results from the power of an underlying myth, realized in actual mythology, ritual, and even literature. At this point the theory has morphed into *mythocritique*, and it might as well be evoking a Jungian archetype, that will account for Frodo's triumph in Tolkien's *Lord of the Rings* as well as for Sophocles' *Philoktetes*. What, then, of the theories of Georges Dumézil (above, p. 6)? Shall they be exaggerated statements of the commonplace, or shall they make clear the thought of ancestral Indo-Europeans, inherited by their successors such as the Greeks and Indians? But maybe there is a third possibility: the addition of the fourth function to his system (Allen, CH. 18) may, after a little more work, join up initiation theory and psychoanalysis.[36] If myth is to be interpreted (and that is everyone's supposition, without which this volume and hundreds of others would be wholly pointless), then that is because there is a level of thought and a type of thought that all these approaches imply, maybe unwittingly, or explore.

Omissions and Controversies

It is customary for authors to beg the reader's forgiveness for whatever defects remain after they have received advice they were unable in their human frailty fully to implement. Our omissions are worse. From antiquity we have not really covered the rise of commentary (300–100 BC), except briefly (Mori, CH. 12; Graf, CH. 17); or the exciting period in the first centuries BC and AD when myth at times became a free-for-all and some took Homer to task for his inaccuracy;[37] or the role of myth in the rhetoric and imagination of the Second Sophistic (AD 100–300), when Greek culture reigned supreme in a Roman empire.[38]

From the modern period it will become apparent that mythology is a rich part of European tradition and identity (see above), and there is much more discussion than we can present here. The interplay of the myth of the wise Orient with the study of classical literatures at the end of the Enlightenment is worth a lifetime's study in itself; and it is this that leads to the remarkable authority in the second half of the nineteenth century of Max Müller, reinvigorating Greek mythology from the Sanskrit *Rig Veda* with a romanticism inherited from his poet father Wilhelm Müller, author of the *Winterreise*. Sadly, though we talk about initiation (Dowden, CH. 26) and about the 'structural' anthropologist Lévi-Strauss (Calame, CH. 27), we have little time to sketch in the imperial mission of nineteenth-century powers, above all Great Britain, and the competing ethnologies that they led to. Every paragraph of Bremmer's chapter encapsulates something worth study in its own right as part of the history of Greek mythology and part of the ideas we and our modern intellectual forebears have lived through in order to build, or maybe weave, the subject we now study.

It may seem to some readers that the history of a subject like mythology is a history of its errors and mistakes, of ideas now exploded. But every exploded idea teaches us something and forms part of the fabric. It is a shame that we have not in this volume confronted J. J. Bachofen (1815–1887), with his supposition of matriarchal societies.[39] Matrilinearity, certainly. But matriarchy? – the evidence is not there, and the Amazons (Lewis, CH. 23) constitute ideology, male ideology at that, not historical testimonial (Dowden 1997). That is not to say, however, that these myths cannot speak to our own times: Euripides' *Trojan Women* can tell us through the power of myth about Iraq or Afghanistan; Amazons can speak archetypally to those concerned with women's proper place in twenty-first century society – the fact the myth did not mean that to ancient Greeks does not imply that it is illegitimate in a different society to hear a different voice; and issues of race and the relative role of cultures supreme in European education compared with the worlds that Europe has exploited are worth new consideration provided we do not lose our critical instincts. The time has come to digest Bernal's *Black Athena*, or find an alternative path – as is done by Rutherford in CH. 24.

It is delightful to see what huge passions can be aroused by the theory of mythology. The theories of Bernal led to a furore of controversy.[40] Dumézil was denounced in his time for some fascist sympathies, but really reviled for constructing a theory that was too ambitious for the digestive tract of scholars (cf. Allen, CH. 18). In the 1980s, in Dowden's hearing, Carl Kerényi (see above), little cited in this volume, was denounced by a leading mythologist, also little cited here, as having done 'great damage' to the study of mythology. Lévi-Strauss almost whimsically conducted, in implicit contradiction of Freud, a counter-analysis of the Oedipus myth in an algebra which at once appalled empirical scholars and enticed them into imitating him,[41] and led even the magisterial figure of Walter Burkert to pronounce that 'I do not think Lévi-Strauss has proved anything' (1979: 11), but not without somehow reflecting the method himself (1979: ch. 1). Dowden has learnt that the wickedness of initiation theory is to propose an almost 'Kuhnian paradigm',[42] but perversely has come to the view that the theories of Kuhn (1996) – about scientific revolutions and 'paradigm shifts' – are not at all a bad way of viewing the sudden shifts in the kaleidoscope of thought about myth as one generation of scholars succeeds another (Dowden 2011). We need to understand how theories are made, how they decay, and why they so engage our energies. Mythology is arguably the finest scenario for this Kuhnian drama.

But it is perhaps psychoanalysis – not just in the study of mythology – that has roused the strongest passions, particularly with the publication of the withering 1,000-page French volume of 2005, *Le Livre noir de la psychanalyse: vivre, penser et aller mieux sans Freud* ('The black book of psychoanalysis: live, think and do better without Freud'),[43] full of articles like 'Freud: Profit, and

Taking Advantage of Weakness', or 'Why is Lacan so Obscure?', or a particularly cruel piece on the psychoanalyst of fairy-tales (Bettelheim 1976), 'Bettelheim the Imposter'.

This volume aims to provide a more civil and more liberal approach to the great variety of a hugely exciting and challenging subject. Mythology underpins all our lives at all times, and Greek mythology, because of its unique inner force (however one understands it), has pride of place amongst mythologies even today. It is worth understanding, and perhaps this volume will give some sense of how much there is to understand and of some of the routes by which that understanding may be reached.

FURTHER READING

On the nature of Greek mythology see especially the systematic books of Dowden (1992) and Graf (1993a); Buxton 1994 is more sensitive to 'feel' and context; a fresh, distinctly theoretical, approach (as in CH. 27) is deployed by Calame 2009a. Stimulating collections of essays include Bremmer 1987, Edmunds 1990 and Woodard 2007. On the history of the study of mythology see the helpful handbook of William G. Doty (2000) and the penetrating study of Von Hendy (2002), as well as, naturally, Jan Bremmer's overview of the history of the study of the subject in this volume (CH. 28).

NOTES

1. Assmann (1992: 49), building on work of Jan Vansina.
2. See Sauzeau: online.
3. For all these strands, see Dowden (2001).
4. Cf. Dowden (2004: 196–204).
5. On the way Pindar contends with the negative connotations of 'professional' poetry see Nagy 1989.
6. Even 'the most Indo-European of Greek poets' (M. L. West (2007: 15, quoting Calvert Watkins)). For discussion of myth in earlier Greek lyric see, for example, Nagy (2007) and chapters in Parts One and Two of Budelmann (2009).
7. Myth, and Homeric myth in particular, was clearly an important ingredient in the works of the early comic playwright Epicharmos (active in the Syracuse in Sicily in the early fifth century BC), who wrote plays with titles like *Odysseus the Deserter*, *Kyklops*, and *Sirens*, as well as a *Prometheus* or *Pyrrha*. Sadly, only meagre fragments of his works survive.
8. For the ongoing debate about the extent and nature of connections between drama and the social and political institutions of the democratic city see, for example, Goldhill (1987); the essays in Winkler and Zeitlin (1990); Cartledge (1997); Saïd (1998); Griffin (1998); Seaford (2000); Goldhill (2000); Rhodes (2003); Finglass (2005).

9.   Exceptions: Aeschylus' surviving *Persians*, presenting a version of very real and recent events but providing distance through its setting in the far-off Persian capital (and Xerxes, his mother Queen Atossa, and the shade of his dead father Dareios are 'mythical' figures enough from the perspective of an Athenian citizen); and Phrynichos' lost *Sack of Miletos*, which, Herodotos tells us, caused offence to the Athenians by presenting, in the recent fall of a great Greek city to the barbarians, sorrows which were too close to home. Then there is the odd case of Agathon's *Antheus*, also lost, but tantalisingly mentioned by Aristotle (*Poetics* 1451b21) as unusual in having both an invented subject and invented characters; a significant departure from tradition, then, but not necessarily a non-mythical setting: Agathon may have 'found' new figures in established mythical family trees.

10. Sourvinou-Inwood (1989: 136).

11. Cf. Wendy Doniger's idea of 'telescopic' and 'microscopic' functions of myth (Doniger 1998: 7–25); Jean Alaux in CH 7 uses the metaphor of the prism.

12. Antiphanes F189, from a play called *Poiēsis* ('Poetry' or 'Composition'): for text, translation, and discussion of the fragment's implications for comedy as 'fiction', see Lowe (2000: 260–9); also Olson (2007: 154 f. (text), 172–5 (commentary), 437 f. (tr.)).

13. Walcot (1976).

14. Not all tragedies are set in cities (Sophocles' *Philoktetes* and Euripides' *Hecuba*, for example, are not), but most are. Satyr plays, by contrast, seem often to have been set in the wilder places where the part-human, part-animal followers of Dionysos who formed their chorus were at home.

15. And, as Roland Barthes persuasively suggested (1957), there is a sense in which brands and advertising *are* the modern world's mythology: see further below.

16. It is interesting to speculate, but impossible to know, how much effort Euripides' production team made to realize the spectacle of Apollo's temple visually in the theatre.

17. On Isocrates' Panhellenic project see, for example, Livingstone (1998).

18. On the Alexander myth in the Roman world see Spencer (2002).

19. For a brief, clear discussion of *koinē*, see Colvin (2007: 63–6) ('essentially an expanded, international variety of Attic, heavily influenced by Ionic', 65). On Hellenistic education (a narrower field than *paideia*), see Cribiore 2001, and on literature and social identity, including questions of the availability or otherwise of *paideia* to non-Greek elites, Shipley (2000: 235–70); on the later legacy of Hellenism under Roman rule, see Swain 1996, Whitmarsh 2001, and essays in Borg (2004).

20. On how citizens of other Hellenistic *poleis* used myth to make themselves at home both in new locations 'abroad' and within a Panhellenic framework see Scheer (2003) and Graf in CH. 11.

21. On Hellenistic poets' use of myth see Fantuzzi and Hunter (2004, for example, 43–88 (Callimachos' *Aitia*), 224–45 (Aratos' *Phainomena*)).

22. On the relationship between Hellenistic and Roman literature see Fantuzzi and Hunter (2004: 444–85).

23. Less than fifty-three years according to a famous musing of Polybios in the opening of his *History* (1.1.5), but actually much longer: see Shipley (2000: 368–99).

24. On the 'Greekness', or at any rate non-Otherness, of the Trojans in Homer and in the Archaic period in general (by contrast with their later 'orientalization') see J. M. Hall (2007b: 346–50).

25. On Dionysios' approach to myth and history see Fox and Livingstone (2007: 555 f.), and on 'Aeolism', the theory of Latin as a dialect of Greek, Stevens (2006–7).

26. Though, Fox reminds us, Plutarch is also well aware of the oddness and Otherness to the Greek mind of many Roman traditions, as his work *Roman Questions* demonstrates (see pp. 252–3).

27. Athenaios, *Deipnosophists*, Epitome 2.1 p.164.

28. Art: Reid (1993); Hunger (1959).

29. Opera: Poduska (1999); Hunger (1959).

30. Barthe (1957: 'Le Mythe, aujourd'hui' ('Myth today')).

31. Lévi-Strauss and Eribon (1998: 107).

32. Frye (1957, 1963).

33. Cf. Durand (1992: 35–7).

34. For example, Jung and Kerényi (1951).

35. See Kerényi (1976a, 1976b).

36. See the ingenious solution of Sauzeau (2010).

37. Dowden (forthcoming). 'Fact and fiction in the New Mythology: 100 BC–AD 100', in J. R. Morgan, I. Repath (eds), *'Where the Truth Lies': Lies and Metafiction in Ancient Literature*, Groningen.

38. See Borg (2004), in which several essays are of interest to the student of mythology.

39. Bachofen (1861, 1967).

40. Lefkowitz and Rogers (1996), and the riposte of Bernal (2001).

41. Kirk (1970 and especially 1974); Leach (1974: ch. 4).

42. Dodd and Faraone (2003: xiv).

43. This is Meyer *et al.* 2005

PART I

ESTABLISHING
THE CANON

CHAPTER TWO

Homer's Use of Myth

Françoise Létoublon

Epic and Mythology

The epics of Homer[1] are probably the oldest Greek literary texts that we have,[2] and their subject is select episodes from the Trojan War. The *Iliad* deals with a short period in the tenth year of the war;[3] the *Odyssey* is set in the period covered by Odysseus' return from the war to his homeland of Ithaca, beginning with his departure from Kalypso's island after a seven-year stay.

The Trojan War was actually the material for a large body of legend that formed a major part of Greek myth. But the narrative itself cannot be taken as a *mythographic* one, unlike the narrative of Hesiod (see CH. 4) – its purpose is not to narrate myth. Epic and myth may be closely linked, but they are not identical, and the distance between the two poses a particular difficulty for us as we try to negotiate the mythological material that the narrative on the one hand *tells* and on the other hand only *alludes to*. 'Allusion' will become a key term as we progress.

The Trojan War, as a whole then, was the material dealt with in the collection of epics known as the 'Epic Cycle', but which the *Iliad* and *Odyssey* allude to. The Epic Cycle, however, does not survive except for a few fragments and short summaries by a late author, but it was an important source for classical tragedy, and for later epics that aimed to fill in the gaps left by Homer, whether in Greek – the *Posthomerica* of Quintus of Smyrna (maybe third century AD), and the *Capture of Troy* of Tryphiodoros (third century AD) – or, in Latin, Vergil's *Aeneid* (first century BC), and Ovid's '*Iliad*' in the *Metamorphoses* (first century AD). It also fuelled the prose accounts of 'Diktys of Crete'

A Companion to Greek Mythology, First Edition. Edited by Ken Dowden and Niall Livingstone.
© 2014 John Wiley & Sons Ltd. Published 2014 by John Wiley & Sons Ltd.

(first century AD) and 'Dares of Phrygia' (unknown date AD), allegedly eye-witnesses to the Trojan War and particularly popular from the Middle Ages to the seventeenth century. So our task is to study how Homer *uses* Greek myth even though we have no direct evidence of Greek myth before Homer, rather an uncomfortable and paradoxical challenge.

Evidently, a body of Greek myth did exist in the oral tradition before the time when the *Iliad* and *Odyssey* were in the process of composition, and the oral tradition itself may be seen depicted in the epic through such figures as Demodokos. The epics even show us that some divergent traditions circulated about some episodes of the Trojan War: the *Odyssey* alludes to a quarrel between Odysseus and Achilles (8.75)[4] instead of the *Iliad*'s quarrel between *Agamemnon* and Achilles; an expedition of Odysseus with Diomedes to the town of Troy is alluded to in the *Odyssey*, but is rather different from the spy mission to the camp of the Trojan allies of *Iliad* 10, where the Trojan spy Dolon and the king Rhesos are killed and Rhesos' horses stolen.

Scholars such as Kakridis (1949) and Severyns (1928)[5] paved the way for the critical approach we refer to as 'Neoanalysis' (see further CH. 22), which is based on the idea that Homer already knew the traditions which later authors told – in the *Kypria*, *Aithiopis*, *Iliou Persis* and other cyclic epics. This means that he may be *alluding* to 'texts' we do not know, for instance an *Argonautika*, as we can see from the *Odyssey*'s mention of the ship Argo, *pasi melousa* 'known by everybody' (*Odyssey* 12.69–70). A significant proportion of this mythology may only be known to us in written form through late texts, but its presence in vase paintings guarantees that it was already told in the Archaic Age.

So this chapter starts from the mythological material which the *Iliad* and the *Odyssey* exploit and begins with the episodes of the Trojan War in chrono-logical order (as known from the whole ancient tradition, from the summary of the Epic Cycle by Proclus, via the Byzantine patriarch Photius in the ninth century AD, to Tryphiodoros and the Latin authors mentioned above). At the same time we will do well to remember that there is a certain methodological inconvenience in this approach: we are not sure that such or such events were told in one part of the Cycle rather than in another. Furthermore, it is not even agreed that the different parts of the Epic Cycle – whether oral or written – existed in the Archaic Age (before the *Iliad* and the *Odyssey*) in the form that they later took and that we know.

Cosmogony and Beginnings

The difference between how Homer and Hesiod narrate myth can best be seen in their presentation of cosmogony and cosmology. In Homer, because her son Achilles needs her help, we 'see' the goddess Thetis living in the sea with her aged father (the 'Old Man of Sea') (*Iliad* 1.357–63). Then we learn from her that Zeus is not currently in his usual home on Mount Olympos, but engaged in a twelve-day feast amongst the Ethiopian people (1.423–4). Later, when Hera gives an excuse to Zeus for going to the limits of the Earth, we discover that Okeanos (Ocean) is the 'origin (*genesis*) of the gods' (14.201) and is constantly quarrelling with his wife Tethys (14.205). This is an alternative cosmogony to that told in the *Theogony* (106, see CH. 3): Okeanos has taken the place of Ouranos, and Tethys that of Gaia.

In Book 15, Zeus's commands to Poseidon through the messenger Iris and Poseidon's answer (15.158–67, 185–99) remind the audience how the three sons of Kronos once parted the world, 'but the earth and Olympos' heights are common to us all' (193, tr. Fagles 1990), which scarcely seems consistent with the account of Zeus's law on Earth in Hesiod's *Theogony*. One may suspect that the needs of the argument influenced Poseidon's discourse. Another mythical variant may be found in the *Iliad*'s account, in a simile, of Earth suffering from Zeus's onslaught on Typhōeus (*Iliad* 2.780–3, told somewhat differently at Hesiod, *Theogony* 821–46).[6] In any case, we find ourselves here in territory with a seriously Near Eastern feel and most scholars now think in terms of borrowing from Near Eastern tradition rather than the common Indo-European inheritance (on these possibilities, see Part IV of this book).[7]

Preliminaries to the Trojan War

It is not easy to decide how Homer's narrative relates to pre-existing myths of Troy, not least because the poems have their own narrative strategy, one focusing on the anger of Achilles and the plan of Zeus, the other on the return of Odysseus. This strategy does not follow the events of the Trojan War, or only a very limited part of them. Rather, the poet treats those events, well known to his audience, as a kind of mental map for locating the places, the people, and the events of his narrative – they are situated relative to the whole Trojan myth. The narrative is concerned with chronological order only in respect of Homer's own epics: the chronology of the *Iliad* begins with the anger of Apollo and ends with the burial of Hektor. The mythic elements are only taken into account when they are useful for the frame of the narrative itself. Of course, if we take Hesiod's *Theogony* as the standard for Greek mythology, we might speak of a Homeric 'deviation' from the traditional narrative concerning the first ages of the world. The myth of the ages of mankind explicitly told in Hesiod (*Works and Days* 109–201), usually considered as a borrowing from Near Eastern myth (see M. L. West 1966, 1997), may rather correspond to the Homeric evidence if we believe Most (1997).

Turning to the events before the war, we know through other texts that Zeus took the form of a swan to seduce Leda, who then gave birth to Helen, Klytaimestra, and the Dioskouroi, be it from one or several eggs. We find no mention of these specific details in Homer, but Helen is sometimes called 'Zeus's daughter': she is (in rather archaic Greek) *Dios ekgegauia*, 'sprung from Zeus' (*Iliad* 3.418) or *kourē Dios aigiochoio*, 'the maid of aegis-bearing Zeus' (3.426).[8] So we may suppose that Homer does know the myth of Helen's birth but does not need to mention it explicitly, probably because it was generally known. It is not that it is suppressed by Homer in order to avoid extraordinary details, as some scholars have thought, but rather that he does not foreground magical and fantastic detail (see Griffin 1977b) or, more generally, irrational events.

The foundation of Troy was probably an important part of the myth, given the number of allusions to it in Homer. The whole genealogy of its kings is proudly uttered in Aeneas' challenge to Achilles (*Iliad* 20.215–40). First, Dardanos founded Dardania in the mountains; then he was succeeded by Erichthonios, whose name seems to imply a myth (one of birth from the Earth itself: a *chthonic* myth) parallel to the Athenian myth.[9] Next comes Tros whose name clearly points to the name of the Trojan land, *Troiē*, whereas his son's name Ilos points to the city, *Ilios* or *Ilion*; then, after Ilos, comes Laomedon, Priam's father – and Aeneas' great-grandfather (see below for the use of this genealogy in argument). The walls of Ilion (we tend, inaccurately, to call the city Troy) play an important role in the narrative, even if the war is not shown as a siege: if the enemy enters the city, it is thereby lost, as is shown by Andromache when she learns that Hektor is dead and throws her veil down (*Iliad* 22.467–72). The building of these walls of Troy by the two gods Apollo and Poseidon employed as *thētes* (serfs) by King Laomedon is told by Poseidon (*Iliad* 21.441–60), again to buttress an argument (see below). Earlier in the *Iliad* (7.452–3) we find another allusion to their building of the walls of Troy for Laomedon, again in a speech by Poseidon, where the fame of these walls is threatened by a new construction, this time by the Greeks – which Zeus encourages Poseidon to overwhelm by sea and sand after the Greeks return home (459–63).

Homer mentions the abduction of the beautiful youth Ganymede to become the wine-bearer on Olympos and the horses given as compensation (*Iliad* 20.232–5). In comparison with later poetry and literature (symposium poetry, Socratic dialogues, Hellenistic epigram, and pastoral), Homer seems as discrete about homosexual love as he is about magic.

The topography of Troy shows, amongst other landmarks, the Skaian gates and the fountains where Trojan women used to wash the linen in peacetime – and Hektor prophesies that Achilles will be killed there (*Iliad* 22.360). We also see the tomb of Ilos (the king who gave the city its name *Ilios* or *Ilion*) used in the narrative as a landmark. Thus we meet formulae (standard units of Homeric verse) such as[10]

* *para sēmati Īlou* ('by the tomb of Ilos', *Iliad* 10.415)
* *par' Īlou sēma palaiou Dardanidāo* ('by the tomb of Ilos the ancient son of Dardanos', *Iliad* 11.166)
* *epi tumbōi | Īlou Dardanidāo* ('on the tomb | of Ilos son of Dardanos', *Iliad* 11.372).

The story of Paris, son of Priam and Hekabe, which we know from later authorities (especially Apollodoros 3.12.5 §§ 147–50), is not mentioned explicitly by Homer. In this story, his mother Hekabe dreams she gives birth to a flaming torch,[11] and the seer Aisakos then interprets this as foretelling the downfall of Troy, declaring that the child will be the ruin of his homeland. But, instead of killing him, his parents decide to abandon the child, and a herdsman exposes him on Mount Ida, hoping he will die there. He is, however, suckled by a she-bear. Though Homer does not mention this story, frequent allusions[12] in the *Iliad* show that a curse is acting against Troy: Paris should have perished as a child, long before abducting Helen.

Moving now to Greece, we can start with Phthia (a district of the later Thessaly). Since the gods know that a son born of the goddess Thetis would be stronger than his father, none of them are willing to marry her.[13] Instead, they choose a mortal husband for her, Peleus. This was a famous wedding, as was the list of wedding-gifts. We know it best from Catullus 64 (mid-first century BC), but it was known long before that, and even the *Iliad* alludes to it, talking of the immortal horses given to Peleus (18.443–55) and the presence of the gods there (as mentioned by Hera at 24.62). Some later authors have the beauty contest between the three goddesses planned at this wedding. We can also see the wedding depicted as early as the sixth century BC on the François vase:[14] here we see Cheiron leading the procession of the gods, holding Peleus' hand while Thetis sits waiting inside the house.

Homer's narrative says little of Achilles' childhood: if we can trust *Iliad* 11.831–2, he was taught by 'Cheiron, the most just (*dikaiotatos*) of the Centaurs', but in *Iliad* 9, Phoinix seems to have been the main teacher. Thetis mentions twice that she nourished him so that he grew up like a young plant (*Iliad* 17.56; 18.437), but she never talks about how she tried to make him immortal, quite unlike, for instance, Apollodoros.[15] On the paternal side, we learn of Achilles' descent from Peleus, then back to Aiakos and eventually Zeus (*Iliad* 21.188–91). Patroklos confirms Achilles' ancestry by denying it, when he focuses on his disregard for the sufferings of their companions (*Iliad* 16.33–5):

> Cruel! Your father was not the horseman Peleus,
> Nor Thetis your mother – the grey sea bore you
> And the towering rocks, so sheer is your mind!

Patroklos has a history too. As Achilles sleeps, Patroklos' shade reminds Achilles of the time when he came to Peleus' court with his father Menoitios after he had killed another boy he was playing knucklebones with – alluding then to their common childlessness, games, and learning (*Iliad* 23.83–90).

The origins of the war are well known, above all the Judgement of Paris between the three goddesses, Athene, Hera, and Aphrodite. Because Paris judged Aphrodite to be most beautiful and gave her the apple she took the part of the Trojans, supported the Greeks. The *Iliad* knows this episode well enough, as can be seen from the fleeting allusion in the last book of the *Iliad*, where most of the gods pity Hektor

> But not Hera, Poseidon or the girl with blazing eyes.
> They clung to their deathless hate of sacred Troy,
> Priam and Priam's people, just as they had at first
> When Paris in all his madness launched at the war.
> He offended Athena and Hera – both goddesses.
> When they came to his shepherd's fold he favored Love
> Who dangled before his eyes the lust that loosed disaster.
>   *Iliad* 24.26–30 (tr. Fagles 1990).

Athene is the city-goddess of Troy (something the epics do not explain), as can be seen in the prayer Hektor has his mother make in Book 6. This can also be seen in the legend of the Palladion, the talismanic statue of Pallas Athene kept in Troy: as long as the statue remains in the sanctuary, the city will be safe. Nevertheless, Athene is constantly opposed to Troy, whereas Apollo is, with Aphrodite, the sole god constantly defending the 'Holy city'.[16]

Aphrodite's reward to Paris is, of course, the most beautiful woman in the world, Helen. And so it is that Paris, the guest of Menelaos in Sparta, seduces Helen, carries her away on his ships and sleeps with her for the first time on the little island of Kranaë, then takes her to Troy. This was told in the *Kypria*, and is well known in Homer (*Iliad* 3.46–51, 443–5 by Paris; 24.765–7 by Helen).[17]

Agamemnon and Menelaos now call their allies and gather the ships at Aulis,[18] but the winds and sea prevent them setting out. The seer Kalchas reveals Agamemnon must sacrifice his daughter (Iphigeneia), but Homer only refers either to the gathering at Aulis, a prodigy and a prediction by Kalchas that the siege would take ten years (*Iliad* 2.301–32); he also has Agamemnon offer Achilles his daughter 'Iphianassa' as a wife (*Iliad* 9.145, 287), where the name looks as though it may be influenced by 'Iphigeneia'. All mention of the sacrifice is omitted or avoided in Homer, though we may see an allusion in Agamemnon's

Table 2.1 Homer's allusions to the mythology of the Trojan War as presented in the Epic Cycle.

Plot	*Iliad*	*Odyssey*
Kypria		
The beginnings: the Judgement of Paris	24.26–30	
Paris abducts Helen	6.292	
Agamemnon and Menelaos call their allies and gather the task force at Aulis	2.303–4	
Achilles hidden on Skyros (whence Neoptolemos' birth)	19.326–7	11.506
Odysseus does not want to leave his young wife and son; he feigns madness, but is recognized		
The ships becalmed at Aulis (during the first, or the second, gathering of the Achaeans there – see n.19)	2.303	
The seer Kalchas prophesies that the goddess Artemis wants a sacrifice, and Agamemnon gives his daughter Iphigeneia, whence the revenge of his wife Klytaimestra	1.106–8?	
The journey: the ships leave Aulis. Philoctetes wounded by a snake and abandoned on Lemnos with his bow	2.717, 721–4	
The (nine) years of War (before the beginning of the *Iliad*): Protesilaos, the first to die	2.698, 706, 708; 15.705–6; 16.286	
Aethiopis and *Little Iliad*		
After Hektor's death, and after the end of the *Iliad*, encounters of Achilles with Penthesileia, and with Troïlos and Polyxena		
Antilochos' death, defending his father Nestor; Memnon's death, killed by Achilleus		4.187–8
Achilles shot in the mortal part of his foot by Paris	22.359–60	
The quarrel of Odysseus and Ajax over the arms of Achilles Ajax's madness		11.543–8, 24.20
Odysseus and Diomedes enter Troy and steal the Palladion		4.244–58 (indirectly)

Continued

Table 2.1 Cont'd

Plot	Iliad	Odyssey
Iliou Persis		
Odysseus devises the means of taking the city, and Epeios builds the Horse, in which the warriors hide; it is left on the beach		4.274–89, 8.492–8
Aeneas leaves the city		
Fall of Troy: death of Priam, death of Astyanax, the city razed to the ground	22.484–507, 24.731–6	
Trojan women taken as captives by the Achaeans: Andromache, Cassandra, Hekabe	6.410–32, 22.485–511, 24.725–34	
Nostoi		
The return home of the Achaean warriors		3.162–83
Agamemnon killed by Aigisthos and Klytaimestra		1.35–40, 3.262–322, 4.512–37, 11.397–439, 24.20.
Orestes' revenge		1.298–300, 11.459–61?
Ajax, son of Oïleus, dies after offending Athene and the gods		4.499–510.
Menelaos goes to Egypt with Helen		3.318–22, 4.83, 228–32, 352–9, 581
Telegony		
Odysseus killed by Telegonos, his son by Circe		

denunciation of the seer Kalchas for 'never saying anything good' (*Iliad* 1.106–8), a thought which also occurred to ancient commentators.[19]

At about this time in the legend, Thetis has hidden Achilles on the island of Skyros, at the court of its king, Lykomedes. No mention of this occurs in Homer, but his son Neoptolemos, who is notably living on Skyros, is important in Achilles' mind.[20]

Presently, during the journey from Aulis to Troy, the hero Philoktetes is bitten by a snake; his infected wound produces an unbearable smell, and his companions abandon him on the desert island of Lemnos with his bow. Though we know this mainly from Sophocles' play *Philoktetes*, this story is already known to Homer, who takes the trouble to account for the hero's absence in the 'Catalogue of Ships' (*Iliad* 2.721–5).

The Trojan War Itself

The war is already in its tenth year when the *Iliad* begins. We have no traditional narrative of the previous years, only allusions to a few prominent events. Protesilaos ('first of the army') was the first man in the Greek army to die; we do not know how, but his ship is mentioned as a landmark in the fighting (*Iliad* 15.705–6; 16.286). The Achaians sack several towns in the vicinity, kill numerous warriors, share out spoils, and take women and children away as slaves. Chryse is where Agamemnon took Chryseis ('she of Chryse', the priest Chryses' daughter); and Thebes Hypoplakiē ('beneath Mount Plakos') is where Andromache's father, king Eëtion, was killed by Achilles together with her seven brothers (*Iliad* 6.414–18). Lesbos and Syros are the scene for the capture of Diomēdē and Iphis, who are given to Achilles and Patroklos respectively (*Iliad* 9.664–8). And it is at Lyrnessos on Lesbos that Achilles takes Briseis (*Iliad* 19.60), according to Homer the daughter of 'Briseus' (*Iliad* 1.392).[21]

After the *Iliad* ends, Antilochos will be killed defending his father Nestor, who recalls this fight when talking to Telemachos (*Odyssey* 3.103–12). The killer turns out to have been Memnon, son of Eos (Dawn).[22] The Aithiopis *Aithiopis* told this episode and also told of Memnon's death at the hands of Achilles, and Eos' mourning. Antilochos is still living in the period told by the *Iliad*, and indeed he is seen participating in the chariot-race in the games for Patroklos in Book 23, following the instructions Nestor gives him.

Achilles will be killed by an arrow fired by Paris – at the mortal part of his foot according to later tradition.[23] This death at Paris' hands is of course not part of the *Iliad*'s narrative, but it is prophesied by Hektor at *Iliad* 22.359–60, and Hektor even locates the scene precisely, at the Skaian gate. The quarrel over Achilles' arms and the madness of Ajax, known through a number of Greek and Latin texts since Sophocles, is alluded to in the Nekuia (*Odyssey* 11.543–67), and Achilles may be found addressing Ajax in the Underworld in the 'second Nekuia' (*Odyssey* 24.20).

There are several prophecies of which the Trojans and the Achaians are aware concerning the fall of Troy. First, it needs Philoktetes to be there with his bow; secondly it needs the Palladion, the statue of Athene which had once fallen from the sky, or rather had fallen from Zeus,[24] to be removed from the sanctuary it was kept in, away from mortal sight. We know from later texts that Odysseus and Diomedes went together inside Troy and stole it, with some details which are not to Odysseus' credit. Neither the *Iliad* nor the *Odyssey* mention this, but in the *Odyssey*, Helen tells of an expedition by

Odysseus disguised as a beggar, in which she alone recognized him and talked with him about the future (4.244–58).[25] The incident also seems to be reflected by the spying mission of Odysseus and Diomedes in *Iliad* 10, the *Doloneia*.[26]

Better known is the stratagem for taking Troy, the Wooden Horse. It is an idea of Odysseus', executed by the craftsman Epeios. Two different passages in the *Odyssey* evoke this episode: in one Menelaos tells the story of how the Achaians inside the horse hear Helen imitating their wives' voices, but Odysseus prevents them from going out (4.274–89); in the other Demodokos sings the episode (8.492–8). What follows is the Sack of Troy, not told in the *Iliad*, of course, but in the lost *Iliou Persis* ('Sack of Troy'). Nevertheless, several episodes are anticipated in the *Iliad*: Astyanax' fate is foreseen in the meeting between Hektor and Andromache on the walls of Troy, in *Iliad* 6, and in Andromache's words of mourning (22.485–500; 24.726–45). The latter reference also anticipates the Astyanax being cast from the walls of Troy. And other moments are recalled in the *Odyssey* (22.484–507; 24.731–6).[27]

Turning now to the Returns (*Nostoi*) of the Greeks, the *Odyssey* alludes several times to Agamemnon's tragic return and Orestes' vengeance (1.35–41, 298–300; 3.234–8; 4.512–37; 11.397–439, 459–61; 24.20). Nestor's return is told in Book 3; and Menelaos' journey with Helen to Egypt receives extensive treatment in Book 4, where we also learn that Ajax, son of Oïleus, died because he offended the gods (*Odyssey* 4.449–510).

Other Myths

Apart from the Trojan War and the events following it, we see many allusions to other myths in Homer. From Theban material, the Labdakids, Oedipus and his sons are mentioned briefly. We hear for instance of Oedipus marrying his mother (*Odyssey* 11.271–80) and his funeral games (*Iliad* 23.679–80).[28] We know about Tydeus at Thebes both before the expedition of the Seven against Thebes and during that siege (*Iliad* 4.371–87, 399; 10.285–90). At Kalydon in Aitolia, the monstrous boar sent by Artemis, the hunt, and the hero Meleager are evoked briefly at *Iliad* 2.640–2, and more extensively by Phoinix in Book 9 (see below). No woman is mentioned as present at the hunt, though Atalanta (later mentioned by Ovid) is already seen on the frieze of the François Vase, with her name clearly legible alongside.

Herakles is probably Homer's single-most referenced non-Trojan hero, from his birth to his labours and other adventures, such as his quest for the 'dog of Hades' (*Iliad* 8.366–9). At *Iliad* 19.91–129 a rather long tale recalls how Zeus was mislead by Hera and Atē, when Alkmene was about to give birth to Herakles. Zeus swore that the baby born would be king and

Hera therefore caused Eurystheus' birth to take place ahead of Herakles'. His death, through the will of Zeus, is alluded to at *Iliad* 18.116–18. His labours are alluded to in *Iliad* 8.363 ('the *athla* for Eurystheus') and the mention of a man that Eurystheus used as a messenger to him may well allude to them (15.635), as has been thought since ancient times and translations often add the word *labours* (for instance, Fagles 1990). Indeed, it has been thought that the episode refers to the scene where Eurystheus hides in a jar (Gantz 1993:415). Above all, the way his offspring Tlepolemos addresses the Lykian ally of the Trojans, Sarpedon, said to be the son of Zeus, shows he was actually a model for Homer's heroes:[29]

> 'Why, think what they say of mighty Herakles–
> there was a man, my father,
> that dauntless, furious spirit, that lionheart ...'
> 5.638–9 (tr. Fagles 1990)

Tlepolemos proceeds to recount Herakles' expedition against Laomedon's Troy (several generations earlier if we follow Aeneas' account of his own noble descent), showing that the War between Achaians and Trojans is a quasi-hereditary one, or that the noble sons are walking in their fathers' footsteps. The same expedition is visible at *Iliad* 20.145 where Homer mentions Herakles' wall. Meanwhile, the *Odyssey* recalls through the history of Eurytos' bow the siege of Oichalia – mentioned briefly when Odysseus boasts of his prowess at the bow (8.224). But it also appears in detail when the narrator recalls how Eurytos' bow came into Odysseus' hands via his son Iphitos (*Odyssey* 21.22–38). It is true that Herakles is not at his best in this passage, since he is said to have killed the man he had welcomed as a guest in his home, a *xenos*, and to have kept the mares Iphitos came to reclaim; but it does also mention Herakles' 'great deeds' (21.26).

Homer presents many details from the gods' 'biographies'. For instance, Lykourgos pursues the young Dionysos and his nurses on Mount Nysa (*Iliad* 6.130–43), and Dionysos takes refuge with Thetis in her sea cave; Lykourgos' punishment is to be blinded. Another god received and nursed by Thetis is Hephaistos, whom his mother Hera had thrown from Olympos (*Iliad* 18.394–408); this will entitle Thetis to ask him to forge new arms for her son. The whole action of the *Iliad* is set in motion by the debt Zeus owes to the goddess Thetis since she helped him against the other gods – and by Hera's wrath.[30]

In the *Odyssey*, to understand the difficulties faced by Odysseus in his return we need to know about Poseidon's anger, which is justified by Polyphemus' curse on Odysseus at the end of *Odyssey* 9. We will see further instances as we analyse the different uses of myth in Homer.

Uses of Myth in Homer

Myth as knowledge of the world: the Homeric encyclopedia

The formulaic style of the Epics was well suited to deliver a kind of encyclopedic knowledge in various fields.[31] This knowledge seems to depend on techniques of remembering and often occurs in form of catalogues:[32]

Geography

Spatial knowledge of the Aegean islands and the sea routes from Greece to Troy in the *Iliad*; routes to the Ionian Islands and visits to new worlds in the *Odyssey*.[33] Knowledge of mountains (*Iliad* 14 225–30; *Odyssey* 6.102–8: Artemis in the mountains). The 'Catalogue of Ships' (*Iliad* 2.441–760) provides a sort of statement of the geography and population of Greece in the Geometric period.

Products and properties

Knowledge of the various products, metals, plants, and of technologies, for example, 'Alybe, where silver originated' (Iliad 2.857); the skill of Maionian and Karian women in colouring ivory with purple (used as a simile for blood on skin, Iliad 4.141–5); shipbuilding (*Odyssey* 5.233–61).[34]

Meteorology and climate

Meteorological and practical knowledge for seamen: where one can expect storms (Cape Maleia was known as especially dangerous: *Odyssey* 3.287; 4.514; 9.80; 19.387; Homeric *Hymn to Apollo* 409). Myths often give explanations for natural phenomena, day and night, the seasons of year, storms and other extraordinary events (*Odyssey*, e.g., 3.320–2; 5.269–322; 365–493; 10.48, 86; 12.405–9, 415–16).

Ethnography

The *Odyssey* almost serves as a guide to the world in antiquity,[35] though some strange absences may be noted. There are few mentions of Crete, though Homer mentions numerous towns: its king, Idomeneus, is not amongst the greatest heroes in the *Iliad*; the labyrinth built by Daidalos at Knossos is mentioned at *Iliad* 18.590–3. Crete is most used as a backcloth for Odysseus' lying tales and false identities (especially *Odyssey* 19.172–84).[36]

Cosmology

In addition to the cosmological passages mentioned at the beginning of this chapter, the Shield of Achilles (*Iliad* 18) shows how the Greeks in Homer's time imagined the sun, the stars, and the constellations in the middle of the cosmos, thought of as a circle limited by the Okeanos (*Iliad* 18.483–9).[37] But before this, we see Thetis enter Hephaistos' house, which he built himself with a gold-nailed vault: this, then, is a rounded and enterable image of the cosmos, where the shield seems more like a flat map. Homer also alludes to cosmogonies: we saw earlier how Hera invokes the quarrels of Okeanos and Tethys as an excuse for her journey; other passages refer to a war between the gods and the Giants, and a war between the Centaurs and the Lapiths.

To this list we may add the whole area of theology and politics on Olympos.[38] Because he is close to the gods through the medium of the Muses, the poet knows much more about gods than humans usually do. Sometimes he alludes to words used by the gods, fragments maybe of a whole language.[39] And instead of eating and drinking like humans, it is well known that they have *nektar* and *ambrosia*. Their physiology is different too: the passage where Aphrodite is wounded by Diomedes reveals they have *ichor* in their veins, not blood (*Iliad* 5.339–40, 416).

However, the most visible part of theological knowledge concerns the powers of the gods. The Olympian gods seized power from the Titans, and they once shared out the world, as we saw above between Zeus, Poseidon, and Hades. Other versions show a number of the gods involved in the distribution.[40] Amongst the other gods, we sometimes see allusions to their particular power and honours, and to the quarrels that derive from them: Athene, Poseidon, Apollo, Artemis, and Hera, take part in the battle at Troy, though Zeus strictly forbids it. The loves of the gods form an important part of mythology, and a few allusions are known in Homer, though he does not seem particularly to appreciate this genre: Zeus himself lists a catalogue of women whom he loved (Ixion's wife, Danaē, the daughter of Phoinix, Semele, Alkmene, Demeter, and Leto) as an argument for his wife Hera to have sex with him, since he never before felt such a strong erotic desire (*Iliad* 14.317–27). It is interesting that Leda is not mentioned here, despite Helen's importance in the *Iliad*.

Male gods are known as seducers, sowing the world with their glorious offspring. The goddesses have a less happy fate. Thetis does not seem to have stayed long in Peleus' house in Phthia, since the *Iliad* shows her living with her sisters the Nereids in sea caves. In *Odyssey* 5.118–27 another goddess, Kalypso complains about the female lot, when she learns from Hermes that she must allow Odysseus to return to Ithaca, and lists various instances of goddesses who slept with a mortal without obtaining lasting happiness – Eos with Orion, Demeter with Iasion – which constitutes an interesting parallel to the Homeric *Hymn to Aphrodite*, where Aphrodite herself tells Anchises how Zeus' abduction of Ganymede (202–6) contrasts with the loves of the goddesses, whose paradigm is provided by the case of Eos (Dawn) and Tithonos (218–38): she obtained immortality for him but not eternal youth.

Apart from love affairs, the gods also experience some trouble with human beings: at *Iliad* 5.370–417, Aphrodite goes to her mother Dione (another difference from Hesiod's *Theogony*) to complain about her wounding by Diomedes. Her divine mother, as a consolation, then tells a catalogue of other occasions where the gods have suffered wounds at the hands of mortals: Ares from Otos and Ephialtes, Hera from 'Amphitryon's son' (Herakles), Hades also from Herakles, but this time called the son of Zeus.

Myth as paradigm

Myth is frequently used, mainly in speeches, as a 'paradigm' (example) in the context of an argument: since this or that event in myth turned out in a particular way, so the addressee should take care to behave in the same/opposite way as the comparable figure in the myth.[41]

Thus, in *Iliad* 9, Phoinix presents Achilles with Meleager as a model for relenting in one's anger; Achilles is not swayed by this and remains wrathful and rejects the conciliation proposed by the embassy.[42] Later, in *Iliad* 24, Priam presents Achilles with Niobe as a model to justify eating despite his sorrow (somewhat oddly, see CH. 6, pp. 127–9). We saw above how Kalypso's catalogue of goddesses in love helps her to accept her female condition, and how Dione's list of wounded gods seeks to console Aphrodite. There are also several instances of Herakles being used as a model (particularly for Tlepolemos). In the *Odyssey*, Penelope uses Aēdon ('Nightingale')[43] as a model for her nights passed in weeping. Aēdon in myth mourns for the son Itylos whom she killed through *atē* (error, or possibly madness). Penelope is mourning for her husband, absent for twenty years, but maybe she feels guilty about her own son Telemachos, to whom she cannot give the protection against the suitors that he needs.

In *Odyssey* 21 (295–304), when the suitor Antinoös gives the parallel of the Centaurs and their leader Eurytion, who was misled by wine and killed his host Peirithoös, the argument seems to have a meaning quite contrary to its aim: the suitors are, after all, eating and drinking Odysseus' wealth (Edmunds 1993: 37–8). Is this parallel put ironically in the mouth of Antinoös?[44]

Myth enhancing character

Homeric poetry seems also to use myth to amplify character: so Diomedes' glory (*kleos*) is enhanced by the magnificent deeds of his father Tydeus, recalled by himself (*Iliad* 10.285–94) and by other characters who knew him or know about him – such as Agamemnon, who did not, he says, actually meet him (4.370–400), or Athene (5.801–13), who did.

Nestor's numerous complaints about the fading of his youth and vigour lead to narratives of his glorious past, and in his own memory he becomes a hero of a former generation (*Iliad* 1.262–70; 4.319–20; 7.134–60; 11.671–803).[45] Heroes usually die young, as some do in the *Iliad* itself – Sarpedon, Zeus' son, at the hands of Patroklos, Patroklos at the hands of Hektor, Hektor at the hands of Achilles. And we all know that Achilles will die soon after he kills Hektor, as on various occasions Patroklos, his horse Xanthos, his mother Thetis, and the dying Hektor all predict and remind him. Nestor, on the other hand, has exceptionally survived his own time for being a hero; furthermore, he survives his own son Antilochos, as can be seen from his nostalgia in front of Telemachos in *Odyssey* 3 and from the words there of his son Peisistratos.

Odysseus will finally narrate his own glorious past, to the Phaiakes on Scheria and to his family in Ithaka, or hear it narrated to him by an *aoidos* (bard). He and Nestor form the exceptions to the rule that the hero does not survive his glorious deeds to narrate them; on the contrary, his death is the condition for those deeds to become the strange thing we were looking for, myth. Thus, the narrator shows Achilles, the 'best of the Achaians', in front of a silent and meditative Patroklos, singing the 'deeds of heroes' (*Iliad* 9.189) – past deeds, of course, not his own. And Hektor's last wish is that future generations will hear about his actions and glorious fighting and death (*Iliad* 22.304–5).[46]

Though the main characters are not presented as mythical in the narrative, the density of allusion in the Epics tends to insert them in a general mythical frame: Achilles particularly already shows mythical features in the *Iliad*; for instance, when the poet tells us first in Book 16 that Patroklos does not take the ash-spear Cheiron gave once to Peleus, then in Book 19 that Achilles takes it, with a pair of nearly identical lines (Létoublon 2001: 26, and 2007: 223–4). The allusion to Cheiron and Mount Pelion calls to the audience's mind the memory of the mythical education of Achilles in the mountain caves by the Centaur. And the whole mythical biography comes to mind in the *Odyssey* when Odysseus meets in the Underworld with Achilles' shadow asking for news of his father Peleus and his son Neoptolemos.

Opposite trends in the study of Homer, neoanalysis (concerned with the influence of predecessors on Homer) and the study of oral poetry (concerned with a constant re-creation of epic, anew, by the improvisation of the oral performer), may perhaps be profitably combined in the case of myth. The characters in Homer can be viewed as built on an older *mythical* frame but set in a story that did not belong to this traditional frame, and in some cases either totally invented or at least inflated far beyond their primitive form. So, for instance, it has been suggested in the neoanalytic school that Patroklos and even Hektor could be characters newly invented for the *Iliad* (see CH. 22 n. 9). This cannot be absolutely proved, but several details suggest it. If so, Homer could prove a 'deviant' poet in comparison, maybe, with the poets of the lost Epic Cycle.

Myth thus has a typically epic effect since it models human beings into heroes by giving them a kind of traditional aura. Nagy (2007: 62–3) speaks of the poetic function of similes: the volume of mythical allusions in both the *Iliad* and *Odyssey* enhances this poetic function still more.

The Complexity of Myth

We may conclude by observing that the origins of the Trojan War can act as a model of how mythical tales unfold the complexity of the world we live in. What gave rise to the war, after all? At first sight, the war begins with Menelaos asking Helen's former suitors to form an army against Paris the abductor of Helen. But if we believe the story of the Judgement of Paris, the apple thrown by Eris could be the actual cause of the war. Or is it the flame Hekabe saw in her dream before Paris's birth? Or else the egg laid down by Leda giving birth to Helen and Klytaimestra? Later texts seem to compete in giving several explanations, and thus seem to recognize that none of them constitute the main cause of the conflict – except perhaps that war is the natural condition of mankind.[47]

FURTHER READING

Translations

Amongst the many English translations of Homer's works, those of Richmond Lattimore and Robert Fagles may be particularly recommended: R. Lattimore, *The Iliad of Homer* (Chicago 1951); *The Odyssey of Homer* (New York 1967); R. Fagles, *The Iliad* (New York 1990); *The Odyssey* (New York 1996). For the summaries of the cyclic epics and the fragments of those poems and of other epics, see M. L. West, *Greek Epic Fragments* [Loeb Classical Library] (Cambridge MA 2003).

The text in detail

For information about the text in detail, we have at our disposal a rich variety of commentaries: For the *Iliad*, G. S. Kirk (ed.) *Commentary on the Iliad*, 6 vols (Cambridge): Kirk 1985, Kirk 1990, Hainsworth 1993, Janko 1992; Edwards 1991; Richardson 1993. For the *Odyssey*, A. Heubeck, S. West, J. B. Hainsworth (eds): *A Commentary on Homer's Odyssey* 1 (Oxford 1988); A. Heubeck and A. Hoekstra (eds) *A Commentary on Homer's Odyssey* 2 (Oxford 1989); *A Commentary on Homer's Odyssey* 3 (Oxford 1990). And for a narratology of the *Odyssey*, de Jong 2001.

Myth

For myth in general and as it affects Homer, see Dowden (1992); Edmunds (1990, 1993, 1997); Nagy (1990); Gantz; Richir (1998); Hansen (2002); Hurst and Létoublon (2002); Létoublon (2004); Alaux and Létoublon (2005). On the *nature of the epic genre*, see Ford (1997), and J. M. Foley (2005).

On *Relations between Greek religion and myths* see Ogden (2007, especially Dowden (41–55), Larson (56–70), and Ekroth (100–14)).

For *Homer* and his authorial methods, see Kakridis 1949, 1971; Kullmann 1981, 1992; Dowden 1996; Létoublon 2001, Minchin 2001. On the *Iliad* specifically: Kullmann 1960; Willcock 1964, 1977; Nagy 1979; 1992; Schein 1984; Edwards 1987; Slatkin 1991; Cairns 2001. On the *Odyssey*: Germain 1954; Stanford 1968; Clay 1983; M. Katz 1991; Peradotto 1991; Felson-Rubin 1993; Murnaghan 1987; Schein 1996, 2002; Danek 1998; Dougherty 2001; Létoublon 2006. On the Epic Cycle: Severyns 1928; Burgess 2001; 2005.

On the *Trojan War*: Scherer 1963, Andersen 1990, and Hertel in this volume (CH. 2). For Homer as *oral poetry*, and, for example, *formulae*, we may turn to M. Parry 1971; Lord 1960, 1991, 1995; Havelock 1963; J. M. Foley 1991, 1997; P. W. Rose 1992; Edwards 1997; Russo 1997.

For *Near Eastern parallels and influences*: Walcot 1966, Burkert 1992 (discussed in Haubold 2002), M. L. West 1997, and CHS 19 and 20 in the present volume; likewise CH. 18 for the *Indo-European* dimension.

NOTES

1. By 'Homer' I mean simply the poet or poets of the *Iliad* and *Odyssey*.
2. The Linear B tablets of the Mycenaean age are in no sense literary and, apart from presenting us with certain names of gods or heroes, contain no mythological matter. Otherwise Homer's epics are the oldest Greek text altogether, provided we follow the traditional chronology rather than, for instance, M. L. West (1966: 41; see also 1995).
3. On the chronology of the war, see *Iliad* 2.134 ('nine years of great Zeus have gone'), 2.295, and cf. Kalchas' prophecy at 326–9.
4. Cf. *Iliad* 9.347 with the scholia ad loc.
5. See also works of Willcock, Kullmann, Andersen, Schein, Danek, and Burgess cited in the reference section.
6. See Gantz (48–51).
7. Walcot (1966), Burkert (1992), Most (1997), M. L. West (1997), Haubold (2002: 1–19), Woodard (2007: 92–104).
8. See also *Odyssey* 23.218.
9. See Alaux and Létoublon (2005).
10. Cf. *par' Ῑlou Mermeridāo* ('from Ilos son of Mermeros', *Odyssey* 1.259). Another grave, this time anonymous, is also used as a landmark at *Iliad* 23.331.
11. Scholiast D on *Iliad* 3.325; Hyginus, *Fabula* 91.

12. Scholiast D on *Iliad* 3.325 and Apollodoros 3.12.5 Section 148 place Hekabe's dream before his birth; Helen's or Hektor's formulas like 3.428 'I wish you had died there and then' (also 7.390, 24.764), see also the vocative *Dyspari* ('mis-Paris') used by Hektor addressing his brother in Il. 3.39 and 13.769). Sophocles and Euripides both wrote tragedies called *Alexandros*, referring to Hekabe's dream and to the baby abandoned on Mount Ida and nourished by an animal.

13. See Slatkin's argumentation with the evidence from Pindar, *Isthmian* 8.29–38 and [Aeschylus], *Prometheus* 755–8: Slatkin (1991: 70–8).

14. This vase, Florence 4209, is copiously illustrated on the web (search for: Francois vase).

15. Apollodoros, *Library* 3.13.6; on Achilles' diet as a baby, see Hanson (2003: 187–8).

16. Scully (1990: 16–40).

17. For the Judgement of Paris, see Gantz (567–71); the abduction of Helen, 571–6.

18. Homer mentions only one mobilization at Aulis, whereas later texts (*Kypria* and *Ehoiai*) seem to imply that Iphigeneia's sacrifice occurred during a second stay there (Gantz 582–8).

19. Scholiast on *Iliad* 1.108.

20. *Iliad* 19.326–7; see also *Odyssey* 11.506–9. Apollodoros resumes the anecdote in *Library* 3.13.6. The tradition of Achilles' being dressed as a girl and Odysseus' cunning and dramatic uncovering of his identity may be a later story; it certainly appealed to painters.

21. Zarker (1965: 110–14); Taplin (1986: 15–19), and P.V. Jones (1995: 101–11). [Maybe originally she had been the 'maid of Brise', or Brēsē, a promontory on Lesbos with a temple of Dionysos Brisaios, see Wilamowitz (1916: 178 n. 1); Androtion *FGrH* 324 F56; Stephen of Byzantium s.v. Brisa. KD]

22. *Odyssey* 4.187–8.

23. The first allusions to Achilles' tendon seem to occur in Hyginus *Fabula* (107) and Statius *Achilleid* (1.133–4); Apollodoros refers rather vaguely to his foot (*Epitome* 5.3): Gantz (625–8).

24. The statue is qualified in both Apollodoros and Dionysios of Halikarnassos as *diipetes* – 'Zeus-fallen', with the name Zeus apparently in the dative as though he had *caused* it to fall.

25. See Heubeck and West (1988) on the passage: 'she held Odysseus at her mercy, but did not betray him because she had come to see the folly of her desertion and longed for a Greek victory.'

26. As explored by Dowden (2010: 112–14).

27. On allusions in the *Iliad*, see the synthesis given by Cairns (2001: esp. 38–43, and particularly, on Astyanax's fate, 41 with n. 148).

28. See Edmunds (1985: 7, 20).

29. See Galinski (1972: 9–22) (on the 'Archaic Hero') for a different view.

30. See Slatkin (1991: 53–84).

31. See Havelock (1963: 134–44). For techniques of memory, see Minchin (2001: 11–31).

32. On catalogues as a form of communication, see Perceau (2002).

33. See Germain (1954), C. Segal (1994), Malkin (1998), Dougherty (2001).

34. On shipbuilding and songbuilding, see Dougherty (2001: 27–37).

35. Again, Dougherty (2001: 27–37).

36. See Murnaghan (1987); Peradotto (1991).

37. See Létoublon (1999) with bibliography.

38. See the title of Clay (1997a, *The Politics of Olympus. Form and Meaning in the Major Homeric Hymns*).

39. Létoublon (1985).

40. *Iliad* 15.185–93, Cairns (2001: 37).

41. The classic study is Willcock (1964, 1977). See also Nagy (1992 and 2007: 63–6).

42. On the role of anger in the plot of the *Iliad*, see Muellner (1996: 94–175).

43. Or *aēdon* ('a nightingale') – see Létoublon (2004: 83) on this ambiguity.

44. For ironic use of features of the tradition in the *Odyssey*, cf. the reversed similes analysed by H. Foley (1978) and the discussion of Felson and Slatkin (2004: 91–114).

45. Cf. Dickson (1995: 10–20) on this extraordinary longevity.

46. Cf. Vernant (1991: 50) and the whole chapter.

47. [Cf. Thomas Hobbes, *Leviathan*, ch. 13. KD].

CHAPTER THREE

Telling the Mythology: From Hesiod to the Fifth Century

Ken Dowden

Introduction: Mythology and Mythography

'Greek mythology' can be seen as a collection of stories ('myths') that can be presented alphabetically in a dictionary, or – remarkably – that can be told from the beginning (the origin of the gods) to the end (the Trojan War and its aftermath) as though it was a history. To write a body of mythology, especially in this continuous story mode, is to be a 'mythographer', and what a mythographer engages in, not unnaturally, is 'mythography'. This chapter is about the origins of mythography and its development first in verse and then in prose up to the classical period of Greece. This activity served to record tradition every bit as much as history finally did; indeed, history was something that emerged from mythography. Tellings of myth, too, could be regarded as true or false, as authorized or not, as making sense or not. The Muses that appeared to Hesiod (so he tells us in the proem to his *Theogony*) told him:

> We know how to pile up falsehoods that look genuine;
> But we know when we wish how to utter truths.
> (Hesiod, *Theogony* 27–8)

Myths have their own sense of authority.

A Companion to Greek Mythology, First Edition. Edited by Ken Dowden and Niall Livingstone.
© 2014 John Wiley & Sons Ltd. Published 2014 by John Wiley & Sons Ltd.

Hesiod and 'Hesiod' (seventh–sixth centuries BC)

Where each god was born from – whether they always existed, all of them, and what they were like in appearance, was not known until, one might put it, yesterday or the day before. Hesiod and Homer were I think 400 years older than me, no more than that. They are the ones who created the theogony for the Greeks, gave the gods their titles, distinguished their roles and skills, and indicated their appearance. (Herodotos, *Histories* 2.53)

This is a statement of a fifth-century BC man. For him, there is a fairly definite view of the gods, which is a significant part of mythology, and it was Homer and Hesiod – who in our chronology were composing their works not much earlier than 700 BC, if at all – who created this authoritative view. The truth was not quite like this and Hesiod, like Homer, was part of a longstanding and continuously evolving tradition of poetic creativity, one which had vanished by Herodotos' times.

The epic tradition that was embodied in the works of Homer and the cyclic poets, as we saw in CH. 2, was only part of the story, if a very influential one. Its purpose was to recount heroic mythology, centring on wars (the Trojan War and the wars against Thebes) or on other heroic exploits (the voyage of Argo, possibly cattle-raiding stories, and difficult returns like that of Odysseus) and, in a different register, the exploits of superheroes such as Herakles and presently Theseus.

Hesiod (c. 700 BC) is known for two works which are believed to be genuine (for the most part) and have survived complete; but there is also a plethora of works which are not genuine but go under his name (so they are by 'Pseudo-Hesiod', or are noncommittally 'Hesiodic'). Of these mostly only fragments survive, though rather a lot of them, given the importance of this body of literature (mainly of the seventh–sixth centuries BC) to later tradition. 'Hesiod', in this wide sense, is the foundation of Greek mythology as we know it, much more so than Homer. Hesiod often seems to *tell* the mythology, where Homer assumes you already know it and composes a descant on it.

The two complete poems are the *Theogony* and the *Works and Days*. Both are highly individual compositions, and both go well beyond plain statements of authentic mythology. They are also fashionable for their day, and behind the façade of a righteous, sometimes grumpy, narrator lies an author drawing on the resources of Near Eastern mythology and poetic forms, as we can see in more detail in CH. 19.

A theogony is an account of the *gods* (*theoi* in Greek) and how they were *begotten* or *came into existence* (the Greek root is *gon-*). Hesiod presents his *Theogony* as the sort of performed tribute to the gods (*hymnos*) that the Muses themselves sing (*Theogony* 11–21); and it is they who accredit him to sing it too. The gods may be described as 'the holy race of immortals who always exist' (21, 105, and cf. 33) but all the same, Hesiod will tell (106) how they were sprung ultimately from Earth (Ge) and Heaven (Ouranos), and how they divided up their roles (112), the act which Herodotos (above) trans-ferred to Hesiod himself. There is thus, from the beginnings of theogonies in Greece, a contradiction between the eternity of the gods and the myths of their coming into existence, one which will eventually even encompass Plato's own myth of the creation in the *Timaios* (see CH. 9) and would raise the issue for later interpreters (such as Plutarch) of whether Plato had meant the crea-tion to be in time or whether it was a way of expressing views about the world and its dependency on the divine.

As Hesiod reaches for the beginnings of the divine, and for the beginnings of our own universe, this pre-world is populated very much by personifica-tions (116–46) – by the Gap (*Chaos*) from which the Darkness (*Erebos*) and Night (*Nyx*) first sprang, and by Night's children Ether (*Aither*, the bright upper air) and Day (*Hemera*). We meet Earth, Heaven, and the primal force of Love too. Some of this relates to Near Eastern conceptions which make their appearance also in Genesis 1 (cf. CH. 19). As proliferation becomes pos-sible, now collective groups arise – mountains, and nymphs to go with them; Titans, and Kyklopes (to forge Zeus's thunderbolt; no mention of Polyphemos and Odysseus at this cosmic level – that may be a distinctive, and wilful, crea-tion of Homer's). The plot is now sufficiently developed for tensions to set in. The monstrous Hundred-Handers, loathed by their father Heaven, are buried in the Earth, in effect being *un*-born. Earth in revenge makes the great ada-mant sickle which the youngest Titan, Kronos, agrees to wield, and Earth and Heaven are separated by the castration of his father Heaven, the final separa-tion of Heaven and Earth, but also a terrible act which would send shock-waves through later interpreters of Greek mythology.

The *Theogony* is a work very rich in proper names of divine beings and con-stantly tempts those so disposed to draw family trees connecting all these fig-ures. But the key point of the work is to celebrate the victory of Zeus and the gods who live on Olympos. Zeus overthrows Kronos and the Titans; Zeus becomes distant from men because Prometheus' attempt to help man back-fires; the institution of sacrifice is explained (535–69); and Zeus has Hephaistos create woman to be a bane to men. Together with his fellow Olympians he fights the Titans (the 'Titanomachy', 617–735), wielding awesome lightning and thunder. The Titans are cast into the depths of Tartaros and locked up there. And finally (820–80), he defeats one last monster, Typhon, an emblem-atic compound of horror and confusions.

From this point, the *Theogony* goes downhill. The new regime is established and the wives and offspring of the gods are briefly recounted (886–929), though the style of the poem seems by now to be wandering from that of the real Hesiod. Suddenly, there is a transition (963–8) to present goddesses and their liaisons with mortal men (969–1018). But the *Theogony* ends with another transition (1019–22) – to a highly significant work of which Hesiod, however, is agreed not to be the author, whose function it is to tell of liaisons of gods with mortal women. This large-scale work bears the title *Catalogue of Women*, though ancient writers often referred to it as the *Ehoiai*, the 'Or-likes', from the formula that introduced each named women:

> Or like her in Phthia with the beauty of the Graces,
> she who dwelt by the waters of the Peneios, Kyrene.
> (Pseudo-Hesiod, *Catalogue of Women*
> F 215 MW (F 158 Most))

It is difficult at first to envisage the scale of this lost work, or indeed its significance. But, looking at the fragments, it becomes clear that a very large portion of Greek mythology was to be found here and that its organizational principles may have been defining for Greek mythology as we know it. It might seem that a work where every incident arose from a mortal woman who was impregnated by a particular god would be miscellaneous and episodic. And it does give the impression (F 1 MW/Most) of being organized god by god, much like *Theogony* 886–929, though on a huge scale. But in fact the *Catalogue* seems to have proceeded region by region, descent group by descent group. And its whole principle of organization, and indeed its contents, are generally thought to be mirrored in a text that does survive and is much used by modern students of mythology, the *Library* of Apollodoros (of which more at the end of this chapter). In turn, then, Apollodoros underpins most modern continuous (as opposed to alphabetical) accounts, such as that of Robert Graves.

We cannot know on what earlier work the perhaps mid-seventh century BC *Catalogue of Women* was based, though it is suggestive that Homer includes a listing of women in Hades for Odysseus to witness (*Odyssey* 11.225–329), perhaps in tribute to a predecessor of this work. Mythology must originally have been told on an area, or family, basis, not least because the systems of mythology emerge from the heritage of particular areas of Greece and can only have been combined by poets travelling from area to area and producing compromises and syntheses. The end of the geometric period and beginning of the archaic age was one in which travel and trade were vibrant, and systematic multiregional mythologies must by this point have been long in existence. But the *Catalogue of Women*, with its 'Or-like' approach, became the definitive collection of the national mythology. It is a tragedy that it does not survive intact. Glenn Most speaks with justice of 'an idiosyncratic, original work of art' and of a 'human counterpart to Hesiod's *Theogony*'.[1]

Table 3.1 Ps.-Hesiod, *Catalogue of Women* (following Most (2006: lii–liii)).

Bk	Contents	Region	= Section (Table 3.6) of Apollodoros
1	Descendants of Deukalion, Hellen, Aiolos	north Greece	B
2	Aiolids (end)	north Greece	B
	Descendants of Inachos	Argolid	C
3–4	Descendants of Agenor	Crete; Thebes	D
	Descendants of Pelasgos	Arkadia	E
	Atlas' daughters: the Pleiades	Arkadia; Troy; Thebes	E, F, D
	Pelops and his descendants; Herakles	Argolid	I, C
	Asopos and offspring; Peleus	uncertain; Aigina;	G
	Kekropids and Erechtheids	Phthia Athens	H
5	Suitors of Helen; Zeus's plans for the Trojan War		I

The *Catalogue* extended over five books – a long follow-up to the *Theogony* in just one book, but nowhere near an *Iliad* with twenty-four. Its contents can be reconstructed given that they seem to have determined the design of Apollodoros' *Library of Greek Mythology* (see Conclusion in this chapter). So, as reconstructed by Most,[2] its material was distributed as in Table 3.1. Key figures originate the mythology for particular sections: so, for instance, Aiolos (eponym of the Aiolian Greeks) drives much of Book 2, and 'Aiolids' are his descendants.

Though the first four books trace genealogies, the fifth book is the most remarkable in the structure, serving as it does not only to close the *Catalogue* but also to close Greek mythology. I have spoken elsewhere of 'the Trojan War, with which myth ends'.[3] This is a matter of design in the *Catalogue*, and indeed is integral to the plot: Zeus has specifically planned the end of the heroic race through the medium of the Trojan War (F 204 MW, F 155 Most, 96–123). And mythology, which began with a theogony depicting the prehistory, the time of the gods and their beginnings, continues as a sort of history through the main part of the *Catalogue* until the end comes. There was a logic in presenting Hesiod's *Theogony* as the prelude to this work.

This panorama of gods and men is brought down to the present day by Hesiod's *Works and Days*. This remarkable composition has as its principal subject the nature of the world in which we humans live and how we are to respond to it, particularly through unremitting toil. But it also sets this in the context of the *Theogony* (by the real Hesiod too) and in the context of at least the subject matter of the *Catalogue*, a poem which on most scholars' assumptions was composed significantly later than Hesiod. It links into the *Theogony* by recapitulating the story of Prometheus – how he stole fire and how, in revenge, the first woman, Pandora, was created. But now she has 'Pandora's box' to open, unleashing plagues and grief upon men (90–105, on which see CH. 23). But it also links into the *Catalogue*, through the 'Myth of the Races' (109–201). Zeus creates mankind five times over, and each new creation is worse than its predecessor – Gold to Silver to Bronze to the Heroes and finally to us, an age of Iron. The sequence is *interrupted* by the race of Heroes, both because they are not labelled after a metal, and because that race is 'more just and better', indeed 'divine' (158–9). Some even live on by the Ocean on the Isles of the Blest. But their function is to fight and die at Thebes, and at Troy for the sake of Helen, as part of Zeus' plans for the world. This is a return to the closure of the heroic, mythical world that we see in the *Catalogue*. Once that world too is over, we are left only with the age of modern men, the real subject of the poem – the harsh justice of Zeus, the work that must be done in all its detail, and the few clues one can learn from heavenly signs or from observance of dates that will make one's lot a little better than it would otherwise have been. But the two ages of mythology, the age of the gods and the age of the heroes, are the context in which we understand the harsh realities of modern life.

Beyond these systematic works, the body of traditional poetry that goes under the name of 'Hesiod' exploits all sorts of mythological subjects. The *Catalogue* appears to have inspired elaborations: a surviving poem, the *Shield of Herakles*, starts with a fifty-six-line 'Or-like' from the *Catalogue*:

> Or like her, leaving her home and fatherland,
> who came to Thebes to join warlike Amphitryon,
> Alkmene.
>
> (Pseudo-Hesiod, *Catalogue* F 195 MW
> (F 138 Most) 8–10 (= *Shield* 1–3))

Fifty lines later, she has given birth to Herakles. Together with this, the poem packages a description of Herakles' defeat of Kyknos ('Swan'), son of Ares, most notable for its description of Herakles' shield (a virtuoso turn also practised by Homer in the case of Achilles' shield, *Iliad* 18.478–608). It depicts ferocious personifications – Fear, Strife, Slaughter, and suchlike – and ferocious animals to match; then there are Lapiths and Centaurs, Perseus and Gorgons, and scenes, rather like Homer's, of war and peace, with the ocean (just as in Homer's) bounding the micro-universe that this shield displays.

There was also another poem, the 'Great Or-likes' (*Megalai Ehoiai*), some sort of large-scale variant containing yet more detail.[4] And then there were such works as *The Wedding of Keyx*, an apparently obscure subject: Keyx is presumably the King of Trachis, father-in-law of Kyknos (*Shield* 356); it is doubtful whether he is the same as Ovid's Ceyx, on whose death he and his beloved wife Alcyone are turned into birds (Ovid, *Metamorphoses* 11.710–48). Poems about weddings are found elsewhere too: Catullus 64 'celebrates' the wedding of Peleus and Thetis; and in the Bosnian tradition, one of the poems studied by researchers was Avdo Medjedović's *Wedding of Smailagić Meho*. Perhaps poems about mythic weddings are good for singing at actual weddings. Perhaps 'Or-likes' about mythical mothers also suit that environment.

And beyond this lies a further miscellany of poems: one about the mythic prophet Melampous ('Blackfoot'), the *Melampodia*, another about the *Descent of Peirithoös* into the Underworld, another about the *Idaian Daktyls* (whose magic invented metalworking and mystery religions), and another about the origin of constellations, the *Astronomy*. If you needed more advice than you could find in the *Works and Days*, you could always turn to the *Precepts of Cheiron*, where the noble, educational Centaur who tutored Achilles and Jason would helpfully tell you:

> Now give all this full consideration in your thought-packed minds:
> first, whenever you enter a house
> always do fine sacrifice to the immortal gods …
> (Pseudo-Hesiod F 283 MW (F 218 Most))

Mythology was integral with the stages of life, its special moments, and its values. In a real sense, Greeks of the Archaic Age lived the mythology. That is why the plots of tragedy could in the end be largely restricted to the mythology.

Other Poets of the Seventh–Sixth Centuries BC

Poets were busy with the mythology in their societies in the seventh century and much of the sixth century, mythologies that existed in all sorts of different cities and regions, amongst them, Corinth. Some significant poems in the Corinthian tradition that were still known in Roman times, went under the name of Eumelos. The *Titanomachy* ascribed to him told in more detail than Hesiod, and not always the same detail, of the times long ago when the Olympian gods, and in particular Zeus, were still establishing their power and had to confront gods of an earlier generation, the Titans, and defeat them. Seventh-century art tended to pick up a similar conflict, the Gigantomachy, the battle with the Giants, which perhaps had more pictorial possibilities. Whatever the particulars, it is clear that the age of the beginnings were of special interest at this time, and this may reflect the fact that mythology of beginnings was relatively new to the Greek tradition and rather more fluid, more exposed to authors who wished to make an original account. Where Homer's heroic epic in effect represents the culmination of a long-standing tradition, however original and personal his take on it, Hesiod was actually bringing something new to Greece, perhaps in large part from the Near East, which only gradually became something standard and central to Greek tradition. Indeed, he never wholly drove out the capacity for thinking of theogony in different ways.

'Eumelos', rather like the Epic Cycle (see CH. 2) gives the appearance of presenting some of the back story to Hesiod and Homer, though in fact they must draw on him or his predecessors. Mēkōnē, an obscure place (supposed to be the same as Sikyon near Corinth), is named by Hesiod as the place where Prometheus tricked the gods into taking the inedible parts of animals as their portion in meals then shared with men, and later in sacrifices; this is what leads to the final division of men from gods. But why at 'Mēkōnē'? It looks as though this may have been where Eumelos situated an episode after the Gigantomachy where the gods cast lots for which part of the world they would rule – heaven, sea, and Tartaros.[5] This casting of lots is referred to by Homer (*Iliad* 15.187–93), but without any context. It is only really in the account of 'Eumelos' that this major event gets its logical context and a place to happen – in the vicinity of a village interestingly called Titane,[6] and near the Corinth that Eumelos came from. And similarly, the helpful deeds of which Achilles thinks Thetis should remind Zeus (*Iliad* 1.394–407, rather an offbeat account it must be said) include a reference to Thetis' summoning of the hundred-handed creature Aigaion or Briareos to the side of Zeus. She must have summoned him from the sea, which is her special domain; it was there, according to Eumelos (F 3 West), that Aigaion, a son of the Sea (Pontos), had his home. Thetis' story (or Achilles') is evidently not based on Hesiod's version (*Theogony* 617–28), where Briareos is instead son of Heaven and summoned by Gaia (Earth).[7]

Another mythographic poem of this era was the *Phoronis*, a poem from Argos in which the first man was called Phoroneus and he (not Prometheus) was responsible for the introduction of fire.[8] This also told of a mythical first priestess of Hera at Argos, 'Kallithoē … she who first decorated the Lady's (i.e., Hera's) tall pillar round about with wreaths and tassels' (F 4, tr. M. L. West). Regionalism was doubtless not the whole story: this author could tell you details about the Idaian Daktyls (the first metalworkers) and the Kouretes, who according to him played the double-flute and came from Phrygia. This is doubtless the tip of an iceberg of local traditions now lost to us, but poems like those of 'Eumelos' and the *Phoronis* were those that went into the melting-pot of the sixth century BC from which a more standard mythology emerged.

Towards the end of the sixth century, less standard mythologies also came into existence, including mystical ones supposedly written by the legendary Orpheus – or the no less legendary poet Mousaios, or the primal hierophant of the Eleusinian Mysteries, Eumolpos. Some of these are dealt with in CH 4.

Obviously, many poets in this period (600–400 BC) are significant for the history of myth but are not in themselves mythographers. Possibly the most important of these outside epic and tragedy are Stesichoros, Bakchylides, and Pindar (CH. 5).

The Prose Tradition, Fifth Century BC

By the mid-sixth century the age of prose was beginning. What had once only been a medium for records, correspondence, and the emerging notion of law codes (and the plethora of public documents – inscriptions – that would follow), now became a way of setting down a view of the world. Before Herodotos set down what we regard as the first *History* (c. 430 BC), others set down philosophy and mythology. Mythology is very like history and the compulsion to write down the mythology (the act of 'mythography') has some of the same sense of recording a definitive narrative account of the past in which your readers may place their trust.

Akousilaos (Acusilaos) of Argos

The first prose mythographer of whom we know was Akousilaos of Argos, who wrote his *Genealogies* in three books around 500 BC. Though his work is lost except for fragments, we know he began with a theogony and ended with the Trojan War and its aftermath, thus conforming to the design of 'Hesiod' and helping make this the definitive shape of Greek mythology. The lovely story that he based his work on bronze tablets that his father uncovered while digging in the garden (T 1), if it is not a later invention, will have appeared in his introductory section to bolster the authority of the traditions he now set down.

In passing on 'traditions', writers sometimes opted for the conservative, sometimes for the innovative. Conservatism was denounced centuries later (in the second century AD) as plagiarism by the Christian Clement of Alexandria: 'Hesiod's material was converted into prose and issued as their own by the historical [!] writers Eumelos and Akousilaos' (Clement, *Stromata* 6.26.7 (Eumelos, T 2 West)). Josephus on the other hand (first century AD) regards it as a chore to list 'all the points on which Akousilaos corrects Hesiod' (Akousilaos F 6). Degrees of innovation are recorded too by the philosopher

Table 3.2 Akousilaos' *Genealogies* (*FGrH* 2 F esp. 1–4).

Book	Known, or plausible, contents	= Section (Table 3.6) of Apollodoros
1	Okeanos and the origin of rivers; theogony (and Phoroneus?)	A
2	?	
3	A contemporary of Agamemnon (Echepolos of Kleonai)	I
uncertain	Phaiakes (and return of Odysseus?)	C
	Phoroneus, Niobe; Io and 'All-seeing' Argos; Proitids; Herakles: deeds and death	
	Deukalion and Pyrrha; Aktaion; Apollo kills Kyklopes; Asopos; Kaineus; Trojan War	B, D, E, G, H, I

Philodemos (first century BC): 'In certain authors the universe is said to have begun with Night and Tartaros, in some with Hades and Ether [*Aither*, the divine upper atmosphere]. The author of the *Titanomachy* ['Eumelos', then] says it began with Ether. But Akousilaos says everything started with Chaos ['the gaping emptiness']. In the work ascribed to Mousaios it says 'Tartaros first ... Night' (Akousilaos F 2). So, varying conceptions existed of what it was like before the universe was created, as these early pre-philosophers struggled to depict the nature of emptiness through mythological personifications. There was just air, no light, just emptiness.

The material of theogony and genealogy was particularly receptive to thoughtful variation, as we can see from this scholion (note by an ancient Greek commentator):

> Akousilaos in Book 3 says that it so happened that *rhanides*, i.e. droplets, fell to earth from the castration of Ouranos, from which the Phaiakes were born, but others [namely Hesiod, *Theogony* 185!] say it was the Giants. Alkaios [the poet from Lesbos, c. 600 BC] says that the Phaiakes have their descent from the droplets of Ouranos. And Homer [*Odyssey*, e.g., 5.35] says the Phaiakes are related to the gods because of their descent from Poseidon. (Scholion on Apollonios, *Argonautika* 4.992 (Akousilaos F 4))

The Phaiakes (Phaeacians) are the people Homer has Odysseus meet in the *Odyssey*: they receive him hospitably and convey him home with gifts. They seem to our eyes to be an epic transposition of a people like the Phoenicians, who would have been familiar seafarers in Homer's times. But this is not how Greeks later viewed it, and it is revealing for the nature of Greek belief in their mythology to adopt their priorities: it was an object of genuine interest where the Phaiakes came from and how divine they were, and whether they were sprung from the blood of castrated Ouranos, and if not them, then who was? Correction of genealogies and new explanations of events were the preoccupation of successive mythographers. So doubtless Akousilaos' *Genealogies* were packed with such detail and did indeed seek to improve, particularly in the opening book, on Hesiod. We do not, however, hear of more than three books, and the coverage, which looks quite similar to Hesiod's *Theogony* plus-*Catalogue*, may have been organized in the same way but been more compressed or selective.

But why did Akousilaos write this work? It may seem an obvious thing to write books outlining Greek mythology, but in our times that is because Greek mythology is something we need to learn. The overwhelming quest amongst Greeks seems to have been to record mythology correctly and fully, much as authors would presently be concerned to set down a correct and complete history. Akousilaos is by no means as idiosyncratic as his contemporary Hekataios was (as we shall see later in this chapter), but his motivation was similar: this is why he 'corrects' Hesiod. And in following ages, it was this sort of limited 'correction' that was valued: what commentators, scholars, and poets wanted was a reliable, traditional mythology containing the most correct account possible. 'Correctness' here combines two different approaches: (i) the *historicizing* approach: the story told is what actually happened (as though myth were history); (ii) the *authoritative* approach: the story told is based on the best, and probably oldest, authors.

One area that authors persistently corrected and filled out was the story of the Trojan War, where the back story to Homer was attested by figures of weaker authority than Homer (the cyclic epics, see CH. 2) who were therefore ripe for correction. Sometimes, too, one might report (or make up) the events that Homer passed over in his own account. Take, for instance, the cause of the Trojan War. The prevalent account is, and was, the story centring on the Judgement of Paris, but Akousilaos developed an ingenious variant *explaining* the reference Poseidon makes in *Iliad* 20.306–7 to the fact that Zeus now detests the clan of Priam and that soon Aeneas (and his descendants) will rule over the Trojans. We find this reported in the scholia on Homer:

> In the light of an oracle to the effect that Priam's reign would end and the descendants of Anchises would be kings over Troy, Aphrodite made love to Anchises, though he was past his prime. She gave birth to Aeneas and, in order to construct a reason for the downfall of the Priamids, created in Paris a longing for Helen and after the abduction gave the appearance of supporting the Trojans (whilst in truth she counselled their defeat) so that they would not completely despair and return Helen. The story is in Akousilaos. (Scholion on Homer, *Iliad* 20.307 (Akousilaos F 39))

Thus Akousilaos produces a picture of elaborate long-term diplomacy on the part of the goddess. This is not quite reducing myth to history (it still has a goddess in it), but it does assign more historically plausible motives. It is therefore *historicizing*, even if it is a new account and therefore technically lacks authority.

A simpler case of filling out the story (it may even be what Homer was thinking of) results from Akousilaos' reading of a problematic line of Homer's *Odyssey* (11.520–1) where Homer refers to Achilles' son Neoptolemos having killed one Eurypylos, son of Telephos, and lots of his comrades 'because of a woman's presents'. Here the scholion tells us,

> Eurypylos – the son of Astyoche and Telephos, son of Herakles – took over his father's domain of Mysia and became its leader. Priam learnt about his acquisition of power and sent to him to come and join the Trojan side. Since he replied that he could not because of his mother, Priam sent his mother as a gift a golden vine. And she accepted the golden vine and sent her son to war, and he was killed by Neoptolemos son of Achilles. The story is in Akousilaos. (Scholion on Homer, *Odyssey* 11.520 (Akousilaos F 40))

Akousilaos probably said more than this. Telephos is wounded by Achilles at the beginning of the war when, in a false start, the Greeks invade Teuthrania (Mysia), thinking it is Troy (a story not from Homer but from the Epic Cycle). He is at the centre of an elaborate mythology which we do not have time to go into here, though his healing by Achilles and a melodramatic scene in a lost play of Euripides (the *Telephos*, mercilessly parodied by Aristophanes) are part of this story. Here we enter a mirror scene where Telephos' son is killed by Achilles' son, perhaps because Telephos had sworn that his family would not enter the war. His mother Astyoche is, in fact, Priam's sister. And the golden vine, it transpires, is actually the one given by Zeus to Ganymede (as we can see in the cyclic epic, the *Little Iliad*, F 6 West). These mythographies, as recorded by Akousilaos and others like him, serve to show that Homer's mythology is the tip of an iceberg, part of a complex and rich tapestry of stories, often conflicting with each other, but all creating a body of knowledge too large for us to master if we do not have our Akousilaos to hand. It is revealing too that this story of the death of Eurypylos furnished the subject for a play by Sophocles where a surviving fragment seems to provide a report of Priam lamenting over his dead body (Sophocles, *Eurypylos* F 210.70–85). From the perspective of mythography it may seem that one of the conditions for the possibility of the tragedy we know was in fact the development, and recording, of a sufficiently rich and complex mythographic tradition. It is no coincidence that Akousilaos stands at the head of the fifth century, drawing together, organizing, and completing the ancient traditions of epic poetry.

We should not, however, leave Akousilaos without noting the role he assigns to his local *polis*. Like the *Phoronis* (above), he claims that Phoroneus was the first man, a son of the river Inachos and the first king of Akousilaos' native Argos (F 23). Autochthony, the quality of always having been there, not having arrived from some other place, having even sprung from the ground itself – like the Athenian Erichthonios – was always valued by Greek societies that had been there before the tribal movements ('Dorian invasion') at the end of the Bronze Age. Argos, then, made that claim, and the poet of the *Phoronis* and Akousilaos were at different times its mouthpiece.

Hekataios (Hecataeus) of Miletos

At much the same time, Hekataios, whose work was the key predecessor to Herodotos' *Histories* was laying down the foundations for geography and ethnology, themselves vital components of history, but he also wrote a work usually referred to as *Genealogies*. Its beginning famously ran, 'This is the account of Hekataios of Miletos. I write the following in the way that seems true to me – the stories of the Greeks are many and laughable, as it appears to me' (Hekataios F 1). So, where he felt they were too foolish, Hekataios proceeded to rewrite myths in order to bring them within the bounds of historical possibility. Logically, this is the *historicizing* approach, which is taken at the cost of authority. In a sense, though, this has mutated into a third approach, (iii) the *virtuoso* approach, in which the intellect of the author is admired for the ingenuity displayed in reconstructing history from myth (without regard to its plausibility or authority). This reduction of myth to history is generally known as *rationalization* of myth (that is, making it rational so that it could actually have happened), but that maybe gives too little credit to the applause invited by these stunts of interpretation. And they would become commoner later.

One instance concerns Cape Tainaron (south of Sparta), where there was a cave …

> … and in certain Greek poets this is where Herakles brought up Hades' dog – even though there is no road leading through the cave beneath the earth and even though it is hard to believe that there is some underground settlement of the gods where souls gather. Hekataios the Milesian has found a likely explanation, when he says that a terrible snake lived at Tainaron and that it was called the Dog of Hades because anyone it bit automatically died immediately from the poison. Herakles, he continues, brought this snake to Eurystheus. (Pausanias 8.25.5 (Hekataios, *FGrH* 1 F 27))

Pausanias (or Hekataios?) proceeds to argue that Homer referred to the 'dog of Hades' but did not *name* it or describe its appearance – the idea that it was

Table 3.3   Hekataios' *Genealogies* (*FGrH* 1 F 13–32).

Book	Contents	= Section (Table 3.6) of Apollodoros
1	Deukalionids, Argonauts	B
2	Danaids	C
	? Herakles and the Heraklids	
3	? Theban mythology	D

a three-headed dog called Kerberos came later. So we can see again that Homer (*Iliad* 8.368, *Odyssey* 11.623) lies at the root of this discussion, and Homer's economy and allusiveness leaves room for ingenious filling out of detail. And once again we see the continuing fascination of those committed to the heritage of mythology, in this case Pausanias in the second century AD, for the pioneers of prose mythography like Hekataios around 500 BC. It is interesting that the text of Hesiod was adjusted at some stage to contain the offspring of the viperous Echidna, including a named 'Kerberos' with no less than fifty heads (*Theogony* 311–12).

We should not, however, develop an exaggerated idea about rationalization in Hekataios. It was a tool he sometimes turned to, but on other occasions it would be left for later authors to intervene. This is what happens when Phrixos, son of King Athamas of Orchomenos, is rescued from sacrifice by the ram with the golden fleece and he flies off on it with his sister Helle, who, alas, falls into the sea (*pontos*, thus naming the *Helles*-pont). Should he stop? At this key moment, the ram speaks to assure him to go on: 'The story that the ram spoke is in Hekataios. But others say he sailed in a ram-prowed boat. And Dionysios [Skytobrachion, possibly early third century BC] in Book 2 says Ram was the tutor of Phrixos and sailed together with him to Kolchis' (Scholion on Apollonios, *Argonautika* 1.256 (Hekataios F 17)).

Turning from the manner to the scope of Hekataios' *Genealogies* we can see that its contents were arranged rather as in Table 3.3. At first sight, this is the standard mythology in the standard order, a replica almost of Akousilaos (or vice versa). But there is a key difference: there is no evidence that Hekataios included theogonic material. This was maybe beyond the scope of a sensible account and that attitude, together with some rationalization and his geographical interests and activity as a politician, in a way make him the first historian. Herodotos (writing c. 440–420 BC), otherwise the first, follows in his footsteps but may be viewed in comparison as setting aside the mythic period altogether (cf. Herodotos 1.1–5 and 1.6 *init.*).

Table 3.4 Pherekydes' *Histories* (*BNJ* 3 esp. F 1–41).

Book	Contents	= Section (Table 3.6) of Apollodoros
1	Peleus; Koronis and Ischys	G, E
2	Argolid: Perseus and Danae; Herakles	C
3	Herakles (contd.), Heraklids	C
4	Agenor, Kadmos	D
5	Kadmos founds Thebes, the *Spartoi* ('Sown Men')	D
	Protogeneia, daughter of Deukalion	B
6	Argonauts	B
7	Argonauts (contd)	B
	Aiolids; Melampous and Iphikles	B
	Kephalos and Prokris	H
8	Asklepios; Apollo serves Admetos	E
	Ankaios (Kalydonian Boar)	B
	Pelops and Oinomaos	I
	Niobe's tears	D
9	Elatos, son of Ikarios, father of Tainaros	E (3.9 or 3.10)
10	Pelops, descent	I
	Thebes: Amphion and Zethos; the Phlegyes	D

Pherekydes of Athens

One final key mythographer was writing perhaps in the 470s BC – between Hekataios and Herodotos. This was Pherekydes of Athens, whose *Historiai* ('Researches', the same title as Herodotos) reached later authorities in ten books. It is perhaps worth emphasizing at this point that it is generally believed that, rather than forming part of the original design of earlier authors, book divisions arose in the Hellenistic age, in the third century BC, as a convenience for scholars. Regardless of this, they are useful for describing the sequence of events in our mythographers.

From Table 3.4 it can be seen that Pherekydes ventures rather further from the traditional organization of mythology than his predecessors seem to have done. That is not to say that he ignores it: Book 2 to the first half of Book 5 follows the traditional sequence; and from there to mid-way through Book 7 appears to mop up the earlier material. Our impression, however, of the remainder is that Book 1 is more concerned to promote the mythology of the Aiakids, who as they originate on the island of Aigina, create an interest – and an agenda – for his Athenian audience. But the last books are more miscellaneous, unless his principle of organization (which is much contested) eludes us. It does however seem that he, like Hekataios, allowed no place for a theogony.

Be that as it may, his name appears constantly in later literature and in particular in the scholia on Homer – seven times, in something of a catchphrase, 'the story is in Pherekydes' (*he historia para Pherekydei*). There are 180 arguable quotations from, or allusions to, his work, contrasted to the 46 for Akousilaos and 23 for the *Genealogies* of Hekataios.

There are some signs that Pherekydes promoted particular Athenian agendas. For instance, we read,

> Philaios son of Ajax made his home in Athens. He had a son Aiklos, who in turn had Epilykos, who had Akestor, who had Agenor, who had Oulios, who had Lykes, who had ?Tophon, who had Philaios, who had Agamestor, who had Tisandros – in whose archonship in Athens *<something or other happened>*, who had Miltiades, who had Hippokleides – in whose archonship [566/5 BC] the Panathenaia was established – who had Miltiades who colonised the Chersonese [c. 520 BC]. (Pherekydes F 2)

Ajax belonged in Salamis, whose ownership Athens had once disputed with Megara. He was the son of Aiakos, who belonged on the island of Aigina, with which Athens had fraught relations. This genealogy clearly prepares the ground for propagandist use. Furthermore, the Philaids were an important clan in the politics of Athens and it is hard not to discern in the background the figure of Kimon, the son of the Miltiades 'who colonised the Chersonese' and who was the leading politician of the 470s and 460s. This is why we date Pherekydes in the 470s or so (the only evidence we have otherwise is a later chronologist who says he 'flourished' in 455/4).[9]

Pherekydes, like earlier mythographers, fills out missing details in the genealogy and mythology. Who was the eagle that was sent to gnaw at Prometheus' liver? Why, none other than the offspring of Typhon and Echidna (F 7b) – like the Kerberos we earlier saw added to Hesiod and which was known to Akousilaos. His style appears to have been very simple, and something of this 'story-telling supplement to the mythology you already know' can be seen in the following report of his account of the Perseus story in Book 2, where our source, a Scholion on Apollonios *Argonautika* 4.1091, appears to quote him word for word:

> In what follows he also talks about the death of Akrisios, to the effect that 'After the *apolithosis* ['turning into stone'] of Polydektes and those with him using the head of the Gorgon, Perseus leaves Diktys behind on Seriphos to rule over the remaining Seriphians, but himself went off by ship to Argos together with the Kyklopes, Danae, and Andromeda. And when he gets there he does not find Akrisios in Argos: he had gone away in fear of him to the Pelasgians in Larissa. So, not finding him, he leaves Danae behind with her mother Eurydike, and Andromeda and the Kyklopes too, and himself went to Larissa. And on

arriving he recognizes Akrisios and persuades him to come with him to Argos. But when they were about to go, he comes across a competition of young men at Larissa. He strips for the contest, and takes a discus and throws it. It was not the pentathlon but they were contesting each of the events individually. The discus, however, lands on Akrisios' foot and wounds him. Suffering from this, Akrisios dies there in Larissa, and Perseus and the Larissans bury him in front of the city, and the locals make him a *heroion* [shrine where he may be worshipped as a hero]. And Perseus leaves Argos.' (Pherekydes F 12)

So this is what happened to Danae's father Akrisios (a question we perhaps never thought to ask). Perseus kills him, which is good. But not deliberately, which would have been bad, as Akrisios is Perseus' maternal grandfather. We have no idea what the Kyklopes are doing in this story, but doubtless there was a fascinating reason. And Diktys the fisherman becomes king of Seriphos. If there were more of Pherekydes, we might even find out what happened in the end to Andromeda.

Countless questions are answered by Pherekydes, which is why he is required reading for ancient commentators (scholiasts). If Ares and Harmonia are the parents of the Amazons, where did they have sex? – in the Akmonian Grove, which is near the distant River Thermodon (F 15a). What was the origin of the Golden Apples of the Hesperides that Herakles had to fetch? – they were produced by Ge (Earth) on the marriage of Hera (F 16a). And the Hesperides, in case you are wondering, are the daughters of Zeus and Themis (F 16d). Where did Herakles get the advice on how to win the apples? – from the nymphs by the River Eridanos (F 16a). Pherekydes may have introduced this distant north-western river Eridanos, later identified with the Italian river Po, into Greek mythology altogether (F 74). But he did not persuade Herodotos, a generation later, who denied it even existed (3.115).

Rationalization does not seem to be an interest of Pherekydes. His Niobe prays to Zeus to be turned into stone. And she is (F 38). There is no attempt to eliminate the miraculous nature of this story which is, in the end, about a natural feature of a rocky landscape. He has no problem with the Kerkopes, opponents of Herakles, being turned to stone, either (F 77). Indeed, *apolithosis* (turning to stone) plays a remarkable role in Pherekydes.

Pherekydes tells versions of some of the obscurer stories which appear in the tragedians (Aeschylus was his contemporary, after all). Neoptolemos' death in Delphi and Orestes' marriage to Menelaos' daughter Hermione, scarcely a central part of the tradition, may have driven Sophocles' lost play, *Hermione*, and are referred to at the end of Euripides' *Orestes*, apparently based on Pherekydes (F 64a–b, 135A). The earliest reference to Neoptolemos' death has been held to be in Pindar, but the particular poems in question (*Paean* 6, *Nemean* 7) may well date from the period 478–460 and therefore be contemporary with,

or derived from, Pherekydes.[10] The way *Nemean 7* is addressed to Sogenes of
Aigina and takes the Aiakids into consideration, it looks as though Pherekydes'
first book is in Pindar's mind.

Patroklos' killing of a youth led to his arrival at Peleus' court (*Iliad* 23.87).
His name was 'Kleisonymos', Pherekydes helpfully informs us (F 65).
The same story later, amongst the Alexandrian poets, became the subject of
the *Astragalistai* ('knucklebone players'), a play by the then celebrated tragedian Alexander of Pleuron. Given our fragmentary remains both of the prose
mythographers and of the extensive output of tragedians, it is probably best
to take the view that tragedians were men of their times and, as part of their
culture, read all the mythographical literature available to them, just as
Herodotos doubtless did. Aeschylus may have claimed that his plots were
'slices' of Homer, but in fact few tragedies owe their origin to the *Iliad* and
Odyssey. The broader tradition of the cyclic epics and of the works discussed
in this chapter provided an enormously wealthier range of possible plots to
dip into.

Hellanikos of Lesbos

With the *Historiai* of Pherekydes the work of mythographers, in the sense of
those who tried to write a complete mythology, was apparently done. But
this really only marked the beginning of the Greek tradition. What followed
was more detailed work, something which in our sense was rather more
'scholarly'.

Hellanikos is usually viewed as a historian (his scope is in fact not unlike that
of Hekataios). He was a younger contemporary of Herodotos and an older
contemporary of Thucydides, and lived to the ripe old age of eighty-five. He
was responsible also, however, for some key mythographic studies and what
immediately catches the eye is the two-book *Phoronis*. The title of this work
makes clear that Hellanikos must have accepted the somewhat deviant account
of Akousilaos (and the earlier poetic *Phoronis*) according to which the beginnings of human genealogy lay in Argos itself, with the first king, Phoroneus,
whose son was Pelasgos (the eponym of the people who in myth precede the
Greeks in Greece). Phoroneus is mentioned by Hesiod (F 10b) and Apollodoros
(2.1), but he is given only second position in the series of accounts of the origins of humanity (Section C, not B in Table 3.6) and has little impact. For
Hellanikos, on the other hand, Phoroneus was evidently the key to the tight
genealogical organization of his monograph on the mythology of the Argolid
and Thebes. This exercise is repeated for a new and apparently separate monograph on the Ionian peoples and their perceived relations in the time of myth,
which starts from Deukalion in a more conventional way, as we can see from the

Table 3.5 Hellanikos' various mythographic works (following Jacoby, *FGrH* 4).

Book	Contents	= Section (Table 3.6) of Apollodoros
Phoronis 1	Theogony?	A?
	Phoroneus, and the Pelasgians	C, E
	Agenor and Kadmos. The 'Sown Men' (*Spartoi*)	D
	Polyneikes and Eteokles.	D
Phoronis 2	Herakles and his labours	C
Deukalionis, 2 bks	Agenor, Kadmos	D
	Deukalion and Pyrrha; beginnings of Aitolia	B
	Neleus (Pylos); Kodros (Athens), Boiotia	B; I, D
	Jason and the Argo	B
Atlantis (2 bks)	Atlas – the Pleiades and, for example, Hermes; sons of Atlas	E
Asopis, 1 bk	The R. Asopos	G
	Genealogy of Miltiades?	
Troika, 2 bks	Genealogy and geography of Troy	F, I
	Myths of Troy	
	Achilles and the swollen Skamandros	
	The Wooden Horse and fall of Troy	

coverage of Apollodoros (Book 1) and from the very starting point of the Hesiodic *Catalogue of Women*.

However much Hellanikos refines the organization of the mythographic works, their real significance lies in the 'improvement' in detail, not just in the assertion of new or variant genealogical information but also in the references to actual places in the Greek world: it is as though he improves the reality of the mythology, this time not by historicizing it, but by 'geographizing' it. All the same, his books dedicated to the *Troika* do seem to have helped the illusion that the Trojan myth was history, something which would reach completion towards the end of the first century AD when someone wrote the war memoirs of Diktys of Crete, supposedly an eyewitness of the war itself. So it is that Hellanikos addresses the problem of the battle conducted by Achilles with the river Skamandros (*Iliad* Book 21):

About this time god rained on Mount Ida. As a result the Skamandros overflowed its banks due to the storm water and overran the area that had hollow places. Achilles met with this torrent first because he was at the head of the army and, concerned that the torrent might do him some harm, took hold of some elms that were growing on the plain and hoisted himself up. The others, seeing the torrent in time, turned wherever each individual one of them could and climbed the hills that overlooked the plain. (Hellanikos F 28)

So far we have seen the fabulous matter of theogonies excluded from more hard-headed accounts of mythology. But a determined segregation of myth as a whole from history, though a long time growing, would only arrive in the following generation when Ephoros created 'universal history' but excluded from it the entire mythical period: he began at the sack of Troy (T 1) and the return of the Heraklids (T 8). For the time being, mythography would be a matter for specialists and for those who in succeeding centuries would seek to explain great works of literature, the epics and the dramas.

Conclusion: Apollodoros, *The Library*

It is, however, worth showing where this picture culminates for us. Our principal account of mythology from antiquity is, of course, none of the lost texts we have discussed above, though maybe they would be if we had them. Instead we resort to a text about which we know very little, the *Library* (*Bibliothēkē*) of Apollodoros. This text aims to give a systematic, continuous account of the mythology in as accurate a version as is possible, quite often stopping to cite its sources (often the lost authors discussed in this chapter). It is later than around 60 BC because he mentions the author Kastor of Rhodes (at 2.1.3) whose work goes that late. It is generally thought that 'Apollodoros' is a pseudonym or an incorrect attribution, referring to the relatively famous second-century BC annalist and scholar Apollodoros of Athens, who also wrote an *On the Gods*. This is an unnecessary supposition and he does seem as entitled to the name 'Apollodoros' as the other 1,314 that are known currently in the Oxford *Lexicon of Greek Personal Names*.[11]

My own view is that this is a mid-/late first-century AD authority who is trying to stabilize Greek mythology at a time when ever more preposterous alterations are being suggested for it – often to prove Homer wrong, rather as a sport or a party game.[12] But, whether this is true or not, it is the nearest we are going to come to a reliable and complete mythology from antiquity. Fortunately, though part of it is lost, we do have versions of an abridgement (*Epitome*) of the work. Its contents, as we have now seen, follow quite closely the order of the combination of Hesiod, *Theogony* and the Hesiodic *Catalogue of Women*. The organization, as can be seen from Table 3.6, is by genealogy and region till we reach the Trojan War, where the illusion of history and chronology is practically complete.

Table 3.6 The *Library* of Apollodoros.

	Chapter	*Contents*
A Book One 1–6: the gods (scene: divine geography)	1	Theogony; the Titans; the birth of Zeus
	2	Zeus defeats the Titans. The offspring of Titans, and various monsters and sea-creatures
	3	Zeus and the birth of the Olympian gods
	4	Deeds of Apollo and Artemis
	5	Pluto, Persephone, and Demeter
	6	The gods' battles with giants and with Typhon
B Book One 7–9: the descendants of Deukalion (scene: Thessaly and neighbouring areas)	7	Prometheus (creation of men; gift of fire) Deukalion and the Flood Deukalion's son Hellen ('Greek') and his sons Doros ('Dorian'), Xouthos, and Aiolos ('Aiolian') Aiolos' descendants (THESSALY, AITOLIA, and ELIS)
	8	The boar hunt of Meleager at Kalydon (AITOLIA); the hero Tydeus
	9	Athamas (BOIOTIA), Phrixos, and the Golden Fleece Sisyphos, Prokris, and Eos, Salmoneus' impiety (THESSALY, ELIS), Melampous Admetos and Alkestis (THESSALY) the Argonauts (Iolkos in THESSALY)
C Book Two: the descendants of Inachos (scene: mainly the Argolid; some remote lands)	1	Inachos (ARGOLID), his son Phoroneus, and Niobe, mother of Argos and Pelasgos Agenor (see Bk 3) and his son 'All-seeing' Argos Io – seduced by Zeus, wanders the world. EGYPT and LIBYA The Danaids murder their husbands. Amymone and Nauplios
	2	Akrisios and Proitos, warring twins TIRYNS; madness of the Proitids, cured by Melampous
	3	Bellerophon and Stheneboia; Pegasos, and the Chimaira (LYKIA) Bellerophon and the Solymoi, and the Amazons
	4	Danaē and Perseus; the Gorgon Medusa; Andromeda (AITHIOPIA). Amphitryon and the Teleboai (on Taphos); Alkmene; Herakles and Eurystheus; deeds, and madness of Herakles

Continued

Table 3.6 Cont'd

	Chapter	Contents
	5	The Labours of Herakles
	6	Herakles and Iole; his murder of Iphitos; recovery of Alkestis; servitude to Omphale
	7	Miltary deeds of Herakles; Auge (TEGEA); his wife Deianeira (KALYDON)
		Aigimios; Kyknos
		Capture of Oichalia (and Iole); the poison cloak; death on Mt Oita; immortality
	8	Flight of the Heraklids (e.g., Hyllos) from Eurystheus; return of the Heraklids to the Peloponnese
		Various oracles and soothsayers; division of the Peloponnese
D Book Three 1–7: the descendants of Agenor (scene: mainly Thebes, with orientalizing start)	1	Agenor's children, e.g., Europa and Kadmos (PHOENICIA)
		Europa and the bull (Zeus); Kadmos goes in search of her
		Her son Minos. Pasiphaē and the bull; the Minotaur (CRETE)
	2	Katreus, son of Minos; Katreus killed by his son Althaimenes
	3	Glaukos raised from dead by seer Polyidos
	4	Kadmos follows cow, founds THEBES, defeats the Sown Men (*Spartoi*)
		Kadmos and Harmonia
		Zeus, Semele, and Dionysos; Ino and Melikertes. Aktaion
	5	Dionysos, and Lykourgos in Thrace; India; Thebes (Euripides' *Bacchae*)
		Etruscan pirates (Homeric *Hymn to Dionysos*); brings Semele from Hades
		Theban stories: Antiope, her twin sons Amphion and Zethos; the death of Dirke
		Niobe enrages Apollo and Artemis
		Laios, Jocasta, Oedipus (Sophocles' *Oedipus Tyrannos*)
	6	Eteokles and Polyneikes; the Seven Against Thebes
	7	Kreon and Antigone; Sons of the Seven, the *Epigonoi*

Table 3.6 Cont'd

	Chapter	Contents
E Book Three 8–11: the descendants of Pelasgos; and of Atlas (scene: Arkadia and its neighbour Lakedaimonia [Sparta])	8 9 10 11	Children of Pelasgos; Lykaon offers cannibal meal to Zeus (SW ARKADIA) Kallisto, and her son Arkas (ARKADIA) Auge and Telephos (TEGEA, S ARKADIA; MYSIA) Atalanta and the golden apples Atlas' daughters, the Pleiades (ARKADIA) Birth of Hermes (N ARKADIA). Steals cattle of Apollo LAKEDAIMONIA; Apollo kills Hyakinthos; Dioskouroi and the Leukippides Deeds of Apollo: kills Koronis; kills the Kyklopes over death of Asklepios Tyndareus, Helen, Klytaimestra, Penelope; suitors of Helen End of the mortal life of the Dioskouroi
F Book Three 12: the descendants of Elektra (scene: Troy)	12	Elektra (one of Pleiades, cf. 3.10): sons Iasion and Dardanos; Demeter and Iasion; the founders of Troy (Teukros, Dardanos, Ilos, Tros); the Palladion; Eos and Tithonos; Priam, Hekabe, Helen, Paris, Andromache.
G Book Three 12–13: The descendants of Aiakos (scene: Aigina and alleged daughterlands)	12 13	R. Asopos seeks Aigina (abducted by Zeus). Aiakos; men from ants; keys of Hades; son Telamon goes to SALAMIS Son Peleus goes to PHTHIA; early adventures; marriage to Thetis Thetis nearly immortalizes Achilles. Achilles on Skyros. Patroklos.
H Book Three 14–16/*Epitome* 1: (scene: Athens)	14 15 16 1.1–4	Kekrops (ATHENS); Athene and the olive-tree; daughters of Kekrops; Kephalos and Prokris Adonis; Athene and Hephaistos. Erichthonios; Tereus and Prokne Boreas abducts Oreithyia Kings of Athens: Erechtheus, Pandion, Aigeus Nisos and Skylla (MEGARA) The Minotaur and the Labyrinth (KNOSSOS) Deeds of Theseus *rest of text is lost: we now turn to the Epitome (abridgement), which does survive* … deeds of Theseus

Continued

Table 3.6 Cont'd

	Chapter	Contents
	1.5–15	Theseus and the Minotaur; Ariadne; suicide of Aigeus; flight (both senses) of Daidalos and Ikaros; death of Minos
	1.16–24	Theseus and the Amazons; Phaidra and Hippolytos; Ixion and Hera (whence the Centaurs)
		Theseus and Peirithoos; Lapiths and Centaurs; Kaineus; Helen.
I	2.1–2	Tantalos; Broteas and Artemis
Epitome 2–7: The descendants of	2.3–9	Pelops (son of Tantalos), and Poseidon, and Hippodameia
Tantalos; the Trojan War and	2.10–16	Sons of Pelops; Thyestes and Atreus and the kingship of Mycenae
aftermath		Agamemnon and Menelaos; Klytaimestra, Helen
	3	The Trojan War: preliminaries, and up to where the *Iliad* begins
	4	The plot of the *Iliad*
	5	Events after the *Iliad*, the capture of Troy
	6	Returns, and subsequent fates of, the Greeks who went to Troy
	7	The *Odyssey* and the end of Odysseus' story

In Table 3.6, which obviously cannot itself tell the mythology,[13] I have attempted to show the articulation of the mythology. (A) deals with beginnings and gods. (B) deals with mythology about (and which therefore originated in) Thessaly. It will be seen that this mythology is not quarantined to Thessaly on the map, but spreads, as culturally it will have done, to Boiotia to the south and Aitolia to the south-west of Thessaly. This beginning also serves to deal with the Greeks as mythology systematized them in their entirety, as the sons of Hellen.

With (C) we move to the Peloponnese, and specifically to the Argolid. Lykia, Libya, and Egypt mark how gradually mythology came to map the rest of the world relative to the home-base for that mythology. Aithiopia is a practically ideological place, rather than a real one (see Rutherford, CH. 24); the myth of Andromeda when located more 'realistically' usually found itself at Joppa (Jaffa). The first half of Herakles' labours are in or near the Argolid, and his map does seem to draw a picture of the influence of the Argolid over the Peloponnese, probably in Mycenaean times (the formative age for the mythology). The location of Oichalia is quite uncertain – it may be in the south-west Peloponnese, in Messenia, or else as imaginary as the damsel Iole.

(C) not only enshrines Argive stories. It *competes* with other parts of the mythology. Phoroneus is the first man – he is autochthonous, and Niobe is the first woman with whom Zeus coupled. If authors such as Apollodoros and Hesiod actually accepted this, then the story would have to be told at the beginning of the account of humanity – as section (B) instead of Thessaly. Hellanikos' *Phoronis* did adopt this perspective, as doubtless the archaic *Phoronis* had. And it is hard to believe that Akousilaos would not have done. The same thing happens in other areas, too. In (D) Kadmos must defeat the Sown Men, an emblem of autochthony (birth from the earth). In (E) Pelasgos is autochthonous on Hesiod's account, but made a son of Zeus and Niobe by Akousilaos to re-skew the genealogy to Argive primacy.[14] In (G) Aiakos is on his own at the beginning and needs men to be made out of ants; that done, a dispersion can follow and places like neighbouring Salamis and (outrageously) Phthia, effectively in Thessaly, can be derived from Aigina. In (H) Athens has its own autochthonous characters, bearing the name 'from the very earth' – Erichthonios/Erechtheus – the latter born of the semen of Hephaistos, falling to Athene's disgust on her leg and wiped thence to the ground (Apollodoros 3.14.6). Somehow related is the theme of cannibalism and dismemberment: Pelops (I) needs to be reassembled, but others are merely eaten or merely offered: Lykaon's impious feast in Arkadia (E) and the banquet where Atreus serves Thyestes' children (I). These are not so much matters of recurrence as realizations of very similar mythologies in different landscapes. The trick of the mythographer is to piece them together as though they were independent stories which somehow can be mapped together.

The structure creaks somewhat at (F), where the need to establish Troy so that it may play its full mythical part in the story later leads to the creation of a tradition as though Troy, too, had contributed its local mythology to the system. That is, of course, an illusion. There is no Trojan mythology – in the sense of a mythology told by Trojans to each other that becomes incorporated in 'Greek mythology'. It is perhaps desperate to deploy 'Elektra', one of the Pleiades, to make (F) possible. It is redolent of how, later, Romans had to be accommodated in the mythic system (see Fox, CH. 13).

The Athenian mythology (H) seems unusually separable from the main body of Greek mythology and makes its best connections with outside through the Herakles-like modelling of Theseus and his close association with a Lapith. But it may be, to speculate, that Athens was rather outside the main cultural circles of late Mycenaean mythology.[15]

Finally (I). This section starts with sinners against the gods, and is not without them as the story progresses (particularly Lokrian Ajax and his terrible offence against Athene). But in the end it is about establishing the place of the treasured epics of Homer in the mythographic tradition. Homer, indeed, did not intend to tell mythology (cf. Létoublon in CH. 2). But as the centuries passed he seemed to have done so, and it becomes the duty of the mythographer to enshrine his 'histories', as they can seem, in a genealogical and regional mythology that has dominated this chapter.

FURTHER READING

Hesiod the mythographer is not specially well served in the English language. A good sense of his character and some modern debates can be obtained from Lamberton 1988; J. S. Clay 2003 gives us Hesiod the thinker. More severely traditional (lots of Greek in the text) are West's commentaries on the *Theogony* (1966) and *Works and Days* (1978) but they are where the serious information is. Beyond that, one may turn to Most's excellent and extensive introductory material (2006–7: vol. 1).

Books on mythology have difficulty finding space for archaic and classical mythography. Graf deals primarily with theogony and cosmogony (1993a: ch. 4) and deals a little with the *Catalogue of Women* as genealogy (126–8). Dowden 1992 is rather lacking on Hesiod but better on Akousilaos and such mythographers (1992: 42–5). Pearson 1939 must still be pressed into service until such time as Robert Fowler produces Vol. 2 of his *Early Greek Mythography* (cf. Fowler 2000), with its mythological half of the commentary, and until the *BNJ* commentaries are complete (see below).

It is best to read the texts for oneself. The only anthology, though of rather wide scope, is Trzaskoma *et al.* 2004. *BNJ*, currently only online in significant university libraries, will soon provide translation of, and commentary on, all fragments of such authors as Akousilaos (see 'Less Easily Found Texts' in the bibliography).

The story beyond the fifth century BC is taken up by Carolyn Higbie in Woodard 2007 (ch. 7).

NOTES

1. Most (2006–7: liii).
2. Most (2006–7: lii–liii).
3. Dowden (1992: 46).
4. Clearly, it was a separate poem: see D'Alessio (2005a).
5. Kallimachos, *Aitia* F 119 with M. L. West (2002: 115–16).
6. M. L. West (1966, online 536).
7. M. L. West (2002: 111).
8. Pausanias 2.19.5.
9. Pherekydes, *BNJ* 3 T 6, and W. S. Morison's commentary; Huxley (1973).
10. Gantz (1993: 690) (earliest references in Pindar); Finley (1951).
11. http://www.lgpn.ox.ac.uk (accessed 1 August 2010).
12. Dowden (forthcoming a).
13. It builds, of course, on Frazer (1921 1.xlv–lviii).
14. Apollodoros 3.8.1 (Hesiod F 160 MW, F 110 Most; Akousilaos *BNJ* 2 F 25).
15. This might make sense in the light of the interesting theories of Margalit Finkelberg about the development of Greek dialect groupings in this period (Finkelberg 2005: 138).

CHAPTER FOUR

Orphic Mythology

Radcliffe G. Edmonds III

What Orphic Mythology?

There was no such thing as Orphic mythology in the classical world. That is
to say, there was no set of stories that could be found exclusively in the poems
attributed to Orpheus or associated only with the rituals he was thought to
have founded; and there was no separate Orphic myth of Dionysos, and no
special Orphic cosmology setting out peculiarly Orphic doctrines.[1]

All the myths found in the 'Orphika' (see next paragraph) appear in other
contexts as well; the name of Orpheus was used, in different ways at different
times, to lend authority to poems and rites that drew from the same traditional stock of Greco-Roman mythological tradition that other poets used.
Nevertheless, it is worth examining the tales with which the name of Orpheus
was associated, since the collection shows what criteria the ancient Greeks and
Romans used to define the category of 'Orphic' for certain extraordinary religious phenomena, both rituals and myths.

As recent scholarly efforts in reconstructing the ancient category of 'magic'
have shown, the reconstruction of the ancient category of 'Orphic' must begin
with the recognition that the label 'Orphic' is also, in some sense, an ancient
cultural classification as well as a modern scholarly category.[2] The ancient
Greeks recognized a category of texts and religious actions that could be
labelled *orphika* and people who could be labelled *orpheotelestai* (practitioners
of rites) or even *orphikoi* (authors of *orphika*). However, to limit the ancient
category of Orphic only to those things 'sealed with the name of Orpheus', as
Linforth once did, would be to exclude people and things that the ancient

A Companion to Greek Mythology, First Edition. Edited by Ken Dowden and Niall Livingstone.
© 2014 John Wiley & Sons Ltd. Published 2014 by John Wiley & Sons Ltd.

Greeks would have classified together.[3] A text, a myth, a ritual, might therefore be 'Orphic' because it is explicitly so labelled (by its author or by an ancient witness), but also because it was marked as extraordinary in the same ways as other things explicitly connected with the name of Orpheus and grouped together with them in the ancient evidence.

The 'Author' and His (Strange) Work

Nevertheless, the starting point for a definition of an Orphic myth would simply be a myth found in a poem attributed to Orpheus. The people of the Greco-Roman world attributed to the mythical poet Orpheus a number of poems composed in the dactylic hexameter and poetic language most familiar from Homeric poetry, as well as crediting him with the foundation of a number of rituals. Orpheus was the child of a Thracian king and a Muse (or of some similar semi-divine background), and his skill at poetic song was unrivalled by any – even the beasts and the trees drew near and listened when he played.[4]

As an Argonaut, he took part in one of the earliest heroic ventures, several generations before the war at Troy; thus his poetic authority preceded even that of Homer. As Redfield has pointed out, to connect the name of Orpheus to a story or ritual is 'to bypass tradition and claim (as it were) a fresh revelation', to claim the authority, not of the familiar cultural tradition, but of a specially privileged individual.[5] Such authority provided the incentive for many poets to circulate their poetry under the name of Orpheus, just as the work of many poets went under the name of Homer. Later scholiasts identify authors, starting around the sixth century BC, who wrote works under the name of Orpheus; and over a millennium later in the fifth century AD, the Orphic *Argonautika* styles itself a work of Orpheus. Certain features of the verses, such as an address to Mousaios, the pupil of Orpheus, or the familiar *sphragis* (signature) line, 'I speak to those of understanding; close the doors of your ears, ye profane', serve as evidence within the text that it comes from Orpheus.[6]

Not only can a pseudepigrapher (a person writing under an assumed name) thus apply the label 'Orphic' to his own text, but, even without such self-labelling, others might also attribute a text or ritual to Orpheus. Modern scholars have tended to make such attributions on the basis of supposed Orphic doctrines (of the immortality of the soul, of its stain by an original sin of the Titans' murder of Dionysos, and of its purification through a cycle of reincarnations), but the ancients made no such doctrinal classifications.[7] Rather, the ancient label 'Orphic' was more like the contemporary term 'new age', which is associated, not specifically with particular religious ideas or organizations, but more vaguely with a set of ideas loosely defined by their distance from mainstream religious activity, especially by claims to extraordinary purity, sanctity, or divine authority.[8] Like 'new age', the association with Orpheus can be positive, indicating special inspiration that goes beyond the ordinary, but often is negative, implying a holier-than-thou attitude that is either ludicrous or hypocritical. Euripides' Theseus accuses his son, Hippolytos, of being a fraud, pretending to extreme purity while secretly making advances on his step-mother:

> Continue then your confident boasting, take up a diet of greens and play the showman with your food, make Orpheus your lord and engage in mystic rites, holding the vaporings of many books in honor. For you have been found out. To all I give the warning: avoid men like this. For they make you their prey with their high-holy-sounding words while they contrive deeds of shame. (Euripides *Hippolytos* 952–7 (tr. Kovacs))[9]

Therefore, whenever something is labelled as Orphic, it is always important to determine who is applying the label and in what context, and whether it is self-applied or applied by another. The label may be positive or negative, indicating something extraordinarily good and authoritative or extraordinarily bad, either revolting or ineffectual, but it always indicates something out of the ordinary.

The ancient sources attest in many ways to this stamp of strangeness that characterizes the Orphic poems. Often, this characterization is negative: the Orphic poems are full of horrible stories that offend the sensibilities not just of later Christian authors but even of classical authors like Plato and Isocrates. Isocrates, indeed, claims that while other poets such as Hesiod and Homer may tell offensive stories about the gods, Orpheus is really extraordinary.[10] Such unusual tales may also be viewed in a positive sense, as the vehicles of sublime truths inexpressible in other ways. The unknown author of a work that discusses an Orphic poem argues that Orpheus' bizarre tales actually compel the reader to seek for their hidden meaning. In his discussion, preserved on the earliest papyrus surviving from Greece, probably dating back to the fourth century BC, the author claims that Orpheus recounts 'sound and lawful things', even though 'his poetry is something strange and riddling for people. But Orpheus did not intend to tell them captious riddles but momentous things in riddles.'[11] Orpheus reveals more profound truths in his myths than Homer and Hesiod, precisely because of the strangeness of the way he expresses them.

This strangeness often manifests in an attribution to a foreign source. Orpheus himself is often called a Thracian, not a Greek but a member of a half-civilized tribe in the northern border regions of Greece. The myths he tells, and the rituals to which some of these myths pertain, are at times also labelled as foreign, deriving from some non-Greek source. Some of these mythic elements may actually have been foreign, but the name of Orpheus is often used as a way to mark things within the Greek tradition as strange or extraordinary where there is no real indication that they derived from another cultural tradition. The rites of Dionysos, for example, are consistently portrayed in the ancient sources as coming from without, alien intrusions on the normal religion of the Greek city state, but they were nevertheless part of Greek religion from the Mycenaean period (and perhaps before).[12] So too, myths tell of the introduction of the rites of the Mother of the Gods from various places in Asia Minor, and even the ritual of Demeter that seems most widespread across the city states of Greece, the Thesmophoria, is usually given a foreign origin, brought from Egypt by some extraordinary religious figure like Melampous or Orpheus.[13] Even if some of these elements might, historically speaking, actually have first been introduced into the Greek tradition from other sources (e.g., Phrygian, Egyptian, Thracian), the choice to refer to that foreign origin or to associate these elements with Orpheus is in itself a sign that their alien and extraordinary nature is being emphasized.[14]

The Myths of Orpheus

The Greek mythic tradition works by *bricolage*, to use Lévi-Strauss's metaphor of the rag-bag man who takes old pieces of things and patches them together to make new creations,[15] and the pieces used by the authors of the Orphic poems come from the same stock that every other mythmaker uses. Of course, not every subject found in the whole mythic tradition appears in Orphic poems, but every subject found in Orphic poems also appears elsewhere in the mythic tradition. It is the way the pieces are combined and the way the construct is framed that marks them as Orphic.

A survey of the surviving evidence provides the range of stories and themes that appeared in Orphika, but several late lists of the works of Orpheus also provide a glimpse of works attributed to him – though they are all, of course, in the characteristic dactylic hexameter, Orpheus' works include hymns to the gods, didactic poetry, and even epic narrative.[16] Unfortunately, only a few late works survive in any form more comprehensive than fragmentary quotations in other authors: the epic narrative of the Orphic *Argonautika*, the *Lithika* – a didactic poem on the properties of stones, and a collection of Orphic *Hymns*.[17] Fragments and allusions to earlier works, however, suggest a long and creative tradition of forging works in Orpheus' name.[18] The earliest testimonies suggest hymns to the gods and cosmological material starting possibly as early as the end of the sixth century BC. In the Hellenistic period, Orpheus' didactic repertoire may have expanded to include lithika and astrologika, as well as other special knowledge, and new hymns and cosmogonies appeared reflecting the new theological and philosophical developments of the era. Sometime around the first century AD, however, much of the extant Orphic poetry was compiled into a collection of twenty-four Rhapsodies, on the model of the Homeric poems, which themselves had been arranged into the twenty-four Rhapsodies (our twenty-four 'books') of the *Iliad* and the *Odyssey* by scholars in Pergamon and Alexandria around the first century BC.[19] This collection, which survives primarily in quotations by the Neoplatonist philosopher Proclus and his successors, seems to have been the form in which most of the later classical world (from whom the majority of our evidence stems) knew the Orphic tradition.

The *Rhapsodies* have at times been imagined as a coherent poem on the model of Hesiod's *Theogony*, structured as a genealogical account of the creation of the world from first principles through the gods and culminating in mankind. But in fact they were more likely to have been a loose collection of Orphic poetry, made up of a variety of poems that had been composed – and reworked – over the centuries by a number of different bricoleurs.[20] Like the *Sibylline Oracles*, another collection of hexameter verse poetry attributed to a mythical author but composed in different periods by different poets, the Orphic *Rhapsodies* probably contained material that overlapped with and contradicted other parts of the collection.[21]

While the late lexica list titles of Orphic works, perhaps the best indicator of the range of myths associated with Orpheus comes from the Orphic *Argonautika*. This late work begins with a proem that serves to authenticate this poem in the tradition of Orphic poetry, adopting the familiar Orphic style of an address to Orpheus' pupil Mousaios. Orpheus begins by listing all his previous themes before announcing that he will now sing of his own expedition on the Argo in the quest for the Golden Fleece.

Now it is for you, master of the lyre, to sing that dear song which my heart incites me to recount, the things that never before have I uttered, when driven by the goad of Bacchus and lord Apollo I revealed the terrifying afflictions, the remedies for mortal men, the great rites for the *mystai* [initiates].

First, then, the implacable necessity of ancient Chaos, and Chronos [Time], how he brought forth by his immeasurable bands Aither and resplendent Eros, of double nature, facing all around, the famed father of everlasting Night, whom indeed brief mortals call Phanes – for he was first made manifest. And the offspring of powerful Brimo, and the destructive deeds of the Earthborn, who dripped painfully as gore from Heaven, the seed of a generation of old, out of which arose the race of mortals, who exist forever throughout the boundless earth. And the nursing of Zeus, the cult of the mountain-running Mother, the things she devised on the Kybelean mountains for maiden Persephone concerning her father, the invincible son of Kronos, the famous rending of Kasmilos and of Herakles, the rites of Ida, the mighty Korybantes. The wandering of Demeter and the great grief of Persephone and how she became Thesmophoros. And then the glittering gifts of the Kabeiroi, and the ineffable oracles of Night concerning lord Bakchos, and most holy Lemnos and sea-girt Samothrace, steep Cyprus and Adonian Aphrodite, the rites of Praxidike and the mountainous nights of Athela, and the laments of the Egyptians and the sacred libations for Osiris.

You have learned the much-practised paths of divination from beasts and birds, and what the arrangement of entrails is, and what is presaged in their dream-roaming paths by souls of ephemeral mortals struck to the heart by sleep; the answers to signs and portents, the stars' courses, the purification rite, great blessing to men, placations of gods, and gifts poured out for the dead.

And I have told you all I saw and learned when at Tainaron I walked the dark road of Hades trusting my *kithara*, for love of my wife, and the sacred tale I brought forth from Egypt when I went to Memphis and the holy towns of Apis, that the great Nile garlands around. All this you have learned truly from my breast. (Orphic *Argonautika* 7–46, my translation)[22]

Many of these allusions to the Orphic mythic tradition remain enigmatic, but several basic themes emerge. First is cosmology, accounts of the creation and nature of the universe. After cosmology comes a collection of myths involving figures associated with Demeter and Dionysos, as well as the bands of ecstatic dancers known as Kouretes and Korybantes. The various didactic themes, instructions for divination and other ritual practices, offer little in the way of mythic narrative, but the list concludes with stories from Orpheus' own life, his journey to the Underworld in search of his wife, as well as his journey to Egypt, which lead up to the announcement of his new theme, his journey on the Argo. It is worth examining the evidence for each of these themes in turn to get a sense of what myths the ancient Greeks and Romans, from the earliest archaic evidence up to late antiquity, might have associated with Orpheus, what might be called Orphic mythology.

Cosmogony

The first mythological theme the Argonautic Orpheus recounts is *cosmogony*, the 'birth' of the universe. He describes the actions of the first principles – Chaos, Chronos, Night, and Air, as well as the manifestation of the principle of generation, Eros. Several late sources summarize cosmogonic myths derived from the poems of Orpheus, and numerous quotations of various Orphic poems involve cosmological material. This mythological material is, for the most part, taken from the common stock, with only a few strange names and epithets not attested elsewhere. So the label 'Orphic' (applied by the pseudepigraphic authors or by other witnesses) derives not from the content of the poems, but rather from the way in which the mythological content is framed and manipulated.

In some sense, Orphic poetry was always marginal: either its claims to antiquity and direct revelation were accepted, putting its authority higher than Homer and Hesiod, or it was rejected, making it a spurious and later invention, deviant from the familiar and accepted tradition.[23] This very characteristic of deviance from the expected norm, however, makes Orphic poetry a suitable medium for innovative thinkers trying to develop new cosmological ideas. Traces therefore remain of thinkers who tried to work out cosmological problems, such as how something can come from nothing, or how the cosmos can be both a unity and a multiplicity. Of course, these issues are the standard problems that all so-called Presocratic philosophers were grappling with, as well as all the thinkers that followed them in the Greek scientific and philosophical tradition. The extant evidence, however, shows that not only did some of these thinkers choose to articulate their ideas in the form of Orphic poems, but that many of these ideas, even if expressed under the name of Empedokles or Pherekydes, were later classified as Orphic simply because of their strangeness, their distance from the normal ideas (ever-changing though they might be from generation to generation) of the nature of the cosmos.[24] A few particular formulations, notably the cosmic egg and Zeus' swallowing of the cosmos, stand out as ways in which traditional elements are manipulated in Orphic texts, but the evidence, as always, is fragmentary and difficult to interpret.

The first piece of evidence included by Kern in his 1922 collection of Orphic fragments is, quite literally, a joke, and it illustrates perfectly the problems with the evidence. In Aristophanes' comedy *Birds*, the chorus of birds sings of the creation of the world, recounting a myth that puts the birth of the race of birds before the race of the gods – thus justifying the later action of the comedy in which the birds take over the universe from the gods:

> Weak mortals, chained to the earth, creatures of clay as frail as the foliage of the woods, you unfortunate race, whose life is but darkness, as unreal as a shadow, the illusion of a dream, hearken to us, who are immortal beings, ethereal, ever young and occupied with eternal thoughts, for we shall teach you about all celestial matters; you shall know thoroughly what is the nature of the birds, what the origin of the gods, of the rivers, of Erebus, and Chaos; thanks to us, even Prodicus will envy you your knowledge.
>
> At the beginning there was only Chaos, Night, dark Erebus, and deep Tartarus. Earth, the air and heaven had no existence. Firstly, blackwinged Night laid a wind egg in the bosom of the infinite deeps of Erebus, and from this, after the revolution of long ages, sprang the graceful Eros with his glittering golden wings, swift as the whirlwinds of the tempest. He mated in deep Tartarus with dark Chaos, winged like himself, and thus hatched forth our race, which was the first to see the light. That of the Immortals did not exist until Eros had brought together all the ingredients of the world, and from their marriage Heaven,

Ocean, Earth and the imperishable race of blessed gods sprang into being. Thus our origin is very much older than that of the dwellers in Olympus. (Aristophanes, *Birds* 685–703 (tr. O'Neil))

What is Orphic about this passage? Later cosmogonies attributed to Orpheus include an egg in the same intermediary position between first principles and the generations of the gods, whereas there is no egg in Hesiod's more mainstream *Theogony*. The fifth-century AD Neoplatonist Damaskios, in his survey of cosmogonic principles, attributes to the Orphic *Rhapsodies* a cosmogony in which Chronos produces an egg amidst Aither and Chaos, while he mentions another Orphic cosmogony in which water and earthy matter produce a monstrous Herakles-Chronos, who produces an egg.[25] In the *Rhapsodies*, the egg produces the monstrous hermaphroditic form of Eros-Phanes, whereas in the other tale, the egg splits in two, producing Heaven and Earth, the gods who give birth to the succeeding generations.

Damaskios, however, also attributes the egg to the cosmogony of Epimenides the Cretan, another mythical poet and religious specialist, associated particularly with the purification of Athens from blood guilt around the time of Solon. Damaskios cites the fourth-century BC Peripatetic Eudemos as recording that Epimenides has Air and Night produce an egg, along with Tartaros. There was a revival of interest in Epimenides in Athens around the beginning of the Peloponnesian War, and Aristophanes and his audience may well have associated the cosmic egg with Epimenides in particular, rather than Orpheus.[26] To make Aristophanes the earliest witness to an Orphic cosmogony is thus problematic; Aristophanes is parodying something, but what is not clear.

Whatever Aristophanes' audience may have thought, later Greeks associated the egg with Orpheus, whether the verses of Epimenides were later attributed to Orpheus or whether some later Orphic poet simply borrowed the imagery from Epimenides (or even from Aristophanes). Plutarch indeed connects the egg as the symbol of generation with Orphika, recounting that some of his friends joked that he was following Orphic or Pythagorean precepts when he abstained from eating eggs at a party. The joke leads to a discussion of which came first, the chicken or the egg, and one person quotes the characteristically Orphic opening line:

'What is more', he added with a laugh, 'I shall sing for those of understanding' the sacred and Orphic account which not only declares the egg older than the chicken, but also attributes to it the absolute primordiality over all things together without exception ... It is therefore not inappropriate that in the rites of Dionysos the egg is consecrated as a symbol of that which produces everything and contains everything within itself.' (Plutarch, *Symposiaka* ('Table Talk') 2.3 636de)[27]

For Plutarch and his contemporaries, the egg is linked, not just with Orphic cosmogony, but also with Dionysiac rituals of the sort founded by Orpheus. The Orphic tagline he quotes, marking the revelation as special wisdom intended only for the privileged, recalls the way the *Birds* chorus frames their revelation as surpassing the knowledge of ordinary mortals, even the sophisticated (and sophistic) Prodikos.[28] It is precisely this kind of claim to extraordinary wisdom that might cause the *Birds* chorus to have been classified as Orphic in some way by Aristophanes' audience and later audiences, whether or not the image of the egg was originally attributed to Epimenides.[29]

The same tag, which Bernabé makes the first fragment in his 2004 collection of Orphic fragments, shows up in the Orphic poem in the Derveni Papyrus. This poem, preserved in quotations in the fragmentary treatise, appears to be a hymn to Zeus that recounts how he became the supreme power in the cosmos.[30] The myth neatly resolves the problem of how a god born so late in the succession of generations can legitimately be hailed as the primary power by having Zeus incorporate all of the cosmos into himself and then bring it back into existence from him.[31] In the Derveni poem, it appears that Zeus swallows the phallus of Ouranos, which has been floating about in the aither ever since Ouranos was castrated by Kronos.[32] Later authors quote Orphic poems (probably from the Rhapsodic collection) that have Zeus swallowing the first-born (Protogonos) Phanes and then giving birth to the whole cosmos anew.[33] In either case the idea is the same: Zeus incorporates within himself the generative principle, whether it is the hermaphroditic Phanes, who generates the other gods by copulating with himself/herself, or the generative member of the oldest god, Ouranos.

Although Hesiod's cosmogony has its fair share of castrations and swallowings, the Orphic tale makes even more elaborate use of these motifs, provoking increased outrage as well as prompting more profound interpretations. Whereas Hesiod has Zeus come to supreme power like an archaic *tyrannos*, by overthrowing the old aristocracy of the gods (the Titan children of Ouranos) and setting up a new order based on the principle of Justice (*Dikē*), redistributing the honours and authority (*timai*) to those who aided him in his coup, the Orphic story focuses on Zeus' omnipotence, his supreme transcendence of the cosmic order: 'Zeus was the first, Zeus last, of the bright lightning's bolt, Zeus head, Zeus middle, from Zeus are all things made. Zeus the king, Zeus the beginning/ruler of all, of the bright lightning's bolt.'[34] While an early version seems known to Plato, later Orphic poets seem to have embellished this theme in various ways, adding epithets particularly appropriate for Stoic, Neoplatonic, or even Jewish theology.[35]

The cosmogonic myths found in the Orphika, then, seem to play at *bricolage* with the same pieces of the mythic tradition found in Hesiod, but the Orphic combinations are characteristically weirder, even more full of monsters and perversions of the generational succession. The egg or the bizarre multi-headed, double-sexed Phanes serves to begin the process of generation, creating something out of nothing. Zeus' swallowing and re-producing the world likewise makes the cosmogonic process an endless loop, as the youngest god becomes the oldest, last becomes first. While the later cosmogonies put the figure of Chronos ('Time', but also echoing the name of Zeus's father Kronos) at the beginning of all in place of Night, Chronos does not seem to be marked as a particularly Orphic feature (like the egg) in any of the evidence.[36] Moreover, although previous generations of scholars have hailed the Orphic cosmogonies as originating the idea of a creator God, even the notion of Zeus swallowing and re-producing the world does not really fit in with the God of *Genesis,* or even the demiurgic creator of Plato's *Timaios.*[37] Orphic poets may have used the medium of Orphic poetry to put forth new and extraordinary philosophical and theo-logical ideas, but they did so using the same traditional mythic figures and schemas found in other cosmogonies. Even the egg and Zeus' swallowing were not part of all Orphic cosmogonies, and, when Apollonios of Rhodes in his *Argonautika* (1.496–511) portrays Orpheus reciting a cosmogony, he includes neither of these features.[38]

The fragments of Empedokles, as scattered and problematic as they are, probably provide the best insight into the nature of other Orphic cosmologi-cal writings, of which little more than the titles are preserved. Empedokles' didactic hexameters, describing the nature of blood, bone, and flesh or the four elements that make up all perceptible matter, show how an innovative thinker can use the traditional medium of dactylic hexameter verse and the traditional mythic figures like Zeus, Hephaistos, and Aphrodite to put forth new ideas about the nature of the cosmos.[39] Empedokles claimed his own authority for his revelations, but others preferred to use the name of Orpheus, whether the Pythagoreans of the archaic and classical age, like Brontinos and Zopyros, to whom the *Net,* the *Robe,* the *Krater,* and other *Physika* are attrib-uted, or the Neopythagoreans of a later era who composed the *Lyre* and the *Hymn to Number.*[40]

Amongst the myths found in Orphic poems, then, cosmogony and cosmol-ogy took a prominent place, and thinkers who wished to propagate their own ideas found in Orphic poetry an effective vehicle for expression.[41] Hymns to the gods, like the Orphic hymn to Zeus in the Derveni papyrus as well as the Homeric *Hymns,* provided the occasion for numerous and rich mytho-logical narratives, while didactic poetry could elaborate physical and cosmo-logical themes using the traditional elements of the mythic tradition. These cosmologies did not form a coherent or consistent whole, much less an iden-tifiable Orphic doctrine about the nature and history of the cosmos.[42] Rather, the Orphic cosmological myths were marked by the extraordinary manner in which they employed the traditional mythic material, the peculiar perversions of the successions of generations, whether through castration or swallowing or even the production of a generative god from an unfertilized wind egg.

The Poetry of Ritual

The cosmologies, however, are not the only or even best known myths with which Orpheus is associated. Orpheus is, first and foremost, a poet of the sacred rites, and he is credited with founding or providing the songs for many different rites honouring a selection of deities.[43] The list in the Orphic *Argonautika* again provides an overview that tallies with the evidence surviving elsewhere; Orpheus founds rituals for Demeter or similar Great Mother figures and for Dionysos or similar Bacchic figures. The myths of his poetry thus relate the tales of these divinities, honouring them for their vicissitudes and celebrating their power in overcoming them.[44]

Perhaps the best-known mythic theme from the list in the *Argonautika* is the wanderings of Demeter and the grief of her daughter Persephone. One Orphic poem even begins, 'Sing, goddess, of the wrath of Demeter of the gleaming fruit', just as Homer's *Iliad* begins, 'Sing, goddess, of the wrath of Achilles son of Peleus.'[45] Many sources associate Orpheus with the myths and rituals connected with an aggrieved goddess, be it Demeter, angry and mourning over the loss of her daughter, or Persephone, grieved over her abduction, or even some other variation on the theme. Such aggrieved goddesses must be appeased, and these myths often conclude by telling how the goddess gains new honours amongst the gods as well as honours from mortals by the institution of propitiatory rites. Again, many such stories appear in the mythic tradition, but the Orphic versions bear some stamp of strangeness that mark them as extraordinary.

Of course, as with most Orphic poetry, only fragments remain to attest to the peculiarities, but a papyrus from the mid-first century BC preserves portions of a hymn to Demeter attributed to Orpheus and marked as Orphic by an address to Mousaios.[46] In this myth, Persephone, daughter of Demeter and Zeus, is abducted by Hades, lord of the Underworld, while she is picking flowers amongst a group of Oceanid nymphs and other maiden goddesses. The abduction was arranged by Zeus and Hades without the knowledge of Demeter, and Zeus even prevents Artemis and Athene from interfering.[47] Demeter wanders the earth, searching for her child, waving torches and raving in her wrath and sorrow.[48] Finally, she comes to Eleusis, where, disguised as an old woman, she meets a mother and her daughters. In a scene missing from the fragmentary papyrus but reported elsewhere, the mother, Baubo, cheers the mourning Demeter by joking and exposing her genitals, and she gets the goddess to break her fast by drinking the *kykeon* (a ritual mixture).[49] The goddess then agrees to become the nurse of the child. Demeter attempts to make the child immortal by anointing him with ambrosia and putting him in the fire, but she is interrupted by the mother and the child is burned to death.[50] Demeter then reveals her divinity, castigating mortals for their foolishness and asking if anyone knows who has abducted Persephone. Although the papyrus breaks off shortly after this point, the tale can be reconstructed from other references to Orphic tellings of the myth. Some of the local inhabitants of Eleusis have witnessed the abduction of Persephone, and Demeter rewards Triptolemus, Eumolpus, and Eubouleus for their information by giving special agricultural wisdom, whether it is the gift of grain for the first time or some similar benefit.[51] The ending of the story seems to have varied; in some versions Demeter or Hekate (as her daughter or friend) goes down into Hades to seek Persephone, and in some variants Persephone herself chooses to remain in the Underworld.[52]

The aggrieved goddess, who has lost both her daughter and her own honour through the violation, must be appeased, and the polemics of the early Christian apologists make clear that these tales were associated with rites that honoured the goddesses, both mother and daughter. Unfortunately, these polemicists are little concerned about precision of detail, so it is impossible to sort out which versions of the myths are connected with which rituals and how.[53] Nevertheless, the tale of Demeter and Persephone was associated first and foremost with the Thesmophoria festival, which was celebrated all over the Greek world, as well as with the Eleusinian Mysteries, the local Athenian festival which was the most prestigious target of the polemics.[54] Demeter seems to be celebrated primarily as the mourning mother, lamenting and searching for her lost child, and this focus on her mourning causes this tale to be grouped, in the ancient sources, with other myths of a mourning goddess, like Isis seeking Osiris, Aphrodite mourning Adonis, and Kybele bewailing Attis. Even though, in these tales, the goddess is lamenting the loss of a lover rather than a daughter, the imagery of the goddess roaming the world seeking or bewailing her lost one is similar, and it is the laments that seem to have been the focus of the rituals.[55] Although we have no more than mere references, Orpheus is credited with poems on all these myths, so this theme of the mourning goddess seems particularly associated with Orphic poetry.

Not only must the anguish of the mother be appeased, but the ravished maid herself must be compensated for her griefs. Persephone's new role as queen of the Underworld brings her new honours, both amongst the gods and from mortals, that serve as recompense for her experience.[56] However, other variations of the myth present a different kind of story, where the Korē (Persephone) is raped by her father Zeus, often in the form of a chthonic snake, either before or after her marriage to Hades.[57] An Orphic *Hymn* celebrates the otherwise unknown Mēlinoē, who is described in terms reminiscent of Hekate and the Erinyes, as a daughter of Persephone by Zeus, who came disguised as Plouton (Hades).[58] The identity of the victimized daughter sometimes varies as well. Misē, for whom rites similar to those celebrated for Korē (Persephone) were performed, is described in the Orphic *Hymn* as the daughter of Demeter at Eleusis, of Meter in Phrygia, of Cythera in Cyprus, and Isis in Egypt – that is, she is the daughter of the mourning mother in whatever aspect she might appear.[59]

In some versions, the aggrieved mother herself is the rape victim. The wrath of Demeter might come from her violation by Zeus, who is either her brother or, when she is identified with Meter or Rhea, actually her own son. Clement associates Zeus' rape of his mother with the wrath of Demeter as well as with the rites of Kybele.

> Then there are the mysteries of Demeter, and Zeus's wanton embraces of his mother, and the wrath of Demeter; I know not what for the future I shall call her, mother or wife, on which account it is that she is called Brimo, as is said; also the entreaties of Zeus, and the drink of gall, the plucking out of the hearts of sacrifices, and deeds that we dare not name. Such rites the Phrygians perform in honour of Attis and Kybele and the Korybantes. And the story goes, that Zeus, having torn away the testicles of a ram, brought them out and cast them in the lap of Demeter, paying thus a fraudulent penalty for his violent embrace, pretending to have cut out his own. (Clement, *Protr.* 2.15.1–2 (tr. Wilson, modified))

While Clement is undoubtedly mixing up different rites and emphasizing the most obscene elements in his polemic, the author of the Derveni papyrus also refers to the rape of Demeter[60] – as well as Zeus' desire for his own mother, which he characteristically explains as a profound allegory.[61] While this earlier Orphic poem may not have narrated the rape itself or gone further to describe Zeus' other erotic pursuits, the Christian polemicists can pick out a succession of rape stories, perhaps from the Orphic Rhapsodies, in which Zeus rapes first his mother and then the daughter he produces from this union. Athenagoras and Clement describe how Zeus first violated his mother in the form of a serpent, producing a child so monstrous that her mother would not nurse her.[62] This child, Persephone, he later raped, again in the form of a serpent, and this union produced Dionysos.[63] These incestuous rapes in every case produce offspring from the angered goddess, which may be the meaning of the reference in the *Argonautika* list to the offspring of Brimo, since Clement understands Brimo as a name signifying the goddess' anger.[64]

All this violence demands recompense, and the mystery rites seem to have been the special ceremonies by which the goddess' grief and anger were celebrated and appeased. Whether these were Eleusinian rites for Demeter and

Persephone, Phrygian rites for Meter or Kybele, Phlyan rites for Megale, or the rites of another figure like Hekate, Praxidike, or Athela, Orpheus was often (but not always) associated with them, as founder or simply as the singer whose hymns were part of the ritual or told the related myths.[65]

In addition to the cult of the mountain-roaming Mother, the Argonautic Orpheus mentions the nursing of Zeus as one of his previous themes, and the mythic pattern of a threatened infant god, be it Zeus or Dionysos or some other, appears in various ways in the evidence for the Orphic poems. When the infant god is born, since he is a potential heir to the kingship of heaven, he is hidden away with special nurses and with a special band of male guardians to protect him. He re-appears from hiding or destruction as an adult to assert his power against the forces of the earlier generation and claim his place amongst the gods.

Little survives of any Orphic tellings of the infancy of Zeus, but the myth found in other sources recounts how Rhea hid Zeus away from Kronos, who was swallowing all the children Rhea bore to prevent them from overthrowing him. He was nursed by nymphs or bees or a goat and protected by the Kouretes or Korybantes, who did their characteristic ecstatic armed dance around the cave in which the god was hidden, drowning out his infant cries with the clashing of their arms. Zeus grows up and defeats his father Kronos and the Titans in a mighty battle, having first tricked his father into vomiting back up the other children he has swallowed and then having obtained other divine allies.[66] Quotations or references to Orpheus in Neoplatonic authors confirm that some version of this tale appeared in the Orphic Rhapsodies, but it is difficult to tell what version or versions were recounted or how early any of these stories were recounted under the name of Orpheus.[67]

The infant Zeus has little trouble evading the threat of his father and becoming master of the universe, but other infant deities face more serious threats. Various sources attribute to Orpheus myths of the infancy of Dionysos, who goes through the same pattern of threat and return, although different versions have radically different elements in each part of the tale. Whereas Rhea always gives birth to Zeus, Dionysos has many births – from the ashes of Semele, from the thigh of Zeus, from Demeter, from Persephone, from the collected pieces of his own dismembered body. Some systematizing mythographers attempt to reconcile these births into a sequence, like that found in Nonnos, in which Dionysos Zagreus, the child of Persephone and Zeus, is reborn after his dismemberment as the child of Semele. It is important to note, however, that this sequence does not hold in all of the evidence and that it creates other problems in narrative chronology, suggesting that the different tales coexisted in the tradition, however troubling the inconsistencies might be to tidy-minded scholars, both ancient and modern.[68] Nor was any version peculiarly Orphic, since various sources attest to Dionysos as the child of Semele, Persephone, and Demeter in different Orphic myths.[69]

After his birth, from whatever mother (or father), the infant god is entrusted
to the care of women (whether to nymphs of some sort or to a nurse like Ino,
Hipta, or even Rhea) and to the protection of male guardians (satyrs, Kouretes,
or Korybantes).[70] The forces of the older generation, however, try to destroy
the child, whether a jealous Hera incites his adult protectors to violence or
whether some band of attackers slips past the defenders.[71] The Christian
polemic of Clement preserves the most detailed account of an Orphic version
of this attack:

> The mysteries of Dionysos are perfectly inhuman. While he was still a child, the
> Kouretes danced around with clashing arms, and the Titans crept up by stealth and
> deceived him with childish toys. Then these Titans dismembered Dionysos while
> he was still an infant, as the poet of this mystery, the Thracian Orpheus, says:
>
> > *Top, and spinner, and limb-moving toys, And beautiful golden apples from
> > the clear-voiced Hesperides.*
>
> And it is not useless to put forth to you the useless symbols of this rite for con-
> demnation. These are knucklebone, ball, hoop, apples, spinner, looking-glass,
> tuft of wool. So, Athene, who abstracted the heart of Dionysos, was thus called
> Pallas, from the palpitating of the heart. The Titans, on the other hand, who
> tore him limb from limb, set a cauldron on a tripod and threw into it the limbs
> of Dionysos. First they boiled them down and, then fixing them on spits,
>
> > *held them over Hephaistos* (the fire).
>
> But later Zeus appeared; since he was a god, he speedily perceived the savor of
> the cooking flesh, which your gods agree to have assigned to them as their por-
> tion of honor. He assails the Titans with his thunderbolt and consigns the limbs
> of Dionysos to his son Apollo for burial. And Apollo, for he did not disobey
> Zeus, bearing the dismembered corpse to Parnassus, deposited it there. (Clement,
> *Protreptikos* 2.17.2–18.2 (*OF* 34K, *OF* 588iB), tr. Wilson, modified)

The toys by which the Titans distract the child become the tokens of a mystery rite that celebrates and propitiates the deity who has suffered this vicissi-
tude, and a third-century BC papyrus from Gurôb refers to these tokens, along
with invocations of the Kouretes, Pallas, Brimo, Demeter, Rhea, and
Dionysos.[72] The role of Apollo in gathering the pieces probably reflects the
influence of Platonic allegorizing on the myth, since the Platonists understand
the dismemberment as the cosmic process of movement from One to Many,
and Apollo, read as *a-pollon*, Not-Many, is the principle that restores Unity.[73]
Other Orphic versions feature Demeter/Rhea in the role of collector; under
her care he is restored to life in some fashion.[74] This version is often connected
with the myth of Isis and Osiris, another of the themes of Orpheus, even
though the restored Osiris seems to remain in the Underworld, while the

revived Dionysos goes on to establish his power as a god in the lands of the living.[75] In some versions, Dionysos is restored from his collected limbs or from the heart that Athene managed to take away from the Titans; in a few variants, this heart is ground into a potion that is fed to Semele, who gives birth to a new Dionysos.[76] In any case, a restored Dionysos emerges after the dismemberment to claim his honour as a god.[77] Other vicissitudes, such as being healed by Rhea/Kybele of madness inflicted by Hera or escaping from some threat by plunging into water and coming back out again after care from Thetis or the like, appear in other sources and may have appeared in Orphic versions as well.

Many myths of Dionysos, in sources throughout the tradition, tell of his entry into some community, the resistance to him and its consequences, culminating in the acknowledgement of the god's power and divinity.[78] Such myths would naturally have been appropriate themes for poetry linked with rituals honouring Dionysos, and Orpheus would certainly have been an authoritative name for such poems, but little evidence survives of such poetry. Nonnos makes Dionysos' victories in a Gigantomachy a triumph parallel to Zeus' victories in the Titanomachy, and the Argonautic Orpheus mentions the destructive deeds of the earthborn Gigantes, born from the blood of Heaven, as one of his previous themes.[79] The systematizer Diodoros, on the other hand, complains that, although everyone knows that Dionysos took part in the Titanomachy, it is very difficult to get the chronology to work out right, and it is likely that conflicting stories were used by different mythic *bricoleurs*, both Orphic and non-Orphic, as they composed their tales for different audiences and occasions.[80]

The confusion between Gigantes and Titans is only part of a wider conflation of similar bands of primordial races; these earthborn men are at times associated with other primeval autochthons, not just the Kouretes or Korybantes who protect the infant god from their assaults, but also the Telchines, Daktyls, Kabeiroi, and even satyrs.[81] The fundamental ambivalence of these figures is clear from the versions in which the protective group is infiltrated or replaced by a group of assailants, as the Kouretes are by the Titans in Clement's version, as well as from the stories in which the Kouretes themselves are the killers.[82] The Kabeiroi, often identified with the Kouretes and Korybantes, appear in the Argonautic Orpheus' list not only in the references to their cult sites of Lemnos and Samothrace but also in the tale of the rending of Kasmilos, one of the names given to the Kabeiroi in Samothrace.[83] The myth remains obscure, but Kasmilos may here be the younger Kabiros, often assimilated to Dionysos Sabazios, or perhaps the third Korybantic brother killed by the other two, whose remains became the object of cult.[84] All of these types, as Strabo tells us, are terrifying figures who dance ecstatically with weapons to the accompaniment of the flutes and cymbals in the train of the mother goddess.[85] Orpheus, as the poet most associated with such rituals, seems often to have been credited with poems that recount myths involving these figures.[86]

In addition to cosmological myths, then, myths associated with the festivals of Demeter and Dionysos and their attendants were the subject of Orphic poems. Many of these rites involved lamentation of the deities' vicissitudes (such as loss, rape, or dismemberment), as well as ecstatic celebration (wild dancing with characteristic flutes, cymbals, and drums), and these festivals served to win the favour of these deities for the mortals propitiating them.[87] Obviously, not all the songs performed at all these rituals throughout the Greek world were attributed to Orpheus, just as Orpheus was not credited with founding every one of these rites, but Orpheus was the most prestigious author of rite or poem for such festivals, and many must have been credited to him. Pausanias, it may be noted, dismisses most of this mass of poetry as not truly by Orpheus, with the single exception of the Orphic hymns for the mysteries of Megale, the Great Goddess, celebrated by the Lykomidai at Phlya, which he describes as receiving great honor from the gods, although relatively short and inferior in beauty to the Homeric *Hymns*.[88] While the mythic narratives may not have been as compressed as those in the extant Orphic *Hymns*, the Homeric *Hymns* provide a better analogy for the form in which the myths of Orpheus appeared than the epic narratives of Hesiod.[89] Such hymns propitiate the divinity by a brief and allusive recounting of a myth that highlights in some way the honours of the deity, and this kind of poetry, whether in hymnic or other form, may have been performed in religious contexts along with sacrifices and other rituals.[90]

While the Homeric *Hymns* celebrate, for example, Apollo at his Delian festival, a celebration that unites all the Ionian Greeks, the label 'Orphic' is attached to more exotic myths, tales that mark their distance from the common stream. Demeter and the Mother of the Gods may be as Greek as Dionysos, but the myths associated with Orpheus seem to emphasize the alien nature of the gods – the Cretan Dionysos or Zeus or Phrygian Sabazios, the Phrygian Kybele or the Egyptian Demeter, the Kabeiroi of Samothrace. Regardless of the actual origin of such cults, they were marked as alien elements present in Greek religion in the fifth century BC and the Orphic label appears as early as the fourth century.[91] No doubt the number of Orphic poems on these subjects grew with the increasing popularity of such cults in the Hellenistic and later periods, since Orpheus' name signified not only expertise on these topics but also the authority of great antiquity for these newly developed rites. The mythic patterns repeated across generations – the infancy of Zeus and Dionysos or the rape of Rhea/Demeter/Persephone – permitted innovation within familiar storylines, and, although such repeating patterns cause difficulties for systematizers ancient and modern, the twists of intergenerational relations create shocking tales – full of mystic significance for the initiates guided by allegorizers like the Derveni author, or marks of pagan degeneracy for the Christian polemicists who preserve so much of the material.

The Life of Orpheus

The last group of mythic themes for Orphic poetry comes from the life of Orpheus himself. Although the expedition of the Argo and Orpheus' descent into the Underworld in search of his wife appear in many forms in other tellings throughout the mythic tradition, there is little evidence for Orphic poems on these subjects, beyond the surviving Orphic *Argonautika*. While it is not impossible that earlier poems claiming to be by Orpheus had recounted the Argonautic legends, the myths of the heroes (Trojan, Theban or otherwise) are not elsewhere attributed to Orpheus, and there is no surviving evidence for such a poem – even the Byzantine *Souda* does not include an *Argonautika* in its long list.[92]

The *Souda* does mention a *Katabasis* ('Descent to the Underworld') attributed to Herodikos of Perinthos, but this Orphic work does not seem to have had the impact on the mythic tradition that other versions of Orpheus' descent had.[93] Indeed, when ancient authors refer to myths of the Underworld, Orpheus himself does not make the list.[94] Despite the assumption in much modern scholarship that Orphic doctrines about the soul must have come from a *katabasis* poem narrated by Orpheus himself, no ancient source ever credits Orpheus with special knowledge about the soul and its fate on the basis of his own descent to the Underworld.[95] Even the Orphic fragments quoted, in Proclus and others, about the soul and its fate show no signs of coming from an autobiographical account, while the instructions for the Underworld journey on the gold sheets resemble more an oracular response than an excerpt from a narrative *katabasis*.[96] The evidence from Diodoros suggests that descriptions of the Underworld and the fate of the soul might have been framed as revelations which Orpheus brought back from his trip to Egypt, but it is impossible to know what other tales might have mentioned such ideas.[97]

Conclusion

The myths of Orpheus are exotic tales within the Greek mythical tradition. They tell of familiar gods, like Zeus or Demeter or Persephone, doing strange things, or they tell of strange gods, like Sabazios or Kybele or Misē, doing familiar things. Orphic mythology – that is, the myths attributed to Orpheus – draws on the same stock of mythic elements and patterns as the rest of Greek mythology, but the label 'Orphic' was not applied to ordinary and common myths of familiar gods or heroes doing familiar things. A poet might put the name of Orpheus on his own work – or a city might claim that Orpheus founded their local ritual – because that name would carry the authority of antiquity and direct divine inspiration, just as a poem or rite deemed exceptionally holy might be attributed to Orpheus by later observers ignorant of the true author. On the other hand, the label of Orpheus' name might be applied by ancient thinkers to classify texts or rites that were exceptionally strange – alien rites or tales of perverse and horrifying deeds by the gods. While in earlier periods, other names, such as Epimenides or Mousaios, might be used for such things, starting with the Hellenistic period the name of Orpheus becomes the dominant label, absorbing the others as later thinkers classify their works as 'Orphic' or even attribute their poems to Orpheus.[98]

A survey of the mythic themes in Orphic poems shows that myths associated with the mysteries of Demeter and Dionysos, in their various aspects, names, and forms, are the most likely to be attributed to Orpheus, although cosmogonies also had their place. The mourning mother goddess, whether Demeter seeking Persephone or the mountain mother Kybele with her attending train of Korybantes, is celebrated in many myths attributed to Orpheus, as are the griefs of Persephone. The births of Dionysos or Zeus, as well as the threats the young god must overcome, form another theme, while tales associated with the attending Kouretes are also seen as characteristic of Orpheus. Orpheus also relates myths like that of the cosmic egg or of Zeus' swallowing the cosmos, and his tales are populated by strange creatures, multiformed monstrosities who nevertheless behave less strangely than some of the more familiar gods.

These exotic myths, many ancient thinkers felt, must contain the most sublime truths, and Orpheus' myths are continuously the subject of exegesis, from the earliest commentaries found in the Derveni Papyrus to the complex allegories of Neoplatonists like Proclus and Olympiodoros. These interpretations shape the myths, as the meanings are built into the story by each successive generation of poets who use the name of Orpheus. These *bricoleurs* weave new myths from the patterns and themes of the old, validating their innovations with the legendary antiquity and authority of the oldest and most inspired of poets. There was no fixed set of Orphic myths or doctrines, no Orphic mythology, just a bewildering array of rituals and myths to which different ancient authors and audiences, at different times and for different reasons, gave the magical name of Orpheus.

FURTHER READING

The study of Orphika is fraught with controversies that date back even before the great clash of Creuzer and Lobeck in the nineteenth century. In the middle of the twentieth century, Guthrie (1952) and Linforth (1941) both examined the evidence and came up with radically different reconstructions. Guthrie provided a synthesis of all the Orphic materials that depicted Orphism as a coherent religious movement with distinctive myths and theologies. Linforth, on the other hand, systematically reviewed the evidence and concluded that there was no consistent pattern of things Orphic. Both studies are still worth reading for their comprehensive reviews of the material.

The late twentieth century, however, saw the discovery of several new and significant pieces of evidence. The most important of these is undoubtedly the Derveni Papyrus, but the discovery of the bone tablets at Olbia and an increasing number of funerary gold tablets also reinvigorated the study of Orphic materials. M. L. West (1983) incorporates this new data into his reconstruction of the Orphic poems. Despite the fact that his reconstruction is premised on the mistaken idea that these poems can be charted in a textual stemma, there is a wealth of erudite and fascinating material in West's study. Perhaps the best recent overview is provided by R. Parker (2005), who briefly reviews the materials and the significant questions in the study of Orphism.

With regard to specific works, the Derveni Papyrus is the most crucial piece of new evidence for understanding not just cosmological ideas circulating under the name of Orpheus but also the ritual practices connected with that famous name. Although a formal edition and commentary has finally appeared in Kouremenos, Parassoglou, and Tsantsanoglou 2006, the best study of the papyrus as a whole remains the Betegh 2004. Morand 2001 is the best study of the collection of Orphic Hymns, while the latest trends in the scholarship on the gold tablets are represented in the essays in Edmonds 2010b. Although both Riedweg (1993) and Holladay (1996) have written on the Hellenistic Testament of Orpheus, little scholarship has been devoted to the late Orphic *Lithika* and Orphic *Argonautika* beyond the editions of Halleux and Schamp (1985) and Vian (1987). Too little has been done to contextualize the fragments of Orphic poetry within the Neoplatonist philosophers, who are our main sources for Orphika, but the collection of Brisson's essays in Brisson 1995 provides the most substantial work in this area.

Bernabé's edition (2004–7) of the Orphic fragments contains far more material than the older edition of Kern (1922), but the basis for the selection is Bernabé's idea of the essential core of Orphic doctrines, rather than the ancient categories of things labelled Orphic. Particularly problematic is the centrality, in Bernabé's classification, of the myth of Dionysos Zagreus. For the controversy, see Edmonds 1999, Bernabé 2002a and 2003, and Edmonds 2008b. Bernabé's massive collection (Bernabé and Casadesús 2008) provides essays in Spanish on a wide variety of topics relating to Orpheus and Orphism, which, if treated with methodological caution, provide a good overview of the evidence.

NOTES

1. Contrast the discussions in, for example, R. Parker (1995) of 'the Orphic cosmogony' and 'the Orphic myth' of Dionysos, in R. Parker (2005: 358) of 'that alternative Dionysos who in Orphic myth was a key eschatological figure', or in Sourvinou-Inwood (2005: 169–89), of 'Orphic mythology' and the 'Orphic Dionysos' that infiltrate the mainstream polis cults and myths.

2. This idea is developed at greater length in Edmonds (2008a) and will receive full treatment in a new book which I am writing under the working title 'Redefining Ancient Orphism'. Such a reconstruction differs from earlier scholars, such as Guthrie (1952), who imagined an Orphism with identifiable believers and doctrines, as well as from contemporary scholars, such as Bernabé, who define Orphism as a current of religious ideas defined by certain doctrines (see n. 7).

3. Linforth (1941, xiii). Linforth rightly warns of the slippery slope encountered once one goes beyond this single criterion; however, attention to ancient ('emic') acts of classification, rather than to (modern 'etic' categories of) doctrines or mythic motifs, provides a more secure methodology. Certain myths include the name of Orpheus as a character (e.g., his journey on the Argo, or his journey to the Underworld in search of his wife), but such myths are only Orphic when they are explicitly framed as the tellings of Orpheus himself.

4. Bernabé has compiled all the testimonies to the life of Orpheus in the ancient materials as F 864–1095 in his edition of the Orphic fragments (Bernabé 2004, 2005, 2007), surpassing the collection in the older edition of Kern (1922). References to Bernabé's collection will be in the form, for example, *OF* 867B, with corresponding references to Kern's edition, either *OT* 5, for the testamenta, or *OF* 317K, for the fragments. References to the Orphic *Argonautika* (*OA*) are from Vian (1987), to the Orphic *Hymns* (*OH*) from Morand (2001). Although the official editio princeps of the Derveni Papyrus has come out in Kouremenos, Parassoglou, and Tsantsanoglou (2006), I cite the text and translation in Betegh (2004).

5. Redfield (1991: 106). Of course, the potential for putting forth a new claim to religious authority was assisted by the medium of writing, which allowed for the multiplication of poems under the name of Orpheus, each of which could present a new alternative to the current norms. The caricature in Plato *Republic* 364b2–365a3 (*OF* 3K, 573B) and Euripides *Hippolytos* 948–57 (*OT* 213, 627B) of the hubbub of books connected with Orpheus shows the effect that this use of texts had on the contemporary audience. Since written texts attributed to an authority such as Orpheus were a useful device for religious innovators (or deviants) to urge their claims, such texts could be associated with deviants or innovators like Hippolytos even though he did not make use of such books.

6. Bernabé has collected the uses of the *sphragis* line in *OF* 1B. Addresses to Mousaios appear in *OA* 7, 308, 858, 1191, 1347; *OH*, proem 1; *the Testament of Orpheus* (Διαθῆκαι) (Ps.-Justin, *Exhortation to the Greeks* 15.1 = *OF* 245K, 377iB);

Clement, *Exhortation* 7.74.3 (*OF* 246K, 337iiB); Eusebios, *Preparation for the Gospel* 13.12.4 (*OF* 247, 378B); *Ephemerides* (Tzetzes, *Prolegomena to Hesiod* 21 Gaisford, *OF* 271K, 759B); *On Earthquakes* (*OF* 285K, 778B); cf fragments of Mousaios in Bernabé 2007.

7. Bernabé (1998a: 172) : 'El creyente órfico busca la salvación individual, dentro de un marco de referencia en que son puntos centrales: el dualismo alma-cuerpo, la existencia de un pecado antecedente, y el ciclo de trasmigraciones, hasta que el alma consigue unirse con la divinidad.' ('The Orphic believer seeks individual salvation within a frame of reference in which the following are the central points: soul–body dualism, the existence of original sin, and the cycle of rebirth until the soul achieves union with the divine', tr. KD); cf. Bernabé (1997: 39) and Bernabé (2004b: 208–9). Guthrie (1952: 73), puts the same ideas in less guarded terms: 'The Orphic doctrines included a belief in original sin, based on a legend about the origin of mankind, in the emphatic separation of soul from body, and in a life hereafter.'

8. For a study of the 'New Age' in the twentieth century, see Sutcliffe (2003).

9. This passage is *OT* 213, *OF* 627B. Redfield (1991: 106) notes the unusual collection of elements in Theseus' condemnation: 'Probably the Greeks themselves were vague about the category; Theseus assumes that since Hippolytos claims to be chaste (a claim not characteristic of the Orphics) he must also be a vegetarian and read Orphic books. All three would be tokens of a rejection of the world, and therefore mutually convertable.' The vagueness of the associations is striking here: Hippolytos the obsessive hunter displays no hint of vegetarianism. Nevertheless, vegetarianism is one of the peculiarities often linked with Orphic things, and Euripides' audience would have understood the kind of categorizing that lumps all of Theseus' charges together.

10. Isocrates 11 (*Busiris*), 39 (*OF* 17K, *OF* 26iiB). Plato, *Euthyphro* 5e (*OF* 17K, 26iB), claims to know stories even more astounding than the bindings and castrations generally attributed to Homer and Hesiod. In his critique of pagan religion in the beginning of the third century AD, the Christian writer Origen (*Contra Celsum* 54) claims that Orpheus said much worse things than Homer about the gods, while his slightly later contemporary Diogenes Laertius, in his biographies of philosophers (1. 5, *OF* 1046ii + 8iii B, *OT* 125K), disputes with those who attribute to Orpheus the beginning of philosophy: 'But if one ought to call a man who has said such things about the gods as he has said, a philosopher, I do not know what name one ought to give to him who has not scrupled to attribute all sorts of human feelings to the gods, and even such discreditable actions as are but rarely spoken of among men.'

11. Derveni Papyrus col. vii. 2, 4–7 (tr. Betegh). Plutarch later credits Orpheus with the same profundity (F 157, Eusebios, *Preparation for the Gospel* 3.1.1, *OF* 671B).

12. Contrast Rohde (1925). Detienne (e.g., 1979 and 1986) has developed the idea of Dionysos as a structural outsider by nature, and Versnel (1990: 96–205) explores the idea in interesting ways; for an overview, see Isler-Kerényi (2007: 232). 'Normal' religion is, of course, a controversial term, since what seems normal may vary from age to age, from speaker to speaker, and from situation to

situation. See Edmonds (2008a) for more discussion of the categories of 'normal' and 'abnormal' religion.

13. On the Thesmophoria, see Versnel (1993: 229–88). As R. Parker (1995: 502) notes, 'The mythological mind often treats what is abnormal as being literally 'alien', of foreign origin. So too does the scholarly mind, and exotic origins for these exotic phenomena have been sought and found: the tradition goes back to Herodotus, who in the long text of 2.81 says that the 'so-called Orphic and Bacchic mysteries' are in reality "Pythagorean and Egyptian".'

14. R. Parker (1995: 502) again puts it well, 'The case for particular borrowings has to be considered, and is occasionally good, but "influence" or "borrowing" can never provide more than a partial explanation for cultural change. Foreign thought is not picked up irresistibly, like a foreign disease; and the decision to take up this or that idea always requires an explanation. In fact, all that can plausibly be claimed is that particular elements in Orphism may have been borrowed; the synthesis is Greek, and must be explained in terms of Greek society.'

15. Lévi-Strauss (1966: 16–36).

16. *Souda* s.v. Orpheus o 654 (*OT* 223d, *OF* 708B).

17. All these works date from the Roman imperial era; the *Hymns* may be perhaps as early as the second century AD, while the *Lithika* and the *Argonautika* may be as late as the fifth century AD. For the Orphic *Argonautika*, see Vian (1987); for the *Lithika*, see Halleux and Schamp (1985); for the *Hymns*, see Morand (2001) and Ricciardelli (2000).

18. M. L. West (1983: 7–15) summarizes the testimonies for early Orphika. The fragmentary nature of the evidence makes dating individual themes and elements very difficult, and it is often necessary use a composite of evidence from different sources of different eras to reconstruct the patterns of a story. It is important to note, however, that the particular details and combinations in each piece of evidence are the products of mythic *bricolage* in particular circumstances and cannot be extrapolated for other times and sources.

19. M. L. West (1983a: 247–51) locates the collections of the *Rhapsodies* in Pergamon in the first third of the first century BC, but Brisson (1995: 5) prefers a date in the first century AD. Brisson's argument that Chronos could not have been added to the cosmogony before the spread of Mithraism in the first century AD is not persuasive, but West's date relies on his unconvincing interpretation of the reference in Cicero (*de nat. deor.* 1.107, *OT* 13, *OF* 889iB) to provide a *terminus ante quem*. Cicero's testimony does not imply that he knew of only one canonical Orphic poem, but rather suggests that he had access to the same treatise of Epigenes cited by Clement that raised doubts about the authorship of Orphic poems.

20. M. L. West (1983) provides an elaborate account, tracing all the pieces of evidence to their imagined place in this grand scheme, creating a stemma for the different variants to account for any discrepancies. His whole account, however, depends on the assumption that a variety of myths can be charted like varying readings in a manuscript tradition, rather than being the products of *bricolage* that combine and recombine the same pieces in many different ways and forms.

21. Buitenwerf (2003: 65–91), traces the development of the *Sibylline Oracles* collection. Like the Orphika, the *Sibylline Oracles* seem to have been collected in the first century as a repository of ancient wisdom, since the Sibyl, like Orpheus, was imagined to have predated the Trojan War and had direct access to the divine.

22. I have followed the *TLG* text, adapted according to Vian (1987).

23. Cf. Herodotus' famous claim (2.53, *OT* 10, *OF* 880B) that Homer and Hesiod first laid out the names, genealogies, and honours of all the gods for the Greeks, which also disparages the claims of other poets (such as Orpheus) to be older and more authoritative. By contrast, Pausanias (9.30.12, *OF* 304, 531iiB) rates the real Orphika as more loved by the gods than the Homeric, even if not quite as beautiful.

24. Bernabé collects the testimonia for the identification of Empedokles as an Orphic (*OF* 1108, Diogenes Laertius 8.53; Syrianos, *in Arist. Met.* 11.35, 43.11) as well as listing the fragments in which he detects ideas similar to those found in the Orphika (*OF* 447–53). M. L. West (1983: 7–15), looks at the various fifth- and sixth-century authors to whom Orphika were attributed, probably in the fourth-century BC treatise of Epigenes.

25. Damaskios, *On First Principles* 123–4 (1.316–19 Ruelle, *OF* 28 +54 + 60K, 69 +75–89B). Athenagoras (18.3, *OF* 57K, 75–89B) attributes to Orpheus the second cosmogony, which Damaskios describes as 'the one according to Hieronymus and Hellanicus, if they are not the same person.' On this question, see M. L. West (1983: 176–8).

26. M. L. West (1983: 50–1) points out that in 432/1 BC, the stain on the Alkmaionids from the Cylonian coup was brought back into prominence when the Spartans brought it up against Pericles. The purification of Delos in 426 may also have been modelled on the Epimenidean purifications.

27. Loeb translation, with modifications; cf. 635ef.

28. This frame resembles other revelations from Orpheus or other figures claiming such extraordinary insight (cf. *OF* 233K, 337B; Ps.-Pythagoras, *Golden Verses* 54–60; as well as Epimenides F 1 DK, *Isaiah* 6.9, Parmenides F 6 DK, Emped. F 2 DK; Ovid, *Met.* 15.153; Hom., *Hymn Dem.* 256–62; cf. Richardson (1974: 243–4) and Dunbar (1995: 429–32)).

29. Aristophanes may also be parodying various ideas that his audiences would have associated with thinkers, like Empedokles, who made similar claims to extra-ordinary wisdom. The role of Eros (700) in bringing all things together recalls the role of Empedokles' *Philotēs* (usually translated 'Love'), while the whirlwinds (697) recall Empedokles' *dinē* ('swirl' that brings together all the elements). See further Dunbar (1995 *ad loc*). So too, Night produces the wind egg (that is, an unfertilized egg) with the help of Air, perhaps an allusion to the role of Air in the cosmologies of thinkers such as Anaximenes and Diogenes of Apollonia, but also to the idea, attributed to 'the so-called Orphic poems' by Aristotle, that the soul enters the body blown in on the winds (Arist., *de anima* 410b27, *OF* 421B, 27K).

30. Whereas M. L. West (1983: 69) sees it as an abridgement of a hypothetical earlier Orphic cosmogony he calls the 'Protogonos Theogony', Bernabé (2002c: 94–5), identifies its form as more closely resembling the Homeric *Hymns*.

31. A version in the *Rhapsodies* portrays Zeus asking Night, 'Mother, highest of the gods, immortal Night, how am I to establish my proud rule among immortals?' and 'How may I have all things one and each one separate?' (Proclus, *On Plato, Timaios* 1.206.26 = *OF* 164K, *OF* 237i–iiB; cf. *On Plato, Timaios* 1.313.31 = *OF* 165K, *OF* 237ii–vB).

32. Derveni Papyrus col. 13.4 He swallowed the phallus of [...], who sprang from the aither first (αἰδοῖογ κατέπινεν, ὃς αἰθέρα ἔχθορε πρῶτος). The Derveni commentator interprets this phallus as the sun, which is responsible for all generation. By contrast, M. L. West (1983: 85) argues that Zeus swallowed the revered (αἰδοῖον) Protogonos, rather than his phallus (αἰδοῖον), and commentators have been divided whether the Derveni Papyrus matches the later Rhapsodic version in this way or represents a different version. I have followed the cogent arguments of Betegh (2004: 111–22), who reviews the controversies, emphasizing amongst other things the parallels with Hittite Kumarbi raised by earlier commentators.

33. Proclus, *On Plato, Timaios* 1.324.14 (*OF* 167K, *OF*241B): 'Thus then engulfing the might of Erikepaios, the Firstborn, he held the body of all things in the hollow of his own belly; and he mingled with his own limbs the power and strength of the god. Therefore together with him all things in Zeus were created anew, the shining height of the broad Aither and the sky, the seat of unharvested sea and the noble earth, great Ocean and the lowest depths beneath the earth, and rivers and the boundless sea and all else, all immortal and blessed gods and goddesses, all that was then in being and all that was to come to pass, all was there, and mingled like streams in the belly of Zeus' (tr. Guthrie). Cf. Athenagoras, *Embassy for the Christians* 20.4 (*OF* 58K, 85B), Proclus, *On Plato, Timaios* 3.101.9 (*OF* 2K, 240viB), Proclus, *On Plato, Kratylos* 62.3 (*OF* 129K, 240iB).

34. *OF* 14B reconstructed from Derveni Papyrus col. xvii.6, 12; xviii.12–13; xix.10. Bernabé postulates another line mentioning *moira* ('fate') because of the discussion of *moira* in col. xviii.

35. Plato, *Laws* 715e, with scholiast (*OF* 21K, 31iii–ivB). The Stoic version appears in Ps.-Aristotle, *de mundo* (*OF* 69K, 31iB), while Porphyry preserves a later Platonic one (Porphyry, *On Statues* F 354, *OF* 243B, *OF* 168K, Eusebios, *Preparation for the Gospel* 3.8.2). Indeed, this theme of the transcendent Zeus, without the story of his swallowing Phanes or the phallus, appears in the so-called *Testament of Orpheus*, an Orphic poem that portrays itself as Orpheus' conversion to monotheism and his recantation of all his previous themes. Cf. the studies by Riedweg (1993) and Holladay (1996). The *Testament of Orpheus* played an important role in the later reception of Orphika, since it put him amongst the figures of classical antiquity that prefigured Christian truth.

36. In contrast, M. L. West (1983: 263) claims that Orphic mythology provided the main channel for the transmission of the Time-cosmogony. Brisson (1995: 5) argues to the contrary that Chronos did not enter the cosmogony until the first century AD. Betegh (2004: 157–8) sums up the controversies over Chronos (esp. n. 117). None of these controversies takes into account the absence of any

evidence marking Chronos as pertaining peculiarly to Orphika, in the way that
Plutarch's evidence marks the egg.

37.   Cf. Guthrie (1952: 106): 'The conception that seems to me to have the best
right to be called an Orphic idea is that of a creator.' Betegh (2004: 180–)
argues that the poem used the verb μήσατο ('devised', cf. col. 23.4) to describe
Zeus' re-production of the world as a conscious devising of the cosmos, rather
than 'simply spew[ing] up the previously swallowed entities.' Nevertheless, the
verb may have only described Zeus' plan to swallow and spew back up, since
the poem contains no references to the kind of demiurgic planning and creating
that appears in other kinds of accounts.

38.   Rather, he seems to incorporate other ideas that seem to come from thinkers like
Empedokles and Pherekydes of Syros; cf. the role of deadly strife as a creative
principle in Empedokles and the intervention of a generation of Ophion and
Eurynome in Pherekydes. Both of these thinkers, of course, are later associated
with Orpheus and Orphika. For Pherekydes, cf. *Souda* (*OT* 228, *OF* 1127B);
Empedokles, see n. 24 above.

39.   Empedokles F 6, 96, 98 DK.

40.   Cf. M. L. West (1983: 7–15, 29–33).

41.   The evidence for the specific content of any of these poems is problematic, however, since most of it comes from fragmentary quotations in very late sources.
The dangers of speculative reconstruction are aptly illustrated by comparing
what Damaskios says about the cosmogonies of Homer and Hesiod with those
he attributes to Orpheus. His summary of Homer's cosmogony would lead us
to expect as full and detailed a narrative as that of Hesiod, if the full content of
those poems did not survive, and there is no reason to suppose that the cosmological material in the Orphic *Rhapsodies* or any other poem followed as comprehensive a narrative as Hesiod's rather than comprising a set of allusions to
cosmogonic figures in the manner of Homer. Damaskios 319.7–320.5 spends
equal time on Homer and Hesiod, and his references to Eudemos show that the
systematization of the cosmologies of the poets dates back to the fourth-century
Peripatetics, if not earlier. Ps.-Justin (*Exhortation to the Greeks* 2 BC) likewise
attributes a canonical, systematic cosmogony to Homer, on the basis of the same
line that Damaskios cites, *Iliad* 14.302. The elaborate reconstruction of the
Orphic theogony in M. L. West (1983) depends on the assumption of a comprehensive narrative from first principles to the affairs of men of a scope surpassing even Hesiod's *Theogony*.

42.   Even the idea, based on the fragment of Orpheus from Plato, *Philebus* 66c
(*OF* 25B), that the standard Orphic theogony had six generations is misguided.
Even if Plato is referring to a theogonic poem that covered six generations (by
no means a certainty, given the context of Plato's allusion), other Orphic poems
may have detailed fewer (or more) generations. While Proclus does cite six
(*Tim.* 3, 168.15 = *OF* 107K, *OF* 98iiiB), Olympiodoros, for example, cites an
Orphic theogony of only four generations (*On Plato, Phaedo* 1.3 = *OF* 220K, *OF*
174 viii + 190 ii + 227 iv + 299 vii + 304 i + 313 ii + 318iii + 320 iB), and much
needless scholarly effort has been expended in the attempt to make all the

evidence for Orphic theogonies conform to the six generation model (see the notes in Bernabé on *OF* 25B).

43.   Bernabé collects the testimonies to Orpheus as the originator of mysteries and rites in *OF* 546–62B (more comprehensive than Kern *OT* 90–104, 108–10).

44.   Bianchi (1965) sets out the category of deities who suffer 'vicissitudes', such as rape, dismemberment, or death, and importantly points out that the meaning of these vicissitudes to the worshippers could vary enormously in different contexts.

45.   Ps.-Justin, *Exhortation to the Greeks* 17.1 (*OF* 386B. 48K), cf. *Iliad* 1.1. While the mythic pattern of the wrath of the aggrieved goddess is certainly more ancient even than Homer, appearing in earlier Near Eastern and Indo-European sources, there is no reason to believe the early Christian apologist who sees Homer as trying to outdo his earlier rival, Orpheus; the traditional formula was more likely adapted by an Orphic *bricoleur* at some later point precisely to contrive the effect of poetry older than Homer. Cf. Sowa 1984: 95–120, Nickel 2003 on this pattern.

46.   *P. Berol.* 13044 (*OF* 49K, *OF* 383 + 387 + 388 + 389 + 392 + 393 + 396 +397iiB). This papyrus has received little attention in recent years and has mostly been relegated to the role of supporting evidence for the Homeric *Hymn to Demeter*, cf. Richardson 1974: 66–7, 77–86. While this hymn may have begun with the Homeric 'Sing, goddess, the wrath …', it also includes a number of lines that appear in the *Homeric Hymn to Demeter*.

47.   Cf. Euripides, *Helen* 1314–18; Claudian, *Rape of Proserpine* 2.204–46.

48.   Euripides (*Helen* 1301–69) depicts the wandering Demeter like the Phrygian or Cretan Mother of the Gods, accompanied by rattling castanets and finally appeased by Bacchic ceremonies with drum and flute, just like those associated with Kybele.

49.   Clement, *Exhortation* 2.20.2–21.1 (*OF* 52K, *OF* 391ii + 392iii + 394i + 395B). On Baubo, see Olender (1990). Cf. the role of Iambe in the Homeric Hymn 200–5, with the comments of Richardson (1974, 213–17).

50.   Although the child is saved in the Homeric *Hymn*, Apollodoros 1.5.1 also relates the death of the child. Thus, although the fate of the child is obviously of crucial importance to each particular telling, the general pattern of the myth could admit either alternative.

51.   Clement refers to them as γηγενεῖς, autochthonous or primordial peoples born from the earth, and designates Triptolemos a cowherd (*boukolos*), Eumolpos a shepherd, and Eubouleus a swineherd. The title *boukolos* appears in a variety of Bacchic mysteries, and the swine of Eubouleus, which fall into the chasm out of which Hades appears, are associated with the piglets offered at the Thesmophoria. The gift of grain became a major theme in Athenian imperial propaganda, but the Homeric *Hymn* omits this episode, substituting a temporary famine, which Demeter ends when appeased.

52.   Demeter's descent: Orphic *Hymn* 41.5, cf. Claudian, *Rape of Proserpine* 3.105–8. Hekate: Callimachus F 466 (*OF* 42K, *OF* 400iiB). Persephone not returning: Vergil, *Georgics* 1.39 and Servius *ad loc.*; Columella 10. 269–74; Lucan, *Civil War* 6.698–9, 739–42.

53. Clement, *Exhortation* 2 provides a comprehensive overview of and attack upon the Greek mysteries, and his polemic served as a source and model for many later ones.

54. Orpheus as founder of the Eleusinian Mysteries (*Marmor Par. IG* XII 5.444 = *OF* 379 + 513B, *OT* 221; Clement, *Exhortation* 2.20.1–21.1 (*OF* 52K, *OF* 515B); Aristid., *Or.* 22.1 (*OF* 516B); Proclus. *in Remp.* 2.312.16 (*OT* 102 K, *OF* 517iB), *Plat. Theol.* 6.11 (*OF* 517iiB); Theodoret, *Remedy for the Diseases of the Greeks* 1.21 (*OT* 103, *OF* 51iB); cf. also Aristophanes, *Frogs* 1032 (*OT* 90, *OF* 510B), Euripides, *Rhesus* 938–49 (*OT* 91 = *OF* 511B; [Dem.] 25.11 = *OT* 23, *OF* 512B; Diodoros 4.25.1 = OT97, *OF* 514). Theodoret also attributes the Thesmophoria to Orpheus, but other sources, starting with Herodotus (2.49.1 = *OF*54B), sometimes credit Melampous with importing both Dionysiac and Demetriac rites from Egypt (cf. Clement, *Exhortation* 2.13.5 = *OF* 385B; Diodoros 1.97.4 = *OF* 56B). On the Thesmophoria, see Chlup (2007); Versnel (1993: 228–88); R. Parker (2005: 270–83).

55. As Roller (1999: 252) notes, with many examples of myths and rites associated with such goddesses, 'The tone can be solemn or humorous, respectful or critical, but the mourning rite is always the central core of the narrative.' Here, indeed, attending to ancient acts of classification proves methodologically significant, producing a grouping of mother mourning child with goddess mourning lover that is unexpected from a modern scholarly perspective.

56. Pindar F 133 (in Plato, *Meno* 81bc, *OF* 443B) refers to the ποινή ('penalty, fine') that Persephone accepts from mortals for her 'ancient grief' (παλαιοῦ πένθεος), and Hades consoles her in the Homeric *Hymn to Demeter* (362–9) with the promise of the honours she will receive from every mortal; cf. Claudian, *Rape of Proserpine* 2.277–306. I have explored this theme in greater detail in Edmonds (forthcoming).

57. A detail preserved not only in early Christian polemic (Athenagoras, *Embassy for the Christians* 20.3 = *OF* 58, *OF* 87–89B; cf. *OF* 153K, *OF* 276i + 281iiiB) but also narrated with characteristic relish by Nonnos 6.155–64. A similar myth is told of the Roman Bona Dea, raped by her father Faunus in the form of a snake, and Plutarch compares this tale to the Orphika (*Caesar* 9 = *OF*584B; Macrobius, *Saturnalia* 1.12.20–9). See Versnel (1993, 228–88), on the similarities of the Bona Dea festival to the Thesmophoria complex.

58. Orphic *Hymn* 71 to Melinoē;. On the difficulties with this text, see Morand (2001: 181–8), and Ricciardelli (2000: 494–9), who also discuss a lead tablet on which the name Melinoē appears associated with Persephone.

59. Orphic *Hymn* 41 to Misē, which also describes her as a feminine aspect of Iacchos. Asklepiades of Tragilos (*FGrH* 12 F 4) makes 'Misa' the daughter of Dysaules and Baubo at Eleusis, and Mismē receives Demeter in her wanderings in Antoninus Liberalis 24. The Kathodos festival of Misē is mentioned in a mime of Herodas (1.56), and an inscription from Aeolic Kyme (*IGSK* 5, 38) identifies her with Korē. Hesychios preserves two more pieces of information about Misē, that she has something to do with Mētēr ('Mother' sc. goddess) and oaths, and that she is connected with feminine insatiable desire, quoting a fragment of the

comic poet Kratinos to the effect that women who are '*misētai*' use dildos (F316 = Hesychios 1442, 1450).

60. Derveni papyrus, col. 22.12–13 equates Demeter, Rhea, Ge, Meter, Hestia, and Deio and explains the name Deio from the fact that she was ravaged (ἐδηιώθη) in intercourse (not parturition, as Kouremenos, Parassoglou, and Tsantsanoglou (2006) take it). The parallels with the rapes of Demeter mentioned in Pausanias suggest sexual violence that leaves Demeter with a wrath that must be propitiated. It is notable that at both Thelpusa and Phigaleia, Demeter bears a daughter from this rape who corresponds to Persephone (even though the rapist in the local stories is Poseidon as a horse rather than Zeus as a serpent), and that mystery rites with the familiar torches and mystic *cista* (box) are instituted to propitiate her (Pausanias 8.25.6, 8.42.2–3). Ovid (*Metamorphoses* 6.114–19) has Arachne depict Jove's rape of Deo in the form of a snake and Neptune's of Ceres in the form of a horse.

61. Derveni Papyrus col. 26. 8–13 The Derveni author explains that Orpheus meant that Zeus desired to have sex, not with his own mother (μητρὸς ἑαυτοῦ) but with the good mother (μητρὸς ἑᾶς – as if ἑᾶς were the equivalent of ἑάων), a piece of etymologizing that has won him perhaps more gratuitous condemnation from modern scholars than anything else in the treatise.

62. Athenagoras, *Embassy for the Christians* 20.3 (*OF* 58K, *OF* 87–9B). Athenagoras relates that, because Rhea/Demeter would not give this four-eyed, two-faced, horned infant the breast (*thēlē*) to suckle, she was called Athēla the maiden (Korē), not to be confused with the maiden Athēnē. Cf *OA* 31 ὀρεινῆς νύκτας Ἀθηλῆς.

63. Clement, *Exhortation* 2.16.1–3; Clement associates the symbolon of the Sabazian mysteries and its 'god in the lap' with this rape in serpent form. This symbolon appears also in the Gurob papyrus (*P. Gurob.* 1.24 = *OF* 31K, *OF* 578B).

64. *OA* 17. Hippolytos, *Refutation of All the Heresies* 5.8.41 claims that the Eleusinian Mysteries culminated with the pronouncement that 'Brimo has born a son, Brimos', but he understands Brimo as 'mighty' rather than 'wrathful'. Brimos might be identified with Iakchos/Dionysos, but, as the Orphic *Hymn to Misē* shows, even the gender of the offspring seems to have been fluid in these myths.

65. Linforth (1941: 262–3) lists the rites Orpheus is said to have founded; Bernabé *OF* 510–535 includes more testimonies, not all relevant.

66. Apollodoros, *Library* 1.1.5–1.2.1, but different details appear in various sources. For an overview, see Gantz (1993: 41–5).

67. To defeat the previous generation, Zeus receives oracular advice from the primordial goddess Night and binds his father Kronos, having made him drunk with honey. The regurgitation of the other gods and the Titanomachy may follow, but Zeus also apparently learns from the defeated Kronos that he must swallow Phanes to become the supreme ruler of the cosmos. M. L. West (1983: 72) tries to reconstruct the story with reference to the fragments.

68. Some of the versions have the dismemberment occur after the birth from Semele, including one of the earliest in date, Philodemus' reference to Euphorion

(*P.Herc.* 247 III.1 = *OF* 59B), which lists the three births of Dionysos as first from his mother, second from the thigh, and third after his dismemberment. Note that Diodoros (3.62.6 = *OF* 301K, *OF* 59iiiB) also makes the birth after the dismemberment the third, not the second. Diodoros expresses his dismay at the conflicting traditions about Dionysos (3.62.2, 3.74.6). Bernabé (1998b) tries to reduce all the versions to two variant story-lines, both of which contributed elements to the *Rhapsodies*. The 'primary version' has Dionysos born of Persephone, torn apart by the Titans, and then reborn from Semele, while the 'secondary version', which he associates with Egypt and Osiris, has Dionysos born of Demeter/Rhea and reborn from the re-assembled pieces collected by her after his dismemberment. Apart from the methodological problems of reducing mythic variants to simple stemmata, Bernabé's hypothesis founders on the fact that the sequence of mothers from Persephone to Semele does not hold in all the evidence.

69. Despite the assumption, in much modern scholarship, that the son of Persephone is the 'Orphic Dionysos', Diodoros 1.23 (*OF* T95, *OF* 327ivB) shows that the Orphic rites were celebrated in honour of the son of Semele rather than the son of Persephone. However, he also attributes the version that Dionysos' mother was Demeter to the Orphika (3.62.8 = *OF* 58B); cf. Cicero's catalogue of different Dionysoi at *On the Nature of the Gods* 3.58 (*OT* 94, *OF* 497iB), and note other testimonia from later authors probably indebted to Cicero in *OF* 497B. The fourth Dionysos is the child of Jove and Luna (probably arising from a confusion of Semele and Selene), and it is in his honour that Orphic rites are celebrated, not the son of Jove and Proserpine, who is first on the list. Bernabé (1998b: 34–6) presents the evidence for Semele as part of the Orphic tradition.

70. Again, while the variant mothers, nurses, etc. are important for each particular telling, the concern here is for the general pattern, since not enough evidence survives to analyse the nuances of particular tellings. Hipta as the nurse of Dionysos Sabazios appears in *OH* 49 (*OF* 199B). Nymphs and satyrs, the familiar companions of Dionysos, appear in *OH* 51.3 and *OH* 54.1, Ino Leukothea in *OH* 74.2. Apollodoros (3.4.3) puts them in sequence, with Dionysos going to the nymphs after the disasters in Ino's house, while Nonnos (9.1–169) reverses the sequence, having Hermes bring Dionysos to Ino after the nymphs go mad and start chopping up babies. The god is nursed there by Mystis before being brought to Kybele. The Kouretes appear in Clement (*Exhortation* 2.17.2–18.2 = *OF* 34K, *OF* 588iB), and Proclus (*Platonic Theology* 5.35 = *OF* 151K, *OF* 278iiB). Pausanias (3.24.3–5) preserves a peculiar local version in which Dionysos is put in a chest like Perseus and nursed by Ino when washed ashore. He notes that the spot is marked by statues of Korybantes (or Dioskouroi) with Athene.

71. The similarity between the groups of adult women or men who are supposed to be protecting the child and those who attack the child is striking – the nymph nurses who become child-menacing mainads or the protective Kouretes who are replaced by attacking Titans. In some myths, the Kouretes themselves become the killers, as in Apollodoros' tale of Epaphos (2.1.3); cf. Edmonds (2006: 353–8).

72. *P. Gurob* 1 (Pack² 2464) (*OF* 31K, *OF* 578B). The text may contain instructions for a ritual, as well as poetic texts to be recited, but its fragmentary state makes it difficult to reconstruct. See Hordern (2000) for details of this text.

73. Cf. Plutarch, *de Ei* 388e. The Platonic interest in this myth as signifying the Many and the One accounts for the disproportionate number of references preserved in the Neoplatonists to the dismemberment story. For the role of Neoplatonic allegorization in transmitting and shaping the myth, see Edmonds (2008b and 2009).

74. Diodoros 3.62.6 (*OF* 301K, *OF* 59iiiB) lists his rebirth after his members are collected by Demeter as the third birth of Dionysos and claims (3.62.8 = *OF* 58B) that this version agrees with the Orphika; cf Cornutus 30 (*OF* 59ivB).

75. Plutarch unhesitatingly identifies Dionysos and Osiris (*de Is.* 364e–365a), but Herodotus too seems to draw a connection (2.24.2, 59.2, 144.2, 156.5). Cf Burkert 2004: 72–4. The myth of Epaphos, the son of Zeus by Io, may provide the link between Dionysos and Osiris. Io, who appears in Egypt as a cow, is often assimilated to Isis (cf Akousilaos *BNJ* 2 F 26–27; Pherekydes *FGrH* 3 F 67; Hdt. 1.1, 2.41, 3.27), and Diodoros lists Epaphos as the Egyptian Dionysos who is responsible for the Dionysiac rites there (3.74.1). Moreover, Apollodoros (2.1.3) recounts that Epaphos was by the Kouretes at the behest of Hera, while Hyginus, *Fabulae* 150 preserves the tale that Hera tried to get the Titans to kill Epaphos.

76. Cf. Hyginus, *Fabulae* 167; Proclus, *Hymn* 7. This variant bears the marks of systematizers creatively trying to get all the different versions to line up. Firmicus Maternus (*Error of the Profane Religions* 6.1–4 = *OF* 214K, *OF* 304iii + 309vii + 313iii + 314iv +318v +325 + 332B) provides a Euhemerized version in which a plaster model is made into which the heart is placed.

77. The creation of mankind from the remains of the Titans does not follow the dismemberment of Dionysos, as many modern scholars continue to imagine. An anthropogony is a common sequel to the myth of the Titanomachy or Gigantomachy, but only the sixth-century AD Neoplatonist Olympiodoros (*on Plato, Phaedo* 1.3 = *OF* 220K, *OF* 174 viii + 190 ii + 227 iv + 299 vii + 304 i + 313 ii + 318iii + 320 iB) combines the myth of the dismemberment with the anthropogony, drawing on a tradition of Neoplatonic allegorizing that reads both the Titanomachy and the dismemberment as signifying the opposition of unity and multiplicity (cf. Proclus, *On Plato, Republic* 1.90.7–13). I have discussed Olympiodoros' innovation, as well as its consequences in modern scholarship, in Edmonds (1999, 2008b, and 2009), *contra* Bernabé (2002a, 2003).

78. Cf. Detienne (1986). Sourvinou-Inwood (2005: 149–240) discusses the mythico-ritual complex of Dionysos' arrivals. After the conquests of Alexander, the myths of the conquests of Dionysos shift from the scale of the individual polis to the whole oikoumene, but the pattern remains much the same.

79. Nonnos, *Dionysiaka* 48.1–89. These destructive deeds are more likely to be the war against the gods, with its many battles and episodes, than the murder of the infant Dionysos, although the Gigantes are sometimes the perpetrators in that episode, particularly when the earthborn are interpreted as earth-working farmers tearing apart Dionysos the vine to produce wine. Cf. Diodoros 3.62.6–7

(*OF* 301K, *OF* 59iiiB). The birth of the giants as the race of mortals born from the earth and blood of heaven is found even in Hesiod (*Theogony* 183–7) and becomes a common anthropogony in the mythic tradition. See Edmonds (2008b and 2010a) and Yates (2004) as well as Clay (2003: 96–9). One of the few references to a specific book of the Orphic *Rhapsodies* (Book 8) also refers to the race of Gigantes, born from Earth and the blood of Heaven (*Etymologicum Magnum* 231.21 s.v. Γίγας = *OF* 63K, *OF* 188B).

80. Diodoros 3.62.8 (*OF* 58B).

81. Not only do the Kouretes or Korybantes guard the infant Zeus and Dionysos, but, in some Orphic tales, they are protecting the young Korē before her abduction by Hades. Proclus, *Platonic Theology* 6.13 (*OF* 191K, *OF* 279iB). Proclus frequently discourses at length on the protective function of the Kouretes and Korybantes as a cosmic principle in his Neoplatonic system, for example, *On Plato, Kratylos* 396b 58.1 Pasq. (*OF* 151K, *OF* 198iB), *On Plato, Timaios* 28c 1.317.11 (*OF* 213iiB), *Platonic Theology* 5.3, 5.35 (*OF* 198iiB). Athene seems to be designated the leader of the Kouretes in some Orphic texts (Proclus, *On Plato, Kratylos* 406d 112.14 Pasq. = *OF* 185K, *OF* 267iB; *Platonic Theology* 5.35, *OF* 267iiB). Cf. the statue of Athene with Korybantes in Pausanias 3.24.5

82. Cf. the killing of Epaphos by the Kouretes in Apollodoros 2.1.3, replacing the Titans in Hyginus 150, see n. 75 above.

83. Scholiast to Apollonios 1.917 (p. 78 Wendel), who identifies Kasmilos as Hermes and the others as Demeter, Hades, and Persephone. Herakles, also mentioned in *OA* 24, is sometimes identified as one of the Idaian Daktyls; cf. Strabo 10.3.22.

84. Clement, *Exhortation* 2.19.1; cf. Firmicus Maternus, *Error of the Profane Religions* 11. Clement assimilates the Kabeiroi to the Korybantes and claims that the rites have to do with the head of the murdered brother or with the phallus of Bacchus (here perhaps identified with the brother), which the brothers take to Etruria.

85. Strabo 10.3.7 describes Kouretes, Korybantes, Daktyls, Telchines, and Kabeiroi as all the same types; in 10.3.19 he adds satyrs as similar Bacchic figures who protect the infant Dionysos, even though they are not armed dancers. Lucian (*On dancing* 79.15) interestingly groups Titans with Korybantes and satyrs.

86. Works on the Kouretes and Korybantes are also attributed to Epimenides (Diogenes Laertius 1.113), a figure who, like Orpheus, was associated with mystery rites (cf. Strabo 10.4.14 and Plutarch, *Solon* 12.7). In the Hellenistic period and later, the poems of Epimenides may have been credited to Orpheus, just as the work of many other lesser-known poets with similar themes seems to have been classified as Orphic. Such fusion of attributions may account for the Argonautic poems attributed to Epimenides. M. L. West (1983, 39–61) remains the best treatment of such figures, although the fragments are collected in Bernabé' final volume of *Poetae Epici Graecae* (Bernabé 2004–7).

87. West's model of initiations into a group unduly restricts the scope of the Orphic poetry, and his derivation of such societies from shamanistic practices lacks historical credibility. 'What the myth itself suggests is a ritual of initiation into a

society – presumably a Bacchic society – which has taken on, at least at the mythic level, the special form of the shaman's initiation.' (M. L. West 1983: 150). Such private Bacchic associations certainly existed in the Hellenistic and Imperial periods, but even in those periods they must have represented only one context in which these myths were deployed. The spectrum ranged from itinerant specialists with individual clientele to civically sponsored ceremonies, and, while the details of a particular telling might help uncover the social and religious context in which it was performed, the general pattern of the myth cannot indicate a limitation to any particular point on the spectrum.

88. Pausanias 9.30.12 (*OF* 304, *OF* 531iiB), cf 9.27.2 (*OF* 305, *OF* 531iB). Hippolytos provides the information that these mysteries are for a goddess Megale, clearly some form of Magna Mater (Hippolytos, *Refutation of All the Heresies* 5.20.4 (*OF* 243K, *OF* 532B). Pausanias denies that any other Orphika are authentic besides the hymns of the Lykomidai, and his habit of referring to Orphika he considers spurious as works of Onomakritos has caused much confusion amongst scholars, especially when they take such references as evidence of a sixth-century BC date.

89. All these poems drew on a common stock of hexameter poetic language and formulae from the oral poetic traditon. In addition to the shared language between the Homeric *Hymn to Demeter* and the Orphic poem preserved on the Berlin Papyrus (see note XX), line 7 in the Homeric *Hymn to Herakles* also appears in the Orphic poem in the Derveni papyrus (col. 12.2). The Derveni poem also uses lines that appear in the larger Homeric epics (*Odyssey* 8.335 ≈ Derveni 26.4; *Iliad* 24.527–8 ≈ Derveni 26.6–7).

90. The extant Orphic *Hymns* each begin with instructions for a sacrificial offering of some kind of incense, but it is difficult to reconstruct fully the ritual contexts in which they might have been performed. Such a task is obviously even more difficult for poems that are no longer extant. The connection between the Homeric *Hymns* and ritual is even less clear, although they too must have been performed in the context of some religious festival, that is, a ritual setting.

91. Euripides' *Cretans* refers to the initiates of Idaian Zeus and Zagreus Nyktipolos, as well as the rites of the Kouretes and the Mountain Mother, although there is no indication that these rites were labelled Orphic, even by Porphyry, who preserves the fragment (Euripides, *Cretans* F 472 = Porphyry, *On Abstinence* 4.56, *OF* 458B); cf. Versnel's reading of Euripides' *Bacchae* in the context of such alien cults (Versnel 1990: 96–205). Plato and Isocrates seem to be aware of Orphika devoted to such myths, cf. Isocrates, *Busiris* 11.39 (*OF* 17B).

92. *Souda* s.v. Orpheus (Adler o 654). In the briefer o 657, Orpheus (of Kroton) is credited just with an *Argonautika* and 'some other stuff'. Note, however, that Diogenes Laertius does attribute Argonautic poems to Epimenides, so Argonautic material may have been in the Orphic repertoire. For the prehistory of the Orphic *Argonautika*, see Vian (1987).

93. The earliest reference to Orpheus' descent comes in Euripides, *Alcestis* 357–62 (*OT* 59, *OF* 980B), but it is clearly a familiar story in the mythic tradition before then and is developed in many ways by various authors. Bernabé collects

all the testimonies *OF* 978–99B (and see the notes at Bernabé (2004: 445–7)).

94. Plutarch, *How a young man should listen to the poets* 17b7 mentions Homer, Pindar, and Sophocles as authors who tell of the Underworld, while Pausanias 10.28.7 compares the Underworld vision in Polygnotos' painting at Delphi with the well-known *katabaseis* in Homer and the (lost) epic *Nostoi* and *Minyad*. By contrast, Orpheus is often listed as an expert in rites and purifications, as well as oracles and other special divinatory knowledge.

95. Contra R. Parker (1995: 500): 'Orphic poetry can almost be defined as eschatological poetry, and it was in such poems perhaps that "persuasive" accounts of the afterlife – accounts designed, unlike that in *Odyssey* xi, to influence the hearer's behaviour in the here and now – were powerfully presented for the first time.' M. L. West (1983: 12) supposes that the references to the *Katabasis* must be to a poem 'in autobiographical form'. The lack of emphasis on ideas of the soul in Orphic literature renders even more problematic Bernabé's definition of Orphism in terms of doctrines of the soul (cf. Bernabé 1998a: 172, and n. 7 above).

96. Bernabé collects (*OF* 337–350B) the fragments quoted from Orphika that pertain to the fate of the soul. The gold tablets or *lamellae* can only be considered Orphic in that they claim a special status for the deceased on the basis of her purity or divine connections, since the name of Orpheus appears nowhere in any of the texts. See Edmonds (2004). Riedweg (1998, 2002, and 2010), tries to reconstruct, in a fundamentally misguided attempt, an Orphic *katabasis* poem from which all the tablet texts derive. For the semiotic features that suggest a resemblance between some of the tablets and oracles, see Edmonds (2010b).

97. Diodoros 1.96.1–97.6, includes *OT* 96, *OF* 61–62B; cf. *OA* 43–5 on the sacred tale brought back from Egypt.

98. As Burkert (1972a: 131) says of Pythagoras, 'Whoever wanted to find a tangible personality in the chaotic mass of Ὀρφικά hit upon Pythagoras, and those who wanted to cast doubt on his originality used Orphism for this purpose.' While this point is applicable to many authors to whom Orphika were attributed, Pythagoras himself is a special case, for two reasons. First, Pythagoras himself was reputed not to have written anything, so pseudepigrapha in his name were less common. Second, the Neopythagorean movement in the first century BC revitalized the authority of Pythagoras himself in a way that Epimenides, Mousaios, Linos, and others never benefited from. Iamblichos (*Pythagorean Life* 146–7), at the end of this Neopythagorean movement, recounts that Pythagoras derived his most profound ideas from the most mystical works of Orpheus, even quoting a line of Pythagoras which claims he received the idea of number from the initiator Aglaophamos, who derived it from Orpheus.

PART II

MYTH PERFORMED, MYTH BELIEVED

CHAPTER FIVE

Singing Myth: Pindar

Ian Rutherford

Myth in Choral Song

Choral song, of which Pindar was regarded as the supreme exponent, was perhaps the most widespread form of song and poetry in ancient Greece, which has been characterized as a 'song-culture' (Herington 1985). The main forms of choral song were the hymns and cult songs, such as the paean, or maiden-songs (*partheneia*); songs in honour of men, such as victory-odes (also known as 'epinician odes': Greek *epinikia*); and narrative dithyrambs performed in competitions. Of Pindar's poetry, four books of victory odes have survived (the *Olympians*, *Pythians*, *Isthmians*, and *Nemeans*) along with fragments of works in other genres. Most Greek choral lyric songs seem to have contained a narrative, usually drawn from the world of heroic mythology, occasionally from what we would regard as history (e.g., Pindar, *Isthmian* 7; Bacchylides 3). This is a distinctive feature of Greek choral poetry, and comparable forms of performance in other cultures, such as the Psalms (Hebrew *Tehillim*) of the Hebrew Bible, seem not to have featured such narratives so much, if at all.

Scholars of Greek lyric poetry usually call these mythological narratives within songs 'myths' for convenience. For instance, Young (1971) defines the 'myth' in the epinician as 'the major connected narrative, whether composed of one or more stories, that formally assumes the greatest digressive proportion in an ode'. This is in spite of the fact that most would probably reserve the term 'myth' in the strict sense for stories that exist outside of any particular literary formulation, or that can be abstracted from all such formulations.

A Companion to Greek Mythology, First Edition. Edited by Ken Dowden and Niall Livingstone.
© 2014 John Wiley & Sons Ltd. Published 2014 by John Wiley & Sons Ltd.

It is important to remember, though, that a myth at this period is essentially a traditional narrative, and that the experts in traditional narratives in the archaic world are, above all, the poets. It follows that the 'myth' sections of choral songs have a claim to be considered as 'myths' in every sense of the word.

Functions of Myth in Choral Song

Myths have several different functions:

1   One important function, at last in epinician odes, is to *provide an exemplum* relating to the life of athletic victor or his family or city, or a prediction of their future. (On mythological *exempla* see CH. 6.) Since mythical subjects are inherently exalted, the effect of comparing the victor to the heroic past is to approximate his life to that same exalted status. Exact correspondences are probably less important than general ones, such as 'nature is important' (see, e.g., Erbse 1999). Specific correspondences are rarer. For example, in Pindar *Pythian* 6 the myth of Nestor and Antilochos provides a parallel to Thrasyboulos, son of Xenokrates. Pindarists have, in the past, spent a great deal of time trying to prove whether or not a given 'myth' relates to the victor. They did so on the mistaken assumptions that (i) only thus would the song achieve unity and (ii) unity is a necessary feature for an ancient choral song (see, e.g., Young 1964, Heath 1986).

2   Myths may *teach moral or cosmic lessons* such as 'disasters are sometimes followed by happiness' (e.g., Pindar *Olympian* 2.20), or 'mistakes can work out all right in the end' (e.g., *Olympian* 7), or 'repay your benefactors' (e.g., Ixion in *Pythian* 2, cf. Doniger 1999). They may simply illustrate the human condition in general (e.g., *Pythian* 3). A whole song could be devoted to such a mythological argument; for example, F 169 where the Labours of Herakles support the thesis that 'law is king of all'. Often, such mythological arguments are quite short, and here the term 'mythological paradigm' is used, a feature that goes back to Homer. An example is the story of Niobe as told by Achilles in *Iliad* 24 ('eat: even Niobe ate'; on this and other examples see CH. 6). With this we may compare the story of Philoktetes at *Pythian* 1.50–7, or the warning words of Jason's admirers at *Pythian* 4.86–92.

3   Myths may *justify a political situation*: these are 'charter-myths', to use Malinowski's terminology.[1] Pindar's myths of colonization belong in this category. Herakles (a frequent theme in Pindar: see below) may sometimes function as 'pre-colonizing' barbarian enemies, in his struggles against Geryon (to the west), Antaios (to the south), the Meropes (to the east), and Diomedes and Alkyoneus (to the north). The ancestors of Theron of Akragas

came from Thebes via Rhodes (*Olympian* 2; F 119), and those of Aristagoras of Tenedos came from the Peloponnese and Thebes, participating in the 'Aiolian migration' (*Nemean* 11). The Cycladic islands were colonized from Athens (*Paean* 5), though Keos was still proud of its Minoan heritage (*Paean* 4).

4   A myth may *explain a ritual or festival*, providing either an aetiology for it or a verbal counterpart to what goes on in the ritual, a *legomenon* (thing said) corresponding to the *drōmenon* (thing done). In such cases, the myth may be perceived not as an event of the distant past but as happening now in ritual space. It is worth remembering that Jane Harrison's theory of ritual took as its initial example a choral poem with a ritual background: the *Diktaian Hymn to the Kouros*.[2]

In Pindar, the ritual function of myth is found particularly in the non-epinician genres. For example, *Paean* 15 (in fact a *prosodion*, a processional song) seems to describe the action of a ritual. *Dithyramb* 1 (F 70a) relates the myth of the conflict between Dionysos and Perseus at Argos and seems to be tied to a festival context at Argos.[3]

Such ritual functions do, however, seem to occur in some *epinikia* as well. For instance, Eveline Krummen has argued that some details of the myth in *Pythian* 5 reflect the festival context of performance. Thus the narrative of the arrival of the sons of Antenor from Troy seems to imply a ritual where they are still ritually received at a sacrifice (83–93, cf. Krummen 1990: 128). Again, in *Isthmian* 4 both the narrative and the ritual context have to do with Herakles and his children. For ritual and myth in *Olympian* 1, see below (pp. 112, 114–15).

5   Myths have a *connective function*, both over space and over time, and often in both dimensions together. In *Paean* 6 the religious histories of Delphi and Aigina are woven together in a continuum spanning many generations. *Olympian* 6 manages to connect Syracuse (contemporary) with Olympia (ancient and contemporary), Arkadia (ancient), and Thebes (contemporary). According to F 58, the oracles of Zeus at Dodona and the Siwa Oasis in Libya are united by the fact that they were both founded from Egyptian Thebes.

6   One function of the use of myth in choral songs is surely to *entertain*, to excite and to delight. In the case of narrative dithyrambs designed for competitions, this function would be the only one.

7   Mythocriticism: Pindar is not a naïve storyteller, and when he relates a myth, part of his aim is to stamp this particular version as his own. This *corrective function* is explicit in the case of the story of Pelops in *Olympian* 1 (37–93), but also in other odes where the poet underlines a novelty or correction.

The use of myth varies from genre to genre:

1   In cult hymns, the mythological narrative seems to have served as an illustration of the *accomplishments of the deity* being praised, or as an aetiology of the cult.

2   In victory odes, the mythological narrative may illustrate the *prowess of the victor*. Myths may also sometimes provide *aetiologies for the festival*. An example of this is the various odes in which Pindar presents aetiologies for different aspects of the Olympic Games. The festival at Olympia was founded by Herakles after he defeated Augeias (*Olympian* 10); on a different occasion Herakles brought the sacred olives from the Hyperboreans (*Olympian* 3); but the hero most closely associated with the foot race and the chariot race was Pelops (*Olympian* 1), while the priestly genos of the Iamidai can be traced back to Iamos (*Olympian* 6).

3   In competition dithyrambs, the whole content was 'mythological narrative'. Examples of this can be found in Bakchylides' dithyrambs, but not amongst the surviving works of Pindar.

Poets tend to use a different myth for every song. For example, while most of the Aiginetan victory odes focus on the history of the Aiakidai (the descendants of the island's founding hero, Aiakos), they always deal with a different episode from that history. Repetitions are very few: the myth of Neoptolemos at Delphi (*Paean* 6, *Nemean* 7); the birth of Herakles (*Isthmian* 1, "*Paean*" 20); the story of Bellerophon (*Isthmian* 7, *Olympian* 13); the origin of Delos (F 33c–d, *Paean* 7b).

In many cases, the same 'myth' serves several different functions. Entertainment and ornament are presumably always part of the point. In *Olympian* 1 the myth of Pelops is told as the aetiology of the ritual of two events at the Olympics. It is also, however, an exemplum of Hieron's victory in the horse race and a prediction of the future victory that he hopes to win in the chariot race. (It may also provide an exemplum for the right and wrong way to conduct a feast; see D. Steiner 2002). It is not a particularly 'connective' myth, because the family of the victor being celebrated, Hieron, has no link to Pelops, and his city, Syracuse, has none to Olympia. In *Olympian* 2, the myth of the family of Kadmos illustrates the principle that disaster may be followed by happiness later on, and also connects Theron and Akragas to the heroic world of Thebes.

Innovation

Pindar on mythos

For Pindar, the word *mythos*, which he does use occasionally, means a false story. For 'mythological narrative' in our sense Pindar has no term, and it is not even clear that he would have distinguished between narratives drawn from what we regard as the distant mythological 'past' and narratives drawn from quite recent history (such as the narrative of Kroisos in Bakchylides 3). For Pindar, the crucial distinction is between true stories and false ones, and he aims, by eliminating false traditions, to get back to the truth (for a good account of this process, showing parallels with contemporary historiography see Loscalzo 2001). The criteria on which stories are categorized as false seem to include:

1   Attitude to religion: the stories represent the gods, and possibly heroes as well, as behaving immorally. This is explicit in *Olympian* 1, where the poet comes up with his own preferred version; it is implicit in *Olympian* 9, where he does not. Sometimes he begins a myth and then breaks off from a full narration (on such 'break-offs', see Race 1989). Many other cases have been detected where Pindar seems to ignore a version of a myth that represents a hero as barbaric or a god as limited in power or knowledge (Robertson 1940). As George Huxley puts it, 'Pindar moralises, amending traditional mythography in the light of his own *semnotēs*, [the Greek word for] the sense of what is reverent and fitting' (1975: 14).

2   Motivation: the stories are the result of slander spread by people who are jealous of someone, such as the 'jealous neighbours' at *Olympian* 1.47. Thus, the true myth is analogous to the true praise that the epinikian poet bestows on his patron, and is perhaps indistinguishable from it. A variant on this may be seen in *Nemean* 8, where Ajax is brought down by the corrupt decision, motivated by envy, which deprives him of the armour of Achilles: here, instead of envy creating a false myth, envy operates *within* the myth to create a 'false' outcome in which honour is not given where it is due.

3   Deceptive skill of earlier poets: the stories are the result of the skill of a clever poet, as in the case of the story of Odysseus as told by Homer: 'his skill deceives with misleading tales [*muthois*]' (*Nemean* 7.20–2). The story of Palamedes and Odysseus in F 260 seems to have been another case of this. Poetic skill can be used to mislead: it is seen as amoral, as in Hesiod (see *Theogony* 26–8 and CH. 3). Again, an analogy can be made with the deception *within* the mythological story that causes Ajax's suicide in *Nemean* 8 (see especially lines 32–4b).

It follows from (2) and (3) that Pindar's notion of myth is dynamic: the narrator's attitude to his subject matter is crucial. For Pindar, mythmaking is linked to praise, and contrasted with blame and envy. It will tend to exalt the subject. This is the correct course, and that chosen by Pindar (the earlier poet Archilochos, notorious for abusive blame-poetry, is mentioned as an example *not* to be followed at *Pythian* 2.55). The only figures who do not deserve praise are the enemies of the gods, such as Typhon, Ixion, and

Tantalos. Thus, the narrative of the myth should in general gloss over episodes that reflect badly on their subjects, not so much mirroring the events as redeeming them (see, for instance, the poet's elaborate defence in *Nemean 7* of his treatment of the story of Neoptolemos). Time has the same effect, both because it makes us forget, and also because it puts things right (for reflections on this principle and its limits see, for example, *Olympian 2*).

Pindar as mythmaker: the case of Olympian 1

An important methodological question is whether Pindar himself creates variants of myths or simply selects between variants which already exist. A key test case is the myth of Pelops in *Olympian 1*, where he rejects the version which he himself reports – that at a feast attended by the gods Tantalos served up his son Pelops in a cauldron, that Demeter ate his shoulder, and that after the revolted gods had brought Pelops back to life they gave him an ivory shoulder in its stead. This sounds like a van Gennepian initiatory schema, in which the transition from boyhood to manhood is marked by a symbolic action which resembles killing followed by rebirth with a new identity (see further, Hubbard 1987b). Pindar's preferred version includes both cauldron and feast, but separates them out. This time, Poseidon fell in love with Pelops when he emerged from the cauldron (a birth ritual?) with his ivory shoulder (with which he was born?) and took him to Olympos (just as Zeus took Ganymede). The feast takes place and Tantalos steals nectar and ambrosia; in punishment for his father's crime, Pelops is returned to earth. When he comes of age, he wishes to attempt the chariot race set by King Oinomaos as a test for suitors of his daughter Hippodameia. Pelops prays on the seashore to Poseidon (rather as Achilles prays to Thetis in the *Iliad*) for assistance and a team of horses. Having obtained these, he wins the race, takes the kingdom, and is still honoured in Olympia today.

Although Hieron's victory was in the single horse race (*kelēs*), the myth looks forward, as Köhnken (1974) points out, to the even more prestigious chariot victory he was aiming to win later. Pindar presents his own version as true, and the other version as the result of the charm of fiction (28–30) and envy (47). It seems likely that Pindar's 'true' version is his own creation, even though the story of Pelops' victory over Oinomaos must be older. Nagy (1986) seems to argue that the whole of Pindar's preferred version predates him. Specifically, he suggests that the two versions of this myth represent myths attached to the two principal competitive events at Olympia, namely the foot-race (*stadion*, said to have been the first and for some time the only event) and the chariot race. Thus, Pindar's rejection of one version of the myth in favour of the other is simply another way of telling the story of how the chariot race was introduced at Olympia and eventually replaced the footrace as the defining event. But even if Pelops' role in the aetiology of the chariot race is indeed earlier than Pindar, Pindar's revision of the 'cooking' myth would not have to be: the reassembled Pelops, ivory shoulder and all, could perfectly well have won the race without support from his former lover, Poseidon. In this case, then, it seems likelier that Pindar does innovate, although he presents himself, and may have seen himself, as establishing the authentic version.

How much innovation?

Partly because of his explicit statements about mythology, the central questions in discussing Pindar's poetic use of myth, or mythopoetics, must be, How much innovation is there, and why does he innovate? Assessing the extent of Pindar's contribution is difficult for the obvious reason that features that seem to us to be new may in fact be modelled on sources now lost to us. Since there are some cases where we know that a myth treated by Pindar also featured in an earlier work, such as the Hesiodic *Catalogue of Women* or a poem by Stesichoros, and since our knowledge of early Greek poetry is incomplete (as was that of Hellenistic scholarship), it follows that there is a high risk that we may underestimate Pindar's debt to the past.

Pindar's account of his poetic processes in *Olympian* 1 is unusually explicit. Elsewhere he occasionally implies that he is singing 'new songs' or 'correcting' the discourse of myth (for example, in *Olympian* 9 and *Olympian* 7), but it is difficult to know what such statements mean. Many cases are very uncertain. For example, it has been argued that Pindar changed the tradition of the founding of the Olympic Games. He attributes the foundation to (the famous) Herakles: see, for example, *Olympian* 10.43–59. The argument goes that in so doing he rejects an earlier tradition that it had been founded by the Idaian Daktyls (*Daktyloi Idaioi*: diminutive mythical inventors of metalwork dwelling on Mount Ida), who had been looking after the baby Zeus at Olympia (which was already a sanctuary of Kronos in this version). In this version, one of the Daktyls was apparently called Herakles, and it was he who fetched the wild olive tree which furnished the victors' crowns from the land of the Hyperboreans (Pausanias 5.7.7; see also Huxley 1975). There is no compelling reason, though, to believe that the version told by Pausanias is older than Pindar's.[4]

Many other possible cases of innovation have been catalogued by Roberston (1940) and Huxley (1975). There are two cases, for example, in *Nemean* 3. At line 34, Pindar has Peleus capture Iolkos 'alone without an army', which seems designed to counter the tradition that Peleus leads his army in through the two halves of the body of the wife of Akastos (Apollodoros 3.13.7; Huxley 1975: 18; for an Anatolian equivalent to the rite, see Masson 1950). Again, at lines 48–9, Pindar has the young Achilles bring the 'panting' bodies of animals to Cheiron, but it seems likely that the original point was that Achilles ate the animal's living marrow.[5]

In some cases, Pindar seems to correct the *Catalogue of Women*. For example, in the *Catalogue* Apollo learnt of Koronis' infidelity from a crow F 60 MW (F 239 Most), but Pindar both alludes to and rejects this version: '[Apollo was] informed by his surest confidant, his all knowing mind, impervious to lies' (*Pythian* 3.27–8). It has been suggested that an episode in the Kyrene story in *Pythian* 9 (39–51) where Cheiron has to remind Apollo that he is omniscient is also a correction of the *Catalogue* (Huxley 1975: 15). *Olympian* 9 tells the genealogy of Opous, eponym of the principal city of Eastern (or Opuntian) Lokris. Pindar recounts that Opous' father was Zeus, while his mother was the daughter of an Epeian who was also called Opous. (The Epeians were, according to tradition, the early inhabitants of Elis: *Odyssey* 13.275.) Zeus gave this woman as wife to her father's brother, Lokros, childless ruler of the kingdom of Lokris. King Lokros adopted her child, named him Opous after his maternal grandfather, and put him in charge of the city, which in turn came to be named Opous after him. Pindar's poem appears to indicate that he is innovating here, since he talks about 'new songs' (47–8). The motivation seems to have been to obliterate the story, attested as having been told in the *Catalogue*, that Lokros was driven out of Eastern Lokris by his son Opous and went on to found Western Lokris (Huxley 1975: 31–3; Gerber 2002: 51–2; Mann 1994: 324; D'Alessio 2005b: 224–6).

In other cases Pindar corrects unsavoury versions of myths relating to his own city, Thebes. In *Isthmian* 4, for instance, Pindar calls the children of Herakles and Megara 'bronze-armed' (line 69), thus indicating that they were not in fact killed as children (Huxley 1975: 17). Similarly in *Nemean* 9.24 and *Olympian* 6.15, where seven pyres are said to burn after the fall of the Seven against Thebes (line 24), it has been suggested (Hubbard 1992) that the poet is subtly correcting the story that the Thebans deprived the dead of funeral rites.

The account of the battle between the Dioskouroi and Idas and Lynkeus in *Nemean* 10 also seems to represented a radically streamlined rendering of earlier versions. The version attested for the Cyclic *Kypria* is such an example,[6] in particular, the point at which in the *Kypria* Lynkeus' x-ray vision enables him to see the Dioskouroi as they lie in ambush in a tree trunk – Pindar keeps the tree trunk (line 61), but dispenses with the ambush.

Aiginetan mythology

One case where great uncertainty remains is Pindar's account of Aiginetan mythology, focused on the Aiakidai, whom Pindar regards as Aiginetan in origin (Burnett 2005). There is no sign of this association in Homer's writings

(Homer also ignores the family connections of Ajax, Achilles, and Patroklos), and it may be that this family was originally associated with South Thessaly, though Ajax's association with Salamis is Homeric. The Aiginetan associations may have already appeared in the *Catalogue of Women* and a poorly-attested archaic epic, the *Alkmaionis*. The role of the Aiakidai is taken to its extreme in *Olympian* 8, where Aiakos helps Apollo and Poseidon build the walls of Troy, which is to be sacked twice, by his son and great-grandson. This may be compared with the analogous correlation between Aiakos, his great-grandson Neoptolemos, and Delphi outlined in *Paean* 6. It is tempting to speculate that Pindar's close connection with his Aiginetan patrons led him to innovative here, but we cannot be certain (see Hubbard 1987a). On the other hand, it is also possible that Pindar's Aeginetan mythology is an old tradition which was, for some reason, excluded in the Homer poems (Nagy 1990).

Motives for change

I said earlier that Pindar avoids myths that show disrespect for gods or heroes. Pindar rarely speaks ill of the gods. According to F 283 he is supposed to have reported that Hera was imprisoned by Hephaisto, but we do not know the context. According to F 91 the gods disguised themselves as animals when they were chased by Typhon, possibly a borrowing from Egyptian mythology (J. Gwyn Griffiths 1960). Pindar's version of the myth of Ixion avoids the implication that Ixion actually slept with Hera (just as Stesichoros' palinode avoids the implication that Helen was an adulteress; see Doniger (1999) on parallels for such splitting of identity). Plato does not criticize Pindar for impiety, merely for immorality (see, for instance, *Republic* 365b on F 213). The only exception to this is *Republic* 408b, commenting on the implication at *Pythian* 3.52–4 that Asklepios took bribes,[7] but perhaps that passage merely shows that for Pindar Asklepios was not a god.

Usually Pindar does not reject myths on the grounds that they are inherently implausible. In *Pythian* 10.48–51 he says that he believes even the story of Perseus and the Gorgon. Compare F 233: 'nothing is believable to those who do not believe'. On the other hand, at *Paean* 7b.45 he (or the chorus leader) seems to say that he doesn't believe something 'unbelievable' (Gk *apiston*).

Politics will, of course, have been another factor. The Aiakid adventures in the Aiginetan odes are ultimately an expression of Aiginetan self-aggrandizement at this period. Similarly, Hubbard (1992) suggests that Pindar's attribution of the foundation of the Sikyonian Pythia to Adrastos rather than to Kleisthenes reflects the ascendancy of a pro-Argive political faction at Sikyon in this period.

Mythopoetics and genre

The accident of their survival means that our view of Pindar's treatment of myth is heavily biased towards the epinicians, but it is worth remembering that other genres may have approached it differently. The contrast between the telling of the myth of the death of Neoptolemos in *Paean* 6 and *Nemean* 7 is essentially that between ritual and praise. *Paean* 6 seems to have presented the Delphic festival of the Theoxenia as tied to the Aiakidai of Aigina. Delphic Apollo saved Greece when he instructed them to use Aiakos as an intermediary to ask Zeus to end the great drought afflicting Greece, and it is this act of grace that the Theoxenia commemorates. Three generations later, however, it was Apollo too who killed Aiakos' great-grandson Neoptolemos after Neoptolemos had slaughtered Priam at the altar of Zeus Herkeios during the sack of Troy. Neoptolemos now has a cult at Delphi beside the temple of Apollo. Pindar deals with the same myth in a much more oblique and diplomatic manner in *Nemean* 7, written in honour of a boy victor from Aigina. He omits the detail that Neoptolemos killed Priam, and Neoptolemos' killer is named as 'a man' (line 42) rather than Apollo. The generic convention that the myth ought to provide an *exemplum* for the victor requires that the story of Neoptolemos be presented in a form which offers him praise.

Organization of narratives

Even if we cannot be sure about originality, Pindar certainly shows skill in organizing mythological narratives. Two good examples are

1   The presentation of Rhodian mythology in *Olympian* 7,[8] which is sketched in three stages, going back in time: (i) the founding of Rhodes by Tlepolemos after he murdered Likymnios in Tiryns; (ii) the institution of the fireless sacrifice in honour of Athene at Rhodes (thus successfully pipping the Athenians to the post in honouring the newly born goddess);[9] (iii) in deep mythology, the process by which Rhodes came to be assigned to the god Helios. So in correct order, the three stages are: the emergence of the island and Helios, the cult of Athene at Lindos, and the Dorian colonization. Each of the three stages involves a mistake which turns out well (*felix culpa*, to use Thomas Aquinas' Latin term).

2   The myth of the foundation of Kyrene, as told in the semi-epic *Pythian* 4. This mythical narrative, easily the longest and most sophisticated in the works of Pindar, presupposes a division of time into three stages: Stage 1, Medea, returning from Kolchis with the Argonauts at Thera, prophesies the future foundation of Kyrene following Euphamos' loss of the sacred clod of earth; Stage 2, seventeen generations later, Delphi tells Battos to found Kyrene; and Stage 3, eight generations later, the present. Stage 1 is made more complex by

the fact that Medea makes it clear that, if Euphamos had taken the clod back to Sparta as he was supposed to and had thrown it into the mouth of the Underworld at Tainaros, the colonization would have happened directly from the Peloponnese just four generations later (that is, after the Trojan War), in which case Kyrene would have been non-Dorian. So the present situation is again the result of a mistake.[10]

Panhellenic and local

Pindar probably ranges from the local to the Panhellenic in the scope of his myths, from relatively local mythology that would probably be easiest to find in cult songs for local sanctuaries and festivals – the birth of Teneros in *Paean* 9, or the myth of Herakles on Paros in F 140b, for example – to those relating to Panhellenic sanctuaries, of which *Paean* 6, relating to the Theoxenia and including a sacrifice 'on behalf of all of Hellas', is a good example.

More commonly, Pindar weaves connections between the Panhellenic and the local. A primary mechanism here is genealogy. Thus, *Olympian* 6 is written for Hagesias of Syracuse, a member of the Iamid family of Olympic priests whose family had connections with Stymphalos in Arkadia. Pindar recounts the myth of the birth of the Iamids' ancestor, Iamos, in Arkadia, and himself claims to have a genealogical link with Arkadia in that Thebe, the nymph who is the eponym of Pindar's native Thebes, was the daughter of Metopa who, in turn, originally came from Stymphalos. In *Olympian* 9 the rather obscure local mythology of Eastern Lokris is broadened out and given potentially Panhellenic significance by incorporating a character from Elis and by including Patroklos amongst his descendants. Aiginetan mythology is slotted into the Panhellenic matrix not only by stressing the role of the Aiakidai in Panhellenic events (e.g., in the Trojan War), but also by describing the Aiakid diaspora that took members of the family as far afield as Molossia and Cyprus.

Myths told in Homer are not well represented in Pindar, at least not in the epinicians poems. It is possible that part of the reason for this is that Pindar did not want to use for victory songs themes that were already established at the Panhellenic level (Mann 1994).

Themes connecting across time

Many of Pindar's myths are concerned with origins of one sort or another;[11] deaths are much less common than births. The extant songs do not say much about the origin of the universe, though that seems to have been touched on in the *Hymn to Zeus*, which described the origin of at least some of the gods.[12] So too, *Olympian* 9 describes the repopulation of the earth by Deukalion and

Pyrrha after the Great Flood. The birth of Apollo was narrated at least once (in *Paean* 12) and probably elsewhere as well; we have the birth of Herakles in *Nemean* 1, of Iamos in *Olympian* 6. The island of Rhodes is born from the sea in *Olympian* 7.62–71; the *Hymn to Zeus* describes the rooting down of the island of Delos to the seabed (F 33c); the foundation myth of Kyrene set out at *Pythian* 4.13–57 hinges on the sacred clod of earth that determines the future fate of Libya.

Pythian 1 presents the historical foundation of the city of Aitna by the poem's dedicatee, Hieron, in mythical terms, as the continuation of the long Dorian migration (lines 61–6) and as a symbol of the triumph of divine order and divine music over Typhonic chaos (lines 1–28). *Olympian* 10 narrates the origin of the Olympic Games, presenting it as 'birth rites', with the Fates (Moirai) in attendance (53–4). The origin of the Delphic oracle is perhaps touched on in *Paean* 8.

One of Pindar's hymns told the story of the creation of the Muses: when Zeus asked the gods whether they needed anything, they replied, someone to praise his deeds and accomplishments in music (F 31). *Pythian* 12 tells the aetiology of one particular melody, the 'nome of many heads', in imitation of the death cries of the Gorgons. In F 139, from a lament (Greek *thrēnos*), a number of distinct forms of lamentation are traced back to the mythological singers whose deaths they originally honoured. Pindar gives varying accounts of the origin of the dithyramb: in Naxos (F 115), or in Thebes (F 71, cf. *Olympian* 13.25).

Pindar uses myth to stress relationships between the generations within a family. Thus, Antilochos sacrifices himself for his father, Nestor, in *Pythian* 6.28–42; the sons of the Seven against Thebes, known as the Epigonoi ('Afterborn'), redeem the failure of their fathers in *Pythian* 8.39–55; Amphiaraos gives advice to his son Amphilochos in F 43); and in *Olympian* 8.42–6 we learn that the walls of Troy, having been built by Aiakos, will be torn down by his descendants in the second and fourth generations.

Myth forges connections between the heroic past and the present. Thus, Theron of Akragas is descended from the family of Polyneikes, a clear example of good fortune succeeding bad in the same line (*Olympian* 2.46); Hagesias of Syracuse is a member of the Iamid family (*Olympian* 6); Arkesilas king of Kyrene is descended from Battos (*Pythians* 4 and 5); and Aristagoras of Tenedos has heroic ancestors (*Nemean* 11.33–43). Such connections cannot always be made: the Aiakidai have left no descendants on Aigina, for example, although Neoptolemos did found the royal line of Molossia (*Nemean* 7).

Thebes

As a Theban, Pindar naturally stressed Theban mythology. He surveys various themes at the start of *Isthmian* 7: Dionysos, Herakles, Teiresias, Iolaos, the Sown Men (*Spartoi*), the Seven against Thebes, and the Aigeidai who helped

Sparta take Amyklai (significantly not Oedipus!); *Pythian* 11 similarly invokes a long sequence of Theban myths, as does F 29, from the *Hymn to Zeus*. *Olympian* 2 surveys the daughters of Kadmos, touching on Semele, Ino, Oedipus, and Polyneikes, spinning the disasters as evidence that everything works out in the end. *Paeans* 7 and 9 seem to have told the stories of local Boiotian prophets.

Of those, the most important in the extant poems is Herakles, by genealogy an Argive hero (as in *Nemean* 10.16–18) but transplanted to Thebes. Of the canonical Labours of Herakles, six are mentioned: the Keryneian Hind in *Olympian* 3.28–30, the Stables of Augeas in *Olympian* 10.28–30 (coupled with the defeat of the sons of Molione), the Mares of Diomedes in F 169, Laomedon and Hesione in F 140a, the cattle of Geryon in F 169a, and Kerberos in *Dithyramb* 2 (F 249a; presumably implied in F 70b). It may be noticed that these six are predominantly the more Panhellenic of the labours, rather than those narrowly confined to the Peloponnese.

Other achievements of Herakles are also mentioned: his defeat of Alkyoneus at Phlegra and the war on the Meropes (*Nemean* 4.26–7, *Isthmian* 6.33), assisting the gods against the giants (prophesied by Teiresias, *Nemean* 1.67–9; cf. *Nemean* 7.90), the defeat of Antaios (*Isthmian* 4.52–5; also the probable subject of F 111), and the battle with Kyknos (*Olympian* 10.15–16)[13]. *Nemean* 1 focuses on the feat of strength he performed as a newborn baby (cf. also "*Paean* 20"). *Olympian* 9 talks of a battle at Pylos between Herakles and Poseidon, between him and Apollo, and between him and Hades. If this is all one event (so Gerber 2002: 36), we have no other reference to it, but it might be three: first, Herakles' attack on Pylos, second the stealing of the Delphic Tripod, and third the Kerberos labour (see Gantz 455). Herakles also founds cults and competitions: he brings the olive to Olympia and sets up the Olympic Games (*Olympians* 3 and 10), and F 346, in part known only since 1967, shows Herakles founding the sanctuary at Eleusis, having undergone an initiation.[14] In another fragment (F 140b) he founds the Delian sanctuary on the island of Paros. In two odes Pindar presents a mini sequence of labours carried out by Herakles and Telamon together: sacking Troy (with Peleus in F 172), waging war on the Meropes, and killing Alkyoneus (*Isthmian* 6 and *Nemean* 4). At the opening of *Pythian* 10, Herakles is hailed as an ancestor figure both for Lakedaimon and for Thessaly.

Several features are worth noticing:

1   Shaping of myths: *Isthmian* 4 (for a Theban hero) describes his defeat of Antaios, his achievement of immortality, and his marriage to Hebe, but omits his death and seems to alter the story of the murder of his children.

2   Herakles and 'Law': F 169, perhaps from a dithyramb, described two violent labours – the cattle of Geryon (cf. F 81) and the horses of Diomedes –

presenting these, somewhat paradoxically, as illustrating the principle that 'law' (*nomos*) is king of all. Pindar must have meant the Law of Zeus. Herakles is presented as a civilizing power, an agent of divine law enforcement.

3   In several poems Herakles is a symbol for the ultimate lengths to which one can go. Thus, in *Olympian* 3, after telling of Herakles' journeys to the Danube and the land of the Hyperboreans, Pindar uses the Pillars of Herakles at the end of the poem as a metaphor for the limiting pinnacle of human achievement. The same metaphor appears at *Nemean* 3.19–26 and *Isthmian* 4.7–13.

The story of the Seven against Thebes has less prominence than might be expected. The fullest version appears in *Nemean* 9, where the expedition is presented as ill-omened, with the focus on the death of Amphiaraos (an event also described in *Olympian* 6.12–17. As has been seen, Hubbard (1992) suggests that the detail of the 'seven burning pyres' in both *Nemean* 9 and *Olympian* 6 is there to counter the alternate tradition that the Thebans denied the bodies burial. *Pythian* 8.35–60 has the dead Amphiaraos make a prophecy on the occasion of the arrival of the second expedition against Thebes by the Epigonoi; this leads up to a statement by Pindar that he has a special relationship with Amphiaraos' son Alkman. In a fragment (F 43) Amphiaraos advises another son, Amphilochos, to imitate a sea creature, changing to suit the situation.

Conclusion

To sum up, three points can be made:

1   In Greek lyric poetry, of which Pindar's work happens to be the best surviving example, myth was not, for the most part, abstract narrative, but a tool to be used for a purpose: to glorify, to teach, to explain, and to some extent also to entertain.

2   Pindar comes at the end of this tradition, in a period when there was increasing scepticism about the claims and truth value of myth, at least in intellectual circles; simply by continuing to use myth in the traditional way, he was taking a conservative stance. The same point could be made about his attitude to religion, for example, his embrace of a theological interpretation of an eclipse (*Paean* 9).

3   At the same time, Pindar's attitude towards the traditions of mythology was critical: he seems to have seen it as one of his functions to sort myth out, eliminating false traditions and returning to the truth. And in this respect, it may well be that he is to some extent reflecting the intellectual trends of his time (cf. CH. 3).

FURTHER READING

There is no general guide to myth in Pindar in English, although there is one in German (Köhnken 1971). The long narrative of the *Pythian* 4 is explicated by C. Segal's virtuoso work, *Pindar's Mythmaking* (1986b), and by Calame (2003), who also deals with *Pythian* 5 and *Pythian* 9. General surveys include Bowra 1964: ch. 7, as well as Mann 1994 and Segal 1986c. Valuable discussions of specific poems include Köhnken 1974 and Nagy 1986 on *Olympian* 1 and Sfyroeras 1993 on *Olympian* 7.

NOTES

1. For the approach to myth of the influential Polish anthropologist Bronislaw Malinowski (1884–1942) see Malinowski (1948); for a recent overview, Csapo (2005: 140–5).
2. Discovered in a Roman-period copy of an earlier Greek inscription at Palaikastro in Crete in 1904. On the poem, see, for example, M. L. West (1965) and Perlman (1995), and on Harrison's interpretation of it, Csapo (2005: 146–9).
3. See lines 11–15, with Lavecchia (2000: 93 and further references cited there).
4. See Jouanna (2002).
5. Philostratos, *Heroikos* 19.2 (p. 730 Olearius); Statius, *Achilleid* 2.96–100; Huxley (1975: 19).
6. F 15 *PEG*; see also D.C. Young (1993), Gantz (325–7).
7. See Gantz (91–2).
8. See Barrigon (2002).
9. Sfyroeras (1993).
10. On the mythical themes of *Pythian* 4, see further C. Segal (1986a), Calame (2003).
11. C. Segal (1986c).
12. D'Alessio (2009).
13. This alludes to Stesichoros, cf. Hubbard (1989).
14. Perhaps to be linked to *Dithyramb* 2, the *Katabasis of Herakles*, or *Kerberos*, for the Thebans, as Lavecchia (2000 ad loc.) suggests.

CHAPTER SIX

Instructing Myth: From Homer to the Sophists

Niall Livingstone

Instructive Functions of Myth

In what sense is myth instructive? From its earliest appearances, the Greek word *mythos* can indicate, amongst other things, a public utterance expressing the authority of its speaker. Thus, at the beginning of the *Iliad* Agamemnon sends the prophet Chryses away contemptuously and places 'a strong *mythos* upon him' (1.25); Achilles is famously trained by Phoinix to be 'a speaker of speeches and a doer of deeds' (9.443), and 'speeches' here are *mythoi*.[1] Myths in the later sense of the word that we inherit are also more than just stories: they encapsulate something about the way the world should (or should not) be. They are exemplary, 'paradigmatic' (we will shortly encounter the semi-technical use of the Greek word *paradeigma*, 'example'). Myth also helps to crystallize belief and to fashion thought patterns, which is why, as Penny Murray says (CH. 9), Plato thinks it too important to be left in the hands of the poets.

Sometimes the exemplary quality of a myth is fairly evident. The mythical characters Herakles and Odysseus are models of different kinds of endurance, Achilles of youthful courage, Penelope of loyalty and prudent wisdom, Theseus (in tragedy at least) of human solidarity and protection of the weak, and so on. Klytaimestra, Medea, and other terrifying female figures can be understood as warnings, or as reaffirming, by the power of contrast, the security and order of the real patriarchal family. Stories like the Gigantomachy and Titanomachy symbolize the victory of Order over Chaos; the tales of wrongdoers who get their comeuppance from Herakles or Theseus are also easily moralized.[2]

A Companion to Greek Mythology, First Edition. Edited by Ken Dowden and Niall Livingstone.
© 2014 John Wiley & Sons Ltd. Published 2014 by John Wiley & Sons Ltd.

Other stories do not lend themselves to such straightforward explanations: Danaos, his many daughters, and their disastrous marriages, for example, or the inexorably unfolding career of Oedipus.[3] Nevertheless, in general, myths impress audiences both ancient and modern with a sense of a significance beyond the mere fact of 'what happens'. With myth, there is no equivalence between what you see and what you get.

As can be seen later in this volume (CH. 11), myth was also crucial in defining Greek identity, serving something of the same function as the ideological apparatus of the modern nation state (such as anthems, national holidays, commemorations, national heroes or founder figures); myths embodied the sense that Greek-speaking peoples had a shared (mythical) past and thus in some sense, in spite of all conflicts and divisions, a shared destiny and duty of mutual respect. The corpus of myth thus constituted a powerful education in religion, ethics, and civics. This chapter explores some of the ways in which this educative power of myth was realized or harnessed in literary texts of all kinds from Homeric epic to late antiquity. It will thus range widely, frequently connecting with themes of other chapters in this volume, and in places providing the reader with only the briefest pointer to further reading.

Mythic *Paradeigmata* in Homeric Epic

Myth is (sometimes) paradigmatic in presenting a model of how things should be. The Greek word *paradeigma* (plural *paradeigmata*) and its Latin equivalent *exemplum* (plural *exempla*), both meaning 'example', are sometimes used in a more technical sense: a story of how someone behaved on a previous occasion told in order to persuade someone else how they should behave now (see p. 40).[4] Often their function is to comfort (consolatory: 'X was in a worse situation than yours, but got through it, so you will get through this') or to encourage (exhortatory: 'X persevered through harder times than yours, so you should persevere'). Often there is a bit of both.[5] *Paradeigmata*, in Homer and in later authors, may feature 'historical' characters, but they are often drawn from myth. An interesting case is the *paradeigma* by which Nestor tries, unsuccessfully, to persuade Agamemnon and Achilles to listen to his advice in his speech at *Iliad* 1.253–86: it is taken from his own long life, but goes back to a time when he fought the Centaurs alongside heroes such as Theseus, a time which has mythic distance even from the perspective of the Trojan battlefield.[6] It is not so very different when Odysseus exhorts himself to a supreme effort by reference to one of his own 'mythic' experiences:

'Endure, my heart! You have endured worse than this
on the day when the Kyklops whose drive is unrestrained devoured my
strong companions; but you bore it, so that wit
brought you out of the cave though you thought you would die.'

(Odyssey 20.18–21)[7]

The power of a *paradeigma* consists more in the very act of comparing
the addressee's situation with a mythic one than in the real closeness of the
comparison. This may be illustrated by examining a famous example at one of
the most emotionally charged moments of the *Iliad*. In Book 24, Priam enters
the Greek camp at night and comes to Achilles' tent in order to beg him to
accept a ransom in exchange for the body of his dead son Hektor. In an intense
scene, the two men weep together: Priam for his dead son, Achilles for his dear
friend Patroklos and for his father, Peleus, whom he will never see again. Achilles
offers Priam stark consolation in the form of reflections on the dispensation of
Zeus for humans: no mortal life is free from pain (24.468–551). He accedes to
Priam's request and leaves his tent to prepare Hektor's body to be sent home
for burial. When he returns he proposes a shared meal (a powerful symbol of
reconciliation, however brief) and once again offers consolation, this time combined with exhortation and in the form of a mythological *paradeigma*:

> Now let us turn our thoughts to a meal.
> Even Niobe of lovely hair turned her thoughts to food
> although twelve children of hers had died in her palace,
> six daughters, and six sons in the prime of youth.
> Apollo killed her sons with arrows from his golden bow   605
> in anger against Niobe, and Artemis the archer her daughters,
> because she claimed she was equal to Leto whose face is beautiful:
> she said Leto had borne two children, but she herself had borne many;
> but Leto's, though only two, put all of hers to death.
> For nine days they lay in their blood, and there was no-one   610
> to bury them, since Kronos' son had turned the people to stones,
> but on the tenth day the Heavenly Gods buried them.
> And she turned her thoughts to food, when she stopped shedding tears.
> Now among the rocks, it seems, in the lonely mountains
> on Sipylos, where they say the beds are of the goddess   615
> nymphs who dance around Achelōos,
> there, stone though she is, she broods on her god-sent pain.
> Come then, glorious old man, we too should attend
> to food.

(Iliad 24.601–19)

The example is obviously apt. Things could be worse: Niobe lost twelve
children at once, Priam has (on this occasion, at least) lost only one. The grim

interlude when the corpses are left to lie in their blood (not mentioned in other versions of the story) provides an analogue to something which Achilles obviously cannot mention directly, his own mistreatment of Hektor's corpse. In another respect, though, it is very clearly not apt. Niobe's fame in myth is simple (the fullest version is in Ovid, *Metamorphoses* 6.146–312). Unwisely, she boasted that her children were more numerous than Leto's. Leto's two children were the gods Apollo and Artemis, and they killed all of hers. Niobe's grief was such that she wept until she turned to stone (and her tears became a stream). The number of children varies according to version. Sometimes one of them survives. The exact terms of Niobe's insult to Leto vary too. But there is never, except here, any suggestion that she pauses from her weeping to eat. It destroys the essential logic of the story: unremitting grief transformed to numbness, the woman and her tears transformed to stone and water. In short, Niobe's meal is a free invention by the poet – or by the character Achilles, who, being trained as we have seen as a 'speaker of *mythoi*' as well as a 'doer of deeds' (*Iliad* 9.443), should understand the persuasive use of myth.

Ever since antiquity, scholars have been troubled by this lapse of narrative logic, and have felt tempted to fix it. One solution is to delete lines 614–17. An ancient commentator (scholiast) writes:

> [These] four lines are removed, because they do not follow on from 'And she turned her thoughts to food ...' Because if she was turned to stone, how could she consume food? And the consolation is ridiculous: 'Eat, because Niobe ate, and she was turned to stone.' (The 'A' Scholia on *Iliad* 24.614–16)[8]

This proposed deletion creates a new version of the story in which, after nine days of weeping, Niobe eats and then (presumably) gets on with her life: something of an anticlimax. This approach is too literal-minded and logical-minded. This is not how mythic argument works. Since everyone knows that Niobe wept until she was turned to stone, creating a version in which she ate and recovered instead does not make her a good example in a literal sense. The whole point is that Achilles invokes her in spite of the fact that she is a bad example. He does violence to her myth by saying, for the sake of his argument, that she ate when we all know she did not, and then actually underlines this distortion by returning to the traditional turning-to-stone story even though it no longer makes sense. Here and often, mythological *paradeigma* works on the one hand by creating a connection between the present situation and a mythical one (Priam is like Niobe in that he has suffered an incalculable loss), and on the other hand by emphasizing the distance and lack of correspondence between myth and reality.[9] Niobe wept until she turned to stone because she is part of the world of myth, a world of absolutes: a world in which, for instance, a man could not see in his enemy the image of his own father, and a father could not set aside for a moment his hatred of his son's killer.[10] Niobe would eat if she were part of our world; Priam should, and will, eat because he is. The mythological comparison brings out both how the extremity of his distress reaches beyond the limits of imaginable experience and how, nonetheless, it remains rooted in it. Priam will eat, but he will not then, like the Niobe of the scholiast's 'tidied' version, simply be able to move on from his sorrow. As Achilles' next words acknowledge, there is much grief yet in store (619–21):

> we too should attend
> to food. After that, it may be that you weep again for your dear son,
> when you have brought him into Troy. He will cause you many tears.

Achilles' anomalous version of Niobe's story makes evident the fact that equivalences with myth are never complete. Comparison with myth puts real experience – in this case, Priam's grief – in perspective: on the one hand, it has limits; on the other hand, it is (within the terms of the poetic fiction) all too real.

An interesting counterpoint to the effect of the Niobe *paradeigma* may be seen in a famous episode in the *Odyssey*, when Odysseus is being entertained amongst the Phaiakians at the court of King Alkinoös in Scheria. Here the bard Demodokos unintentionally makes Odysseus cry by singing of episodes from the Trojan War. At first Odysseus hides his tears (8.83–95). When Demodokos tells the story of the Wooden Horse and the sack of Troy itself, though, he no longer hides his tears, and is likened in a striking simile to a woman lamenting her husband who has fallen defending his city (8.521–31). By contrast with the distancing effect of mythological *paradeigma*, this story from Odysseus' own 'history' results in intense identification, not just with his own past self but with the victims of his past actions.[11]

Hesiod

Hesiod's mythography is discussed elsewhere in this volume by Ken Dowden (CH. 3). But his work requires particular, if brief, discussion here. He is the first Greek poet to combine narration of myth with an explicitly didactic stance: he is telling his audience both how things came to be (in the *Theogony*) and what we should do now (in the *Works and Days*). The opening passages of the *Works and Days* are of particular interest for our discussion of the instructive use of myth. The poet deploys myth in a variety of ways to drive home his insistent, urgent message that work, however disagreeable and unrewarding, is the appropriate and necessary response to the hardness of human life.

After invocation of the Muses (1–10), the poem begins with a mythical or theological 'correction' of its sister-poem, the *Theogony*. There is not, as stated at *Theogony* 225, a single goddess Strife (*Eris*). In fact there are two. One is destructive and encourages war; today we might call her Conflict. The other is beneficial and drives people to work harder; we might call her Competition (*Works and Days* 11–26). The poet thus asserts his authority to manipulate myth or to discover new mythological 'truths', in line with the creative role in organizing myth which is assigned to Homer and Hesiod by Herodotos (see p. 48). This newly revealed goddess *Eris*, who pits worker against worker and indeed poet against poet (26; an idea not lost on later poets who imitated Hesiod) in their efforts to outdo each other, is the presiding deity of Hesiod's poem – alongside *Dike* 'Justice', whom Hesiod's brother and addressee, Perses, has offended by seeking an unequal distribution of their inheritance.

Human beings are all too able to dream of a godlike life of ease and leisure, but this must not blind us to the real hardness of the world we live in. In this sense the *Works and Days* could be said to be 'anti-soteriological' (cf. CH. 15): its message is that our only hope lies not in any imagined otherworld, but in making the best of this one. This point is driven home by two related myths in the long section 42–201: the story of Prometheus and Pandora, and the Myth of the Races. The premise of the first is that the life of ease *is* possible for humans, at least theoretically, if it were not for the fact that the gods have chosen to 'hide' the means of life (42). The explanation for this takes us back to Prometheus' attempt to deceive Zeus and the gods' revenge in the form of the creation of the first woman, Pandora, already narrated in *Theogony* but told here (CH. 3) with the added element of Pandora's Box (90–105). When she releases all the evils into the world, all that is left behind is Expectation (*Elpis*). This human reliance on Expectation provides the rationale for Hesiod's poem, a guide to what we may reasonably expect and thus to uncovering, by agricultural toil, the livelihood which the gods have hidden.

The Myth of the Races starts from a slightly different premise: human beings once *did* live a life of ease just like the gods (112–3), in the time of the Golden Race (ancestor of the enduring idea of a 'Golden Age', in Greco-Roman literature and beyond). Since then, however, they have progressively degenerated as a series of new races were created, each of a baser metal than the last – with a blip, as was noted in CH. 3, for the Race of Heroes, non-metallic and superior to the Bronze Race who came before them. We ourselves are the Race of Iron, a metal symbolizing both cruelty and hard work. We can still expect some good things as well as bad (179), but one day, when force completely takes the place of justice in human relations and all sense of reverence is lost (192–3), Zeus will destroy us too (180). The myth thus drives home the other key theme of *Works and Days*: justice as well as work is necessary for human survival.

I conclude this section with a brief look at Hesiod's next story, not a myth but an example of a genre related to myth: the fable.[12] A nightingale cries pitifully as she is clasped in the claws of a hawk. The hawk reproaches her, say-ing in essence: 'I am stronger than you and will do what I like with you. It is a waste of effort to resist superior force' (202–12). The moral is probably twofold. On the one hand, the gods have made life hard for us, but they are stronger than us and it is useless to complain: we should accept our lot and get on with it (underlining the theme of work). On the other hand, the ugly image of the songbird in the claws of the hawk points to the cruelty and arbi-trariness of force, and the desirability of a better way of resolving differences (underlining the theme of justice). It also seems likely that we are invited to see in the nightingale the figure of the poet himself, wronged by his brother and seeking redress, and a better social order, through his poem.

Philosophical Critique and Adaptation of Myth

The ancient commentator's attempt to 'tidy up' Achilles' Niobe-story which we encountered above is related to another important ancient reaction to myth as a body of stories which are, or should be, instructive. Many ancient readers of myth (particularly, but not exclusively, myths relating to the gods) were troubled not by the logic of the stories but by the bad moral example they present. In the sixth century BC, the philosophical poet Xenophanes of Kolophon wrote that

> Homer and Hesiod have attributed to the gods everything
> that brings disgrace and censure among humans:
> thieving, adultery, and deceiving one another.[13]
> (Xenophanes 21 B 11 DK)

It is easy to see Xenophanes' point: examples are not far to seek. The story of Hermes' theft of Apollo's cattle is related in the *Homeric Hymn to Hermes*. The adultery of Aphrodite and Ares and its exposure to the other gods is humorously presented by the bard Demodokos at *Odyssey* 8.266–366 (to say nothing of the gods' innumerable affairs with mortal women). Hera famously deceives Zeus in order to distract his attention from the Trojan battlefield in the *Iliad* (14.153–351). Xenophanes concludes that people in general, and Homer and Hesiod in particular ('everyone has learned from the beginning according to what Homer says', 21 B 10), have made the gods in a human image. After all, foreign peoples think their gods look like them; if animals had gods, they would look like animals (21 B 15–16). Xenophanes concludes that poetic theology is false. Euripides has his tragic hero Herakles, unable to com-prehend the hatred that has led Hera to make him go mad and kill his family, take refuge in a Xenophanean viewpoint:

> That the gods choose beds which are forbidden
> I cannot believe, or that they fasten each others' hands in chains.
> I have never thought it, and will not be convinced;
> nor that one god is born to be master over another.
> If god is truly god, then he has need
> of nothing. These are the miserable stories of poets.
>   (Euripides, *Madness of Herakles* 1341–6)

Xenophanes' solution is simple and radical: he rejects the traditional pantheon and claims that there is one deity, who bears no resemblance whatsoever to humans (21 B 23). Another way of solving the problem of divine and heroic immorality is the kind of radical censorship proposed in Plato's *Republic* (see CH. 9). Others sought to solve this problem in ways which preserved the authority of poetic myth, and the most important method of doing so is *allegorical interpretation* (which is discussed in various other chapters, especially CHS 10, 15, and 17).[14] This is interpretation based on the assumption that, while talking about one thing on the surface, at a deeper level these works are talking about something else (like George Orwell's *Animal Farm*, apparently telling the story of a farm taken over by the animals but 'really' satirizing the Stalinist regime in the Soviet Union). A leading exponent of allegorical interpretation of Homer was Herakleitos 'the Grammarian' or 'the Allegorist' (on whom see also CH. 15), writing perhaps in the first century AD but drawing on the work of much earlier scholars. For Herakleitos, it is an easy conclusion that Homer expresses himself allegorically. His treatise *Homeric Problems* begins (in Russell and Konstan's translation):

> It is a weighty and damaging charge that heaven brings against Homer for his disrespect to the divine. If he meant nothing allegorically, he was impious through and through [a memorable 'sound bite' in the Greek: *panta gar ēsebēsen, ei mēden ēllēgorēsen*, literally 'he blasphemed in everything if he allegorized nothing'], and sacrilegious fables, loaded with blasphemous folly, run riot through both epics. (tr. Russell and Konstan 2005)[15]

This cannot of course be true. Homer is our life-blood, our mother's milk, our very being, as Herakleitos makes clear:

> From the very first age of life, the foolishness of infants just beginning to learn is nurtured on the teaching given in his school. One might almost say that his poems are our baby clothes, and we nourish our minds by draughts of his milk. He stands at our side as we each grow up and shares our youth as we gradually come to manhood; when we are mature, his presence within us is at its prime; and even in old age, we never weary of him. When we stop, we thirst to begin him again. In a word, the only end of Homer for human beings is the end of life.

Just as Samuel Johnson made clear his own identity and allegiance in his aphorism 'when a man is tired of London, he is tired of life', so Herakleitos here sets out the centrality of Homer to the identity of an educated Greek. So if Homer appears to be presenting morally dubious stories, the fault must lie with us: we are failing to understand him correctly. Happily, Herakleitos is able to relieve us of all such misapprehensions.

His technique is nicely illustrated by his treatment of Homer's account of the 'deception of Zeus' (Greek, *Dios apatē*) by Hera in *Iliad* 14, an episode which is likely to have been at the forefront of Xenophanes' mind when composing the lines quoted above. In order to distract her husband, Zeus, from the battlefield machinations of the pro-Greek gods, the queen of the gods borrows from Aphrodite her magic girdle (which embodies 'affection, yearning, and flirtatious persuasion, which deceives the minds even of the most strong-witted', *Iliad* 14.216–17) then uses it to induce her husband to have sex with her, and thus lulls him to sleep. According to Herakleitos,

> this is an allegorical way of speaking of the spring, the season when all plants and grasses emerge from the ground as the frost and ice gradually melt ... He also represents Hera, that is to say the air, as still glum and gloomy after the winter [probably a reference to 14.158, where Hera is said to find her watchful husband 'hateful'] ... The rich and fertile season, with its sweet scent of flowers, is suggested by the kind of ointment with which Hera anoints herself ... He also puts into the lap of air the strap or *kestos* [the girdle of Aphrodite mentioned above] 'wherein is love, desire, and company', because this season of the year has as its portion the greatest delights of pleasure, for we are then not chilled by cold or heated too much, but our bodies enjoy the comfort of middle ground between the two disagreeable extremes. (*Homeric Problems* 39, tr. Russell and Konstan 2005)

And so on. The ensuing Chapter 40 sorts out another problematic passage, *Iliad* 15.18–21, where Zeus wakes up, realizes he has been deceived, and threatens Hera, reminding her of a previous domestic incident when he hung her in chains from the sky with anvils attached to her feet. This, it turns out, is 'a theological account of the creation of the universe'. Where *paradeigma* deploys myth as a vehicle for an ethical message, allegorical interpretation makes it possible to rewrite myth as an exposition (on the highest authority) of one's own pet philosophical or natural-scientific theories.

Myth and Praise: Pindar and Isocrates

Pindar's use of myth in his poems celebrating victorious athletes, discussed by Ian Rutherford in the previous chapter, provides a model for the rhetorician Isocrates (born in the fifth century BC but writing mainly in the fourth century).

Isocrates writes polished political speeches on edifying subjects, his recurrent
theme being the need for the Greeks to unite amongst themselves and fight
against non-Greeks ('barbarians'), primarily the Persians: the 'Panhellenic
project'. In the speech which made his name, the *Panegyricus* ('Festival
Oration'), the foundation of the Eleusinian Mysteries is marshalled alongside
the Persian Wars as justification for Athens' claim to leadership of the Greeks
in Isocrates' planned Panhellenic enterprise. At the very end of his career, in
the *Panathenaicus* (written, so Isocrates tells us, at the age of ninety-four),
Isocrates makes Agamemnon (king of Argos) the standard bearer of the
Panhellenic project. This is appropriate in a speech which, while once again
championing Athens, gives serious consideration to Sparta's rival claim for
leadership of the Greek world.

In Isocrates' speeches we see the beginning of a significant trend whereby,
as myth becomes historicized, history too becomes mythicized. This trend is
in a sense anticipated when historians such as Herodotos and Thucydides seek
to incorporate the Trojan War and other 'mythic' material in their accounts:
see, for instance, Alan Griffiths' discussion (CH. 10) of their different views on
whether Minos of Crete was the first ruler to establish naval dominance (Greek
thalassokratia). In Isocrates' speeches, solemn historicizing treatments of
myth converge with solemn mythologizing treatments of history. The Greek
victors of the Trojan and Persian Wars become equally heroic and, in a way,
equally fantastical, as indeed they – and even Gauls – would later in the art of
Pergamon.[16]

Myth in Teaching: Mythological Epideictic

The study and learning of Homeric and other poetry is central to Greek education from the earliest times: Achilles, the 'speaker of words and doer of
deeds', is also a singer of the 'famous deeds of men' (*Iliad* 9.189). Active
manipulation of myth, on the other hand, starts to find its place in formal
teaching in the fifth century BC amongst the so-called sophists. The sophists
were travelling teachers offering instruction in a variety of subjects, often
including techniques of persuasion ('rhetoric') for which, controversially and
much to the disgust of aristocratic writers like Plato, they charged fees. Their
success was rooted in the demand created by a new inclusiveness in government. Under democracy and related systems of government, personal ability
and persuasive skills now became an increasingly viable route to political success, though noble birth and wealth remained, then as now, extremely important. Athens, inevitably, was a major centre of their activities, though few
sophists were themselves Athenian citizens. Sophists gave public performances to show off their skills and attract pupils; this sort of performance was

known as a 'display' (Greek *epideixis*, plural *epideixeis*). Speeches composed for such displays became known as 'epideictic' speeches, a category which was then extended to include other speeches whose function was more honorific than practical, such as funeral orations. For Aristotle, and then throughout antiquity, epideictic was, together with forensic and deliberative, one of the three genres of rhetoric.[17]

One popular form of *epideixis* was a persuasive speech in a fictional situation derived from myth (the Trojan War being a particularly popular setting), which is therefore 'mythological epideictic'. Thus the famous fifth-century BC sophist Hippias of Elis gave a performance imagining a situation in which, after the fall of Troy, Achilles' son Neoptolemos asks wise old Nestor what is the best way of life to achieve a glorious reputation, and Nestor duly gives his advice. This performance was apparently a big hit in Sparta, presumably because of its traditional content, but rather startlingly in view of the Spartans' reputation for prizing brevity.[18] Similarly, Hippias' contemporary Prodikos of Keos performed a well-received *epideixis* on the theme of 'the Choice of Herakles', preserved (unlike most sophistic writings) because it is quoted or paraphrased at length by Xenophon in his *Recollections of Socrates* (usually known by its Latin title, *Memorabilia*). In it, the young Herakles is unsure what path to take in life; two female figures appear to him, both of course impersonated by the sophist himself. One is Vice personified, who tries to seduce him with the pleasures of a life of self-indulgence. The other, who is Virtue personified, warns him of the emptiness of such superficial pleasures and praises instead the rewards of a life well lived.[19]

The best-known, and probably most influential, piece of mythological epideictic is the speech *Helen* composed by Gorgias of Leontinoi in Sicily, the most famous fifth-century teacher of rhetoric.[20] Its stated aim is to praise Helen, but in fact it does this by defending her, or rather by refuting the arguments of those who blame her. The character of Helen may be sympathetically treated in the Homeric epics, but in general she had a very bad press in Athenian tragedy, where she tends to be a hate figure both as an adulterous woman and as the cause of the Trojan War. Gorgias' line of defence is to claim, not that Helen did not commit adultery with Paris, or that she was justified in doing so, but rather that she had no choice and therefore cannot be held responsible. Something must have made her do it, Gorgias argues: fate or divine will; or physical force; or persuasion; or love. He discusses each possibility in turn, arguing that she could not be expected to resist any of them and is therefore free from guilt. The centrepiece of the speech is a gloriously florid evocation of the irresistible power of persuasive speech: 'speech is a mighty lord, which, though its substance is most miniscule and quite invisible, accomplishes truly divine feats: it can dispel fear and relieve grief and instil joy and inspire pity' (Gorgias 82 B 11 DK Section 8).

It seems likely that the influence of Gorgias' *Helen* is at work in the clever speech which the character Helen makes in her own defence in Euripides' *Trojan Women* (914–65), in which she transfers the blame for her elopement and the ensuing war first onto Hekabe for giving birth to Paris (919), then onto Priam for not destroying the child as the omens indicated he should (921), then onto Aphrodite as goddess of love (948), and finally onto the gods in general (965–6).

Another surviving mythological epideictic work by Gorgias is the *Palamedes*, a defence speech for the hero when falsely accused by Odysseus of treachery during the Trojan War. This episode was also the subject of Euripides' lost tragedy, the *Palamedes*, which formed part of the same tetralogy of plays on connected subjects as the surviving *Trojan Women*. It is tempting to see a thread of Gorgianic influence. Gorgias' *Palamedes* certainly set a trend which continued into the fourth century. There is a companion-piece, a speech in which Odysseus makes the case for the prosecution, attributed to the fourth-century rhetorician Alkidamas of Elaia, who was said in antiquity to have been Gorgias' pupil (though not much store should be set on such claims). There is also a pair of speeches, *Ajax* and *Odysseus*, attributed to the versatile philosopher-cum-rhetorician Antisthenes. Here the two heroes present their rival claims to be awarded the armour of Achilles after his death. We can also see the popularity of mythological themes from other titles of lost works: a *Praise of Bousiris* by the (untypically) Athenian sophist Polykrates; and an anonymous *Praise of Thersites*, famous as the ugliest man in the Greek army at Troy (*Iliad* 2.216)!

Why did rhetoricians choose mythological themes? The instructive content of these speeches is to a fair extent independent of the details of the particular myth. Gorgias' *Helen* is a reflection on human free will and responsibility, a display of Gorgias' written style at its richest, and above all an advertisement for the power of rhetoric. Helen is a fitting subject as the symbol of another mesmerizing force capable of bypassing the rational faculties, sexual attraction. The *Palamedes* is a lively demonstration of standard moves in any defence speech (e.g., I had no motive, I had no opportunity, it's not in my character), while Alkidamas' *Odysseus* is essentially an exercise in character assassination.

It is, however, fairly easy to see more general reasons for the appeal of myth. First of all we may imagine a crowd gathering around a sophist performing an *epideixis*. If a newcomer arrives and asks someone what's going on, the answer 'he's being Odysseus prosecuting Palamedes' is more likely to keep him in the audience than 'he's demonstrating rhetorical techniques of incrimination in the absence of hard evidence'. Myth allowed rhetorical teaching to associate itself with other popular genres such as tragedy (and comedy, which in the fourth century made increasing use of mythological plots). The memorable quality of the mythological stories, and the familiarity of characters such as Odysseus, probably helped people to remember the rhetorical moves.

But mythological epideictic was also very much a means for sophists to define the relationship between the education they offered and the traditional education based on the Homeric poems: it was part of the same tradition, but it was intriguingly original and innovative. The sophists sometimes appear as characters in Plato's dialogues and Plato has one of them, Protagoras, make the following controversial but maybe not unrealistic claim: '*I* say that the skill of the sophist dates back to ancient times and that those ancients who practised it, fearing it would be offensive, put up a screen and concealed it; some of them did this with poetry, people like Homer and Hesiod and Simonides, whereas others used rites and oracle-mongering, Orpheus, Mousaios and their ilk'(Plato, *Protagoras* 316d (tr. KD)). Thus sophistic education was inscribed in the complexity of ancient educative traditions, in which mythology played a large, and recurrent, part. This is doubtless why episodes from the Trojan War were particularly popular. And to this can be added that impersonating characters from myth also leant glamour to the sophists themselves, contributing to their image as 'larger-than-life' celebrities.

Conclusion

We have seen how, throughout the archaic and classical periods, myth was deployed for purposes of instruction in a wide variety of ways. Authors took advantage of considerable freedom to adapt, alter, and even invent. Part of what makes myth valuable for instructive purposes is its combination of reality and unreality, its power to make connections between the world we live in and other imagined worlds. Myth helps make instruction memorable. It also imparts authority and glamour.

FURTHER READING

On Homer, see the further reading recommendations of Létoublon, CH. 2, plus Held 1987 on *paradeigmata*; on Hesiod, again see Dowden's recommendations in CH. 3, especially Clay 2003. On fables see above all Holzberg 2002, with illuminating discussion and critique of earlier scholarship. The *Homeric Problems* are translated, introduced, and annotated in Russell and Konstan 2005. On myth and philosophy see Morgan 2000. For a recent discussion of Xenophanes of Kolophon in particular, with references to earlier literature, see Granger 2007; Granger focuses on Xenophanes' choice, which might be considered surprising in view of the trends of his time and of his sharp critique of earlier poets, to present his ideas in verse rather than in prose. On the question, tangential to the topics of this chapter but connected with them, of how prose emerges as an authoritative form of expression, see Goldhill 2002 and the essays in Yunis 2003. Yunis 1988 includes a fascinating discussion of the use to which

Euripides puts Xenophanes' ideas in the *Madness of Herakles*. On Isocrates see Papillon 2007) and Fox and Livingstone 2007: 551–3; on Gorgias, Bons 2007, with useful further reading; on epideictic rhetoric in general, Carey 2007 (246–7 briefly on mythological epideictic). Ford 2002 is a fascinating series of discussions which, while pursuing an argument about the emergence of poetic theory, cut across many themes touched on in this chapter: see, for example, ch. 2 on Xenophanes and the 'ancient quarrel' between poetry and philosophy, ch. 3 on the beginning of allegorical interpretation of epic (Ford does not come down as late as Ps.-Herakleitos, for whom see CH. 26 in this volume), and pp. 172–87 on Gorgias.

NOTES

1. On this earlier sense of *mythos*, see Dowden (1992: 4–5); and cf. Bremmer (1999a: 56 f).
2. In one of his speeches, the Roman-period rhetorician Dio Chrysostom (first century AD) presents the famous Cynic philosopher Diogenes of Sinope (fifth–fourth century BC) interpreting Herakles' adventures as the victories of a strong, healthy man over representatives of a series of vices: Diomedes is a decadent aristocrat, Geryon wealthy and arrogant, Bousiris a gluttonous athlete, the Amazon queen vain of her beauty, and so on (8.29–35).
3. Despite the passage of years, Dodds (1966) remains useful, as well as entertaining, as a critique of some misguided ways of seeking a 'moral' in Sophocles' play *Oedipus the King*. For a more recent attempt, see Ahrensdorf (2004). I leave the reader to decide how successful Ahrensdorf is in avoiding the pitfalls identified by Dodds. For a curious interpretation of the play as containing a *paradeigma* which illuminates US President Bill Clinton's notorious affair with Monica Lewinsky, see Schechner (1999). On the significance of the myth of the Danaids see Sian Lewis in CH. 23.
4. See also M. W. Edwards (2005: 305); and the classic study of Malcolm Willcock (1964).
5. M. Davies (2006: 582–3).
6. See below on the Homeric epics as a borderland between what is and is not 'myth'.
7. Translations are my own unless otherwise stated.
8. The 'A' Scholia, scholarly notes on the *Iliad*, so called because they were written in the margins of a tenth-century AD manuscript now known as Venetus A, were compiled from various works but contain material which goes back to Alexandrian scholarship of the third–second centuries BC. For more on this and on ancient scholarship on Homer in general, see Dickey (2007: 18–28).
9. See also Held (1987: 254) on the sense in which the story of Niobe, because it is not drawn from Achilles' own experience or family history, is more distinctively 'mythic' than most paradigmatic stories in the *Iliad*. On the effectiveness of Achilles' version of the Niobe-story as a *paradeigma* for Priam, see also Schmitz (2001: 151–3).

10. Readers will notice some relativism in the use of the words 'myth(ical)' and 'real(ity)' in this discussion. I treat the Homeric poems as 'myth' when seen from the outside, for example, from the point of view of later literature, but as 'reality' when seen from the inside, from the point of view of their characters. On the (qualified) realism of the *Iliad* and *Odyssey*, see, for example, Dowden (2004: 202) and M. W. Edwards (2005: 305), and on the Trojan War as 'the end of myth', Dowden in this volume (CH. 3).

11. On these episodes, see further, Fox and Livingstone (2007: 545).

12. On ancient fables, see Holzberg (2002: 13) on the hawk and the nightingale, 'the earliest surviving [Greek] fable'. Briefly, and broadly speaking, fables resemble myth in their exemplary and otherworldly quality. They differ in being freely invented, though this is not a hard-and-fast distinction, since on the one hand, as we have seen, authors adapt myths quite freely, and on the other hand, fables become 'traditional'. They also differ in having a definite moral, though, as in the present case, that moral is not always entirely explicit.

13. The idea is expressed again in 21 B 12, perhaps from another passage of the same work. Xenophanes' philosophical fragments are conveniently accessible in Waterfield (2000: 22–31), where B 11 is Waterfield's F6.

14. Dowden (1992: e.g., 24–5, 40–2) briefly presents aspects of allegory in various authors, including Herakleitos. Graf (1993a: e.g., 194–8, and CH. 17 in this volume) gives a real sense of the continuing tradition of allegory in late antiquity and on. See also Subject Index s.v. allegory.

15. See Russell and Konstan (2005) for text and translation of the *Homeric Problems* with extremely helpful introduction, notes, and bibliography.

16. Dowden (1992: 161).

17. Aristotle (*Rhetoric* 1358b) divides rhetoric into three genres (each of which has two interchangeable names in English use, one derived from Greek and one from Latin): law-court speeches ('dicanic' or 'forensic'), political speeches in an assembly ('symbouleutic' or 'deliberative'), and display speeches ('epideictic'; the Latin-derived term 'demonstrative' is less common). He subdivides dicanic into prosecution and defence, symbouleutic into persuasion and dissuasion, and epideictic into praise and blame. The first two divisions make obvious sense, but the third is more problematic: praise (and to a lesser extent blame) is a common theme of epideictic, but as will be seen, fictional law court speeches were also used for *epideixis*. In practice, epideictic came to be something of a rag-bag heading for anything which was not dicanic or symbouleutic.

18. Ps.-Plato, *Hippias Major* 286ab (Hippias 86 A 9 DK, Waterfield 2000: Hippias T2).

19. Xenophon *Memorabilia* 2.1.21–34 (Prodikos 84 B 2 DK, Waterfield 2000: Prodicus F1).

20. Gorgias 82 B 11 DK (Waterfield 2000: Gorgias F1).

CHAPTER SEVEN

Acting Myth: Athenian Drama

Jean Alaux

Introduction: Myth and Theatre

Throughout history, Greek drama, especially Greek tragedy of the fifth century BC, has been so much discussed and so frequently adapted that readers today tend to regard it as the main source of the most celebrated myths of ancient Greece.[1] In fact, all these dramatic works, most of which were performed between 472 and 401, draw on stories that had already inspired epic or lyric poetry. Thus, one of the best known Greek tragedies, *Oedipus the King* by Sophocles, takes up a subject already touched on by Homer (*Odyssey* 10.271–80) and also featured in a lost epic poem, the *Oidipodeia*. Aeschylus had written an *Oedipus* before Sophocles,[2] and we still possess some fragments of a play by Euripides, later than Sophocles' *Oedipus*, in which the hero is blinded by Laios' servants and not by his own hand (F 5 Jouan/Van Looy).

So, for the study of myth the plays of the classical period are a point of reference, but by no means a beginning. They make selections from a vast store of pre-existing material, which they submit to the constraints of the stage with considerable freedom in the treatment and organization of themes. Moreover, the tragic playwrights engage in dialogue both with earlier literary genres and with previous dramas. Even within the *oeuvre* of a single author such as Euripides, considerable variants and differences can be seen in the treatment of a particular story.

As for comedy, which turns around events not set in the remote world of myths but (with some exceptions) in an apparently familiar Athens, it constantly toys with tragic models and also engages in parody of epic (with many

---

A Companion to Greek Mythology, First Edition. Edited by Ken Dowden and Niall Livingstone.
© 2014 John Wiley & Sons Ltd. Published 2014 by John Wiley & Sons Ltd.

mythical allusions). Mention should also be made of satyr plays. These were performed as a tragic playwright's fourth play after three tragedies (three tragedies make a 'trilogy'; the group of four plays, three tragedies plus a satyr play, is a 'tetralogy'). Satyr plays presented light, bawdy depictions of figures from heroic myth, with a chorus of satyrs (hence the name), in a pastoral setting. There are many fragments, but the one satyr play which survives intact is Euripides' *Kyklops*. Its theme is taken from the famous episode in *Odyssey* Book 9, but here Polyphemus speaks like a fifth-century sophist. We also have substantial papyrus fragments of Sophocles' *Trackers* (*Ichneutai* in Greek), inspired by the *Homeric Hymn to Hermes*: Silenos leads the satyrs in pursuit of the infant Hermes, who has stolen Apollo's oxen.

Before even attempting a classification of drama's use of myth, I wish to stress the simultaneously ritual and civic purposes served by theatrical performances in the fifth century. They were dedicated to Dionysos, whose altar (*thumelē*) was placed in the centre of the dancing-floor (*orchēstra*), where the chorus performed. Indeed, one of the forms that may have influenced the beginnings of theatre was the dithyramb, said by Herodotos (1.23) to have been first instituted in Corinth by Arion, in which choral singing in unison alternated with solos by the chorus leader. In Athens, tragedies, satyr plays, and comedies were performed on the occasion of the major Dionysiac festivals (the Great Dionysia, but also the Lenaia and the Rural Dionysia). At the Great Dionysia, four whole days (later three days, from the beginning of the Peloponnesian War) were taken up with play performances, which were in competition with one another and on which a final vote was taken.[3]

To understand the close link between Dionysos and the theatre, the best starting-place is probably one of the last works of Euripides, the *Bacchae*: a play which stands apart from his other works and offers a very distinctive image of Dionysos. In this tragedy, the god himself, disguised as a Lydian, comes to punish the king of Thebes, Pentheus, for denying his divinity and thus also rejecting the dimension of otherness which he embodies. The god, who delights in masks, hides behind a human appearance and at the same time behind the actor's mask.[4] There is thus a twofold analogy between the nature of Dionysos and the nature of theatrical performance. Dionysos is a permanently dual god, being at once Greek and eastern, masculine and feminine. His relationship to human beings is marked through and through by the mystery of an absence and the intensity of a presence. While he is often represented by masks in religious ceremonies, his facial characteristics are nevertheless such that those at whom he directs his gaze are rooted to the spot.

Greek tragedy similarly calls into question and blurs the essential polarities of familial and civic identity by presenting human beings in a troubled light, by raising questions about the relationship between the doer and the deed and between thoughts, words, and acts, and by blurring the boundary between male and female. In addition, its effectiveness depends on the perception of a new space, which is that of fiction, of imitation (Greek *mimēsis*): the masks worn by the actors and by the members of the chorus tell the audience that they are not really the heroes of the play, while at the same time offering a means of projecting voices, which are thus able to convey powerful emotions.[5]

In the case of Euripides' Dionysos in *Bacchae*, the myth reflects the very nature of the performance: it emblematizes it. But this is an extreme case. Most of the time, myth feeds into dramatic poetry at three levels: it is a source of narrative material containing numerous variants on which authors can freely draw; it also exists in specific pre-existing form in the works of earlier authors; and lastly, once reinvented, it offers a binding framework, which provides the actual storyline of the play and its main underpinning structure (see Aristotle, *Poetics* 1450a38–b3). It is here that we see a major difference from the comedies of Aristophanes, whose structure has more a patchwork effect. No play more clearly illustrates this feature than *Oedipus the King*, which unfolds by way of such a measured and skilfully crafted progression that Sophocles has been said to have invented the detective novel.[6]

The Choice of Subjects

The corpus of plays that have come down to us in their entirety is, of course, limited. Those that survive are a tiny proportion of what once existed, the result of a gradual process of selection in antiquity followed by a hazardous process of transmission from antiquity to the present. Aeschylus composed between seventy-three and ninety-one dramas, Sophocles more than a hundred, and Euripides more than ninety; what survives is seven plays attributed to Aeschylus, seven by Sophocles, and nineteen attributed to Euripides (including the satyr play *Kyklops*), before we even consider their numerous competitors whose work is lost. The same is true for comedy. We possess eleven plays by Aristophanes, and one more-or-less complete play and numerous fragments by Menander, the master of New Comedy, but there are traces of more than a thousand titles altogether and some two hundred authors. We do, however, have numerous tantalizing fragments of lost plays, which can help us form a fuller understanding of the uses to which myths were put on the Athenian stage.

When we examine the plays and fragments that have come down to us, we see that there are two groups of myths that enjoy particular favour: the Trojan War and the vicissitudes of the royal family of Argos (some twenty plays by Aeschylus, more than thirty by Sophocles and twenty or so by Euripides); and the legendary history of Thebes (four tragedies by Aeschylus, six by Sophocles, and some ten by Euripides). This latter group, though smaller, includes two surviving masterpieces, Sophocles' *Antigone* and *Oedipus the King*. (See Table 7.1.)

Table 7.1 Classification of extant tragedies by mythological subject.

	Aeschylus	*Sophocles*	*Euripides*
Troy/Argos	*Oresteia* (*Agamemnon, Libation Bearers, Eumenides*)	*Ajax, Philoktetes, Electra*	*Andromache, Hecuba, Trojan Women, Helen, [Rhesus], Electra, Iphigeneia among the Taurians, Orestes, Iphigeneia at Aulis*
Thebes	*Seven Against Thebes*	*Antigone, Oedipus the King, Oedipus at Kolonos*	*Phoenician Women, Bacchae*
Attica			*Children of Herakles, Hippolytos, Suppliant Women, Ion*
Herakles		*Women of Trachis*	*Herakles*
Others	*Persians, Suppliant Women, Prometheus Bound*		*Alcestis, Medea*

In the case of the Trojan War, there are two explanations for its popularity as subject matter. First, it is the subject of the Homeric epics, with which tragic drama is in constant dialogue. Secondly, especially in the plays of Euripides, there is an inescapable parallel with the Peloponnesian War, whose events, tragic for Athens and for the wider Greek world, are vividly recounted by Thucydides. In the case of Thebes, the explanation is more complex. From the time of its foundation to the calamities that afflict the family of Oedipus, it embodies, from the Athenian point of view, a kind of anti-city, where political and familial models are defective: the negative, in fact, of the ideal pursued by Athenian democracy.[7]

Of course, the range of subjects covered extends well beyond these examples. Specifically Athenian myths, concerning, for example, the mythical beginnings of the city and the figure of Theseus and his family, are well represented. Herakles, the great hero who brought civilization to Greece, is the central character of an extant tragedy by Sophocles (*Women of Trachis*) and another by Euripides (*Herakles*). Several plays by Aeschylus, Sophocles, and Euripides were devoted to the legend of the Argonauts and to the story of Perseus. The legend of Prometheus – benefactor of human beings, punished by Zeus – was the subject of a trilogy by Aeschylus. (The authorship of the surviving play *Prometheus Bound* is disputed.)

Aeschylus' *Persians* is an exception in terms of subject matter. This play turns around the announcement at the court of King Xerxes of defeat in the battle of Salamis, an event which took place only eight years before the play was performed. Here, distance in space (and also in viewpoint, since the Greek audience are asked to share from afar in the woes of their enemies) makes up for the lack of distance in time.[8] This is an almost isolated case, however, and the other famous example illustrates why: when Phrynichos put on a tragedy representing, shortly after the event, the destruction of the Greek city of Miletos by the Persians (494 BC), Herodotos tells us that he was sentenced to pay a heavy fine and his play was banned for ever (6.21). The suffering shown was so close in time and in human impact as to engulf the tragic action. In general, it is only through myth that the emotional intensity of tragedy can be appropriately absorbed.

Before investigating the function of myths in the theatre, let us try to identify some shaping principles that underpin this varied body of work. We find a number of recurrent dramatic motifs, topics, and issues – to which various myths will lend themselves in varying degrees. These motifs weave connections between one story and another, and sometimes within the very same story.

Dramatic Motifs

So, for instance, several tragedies hinge on *the return of a king or hero* and the events, usually calamitous, that he triggers, precipitates, or witnesses on his arrival. This is the case in Aeschylus' *Agamemnon*: the central scene in which Klytaimestra at last welcomes her husband home from Troy is followed by his murder inside the stage-building (*skēnē*). In Sophocles' *Women of Trachis*, it is the arrival of Iolē, concubine of the long-absent but now returning hero Herakles, that arouses Deianeira's jealousy and brings disaster. In Euripides' *Herakles*, the arrival of the long-awaited hero sets a dual course of events in motion: first his triumphant punishment of the usurping tyrant Lykos, then the madness in which Herakles kills his own children. In the *Persians*, everything leads up to the final appearance of Xerxes, the physical embodiment of the Persians' defeat. In the case of tragedies dealing with the revenge of Agamemnon's children on their mother Klytaimestra and her lover Aigisthos (Aeschylus' *Libation Bearers* and the two *Electras*), the decisive homecoming is that of the dead king's son, Orestes.

In some of Euripides' tragedies, the *homecoming from barbaric or hostile lands* occurs at the end of the action and offers a happy outcome after everything the hero has gone through. This is the pattern in *Iphigeneia among the Taurians* (c. 414 BC) and in *Helen* (staged in 412 and parodied the following year by Aristophanes in his *Women at the Thesmophoria*), but also in the early play *Alcestis* (438), where the wife who has agreed to give her own life in place of her husband's is returned to Admetos by Herakles, who wrests her from Thanatos (Death). Related but different is the case of Sophocles' *Philoktetes*. Here it is the appearance of the deified Herakles at the end of the play that persuades the hero, abandoned by the Greeks on a lonely island, to go back to the plains of Troy (where his bow is needed for victory), even though his first impulse, when he realizes that he has been tricked by Odysseus and by Achilles' son Neoptolemos, is to go back to his home country. Readers will notice that in the last two tragedies mentioned Herakles appears as a saviour at the end of the action, whereas he himself is the tragic figure in the two plays to which he is central, Sophocles' *Women of Trachis* and Euripides' *Herakles*.

Other plays are built around *rites of supplication*, so important in Greek society and religion.[9] In Aeschylus' *Suppliant Women*, the daughters of Danaos, fleeing Egypt and their violent cousins, take refuge in Argos with King Pelasgos. In Euripides' play of the same name, the mothers of the Argive warriors fallen before Thebes prevail on Theseus to help them recover the bodies of their dead sons. Theseus, the exemplary (if paradoxical) democratic king of Athens, makes a further appearance in Sophocles' last play, *Oedipus at Kolonos*, where he greets the old exile fated to die in the sacred wood of the attic deme Kolonos. In the course of the action, Oedipus must agree to receive his son Polyneikes, who has himself come as a supplicant, but whom he will curse in the end. There are several other plays in which supplication is a dramatic motif: at the beginning of *Oedipus the King*, for example, and in Euripides' *Children of Herakles*, where Theseus' son Demophon grants protection to the children of Herakles, threatened by Eurystheus. It also features at some intensely moving dramatic moments, such as *Andromache* 115–16, *Ion* 1255–83, and *Helen* 64–5 and 528–56.

Another important recurrent motif is *recognition* (see *Poetics* 1452a29–b8 and 1454b19–55a21 for Aristotle's views on its mechanisms and significance). The obvious example, and a good example of the different ways such a scene may be handled, is the recognition between Orestes and Elektra in Aeschylus' *Libation Bearers* and in the *Electra* plays of Sophocles and Euripides. Others include that of Orestes and his sister Iphigeneia, now presiding over the sacrifice of foreigners, in *Iphigeneia among the Taurians*, and that of Kreousa and her son, whom she has tried to poison, in *Ion* (in Euripides' lost *Kresphontes* Merope recognizes her son in similarly extreme circumstances). The most complex case, however, and perhaps the most devastatingly powerful, remains that of *Oedipus the King*. Here the investigation that is the main strand of the action culminates first in Jocasta's discovery that her husband is her son, then in Oedipus' own recognition that he is himself his father's murderer and his wife's son.

Vengeance and the way it is exacted is also a powerful theme in several myths and in the plays they inspire. Often punishment is meted out by gods to those who neglect or defy them, as in Aeschylus' *Prometheus Bound*, where Zeus chains the rebellious Titan to a rock; in Sophocles' *Ajax*, where the hero is pursued by Athene's hatred and afflicted with madness (compare the madness inflicted on Herakles by the vengeful Hera in Euripides' play); in Euripides' *Hippolytos*, where Aphrodite punishes Hippolytos for neglecting her; in *Iphigeneia at Aulis*, where Artemis demands the sacrifice of Agamemnon's daughter; in *Bacchae*, where Pentheus is torn apart by the women of Thebes transformed into bacchants. But vengeance may also be sought by half-divine, half-human figures. In the *Women of Trachis*, the deadly robe given by Deianeira to Herakles is a present from the Centaur Nessos, and posthumously avenges his death at the hero's hands. A comparison may be made with *Medea*, in which Jason's infidelity arouses his wife's terrible and more than human powers. Finally, in *Hecuba*, the queen and her fellow captives, the all-too-human victims of the Trojan War, turn into formidable avengers as they punish the treacherous Thracian king Polymestor.

There is one place more than anywhere else, however, where bloody retribution is exacted: the human family (*oikos*). This is in keeping with Aristotle's remark that 'violences at the heart of alliances' make the best subjects of tragedies (*Poetics* 1453b14–22). The philosopher cites the case of a brother who kills his brother, a son who kills his father, and a mother or son who kill one another, but interestingly omits the case of a father who kills his son, as though such a thing was almost unthinkable for a Greek man (guaranteeing the perpetuation of the line, his male child is in a sense more important than himself). Yet there are tragic heroes who cause the death of their offspring, either indirectly (like Theseus in *Hippolytos*) or under the sway of madness (like Herakles in Euripides' *Herakles*).

Such violence within families is, of course, often linked to faults or errors of previous generations. This is the case in tragedies featuring the Atreidai or Labdakidai (the families to which Agamemnon and Oedipus respectively belong). Interestingly, in plays dealing with the Atreidai, different authors ascribe the origin of the ancestral fault to different generations. For Aeschylus, everything springs from the banquet at which Thyestes was served the flesh of his own children by his brother Atreus, Agamemnon's father. In Sophocles' *Electra*, on the other hand, the hereditary fault goes back to the chariot race in which Pelops, father of Atreus and Thyestes, triumphed over King Oinomaos, thus winning the hand of his daughter Hippodameia but also causing the king's death. In Euripides' play, the origin lies instead with Pelops' father, Tantalos, who butchered his own son and fed him to the gods.[10]

Key Topics and Issues

In addition to the structural motifs that shape the plays, we should also review major issues which are explored on the stage and given a special dimension by the tragic imagination.

Thus the question of burial and of the conflict between purely human laws that forbid it and religious laws that demand it is the subject of Sophocles' *Antigone* and of Euripides' *Suppliant Women*. It also dominates the second part of *Ajax*, which turns upon the fate reserved for the corpse of the hero who has committed suicide and to whom the Greek chiefs wish to refuse the honours of burial. A variant is *Oedipus at Kolonos*, where the issue is not refusal of burial but rather the incorporation of the dead man into the territory of Attica, of which he will become a guardian hero.

Performance of human sacrifice (of and by Iphigeneia, for example) introduces a major dissonance into accepted religious practice, where it is, of course, animals that are sacrificed.[11] It may be added that tragic killing (in particular that of Agamemnon by Klytaimestra) often takes the form of a quasi-sacrificial slitting of the throat (Greek *sphagē*). Sometimes, however, the human victim volunteers for sacrifice, when it is required to save a threatened city: examples are Kreon's son Menoikeus in Euripides' *Phoenician Women*, Herakles' daughter Makaria in the *Children of Herakles*, and Chthonia in the lost *Erechtheus*. A variant is where sacrifice is nobly accepted by the victims even when unjustly imposed from outside, as in the case of Polyxena in *Hecuba*. Such acceptance of sacrifice leads on to the connected theme of tragic suicide, the last recourse of many desperate heroines (such as Jocasta, Antigone, Eurydike, Deianeira, Phaidra, and Evadne). Attention is always given to the method chosen (casting oneself from a height, hanging oneself, cutting one's throat, piercing one's heart), which, as Nicole Loraux demonstrated, always points to the meaning attached to the suicide by the person committing it.[12]

The major polarities in Greek society also find echoes, always indirectly, in the way tragic playwrights address their themes. While the civic identity of Greek men depends largely on the exclusion of all that relates to women, it is a familiar fact that tragedy and comedy alike assign a leading place to women on stage (a trend which develops from one author to another, as may be seen by comparing the degree of authority accorded to female voices in Aeschylus' *Seven Against Thebes* and Euripides' *Phoenician Women*). The tragic imagination is haunted by formidable female characters who assume male roles, even in their command of authoritative speech, or *logos* (Klytaimestra, Medea). On the other hand, it also presents women or groups of women who are victims of war, in other words of men, as in *Andromache* and *Trojan Women*. But the tragic universe is reversible: Klytaimestra falls victim to her son in *Libation Bearers*, and the daughters of Danaos, who flee marriage with their cousins in Aeschylus' *Suppliant Women*, later slit their husband's throats on their forced wedding night.

Central issues in fifth-century thought are also explored on the tragic stage, especially in the plays of Euripides, and sometimes with only minimal transposition to the world of myth. Discordance between thoughts and acts is a recurrent motif in the speeches of the old queen of Troy in *Hecuba* when she is confronted with the cynicism of Odysseus. In *Helen*, the problem of distinguishing appearance from reality is a major theme, closely linked to the plot, which hinges on the distinction between the true Helen, who has remained in Egypt, and her illusory double who has left for Troy. The spectator is left to reflect on how much suffering and how many deaths have resulted from this illusion – and perhaps on whether beauty is indeed anything other than illusion.[13] Already in the works of Aeschylus questions are raised about the relationship between the tragic agent and his action, and the share of responsibility to be borne by an individual who is under a curse, whether directed against him personally or against his race. In *Seven Against Thebes*, for example, Eteokles is cursed by his father Oedipus, but is also led by a fratricidal and suicidal impulse to confront his brother Polyneikes; Albin Lesky speaks of 'the characteristically Aeschylean union of fatal necessity and personal will'.[14]

Variation, Invention, Parody

In its treatment and adaptation of myths, Greek theatre displays considerable freedom. Against the background of traditional tellings such as those of epic earlier dramatic versions by other playwrights (or indeed of their own), and the knowledge and expectations of their audience (shaped in turn by all the above), playwrights are able to weave an ever more complex web of variations.

It has already been stressed that when Euripides deals with episodes in the Trojan War he tends to focus on its victims, usually women and children (as in *Andromache, Trojan Women, Hecuba*): tragedy often takes up the lamentation of the women in the *Iliad*. More generally, the main epic or heroic figures are frequently afflicted, in tragedy, by isolation (Ajax, Philoktetes), bewilderment, and suffering (Herakles in Sophocles and Euripides). Tragedy may also choose versions that depart from the Homeric model: the story that it was not the true Helen but her illusory double who went to Troy and the war is dealt with by Euripides in the play which bears her name, inspired, as has been seen, by Stesichoros and Herodotos. Sometimes the way tragedy handles a myth brings out the dark underside of epic. Thus, the series of domestic murders involving Agamemnon, Klytaimestra, and Orestes makes us very much aware of how allusions to the Atreidai scattered through the *Odyssey* constitute a worrying counterpoint to the relations between Odysseus, Penelope, and Telemachos.[15]

With each year's new plays bringing new tellings of the myths, audiences doubtless relished the effect of surprise. In his *Electra*, Euripides has the title character deride the plausibility of the very clues on which the recognition scene between Elektra and Orestes is based in Aeschylus' *Libation Bearers*. Naturally, this game can operate at several levels and in different directions. The episode of the Argive warriors besieging the city of Thebes in Aeschylus'

Seven Against Thebes (369–719) is taken up and altered in two different places in Euripides' *Phoenician Women* (103–92 and 1104–99). In this play, divergence from Sophocles' *Oedipus the King* is one of the mainsprings of the action. The prologue is delivered by Jocasta who, in Sophocles, hangs herself on learning Oedipus' true identity. In Euripides, her death is delayed; here she dies over her two sons' dead bodies, and by different means, killing herself with a sword. The queen also announces that Oedipus is still in Thebes, where he has been confined to the palace by his sons (64–7), and he will indeed appear, briefly, in the final scene of the play, before he goes off into the exile in which he is doomed to end his days.

Constraints imposed by the characteristic symbolism of a particular work may also play a role in such variations. In Klytaimestra's dream in *Libation Bearers*, Orestes is likened to a snake biting the very breast that suckled it (510–50): the image emphasizes the resemblance between Orestes and his own mother, who herself is often compared to a snake (247–9, 994–6, 1047). The difference from Stesichoros' version, which is less symbolically rich, is revealing. In that version, it is the dead king, Agamemnon, who is imagined as a snake (F 42 *PMG*), and he is to be reincarnated in his son. In the dream as it is recounted in Sophocles, a shoot 'capable of covering with its shadow all the land of Mycenae' springs from the sceptre planted by Agamemnon in the hearth (*Electra* 417–23): here, then, Orestes would appear to be symbolically represented as the son of the king and Hestia.[16]

Cases where the same author gives different versions of the same story are particularly interesting, because the divergences generally have a bearing on the drama. Euripides wrote two tragedies about Phaidra's culpable love for Hippolytos, the son of her husband Theseus. In the first, of which only a few fragments survive, Phaidra is portrayed as a lustful and oppressive stepmother. In the second – surviving – play, two important new roles have been developed: that of the nurse, the heroine's dark double, and that of the goddess Aphrodite herself, with her explicit determination to take revenge on Hippolytos whatever the consequences. The result is to transform Phaidra into a complex, emotionally moving character, in the grip of irresistible forces of passion. Euripides also staged an *Antigone* (now lost) in which the heroine ends up marrying Kreon's son Haimon (by contrast with Sophocles' play, in which her love for her own dead family, her brothers in particular, leads her to forego marriage). On this point, however, Euripides' *Phoenician Women* is completely in agreement with Sophocles: at the end of the play, Antigone even threatens to become one of the Danaids (in other words, to kill her husband on their wedding night) if Kreon tries to force her to marry his son (1675); she prefers to accompany her father in exile. The higher value attached here to ancestry over marriage unions (even between blood relations) tells us a great deal about a significant aspect of Oedipus' family.

   Naturally, comedy also makes use of mythical episodes which have previously been dealt with by epic poetry or tragedy, but does so in a playful mode, with parody being achieved by textual quotation (sometimes direct, sometimes more oblique) and comical stage business. In the parabasis of *Wasps*, the object of Aristophanes' attack, the demagogue Kleon, becomes a hybrid monster (1031–6), and is described in language which quotes from the Hesiod's description of Typhoeus (the giant who threatens established order of Zeus at *Theogony* 824–7), interspersing it with obscenities. In a more poetic vein, the first parabasis of *Birds* uses material both from the *Theogony* and from 'Orphic' cosmogonies when it asserts that the world originated in an egg laid by Night, from which Eros sprang to life and from which the feathered race emerged even before gods and men existed (693–702). In *Women at the Thesmophoria*, the character of Euripides' kinsman assumes two false appearances, first as Helen, whom Euripides-Menelaos tries to set free, then as Andromeda waiting for Perseus to release her (854–928; 1009–135).

   The storyline of a comedy may be based on a mythical situation that has already been treated in tragedy now transposed to a more familiar universe in which care is taken to give it a happy outcome once all cases of mistaken identity have been resolved. In Menander's *Samia*, for instance, Demeas believes that the mother of his son's child, Moschion, is the Samian woman he loves, Chrysis. This theme of love rivalry between father and son, which would later be used both by Ennius and by Plautus in his comedies *Mercator* and *Asinaria*, had already been the subject of Euripides' lost tragedy *Phoinix*. Euripides' play in turn was based on Book 9 of the *Iliad*, in which the old man Phoinix recounts how, in his youth, he very nearly killed his father Amyntor, who had cursed him (447–80). Here a plotline drawn from myth is demythologized in comedy. Sometimes comedy retains explicit mythological apparatus, as in Menander's *Dyskolos*, where the god Pan delivers the prologue and guides the action. On the whole, though, New Comedy replaces figures from myth with representative figures from everyday life (the irascible old man, the young man in love, the cunning slave, and so on); the old mythology gives way to a typology.

Myth in the Theatre: A Prism and Not a Mirror

We have reviewed myth's potential to provide the audience both with recognition of familiar stories and story patterns and, on the other hand, with surprise at innovation on the part of the playwright. Over and above this, what role was played by the acting out of myths – in Aristotelian terms, the *mimēsis* (imitation) of their stories – within the official setting of the great Dionysiac festivals? Behind the mask of the physically present actor, the tragic performance gave voice to a whole distant world, which drew its authority from its very distance from the world of the fifth-century BC Athenian citizen, whom it could nonetheless touch to the quick.

This distance was underscored by the presence of the chorus in the *orchēstra*, which was usually, within the fictive world of the play, composed of members of groups – such as women, old men, slaves, and sometimes also deities – that stand in opposition to the adult male citizens who actually performed. The role of the chorus is to serve as a filter or medium. Vaunting, in the third choral ode (*stasimon*) of *Oedipus at Kolonos* (1224–48), the advantages of 'not being born', the old men of the chorus provide the link between the singular fate of the hero and the common lot of humanity.[17]

'Myth seen with the eyes of the citizen': this often-cited phrase of Walter Nestle pinpoints the twofold movement that occurred as the tragic action unfolded. First, the fiction served to reveal the presence or return of the archaic roots of the individual, the family, and society. Secondly, this decentring by way of engagement with a mythic past made it possible to view the contemporary world with what was no doubt a more lucid gaze. This twofold operation still functions today when Greek tragedies are performed on the modern stage. It is no doubt an aspect of the *katharsis*, the cleansing or purifying effect of tragedy, discussed so enigmatically by Aristotle in the *Poetics*. The myths favoured by tragedy turn on the basic taboos on which civilization is founded, such as incest, parricide, and infanticide. More broadly, they blur the distinctions that ensure the coherence of the family and hence of society itself. Seen from another angle, the specific remoteness of myth allows the questioning of values that nonetheless seemed self-evident to the Greeks. In Aeschylus' *Agamemnon*, the songs of the chorus highlight the horrors and vanity of war. Later, Euripides' Trojan War plays denounce the cynicism of the victors and their abuse of their position of strength. Tragic treatments of the fate of the sons of Oedipus reveal how destructively foreign warfare (*polemos*) overlaps with familial and civil strife (*stasis*). More generally, the stage gives voice to the most radical forms of otherness. It is not by chance that it is a woman and a barbarian, Medea, who, from Euripides to Seneca to Corneille, and beyond, provides one of the most vivid embodiments of the power of tragedy.

The use of myth in the theatre is also a powerful pointer to the conflictual nature of man and society. Conflict is central to tragic confrontation (*agōn*). Sophocles' Antigone and Kreon invoke incompatible laws, which no synthesis can reconcile, as was emphasized by Hegel. At the end of the *Eumenides*, the Erinyes call in the name of blood-right for the punishment of Orestes, who killed his own mother; in response, Apollo and Athene argue that the son is born of the father's seed and that Orestes was therefore right to avenge his own blood (585–673). Even when a trilogy seems to lead to the resolution of a conflict, it is the force of the opposing viewpoints which drives the drama. For example, while at the end of Aeschylus' trilogy on the story of the Danaids Aphrodite delivers a long speech celebrating reconciliation between the sexes and the institution of marriage, the entire action of the surviving play *Suppliant Women* reveals the horror inspired in virgins by the violence of men, a motif which speaks volumes about relations between the sexes. Similarly, the crime imputed to them by the myth sheds light on the way in which the Greek male imagination views the 'race of women'.

Conflict can take place also within the world of the imagination, between the representations shared by the Athenian audience and those invented by tragedy. Treatment of the myth of autochthony is a good example of this. The Athenians claim descent from Erichthonios, who sprung from the earth of the Acropolis and not from a woman's womb. All citizens are called on to acknowledge their origin in that prestigious figure. To do so is to legitimize self-sacrifice in war, since every birth is a debt to the motherland, as is reiterated again and again in funeral orations.[18] It is worth noting that Euripides takes the opportunity to parody such speeches in *Suppliant Women*, where Adrastos is made to sing the praises of Parthenopaios and Tydeus (888–908), in sharp contrast with the disturbing portraits painted of them both in Aeschylus' *Seven Against Thebes* (377–94, 536–47) and in Euripides' own *Phoenician Women* (888–910).

This is not all. When compared with the Athenian civic myth of their first autochthonic ancestor, the account of the origin of Thebes – in particular, the story of the Spartoi ('Sown Men'), who were born from the dragon's teeth sown by the founder Kadmos and kill one another at birth – represents a negative version, one directed towards violent self-destruction. But it must immediately be realized that this is a purely Athenian representation of a rival city's myth of autochthony. We must also wonder what the dramatization of the deadly madness of the Spartoi (and of their descendants who re-enact their story, the sons of Oedipus) may reveal about the negative aspects of the Athenian myth itself, and particularly the exclusion of womanhood and motherhood on which it is predicated.

The choices made by the tragic authors in the myths they simultaneously revisit and rewrite suggest that the cathartic function of the theatre may be understood in two ways. First, the stage serves as a place where, on another plane, transgressions can be committed and desires acted out that are a constant threat to familial and social life. Secondly, and sometimes at the same time, tragic expression offers a means of opening the citizen-spectator to a dimension of otherness that this same familial and social life represses (the female, foreign, barbaric dimension). Even the most firmly entrenched beliefs are disassembled in the tragic prism for the duration of the performance.[19]

Conclusion

This dual function of tragic myth may well provide the reason why the great myths which were staged over and over again in the Theatre of Dionysos only assumed their fullest intensity of meaning in the context of the classical fifth-century BC city. It is true that when the Greek world changed, when Alexander's conquests shook the very foundations of Greek identity and of the relationship between the individual and the community, myths continued to sustain literature, as Hellenistic writers amply testify. Nor did the theatre cease to exercise its power of attraction; from the fourth century BC onwards, tragedy offered food for thought to great philosophers (Plato and Aristotle), increasing numbers of stone theatre buildings were erected, and the great dramatic works were the object of critical editions, painstaking scholarship, and multiple adaptations. In Athens, around 340–330 BC, Lykourgos arranged for official copies to be made so as to guard against increasingly frequent interpolations by actors. But, just as comedy after Aristophanes focused increasingly on the sphere of private, so myth became increasingly a source of literary motifs, which could also be a vehicle for poetic subjectivity. The vanishing role of the chorus, which brought out the political and religious connotations of the plays, attests to this trend. Greek myths became diversified, and also diluted, as they found their way into every literary form, but they ceased to offer such a powerful and collectively accepted way of questioning the world and the individual's place in it, even though, well into the fourth century BC, a philosopher such as Plato did not hesitate to avail himself of them.

FURTHER READING

There is no standard or benchmark set of translations of any of the ancient Greek playwrights into English. This is to be expected: the plays are enduring but also Protean, and engage modern audiences in radically different ways in different times and places; it is also hard for translators to find a path between stilted reverence and distorting or eccentric irreverence, and between archaizing translationese and jarring now-speak. Serviceable versions can be found in a number of established series: Penguin Classics, Oxford World's Classics, the Chicago University Press *Complete Greek Tragedies*, the Loeb Classical Library (where many clunky old versions have recently been replaced by excellent new ones), and the *Cambridge Translations from Greek Drama*.

There are also many freer versions created, often with performance in mind, by modern playwrights and poets. Examples include Ann Carson's *An Oresteia* (versions of Aeschylus' *Agamemnon*, Sophocles' *Electra*, and Euripides' *Orestes*, 2009); Seamus Heaney's *The Cure at Troy* (a version of *Philoctetes*, 1991) and *The Burial at Thebes* (*Antigone*, 2005); Tony Harrison's *Oresteia* (1981) and *Medea: A Sex-War Opera* (1985); Ted Hughes' *Oresteia* (1999); and Liz Lochhead's *Medea* (2000). Interesting versions of Aristophanes are harder to come by; unfortunately, at the time of writing, no published text either of Mary-Kay Gamel's *Julie Thesmo Show* (*Thesmophoriazusae*, 2000: see Gamel 2002) or of Blake Morrison's *Lisa's Sex Strike* (*Lysistrata*, 2007) was available. For a survey of translations (but not, on the whole, 'versions/ adaptations') of Greek drama into English, see Walton (2006).

Baldry 1971 remains an excellent introduction to the world of Greek tragedy. See also chapters in Easterling 1997, and the reference works of A. W. Pickard-Cambridge (1962, 1988). On Aristophanic comedy, see especially Dover 1972, Sandbach 1977, and Moulton 1981.

For an anthropological approach to tragedy and its myths, the writings of J.-P. Vernant and P. Vidal-Naquet are particularly stimulating (1988), as are those of C. Segal (1981, 1986a, 1995) and N. Loraux (1986, 2002). See also Calame 1995, 2009a. The volume *Nothing To Do With Dionysus?* edited by Winkler and Zeitlin (1990) usefully reflects the critical trends of its time.

On the genealogies of Greek myth and the assorted variant versions of the stories, see Gantz. For a sense of the range of subjects treated by the three great tragic dramatists, see Deforge 1986, on Aeschylus; on Sophocles, Jouanna 2007 (esp. 609–76) for a detailed overview of works which survive only in fragments; and, on Euripides, Jouan 1966.

NOTES

1. I would like to offer warm thanks to C. Boulic, N. Boulic, K. Dowden, D. Konstan, and N. Livingstone for their comments and suggestions.
2. Part of the same tetralogy of plays on connected subjects as the surviving *Seven Against Thebes*.
3. See Baldry (1971).
4. From a purely practical point of view, these masks, which expressed a variety of moods, enabled the same actor to perform different roles. Audience members, who might be situated at some distance from the stage, were thus helped to identify the different characters.
5. On the function of the mask, see Calame (2000b: 151–63).
6. For a discussion of reflections of Sophocles' Oedipus story in modern detective (and other) fiction see, for example, Dubois (2005).
7. See Zeitlin (1990).
8. A comparable case is Racine's (seventeenth-century) tragedy *Bajazet*, recounting murderous conflict between brothers at the court of the Ottoman Sultan: events within living memory at the time, but geographically and culturally remote from the play's French audience.
9. See the 2001 reprint with Addendum of Gould (1973); Aubriot-Sévin (1992).
10. See Brunel (1995: 41–112).
11. See Zeitlin (1965).
12. See Loraux (1987).
13. Euripides here draws on Stesichorus (F 192 *PMG*; see also Plato *Phaedrus* 243a–b) and Herodotus (2.116).

14. See Lesky (1983: 21).
15. See M. Katz (1991).
16. See Vernant (1983: 127–76).
17. See Travis (1999).
18. See Loraux (1986).
19. See Loraux (2002).

CHAPTER EIGHT

Displaying Myth: The Visual Arts

Susan Woodford

Identifying Myth

A group of Athenian women arrive in Delphi. They look around them, and in astonishment exclaim 'So, it's not only in Athens that there are beautiful temples to the gods!' Much impressed, they begin to make a closer inspection.

'Just look,' one cries to another, 'there is Herakles, fighting the monstrous Hydra of Lerna.'

'I see that!' her friend replies. 'And next to him a man raising blazing torches. I wonder if it isn't Iolaos, his faithful companion. I once embroidered a cushion with a picture of him.'

Another woman interrupts, 'Oh but do look at this man riding a winged horse and fighting a fire-breathing monster with three bodies!'

A fourth woman cries, 'There is so much to look at! Just look at that raging battle: there's a giant who has fallen, and someone wearing a gorgon head for protection stands over him...'

'That is Athene,' another woman explains.

And then the crowd of women begins to look harder and to name the various defeated giants and the gods who are conquering them: Zeus with his thunderbolt flaming at both ends and Bacchus using his reveller's thyrsos as a weapon ... and so they might have gone on had they not finally noticed the temple attendant standing by and been forced to get on with the drama. For these ladies are not twenty-first century AD tourists on a day-trip from Athens but members of the chorus in Euripides' play *Ion*.[1] The reactions that the dramatist puts into their mouths must, however, have rung true in the ears of

A Companion to Greek Mythology, First Edition. Edited by Ken Dowden and Niall Livingstone.
© 2014 John Wiley & Sons Ltd. Published 2014 by John Wiley & Sons Ltd.

Figure 8.1 Herakles with the Hydra and Iolaos. Attic black-figure neck amphora, 540–520 BC by the Swing Painter.

his fifth-century BC audience. This is a truly vivid example of myths on display, but one may wonder: *how do the women know which myths they are seeing?*

Some features the women describe make the myths easy to identify. Herakles is fighting a unique monster, the Hydra, the main characteristic of which was its multiple heads. Artists confronted with a verbal description of the creature decided that it ought to have snake-like heads, and most thought that nine would be just about the right number. Once you have seen one image of a Hydra, it is easy to recognize another.

The Hydra had the peculiarity that whenever one of its heads was severed, two new ones would grow in its place. This made progress discouraging for Herakles until he discovered that cauterizing the stump of a severed head prevented new growth. He therefore called upon his nephew and faithful companion Iolaos to help him. The story was popular with vase-painters like one who showed Herakles wearing his lion-skin standing to the left with Iolaos on the right (fig. 8.1). The scene was also depicted on sculpted metopes decorating temples.[2]

Figure 8.2 Bellerophon riding Pegasos, attacking the Chimaira. Attic black-figure cup, c. 550 BC.

The winged horse spotted by the third woman is clearly a mythological creature. It must be Pegasos, the mount of Bellerophon when he fought the fire-breathing Chimaira. The Chimaira was triple-bodied; it was basically a lion, but with a fire-breathing goat's head in the middle of its back and a snake for a tail (fig. 8.2). Quite unmistakable.

Such unnatural mixtures – Centaurs that are part man and part horse, sirens with birds' bodies and human heads, a minotaur with a bull's head and a man's body, or a river god with a bull's body and a man's head are all obviously mythological and easy to recognize. Giants can be more difficult. These children of the goddess Earth, whose threat to the gods had to be vigorously fought off, were not necessarily extra-large (though they could be) and for a long time they were represented in art either simply as hoplites (heavily-armed soldiers) or wild men who wore skins and fought with stones rather than man-made weapons (fig. 8.3). In the Hellenistic period some of them were represented with snake-legs (fig. 8.6, below), but before that they could still be recognized by their opponents, that is, the gods whom they fought against. The woman from Athens who pointed out the raging battle knew that it was a fight between gods and giants because she recognized the goddess Athene wearing a 'gorgon head for protection', and others identified Zeus with his 'thunderbolt flaming at both ends' and Bacchus with his characteristic thyrsos. These attributes are very helpful in identifying a god or goddess who might otherwise just be mistaken for an ordinary human being. Thus, the vase painting (fig. 8.3) depicts a similar scene, with Athene shown as a helmeted woman with a leering gorgon's head, a device intended to frighten the enemy, on her *aegis* (a sort of snake-fringed poncho), spearing a giant who looks like

Figure 8.3 Gigantomachy: Athene and Zeus fighting giants. Attic red-figure hydria shoulder, c. 480 BC by the Tyszkiewicz Painter.

a hoplite, while Zeus, a mature man wielding a stylized thunderbolt, slays a wild giant wearing an animal skin and using a boulder as a weapon.

Using such 'attributes', artists could distinguish Herakles by his lion-skin (fig. 8.1), Artemis by her bow, Apollo by his lyre, and so on. There is a brief guide to identifying myths and the characters in them in the appendix at the end of this chapter.

We may assume that the myths the Athenian women admired were sculptures decorating the outside of a temple. This was a prominent location for the public display of myths since many people would be able to see them when they gathered to make sacrifices at the altar, which was usually placed to the east of the entrance to the temple.

Myths in Architectural Sculpture

There were three areas on a temple – or, in fact, almost any Greek public building – that could bear such decorations: metopes, friezes, and pediments (fig. 8.4). In Doric buildings (fig. 8.4 top), there were rectangular (almost

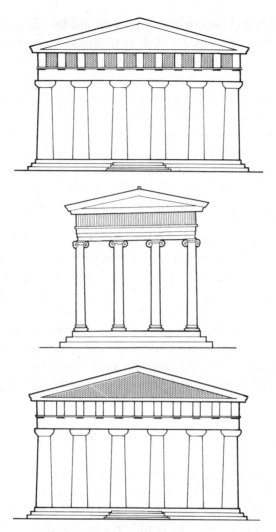

Figure 8.4 Areas for decoration on a temple: metopes (top), frieze (middle), pediment (bottom).

square) metopes, in Ionic buildings (fig. 8.4, middle), long continuous friezes. In both the Doric and the Ionic orders, there was the awkward, low triangle of the pediment (fig. 8.4, bottom). The architecture determined the shape into which decorative sculpture or painting had to be fitted and designers always had to keep this in mind.

The metopes were usually placed on the outside of a building, and had to be decorated with figures made as large as possible in order to be visible from a distance. If the heads of the figures reached the top of the metope and their feet rested on the bottom, there would normally be room for only two, or, at most, three such figures. Presumably the men in charge of constructing the building would have chosen which myths would be illustrated. We have no way of knowing how this was decided. Different choices were made in different places.

On the Parthenon in Athens all fourteen metopes along the front (east side) of the temple were devoted to scenes of gods fighting giants. Sometimes a single god was shown attacking a single giant, at others a single god charging forward in a chariot – a good way to fill the space of the metope, the horses providing an interesting alternative to the more usual two figures. On the three other sides of the building there were other themes.[3]

At Olympia, only the metopes within the porches of the temple were decorated. All twelve (six at the front and six at the back) were carved to illustrate the Labours of Herakles.

In western Greece, several temples were adorned with a sort of compendium of mythological subjects, not necessarily related to a single theme. One metope might show a god struggling with a giant and another illustrate one of the deeds of Herakles, while a third showed Artemis having transformed Aktaion into a stag so that his dogs, not recognizing him, attacked him (fig 8.5). He had offended Artemis either by boasting that he was a better hunter than she or having seen her bathing – either way meriting, she believed, his harsh punishment. On the metope from a temple in Sicily *we* can see Aktaion still in his human form, though obviously the dogs attacking him cannot. This was one way that an artist could solve the awkward problem of showing that someone's real nature was concealed within the shape of an animal. Artists depicting Odysseus' men transformed by Circe faced the same sort of problem.

An artist normally selected some telling incident or event (the beheading of the monstrous Gorgon, for instance, or Europa, entranced by Zeus in his disguise as a bull, riding off on his back) or introduced some obvious attribute or action so that the story would be readily recognizable.

While artists designing metopes had to devise ways of reducing the stories they told to no more than two or three characters, those designing friezes had the opposite problem: they had to find ways to expand whatever myth they were illustrating so that it could fill an extended space. Like metopes, friezes were usually seen from a distance and the figures had to be as large as possible, heads reaching virtually to the top of the available space. Certain subjects lent themselves particularly well to this sort of treatment. Battles, for instance, which were reduced to single combats for metopes, could be expanded almost indefinitely for friezes just by adding more and more fighting figures.

Battles between gods and giants were popular for friezes as well as metopes (fig. 8.6). The base of the Great Altar at Pergamon was decorated with a tremendous extended combat, part of which showed a snake-legged giant at the

Figure 8.5 Artemis and Aktaion. From a metope on Temple E, from Selinunte, Sicily. Museo Nazionale Archeologico, Palermo.

far left confronting triple-bodied Hekate (with multiple arms) beside a handsome human-shaped giant awestruck by the beauty of Artemis who draws her (now lost) bow against him at point-blank range. Between the two lies another snake-legged giant attacked by Artemis' dog. Battles between Greeks and Centaurs and Greeks and Amazons (warrior women) also served well for friezes.[4] All three of these themes could, in theory, be turned into allegories representing the struggle of civilization against barbarism.[5] Processions and assemblies also provided opportunities for artists to keep adding as many figures as they needed, and usually some sort of mythological justification could be found for them.

Figure 8.6 Hekate and Artemis fighting giants. From the Great Altar, Pergamon c. 180–160 BC.

The long low triangle of the pediment (the space left at the front and the back of the gabled roof) could present more problems for the designer. If he was not concerned about presenting a single scene made up of figures on a single consistent scale, he might feel free to introduce hints of a variety of different stories filled with figures whose size was determined solely by the headroom offered by the particular place they occupied in the pediment, those toward the sloping sides being shorter than those toward the centre[6] (fig. 8.7). To illustrate just one myth by means of figures on a unified scale within the pediment was a more challenging task. By the end of the sixth century BC artists had discovered that the challenge could be met most easily by showing a violent conflict. Participants could then all be kept to a single scale but fitted into the slope of the pediment because in the course of the struggle some of them would be standing, while others might be forced down to crouch or even lie flat on the ground.

The battle of the Greeks against the Centaurs was a wonderfully versatile theme: it could be easily reduced to a single combat, as in some of the metopes on the south side of the Parthenon; extended into a running conflict between numerous Greeks and Centaurs, as on a frieze in the Temple of Apollo at Bassai; or organized into a climactic battle presided over by a tall god, as in the west pediment at the temple of Zeus at Olympia (fig. 8.8). In the pediment, the god Apollo occupies the full height of the apex of the pediment, while human heroes on either side of him (shorter than gods) fight Centaurs (who are shorter still). The Centaurs have grabbed women, whose heads do not rise as high as theirs, and, further out from the centre, figures in combat are brought yet lower, so that while they are all on the

Figure 8.7 Herakles and Apollo struggling for the tripod, with Zeus intervening in the centre, and perhaps other stories at the sides. c. 525 BC. Pediment of the Siphnian Treasury, Delphi.

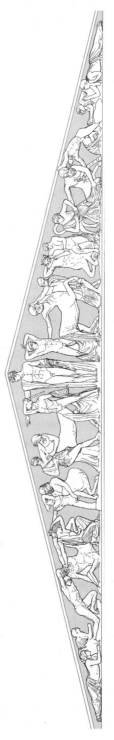

Figure 8.8 Olympia, Temple of Zeus, west pediment. Drawing by Kate Morton.

same scale, the level of their heads is constantly becoming lower – and so conforms to the slope of the pediment.

Statues of the God within the Temple

Because all important ceremonies took place in the open (unlike services in churches, mosques, and synagogues) the sculpted myths decorating the outside of a temple were the ones most frequently seen by the people. Seldom did anyone see the statue dedicated to the god within the temple. Such statues, which could be very large and expensive, were nevertheless sometimes elaborately decorated with mythical subjects.

The huge statue of Athene that stood in the Parthenon, for instance, had its surfaces covered with ivory and gold, ivory for the flesh parts and gold for the clothing. Myths and suggestions of myths were lavishly distributed about the figure: her helmet was decorated by a sphinx in the centre, with two images of Pegasos flanking it. The outside of her shield contained scenes of Greeks fighting Amazons, while on its inner side were represented the battle of gods and giants, and combats between Greeks and Centaurs adorned her sandals. The base of the statue (a long, relatively narrow strip like a frieze) illustrated the birth of Pandora with all the gods in attendance – the sort of assembly that was suitable for the composition of a frieze. We learn all this from authors who saw the statue when it was still extant, and from souvenir copies that were mostly made for Roman tourists.[7]

The celebrated cult statue of Zeus at Olympia, once regarded as one of the seven wonders of the world, was similarly ornamented with images of myths decorating the throne and base of the statue as well as the fencing surrounding it.[8]

Literary Accounts of Mythical Representations Now Lost

Both the statue of Athene in the Parthenon and the statue of Zeus at Olympia were destroyed centuries ago. Many other important works were lost even earlier, particularly paintings. We know of these from writers like Pausanias, who toured Greece in the second century AD and wrote about what he saw, and Pliny the Elder (died AD 79), who included a discussion of works of art in his compendious *Natural History*, as well as from a scattering of other authors. Many of the paintings described were greatly celebrated. Some of them apparently had the sort of subjects we might have expected: Greeks battling with Centaurs and Athenians fighting Amazons in a sanctuary of Theseus;[9] or

Aphrodite rising from the sea by the famed Apelles.[10] Pliny[11] describes a painting by Zeuxis as 'a superb Zeus enthroned amid the assembled gods, with the infant Herakles strangling snakes in the presence of his trembling mother Alkmene and of Amphitryon', surely a visual counterpart to the story told in words by Pindar in his first *Nemean Ode*.

Others are more unexpected. For instance, Pausanias describes at length a large wall-painting that the renowned painter Polygnotos made for the club-house of the Knidians at Delphi in the first half of the fifth century BC. Polygnotos chose to represent the Fall of Troy, but approached it in an unusual way. Instead of showing the horrors of the night of the sack, he depicted, instead, the morning after, with only one warrior still actively involved in killing. Practically devoid of action, there must have been a great stillness in the mural with emphasis placed primarily on emotion and character, traits for which Polygnotos was renowned. To make the identity of his numerous figures quite clear, he inscribed their names beside them, and in order to make his composition interesting, he set some figures higher up and some further down in a multi-level scheme which seems to have been invented by him.[12]

We also hear of particularly ingenious devices invented by painters – for instance, how Timanthes 'being desirous to emphasize, even in a small picture, the huge size of a sleeping Cyclops, painted some Satyrs at his side measuring his thumb with a thyrsos.'[13]

Sometimes painters invented entirely new themes. Lucian describes a mural painted by Zeuxis in the late fifth or early fourth century BC. It depicted Centaurs, monsters who were popular in art in conflicts with men, and normally considered just a group of male adults whose infancy and family life were of no concern to either poets or artists until Zeuxis created

> a picture of a female centaur – and what's more she was depicted in the act of suckling two centaur babies...
>
> The mother centaur was shown with her horse-part lying on some soft grass, and her hind legs stretched out backwards. The woman-part was slightly raised from the ground and propped on its elbow. ... She was holding one of the newborn babies in her arms and breast-feeding it in the normal human manner, but the other was suckling away at the horse-part like an ordinary foal. In the upper part of the picture, on a bit of rising ground, appeared a male centaur, presumably the husband of the lady who was suckling a baby at each end of her anatomy.[14]

These are only a few examples of sometimes rather surprising works of art lost to us. Others that have disappeared without a trace would no doubt have brought further surprises.

Figure 8.9 The Judgement of Paris. Attic white-ground pyxis, c. 460 BC by the Penthesilea painter.

The Evidence from Vase Painting

Although many thousands of vases with painted figures have survived, these form only a very small fraction of what had once existed.

Vase painters delighted in creating images of myths, ingeniously transforming flowing stories into static pictures. This was by no means a straightforward procedure. Vase painters, like sculptors decorating architecture, had to devise ways to make verbal narratives clear in visual terms. Like them they made use of attributes and distinctive monsters (figs. 8.1 and 8.2, above); like wall painters, they could also have recourse to inscriptions (see below discussing fig 8.10).

Vases could be decorated in a variety of different ways. The figures could be painted in black silhouette, with internal markings indicated by incisions (as in figs. 8.1 and 8.2). This technique, called 'black-figure', began to be developed in the seventh century BC and flourished during the archaic period. From the late archaic period (around 530 BC), it was gradually superseded by the red-figure technique in which the figures were left in the natural colour of the clay, the background was painted black around them and the internal markings were indicated by fluid brush strokes (as in figures 8.3 and 8.10).

A third technique, white-ground, consisted of covering the surface of the vessel with a white slip and painting the figures in outline, sometimes adding less stable colours after firing (fig. 8.9). It could produce very charming effects and probably resembled major wall paintings more than any other vase-painting technique, but it was more delicate and easily damaged than the other two techniques. Consequently it was mostly reserved for dedications and funeral offerings, which did not require hard-wearing

Figure 8.10 The Judgement of Paris. Attic red-figured hydria, 420–400 BC, by the Painter of the Carlsruhe Paris.

vessels. Black-figure vase painters particularly enjoyed depicting action scenes and inventing images for monsters. Red-figure vase painters began to explore the emotional overtones of quieter scenes, and increasingly diminished their representations of violence. White-ground vase painters seldom dealt with mythological subjects, but when they did so it was with great refinement.

The Judgement of Paris, the contest of three mighty goddesses for the golden apple, the prize for beauty and the ultimate cause of the Trojan War, was a popular theme. Vase painters could illustrate it relying on a simple formula: three goddesses following Hermes, who leads them to Paris for his adjudication. Lazy artists would barely distinguish the contestants, but more ambitious ones would take the trouble to produce individual characterizations. One artist (fig. 8.9) abjured movement and shows the three goddesses quietly standing by while Hermes explains to Paris, who is seated on a pile of rocks, what is required of him. Though born a Trojan prince, fortune had made Paris a shepherd, and he looks a rustic type with a sun hat on his back and a thin club in his hand for use in hunting or defending his flocks. He must have been astonished by the sudden divine apparitions. The vase painter has identified Hermes by his traveller's hat and his *kērykeion* (special herald's staff). Behind him, Hera, the wife of Zeus, is shown holding a regal sceptre; Athene, next, has her helmet in one hand and a spear in the other, while Aphrodite, quietly confident, brings up the rear, holding a libation bowl in one hand and nonchalantly chatting with her son Eros, a valuable ally in the competition. The goddesses were supposed each to have offered Paris a bribe. Aphrodite's offer of Helen, the most beautiful woman in the world, turned out to be irresistible. The assistance she rendered to Paris in carrying Helen off provoked a Greek expedition to recover Helen and thus began the Trojan War. The bearded man standing behind Paris defies identification: we are not always able to understand every element in Greek art.

A later artist (fig. 8.10) invented a more complex composition with more complex overtones. Instead of lining up the cast on a single ground line, he has scattered the figures up and down across the surface of his vase at different heights, probably in the manner of the wall painter Polygnotos, whose works (see above) are only known to us from descriptions, but which the vase painter had seen with his own eyes. In the centre Paris, attired in an elaborately embroidered exotic costume, is seated with his shepherd's dog at his feet. Hermes stands to the right holding his messenger's staff, addressing Paris. Paris turns towards Hermes, but his attention may well be distracted by the little Eros perched higher up and touching him on his shoulder.

To the left of Paris stands Athene, magnificent in her high helmet, *aegis* with gorgon's head in the centre, a shield in one hand and a spear in the other. A little below her to the left, Hera stands lifting her veil in a bridal gesture and holding a sceptre. One has to hunt for Aphrodite, eventually to find her seated at the far right behind Hermes, her arm around yet another Eros. All the figures are labelled, though the inscriptions, unfortunately, are not visible in the photograph. On the vase itself, however, it is easy to identify the crucial, though partially obscured, figure of Eris, the goddess of discord. It was she who set the contest in motion, having cast the controversial golden apple into the midst of the assembled deities, and here she is shown, head and shoulders appearing right above Paris' head.

The reason why Eris appears only from the waist up is because the artist probably thought of her standing behind a hillock that hides her lower body. He may well have been trying to create a landscape of hillocks and rocks of the sort that would have worked well on the light ground of Polygnotos' wall paintings, but was largely negated by the conventional black background used for red-figure vase painting.

Figure 8.11 Bellerophon riding Pegasos and slaying the Chimaera, 380–370 BC. Pebble mosaic from Olynthos.

Myths in Other Materials

Myths could also be recounted, or suggested, in other materials. The Greeks started to produce figured subjects in pebble mosaics in the fifth century BC. A fourth-century BC example (fig. 8.11) shows a familiar subject, Bellerophon riding Pegasus attacking the Chimaira (see fig. 8.2, above). The elements in the image are easily recognized, but instead of all standing on a single ground line, the hero is placed above the monster. This new arrangement, a sort of metaphor of Good (above) conquering Evil (below), struck such a positive chord that it was perpetuated down the centuries and used, for example, for images of Saint George and the dragon in Christian paintings. The elaborate decorations surrounding the central circular picture here suggest a carpet-like floor-covering, for which the pebble mosaic was no doubt a substitute.

Whereas a mosaic offers a large space for decoration, a coin offers only a small one. But even coins sometimes carried images of myths. For instance, the Thebans, devotees of Herakles, struck some of their coins with a depiction

Figure 8.12   Infant Herakles strangling snakes (silver coin of Thebes). AR stater. Early fourth century BC.

of the infant Herakles strangling snakes. A silver coin of the late fifth century BC (fig. 8.12) shows a hardy infant with a wriggling snake in each hand. This is unmistakably the infant Herakles – for what other hero could display such might so young? The snakes were, according to most sources, sent by Hera to test which of the twins that Alkmene bore was Zeus' son. Herakles made it clear at once! This is, of course, the same story as the one painted by Zeuxis in a more elaborate scene as reported by Pliny (p. 167). On the coin, the baby hero is shown in the centre, while the first two initials of Thebes, the minting city, are placed below him.

   Though very small, a coin provides a pictorial surface on which it is easy to recount a myth. This is far more difficult – and expensive – in free-standing sculpture. However, a group of figures can do the trick. A famous example illustrating a myth is the group of Laokoön and his sons entwined in the snakes sent to punish the priest for inveighing against the wooden horse (fig. 8.13), a scene dramatically described by Vergil in Book 2 of the *Aeneid* (2.40–56, 201–27). Laokoön, rightly as it turned out, warned the Trojans to 'fear the Greeks even when bringing gifts' and had dared to thrust his spear into the suspect wooden horse. As Troy was doomed, Laokoön was not believed but instead was mercilessly destroyed by the gods, for two enormous snakes emerging from the sea attacked both him and his two young sons. The complex stone statuary group, praised by Pliny,[15] was immensely admired when it was first discovered in the Renaissance for its portrayal of pain and suffering.

Figure 8.13 Laokoön and his sons attacked by snakes. First century BC/AD. Probably a Roman copy (or variation) of a Hellenistic original.

There was a certain vogue for mythological statuary groups during the Hellenistic period, and entire or fragmentary Roman copies are preserved of Menelaos with the body of Patroklos, and of Artemis rescuing Iphigeneia by replacing the girl with a deer before the sacrificial knife can fall.

Mythological groups could also be composed of separate statues. Pliny[16] mentions that Myron made 'a Satyr marvelling at the flutes, and an Athene', which some scholars suggest were two separate statues combined into a group illustrating the story that when Athene discarded the flutes she had invented, being disappointed with the appearance of her puffy cheeks when blowing into them, the satyr Marsyas retrieved them, eventually playing them so enthusiastically that he challenged Apollo to a musical competition.

Judicious use of attributes could transform even single isolated statues into ones carrying a mythological message. For instance, a huge muscular Herakles[17] is shown in a statue leaning on his club looking exhausted. One arm hangs limply, hand open; the other hand is behind his back. If you go round the statue you will see that he is holding the apples of the Hesperides in that hand.

This detail alludes to Herakles' many trials and his final triumph, for it reveals how the mighty hero, wearied after completing all his arduous labours, has, by obtaining the apples of the Hesperides, finally come to the end of his trials.

Myths in Greek Art

The human figure was the subject dearest to the hearts of Greek artists, and it was often shown in a mythological context. But much of Greek art was not mythological in content. Most free-standing statues were images of gods or heroes, personifications of abstract concepts, or mortals celebrated for their athletic prowess, poetic genius, or political power, or simply commemorated after their death. Vase painters, as time progressed, became less interested in conjuring up images of myths and more and more interested in illustrating scenes of daily life. Even architectural sculpture sometimes dealt with non-mythological subjects, whether historical scenes of battles and rituals or generic ones – take, for instance, the heated debate as to exactly what the famous Parthenon frieze represents.

Nevertheless, images of myths permeated Greek society on public buildings and in private homes. To the simple they offered the pleasures of recognition, to the sophisticated a challenge to thought. To artists, they were a constant spur to creativity and a stimulus to create increasingly subtle interpretations.

APPENDIX: HOW TO IDENTIFY MYTHS DEPICTED IN IMAGES

This Appendix describes three strategies for identifying images of myths and warns of the pitfalls associated with each.

Identification through Inscription, Attribute or Characterization

A good way to begin is to identify the personages represented.

When a name is inscribed beside a figure, this is usually clear, simple, and convincing, though on rare occasions an inscription may be inaccurate or misleading.[18]

Attributes, too, are generally a reliable guide to the identity of a mythological figure, for instance, a lion-skin and club almost invariably identify Herakles – unless they have been stolen or exchanged so that another figure temporarily possesses them.[19] The usual attributes for the most important gods are as follows:

- Zeus – with thunderbolt or sceptre;
- Hera – pulling aside her veil in a bridal gesture or holding a sceptre;

- Athene – armed with helmet, *aegis* (a sort of snake-fringed bib with the head of the gorgon in the centre) and sometimes also spear and shield, owl and olive;
- Apollo – with a bow or lyre or laurel;
- Artemis – with a bow or accompanied by a deer;
- Hermes – with *kērykeion* (messenger's staff) and traveller's hat;
- Dionysos – with *thyrsos* (pine-cone-topped fennel staff), vines, or drinking vessel;
- Poseidon – holding a trident or fish.

Characterization can also be helpful – for instance, Hera pulling aside her veil in the gesture used by brides, but this gesture is not unique to her, as Helen or Andromache may also use it.

Even the age of a mythological character can vary. Zeus, Poseidon, and Hades are always characterized as mature men, but Dionysos and Hermes, who are bearded in the archaic period, become beardless youths later, and Eros, whose early image is that of a young man, grows ever younger as time goes on, eventually becoming a mere winged baby in the Hellenistic period.

Identification through Conflict with a Unique Monster

Herakles slew the hydra. If one man alone is engaged with a hydra (unmistakable in its configuration), it is highly likely to be Herakles. If there are two men, one is Herakles and the other Iolaos (fig. 8.1).

Perseus slew the Gorgon Medusa. Gorgons have visages so dreadful that merely to look at them is enough to turn a mortal to stone. The horribleness of the Gorgon was represented by means of a frontal face, staring eyes, leering mouth with tusks, snaky curls, and, often, a beard. Perseus was well advised to avert his glance while beheading Medusa, a pose that is in itself telling.

Theseus slew the Minotaur. The Minotaur, fruit of the unnatural union between Minos' wife, Pasiphaē, and an attractive bull that she found irresistible, had a human body but a bull's head (and sometimes a bull's tail).

In such instances the unique features of the monster specify the hero, but the matter is not always so simple; for instance, if the Chimaira is shown attacked by three men, none of them riding Pegasos, it is hard to decide whether any or none of them is Bellerophon or what myth might be illustrated.[20]

Centaurs (with human bodies above and horse bodies from the waist down), though clearly recognizable in themselves, do not have any single adversary, as they were associated with more than one hero: Theseus fought the Centaurs who disrupted Perithoös' wedding feast; Peleus engaged the learned Centaur Cheiron to instruct his son Achilles; Herakles not only slew the ferryman Centaur Nessos who tried to rape his wife but he also fought a group of

Centaurs who gathered uninvited when the Centaur Pholos opened the Centaurs' communal wine jar in order to entertain the hero.

Even Sirens (woman-headed birds) were encountered by more than one hero. Odysseus avoided their fatal lure by having himself tied to the mast of his ship; the Argonauts bypassed these menacing singers by having Orpheus out-sing them.

Identification through Context

Several men poking a stick into the eye of a seated figure is a clear representation of Odysseus and his men blinding Polyphemos. A man clinging onto the underside of a sheep, surely an unusual mode of transportation, must be Odysseus escaping from Polyphemos' cave. But a man *riding on top* of a sheep is Phrixos riding the ram with the golden fleece.

In a scene where Herakles appears to be fighting a hoplite undistinguished by any special characteristics, the hoplite is Kyknos, identified by his adversary. If the scene is expanded to show Athene aiding Herakles and another warrior aiding Kyknos, the second hoplite is Kyknos' father Ares, the god of war, usually distinguished from a generic representation of a hoplite only by context or inscription.

Two women beside a man in a horseless winged chariot are Demeter and Persephone sending Triptolemos on his way to instruct mortals in agriculture.

The activity of fighting Amazons (warrior women) was indulged in by three different heroes: Herakles, Theseus, and Achilles. Herakles can usually be identified by his lion-skin and Achilles by his fatal attraction to Penthesileia, but in the absence of either inscription, attribute, or clear amorous involvement, the conflict remains ambiguous.[21]

FURTHER READING

Woodford 2003 presents a wide-ranging survey of how myths were represented in classical antiquity and is copiously illustrated, as is Carpenter 1991, a useful reference book collecting a rich compendium of images of myths. For the Trojan cycle in particular, Woodford 1993 surveys art and literature with full illustration. A full and scholarly exposition and analysis of images of myths is presented by *LIMC*, an international enterprise with articles in English, French, German, and Italian. It consists of eight large double volumes, of text and illustrations, devoted to mythological iconography with entries arranged alphabetically, each article covering a mythological character (god, hero, or monster) in ancient Greek, Roman, and Etruscan art.

Small 2003 presents an intelligent critical analysis of the relationship of artworks to texts; Schefold 1992 (with plentiful illustration) describes and analyses many images, relating them to literature both extant and lost. For a case-by-case study of the relationship between vase painting and literature, it is helpful to turn to Shapiro 1994, who focuses on a limited number of myths, with many translations, and observes the independence of the literary and graphic traditions. Friis-Johansen 1967 investigates when and where early Greek illustrations can be taken to reflect knowledge of the *Iliad*, but early images are frequently not directly influenced by the Homeric poems, as Snodgrass 1998 carefully demonstrates. For the influence of Athenian tragedy on western Greek vase painting, we can turn to Taplin 2007 (again copiously illustrated). Weitzmann 1947 is still useful for its scholarly study of the relationship of illustrations to texts, with special emphasis on illustrations in books.

NOTES

1. A loose translation/retelling of the first chorus in Euripides *Ion*, lines 184–218.
2. Metopes showing Herakles fighting the hydra appear on the Hephaisteion and the Temple of Zeus at Olympia.
3. The metopes at the back of the Parthenon, the west side, are thought to represent the battle of Athenians against the Amazons; those on the north side, the Trojan War; those on the south (at the ends) a battle of Greeks and Centaurs, while the subject(s) of those at the centre of the south side are uncertain. Most of the metopes, except for the fights with the Centaurs, have been much damaged.
4. Battles with Amazons and struggles with Centaurs were represented on the friezes of the Temple of Apollo at Bassai and on the Mausoleum at Halikarnassos.
5. The Gigantomachy might be thought to have represented violent opposition to the order of the Olympian gods; the Centauromachy, wild nature against civilized restraint; the Amazonomachy, enemy eastern people (and women at that!) against the Greek conception of proper government and behaviour.
6. The pediment of the temple of Artemis at Corfu, for instance, seems to have illustrated three different stories, each on a different scale.
7. A detailed description is given by Pliny, *Natural History* 36.18–19.
8. Pausanias 5.11.1–8.
9. Pausanias 1.17.2–3.
10. Pliny, *Natural History* 35.91.
11. Pliny, *Natural History* 35.63, tr. K. Jex-Blake.
12. Pausanias 10.25.1–27.4.
13. Pliny, *Natural History* 35.74, tr. K. Jex-Blake.
14. Lucian *Zeuxis and Antiochus* 3–4, tr. H. W. Fowler and F. G. Fowler.
15. Pliny, *Natural History* 36.37–8.
16. Pliny, *Natural History* 34.57.
17. The 'Farnese Hercules' in Naples, Museo Archeologico, presumed to be a copy of an original by Lysippos in the fourth century BC.
18. See, for instance, the vase in Leipzig showing Thetis giving armour to *Menelaos* (discussed in CH. 21, p. 416), illustrated in Woodford (2003: 203 (fig. 165)).

19. Herakles' attributes were stolen by mischievous satyrs or aigipans, who naugh-
     tily flaunt them, and the hero was forced to exchange his attire with Omphale,
     when she bought him as a slave; she is therefore sometimes shown wearing his
     lion-skin.
20. Attic black-figure amphora c. 540 by the Swing Painter in the British Museum,
     illustrated in Woodford (2003: 211, fig. 176).
21. von Bothmer (1957).

CHAPTER NINE

Platonic 'Myths'

Penelope Murray

Once upon a time, in the distant past, Athens was home to the finest and noblest race on earth. It was the best governed of all cities, its constitution the most perfect in the world, and its people, endowed by their patron gods Athene and Hephaistos with exceptional wisdom, intelligence, and courage, excelled in warfare. Amongst all its magnificent achievements one great heroic act stood out: its defence of the Mediterranean against invasion by a mighty and arrogant power based on a huge island beyond the 'pillars of Herakles'. These legendary Athenians, though deserted by their Greek allies, stood firm and, with great courage and bravery, repelled the enemy and warded off the hand of slavery from Greece and Asia alike. Soon after this great victory, however, earthquakes and violent floods destroyed all traces of it ever having happened: the entire Athenian army was swallowed up by the earth, and the island empire of the invaders disappeared into the sea. Its name was, of course, Atlantis.

Plato tells the story of Atlantis at the beginning of the *Timaios* and in his unfinished dialogue the *Kritias*. In the *Timaios* Socrates says to his companions, Timaios and Kritias, that he would like to continue their conversation from the previous day, when he had described his ideal state and its citizens. A brief summary of that conversation lets us know that the present dialogue is to be taken as a sequel to the *Republic*, in which Socrates builds up a picture of a perfect society. What would such a state look like in action, particularly when fighting a war? It turns out that this was exactly what his friends had been talking about at Kritias' house last night, and Kritias is prevailed upon to repeat for Socrates' benefit the story that he had missed the night before. It was a very strange story, but absolutely true, vouched for by Solon, the wisest of the

A Companion to Greek Mythology, First Edition. Edited by Ken Dowden and Niall Livingstone.
© 2014 John Wiley & Sons Ltd. Published 2014 by John Wiley & Sons Ltd.

Seven Wise Men of Greece, who had told it to Kritias' grandfather, who in his old age had repeated it to Kritias himself when he was a child (*Timaios* 20d). After some further preamble Kritias recounts the story outlined above, which is said to have taken place 9,000 years earlier (*Timaios* 23e). He notes the amazing coincidence between Solon's account of primeval Athens and Socrates' description of the ideal society, and offers to speak in more detail about those ancient Athenians who seem in fact to be the very same people as the imaginary citizens depicted by Socrates in Plato's *Republic* (*Timaios* 26c–d). But, first, Timaios is going to speak about the origins of the universe, and the remainder of the dialogue is taken up with that subject.

Socrates returns to the story of ancient Athens and its war with Atlantis in the *Kritias*, from which we learn more about these lost societies. In the beginning the gods divided the world up amongst themselves, each ruling over their allotted share without dispute. Athene and Hephaistos presided over Athens, a region which was naturally conducive to intelligence and courage, rich in natural resources, and blessed with a perfect climate. Its people lived a happy, self-sufficient life, its farmers working the land and its warriors living apart from the rest of the population in communal houses. They had everything they needed, but no silver or gold, for which they had no use. As for Atlantis, this was the province of Poseidon, whose descendants, born to him by a mortal woman, ruled the island. It was a remarkably fertile place with an abundance of trees, crops, and animals, both tame and wild. So huge were its pasture lands that it could even sustain elephants, the largest of living creatures. There was an abundance of everything in that sun-drenched island, including minerals, silver, gold, and a precious metal that no longer exists, orichalc. Its fabulous wealth was increased by trade from abroad, its rulers lived in incredible luxury, and its people lived well for generations. But gradually prosperity corrupted them, their happiness destroyed by materialistic ambitions and limitless greed. Zeus, determined to punish them for their wickedness, summoned the gods to a meeting, and addressed them thus ... At this point the manuscript of the *Kritias* breaks off. But we know the end of the story from the *Timaios*: the punishment of Atlantis was its defeat by the model city of primeval Athens.

The story of Atlantis continues to fascinate to this very day. Readers over the centuries have been convinced of its essential truth, and literally thousands of books have been written on the whereabouts of Atlantis. But this story is a myth, an archetypally Platonic myth. No doubt the idea of a lost kingdom taps into some deep-seated need in the modern psyche, such as that which accounts for the popularity of science fiction, a genre which Plato has been credited with inventing. But the appeal of the myth depends largely on Plato's skill as a storyteller, on his ability to make the fabulous seem real.[1] The war between Athens and Atlantis is presented in the form of a historical pastiche, reminiscent in particular of the style of Herodotos. Thus the 'great and wonderful deeds' accomplished by Athens (*Timaios* 20e) recall the 'great and wonderful deeds' of Greeks and barbarians to which Herodotos refers in the opening lines of his *Histories*. The conflict between Athens and Atlantis is assimilated to the great wars between Greece and Persia, but it is also given a Homeric colouring: the utopian paradise of Atlantis in its early days reminds us of Scheria, Homer's semi-mythical land of the Phaiakes (Phaeacians), whose king was also descended from Poseidon. Traditional Greek mythology is also incorporated into the account, with references, for example, to the story of Deukalion and Pyrrha and how they survived the flood (*Timaios* 22b), or to the legendary autochthonous origins of the Athenian people and its early kings (*Kritias* 110a). At the same time, there are parallels in Plato's account with versions of Athenian history in contemporary panegyrics (praise speeches delivered at festivals or at funerals for those killed in war).[2] Details in the 'histories' of both Athens and Atlantis are made to sound familiar, seducing us into believing that they are true. But in reality these places belong to the world of imagination. Though contrasted with each other they also share similarities, both providing models with which to compare the state of contemporary Athens. Beyond that, the myth of Atlantis offers a more general political parable, encapsulating the belief that civilizations are destroyed through greed and the lust for power. The moral dimension of Plato's story is inescapable: like the Old Testament flood, the destruction of Atlantis was a punishment for the wickedness of its inhabitants. And the major themes of the myth tie in with some of Plato's most deeply held philosophical concerns.

Mythos and *Mousikē* in the *Republic*

Myth has an important part to play in Plato's philosophy, and to understand why that should be so we need to turn to the *Republic*. Early on in the construction of the ideal state, which is the theoretical counterpart of the perfect society of primeval Athens depicted in the Atlantis myth, Socrates raises the question of how to educate those who will be in charge of this imagined society, the so-called guardians. It will be sensible, he says, to follow the time-honoured system of education which consists in 'music' for the soul and gymnastics for the body (*Republic* 376e). In the oral culture of early Greece 'music' (Greek *mousikē*) includes poetry, song, and dance as well as music as we now understand it, and it also includes stories (*logoi*). Socrates distinguishes between two types of story, one true, the other false, and makes the rather startling statement that education, in the initial stages at any rate, should be based on false stories. When asked for clarification by his puzzled interlocutor, it emerges that what he is talking about is myth (*mythos*), which he defines as being in general false, but also containing some truth (*Republic* 377a). Since myth is traditionally the province of poets, the myths that they relate, together with the stories told to young children by their mothers and nurses, will have to be carefully regulated to ensure that they accord with the beliefs and attitudes that the founders of the utopian state wish to promote.

In the ensuing discussion what emerges very clearly is the centrality of myth, not only in the education and up-bringing of the young, but also more generally in the shaping of the values of society as a whole. Socrates is highly critical of traditional Greek mythology since in his opinion it inculcates the wrong values and beliefs. He objects, for example, to the famous succession myth of Hesiod's *Theogony* (154–82, 453–506), which told of how Kronos castrated his father Ouranos and then swallowed his own children through fear of being usurped, and how his son Zeus, having escaped this fate, deposed his own father in turn on order to become supreme ruler of the world. This myth should be censored not only because it conveys the wrong impression of the divine, but also because of the bad example it sets for human conduct. Even if a story like this were true, says Socrates, it should not be told, because it would encourage young men to believe that they would be doing nothing wrong in assaulting their own fathers (*Republic* 378a). Similarly, all tales of gods fighting with each other, of battles between gods and giants, and of interfamilial strife amongst gods and heroes should be suppressed. In the ideal state there is to be no strife amongst the citizens, hence story-tellers and poets must be compelled to promote harmony and unanimity by eliminating all tales of quarrels amongst gods and heroes from their repertoire. (In fact, we have already seen Plato himself putting this principle into practice in the Atlantis myth, when, in saying (*Kritias* 109b) that the gods divided up the regions of the world without dispute, he implicitly rejects the well-known tradition of the competition between Athene and Poseidon for possession of Attica).

Although Socrates finds much to criticize in existing Greek mythology, he does not object to myth as such. On the contrary, he sees myth as an essential means of preserving and transmitting values. Hence it is far too dangerous an instrument to be left in the hands of its traditional practitioners, the poets. In the ideal state poets will have to conform to guidelines or 'moulds' (*typoi*) laid down by its founders when they compose their stories (*Republic* 379a). So, for example, poets must depict god as he actually is: since he is good, he cannot be the cause of evil; since he is perfect, he does not change or manifest himself in different guises; nor does he tell lies or deceive human beings (*Republic* 379b–383c). As for human beings, they must be courageous and unafraid of death, so there must be no stories about the horrors of Hades or of heroes lamenting the dead (*Republic* 386a–388d). Instead, poets must depict men who are brave, self-controlled, pious, and free (*Republic* 395c) in order to provide appropriate role models for the future guardians of the state.

The power of myth to mould the beliefs and values of society at large, and not just the young, is exhibited a little later on in the dialogue when Socrates sketches a foundation myth for his society, designed to promote cohesion amongst its members. This is the so-called noble lie, according to which the citizens are to be told that they were all born from the earth. Like brothers born from the self-same mother, they must devote themselves to each other and to protecting the land which gave them birth (*Republic* 417b–e). They may take a little persuading to believe this story, says Socrates, but poets have been telling such tales for centuries. He is alluding here to the well-known myth of Kadmos, who sowed the dragon's teeth from which the Spartoi or earthborn men sprang, a myth to which Plato also refers in the *Laws* (663e) as an example of the incredible stories that people will believe. But we are also reminded of the supposedly autochthonous origins of the Athenians themselves, a motif which also appear in the Athens of the Atlantis myth at *Kritias* 110a (see above). Socrates' earthborn men are to be told, in addition, that god put gold, silver, iron, or bronze into each of them at birth so that they are naturally suited to the different functions that the ideal state demands: rulers, auxiliaries, farmers, and craftsmen. The fact that it is a reworking of Hesiod's myth of ages (*Works and Days* 106–201) gives a veneer of familiarity to this fantastic tale, which Socrates hopes will one day achieve the status of traditional myth (415d).[3] But it is nevertheless a lie (*pseudos*). Modern readers may be shocked by such blatant brainwashing, but for Socrates the end justifies the means; what matters is the moral and social purpose that the myth is designed to achieve. Unlike the myths of the poets, which are, according to Socrates, simply false, the 'noble lie' conveys a truth which is central to the ideology on which the ideal state is founded.

Characteristics of Platonic Myth

Taking this example together with the discussion of myth in the *Republic*, which I have outlined above, we can see the role that myth performs in society. But how does this relate to Plato's use of myth in his own dialogues? It is one thing to say that societies need myths, quite another to make myth an integral part of philosophy. Myths are ubiquitous in Plato's work, from the solemn religious myths concerning the fate of the soul after death to the great creation myth of the *Timaios* and the pseudo-historical account of the war between Athens and Atlantis, and to Aristophanes' enchanting tale of the spherical beings who once populated the earth before they were chopped in two by Zeus in the *Symposium*. There is such variety in these myths, not only in subject matter, but also in length, function, and significance, that no one definition will be adequate. And a proper understanding of Platonic myth would, in

Table 9.1   The principal Platonic myths.

Area	Topic	Text
Life after death and the nature of the human soul	The judgement of souls	*Gorgias* 523a–527e
	The fate of the soul in the afterlife	*Phaedo* 107c–114c
	The myth of Er	*Republic* 614b–621d
	The winged soul	*Phaedrus* 246a–257a
The cosmos, human history, and human society	The demiurge and the creation of the world	*Timaios* 29d–92c
	The cosmic eras	*Politikos* 268d–274e
	Atlantis and ancient Athens	*Timaios* 20d–25d; *Kritias* 108e–121c
	The origin of virtue	*Protagoras* 320c–323a
	Autochthony and the myth of metals	*Republic* 414b–415b = the 'noble lie'
Miscellaneous	The nature of love	*Symposium* 189c–193e, Aristophanes' tale
	The nature of love	*Symposium* 201d–212c, Diotima's account
	Gyges' ring	*Republic* 359d–360b
	Cicadas and the origins of music	*Phaedrus* 259b–d
	Theuth and the origins of writing	*Phaedrus* 274c–275e

any case, depend on a detailed reading of the dialogues in which the individual myths are embedded. But some generalizations are nevertheless possible.

First of all, these myths are invented by Plato. Though they often contain familiar themes and motifs, Plato adapts the traditions of Greek mythology for his own particular purposes. His myths are the product of his own artistic imagination, and, unlike traditional myths which exist in many different versions, they are designed for a specific context. In some respects they constitute a genre of their own in that they are literary and textual rather than belonging to the common stock of stories typical of an oral tradition.[4] Secondly, they are narrative in form, and this is what distinguishes them from other types of imagery, such as metaphor and analogy, which characterize Plato's writing. For example, the famous image of the cave in the *Republic* (514a–517a), although it is often categorized as a myth, is strictly speaking an allegory or extended simile to be taken together with the sun and the line, rather than a mythical narrative: it is explicitly introduced as an analogy for the human condition, and its details are interpreted accordingly. But the difficulties scholars have with the classification of the cave are symptomatic of the deeper problem of drawing the boundaries around Platonic myth, of treating the 'myths' in isolation from their context. In a general sense, however, we can say that the discourse of myth is narrative rather than argumentative, concerned with images rather than abstractions.

Frames and Sources of Myths

When a myth is introduced there is generally some kind of break in the dramatic dialogue, signalling that we are moving into a different register. So, for example, in the *Protagoras* (320c) the sophist prefaces his myth on the origin of virtue with words that highlight the mythical nature of his narrative:

'Would you rather that I showed you [that virtue is teachable] by telling a story (as an older man speaking to his juniors) or by going through a systematic exposition?' Several of those who were sitting around asked him to proceed in whatever way he preferred. 'Well', he said, 'I think that it will be more enjoyable to tell you a story,' [which he then proceeds to do]. 'Once upon a time...'[5]

In the *Politikos* (268d), to take another example, the Stranger, who is the chief spokesman of the dialogue, switches from dialectical to mythical mode, saying that he and his interlocutor had better take a different route in their search for a definition of the perfect statesman:

'We should blend in a bit of light relief, as it were, and help ourselves to a lengthy fragment of a great myth, before returning for the rest of the discussion to the previous method of separating one from another and gaining the summit we're after that way. ... So pay very careful attention to the myth, then, as if you were a child listening to a story'.[6]

The myth that follows is replete with references to traditional stories from Greek mythology: the quarrel of Thyestes and Atreus, which caused the sun to reverse its course; the myth of the Golden Age in the time of Kronos; and the various stories about earthborn men – all of which, according to the Stranger, are misunderstood reminiscences of events which took place in the distant past. In fact the cosmos alternates between periods when god is in control of its revolution, and when he withdraws and the world revolves back on itself. The age of Kronos (whose relationship to the cosmic eras is unclear) immediately preceded the present age of Zeus. In that golden age of peace and plenty when nature produced trees, crops, and fruit in abundance, humans roamed the earth freely without the need for families or any form of social organization. The course of life was reversed from the way it is now: old people grew younger, their grey hair became black, their bearded cheeks smooth, until they became babies again and finally vanished altogether. New life was created not by human reproduction, but by the earth itself, which gave birth to the earthborn race. But eventually the divine helmsman withdrew and the universe rolled backwards, bringing earthquakes and devastation in its wake. A period of stability followed in which the cosmos revolved well of its own accord, but then gradually forgot its course. When god saw the chaos that ensued and the helplessness of men, he intervened to save them with the gift of fire from Prometheus and the skills bestowed by Athene and Hephaistos. After recounting this hugely enjoyable and often fantastical story the Stranger concludes by saying, 'Anyway, I think we should end the myth there and start to put it to work' (274e). In this case the myth is clearly demarcated as a different kind of discourse from the argument that surrounds it. But unlike the traditional tales which it adapts, it has a philosophical purpose.[7]

Another feature of Plato's myths is that they are often attributed to a source other than the narrator. Thus in both the *Gorgias* (524a–b) and the *Phaedo* (108c) Socrates' knowledge of what happens to the soul after death comes from some vague unnamed source. In the *Republic*, the vision of the soul's judgement is put into the mouth of Er, the son of Armenios, a Pamphylian by birth (*Republic* 614b). Some have seen a pun here since *pan phulon* means 'every tribe' in Greek, perhaps making Er a kind of Everyman figure. In the *Symposium* the whole of Socrates' discourse on love, including the tale of Eros' (Love's) parentage and birth (203b), is something he heard from Diotima ('honoured by Zeus'), a woman from Mantinea (*mantis* means 'seer'), who once miraculously warded off the plague from Athens for ten years and was Socrates' teacher in the art of love. The Atlantis myth at the beginning of the *Timaios*, discussed above, is given a very elaborate provenance, beginning with Solon, who had himself heard the story from an Egyptian priest (*Timaios* 22a). The effect of this kind of strategy is to distance the protagonist from the story he is telling and at the same time to exempt him from guaranteeing its truth. It also assimilates these stories to the anonymity of inherited myth, aptly described by Walter Burkert as 'non-factual story telling – the telling of a tale while disclaiming responsibility'.[8] Interestingly, Kritias prefaces his account of the war between Athens and Atlantis with an invocation to the Muses and their mother, Mnemosyne, goddess of Memory (*Kritias* 108c–d) as though he, like a poet, is dependent on some source outside himself for the details of his story.

Truth, Falsehood, and the Limits of Human Knowledge

In terms of subject matter Plato's myths tend to deal with non-verifiable aspects of experience that are beyond ordinary mortal knowledge: the nature of the soul and its fate after death, the divine creation of the cosmos, the distant past where things happened 'once upon a time'.[9] Since myths are concerned with the realm of the imagination rather than with facts, questions of truth and falsehood are not straightforward. These issues are explicitly raised in the *Republic*'s discussion of myth when Socrates says (382c–d) that human beings, unlike the gods, *cannot* know about the distant past. But mythology, and especially myths of origin, can be useful if the falsehood which it inevitably involves is made to look as like the truth as possible. The truth to which Socrates refers here is evidently not factual knowledge of historical events, but moral or ethical truth, such as that contained within the noble lie of the *Republic* (417b–e, discussed above), which is introduced as an example of exactly the kind of useful falsehood (*pseudos*) that Socrates has in mind. The usefulness of myth, again described as 'falsehood' (*pseudos*), in propagating values amongst society at large is also discussed in the *Laws* (663c–664b). But the falsehood of Platonic myth is not usually acknowledged in so blatant a way as it is with the barefaced noble lie. Indeed, in the myth of Atlantis we have the opposite scenario, where Kritias several times insists on the absolute truth of his incredible tale.[10]

More often than not, however, the myths are presented as being neither true nor false, but plausible or likely, the best accounts that humans with their limited knowledge can achieve. Thus the construction of the universe by the craftsman-god, the Demiurge, in the *Timaios* is described as a 'plausible myth' (*eikōs mythos* 29d), a myth which it is reasonable to believe, but which cannot be accurate in every detail because human beings are not gods. Again, in the *Phaedo*, when Socrates has described in graphic detail the various regions of the earth to which dead souls go, and the rewards and punishments that await them there, he says, 'To insist that these things are exactly as I have described them would not befit a man of intelligence. But to think that this or something like it is true ... is fitting and worth risking ... one should repeat such things to oneself like a spell, which is why I myself have been spinning out my story for so long' (*Phaedo* 114d).

Similarly, in the *Phaedrus* (265b) Socrates refers to his great speech on the madness of love and the immortality of the soul as 'a not altogether implausible account' (*ou pantapasin apithanon logon*), which 'perhaps hit upon some truth'. Here, and in the eschatological myths of the *Gorgias* and *Republic*, factual veracity is not an issue: what matters is the religious truth which the myths are designed to convey. As with the cosmological myths of the *Politikos* and the *Timaios/Kritias*, the details of these narratives may be invented, but the stories themselves express ideas about the divine governance of the universe and the destiny of the human soul which Plato believes to be true. In this respect Plato's myths are not unlike the various traditional stories of Greek mythology which serve as a grounding for religious belief, though Plato's conviction that the gods are fundamentally benevolent and rational is totally at odds with traditional Greek theology.

Functions of Platonic Myth

Plato's myths perform a variety of different functions.[11] At the simplest level they can be used as instruments of persuasion, either to exercise social control (as in the case of the noble lie) or to educate those who are unmoved by the abstractions of philosophical argument. Some are aetiological, that is, they purport to offer an explanation of why things are as they are, as for example Protagoras' myth on the origin of human virtue or Aristophanes' playful 'history' of the origins of love. But though they may be a form of play, designed to appeal to children and the childlike part of human nature, that does not mean that they cannot be used for serious purposes. They can also be used to complement or reinforce arguments, expressing in a different way the beliefs and ideas which are subject to rigorous analysis in the dialogues in which they are embedded. Thus, for example, the great eschatological myths which conclude the *Gorgias, Phaedo,* and *Republic* show us in figurative form the paramount importance of living a virtuous life, and thus they underpin the main moral message of these dialogues. Another way of understanding their significance is to say that they go beyond reason, taking over from argument and analysis, and portraying aspects of experience that rational discourse cannot express. So, in the *Phaedrus,* where, significantly, the vision of the soul's adventures is placed in the middle of the dialogue rather than at its end, Socrates says that he cannot describe what the soul actually is (246a). Only a god could do that. Being human, the best that he can do is to offer a likeness, an image of the winged soul with its charioteer and horses, which he elaborates in myth to present as compelling a picture as he can of the nature of the soul. Here the status of the myth is essentially metaphorical in that it seeks to embody truths which analytical language cannot capture, truths which can only be presented pictorially: the graphic and at times bizarre detail which is so a striking a feature of Plato's mythical writing reinforces the sense that what is being portrayed is an imagined world in which he wants us to believe, but which cannot be literally described.

Myth and Philosophy

Any attempt to generalize about the function of Plato's myths is bound to be unsatisfactory, not least because their meanings are to a large extent dependent on context. But one thing that can be said is that Platonic myths are never merely decorative. Unlike the sophists who use myth for illustrative purposes or as exegetical tools, Plato's myths are integral to his philosophy.[12] Indeed the question of what constitutes a myth for Plato is more complicated than it looks, since myth and argument are interdependent, the boundaries between myth and philosophy unclear. While it is sometimes possible, as in the case of the *Politikos*, discussed above, to separate the myth from the argument that surrounds it, Plato's writing in general is so characterized by imagery, storytelling and figurative language that we cannot label one type of expression 'philosophical' and the other 'mythical'. Symptomatic of this blurring is Plato's refusal to make a consistent distinction between *mythos* (myth) and *logos* (rational account). Thus the myth of judgement in the *Gorgias* is described as both a *mythos* and a *logos*, depending on the listener (*Gorgias* 523a); that of the *Phaedo* as a *mythos* (114d); and the ideal city of the *Republic* as the product of 'mythologizing in argument'.[13]

Myth in the *Timaios*

The most extreme example of the interpenetration of myth and philosophy in Plato's work is the *Timaios*. The greater part of this dialogue is taken up with a disquisition on the origins of the cosmos by Timaios, an expert on astronomy who has devoted himself to studying the nature of the universe. He begins with the customary invocation, but rather than appealing, like a poet, to the Muses, he calls on all the gods and goddesses to aid him in what will be, by implication, a far more serious account of the world's creation than those traditionally on offer. In the prelude (*prooimion*, 29d) to his account Timaios makes a basic distinction between that which exists, the eternal, unchanging world of being, and that which comes into being, the world of change and decay that we inhabit. Since our world is so beautiful it must have been made by a divine craftsman (*demiourgos*) who had his eye on the eternal model when he brought order to the chaos of existing matter. Just like a human craftsman, god, the Demiurge, was constrained by his materials (there is no concept here of creation from scratch, *ex nihilo*) but he did the best he could to impose reason on necessity, creating the universe in accordance with the principles of beauty and order that he found in the divine pattern. Fundamental to Timaios' account is the belief that god is good (29a), and that, being good, he wanted all things to be as like himself as possible. He therefore imbued the cosmos with intelligence and soul, making of it a living being like himself, but necessarily subject to the change and corruption that characterize the visible world. This we should accept as a plausible myth (*eikōs mythos*) concerning the origins of the cosmos (29d).

In calling his account a *mythos* Timaios draws attention to its necessarily provisional status: given the limitations of human knowledge only a god could vouchsafe for its complete truth and accuracy. But that does not mean that one myth is as good as another. What is offered here is an *eikōs mythos*,[14] a *plausible* or *appropriate* myth which, even though it may fall short of divine standards of truth, is nevertheless the best that is available to human beings. Unlike the myths of the poets, the *eikōs mythos* of the *Timaios* is based on rational principles, a claim which is clearly implied by Timaios' ironic remarks about traditional mythology at 40d–e. Having described the creation of the cosmos and the heavenly bodies, he says,

> It is beyond our powers to know or tell about the birth of the other gods; we must rely on those who have told the story before, who claimed to be the children of the gods, and presumably know about their ancestors. We cannot distrust the children of the gods, even if they give no probable [*eikotōn*] or necessary [*anankaiōn*] proof of what they say: we must conform to custom and believe their account of their own family history. Let us therefore follow them in our account of the birth of these gods. Ocean and Tethys were the children of Earth and Heaven, and their children were Phorkys and Rhea and their companions; and from Kronos and Rhea were born Zeus and Hera and their brothers and sisters whose names we know, and they in turn had yet further children. (40d–41a)[15]

The repeated emphasis on the plausibility of Timaios' cosmogony[16] contrasts markedly with the lack of 'probable' or 'necessary' proof which characterizes the tales of poets like Orpheus, Mousaios, and the rest of those self-styled descendants of the gods. Some have doubted whether Timaios has any particular theogony in mind here, but his brief summary of the birth of the gods looks very like the Hesiodic version.[17] By incorporating such material into his own cosmogony Plato invites comparison with the poets, while at the same time creating a myth that will transcend all those that have come before. In place of the violent succession myth of the *Theogony*, already a target of Plato's critique in the *Republic* (377e), we have a creator god who brings harmony and order to the universe. In place of the Zeus of Homer and Hesiod, who is responsible for evil as well as good, we have the blameless god of the *Timaios* (42d), concerned only to impart his own rationality and goodness to the human beings he has created.

Theological Myth

The cosmological exposition of the *Timaios* contains much that is technical, including complicated mathematics and abstruse philosophical doctrine that sets it apart from its poetic rivals; but it is nevertheless a myth, and it would be futile to try to distinguish its 'mythical' elements from its 'rational' or 'philosophical' elements. The myth as a whole *is* rational because it is reasonably argued, but it is also an expression of faith in the goodness of god. Part of Plato's project, both here and elsewhere, is to replace what he sees as the false theology of the poets with a truer conception of the divine, and myth is the vehicle that he uses for this purpose. Thus the myth of Er, which brings the *Republic* to a close, reshapes traditional Greek Underworld mythology, transforming familiar ideas to produce a vision of the after-life of the soul which challenges inherited beliefs.[18] Socrates' introductory remark (614b) that this will not be a 'tale told to Alkinoös' (*Alkinou*), but that of a brave man (*alkimou*) invites comparison with the *Odyssey*, where Odysseus' descent to the Underworld, the so-called *Nekyia* (*Odyssey* 11), is one of the most famous of the stories that he tells to Alkinoös (*Odyssey* 9–12). The pun on Alkinoös' name suggests, further, that Plato's myth will encourage bravery in the face of death, in contrast with the cowardice and fear implanted by traditional depictions of the Underworld such as those of Homer, already criticized earlier on in the *Republic* (386a–388d). Er's near-death experience and his vision of the afterlife recalls other Greek heroes who had descended to the Underworld and lived to tell the tale, notably Orpheus, Theseus, and Herakles. And we meet familiar figures in the catalogue of souls choosing their fates (620a–c), amongst them Orpheus, Thamyras, Ajax, Agamemnon, and Odysseus himself. Familiar, too, are the themes of the soul's journey, the judgement of the dead, the grim depiction of the punishments that await the wicked, and the topography of the Underworld with its meadow and river. But despite its Homeric colouring and traditional veneer the main message conveyed by the myth is of a quite different order. The image of the cosmos as a spindle in the lap of the goddess Necessity, together with the Sirens, now transformed from the menacing temptresses of the *Odyssey* into the source of cosmic harmony, depicts a divinely ordered universe, in which the principle of justice itself is embodied. When the souls come to choose the lives in which they will be reincarnated, the moral is clear: *aitia helomenou: theos anaitios* ('responsibility lies with the chooser; god is blameless').[19] These pregnant words, spoken by Lachesis, the daughter of Necessity, encapsulate the central belief of the *Republic* in the goodness of god and the necessity of living a just life.

Conclusion

Plato's myths are unique. No philosopher before or since has used myth in the same way as a form of philosophical expression, no writer combined that inventive capacity with so deep a knowledge of tradition to forge new myths that yet seem old. Myth is as much a part of Plato's philosophy as image-making, dramatic settings, and the dialogue form itself. If his myths still speak to us today it is because Plato was not only a philosopher, he was also a great creative artist.

FURTHER READING

Partenie 2004 is a useful anthology of the major Platonic myths (excluding the demi-urge of the *Timaios*) with bibliography and notes. There is a fuller selection in the classic, somewhat dated, but still valuable study by J. A. Stewart (1905). Partenie 2009 is an authoritative collection of essays on the individual myths, which also includes essays on Plato's myths in the Platonist tradition (J. Dillon) and in Renaissance iconography (E. McGrath). Brisson 1998 provides a detailed overview of Platonic myth, with helpful introduction by Naddaf. On questions of myth and fiction the three articles by Gill (1977, 1979, 1993) can be highly recommended. Morgan 2000 is an excellent study of Plato and the context in which philosophical myth was developed.

NOTES

1. For a general discussion of the myth and its history see Vidal-Naquet (2007). For more detailed analysis see Gill (1977, 1979, 1993).
2. See Morgan (1998).
3. On the 'noble lie' see Gill (1993: 52–5) and Schofield (2007, 2009). Socrates himself refers to Hesiod in connection with this myth at *Republic* 546e. See further, Van Noorden (2010).
4. See further Morgan (2000: 16, 36).
5. Tr. C. C. W. Taylor (1991).
6. Tr. R. Waterfield in Partenie (2004).
7. What that purpose might be is, not surprisingly, a subject of scholarly dispute. See, most recently, Kahn (2009). On Hesiodic motifs in the myth see El Murr (2010) and Rowe (2010).
8. Burkert (1979: 3). On the narrative aspects of Plato's myths see Brisson (1998: 100, 112–15).
9. See further, Brisson (1998: 22–4, 100–11).
10. *Timaios* 20d, 21a, 26e; Gill (1993: 62–6); Morgan (1998: 102–4).

11. See, for example, Brisson (1998: 75–85, 112–21); Morgan (2000: 3–4, 179–84).
12. This point was already made by J. A. Stewart (1905). See also Morgan (2000: 105, 290–1), and Ferrari (2009: 128), who contrasts the 'transparent fables' of the sophists with the 'philosophic piety' expressed in Platonic myths.
13. *Republic* 501e, and cf. 376d. On the deep mythical structure that pervades the philosophical argument of the *Republic* see especially C. Segal (1978). On *mythos* and *logos* see further, Brisson (1998: 7–11, 87–139); P. Murray (1999); Rowe (1999); Morgan (2000: 155–61); Halliwell (2007: 452–5); Clay (2007).
14. For detailed discussion of this phrase see Burnyeat (2009).
15. Tr. H. D. P. Lee (Harmondsworth 1965).
16. For *eikôs* see 44d, 48d, 53d, 55d, 56a, 56b, 56d, 68b, 72d, 90e.
17. See, for example, *Theogony* 132–8, 453–8 and Pender (2010). On Hesiodic echoes in the *Timaios* see also Capra (2010).
18. See C. Segal (1978); Halliwell (2007). On the eschatological myths in general see Annas (1982); Morgan (2000: 185–241); Stalley (2009). On traditional beliefs see especially Edmonds (2004).
19. *Republic* 617e, tr. Halliwell (1988).

CHAPTER TEN

Myth in History

Alan Griffiths

Myth or History?

Before traditions about the past are written down by 'historians' and become 'history', they exist, in partial form, in the brains of every member of every community. They are transferred from brain to brain via mouths and ears. This is 'oral history' – which might just as well be called aural history. And those shared (but various, and competing) traditions about family, clan, tribe, and state, about ancestral friendships and enmities, about space and time, are stored in the same brain-space as what we are in the shorthand habit of calling *mythical* material: stories about gods, demons, giants, heroes, giant heroes, tricksters, ogres, magical objects, flying horses, werewolves, or UFOs.

Of course, these two categories (which may be further subdivided at will into legend, saga, fable, folktale, and so forth), overlap and merge into each other like a Venn diagram. It might be possible to claim x for myth (say, Hephaistos' attempted rape of Athene on the Akropolis) and y for history (the Athenian Tribute Lists, preserved in the same place). But where should we put the *Iliad*'s Catalogue of Ships, or Samson's exploits against the Philistines in Judges 14–16? Or what about Herodotos' story about the Argive youths Kleobis and Biton (1.31), two brothers who are granted an instant, easeful death as a divine reward for filial services to their pious mother? Again: just how and why does the historical figure of Napoleon Bonaparte become transmuted into Boney the bogeyman, invoked to terrify naughty English children back to good behaviour? And how can we reliably distinguish General Dwight D. Eisenhower from the iconic Ike?[1] Will Elvis return like

---

A Companion to Greek Mythology, First Edition. Edited by Ken Dowden and Niall Livingstone.

the Hohenstaufen Emperor Friedrich Barbarossa to bring aid and comfort to his faithful followers?[2]

It is clear that in some texts, at least, the usual and casual categories of myth and history are so fuzzily interfused that all the king's horses and all the king's men couldn't pull them apart again. Nor is this simply a question of terminological definition. Even in languages which don't differentiate 'historical' narratives from other kinds as sharply as English does (consider French *histoire*, German *Geschichte*, Italian *storia*) the problem remains. Is the account of past events which we happen to have before us an accurate, though necessarily selective and abbreviated, account of what really happened (in Ranke's famous formulation: 'wie es eigentlich gewesen', 'how it really was')? Or does it seem to have been so overlaid with powerful, pre-existing patterns from the divine or heroic, or simply folklorish, register that we should not allow ourselves to rely on its veracity?

Categories Ancient and Modern

But would an ancient Greek have recognized, and accepted as valid, the distinctions we are trying to work with? Thucydides, at least, declares in his important programmatic passage at 1.21 that he proposes to exclude *to mythōdes*, 'the novelistic element', from his history of the Peloponnesian War. This can hardly be anything other than a hit at his elder predecessor Herodotos, the charm of whose anecdotal narrative has been appreciated from antiquity to the present day.[3] Thucydides wants to impose a strict limit on the bandwidth of historical narrative as he has inherited it, cutting out the divine dimension and confining himself to a hard-nosed analysis of the human motivation behind political and military events.

And it is true that for Herodotos, as for the fifth-century man in the agora, the gods exist, they influence human behaviour with rewards and punishments, and produce oracles for their guidance. Epiphanies of heroes may still occur on battlefields, heroines like Helen still have power. Thus, Ladike, the Greek wife of the Pharaoh Amasis, prays to Aphrodite for help with her dysfunctional sex life, and her request is instantly granted (2.181). Similarly, Herodotos is happy to refer without qualification to King Minos' journey to the west in search of Daidalos, and Kadmos' attempt to track down Europa (7.170 and 4.147 respectively). The existence of the legendary Athenian king Kekrops (represented as a kind of snake-merman in contemporary art) is taken for granted (8.44). Passages like this, and there are many, might suggest that Herodotos accepted uncritically the general Greek belief in a seamless web of events ('one damn thing after another', as Henry Ford put it)[4] which led from the present back through heroic times to the Olympian and Titan gods – who had, of course, their own dramatic history – and that he regarded all these phases as equally historical.

A closer look severely dents, if it does not quite destroy, this view of Herodotos as, in the old cliché, 'credulous'. His tacit assent to conventional beliefs in passages like these does not imply any strong, positive commitment of his own, any more than allusions to Robin Hood, King Lear, or Cymbeline would in an English-speaking author – or to Parsifal or Siegfried in Wagner. Indeed, he is often careful to distance himself from legendary tradition, ring-fencing his material by ascribing it to informants. It is the Athenians who claim that Kleomenes' suicide was brought on by the goddess Demeter, even if the other two versions (attributed to 'most Greeks' and 'the Argives' respectively) also imply divine vengeance (6.75). At 4.179, the Jason and Triton story is a *logos* he has heard, and it is told throughout in reported speech. The claim of divine assistance from Boreas, the North Wind, is 'an Athenian story' (7.189); and even though the final tale of the posthumous revenge of the Trojan War hero Protesilaos at the conclusion of the Persian Wars suits his compositional purpose to perfection, neatly closing the narrative ring started at 1.1, it is nonetheless kept at arm's length as 'a local Chersonesian story' (9.119). At 8.65, we are even given the source of the tale of the supernatural dust-cloud which portended defeat for the Persian invaders: 'It used to be told by Dikaios, an Athenian exile who had gained some status at the Persian court'.[5]

Moreover, he is prepared to confront the historicity of gods and heroes, giving alternative Egyptian and Greek versions and offering the reader a choice (2.145–6). And in the intellectual climate of the fifth century such an admission of relativity was a dangerous move, the start of a slippery slope. Xenophanes had long ago observed that Ethiopian gods were black and snub-nosed, while those worshipped in Thrace were blue-eyed redheads (F 16 DK, F 168 KRS). So where might that leave the cosmic pretensions of the Olympians? Were they, too, no more than a cultural construct local to Greece?

A final example shows how it is harder than used to be thought to separate the first two great historians' attitudes to myth: whereas Herodotos is inclined to *exclude* Minos from serious consideration as candidate for First Sea Lord (3.122), Thucydides' intelligent survey of pre-history at 1.3 goes into some detail about his supposed naval expertise. And it is Thucydides, after all, who believes that there were more earthquakes, eclipses, and droughts than usual during the Peloponnesian War (1.23). Indeed, more than a century ago Cornford wrote (provocatively), 'If either of the two men is to be called religious, it is Thucydides; if either is sceptical, it is Herodotos. Naivety and artlessness are not terms we should choose to apply to either; something closely akin to cynicism and flippancy is common enough in Herodotos; there is not a trace of either in Thucydides' (1907: 237).

To conclude this section on terminology, a glance at Plato, writing a little later than our two historians. Though his use is not consistent, he does often distinguish between 'true' and 'false' (or 'fictional') modes of discourse, as when introducing his eschatological myth at *Gorgias* 523a: 'you will probably call it a *mythos*, but I say it's a *logos*, on the grounds that I think it's true'.[6] So too at *Politikos* 304d, rhetoric is said to be the skill needed to persuade massed gatherings, using not *didachē* (rational instruction) but *mythologia* (storytelling). Perhaps Plato has fable in mind here – see the famous anecdote about Demosthenes' use of the proverb 'the shadow of an ass' to gain his audience's attention, variously told by the paroemiographer (collector of proverbs) Zenobios (6.28) and by pseudo-Plutarch, *Lives of the Ten Orators* (*Moral Essays* 848a–b).[7]

This mention of public oratory should serve as a reminder that whatever may go on in literary and historical texts – which at this stage are still the preserve of a literate elite – issues of myth and history are firmly rooted in the experience of the Athenian populace at large, who served as jurors in the courts. Speakers or speech-writers like Antiphon or Andokides can refer casually to their opponents as 'a Klytaimestra' or 'an Oedipus' because these characters from myth were well known from the tragic stage – another public arena which those same jurors regularly attended.[8]

Myth as Foundation and Background to the Perception of History

As we have just seen, every Greek (and later many Romans, for they adopted and adapted much of the Greek system) could be relied upon to catch allusions to the world of myth. After all, it was omnipresent, encoded in the ornament of religious buildings and in the cults they housed, based as those were on foundational narratives like the Homeric Hymns. Topography itself reminded people that this was where Aphrodite stepped ashore after her birth in the sea, this was the rock from which the daughters of Kekrops leapt to their deaths.

Above all it was genealogy, which plays such a central role in creating and maintaining a sense of identity in preliterate societies, that connected the Greek present with its past.[9] Miltiades, for example, traced his clan, the Philaidai, all the way back to Aiakos and Aigina, then down through Ajax and his Athenian son Philaios (Herodotos 6.35). Even foreigners were brought into this complex family tree: Persians must be descended from the Greek hero Perseus (Herodotos 7.61, with much detail about Zeus, Danae, Andromeda, Kepheus, etc.), and other significant nations like the Romans had also to be assimilated into the scheme.[10] As for the Greeks themselves, Hesiod laid down the generally accepted structure. In the *Catalogue of Women*, Hellen, the eponymous

Ur-Greek (*Hellēn* being the Greek for 'Greek'), himself a son of Zeus or Deukalion or both, has three sons, Doros and Aiolos, progenitors respectively of the Dorian and the Aiolian ethnic branches of the Hellenes, and Xouthos.[11] Who is this Xouthos? Father of Ion and Achaios, ancestors of the Ionians and Achaians; he is a device for expressing the perception that the last two were more closely related than the other pair. So rather than four brothers we find two uncles with two sibling nephews.

This last example helps make the point that the system was a vehicle for historical analysis; it was dynamic, not static, and thus subject to constant dispute and inventive refashioning according to vested interests.[12] Spartan kings go back to Perseus, according to Herodotos 6.53 – or are they perhaps Egyptians (ch. 54–5), or descendants of Herakles via Hyllos (ch. 52)? The Macedonians, always so eager to claim Hellenic respectability, trace their ancestry back to Argos (see the folktale at Herodotos 8.136), and King Perdikkas used this as a reason for changing his alliances in 418 BC (Thucydides 5.80). The same is true of those who claimed ancient kinship with Sparta,[13] or Ionian descent (Thucydides 3.86, where the people of Leontinoi appeal to the Athenians for help). The inhabitants of Skione not only claim ancestral links to Pellene in the Peloponnese but also explain the location of their polis (in Chalkidike in Northern Greece) by the fact that they were blown off course when returning home after the sack of Troy. This account neatly kills two birds with one stone, establishing both the antiquity of their line and their part in the greatest exploit of the heroic age. They now use this as a reason to revolt from the Athenians and throw in their lot with the Spartan Brasidas (Thucydides 4.120).

Let us pursue this theme of genealogy into various texts where we can trace its use in political argument. The Athenian public enjoyed being reminded by orators and others of their descent from the Marathonomachai, the men who fought at Marathon (see, for example, Aristophanes, *Clouds* 986), and in the *skolia* (drinking songs) of the elite symposium Harmodios and Aristogeiton were 'mythologized' as the Tyrannicides (F 893–6 *PMG*). These are recollections of deeds performed a few generations ago. But such calls to 'remember our ancestors' could be pushed much further back. At Herodotos 7.159, the Spartan Syagros is on a mission to persuade Gelon of Syracuse (another Dorian city) to join the Greek defence against the Persian invaders. Finding his host recalcitrant, he exclaims in hexametric mode 'Yea, how Agamemnon would groan aloud – if he heard you demanding to be made C-in-C as the price of contributing forces!' Here he is clearly donning, or being made to don, the mantle of Nestor, who is the *Iliad*'s regular *laudator temporis acti*.[14] It is also a useful reminder of the malleability of myth that he can implicitly claim Agamemnon as a Spartan, not (as Homer had it) an Argive.[15] A little earlier, at 7.150, the Persians appeal to the Argives on grounds of distant consanguinity and, says the historian, 'the Argives were much impressed by their argument' that they were both descended from Perseus. It was, of course, a convenient justification for the Argives doing what they wanted to do anyway. Similarly, when an oracle told the Thebans to 'seek help from their nearest' (*hoi anchista*), it suited them to understand this Delphic recommendation as meaning not their next-door neighbours, but the Aiginetans – for were the nymphs Thebe and Aigina not sisters, daughters of the river Asopos?[16]

Nor were appeals to the glorious national past limited to rhetorical blather; sometimes they were realized in dramatically effective action, enabling the population at large to take part in physically 'reclaiming their history'. Just as they appropriated Agamemnon,[17] so, in a propaganda coup worthy of Goebbels himself, the Spartans discovered, sometime in the sixth century BC, the bones of his son Orestes buried in the earth of their hated rivals the Arkadians – and repatriated them (Herodotos 1.65). Not to be outdone, in the 470s the Athenian leader Kimon found ('Hey, what's this …?') the skeletal remains of the national hero Theseus buried on the Aegean island of Skyros, and did the same (Plutarch, *Life of Kimon* 8.5–7). But even more important than the bones of your own heroes were those of your enemies: to possess the remains of Oedipus in an undisclosed location on Athenian soil guarantees the security of the Athenian state from Theban attack forever, as Sophocles' last play, *Oedipus at Kolonos*, so powerfully and movingly asserts. This in a play composed during the last phase of the Peloponnesian War, when Athenian defeat seemed likely, if not inevitable.

Myth as Stand-in for History

Since the two nouns with which we are concerned turn out to be so intimately linked, it is hardly surprising to find that when a historian ('or his source', as it is conventional to say) is running short of documentary data, or data of any kind, he ('or his source') is liable to turn to pre-cast patterns of traditional behaviour and action. Myth, including all its subspecies, like folktale and narrative routines which develop in the traditions of epic, provides tempting templates for the moulding of history. Hence the phenomenon of easily transferable 'roving' anecdotes, which may be applied to heroes or villains as appropriate. Herodotos tells two stories about oriental queens called Nitokris at 1.185 and at 2.100; in the latter passage he observes that N^2, the Egyptian, has the same name as N^1, the Babylonian, but he omits to say that both are chiefly remembered for their expertise in hydraulic engineering: their diversion of the Euphrates and the Nile respectively. Clearly this is a wandering tale, of which he has heard two variants in different contexts. The same principle is at work in the variations he presents of the 'holocaust' theme, in which wicked foreigners burn their enemies alive.[18]

But why, in the fifth-century 'age of enlightenment', when free-thinkers like Protagoras and Prodikos were busy deconstructing so much traditional belief, and fabulous creatures like dog-headed men and skiapods were being pushed further and further to the margins of the known world and towards eventual oblivion, should the nascent discipline of historiography be so accommodating to mythical material? Part of the answer, paradoxically, is that it was precisely these new intellectual currents that provided a way of rescuing mythology for serious use and study by means of two new hermeneutic tools. The first of these is rationalism, an approach associated with Herodotos' immediate predecessor Hekataios of Miletos (see CH. 3) and later with a Hellenistic writer called Euhemeros (from whom the English for this phenomenon, 'Euhemerism', takes its name). According to this method of interpretation (and anticipating to some extent the nineteenth-century scholar Max Müller, who called myth 'a disease of language'), myths are the result of a mistaken understanding of what actually once happened in the real world.[19] Thus Aktaion was a profligate hunter who was ruined by the expense of his hounds, and accordingly was said to have been 'eaten' by them. The Hydra was just a big snake. The Trojan Horse was a siege engine that broke a hole in the walls. To take an example from a Roman historian: when Tacitus comes to mention the journey to the Black Sea's eastern shore of the supernatural ram which carried Phrixos, and for part of the way Helle, on its back, he comments 'whether it was actually an animal or rather a ship's figurehead' – thus showing his rationalistic preference.[20] Even gods were perhaps originally ordinary human beings whose exploits were magnified in the telling.[21] In Plato's *Phaedrus*, we hear of the theory that the Athenian princess Oreithyia, far from having been snatched away to the Arctic by Boreas, the god of the North Wind, was just a girl who was blown off a rock on a windy day.[22]

The second of these new 'keys to all mythologies', as George Eliot's Casaubon had it, was the principle of allegory, by which myths were held to encode arcane philosophical truths; each one had embedded in it, if only it could be uncovered, a *hyponoia* or subtext. The prime surviving example of this theory is without doubt the late fifth- or fourth-century BC commentary on an Orphic cosmogonical poem known as the Derveni papyrus (see CH. 4), in which an extraordinary series of mental gymnastics are performed in an attempt to show that the archaic poem is really a kind of scientific treatise wrapped up by Orpheus in layers of poetic obfuscation to conceal its true meaning from the unworthy ignorant.[23]

So now myth had become respectable, and it was worth the historian's while to take this material seriously and make something of it. The very first pages of Herodotos' *Histories* (better, *Researches, Enquiries,* or *Investigations*) show how liberating an effect this had. Io the Argive princess was not turned into a cow by Zeus and whisked off to Egypt, as Greek tradition had it – no, she was abducted by an itinerant Phoenician haberdasher (so, supposedly, the Persian version) or ran off with him when she found herself pregnant (as the Phoenicians themselves are said, improbably, to have told it). And so on.

Herodotos is now free to enrich his narrative by taking up, for example, the myth of Attis the young god who was killed on a boar-hunt, transposing it down into a different key, and reclaiming it for history (1.34–45, Atys the son of King Kroisos of Lydia). Staying in Asia Minor, the interview between Solon and Kroisos in Lydia (1.30–3) creatively recycles the one between Seilenos and Midas in neighbouring Phrygia.[24]

And working from the widespread Greek belief that names and nouns are etymologically significant, not merely conventional, Herodotos feels justified in filling out (let us not say 'padding out') his account of Egyptian Thebes by deporting and rehousing abroad characters and material which the Greeks ascribed to *Boiotian* Thebes.[25] Let us, however, move on to consider a large set of cases where (as announced at the beginning of this section) the historicity of incidents becomes problematic once we recognize that they follow a pre-existing narrative pattern. One example is that of Themistokles who, on the run from Greece, finds himself at the palace of Admetos, king of the Molossians (Thucydides 1.136). He asks for sanctuary from the queen, who tells him to take the royal baby and sit in the ashes as a suppliant till her husband comes home. This is strikingly reminiscent both of the story of Telephos (who *seizes* the infant baby Orestes as a hostage) and of incidents in the *Odyssey* where the hero is instructed by females to plead with other powerful women (7.48–77: the disguised Athene advises him to bypass the king and go straight to his wife, Arete; 12.124: Circe tells him not to expect mercy from Skylla, but to pray instead to her mother, Krataiis). We are therefore entitled to be sceptical about Thucydides' account.[25]

The situation is delicate, though, because sometimes life does replicate art. Here is another example from Thucydides: at 6.46, he tells us how the leaders of the Sicilian city of Egesta conned the Athenian ambassadors into believing that they possessed untold riches by entertaining them to dinner in their houses on successive nights. In each house, at every party, everyone drank from gold and silver goblets. But of course it was the same cups going round and round, set out anew in a different house each evening. We recognize the same folktale pattern here as in the stories of 'Potemkin villages', sham settlements supposedly erected on the orders of a Russian courtier by the name of Potemkin to impress Catherine the Great of Russia as she made a progress through the Crimea. A similar story was told of Mussolini. Apparently he was fooled into believing that money he had disbursed for the construction of fighter squadrons really had been so spent (and not drunk and whored away): when he demanded a series of inspections, the few planes that had actually been built were simply flown from one airfield to the next and parked on the tarmac, pertly gleaming, to await his arrival.[26]

So provisional scepticism is again appropriate. But consider this, from Norman Lewis' account of Naples in the chaotic aftermath of the Allies' arrival in 1944 (Lewis 1978: 117 f.): 'I went to see the Contessa. ... I was shown by a smart little maid into a room furnished with tapestry and antiques, which came as a pleasant change after the majority of Italian country houses, which – even in the case of the upper classes – are usually bare and austere.' Later, he pays a second visit, this time unannounced:

> After hammering on the door for some minutes I was admitted by a half-starved-looking crone into the vast room, now hardly recognisable as it was completely empty. A long wait while the Contessa was found. ... She burst into tears and the truth came out. One neighbour had lent the empty house. Three more had provided the furniture for the single room. Others had chipped in with articles of clothing. Although a member of an ancient aristocratic family, she possessed no more than any other impoverished village girl in her own right.

Things are not simple. Real-world events may repeat both mythology and history.

I end this section with a nice test case, that of Agariste's wedding (Herodotos 6.126–30). Kleisthenes, the tyrant of Sikyon, wants to select the most eligible and advantageous bridegroom for his daughter, and he assembles suitors from all over the Greek world to assess their talents (in both senses). As told by Herodotos, this looks like such a blatant rerun of the legendary contest for the hand of Helen that one may suspect it is a mere literary artefact, cloned by the pseudo-historical oral tradition. But what if Kleisthenes himself had *deliberately* mimicked this prestigious exemplar, as today one might attempt to reconstitute some bogus inauguration ceremony for a Prince of Wales? Can we decide between truth and fiction?

I think in this case we can certainly detect traces of fiction, and point the finger at those who confected it. For whereas all other Greek cities send a single suitor for Agariste's hand, Athens sends two; and the whole focus of the story is on which one of the Athenians, representatives of the Philaid and Alkmaionid families respectively, wins in the end. So whatever ceremonies Kleisthenes may in fact have orchestrated in Sikyon, it is fundamentally an Athenian story.[27]

Conclusion: Myth as Conscious and Unconscious Shaper of Narrative

Thucydides never understood the origin of the [Peloponnesian] war, because his mind was filled with preconceptions which shaped the events he witnessed into a certain form; and this form chanced to be such that it snapped the causal links between incidents, in the connexion of which the secret lies. (Cornford 1907: viii)

At some time in the past it will already have dawned on most readers of this piece that not everything which appears in history books (or in newspapers, which are history books in the making) is true. Some of these untruths are 'innocent', products of the fog of war, or rumour taken as fact. Some are, of course, lies. It is the intermediate terrain which is most interesting: the area where neither writer nor reader are quite in control of their fears, desires, and prejudices, but reach for a story because it seems *right*. Obituaries regularly cite 'possibly apocryphal' anecdotes which are nevertheless felt to encapsulate the essential character of the person memorialized.[28] There is a natural tendency to plump for the best, or sharpest, version of a story. Did Reichsmarschall Hermann Göring say 'When I hear the word culture, I reach for my revolver', or, more wittily, 'When I hear the word culture, I reach for my Browning'? Probably neither, or at least not originally; the second version appears in the first scene of a 1933 play.

So while it is pretty easy to detect the sound of axes being ground, as in the 'Euromyths' so beloved of the British press,[29] it is, and always was, harder to resist the insidious temptation to accept lazy shortcut formulations like 'The Middle Ages' or 'The Twenties'. History is, famously, written backwards, and – once we have seen how things turned out – assimilated to a familiar, comfy pattern. To be apprehensible and comprehensible it must undergo the processes of selection, summarization, and shaping. A 'narrative' must be created.[30] Once the idea takes hold that Egypt is the symmetrical counterpart in the south of the European north, with the Nile mirroring the Danube, even in the detail of its supposed westward turn across the Sahara, everything else follows: the Egyptians must necessarily do everything the opposite way to the Europeans (Herodotos 2.35). And the kind of pre-programmed response that led Athenians to cry 'This man is aiming at tyranny!' (see Aristophanes, *Wasps* 488–99) is allied to the knee-jerk reaction which led to the Watergate scandal spawning a ridiculous proliferation of debased clones on either side of the Atlantic (Squidgygate, Troopergate, Catergate, Irangate, etc.) in the popular press.

A final sentimental–rhetorical comment of the kind that historians make, and which is subject to all the caveats issued above: in calling Herodotos 'the father of history', making him responsible for bootstrapping a whole new genre into existence, Cicero might seem to have been loading an impossible burden on to the shoulders of the writer from Halikarnassos. But he really was a giant, and those shoulders were strong enough for all successive 'historians' to stand on.

FURTHER READING

Because the theme of this paper is such a moving target, with both nouns in its title subject to endless redefinition and dispute, it is even harder than usual to suggest where to go next (except perhaps back to the beginning). What I have tried to offer is no more than a personal perspective on a limitless field, an idiosyncratic snapshot of a fogbound landscape. Something like a sense of a centre of gravity might be obtainable by reading all five contributions in Section V, 'Myth and/or/into History and Ethnography', in Buxton 1999 (167–248). But those editorial slashes in the section title themselves provide an eloquent demonstration of the slipperiness of the entities concerned and of the relationship between them.

NOTES

1. Or an artist from his own self-cultivated image? 'By the 1950s "he got so good at playing the part of Chagall (the Chagall people expected him to be)", recounted his former mistress, "that it was impossible to say whether he was acting or not"' (*TLS* 9 January 2009, 11).
2. I shall intersperse references to ancient texts with modern examples, to make the point that the same issues arise in modern communicative discourse. Most of my sermon-texts will be drawn from Herodotos, because he stands on the cusp of the transition from poetry to prose as a historical medium, but I have tried to show that the fundamental problems apply to later writers too.
3. Most recently by Ryszard Kapuściński (2007) and in Anthony Minghella's 1996 film version of Michael Ondaatje's novel *The English Patient*.
4. Various people are credited with saying that 'history is just one damn(ed) thing after another', including Ford, Harry Truman, and, less probably, the historian Arnold Toynbee. All these attributions may be found on the Web. Elbert Hubbard wrote that 'life is just one damn thing after another' in *The Philistine* 30 (December 1909, 3), another remark that has since been variously attributed.
5. More samples of Herodotos' subtle distancing of his own position from dubious material are 6.61, Helen still active at Sparta (but 'the old woman' is not identified); 6.69 on Astrabakos (but that is the mother's version – see the penetrating article by Burkert (1965)); 4.36, refusal to tell the story of Abaris; 1.86, Herodotos says Kroisos called out to Solon, but the Lydians say that he appealed to Apollo, and rain fell from a cloudless sky; 1.24, Arion does *not*, in his version, appeal to Apollo – the dolphin-lifeboat just happens to be passing.
6. Compare *Republic* 522a, and see Buxton (1994: 12–13). It is Plato, of course, who propounds the concept of the noble lie (*gennaion pseudos*), a false version of human nature and origins designed to keep the lower orders in line (*Republic* 414c–d). On this and on truth claims regarding Plato's myths, see further Murray (CH. 9).
7. Cf. Erasmus *Adages* 1.3.52.
8. Klytaimestra: Antiphon, *Against the Stepmother* 17; Oedipus: Andokides, *On the Mysteries* 129.
9. See Dowden (1992: 74–92).
10. See the classic 1952 article by Elias Bickermann. Herodotos has some fun with his rival Hekataios (of whom we shall hear more below) at 2.143, describing how the latter boasted to the Egyptian priests that he was descended from a god

via only sixteen generations. At this the Egyptians punctured his Greek *amour propre* by demonstrating the great antiquity of their own civilization; they could trace it back through no fewer than 341 generations – and still no god.

11. F9, F10 MW/ Most.

12. Contrast the Hebrew *Torah*, in which who begat whom is something which is unchangeably encoded for all time (even if organizational discrepancies do occasionally arise).

13. See Malkin (1994).

14. See, for example, Nestor's speech beginning at *Iliad* 1.254.

15. Willcock (1964) is an original and beautifully clear exposition of argument-from-myth in the *Iliad*, highlighting the amount of barefaced invention that was allowable – at least from Homer.

16. Herodotos 5.80. Compare the case of Ion and Achaios, above.

17. Syagros' words were reinforced by the Spartan king Agesilaos, who, when setting out to conquer Asia, took care to sacrifice at Aulis, as Agamemnon had done (Xenophon *Hellenika* 3.4.3); see Buxton (1994: 193–8) on such 'Paradigms'.

18. See A. Griffiths (1989: 57–8, with n. 9, and 2006: 138). It is interesting to see that this process is reversible. Thus, Plato's account of Atlantis at *Timaios* 20d–25d and *Kritias* 108e–121c is in fact a brilliant Herodotean pastiche in which history (the attack on Greece by a great eastern power, the Persians) is reverse-engineered into myth: see Vidal-Naquet (1981b).

19. On this rationalizing method see Stern (1996: 1–25) (the introduction to his edition of Palaiphatos' work *On Unbelievable Tales*).

20. *Annals* 6.34. See Kraus and Woodman (1997: 34–5) on this kind of 'loaded alternative'.

21. This was Euhemeros' particular contribution to the line of argument. In fact, though, the fifth-century BC 'sophist' Prodikos had already understood 'Demeter', 'Dionysos', etc. to be no more than abstractions of bread and wine (85 B 5 DK, Waterfield (2000): Prodikos T11).

22. 229c–d (but Socrates is busy mocking the fashion for such reductionist explanations). Two more Platonic examples: according to Aristophanes in *Symposium* 190b, the assault of Otos and Ephialtes on Olympos is no more than a distorted memory of the assault of his (jokingly invented) double-people; in *Timaios* 22c, the Phaithon myth dimly remembers the last *ekpyrosis* (conflagration).

23. See Betegh (2004), with the articles by R. Janko listed in his bibliography. On allegorical interpretation of myth see also CHS 6, 15, and 17 in this volume.

24. Note the shared consonants SLN. This is a trick often used to generate new variants; cf. Kleopatra from Patroklos (KL/PTR = PTR/KL, Palinurus from Elpenor (PLNR = LPNR).

25. A similar case is to be found in the work of Thucydides' Roman disciple Sallust, at *The War with Jugurtha* 79. This story of a boundary dispute recalls not only a reported response of the Delphic oracle (H15 (p. 249) in Fontenrose (1978)), but also, more disquietingly, the myth of Zeus' eagles flying from the ends of the earth to meet at Delphi and thus establish it as the world's 'navel', and the fable

which appears as No. 699 in B. E. Perry's excellent Loeb edition of Babrius and Phaedrus (593 f.).

26. A story which remains politically current in the United Kingdom, being used, for instance, by Jon Gaunt in the British *Sun* newspaper ('Whistlestop Brown on Wrong Track', 9 January 2009) when writing about a selective tour of the country by the then prime minister, Gordon Brown, which, in Gaunt's view, showed him to be even further out of touch with reality than the Italian dictator.

27. See A. Griffiths (2001: 167–8).

28. Any decent left-leaning liberal will naturally be inclined to swallow allegations to the discredit of press barons such as William Randolph Hearst. And in fact Hearst and his rival Joseph Pulitzer have been credited with, or blamed for, a major role in drawing the United States into the Spanish–American War of 1898. One famous story has it that Hearst's correspondent, the artist Frederic S. Remington, sent a telegram from Cuba in 1897 saying 'Everything is quiet. There is no trouble here. There will be no war. I wish to return', to which Hearst replied 'Please remain. You furnish the pictures, and I'll furnish the war.' The earliest source for this story (a version of which appears in the Hearst-inspired Orson Welles film *Citizen Kane*) is the 1901 memoirs of reporter James Creelman, and it is probably quite untrue: see, for example, W. J. Campbell (2000).

29. Examples are numerous. 'British yoghurt will be renamed "fermented milk pudding" if Brussels has its way. Under plans being discussed by EU officials, only yoghurts made using the sour-tasting bacteria according to traditional Bulgarian recipes will be called "yoghurt"' (*Sunday Mirror* 5 March 2006); 'Warning signs are to be put on mountains to let climbers know they are high up. A bizarre new law from Eurocrats is intended to prevent people falling on building sites. But the result is that mountaineers may also have to be warned they are at risk of tumbling off' (*Daily Star* 24 March 2004).

30. See Kraus and Woodman (1997: 45 n. 74) speak of the 'neat dramatic arc' of Sallust's *Conspiracy of Catiline*. And here is Cornford (1907: 197–8): 'Now, we do not deny that these incidents [the deception of Xerxes by the Thessalian Aleuadai and the Athenian Peisistratidai clans] may be historical, not "fabulous"; but it is well to realize that Herodotos' motive for putting them in is that they illustrate one regular link in a chain of mythical ideas. The sequence is so well established that, if the historical facts had been missing, fabulous imagination would have supplied their place'.

NEW TRADITIONS

CHAPTER ELEVEN

Myth and Hellenic Identities

Fritz Graf

The *Local* Character of Myth

Greek mythology is firmly anchored in geography. Its narratives are set in a *specific* region and place inside Greece, specific enough to have suggested to some scholars an origin in the political geography of the Mycenaean Age. This specificity is true for both heroic and divine myths: the major Homeric *Hymns* do not just tell stories about Aphrodite, Apollo, Hermes, or Demeter, they set their narratives in a well-defined locale – Delos and Delphi, Eleusis, the Troad, or the north-west Peloponnese.

What underlies this is that Greek religion was first and foremost *local* religion, articulated in the local performance of a specific cult; and in the same way, mythical narration was tied to local performance, at least in the Archaic Age.[1] During the same era, however, especially successful narratives spread beyond their local setting, and in this a major factor was the success of the Homeric poems that through their very plot had left local ties behind. The Greek fleet that set out from Aulis combined contingents from all over mainland Greece, and the major leaders brought their local stories into this wider context; this is especially visible in the many stories of Nestor that centre on his home, Pylos. This did not cut Greek myths loose from their specific localizations, but made some of them known outside their narrow place of origin. Pindar and Bakchylides did not confine their myths to the home town of the victor or to the myths of a specific contest, of Olympia, Delphi, Nemea, or Isthmia. Although Athenian tragedy is, to a large extent, a reflection

A Companion to Greek Mythology, First Edition. Edited by Ken Dowden and Niall Livingstone.
© 2014 John Wiley & Sons Ltd. Published 2014 by John Wiley & Sons Ltd.

about Athens, most of its heroes are non-Athenian; there are only a few exceptions – a Hippolytos or an Ion.

Still, despite this almost Panhellenic expansion, Greek myths always retained their local roots: down to Pausanias in the second century AD and beyond, Greek myth was mostly concerned with local identity. Local historians and mythographers wrote the story of the foundational past of their own city or region; and at least in the evolutionary understanding of ancient literary historians, their activity preceded the general histories of a Herodotos and a Thucydides; this is not the place to argue whether they were right.[2] This did not change in later ages that were more literary and more cosmopolitan. But it also means that local identities are not all that there was. Local identity was in itself complex, since it formed part of identities determined by clan, profession, or religious group, or was in competition with them. But, in turn, it was an element in larger claims, those of a particular region or of Greece overall; and sometimes the local claims stood in tension with those translocal ones.

Modern research on myth, however, has mostly neglected this approach, concerned as it has been since the days of Heyne (1729–1812, see pp. 532–3) with constructing an essence that should be valid for everybody. This essentialist claim is itself a specific form of the early modern claim that the classical world had set out values that were valid for everybody everywhere. The later reception of ancient myth in European culture reinforced this tendency – or rather it naïvely accepted Ovid's own construction of a translocal Greek mythology as a carrier not only of playfulness and entertainment but also of his specific ideological and poetical, anti-Vergilian, agenda.[3] The one scholar who tried to remedy this situation was Karl Otfried Müller who, in the early nineteenth century, used local mythology for his reconstruction of the prehistory of the Greek tribes. This was a remarkable extension of the general Romantic assumption that myths contained the oldest memory of humanity: if so, they had an origin in a specific group and should retain all local changes that this group had undertaken or suffered. This view implicitly demolishes the belief that myths had a general applicability. But in the same way as his reconstruction remained, in the long run, without resonances, so did his methodology, and we are still left with myth as valid for everybody. The overworked panhellenization that shaped research on early Greek poetry in some quarters is just the most recent offshoot of the assumption that myth must be valid for more than a small group of locals.

In order better to understand the various forces at work in local mythologies, I will first turn to a late construction of a specific regional mythology, that of Elis. Then I will take a rather brief glance at the emergence of Panhellenic mythology.

The Mythology of Elis According to Pausanias

Every time, in his *Tour* (Periegesis) *of Greece*, that Pausanias begins the description of a new landscape he summarizes its history from its very beginnings: it is the past of a place or region that defines its identity. In Book 5, the first of his two books on Elis, after giving a brief analysis of the different ethnic groups that inhabit the Peloponnese, he begins this summary as follows:

> We know that the Eleans immigrated from Kalydon and from the rest of Aitolia; as to their yet more remote past (τὰ δὲ ἔτι παλαιότερα), I have found the following. They say that Aëthlios was the first king in this land; he was a son of Zeus and of Protogeneia, the daughter of Deukalion; Aëthlios' son was Endymion. It was this Endymion with whom, as they narrate, Selene fell in love; and he had fifty daughters from her. But those who hold a more plausible view narrate that Endymion took Asterodia as his wife (others that it was Chromia, daughter of Itonos the son of Amphiktyon, or Hyperippe daugher of Arkas), and that his sons were Paion, Epeios, and Aitolos, and after them he had a daughter, Eurykyde. Endymion organized a foot-race for his sons in Olympia to determine the next ruler: Epeios won and became king, and those whom he ruled were first called Epeians. Of his brothers, some narrate that one of them remained in Elis, but that Paion, angry at the defeat, fled as far as possible, and the country beyond the river Axios was named Paionia after him.[4] As to Endymion's death, the Herakleotans near Miletos and the Eleans do not agree with each other: the Eleans show the grave of Endymion, whereas the Herakleotans narrate that he departed for the Latmos range, and they worship him, and there is a secret sanctuary (*adyton*) of Endymion on the Latmos. (Pausanias 5.1.3–5)

Somewhat later Pausanias adds that Aitolos, the brother of Epeios who remained in the country and succeeded his brother, had to flee because he accidentally killed his opponent in an athletic contest: this explained why he became the eponymous ruler of the Aitolians (5.1.8).

At the outset of this chapter, Pausanias makes a distinction between what is generally known – the immigration of the Eleans from the north, from Aitolia – and the events that preceded this immigration, which he presents as the result of his research: 'we know' as against 'I have found'.[5] In the rest of the book, however, he seems to have lost sight of this distinction: Aitolos, the ancestor of the Aitolians, was an immigrant from Elis.

In the rest of this chapter and the three that follow, Pausanias reviews the subsequent rulers of Elis down to the Trojan War, in a more or less detailed fashion, although few stories are as detailed as Endymion's in the passage translated above, with its divergent variants. Epeios has no male issue, and has some political trouble: during his reign Oinomaos, the son of Alxion or 'according to the poets, of Ares', rules over the neighbouring land of Pisa but is killed by Pelops, a Lydian from Asia who takes over Oinomaos' territory to which he then adds Olympia, taking it away from Epeios; he also builds the first temple of Hermes in Elis (5.1.6–7). But Pelops passes through Elis without founding a royal dynasty: the next king is Epeios' nephew Eleios, son of Eurykyde and Poseidon ('if this is reliable'); his reign is the reason why the Epeians change their name to Eleans. He is succeeded by his son Augeias (who, according to others, is a son of Helios), who receives the longest treatment (5.1.9–5.3.3). Augeias hires Herakles to clean out his stables, with rather complex consequences that are responsible for the fact that athletes from Elis were excluded from the Isthmian games in Corinth (5.2.2–5) and for Herakles' final conquest and destruction of Elis. Herakles hands Elis to Augeias' son Phyleus, who had resisted his father when he tried to cheat Herakles and for this he was exiled to the small island of Doulichion, off the coast of Elis; Herakles now recalls him.[6] And Phyleus restores the power of Elis, sets three rulers over it, and then returns to his island.

With this episode, the story has arrived at the time of Trojan War, one generation after Herakles, and more precisely reached the 'Catalogue of Ships' (in *Iliad* 2): the 'Catalogue' lists four leaders of the Elean contingent, only one of whom, Polyxenos, would return from the war, becoming the next king.[7] His son is a second Eleios, a construction to adjust the chronology: an independent story must have situated the Heraklid takeover under the eponymous king Eleios, the father of Augeias. Under this Eleios, then, the descendants of Herakles return to the Peloponnese and made one Oxylos king of Elis to reward him for his advice on how to conquer the Peloponnese. Oxylos had Elean roots: he was a descendant of Aitolos, the son of Endymion who had left Elis in anger when he lost the foot-race to Epeios. Pausanias dedicates a lengthy narration to the exploits of Oxylos (5.4.1–4) but has to confess that cannot not name any more recent king of Elis than Oxylos' son Laias; so he jumps to Iphitos who lived at the time of the Spartan Lykourgos and renewed the Olympian games to avert a plague and a series of internecine wars that damaged Greece at the time (5.4.5–6). After this, the account gains even more speed: Pausanias quickly looks at the role Elis played during the Persian invasion of 480, the Peloponnesian War, and the expansionist moves of Philip II of Macedon and his successors (5.4.7–9) before dwelling somewhat longer on the local tyranny of Aristotimos at the time of Antigonos Gonatas (5.5.1).

To Pausanias, all these names and events are history; together they constitute the past that has shaped what Elis still is in his time. To make it plausible as history, he rejects, for instance, Endymion's fifty daughters in favour of a more 'reasonable' version with a mere three sons and one daughter (5.1.4). And he distances himself from any divine intervention, such as Selene's love for Endymion (5.1.4), or the divine fathers of Oinomaos (5.1.6) and Eleios

(5.1.8). As early as Hekataios of Miletos (see CH. 3), this is a standard technique for 'cleansing the fabulous with the help of reason,' in Plutarch's phrase, in order to turn it into history.[8]

Identity in this account is ethnic, 'tribal', identity in a regional sense: the myths define Eleans, Aitolians, Paionians. A group is called into existence by the appearance of an eponymous-hero-to-be to provide it with a name; in rare cases, a later eponym has such an impact that an earlier name is changed, without changing the population. Because of the first Eleios, Epeians became Eleans: the new name and its bearer surfaced after the caesura brought about by Pelops' somewhat violent intervention, in what was a sort of second foundation. To Pausanias and his local authors, it is irrelevant that we analytical scholars spot the seams of different traditions that have been stitched together into one local history: what counts is the continuous history that guarantees local identity. They point to markers of memory, still visible, to recall some of these events, and firmly anchor local identity in the landscape: Endymion's grave and, presumably, his hero cult in Elis (5.1.4), the temple of Hermes in Olympia (5.1.7), or the cult of Athene 'Mother' on the river Bady (5.3.2) that commemorates the stratagem to repopulate Elis after Herakles' invasion. Specific institutions make their own contribution, such as the foot-race founded by Endymion at Olympia or the exclusion of Elean athletes from the Isthmia (5.2.2–5); later, when Pausanias retells the history of the Olympian Games, we will learn that there had been a foot-race before that, one instituted by the Kouretes, the guardians of baby Zeus, and that Endymion was amongst several heroes to have organized an athletic contest in Olympia before its decisive renewal by Iphitos, at the time of Lykourgos.[9]

But although the local level is the setting for the narrative it is not the only framework of reference. In the interconnected world of archaic Greece, neighbours contribute to one's self-definition. The chain of actors in Elean mythology begins with Aëthlios, a son of Zeus and of Deukalion's daughter Protogeneia. This genealogy derives the Eleans from the couple who had founded the human race after the Flood, the earliest point in human history one could find; and through her name 'Protogeneia' ('First-born') preserves a claim to be the First Mother of Humans. The same genealogy of Aëthlios is found in the Hesiodic *Catalogue of Women*, although the name of his mother is lost; but barely a century later, Pherekydes of Athens knows her as a daughter of Deukalion and Pyrrha, and Martin West has rightly restored Protogeneia's name in this passage of the *Catalogue*.[10] Protogeneia's name, then, leads the Eleans all the way back to the very beginning of mankind, a claim which in most archaic mythologies outside Greece would normally indicate that the group thinks of itself as the only true humans. In Greece, however, things are more complex. On the other side of the Corinthian Gulf, the Opountian Lokrians claimed that their own founder, Opous, was like Aëthlios a son of

Protogeneia and Zeus; these two claims were reconciled by making Opous and Aëthlios into siblings, although it lead to the consequence that either local claim was much less radical than it might have been meant to be originally, and it inscribes either group in a wider regional context instead of proudly setting off a group from all its 'non-human' neighbours.[11] One of Aëthlios' grandsons is Aitolos, the ancestor of the Aitolians to the north of the Kalydonian Gulf. And Aitolos' mother is either a daughter of Arkas, the eponym of the Arkadians, the neighbours to the south-east, across the mountains, or of one Itonos, who might be the eponym of several cities named Iton or Itone, none of them nearby: one Itone is in Boiotia, another in Epeiros, but the most famous Iton is in Thessaly, home of the sanctuary of Athene Itonia.[12] Whatever the connection is, it ties in with the story that Paion, the third son of Endymion, founded Paionia in Thessaly, and with a story from the Hesiodic *Catalogue* (not present in Pausanias) that Aëthlios married a daughter of Aiolos, the ancestor of the northern Greeks.[13] Whoever reflected on the Eleans was willing to iron out contradictory stories by a compromise that connected them both with their immediate neighbours and with what in the *Catalogue* was the epicentre of action, northern and central Greece.

Not all such claims can be harmonized, especially if they do not concern direct neighbours but places far apart in space. Endymion either died in Elis where he is buried, or he disappeared on the Latmos, on the Eastern side of the Aegean. A compromise is not sought, and is, in any case, perhaps impossible: one has to decide whether the grave in Elis or the cult in Herakleia-under-Latmos carries more weight, and Pausanias seems to have made up his mind in favour of Elis.

Other connections tie local mythology into a wider perspective by other means, bringing in intruders from outside; in the case of Elis, it is Pelops and Herakles. Their own story cycles had only a transitory connection with Elis, but this helped to inscribe the self-definition of the Eleans in a much larger frame, even if it created some stresses for a synchronized chronology. Pelops is the grandfather of Agamemnon, and the Trojan War thus took place in the third generation after Pelops' interference in Pisa; meanwhile Herakles was active one generation before the Trojan War. When Pelops arrived, the Eleans were ruled by their third king, Epeios; Herakles arrived under their sixth king, Augeias, and installed Phyleus as transitory seventh king, and the leaders of the Elean contingent in Troy, Agasthenes, Amphimachos, and Thalpios, ruled together after Phyleus. In order to pack all these kings into only three generations, several of them had to belong to the same generation: two sons of Endymion ruled successively, Epeios and Aitolos (the latter for only a short time, since he had to leave the country as a murderer), as did two sons of Augeias, the transitory Phyleus, and the more permanent Agasthenes, who fell before Troy. We do not know what an Elean king list would have looked like without the necessity of Panhellenic synchronization: presumably it would have been much better spaced out. What matters, however, is that at one point in local storytelling the necessity of synchronization arose as a function of Elean self-definition in a transregional framework.

The main pressure was exercised by the Homeric poems, and especially by the 'Catalogue of Ships', an inventory of Greek states and their local mythologies at the end of the Dark Ages.[14] Once Homer's epic narrations had turned into the canonical account of early Greek history, the list of leaders and their cities became a mandatory chronological framework for any later local mythologies. This meant some tweaking of the local stories, both to fit them into the overall chronology and to accommodate what had originally been independent evidence. Elis sent a contingent with four leaders: the sons of the Aktorione, Amphimachos, and Thalpios, together led twenty ships, whereas Diores, the son of Amarynkeus, and Polyxenos, the son of Agasthenes and grandson of Augeias, led ten each.[15] This established Agasthenes as successor of his father Augeias, and Pausanias' account sets Amphimachos and Thalpios as co-rulers at his side, whereas Diores and his father are at least more than simple private citizens: Pausanias is vague here. Fortunately, Homer narrates how Amphimachos and Diores were killed in battle, which solved some awkward local problems. Polyxenos returned and replaced his father in a regular dynastic succession. This leaves only Thalpios unaccounted for – he must have conveniently died before Troy as well, despite Homer's silence. The sons of the Aktorione and Amarynkeus were less easy to accommodate, since they remain outside the dynastic sequence. They enter the story when Augeias looks for valiant allies to help defend himself against Herakles and offers Amarynkeus, Aktor, and his monstrous twin sons participation in power. There is some justification for this: Amarynkeus was the son of a Thessalian immigrant to Elis, Aktor, a grandson of Epeios on the maternal side, who was ruling one single town in Elis. Chronology is somewhat strained: the twins and Amarynkeus belong to the same generation. Two of Nestor's many stories confirm this, more or less: he tells how in his youth he fought the twin sons of Aktor (*Iliad* 11.750–2) and participated in the funeral games for Amarynkeus (*Iliad* 23.629–31). Elis' mythical history has to fit into the Panhellenic framework established by the Homeric poems.

Arguably Homer's commentators must have contributed much to this work of synchronization and homogenization, and not just in dealing with chronology. A much debated problem was how the Epeioi in the 'Catalogue' were related to Elis: the 'Catalogue' entry begins, 'those who inhabited Buprasion and godlike Elis' (2.615), and later gives the summary that 'many Epeians went' (2.619). The solution Pausanias proposes, that the Eleans were originally called Epeians, is only one possibility: Strabo assumes that the Epeioi originally were a subgroup amongst the Eleans.[16] But it goes almost without saying that part of Elean identity must have been to be part of a Greece that was represented in the *Iliad*, once Homer's narrative had become the standard early history of Greece. Pausanias' account, as far as we can tell, does not depend on the commentators of Homer, but on local historians, though they in turn may have learnt from the Homerists. Thus, the presence of the *Iliad* and its 'Catalogue of Ships' as a firm chronological and prosopographical framework is significant for the Elean construction of themselves, at least during most of their history.

Panhellenic Genealogies

Pausanias anchors his Elean dynastic genealogy in the first couple after the Flood, Deukalion and Pyrrha: the first ruler of Elis was their grandson Aëthlios, born from a union between Zeus and the primordial couple's daughter, Protogeneia. We saw how this parallels the claims of the Opountians on the northern shore of the Corinthian Gulf: their eponymous founder, Opous, was equally thought of as a son of Protogeneia. The Opountians backed their story by pointing out that Deukalion's ark had landed not that far away, on Mount Parnassos, and that after the Flood, the couple had settled in Opous.

From the Hesiodic *Catalogue* onwards, however, the firstborn son of Deukalion and Pyrrha was Hellen, either biologically or at least nominally (if he was biologically the son of Zeus) son of Deukalion.[17] Hellen and his three nephews Graikos (a son of Zeus and the second Pandora), Magnes and Makedon (the sons of Zeus and Thyia) represent three tribal groups on the northern and north-eastern mainland. In historical times. The Magnetes and Makedones were living to the north and to the south of Mount Olympus respectively; the Graikoi however, wherever one imagines their territory, disappeared from view in historical times, and their name has survived only in the Latin name for 'Greeks', *Graeci* (see below).[18] Aëthlios, another son of Zeus and of a daughter of the primordial couple, adds Aitolia and Elis, and thus enlarges the geographical scope towards the south-west, with a strange territorial gap left open between this group and the other male offspring of Deukalion. Given that all these tribal eponyms in the *Catalogue* were thought to be the offspring of Zeus, it is likely that Hellen was too.[19] Hellen's own sons, Aiolos, Doros, and the shadowy Xouthos (Hesiod F 9 MW/Most), originally belonged to a restricted area too – Doros to the landscape of Doris, between Oita and Parnassos, and Aiolos to Thessaly.[20]

At a second stage, this genealogy, hitherto so narrowly focused on northern Greece, was opened up to embrace a much larger area: Dorians and Aiolians are two of the three major ethnical and dialectal groups in Greece. With the addition of the sons of Aëthlios a similar broadening takes place in a somewhat messy area of western Greece. This must have happened before the genealogy of Xouthos was developed. His two sons, Achaios and Ion, add not just the Achaians, but also the Ionians. The Achaians are a rather restricted group in the western Peloponnese wedged in between Aitolians and Eleans, who trace themselves back to Aëthlios. The Ionians include the Athenians, though they are not specifically marked as such in the mythology.

As Achaios and Ion are brothers, this replicates the story that the Ionian migration was triggered by a movement out of Achaia.[21] When the genealogies develop all their ramifications, furthermore, they not only include Kyrene and the Greeks in Africa, but also a vast array of non-Greek peoples, from Egyptians and Arabs to Skythians and Pygmies, allocating the Greeks their own place in a much more vast, 'global' geographical outlook. As it stands, then (or rather, as it can be reconstructed), the *Catalogue* aims at a self-definition of Greece in a perspective that transcends the Panhellenic frame and in a geographical setting that connects Greeks with the non-Greeks around them.

Jonathan Hall (2002) reconstructed the hypothetical development of this genealogy in the context of the history of Archaic Greece. He attributes its construction to the Thessalians as the hegemones (leaders) of the Pylaian–Delphic Amphictyony, the mostly northern league that had its first centre in the sanctuary at Anthela near Thermopylai of Demeter Amphiktyonis (Herodotos 7.200.2), but rather early extended south to incorporate the sanctuary of Delphi. In a further expansionist step, when the Thessalians began to participate in the Olympic Games, the other tribal ancestors were added, in order to present a mythical genealogy of all the Hellenes (Greeks) who had the privilege to be admitted to the Olympic Games. Following a suggestion made by Wilamowitz, Hall understands this genealogical construction as an affair of the aristocrats of Archaic Greece who in this way conceptualized and legitimized their complex relationship and coherence with each other. This explains the somewhat puzzling fact that the Hellenes did not define themselves against their local neighbours, as almost all other myths of ethnic origin do: instead, the genealogy defines the members of the local elites against the commoners who were without splendid heroic ancestors and a 'Panhellenic' network.

This is an attractive hypothesis. But it cannot answer how Hellen came to his dominant position that, in the end, made him the eponymous ancestor of all the Hellenes. Typically, a politically fragmented and decentralized group is named by its neighbours after the first or the most important member of the group with whom they initially come into contact: the Swiss, in their own nomenclature *Eidgenossen*, 'Confederates', were named in early modern Europe after the mercenaries from the tiny city state of Schwyz, a founding member of the confederacy that became rich in late medieval and early modern times with the systematic export of mercenaries; similarly, the *Graeci* must have received their Latin name from the members of the enigmatic *Graikoi*, who were the first to make impact on central Italy, perhaps as pirates or merchants from the eastern shore of the Adriatic Sea. From early on, there are also the *Hellenes* as an individual tribe or inhabitants of a specific territory, *Hellas*: they belong to Achilles' contingent, and Homer consistently places *Hellas* next to the equally shadowy *Phthia*.[22] But already in Homer, the Hellenes have also lent their name to all the mainland Greeks: the '*Panhellenes and Akhaioi*' (in *Iliad* 2.530) must designate the entire Greek army amongst which the Lesser Ajax excels; and in the *Odyssey*, the formula 'whose glory spread wide over *Hellas* and *Argos*, its centre' must again comprise the entire territory inhabited by Greek-speakers to whom the epic story of such and such a hero spread.[23] This tension between the local and the global meaning of the name can be seen as reflecting the contrast between the traditional, mythical information Homer received about a specific landscape and the contemporary use in his time of the group name in a much wider sense. How the former became the latter remains unexplained, and the exact location and importance of the region Hellas and its inhabitants, the pre-Homeric *Hellānes*, has been lost in the murk of the Dark Ages.

It also deserves attention that the *Catalogue* genealogy, as we have observed, does not define the Greeks, the offspring of the first couple Deukalion and Pyrrha, as against non-Greek neighbours, as, for instance, Genesis (10.21) defines the offspring of Shem, the 'sons of Eber', as against those of Ham and Japheth; as far as we can tell, the genealogical analysis of all the non-Greek peoples around them, from the Medes to the Pygmies, is much more complex, inclusive rather than exclusive. This seems to mirror an attitude that predates the painful confrontation with the Persian *barbaroi*.

The construction of the *Catalogue* (see CH. 3) with its overall classification of Greeks, Hellenes, due to an unknown late sixth-century BC poet (an Athenian according to Martin West), remained fundamental when later authors reflected on these things, and must have slowly pushed out other conceptions. We perceive these somewhat different arrangements only in the fifth century BC: Hekataios of Miletos, the first universal historian, reports that Ion was the elder brother of Lokros and son of Physkos (the eponymous hero of a city in west Lokris), connecting the Ionians not with the Achaians but the western Greeks to the north of the Gulf of Corinth. Euripides in his *Ion* describes Aiolos as a son of Zeus and Xouthos as Aiolos' son, whereas Ion is the son of Apollo and Erechtheus' daughter Kreousa.[24] This is markedly different from the *Catalogue* where Aiolos is the oldest son of Hellen and a brother of Kreousa's husband Xouthos and father of Ion, Achaios, and a shadowy daughter, Diomedē; Euripides' genealogy has an unmistakable Athenian twist, explaining also the Athenian cult of Apollo *Patrōios*, 'Ancestral' Apollo. But these are rather exceptions that made no lasting impact: the 'Hesiodic' genealogy was reproduced without changes in the late Hellenistic works of Konon and Strabo, and later in the *Library* of 'Apollodoros'.[25] In the fourth century BC, Hellanikos of Lesbos varied only slightly by adding another daugther, Xenopatra, to Hellen's children.

But for all we can see, the *Catalogue* genealogy remained strictly in the realm of the learned genealogies.[26] Although *Hellenes* became the collective self-designation for all Greeks from Homer onwards, the mythical, genealogical construction is never explicitly used in a political context, as far as we can see: there is no appeal to a common descent from Hellen and his brothers as an argument for Hellenic unity, or a claim to Doric leadership because Doros was a generation older than his nephew Ion. If Jonathan Hall is correct, the genealogy was used in the Archaic Age to define the aristocratic participants in the Olympic Games; but this remains an inference, and it does not seem to have outlived the Persian Wars.

There might be different explanations for this. The genealogy might simply have been too clumsy in its complexity: the *Catalogue* does not strike me as a text easily memorized by all the relevant groups. More importantly, however, the genealogy did not correspond to the kaleidoscope of changing political associations as they shaped themselves in the following centuries: an appeal to unity amongst the descendants of Hellen alone would have left out large parts of northern and north-western Greece, and this was undesirable already in the fifth century BC, even more so later. The appeal to a common military undertaking against the Persians claimed different leadership, but never the Thessalian one that was expressed in the genealogy of Hellen; and the Hellenic unity that began to assert itself in the century-and-a-half after Nero had given freedom back to the Greeks was a cultural unity under Athenian leadership that had no need for any genealogical construction, and certainly not one that emphasized Thessaly. In his Corinthian oration, Nero did not allude to any mythical construction of Hellenic unity, but defined the recipients of his gift locally: it was 'all the Hellenes who inhabit the province Achaia and what up to now has been called the Peloponnese'.[27] In his thanksgiving address for Nero's gift in Boiotian Akraiphia, Epameinondas son of Epameinondas similarly refrained from mythology; if anything, he defined the Greeks by 'the freedom native to their land and belonging to their soil' (τὴν αὐθιγενῆ καὶ αὐτόχθονα ἐλευθερίαν).

Local Genealogies in the Greek East

This abstinence from mythological arguments on a Panhellenic scale contrasts radically with what we perceive on the level of single cities, both in Hellenistic and imperial times, down to the troubled mid-third century AD. These local mythologies, however, become rarely visible: local histories are mostly lost or absorbed in bits and pieces in later works, not the least in geographies like

Strabo's or lexica like the *Onomasticon* of Stephen of Byzantium. However, since the mid-nineteenth century archaeological research has brought an increasing number of local mythological sources to light, from the unassuming inscribed statue base to the impressive official inscription. These documents all show how many cities in Asia Minor claimed Greek descent through their the foundation by a Greek hero, or even connection with Greek divine mythology.[28] Two examples from different epochs and places might suffice.

The recent excavations of the city of Halikarnassos produced a Hellenistic poem in elegiacs, beautifully inscribed in two columns.[29] It details the glory of the city, from its mythology to its famous sons. Baby Zeus, the poem claims, was brought up in Halikarnassos, protected by the Kouretes, who founded the local sanctuary of the god; and similarly, the local nymph, Salmakis, raised Aphrodite's son Hermaphroditos. Neither myth had been attested here before, although some other Karian local mythologies likewise claim the Kouretes and baby Zeus; pride of space is visibly given to Zeus whose four elegiacs open the list; every other entry is shorter. Then follows a chain of Greek heroes who settled here: Bellerophon, 'the tamer of Pegasos,' who was brought by Athene herself 'when she defined the borders of Pedasos', a neighbouring town with an intriguing cult of Athene;[30] Kranaos, 'one of the most shadowy of the legendary kings of Athens' (Hugh Lloyd-Jones) whom other stories have driven out from his city, brought Athenian settlers; Endymion brought Peloponnesians, in only slight disagreement with Pausanias' report (see above). Then the text becomes fragmentary: we glimpse Anthes, a son of Poseidon and founder of Troizen, the mother city of Halikarnassos already in the fourth century BC, who is the ancestor of the local Antheadai, who had been priests of Poseidon Isthmios 'since the foundation of the city';[31] then an unknown son of Apollo, and someone who brought Ariadne; in neither case are we helped by our existing knowledge.

But what we read is enough to form some general conclusions. Local identity ('pride', τὸ τίμιον in the text) is created, as in Pausanias's account of Elis, by a history that relies heavily on myths. As in Elis, some of this history left traces in the present city – the temple of Zeus, the spring Salmakis, the city of Pedasos, the Antheadai and, presumably, a local body of Kouretes like the ones in Ephesos; similarly, the different ethnic origin of settlers must have left traces in the citizen body. But unlike Pausanias' account, this history starts with divine mythology and makes no attempt to rationalize away the more miraculous traits: the birth of Zeus is part of Hellenic identity. The heroic settlers in turn buttress connections with major Greek cities – Corinth (Bellerophon), Athens, Troizen, and the Peloponnese in general. There is also an unexpressed rivalry with other cities: Zeus' birth is claimed by other Karian cities; Pedasos must have claimed Bellerophon as well (or just Pegasos?), Herakleia on Latmos, as we learned from Pausanias, also laid claim the Endymion. Local stories sometimes clashed, and there is no attempt at reconciliation.

Not everyone followed the inclusion of divine myths. The city gate of Perge in Pamphylia contained a series of inscribed statue bases that date to the mid-second century AD which give us some basic information on the statues themselves. They combine Romans who were important in the city's recent history – M. Plancius Varus and his son C. Plancius Varus, both called founders of the city – with several Greek heroes who were active much earlier. Two are mythical seers: Mopsos is described as 'founder, son of Apollo, from Delphi', Kalchas as 'founder, son of Thestor, from Argos'; to them is added Machaon, 'founder, son of Asklepios, from Thessaly, from whom (derives) the sanctuary of Zeus Machanios on the acropolis'.[32] The specific local stories are unknown, but they inscribe themselves into myths that branch out from the Trojan Cycle (Kalchas, Machaon) and the myth of the seer Mopsos which is widespread in south-eastern Anatolia and might have roots that go back to before the Hellenization of the region.[33] In post-Homeric mythmaking, after the Trojan War Kalchas set out on an eastward migration; and in a story made famous by Sophocles, he met his death during a contest with Mopsos in Cilicia.

Four more statues represent Minyas, Rhixos, Labos, and Leonteus, all again qualified as 'founders', all with their genealogy and origin. Leonteus, 'son of Koronos, Lapith' again leads back to the *Iliad* where the Thessalian Leonteus is a companion of Kalchas (*Iliad* 2.745) and accompanied him on his journey. Minyas too, 'son of Ares' son Ialmenos, from Orchomenos', inscribes himself in another famous epic. Although this specific genealogy is otherwise unattested, Minyas is the mythical king of the Minyans of Orchomenos whose daughters were the ancestresses of the most famous Argonauts (Apollonios, *Argonautika* 1.229–30). Rhixos and Labos are more shadowy. The inscription calls Rhixos an Athenian, son of Lykos and grandson of Pandion, and states that 'after him Rhixopous is named' – an isolated detail that may refer to a village in the region of Perge. Labos, from Delphi, is also mentioned because his name lived on in a place-name; the inscription is damaged, and we have no more clues.

This group of statues in the city gate of Perge advertises its twin claims to Greekness and to close links with Rome. Their placement in the gate also indicates that these heroes are protectors of the city. Whereas the connection with Rome is based on recent history, the aspiration to Greekness is buttressed through mythical constructions. Some of them connect the foundation with key epics, the *Argonautika* and the Homeric poems, which together tie Perge to Athens, Argos, Orchomenos, Delphi, and Thessaly. Thessaly, the home of the Lapiths and of Achilles, appears as a landscape of pure Greekness, as it does also in Heliodoros' novel of the third or fourth century, the *Aithiopika*. The same Hellenic claim is made through Athens, Argos, and, surprisingly, Orchomenos. Delphi is vital because of the importance of divination, as are Mopsos and Kalchas: the Pamphylians, like their neighbours the Cilicians and the Pisidians, were famous for the divinatory traditions.[34] But far from claiming a native pride for these traditions and achievements, Perge connects it again with the Greek centre – Mopsos, the Homeric Kalchas, and Delphi, the very centre of Greek divination. Thus, these statues construct an unbroken story of the city, from the Trojan War to the Roman conquest, and guarantee its Hellenic origin, in a move that resonates with the cultural claims of the Second Sophistic.

Conclusions

Thus, we possess rich and only partially explored materials for the ways myth was used to construct Hellenic identity throughout Greek history, in the imperial period no less than in the Archaic Age. What is common to all these ways is the emphasis on local traditions that can be validated on the ground – in sanctuaries, place-names, and social institutions. In the background, there is, at least after the end of the Archaic Age, always the standard provided by the great epic poems, mostly Homer's, that embodies the chronological and genealogical points of reference, and the traditions that one should take care not to contradict. But then they develop in an independent local way and confront us with details that are otherwise unheard of. In clear opposition to this, the one Panhellenic construction, the genealogy expressed in the Hesiodic *Catalogue of Women*, never achieved a similarly binding character and charter status. Until its very end, Greekness, even when expanding eastwards to Anatolia and beyond, remained fiercely local and tied to its kaleidoscope of individual places.

FURTHER READING

Much has been written on how primary the local is for myth since Christiane Sourvinou-Inwood published her seminal paper, 'Persephone and Aphrodite at Locri' (1978). Simon Price's overview (1999) programatically expressed (and somewhat exaggerated) this insight. Local *performance* was exploited highly successfully in Krummen 1990 (in German), though it has not been much reflected in subsequent scholarship; two more recent major contributions are Stehle 1997 and Kowalzig 2007. Otherwise, local mythologies have mostly been exploited as political statements since the days of Martin P. Nilsson (see Nilsson 1951). 'Genealogical thinking' is tellingly explored by Fowler (1998).

From the perspective of expanding worlds, Malkin 1994 examines the role of myth in the 'Spartan Mediterranean'. For later manipulation of mythology, to incorporate new locales (in southern Asia Minor) into the framework of Greek mythology, the most important book (in German) is Scheer 1993; the English reader may usefully turn to López-Ruiz 2009 and to Bremmer's essay 'Balaam, Mopsus and Melampous: Tales of Travelling Seers', most easily available as Bremmer 2008: ch. 8.

NOTES

1. For bibliography on this topic, see the Further Reading section of this chapter.
2. Dionysios of Halikarnassos, *On Thucydides* 5.1; accepted as correct by Fowler (1996); see also Dillery (2005: 505–6).
3. If it suits him, Ovid can free his stories of concrete local ties, as he did with the Cretan story of Leukippos (*Metamorphoses* 9.666–797, cf. Antoninus Liberalis 17) or of Dryope (located at Oitē in Antoninus Liberalis 32, but in *Metamorphoses* 9.324–93 the sister of Iole of Oichalia).
4. The Paiones who dwell around the river Axios appear in the catalogue of Trojan allies, *Iliad* 2.848–50.
5. On this phrase see Pirenne-Delforges (2008: 42).
6. In the Homeric 'Catalogue of Ships', the leader of the contingent from 'Doulichion and the sacred Echinaoi islands who dwell beyond the sea off Elis' is Meges, the son of Phyleus 'who once left his country in anger about his father,' *Iliad* 2.625–9. Here, as elsewhere, local history takes its inspiration from Homer.
7. *Iliad* 2.615–24 gives the four leaders, Amphimachos, Thalpios, Diores, and Polyxeinos. Amphimachos is killed in 13.185–95, Diores in 4.517–25; neither Thalpios nor Polyxeinos reappear after the *Catalogue*.
8. ἐκκαθαιρόμενον λόγωι τὸ μυθῶδες, Plutarch, *Theseus* 1.5; Hekataios *FGrH* 1 F 19 (Danaos' daughters), F 27 (Kerberos, on pp. 59–60 above).
9. Pausanias 5.7.6–5.8.6.
10. Hesiod F 10c (245) MW, see M. L. West 1985: 52; the same genealogy in Apollodoros 1.7.2 (Aëthlios) and 1.7.6 (Endymion, first ruler of Elis). (Note that Protogeneia does not find her way into Most's text, F 10.64, p. 56.).
11. When Pindar, *Olympian*. 9.41–62 turns the Opountian myth into the story that Opous' daughter Protogeneia was seduced by Zeus on the Arkadian Mainalos who then handed the pregnant maiden to Lokros, the claim expressed in the name has become much less totalizing, Protogeneia now being understood as the 'First-born' amongst several siblings. [Graf here follows the view of the scholiast on Pindar, *Olympian* 9.86b–c, that for Pindar Opous' mother was called Protogeneia. For a different view, see p. 116. KD]
12. See the list in Stephen of Byzantion s.v., with more examples.
13. Hesiod F 10c, M. L. West (1983b).
14. I thus firmly side with Visser (1997) against any attempts to understand the 'Catalogue of Ships' as a mirror of late Mycenaean political geography.
15. On the geographical framework that defines Elis in *Iliad* 2.615–24, see Visser (1997: 555–73).
16. See Strabo 8.3.8, following Apollodoros of Athens and Demetrios of Skepsis.
17. The somewhat complex traditions are presented in M. L. West (1985: 51).
18. M. L. West (1985: 55) gives a map on which the Graikoi are rather conjecturally located; see F. Gschnitzer, s.v. 'Graikoi', *BNP*.
19. Hesiod F 2 (F 3 Most).

20. Strabo 8.7.1; Konon *FGrH* 26 F 1.27; Aiolos also Apollodoros 1.51.
21. The sources are in Sakellariou (1958).
22. Achilles' contingent: *Iliad* 2.684; Achilles' home *Odyssey* 11.469; next to Phthia, *Iliad* 9.478.
23. The formula in *Odyssey* 1.344; 4.726, 816; a variation, 15.80.
24. Hekataios *FGrH* 1 F 16; Euripides, *Ion* 57–75.
25. Konon *FGrH* 26 F 1.27; Strabo 8.7.1.; Apollodoros, *Library* 1.7.3. See CH. 3 for a more general account of the Hesiodic *Catalogue*, Hekataios, and Hellanikos.
26. See especially J. M. Hall (2002).
27. *IG* VII 2713 (*SIG*³ 814),12: πάντες οἱ τὴν Ἀχαίαν καὶ τὴν ἕως νῦν Πελοπόννησον κατοικοῦντες Ἕλληνες. This last definition must allude to Nero's unattested plans to rename the Peloponnese, presumably *Nerononnesos*. See Champlin (2003). Epameinondas: line 38 of the same inscription.
28. Scheer (1993) is an important monograph on this subject.
29. Published by Signe Isager (1998); see also Lloyd-Jones (1999a; with corrigenda and addenda in 1999b); Gagné (2006); Bremmer (2009); Graf (2009).
30. Herodotos 1.175, 8.104. See Jameson (2004).
31. See the inscription *SIG*³ 1020.
32. The texts may be found in Şahin (1999: nos 11, 117); see Scheer (1993: 187–200).
33. See Oettinger (2008).
34. Cicero, *On Divination* 1.2: *Cilicum et Pisidarum gens et his finituma Pamphylia, quibus nationibus praefuimus ipsi, volatibus avium cantibusque ut certissimis signis declari res futuras putant* ('The peoples of Cilicia and Pisidia and, bordering on these, Pamphylia, peoples that I myself was in charge of, consider that the future is revealed by the flight of birds and their song, and that these are wholly reliable signs', tr. KD); at 1.25 he asserts that augury, disregarded in his contemporary Rome, is still practiced in these three regions.

CHAPTER TWELVE

Names and Places: Myth in Alexandria

Anatole Mori

Transcendence versus difference

Alexandria was not the only ancient Greek city named after Alexander the Great, but it was the most important. There were roughly a dozen Alexandrias named by (or for) the conqueror, including Alexandria Aria (modern Herat in Afghanistan) and Alexandria Eschate ('Furthest Alexandria', identified as Khujand in Tajikistan).[1] Many of these Alexandrias were comparatively short-lived, and nearly all were probably intended to be little more than fortified centres of Macedonian military control over outlying regions; but the Egyptian Alexandria was situated on a large harbour and seems to have been destined from the start to be a commercial metropolis.[2] Despite, or even because of, its economic success Alexandria would remain culturally distinct from the rest of the country, and in the Roman period its official title was Alexandria-by-Egypt (*Alexandria ad Aegyptum*), a city near but not precisely of Africa that has continued to be more cosmopolitan (or at least more European) down to the present day.[3]

In the fourth and third centuries BC, Alexander and the Ptolemies sought to reconcile the cultural divisions of their new city by emphasizing commonalities between the gods of the Greek and Egyptian pantheons – a move that was certainly facilitated by the polytheistic, inclusive, and combinatory qualities of the two religions. Egyptian mythological narratives, like those of the ancient Greeks, feature elemental divinities associated with earth, sea, and sky and with cyclical, seasonal events – the movements of the sun and moon, the flooding of the Nile, and so on. In their interchangeability and conceptual looseness, the

A Companion to Greek Mythology, First Edition. Edited by Ken Dowden and Niall Livingstone.
© 2014 John Wiley & Sons Ltd. Published 2014 by John Wiley & Sons Ltd.

Egyptian Isis, Hathor, and Horos are easily (and frequently) assimilated with other deities. This is especially true in the case of the sun god, Re, who was not only combined with Amun the creator god, as one might expect, but was also associated with darker powers like Osiris, the rejuvenated god of the dead, with whom Re nightly joined as the composite sun of the Underworld.[4]

Greeks living in Alexandria were easily acclimatized to combinatory divinities like this, as is clear from the cult of Sarapis, which was introduced by Ptolemy I, Alexander's successor to the Egyptian throne. Sarapis was the Greek name for the mummified Apis bull that was worshipped by Egyptians as Osirapis (Osiris-Apis). For many Greeks the dismemberment of Osiris and his being pieced back together would have found a parallel in the death and rebirth of Dionysos.[5] Like Alexander, Ptolemy had supported the cult of the Apis bull at Memphis, the traditional religious centre of Egypt, but he would build a new temple in Alexandria to promote the syncretistic Osiris-Apis-Dionysos-Hades.[6] Within the Sarapeion, as the sacred precinct was called, Greek-style anthropomorphic images of the god mingled with Egyptian-style statues and architectural features, a visual juxtaposition that contrasted 'Greek' with 'Egyptian' even as it united them in a single location.[7]

Ancient Greek myth differs from Egyptian not only in the anthropomorphism of its gods but also in its concern for historical and geographical detail. Greek myths parcel out the world with stories that account for various Hellenic migrations to the east, west, and south. Tales of divine abduction abound: Apollo takes a Thessalian girl to North Africa where she bears a son named Aristaios and then gives her name to Kyrene, one of the larger Greek settlements along the coast.[8] A similar pattern recurs in the misfortunes of Io, priestess of Hera at the Argive Heraion, who was seen by Greeks as the counterpart of the Egyptian Isis (Herodotos 2.41). After Zeus seduces Io, she is transformed into a cow that journeys to Egypt and eventually, recovering human form, becomes mother to Epaphos. Epaphos will found Memphis, and Io will then become grandmother to the eponym Libya, whose descendants, the (Egyptian) sons of Aigyptos and the (Greek) daughters of Danaos, will marry, if with fatal consequences for the sons.[9]

The myths of Kyrene and Io do more than simply conceptualize an exotic other in terms of divine desire. Hesiod's *Theogony* (886–955) presents Zeus as the inheritor of his grandmother Gaia's primordial procreative role: he fathers a fourth generation of gods, from Athene, Persephone, Apollo, Artemis, Ares, Hermes, Dionysos, and Herakles to civilizing divinities like the Fates, the Muses, the Graces, and the Hours (Order, Justice, and Peace).[10] But as the father of Epaphos, Zeus' dynamic influence is shown to exceed the boundaries of the Greek-speaking world, and in a later aetiological myth he is even instrumental in the creation of the zoomorphic Egyptian gods: the rest of the Olympians were thought to have abandoned Zeus to fight Gaia's monstrous son Typhon and to have fled in assorted animal disguises to Egypt where their bestial avatars continue to be worshipped long after the defeat of Typhon.[11] Zeus' procreative power, then, transcends ethnic borders; and from a Greek point of view it was thus perfectly natural for him to be recognized and worshipped by Egyptians as Amun-Re (Herodotos 2.29, 42).

The myth of Kyrene, on the other hand, illustrates the predominantly anthropocentric and local perspective of Greek myth, which is concerned with historical and geographical details because it is primarily concerned with human activity.[12] These stories chronicle the rise and fall of individuals, kings, and communities that are associated with localized, anthropomorphic gods: Argive Hera, Kythereian Aphrodite, Attic Athene, Theban Dionysos.[13] The elite had always traced their own origins back to one or more gods to justify and secure their own political dominance through divine ancestry. Thus, while Zeus' status as a universal father and founder is apparent in the myth of Io, the myth of Kyrene points to Apollo's association with Greece, as the leader of the Muses (*Mousagētēs*) and an icon of poetic tradition and intellectual progress. The foundation story of Apollo and Kyrene was therefore a symbolic vehicle for the cultural ties that endured between mainland Greeks and those who migrated to Egypt and accounted, in effect, for what was *not* Egyptian.[14]

For the Greeks, then, North Africa was a blend of the foreign and the familiar, a sort of kindred other, as all these myths suggest. At the same time, Egypt was recognized as an older civilization and as a source of information about many of the Greeks' own gods and rituals. Herodotos singles out Egypt as the origin of Greek modes of worship (2.58), and according to him Io, Dionysos, and Zeus are all cultural borrowings from Isis, Osiris, and Amun-Re (2.50, 123). Ancient views on the comparative antiquity of these two civilizations are of less interest here than the Greek emphasis on ethnic difference and geographical division, features that are lacking in the Egyptian material. In the mythic imagination of Greece, Egypt was explicitly configured as an exotic and faraway land of strange, bestial gods to which Greek virgins could be transported thanks to Olympian lust (see also CH. 24). Greek myths about Egypt continued to be self-regarding in this way from antiquity down to the early Hellenistic period, when Egypt came under the sway of Macedonian rulers who traced their heritage back to a Dorian hero, Herakles.[15]

Alexander's Mythic Exploits

Parallels between Greek and Egyptian gods were regularly exploited for political purposes by the Ptolemaic kings. However, Egyptian motifs and themes did not predominate in Alexandrian poetry, or rather they were not given the same prominence as Greek motifs and themes. Since the 1980s scholars have advanced the view that Alexandrian court poets were encouraged to promote an Egyptian outlook in their poetry in order to win over elite Alexandrian Greeks who might otherwise have been put off by the Egyptian trappings of the newly founded monarchy.[16] Susan Stephens has persuasively argued that these motifs were deliberately adopted, although the double perspective is not always apparent to us because the Egyptian names appear less frequently in their works. To Alexandrian Greeks, then, the association between Greek and Egyptian myths would have been so close that 'a narrative about the one was predisposed to converge with the other'.[17] I qualify this claim,[18] because such associations, while presumably present to some degree, would inevitably have privileged the Greek side of the equation, ideologically speaking, since Greek authors and audiences were less interested in Egypt for its own sake than in their own heritage – however intangible that might have become. From the political perspective of the Ptolemies, the ancient ties between these civilizations were useful inasmuch as they strengthened the Greco-Macedonian claim to authority, but it is reasonable to conclude that the poets tended to allude to those aspects of Egyptian culture that affirmed their Hellenic origins,[19] with Egypt generally playing a supporting rather than a starring role, as it always had done.

Greeks had certainly been living in Egypt long before Alexander's arrival. Trade with Egypt, which imported wine and silver and exported corn, linen, and papyrus, had been healthy since the archaic period, and from the seventh century onwards Greeks had inhabited the coastal regions of North Africa, in Kyrene and Naukratis and other settlements largely populated by merchants or mercenary soldiers.[20] By the time Herodotos was writing his history in the fifth century BC, a Greek population, while more or less marginalized politically, was scattered throughout Egypt.[21] After the Persian king Kambyses invaded in 525, Egyptian independence from external rule alternately waxed and waned until the arrival of Alexander in 332. Alexander's journey there after his defeat of Tyre and Gaza was largely fuelled by practical considerations; Egypt's resources had to be taken – peacefully enough, as it happened – from the Persian satrap governing at that time in Memphis.[22] Then, too, the wealth of Egypt was legendary and an attraction in itself: in the *Iliad* (9.381–2) Achilles refers to the wealth of Egyptian Thebes ('where the greatest treasures lie') as a measure of his disdain for Agamemnon's offer. Yet Alexander's travels in Egypt, like many of his adventures, were also prompted by his personal rivalry with the mythic exploits of the greatest heroes of Greece.

From boyhood Alexander had seen himself as being in competition with Achilles (Arrian, *Anabasis* 7.14.4), from whom he believed he was descended on his mother's side; and the conquest of Asia was for him a conscious emulation of the Greek war against Troy.[23] Tales of the exploits of Dionysos and the divinized hero Herakles likewise fired his ambitions, drawing him to Egypt and beyond. He travelled to Nysa, the fabled site of Dionysos' childhood, and his emulation of the god would take him as far as India.[24] There he also successfully besieged Aornos, a well-watered mountain citadel (now identified as Pir-Sar in Pakistan), out of a desire to surpass Herakles, who was said to have failed (in the guise of a local god) to take it.[25] Arrian, a historian writing in the second century AD, allowed that while Alexander may have believed that Herakles failed to take Aornos, he himself did not think Herakles had ever travelled to India, and in any case he regarded the story as the typical sort of boastful exaggeration intended to mitigate the failings of lesser men (*Anabasis* 4.27.2). Of course, exaggeration could also be enlisted in support of the achievements of the mighty: Kallisthenes, the court historian who travelled with Alexander, described the miraculous prodigies that preserved the king during his perilous trip through the Libyan Desert to the oracle of Amun-Re in the Siwah Oasis. After losing his way in terrible dust storms Alexander was saved by miraculous rainfall and sent in the right direction by two crows.[26] The first-century BC/AD writer Strabo dismisses these two stories as flattery and court propaganda, but whether they are true or not they attest to the dangers of the expedition,[27] something no native-born Egyptian king had ever attempted, and in fact an army of fifty thousand sent by Kambyses was said to have been destroyed when it did (Herodotos 3.25.3–26.3).

From a pragmatic perspective there was no compelling reason for Alexander to make the trip. The Egyptians had already recognized Alexander's divinity: he was the kingly manifestation of Horos and had assumed all the divine titles associated with pharaonic office (King of Upper and Lower Egypt, son of Re, beloved of Amun, selected of Re, and so on). Alexander being Alexander, the hardships of the journey might have been sufficient to tempt him, but in any case, heroic precedents had been set long ago by Dionysos, said to have originally founded the temple, and by subsequent visits paid to the site by Perseus and Herakles, with whom Alexander claimed kinship.[28] As Bosworth comments, 'The king may have half-consciously connived in the fabrication of the myth of earlier conquests, but for him it was not half-baked hearsay with some basis of probability. It was fact, and he had convinced himself of it.'[29] Alexander accordingly believed (or at the very least acted as though he believed) that the priest officiating at the temple had greeted him as the son of Zeus, an image that Kallisthenes capitalized on, later reporting that before the battle of Gaugamela Alexander was favoured by an eagle omen as he prayed to his father Zeus 'to protect the Greeks if in fact he was born of Zeus' (Plutarch, *Alexander* 33).

From a modern perspective the scepticism of Arrian and Strabo hardly appears unwarranted, but then their opinions do belong to a later era in historical writing: earlier historians of the fourth–third centuries BC were more inclined to accept mythical parallels and wondrous portents, and to exploit them for political ends. Megasthenes, the late fourth-century author of a history of India, extended the parallel between Dionysos and Alexander as conquerors in order to justify Macedonian rule, and his contemporary Hekataios (of Abdera) would adopt a similar approach to the representation of Ptolemy I in Egypt as Osiris:

> Both Megasthenes and Hecataeus had a political agenda and adapted their pres-
> entation of myth to it. For Megasthenes Dionysus' conquest was a justification
> of Macedonian rule in India and an implicit encomium of the men who had cre-
> ated it. For Hecataeus Osiris was a potent image of world empire, the universal
> civiliser and benefactor whose benefactions ensured apotheosis, and behind the
> conquering god was the figure of Ptolemy. In the early Hellenistic period myth,
> even myth deliberately created, was a political force. It represented the current
> rulers as the favourites of the gods, the successors of the gods and the very rivals
> of the gods.[30]

It is not so surprising, then, to find the sophist Anaxarchos referring to Herakles and Dionysos in order to persuade the Macedonians to adopt a ritual greeting (*proskynesis*) that acknowledged Alexander's divinity. Not only would it be right, he claimed, for them to recognize the divine quality of Alexander's extraordinary deeds, which exceeded those of Dionysos and Herakles, but it would in fact be more just because the latter were not Macedonians.[31]

The Case of Kyrene and Other Mythic 'Causes'

But if Alexander's personal rivalry with these heroes was atypical, his fascination with mythic origins was not. At the end of the fourth century BC new capitals like Alexandria and Antioch sought to preserve their cultural heritage with char-acteristically Hellenic civic spaces, religious festivals, poetic performances, and scholarship. The genre called mythography, or 'writing about myths', came into vogue in commentaries and book-length analyses of, for example, the origins of a myth, or its different iterations, or its ties to specific geographical regions. At this time a few writers also began to compile mythological tales in collections about which we regrettably know very little;[32] a later work, Apollodoros' *Library* (dated possibly to the first century AD), gives an idea of the kinds of compendia that would remain popular until the second century AD.[33]

Scholars like Kallimachos, the third-century BC scholar-poet from Kyrene, catalogued lists of natural curiosities and wrote about such *paradoxa*: amazing facts about things animal, vegetable, and mineral. Although Kallimachos was a prolific writer, nearly all of his prose works have been lost, including the ear-liest known example of a paradoxographical catalogue, 'a collection of the wonders of the whole world by location'.[34] Chief amongst the collections of antiquity was the Library of Alexandria itself, and Kallimachos' crowning contribution to it was his annotated inventory of all Greek authors, titled, according to the Kallimachos entry in the *Souda* (a Byzantine lexicon, that is, alphabetical encyclopaedia):

Tables [*Pinakes*] of those distinguished in all branches of learning and their writings in 120 books.

The Library of Alexandria, founded early in the third century by the first Ptolemy, housed thousands upon thousands of papyrus rolls, which made compiling the *Pinakes* no mean feat: the identity and biographical details of each author were established and recorded, together with the genre, length, and first lines of all their works.[35]

Kallimachos' scholarly interest in the rare and unusual is apparent in the remnants of his poetry: six hymns, thirteen iambic poems, some sixty epigrams, a short epic, some experimental lyrics, and the fragments of a badly damaged elegiac catalogue poem, originally in four books, called the *Aitia* ('Causes'). The *Aitia* explores the origins and mythical background of miscellaneous cults, tombs, statues, and festivals. Elegiac verse in the strictest sense was associated with sung laments, but the same meter could be employed for many different kinds of topics and, like epic, had traditionally provided a vehicle for mythical tales and information.[36] Book 1 of the *Aitia*, for example, provided the mythological explanations for a number of curiosities: why the inhabitants of the island of Paros do not play the *aulos* (a type of oboe) during sacrifices to the Graces;[37] why insults and abuse play a role in sacrificial rites honouring Apollo on the island of Anaphe and Herakles on Lindos; why the statue of Artemis on Leukas has a mortar on its head; why a wooden statue of Athene has a bandage on its thigh; and so forth. For Kallimachos, such mythological questions informed the substance of his poetry, while a knowing selectivity, clarity, and witty charm were hallmarks of his style.

Antimachos of Kolophon (fl. 400) likewise combined scholarship with poetic composition, being in this regard a model for the scholar-poets working later in third-century Alexandria.[38] Antimachos wrote a commentary on Homeric epic, but he also wrote an epic himself called the *Thebaid* ('Tale of Thebes') about the assault led by Polyneikes against Eteokles, presumably in twenty-four books like the *Iliad* ('Tale of Ilion'). A long poetic tradition at Kolophon was associated with those genres that were conventionally represented as expressions of the poet's personal voice (iambic, lyric, and elegiac);[39] Antimachos' elegiac catalogue, the *Lyde* (dedicated to the memory of his wife or lover of the same name), was much admired by Kallimachos' contemporaries, and it helped to revive the traditional cataloguing of mythological exempla, especially stories of tragic love, that was modelled after Hesiod's *Catalogue of Women*. The Syracusan poet Theokritos presented similar kinds of doomed love stories in his bucolic *Idylls*, albeit to much greater poetic effect.[40] A fragment attributed to Kallimachos accordingly condemns Antimachos' *Lyde* as a 'fat and unrefined' book (F 398 Pfeiffer i), for while this poem included a number of mythological stories much as the *Aitia* did, it evidently did so in a way that conflicted with Kallimachos' exacting aesthetic standards.

Although Kallimachos was born in Kyrene and apparently spent his life in North Africa (Kyrene and Egypt), he was dedicated to the preservation of *Greek* culture and tradition. Any interest that North Africa held for him seems to have been focused on the origins and current practices of the Greeks who lived there. In this respect his intellectual curiosity recalls that of Alexander, who was mainly interested in Egypt as an exotic backdrop for the achievements of Greek heroes. Blood kinship with Herakles, Dionysos, and Perseus established a parallel and a precedent for his own claim to divinity, as we have seen, but it also asserted a Hellenic ancestral claim on Egypt and Kyrene. In much the same way, Kallimachos' references to Kyrene do more than just celebrate his particular home and communal ties: they serve to draw North Africa as a whole into the Greek cultural ambit, even though Macedonian governance was still little more than two generations old.

Kyrene had been loyal to Alexander, but after his death in Babylon in 323 there was an insurrection. The region was stabilized in 322 after Ptolemy, who had been one of Alexander's generals, took control of Egypt.[41] Acclaimed king by his army in 306,[42] Ptolemy I was crowned as an Egyptian pharaoh two years later. His stepson, Magas, became the governor of Kyrene in 300, and declared himself king after Ptolemy's death. The Egyptian throne passed to another of Ptolemy's sons,[43] and conflicts between this king, Ptolemy II Philadelphos, and his half-brother Magas persisted until the death of the latter (c. 250). In 246 Ptolemy III Euergetes ('Benefactor') succeeded his father and finally united the two kingdoms by marrying his cousin (Magas' daughter Berenike II).[44]

Kallimachos witnessed the conflicts between these two dynasties, and lived long enough to celebrate the rise of his fellow Kyrenean Berenike. Book 3 of the *Aitia* opens with the victory of a chariot team sponsored by her in the Nemean Games (*Victoria Berenices*), and Book 4 ends with the divine *katasterism* (transformation into a star or constellation) of a lock of her hair (*Coma Berenices*).[45] Other Kyrenean references are threaded throughout his poetry. In *Hymn* 3, dedicated to Artemis, the poet refers to the early life of Kyrene as a young girl in Thessaly, and the goddess's friendship with her (*Hymn* 3.206–8). In *Hymn* 2, dedicated to Apollo, he recalls Kyrene's abduction, which leads, as we have already seen, to the foundation of the eponymous Kyrene (*Hymn* 2.75–116). Kyrene is elsewhere represented as a Hellenic community that has been embraced by the local gods. A fragment of Kallimachos' poetry presents an appeal to the Herossai, the heroic nymphs of Libya who dwell along the shores of the Syrtes Gulf, to help 'my living mother' (a metaphor for Kyrene) to flourish (F 602 Pfeiffer i). Amongst Kallimachos' epigrams we find references to several Kyrenians, including Charidas the son of Arimmas of Kyrene (*Epigram* 13 Pfeiffer ii) and Kallimachos' own father, wittily described as 'father and son of Kallimachos of Kyrene' (*Epigram* 21 Pfeiffer ii).[46] Kallimachos focuses on the connections within the city as well: the tragic deaths of Aristippos' two children, Melanippos and Basilo, are said to have convulsed all Kyrene (*Epigram* 20 Pfeiffer ii). These hymns to Olympic gods and appeals to local, anthropomorphic, divinities on behalf of Greek cities reveal that it is not the Egyptian 'other' that fires Kallimachos' imagination, but rather the foundation and continued prosperity of a Hellenic African coast.

This same focus on the Greek colonization of Libya is apparent in the *Argonautika*, an epic poem in four books that was composed by Apollonios, a contemporary of Kallimachos who shared his interest in 'foundation stories' (*ktiseis*). 'Beginning from Apollo', the narrator says (1.1), the poem will recount the adventures of the Argonauts, a group of Greek heroes (including Herakles) who sail to the Black Sea to recover the Golden Fleece. *En route* the Argonauts spend a pleasant sojourn amongst the women of Lemnos, and we learn that as a consequence of this encounter the Argonaut Euphemos' descendants will eventually come to Kyrene and found the Battiad dynasty.[47] Apollonios here reworks Pindar's treatment (*Pythian* 4) of the foundation of Kyrene, and as Green points out, this section likely alludes to Philadelphos' rightful claim on the contested throne of Kyrene.[48] Other features of the epic, such as the pre-eminence of Apollo for the Argonauts and their auspicious stranding in the Syrtes Gulf, clearly echo Kallimachos' own interests in the aetiology of a Hellenic North Africa.[49]

Kallimachos goes beyond Apollonios, however, by drawing explicit parallels, from time to time, between Greek and Egyptian mythic analogues. For example, he refers to the Delian nymphs dancing in honour of Artemis at the springs of the 'Egyptian Inopos', which is mysteriously connected to the Nile via a subterranean connection (*Hymn* 3.171) – an image that reinforces the Herodotean image of Egypt as the ultimate source of Greek cult practices.[50] A fragmentary passage from the *Aitia*, which likely belonged to the second book, describes the poet's encounter with a foreign visitor to Egypt, a man from the island of Ikos (F 178 Pfeiffer ii).[51] Even so, the *aition* in question deals not with Egypt proper but with the Thessalian worship of Peleus, who was the father of Achilles and died on Ikos.

Interestingly, Book 2 deals with the *topos* of 'visitors to Egypt' in Kallimachos' only myth about an Egyptian figure. Bousiris (see CH. 24) was a son of Poseidon and Libya whose practice of sacrificing foreign victims made him synonymous with cruelty and leads to Kallimachos deploying him as an Egyptian model for the apparent subject of the *aition*, Phalaris, the sixth-century BC tyrant of

Akragas in Sicily who roasted his victims in a bronze bull (*Aitia* 2, F 44–47 Pfeiffer i).[52] Strabo (17.1.19) dismissed the story of Bousiris as pure fiction, but nevertheless it is hard to miss its ethnic and political implications, since Bousiris is killed in the end by Herakles (Apollodoros 2.5.11).

Kings of Egypt, Sons of Zeus

Since Herakles was promoted as a Ptolemaic ancestor, the myth of Bousiris offers more than a stereotypical image of heroic Greek dominance over foreign barbarity. During his reign Ptolemy I reissued coins that portrayed Alexander with the characteristic attributes of divine figures like Herakles (club, bow, lion skin), but he also minted similar coins featuring himself in order to emphasize his ties to Alexander and Dionysos as well as to Herakles.[53] Early in his reign a fictitious family tree was introduced which traced the Ptolemaic line back to Herakles and the Argive dynasty of Temenos (a Heraklid, 'descendant of Herakles'),[54] a genealogy that was likewise promoted by Ptolemy II: a cult statuette of Philadelphos (paired with a statuette of Arsinoë II holding her characteristic double cornucopia) depicts him with a club and an elephant headdress.[55] Herakles traditionally carried a club, and his lion skin headdress is here updated with a nod to Alexander's Dionysian travels in India. So too Theokritos' *Idyll* 24 (the *Herakliskos*), reworks Pindar's *Nemean* 1 with an account of the childhood education of a Philadelphos-like Herakles, beginning with his first heroic exploit: the killing of two snakes sent by Hera to destroy the child of Alkmena, one of her (many) rivals for Zeus' affections.[56] And *Idyll* 17, an encomium by Theokritos in honour of Philadelphos, names Herakles as the ancestor (*progonos*) of both the king and Alexander (17.26–7), positing a divine precedent for Philadelphos' incestuous marriage in the union of Zeus with Hera.[57]

The connection with the Dorian Herakles helped to legitimate Ptolemaic rule from the perspective of the Greco-Macedonian community, and it also paved the way toward the deification of the living monarch, something that Greeks and Macedonians were less comfortable with than Egyptians, who had long associated divinity with the office of pharaoh. As Zanker puts it in his discussion of the *Herakliskos*, 'in making Heracles' education as a young man so recognisably Hellenistic, the poet may be trying to impart the impression of normality to matters like deification and marriage to one's sister, an approach observable also in the *Encomium for Ptolemy*'.[58] Official gestures toward deification of a living monarch can be traced back to the first Ptolemy's establishment of a state-run cult for his predecessor Alexander.[59] Philadelphos subsequently honoured Soter with the *Ptolemaieia*, a penteteric (four-yearly) festival,[60] as well as a cult for both parents as the *theoi soteres* ('saviour gods'), before going on to expand Alexander's state cult by adding honors for himself and his sister-wife as the *theoi adelphoi* ('sibling gods').[61]

Although there was an ancient temple dedicated to Herakles at Kanopos, for the most part Dionysos seems to have overshadowed Herakles, despite his genealogical importance,[62] in cult contexts – possibly because Herakles was also claimed as an ancestor by the Antigonids, the Ptolemies' political rivals, who now ruled in Macedonia. No statue of Herakles was displayed during the Grand Procession of Ptolemy Philadelphos,[63] a spectacular parade that lasted for an entire day during a Ptolemaieia festival not long after the death of Soter (the exact date is not certain) and that showcased larger-than-life images of Dionysos, of Alexander (as the new Dionysos), and of Soter. Bosworth points to this intersection of myth and political hegemony:

> The literary record had its visual counterpart in great pageants like the Grand Procession of Ptolemy Philadelphus, which depicted in the most grandiose style the return of Dionysus from India, complete with his triumphal entourage, and shortly afterwards displayed Ptolemy Soter alongside Alexander, both wreathed with artificial ivy crowns and accompanied by women dressed to represent the city of Corinth and the Greek states of Asia and the Islands. Ptolemy is placed on the level of Alexander, and both advertise their association with Dionysus and their emulation of his benefactions, in this case the liberation of the Greek cities under Persian (later Antigonid) rule, which had been the declared object of Alexander's war of revenge.[64]

Kinship ties with both Herakles and Dionysos would continue to be prominently and publicly displayed by the third Ptolemy, who erected a stele in Adoulis (Ethiopia) with an inscription that begins: 'The great king Ptolemy (III), son of King Ptolemy and of Queen Arsinoë, the *Theoi Adelphoi*, the children of King Ptolemy and of Queen Berenike, the *Theoi Soteres*, descended through his father from Herakles, the son of Zeus, and through his mother from Dionysos, the son of Zeus'.[65]

The royal titulature grew longer and more ornate over time, as the generations passed and the dynasty began to deteriorate. The familiar legacy of the era is tragic: with the close of the third century Alexandrian poetry goes into decline, at the end of the first century Kleopatra, the last Ptolemaic ruler, and her Roman consort are defeated, and in the next millennium the great library together with all its holdings will be lost. But the city of Alexandria has survived, and the names and places connected with it have also survived, like mythic outposts of a distant age left behind to mark the passage of the god Alexander. Two impulses, assimilation and differentiation, catalysed the mythic ideology of the Greek diaspora in the fourth and third centuries BC – the one absorbing foreign rites and customs under the aegis of Zeus, the other holding fast to Hellenic tradition and its advances led by Apollo *Mousagētēs*. This polarization of thought may be partially responsible for the destabilization of an icon like Herakles, whose exploits are lightly and even humorously treated by Kallimachos in the *Hekale* and Apollonios in the *Argonautika*, where he appears as a complex and conflicted character: stubborn, choleric, ambitious, loyal, self-centred, and impulsive. If Herakles was the heart of the nostalgic past, glorious, mighty and yet somehow diminished by Alexander's conquest, then Dionysos represented Alexander's vision of a future triumph that always lay just out of reach, beyond the banks of the Indian River Hyphasis.

FURTHER READING

On Egyptian myth, see Hornung 1982b. On Greek myth in the Hellenistic period, see the essays in López Férez 2003. For an introduction to Hellenistic poetry, see Gutzwiller 2007 and Hutchinson 1988; thoughtful and extensive discussions are offered in Fantuzzi and Hunter 2004. On the Egyptian context of Kallimachos' poetry, see Selden 1998 and Bing 1988.

For an English translation of the *Aitia* fragments and Kallimachos' other poems, see Nisetich 2001; for Theokritos see A. Verity, *Theocritus: Idylls*, with notes and introduction by Richard Hunter (Oxford World's Classics 2002). There are several recent translations of Apollonios: R. Hunter's *Apollonius of Rhodes: Jason and the Golden Fleece* (1993) and P. Green's *The Argonautika of Apolloniuos Rhodios* (1997), which has extensive notes, but only in the cloth edition.

On Hellenistic Egypt, see Bowman 1986. Consult Errington 2008 or Shipley 2000 for the history of the Hellenistic period; Chamoux 2003 offers a very readable introduction to the subject. On the formation of the Ptolemaic state, see Manning 2010. There are also a number of excellent collections of essays addressing developments in the Hellenistic era: see Erskine 2003, Ogden 2002, Cartledge, Garnsey, and Gruen 1997, Bulloch, *et al.* 1993, and Green 1993.

NOTES

1. See further Fraser (1996: 171–90).
2. The city boundary was reportedly laid out according to Alexander's directions using milled barley-groats (used for lack of a better marker), a sign, according to the diviners who were part of Alexander's entourage, of the city's future prosperity, particularly in agriculture (Arrian, *Anabasis* 3.1–2.2).
3. Fraser (1972: 1.107–9).
4. Hornung (1982b: 95–6), Stephens (2003: 50–1).
5. For example, Herodotos 2.42, 144.
6. Memphis was the political capital of Egypt until the Ptolemies moved to the palace in Alexandria.

7. Stephens (2003: 15).
8. Pindar, *Pythian* 9; Kallimachos, *Hymn* 2.100–16.
9. Vasunia (2001: 33–74, esp. 40–7); see also Zeitlin (1992).
10. On Zeus the begetter of gods, see Dowden (2006: 41–4).
11. This story is attested for Pindar, F 81 Bowra, but was told at length by Nicander of Kolophon, whose version is preserved in Antoninus Liberalis 28. A similar story appears in Apollodoros 1.6.3.
12. On the local perspective of Greek myth, see CH. 11.
13. Egyptian divinities are certainly attached to regional cults, but there is a stronger tendency toward universalism, and generally speaking Egyptian gods inhabit the sky or the next life (Hornung 1982b: 317–37).
14. Apollo was also paired with the Egyptian god Horos (son of Isis and Osiris), and perhaps Apollo was synonymous with Greek culture in a way that Zeus was not.
15. Macedonians evidently spoke Greek as well as the Macedonian language/dialect, though the southern Greeks became increasingly reluctant to consider them more than barbarians when they became a military threat under Philip II. On the question of Macedonian ethnicity, see further Worthington (2004: 7–8).
16. For discussion and a response to this approach, see G. Zanker (1989).
17. Stephens (2003: 8).
18. Mori (2008).
19. So G. Zanker (1989: 93) 'Egyptian cult, art, and iconography are not at all necessarily binding for the interpretation of Greek art or poetry in Alexandria.'
20 Graham (1982: 134–8).
21 Braun (1982).
22. Arrian, *Anabasis* 3.1–2.
23 Vasunia (2001, 254–5).
24. Arrian, *Anabasis* 5.2.5–7; *Indika* 1.4–7.
25. Arrian, *Anabasis* 4.28.4. See Bosworth (1993: 306–7).
26. *FGrH* 124 F 14a (Strabo 17.1.43).
27. Bosworth (1993: 72). See also Dowden (1992: 89): 'No matter how fictional or artificial local myth seems to us, it is always capable of being treated as strict history by interested parties. Myth, like propaganda, is worthwhile because people will believe it. Enemies must be prepared to counter it within the rules of the games it establishes. Mythic argument is accorded the same respect as historical argument would be in our day – that is, it is persuasive within the limits allowed by the more pragmatic concerns of self-interest and practical politics.'
28. Strabo 17.1.43.
29. Bosworth (2003: 307).
30. Bosworth (2003: 318).
31. Dionysos was Theban and Herakles an Argive (Arrian, *Anabasis* 4.10.6–7, cf. Curtius 8.5.8). Kallisthenes' recognition of Alexander's divinity could only be stretched so far, however, and he rejected Anaxarchos' argument.
32. Possible examples include the *Cycle* of Dionysios of Samos (Ceccarelli, *BNJ* 15; F. Jacoby, *FGrH* 15) and the historian Phylarchos' *Mythical Epitomes*, about

which nothing is known. Satyros, a student of the grammarian Aristarchos, is said to have 'compiled the old myths' (*FGrH* 20 F 1 = Dionysios of Halikarnassos, *Roman Antiquities* 1.68.2). I am grateful to Ken Dowden for drawing my attention to these authors.

33. Higbie (2007). On Apollodoros see pp. 66–72 above.

34. The work itself no longer exists (see Pfeiffer 1968: 134–5), but it is one of many mentioned in the *Souda* entry on Kallimachos; another apparently dealt with similar material: 'On marvels and natural oddities in the Peloponnese and Italy'. These rather lengthy titles were presumably not used by Kallimachos himself. See Blum (1991: 134).

35. On the Library of Alexandria see Fraser (1972: 1.305–35) and Pfeiffer (1968). For ancient testimony about the *Pinakes*, see F 429–453 Pfeiffer i.

36. Elegy is a metrical form written in couplets, of which the first line is an epic hexameter and the second is formed by the opening part of the epic hexameter (the *hemiepes*) repeated twice. See Gutzwiller (2007: 64): 'It seems that longer elegies were typically used for local myths, recounting city foundings and cataloguing legendary ancestors of élite families.'

37. The *aulos* was playing when the Cretan king Minos sacrificed to the Graces and learned of the death of his son. The *Aitia* fragments are badly damaged and only a few lines of this particular aetiology are preserved: the description of Minos' reaction to the news of his son's death is preserved in scholia (interlinear or marginal notes made by ancient commentators, 'scholiasts') on the poem. For this example, see F 7 Pfeiffer i.

38. Pfeiffer (1968: 94–5).

39. Fraser (1972: 1.554).

40. Fantuzzi (1995: 28–9): 'Theocritus took over the use of mythological paradigms into his bucolic poetry; nevertheless he appears to have done so only in order to provoke his readers, who expected to find the standard gnomic value of paradigmatic myths (and of the *exemplum* as a literary practice), but were forced to come to terms with the more ambiguous and disquieting value of Theocritus' stories.'

41. Diodoros 18.3.1; Arrian, *History of the Successors of Alexander* F 1.6.

42. Plutarch, *Demetrios* 18.2.

43. Magas' father was a Macedonian named Philip; his mother was Berenike: after Philip's death Berenike came to Egypt and married Ptolemy, officially titled Ptolemy I Soter ('Saviour'), becoming Berenike I. Their son, Ptolemy II Philadelphos ('Sibling Lover') succeeded to the throne and later married their daughter (his full sister) Arsinoë II. The epithets Soter and Philadelphos were introduced by the younger Ptolemy; see Hazzard (2000: 3–24).

44. On Alexander and the early years of Ptolemaic rule, see Hölbl (2001: 9–46).

45. These two passages recall the allusions to the former queen, Arsinoë II, which frame the first two books of the poem. For the Greek text of the *Victoria Berenices*, see *SH* no. 254; for the *Coma Berenices*, see *Aitia* 4, F 110 Pfeiffer i (with a facing translation in Latin from Catullus 64).

46. Kallimachos was named after his grandfather.

47. *Argonautika* 4.1571–619, 1731–64.
48. Green (1997: 352, 358).
49. This parallelism suggests that Apollonios shared Kallimachos' point of view, but the veracity of the ancient evidence for a quarrel between them is still debated; see further Green (1998); Cameron (1995); Lefkowitz (1980).
50. Cf. the reference to Io as 'the Inachean Isis' (*Epigram* 57 Pfeiffer ii).
51. For its location at the beginning of Book 2, see Cameron (1995: 133–40).
52. See Nisetich (2001: 92–3).
53. Hölbl (2001: 93). Attributes of Zeus and Amun were also depicted in the coinage of Alexander and the Ptolemies.
54. Fraser (1972: 1.45).
55. London, British Museum #38442; photograph in Edgar (1906).
56. On the parallel between Ptolemy Philadelphos and Herakles in this poem: see G. Zanker (1987: 179–81), F. Griffiths (1979: 91–8), and Koenen (1977: 79–86).
57. R. L. Hunter (2003: 8) notes the difference between this self-described *hymnos* and traditional hexametrical hymns which praised the Olympian gods: 'At the heart of this difference lies the fact that the subject of the poem is a man, not (yet) a god, and that just as he and his forebears move smoothly between levels of existence, so the poem in his honor slips between genres.'
58. G. Zanker (1987: 180).
59. Fraser (1972: 1.215–16).
60. A *penteteris* ('five-year') is a cycle of *four* years, because the years were counted inclusively in Greek (and Roman) practice.
61. Hölbl (2001: 94–5); Fraser (1972: 1.217–20). At this point the honorific title for the high priest of Alexander's cult was changed to the 'priest of Alexander and of the *Theoi Adelphoi*'. Alexander's priest was the highest in the land, and this title directly followed that of the king in the dating formulae of all official temple documents. The independent cult of the *theoi soteres* was eventually added to the dynastic cult by Ptolemy IV Philopator.
62. Fraser (1972: 1.208).
63. The procession is described by an eyewitness, Kallixenos, whose account is preserved in Athenaios, *Deipnosophists* 5 197d–e.
64. Bosworth (2003: 318).
65. *OGIS* 54: translation from Burstein (1985 no. 99 (p. 125), with slight modifications). Burstein notes that Ptolemy III was the biological son of Ptolemy II and Arsinoë I, his first wife. See also Fraser (1972, 1: 203).

CHAPTER THIRTEEN

The Myth of Rome

Matthew Fox

'Does a Cave Prove Romulus and Remus are no Myth?'

This headline from 2008 to a article in the online edition of *USA Today* encapsulates a great deal about the essence of Roman mythology. The discovery by archaeologists of a cavernous space decorated with mosaics and buried deep underground on the Palatine hill in Rome immediately raises the possibility that mythical elements of Rome's past may be confirmed as true. As the text of the article itself makes clear, it requires only a little investigation to reveal the absurdity of the connection between Romulus and Remus and any archaeological discovery. However, this does not prevent the archaeologists working in Rome from fostering such associations in the public imagination: they had, after all, claimed the discovery of Romulus' walls in the early 1990s. Why should such connections be made, and why is there such a close link between archaeology and mythology when dealing with Rome? In exploring such questions, we encounter the most important characteristic features of Roman mythology: features that make Roman mythology different from Greek, and go some way to explaining why, in a companion such as this one, Roman myth occupies so small a place. To account for the distinctness of Roman mythology, this chapter adopts two different tactics: it explores scholarly traditions that have shaped the study of Roman myth, to explain why it is so much less the object of scholarly attention than Greek mythology, and it looks in more detail at precisely those issues raised by the *USA Today* headline.

Myth at Rome has a pronounced connection with place. As the title of this chapter suggests, Roman myth is, to a large extent, about providing a mythology for Rome itself, and the geography of the city plays an important part in

A Companion to Greek Mythology, First Edition. Edited by Ken Dowden and Niall Livingstone.
© 2014 John Wiley & Sons Ltd. Published 2014 by John Wiley & Sons Ltd.

most mythological narratives. In addition, there is a pronounced tendency for Roman myths to focus on origins. As in the case of the reversion to Romulus and Remus, myths at Rome are frequently aetiological: explaining the origins of institutions or rituals, or charting the history of buildings or locations back to their earliest use or appearance. And lastly, myth at Rome, more than its Greek equivalent, prompts those telling the stories to think about questions of veracity and historical reliability. Their verification is central to the character of the myths of Rome, and the boundary between myth and history is one that most myths at Rome will in some way challenge. Because of this, consideration of scholarly traditions is particular central to understanding the field. Roman mythology has played a vital part in testing the capabilities of historians and archaeologists as those disciplines have developed over the last two centuries.

Differences between Roman and Greek Myth

Roman myths are not the same as Greek myths. This divergence comes in part from the cultural distinctness of two civilizations, and partly from the manner in which the scholars of the nineteenth and twentieth centuries treated them. There are significant differences between the way myth functions in Greece and in Rome, differences that stem from a distinction that the Romans themselves made: artistic production was a characteristic of Greeks rather than Romans. It was in poetry, and in poetic drama in particular, that Greek myth was transmitted, expanded, elaborated, and analysed. The lack of a strong and early literary tradition gives Roman myth a literary quality: the first time that students of classical literature have, traditionally, come across Roman mythology is in the pages of Livy, whose morally edifying account of Rome from its foundation was an educational mainstay for many centuries. His history provides a very different vision of Roman culture from the excesses of Greek tragedy or the endless proliferation of tales that those same students encountered in reading Homer.

Livy tames the myths and legends associated with early Rome by retelling them in the form of history. Compared to the more fantastic worlds of Homer and the Greek theatre, which, like their Roman counterparts, also deal with Greek prehistory, Livy's account of Rome's earliest years has already been heavily rationalized. That process of rationalization can be easily observed in Greek mythology too, and from its earliest expressions: we need only think of the poet Pindar's argument (in *Olympian* 1) that the story of the dissection and cooking of Pelops by his father, Tantalus, was a malicious invention, and that a more plausible explanation for his disappearance was that he was abducted by Poseidon to act as his 'attendant' (see CH. 5). Similar forms of 'improving' traditional myths by rewriting them can be found in even earlier Greek poets, from Hesiod onwards.

However, the comparatively late development of literature at Rome gives the rationalizations that we find in Roman sources a different character. Pindar still preserves the idea of divine intervention, even though he makes an edifying improvement by distancing the gods from scandalous tales of unwitting cannibalism and instead associates them with the more familiar and acceptable trait of pederasty. In Livy's account of the death of Romulus, the different versions reveal a more elaborate process of reinterpretation. There was one form of the story, he tells us, in which Romulus' inexplicable final disappearance, in a storm cloud that suddenly swept down on a hitherto clear day, was attributed to a group of senators opposed to the monarch.

Much ink has been spilt on the question of the origins of this account of Romulus' death. We can suspect that Livy drew on lost works of an earlier historian for whom the reign of Romulus embodied the same kinds of political struggles as characterized the later stages of the history of the Roman Republic: conflict between different parties in the senate, or between the senate and over-powerful individuals. One favoured candidate for this source is the historian Licinius Macer, who is thought to have fashioned Romulus as a prototypical *popularis* leader. The *populares* were members of a political group that defined itself by ideological appeals to the people and in opposition to the traditional elitist politics of the *optimates* (largely synonymous with the senatorial interest). It is not clear how well-defined such a label was, nor when it came into being; it is certain, however, that it was entirely foreign to whatever political culture existed in Rome in the seventh century BC, the period in which Romulus supposedly ruled. By seeking to explain Romulus' death as the result of a backlash by senators keen to hold on to their power, Macer was deliberately reshaping existing traditions in order to reflect his own political interests. Although we know fairly little either about his career or his writings, we can say with some certainty that he had *popularis* affiliations.

Such a process of uncovering the bias of lost sources upon which Livy drew is known as *Quellenkritik*: this German term translates literally as 'source criticism', but it is used as a loan-word in English to describe a particular strand of scholarship dominated in its early days by work written in German. The methodological problems of this approach are many, and in its pure form it has now fallen out of fashion.[1] It is still important, however, since the search for the original sources in historical accounts is essential for those trying to uncover the myths that might lie behind them. The same process has another form, in which the critic reveals in their true light historical facts that might be disguised by the manner in which they are told as myths. The case of the fourth-century BC Roman general, Camillus, examined below, is a good example of this: in spite of the possibility that Livy's is simply a reasonable historical account (however embellished), that narrative has been thought to conceal a primitive myth.

The process of starting with a rationalized historical source and aiming to reconstruct its mythical or historical antecedents is central to the most prominent trends in modern work on Roman myths. It is a response to the fact that, even in the earliest accounts, the Roman authors are themselves rationalizing these stories and making their myths look historical. Scholars have, understandably, attempted to resist such rationalization and to look, instead, for the original material concealed behind it. Some scholars will be looking for myths; others will be looking for history.

Regarding Romulus, Livy himself is more cautious than the scholars have been. Rather than saying that this is the version given by an earlier historian, he opts for what looks like a formulation intended to avoid clarity. 'I believe there were some people at the time', he says, 'who declared silently that Romulus was done away with by a group of senators,' adding that the obscure rumour of assassination has persisted right down to his own day. It is almost as if he is deliberately trying to prevent the practitioners of *Quellenkritik* from attributing a source to this story: if witnesses to the event thought it was an assassination, they didn't talk about it, nor was that story ever verified. For Livy, the temptation to draw a pointed parallel between the assassination of Romulus and that of Julius Caesar, murdered quite recently at the time when Livy was writing, would be even keener than it is for later readers. As Livy goes on to relate, it was an ancestor of Caesar himself who then provided the verification that Romulus had been transformed into a deity. By writing that the story of an assassination was originally only presented in silence, he refutes the possibility of a reliable written source, and then goes on to define that version of events as a 'rumour' (Latin *fama*).

What may have begun, therefore, as a myth of the same kind that we are used to in Greek literature, with Romulus acting as a demigod-king comparable to Theseus, is already, by the time we encounter it, heavily overlaid with interpretation. Under these circumstances, understanding the 'original' quality of the myth becomes rather an idealistic project. The quest for an original significance, however, played an important part in the retelling of Roman myths in antiquity, just as it has done for modern scholars. The processes of rationalization, and of explaining the myth at the same time as retelling it, is so prevalent within the literary sources for Roman myth that it is helpful to make a clear distinction between two different ways of looking at Roman mythology. On the one hand, the way in which ancient writers themselves rationalize, rework, and explain mythical material provides a rich source for understanding the topic. On the other, there are the continuing attempts by modern scholars, including archaeologists, to find a method of interpreting the 'original' mythical material, and to uncover the 'real' meaning of these stories, divested of their ancient interpretations. Faced with the evidence, this distinction is hard to maintain in practice. But the contrast between the 'real' meaning of the myth, and the rationalizing reworkings of the ancient sources, is central to any engagement with this material.

Naïve or Sentimental? Poetic or Prosaic?

Before going on to consider in more detail the ways in which interpretation and explanation of myth functioned in Rome itself, it is worth exploring further how the literariness of Roman myths, and their perceived difference from the more natural-seeming or spontaneous Greek counterpart, intersects with one particularly influential current in modern thought. If we can appreciate the importance of this way of thinking, it then becomes easier to define our own approach to Roman mythology. The most important difference between myth in Greece and myth in Rome can usefully be framed in terms of the distinction drawn by Schiller at the end of the eighteenth century between 'naïve' and 'sentimental'.

Friedrich Schiller (1759–1805) was an influential German poet and philosopher whose work had a colossal impact on the Romantic movement throughout Europe and beyond. The distinction between naïvety and sentimentality was a way of categorizing literature, specifically poetry, but it developed from an analysis of man's relationship to nature. True poetic genius, for Schiller, was of the same order of experience as unmediated contact with the power of nature. Whereas most poets have to strive to achieve such experience, in the poetry of the greatest geniuses (Homer, Aeschylus, Shakespeare) the power of naïve poetry shines through almost as if the poet were not in control of it.[2] In its blending of human and divine material, of stories that resemble the everyday world of their first readers, and of fantastic and grotesque accounts of the divine and semi-divine worlds, early Greek poetry presents in Schiller's view an archetypal form of mythical literature. While perhaps not so for the original audience, for any readers after the Romantic period, including ourselves, Greek mythology appears as something like a force of nature: a way of thinking about the world that is compelling, but also baffling, and one that, while demanding our interpretation, always leaves an element of awe or power which we accept as being beyond our interpretative capacities.

The first, and most obvious, application of Schiller's categorization to Classical mythology rests on the fact that Roman literature developed later than Greek. Greek mythology, as expressed by Homer and Hesiod, appears in the form of poetry, and poetry which for the most part does not contain authorial comment or criticism of myth. Moreover, both the early Roman poets and the earliest Roman historians are largely lost to us. Whatever similarities or differences between Roman and Greek myth there may originally have been, what we have access to in our sources is, in the case of Greece, early and poetic, and in the case of Rome, late and prosaic. A prose, moreover, which displays all the signs of a long literary tradition of attempting to rationalize myth, comment upon it, and decipher it. Greek mythology therefore looks like a 'pure' form, and Roman like the product of a more critical tradition. In the earliest representations of Roman myth we can observe the work of a critical consciousness, one which has obscured whatever pure, elemental quality the stories themselves may originally have had.[3]

Schiller's ideas intersect with attempts to define the 'sublime', and a wider interest in genius, which were typical of the aesthetic philosophies of Romanticism. The reader may be puzzled as to why I have introduced them into a chapter on Roman mythology. They are relevant, however, because these Romantic categorizations still have a hold on our own way of thinking about mythology, in particular in its relationship to literature. Furthermore, they played an important part in the thinking of the nineteenth-century historians who were the first to attempt the systematic treatment of the earlier periods in Rome's history, and whose work had a lasting effect upon the character of the academic study of the past. It is in Romantic concepts that most of our ways of thinking about myth originate. Myths themselves are often regarded as possessing a pure, original quality, and their rendition in art or literature is, often without thinking, seen as a manifestation of a more sophisticated approach to myth than the one that gave rise to the myth in the first place. Myth is commonly conceived of as a discourse that emanated directly from the 'spirit' of the people who produced it and who continued to perpetuate it in their retellings of mythical stories. The processes of representation, however, in particular literary representations, are seen as less authentic: intellectual attempts to grapple with the mysterious, sometimes disturbing, material of the myth. Rationalizations, in other words, which are an expression of a more sophisticated, better educated, or less 'ancient' way of thinking than was characteristic of the culture in which the myth itself originated. This distinction between different kinds of mythical representation displays the same structure as that between naïve and sentimental.

Furthermore, because many Romantic authors were themselves in the business either of collecting traditional stories or of producing their own myths in order to reanimate mythical values in their own societies, it feels natural to us, even two centuries later, to respond to the contrast between 'literary' myths and 'original' myths in the same manner. The notion that if we had access to the 'original' manifestation of a particular myth we would be able to grasp a deeper truth about the society that produced it is central to almost all scholarly engagement with Roman mythology. This is true even where the approach to myth is to assume not that it is early and original, but rather, late and invented. The problem of naïvety versus sentimentality is not solved; its terms are just rearranged.

A more specific way in which such Romantic thinking is relevant to the study of Roman myth is that it was similar ideas about different kinds of discourse, and their relationship to nature, which gave rise to the most influential modern approach to Roman mythology. Barthold Georg Niebuhr (1776–1831) is often regarded as the founding father of the modern discipline of Ancient History. His development of a critical approach to the sources for that history depended in part upon his theory that the legendary material associated with Rome's origins had started life in a cycle of poetry, now lost, that had found its way, in a manner congruent with Schiller's view of the transition from the naïve to the sentimental, into historical writings about early Rome.[4] Poetry is, in Romantic theory, a discourse generally closer to naïve forms of expression, and Niebuhr's theory of lost Roman folk poetry coincided with a wider interest in folk poetry amongst European Romantics more generally (the example of the brothers Grimm is best known). Furthermore, a number of the most significant scholars of Roman history, particularly in the German-speaking world, were attracted to the notion of a Rome-before-Rome. It presented a culture where myths, even if partially lost, could be found to express the same kind of national consciousness which was essential to the emerging interest in a shared German cultural heritage.[5]

As the study of Roman history became more systematic, so the categorization of the sources for the earlier periods became more firmly established. These sources are late, secondary, and heavily rationalized. They present a particular challenge to the historian, therefore. But properly interpreted, they are more than just the our best hope of reconstructing the city's early history. They are also the repository of our means for understanding the original character of the Roman people, if we follow the common assumption that myths contain particularly profound truths about the communities that produced them. This paradox, that in understanding Roman history we need to decipher myths, has had a determining effect on the kinds of historical analyses that are possible for early Rome. The claim of the excavators to have uncovered structures built by Romulus is an expressive example: if we dig deep enough, the archaeological record itself will prove the truth of a primitive story. Such a claim proves that Niebuhr's paradigms are still central to modern ways of dealing with evidence for early Rome.

To summarize so far: Roman literature came at a much later stage in Rome's cultural development than was the case in Greece. By the time literary sources appear, a kind of secondary intellectual response can be found in them, and they are handed down as part of a discourse concerning Rome's history, rather than, as in Greece, as a collection of stories for which the story itself as the main focus. The distinction between naïve and sentimental goes some way to explaining why, in our own minds, Greek myth represents a purer form of human expression than its Roman counterpart. As a result of the comparative lack of an early artistic culture at Rome, when myths do emerge they contain, more regularly than is so in Greece, some commentary on or interpretation of the myth itself. As we arrive at a period, from the second half of the first century BC, when Roman literature developed greater momentum and from which more of it has been preserved, what we find is a strong trend to reinterpret traditional stories, and for them to serve particular ideological purposes.

Numa's Books

A striking demonstration of the rationalizing trends in the interpretation of myths can be found in the stories concerning the books of Numa. Numa was, tradition had it, the king who was appointed to the throne after the death of Romulus. He is associated from an early stage with all manner of sacred institutions. In his dialogue *On the State* (*de re publica*, mid-50s BC), a work which only survives in a fragmentary form and which contains the first narrative history of early Rome to come down to us, Cicero represents Numa as the founder of a number of priesthoods and rituals which would still have been familiar to his contemporary readers. But in addition to pursuing this idea of the king as a religious founding father, Cicero makes the characters in his dialogue speculate about the source of Numa's religious expertise. They discuss the relative chronology of Numa and Pythagoras, the mystical Greek philosopher who established his school in southern Italy. The speakers are relieved to discover that Numa cannot, in fact, have been influenced by Pythagoras, but rather represented a type of home-grown religious wisdom. This theme was a popular one in Rome at the time, and the question of Numa's relationship to Pythagoras continued to excite interest for later writers. Ovid, for instance, gives a colourful, almost absurd account in Book 15 of *Metamorphoses*, and Plutarch's biography of Numa (in his collection of parallel lives) is credulous in its extreme elaboration of the king's Pythagorean leanings.

In divesting Numa of Pythagorean indoctrination, Cicero was responding to a controversy that he had read about in recently written histories (probably the lost historians Valerius Antias and, before him, Cassius Hemina). Livy, a generation after Cicero, briefly retells the story, drawing at least on Antias as a source. In 181 BC, two stone caskets, sealed with leaded locks, were dug up on the Janiculum hill (Livy 40.29; the story is also told by Pliny the Elder). One casket had, apparently, originally contained Numa's mortal remains, but after such a long time was in fact empty; the other contained books written in Greek and Latin, and in a good state of preservation. They were books of philosophy: they represented religious truths that would have been so damaging to the essence of Roman religion that the senate decreed that they should be burnt. Livy himself is sceptical about Antias' claim that the philosophy in question was Pythagorean. But more important is his picture of a senate in the second century BC debating the value of a particular philosophical interpretation of religion and preventing the circulation of such ideas. The figure of the early king, in essence a quasi-mythical founding figure comparable to many who can be found in Greek mythology, had become the focus of a heated debate about how to organize religious life, censorship, and about the role of senate and magistrates in controlling the circulation of ideas and texts. Central to the story is the figure of the king himself.

It is impossible to find out how this story came into being, what events originally took place when, and how the different sources embellished it. Nevertheless, Numa's books point to an important controversy at Rome concerning how literary or philosophical interpretation could intersect with traditional religious practice. It is this concern which dominates accounts of Numa as a Pythagorean, as much as those (such as Cicero's, or Livy's) in which his remarkable wisdom and piety is attributed to different causes. Livy retells the popular story of Numa's relationship with a wood nymph, Egeria, whose presence can still be detected in several monuments in Rome. But again, he rationalizes: Numa put about the story himself, in order to convince his credulous people that he had a divine power, rather than simply being unusually clever in a human manner – human intelligence was, evidently, not in itself an acceptable basis for rulership.

This ambiguous attitude to religious truth was one that had also occupied Cicero's contemporary and friend, the polymath and prolific collector of all kinds of information relating to the culture and history of Rome, Marcus Terentius Varro (116–27 BC). Although very little of Varro's enormous output survives, he is referred to frequently by Saint Augustine in his *City of God* (early fifth century AD) as the main proponent of a theoretically informed paganism. Roman religion was, to contemporary observers, a disorganized and baffling collection of seemingly arbitrary rituals. For Augustine's attack, the systematization provided by Varro was a convenient target. Varro is accepted as an authority by Augustine, even though we may doubt how representative he was of the actual experience of Roman paganism.

According to Augustine, Varro developed what scholars now call a tripartite theology: a system for describing religion that divided understanding of metaphysical or religious truth into three kinds. There was one way of communicating such truths for the ordinary people, one for priests, and one for philosophers (*City of God* Book 6).[6] The story of Numa's books bears out the same mode of thinking: the senate is concerned to protect religion from the damage that unrestricted access to philosophical truths would cause it. The distinction

Varro made was between different levels of enlightenment, different degrees of understanding to which religion was amenable. The most basic he designated as the mythical or fabulous: in it, latent philosophical truths of a more profound nature could be mediated, through religious practice, or even theatrical presentation, to a wide audience who would be incapable, by virtue of their lack of education, of grasping them in an intellectual manner. The story of Egeria expresses this same way of thinking: Numa used myth in order to add authority to a religious organization that had a deeper, less visible rationale.

We can see in Livy the traces of this earlier story of a king whose philosophical insights surpassed those of his times. Numa himself, in Livy's rationalization, comes across as aware of the tripartite approach to religion: he exploited the mythical in order to provide a form of religious authority that would be accepted by his people. Livy may have been influenced by Varro. In any case, both writers are responding to the arbitrary and fantastic quality of much of Rome's religious practice. They were also working within the same historiographical traditions discussed above: one consisting of fabulous stories which, at the same time, brought with them a long tradition of reinterpretation and rationalization.

Roman Myth and Roman Religion

It is no surprise that a large proportion of the ancient literature dealing with Roman myth comes from works devoted to exploring and decoding Roman religious practice. The two most accessible works where this aim is most prominent are Ovid's late poem the *Fasti*, composed in the first decades AD, and Plutarch's essay *Roman Questions*,[7] written from the perspective a Greek commentator on Rome a century or so later. Both authors devote themselves to explaining what at first sight are evidently rather opaque rituals associated with particular religious festivals or observances. Both are fond of aetiological explanations of these observances. In looking for origins, they frequently retell myths, making a connection between some detail in the story and the ritual they are seeking to explain.

To give a flavour of this kind of writing, here is an extract from Plutarch (tr. Goodwin):

Question 21

Why do the Latins worship a woodpecker, and all of them abstain strictly from this bird?

Answer

Is it because one Picus by the enchantments of his wife transformed himself, and becoming a woodpecker uttered oracles, and gave oraculous answers to them that enquired? Or, if this be altogether incredible and monstrous, there is another of the romantic stories more probable, about Romulus and Remus, when they were exposed in the open field, that not only a she-wolf gave them suck, but a certain woodpecker flying to them fed them; for even now it is very usual that in meads and groves where a woodpecker is found there is also a wolf, as Nigidius writes. Or rather, as they deem other birds sacred to various Gods, so do they deem this sacred to Mars? For it is a daring and fierce bird, and hath so strong a beak as to drill an oak to the heart by pecking, and cause it to fall.

Apart from the fact that Latin worship of woodpeckers is something for which we otherwise have little evidence, this passage is revealing for a number of reasons. We need to remember, of course, that Plutarch was writing from mainland Greece, for a Greek readership, and was profoundly steeped in the cultural and literary traditions of his homeland. He does not shy away from drawing his readers' attention to the bizarre quality of a different set of traditions; indeed, the sensational quality of Roman religion seems to be part of the appeal. He seeks for sources of explanations in a variety of different discourses: mainstream myths (Romulus and Remus); more obscure myths (Picus' metamorphosis, a story inspired by Ovid, perhaps, or by borrowing from the better known Greek stories concerning Tereus), or, in the final explanation, a different kind of interpretation, focusing on the natural behaviour of the bird and integrating it into a devout worldview in which the gods exercise guardianship over different realms of human and animal behaviour.

Like his compatriot Polybios writing over two centuries earlier, Plutarch starts from the assumption that Roman culture was characterized by a remarkable degree of religious observance. Polybios made a direct link between piety, religious organization, and the durability and success of Rome as a growing imperial power. Particularly characteristic of Plutarch's approach is the way different of myths are alluded to as sources of explanation for a feature of Roman religion. To some extent it was automatic for any ancient thinker to look to mythic aetiology for such explanations. In the case of Rome, though, because the myths are directly associated with the origins of the city (whose very existence is thus one of the things to be explained), this aetiological emphasis is especially pronounced.

Plutarch's work is just one example of a strong tradition of Greek writers on Rome. Key figures whose works can still be read are Polybios, Diodoros, and Dionysios of Halikarnassos. All are historians who mediate Rome's history and cultural traditions to a Greek readership, largely from a pro-Roman perspective. For these writers, as for Plutarch, the tools of rationalization are employed in order to decipher religious practice, and to stress the piety and respect for tradition that characterize Roman culture. They provide much of our source material for Roman myths.

Empire, Mythology, and Poetics

Greek prose carries with it a particular style of rationalization, and the Greek account of Rome serves a specific purpose: the explanation to Greek readers of the culture of the conqueror. Such writing is a useful source for those working on Roman myth, but perhaps less central to understanding Rome than the work of Roman authors, especially poets. The prevailing aetiological approach to myth, so evident in prose accounts of Roman religion, also played a crucial part in the cultural shift that accompanied Rome's move to an imperial system of government towards the end of the first century BC. Livy's mention of Julius Caesar in his account of the apotheosis of Romulus is just one tiny piece in a much larger jigsaw, the roots of which lie in the Republic.

The concentration of power in the hands of one man was routinely accompanied by the elaboration of a personal mythology. Like other prominent dynasts, Caesar had made links between himself and the mythical past of Rome, most notably through his supposed descent from Venus. His innovation here was one of degree, rather than of the idea itself. The fragments of a late Republican sculpted frieze from the Basilica Aemilia in the Roman forum that narrate the story of the rape of Sabine women have recently been put on display again in the National Museum of Rome's Palazzo Massimo, near the main railway station: the fragments suggest the possibility that members of the powerful Aemilii family were making similar use of Roman myths to advertise their own power some time earlier. There are several other examples, the simplest being the association of the dynast with a particular mythical figure on coins.

Compared to the remarkable centralization of ideology under Augustus, these are disconnected fragments, but they support one clear conclusion. Origin stories and myths from prehistory could be used to bestow prestige upon living individuals, and to advertise the claims of their families to dominance. This was not simply a matter of individuals emerging as more prominent than their fellow citizens: it was, on the contrary, a form of self-advertisement that was aimed at those same fellow citizens. It demonstrated the power of that individual within the collective consciousness of the city, and while enhancing individual prestige also drew attention to a sense of civic pride, and acted as a celebration of Roman identity. As Roman literature began to gain ground, and become a more central part of the cultural world of the Roman elite, it too became a vehicle for the expression and manipulation of such ideas. In this process, we can see how myths were generated, or came into being, as a means of expressing political power, and that expression came, particularly with the coming of empire, in the form of poetry and historical writing. The influence of Romantic concepts, however, leads us to regard myths in literature as somehow less authentic forms of myth. In this section, I shall devote some space to a discussion of Vergil's *Aeneid*, and show how, once we move beyond a scepticism about the compatibility of literature and myth, we can see Roman mythology in action, during a well-documented historical period.[8]

From one perspective, Vergil's poem can be thought of as the most complete expression Roman mythology: it produces a more coherent mythology for the city than perhaps any other single text or artefact. The poetic elaborations of myth in Vergil's *Aeneid* are a great deal more than a celebration of the Augustan regime. The poem weaves together a large number of origin stories for Rome into a celebration of the city; of Italy; and of its new leading citizen (*princeps*) and father of his country, Augustus. In the *Aeneid*, Rome itself becomes mythologized, and Vergil's great achievement was to build on a sense of continuity present in a mythical tradition already so heavily aetiological. He was able to provide an almost irresistible image of ideological coherence, one in which past and present merge and which made his poem into the standard work for all subsequent writers of epic. But this was not just the work of a poet working in creative isolation. Augustus' monumental reshaping of the city was also a kind of mythologization of the present day. And both the building and the poem should be seen as evolution rather than revolution: they built upon the same traditions of aetiology and political enhancement that existed within the traditions.

Vergil took what he found in Roman lore concerning the origins of the city, in stories from the Italian provinces, and in myths associated with Roman and Italian deities, and knitted it together with the epic literary traditions of Greece. In the process, he created a new sense of symbolic power for Rome, the myth of Rome itself. Vergil's vision of Rome as a city with a destiny, as well as a set of values centred around the imperial house, brought a sense of order to Roman mythology which, as far as we can tell from the remaining evidence, it did not previously possess. This order, of course, is a literary one. It emerges from the epic narrative structures that centre on Aeneas, the refugee from Homer's Troy who starts the process which leads to the foundation of the city by Romulus. He is a composite figure who finds himself in a variety of situations previously occupied by at turns, Homer, Hektor, and Achilles, as well as his other, more unambiguously literary forerunner, Jason, as depicted in the Alexandrian epic of Apollonios.

Servius, one of Vergil's earliest commentators, tells us that the poet's concern was 'to imitate Homer and to praise Augustus'. Regardless of the insufficiencies of this claim as a reading of the poem, there is no doubt that these two poles have a determining effect upon the way in which myths work within the poem. In the imitation of Homer, Vergil is preoccupied with his poetic achievement. In the faulty heroism of Aeneas, the result of Vergil's respect for Homeric prototypes, it is hard to read a credible mythological counterpart to the emperor Augustus. In this sense, the poem does not produce a new myth, or rediscover lost facts about one of the original founders of the city in the way that historians managed with Romulus, Numa, or even some of the lesser known of Rome's kings. But Vergil makes Aeneas a passive, almost unwitting, carrier of Rome's destiny. It is other characters – gods, prophets of various kinds, his dead father – who deliver the messages which bring the theme of Roman imperial destiny into the realm of myth. He is, in this respect, a figure closer to the reader than to those who are themselves gifted with prophetic power: he is a recipient, not a transmitter, of supernatural communication. Of course, we can only make guesses about how effective the poem was in the years after its composition in producing a consensus about the meaning of Rome, and about the connection between the political order and this version of the city's origins. Perhaps Servius' claim that Vergil's second preoccupation was to praise Augustus can be interpreted as a sign of failure: to modern readers, the laudatory quality of the poem is a great deal less visible than the wider ideological content. That said, it seems clear that the traditions of the Roman nobility which linked their families to the period of origin were motivated by a sense of the justified veneration owed to their position. Mythological celebration was one way in which status in the real world could be expressed, even though it was of a more symbolic, even fanciful, quality than the holding of political office or the command of troops or a large retinue of clients.

In endowing Rome with this ideological coherence, Vergil did have forerunners, and some of these would also have been sources for both his ideas and his mythological themes. Ennius' *Annales* (which survives only in short quotations in later authors), was the first epic poem written in Latin (second century BC), and laid a basis for the integration of history with poetic and mythological material. Two of Cicero's poems seem to have foreshadowed Vergil's mythologizing way of celebrating the achievement of great individuals (in one case, Cicero himself) against a background of divine mythology. One is the poem on his own consulship (*de consulatu suo*), extracts of which survive because he quotes them himself in one of his late philosophical dialogues. The other is his lost poem *Marius*, celebrating the achievements of the general and dictator who shared Cicero's home-town. Both poems made advances in poetic technique, and also provided a model for appeals to divine destiny and the role of great individuals in the historical sphere. The collections of myths, aetiologies, rituals, and examination of antiquities by Varro was surely a resource upon which Vergil drew, even if we can only guess to what extent. His lost treatise *On the Trojan Families* is likely to have played some role. It provided genealogies for much of the Italian aristocracy that enabled them to claim an origin in Homer's Troy.

It is largely because of this store of Roman literature that the experience of reading Vergil is very different from that of reading Homer: the portentous, pious atmosphere of the *Aeneid*, redolent of ancestor worship and a fixation on the numinous, is not just the inauguration of a new imperial consciousness. It is also the clearest culmination we have of Republican mythological traditions. In spite, then, of the clearly literary motivation of the epic, Vergil's *Aeneid* shows us myth working effectively in Rome during the historical period. If we define myth as the creation of a symbolically laden narrative containing supernatural elements and depending for its effect upon influencing the beliefs of those who encounter it, then there is no doubt of the *Aeneid's* mythical status. We may still want to think of it as belonging to a secondary, or sentimental, category of myths, as distinct from the primitive mythology of the city, but I hope I have shown that this distinction cannot itself be granted too much weight, and is hard to apply effectively to Roman material.

For students of mythology, there is another key text that merits discussion in this context. Ovid's *Fasti* was for a long time a seriously neglected work, considered of interest only to those attempting to reconstruct Roman religion. Its first great commentator in English was the social anthropologist Sir James George Frazer, author of *The Golden Bough*. The poem's value for an understanding of the mythology of Rome, however, has only recently begun to be explored. Particularly when juxtaposed with the *Aeneid*, Ovid's poem, even on a broad view, tells us a great deal about the ramifications of Vergil's work with myth and about changes in the Romans' own sense of identity in the Augustan period. It is the poem in which Ovid takes on Vergil's worldview most directly, although one can argue that he is never far from sight in any of Ovid's works. But aside from its interest from a literary perspective, Ovid's way of approaching myth, largely aetiological and closely linked to the history of the city, is excellent evidence for the way in which mythology functioned in Rome as an inspiration to literary treatment.[9]

The word *Fasti* refers to the Roman calendar, which concerned itself in particular with defining the days on which certain public actions were religiously permitted (Latin *fasti*). It is the increased codification of the calendar under Caesar and Augustus that provided the impetus for Ovid's poem. Each book deals with one month (although Ovid only completed the first six books), and runs through a selection of feast days and ritual events, adopting an aetiological method of explanation and often digressing into long mythological narratives. The poem represents a different approach to the mythology of Rome from the *Aeneid*. Vergil follows one main narrative strand: the story of Aeneas' journey from Troy to Italy, and the conflict between the newcomers and natives which is the necessary preliminary to the emergence of the Roman people. He uses prophecy and allusion to bind the heroic past to the Rome of his readers' own day. In Ovid, the calendar itself provides this structure: the passage of the Roman year is an opportunity for readers to engage with a panorama of Roman history, in which the present day is a continuous record and celebration of Rome's mythology and history. Ovid's work was facilitated, and probably inspired, by researches undertaken by Verrius Flaccus, a scholar favoured by Augustus and engaged as tutor to his grandsons. Flaccus was responsible for the research behind an engraved version of the calendar, remains of which were discovered at Praeneste (modern Palestrina), not far from Rome, in the eighteenth century. It is thus known as the *Fasti Praenestini*. These fragments too are on show in the Palazzo Massimo museum.

The *Fasti* demonstrates how closely literary and ideological concerns coalesce in the production of a myth-driven vision of Rome. Earlier Roman poets such as Catullus, Propertius, and Tibullus had been much exercised by writing a refined and elegant style of poetry, and had taken as an emblem of this refinement the Greek poet Kallimachos (born c. 310 BC). One aspect of his influence was an interest in aetiology. In his *Aitia* he dealt, in an allusive and learned manner, with a large number of obscure origin stories taken from different parts of the Greek-speaking world, linking mythical origin stories with modern place names, religious institutions, or rituals.[10] Tibullus and Propertius combined Catullus' development of a strong individual poetic voice with this interest in refinement, and in aetiology. Meanwhile, the researches of Varro into the history and prehistory of the city, and into religious and legal traditions, were adding a great deal of detail to what had hitherto been rather disjointed sources, and systematizing the understanding of Rome's history and traditions. With the monumental celebration of Rome's rebirth under Augustus, these different currents came together. The dominance of Augustan poetry in our understanding of Roman myth is thus not just an accident of the survival of these sources and the loss of earlier ones. It was in the Augustan period, with Vergil, Livy, and a little later, Ovid, that Rome developed a coherent sense of its own cultural identity. This was largely because the competing claims of different family traditions which had characterized myth in the republican period were replaced with a centralized authority, linking the city of Rome itself with the ruling dynasty, and weaving together different familial and regional traditions into this over-arching framework centred upon the city and the ruling family. This is not to say that in reading these texts we find two-dimensional propaganda, either for Augustus or for Rome itself. Like most poetic texts, those that deal with Augustan mythology are rich in unresolved tensions. But just as no audience to Athenian tragedy would expect to find the myths of Athens, Theseus, or Perikles to emerge as one-dimensional, so it would be unwise to regard the complexity of Vergil and Ovid as in contradiction to the mythic aspirations of their texts. It is surely a essential aspect of all myths, of whatever age, that they can unsettle their readers, as well as inspire them.

Synchronic v. Diachronic: Roman Myth and the Discipline of History

It has been the aim of this chapter to provide an orientation in the main issues confronting any encounter with myth in a Roman setting. To close the discussion I shall explore a framework for thinking about myth that is particularly helpful in the Roman context. The distinction between synchronic and diachronic was central to the structural analysis of language as pioneered by Ferdinand de Saussure at the start of the twentieth century, and brought to new prominence by the anthropologist Claude Lévi-Strauss (see CH. 17). The adjective 'diachronic' refers to the development of a story or institution through time: when we think of history in general terms, it has a linear, progressive structure, and the history of any particular institution or object (such as the city of Rome) will be hard to pin down to one particular moment. 'Synchronic', on the other hand, indicates focus on a phenomenon at the point in time where it takes place. A synchronic perspective on an event will explore that event in terms of other things occurring at the same time, rather than attempting to explain the event through its antecedents or history. When we read an ancient source, our first experience is of synchrony: it is our reading, located within our own culture. Because of our awareness, however, of the distance in time between the composition of the text, and our encounter with it, we will normally have an awareness of the diachronic dimension: the different conditions under which the text was composed, the shifts in interpretation over time. It is the task of the alert reader or scholar to work beyond the immediate experience of synchrony, to a more diachronic understanding not just of our source or text, but (ideally) of our own act of reading.

There are several ways in which this distinction is useful in the context of Roman myth. To return to the example of the excavations on the Palatine: the structure which seems to be associated with the festival of the Lupercalia can be dated to the Augustan period. Surrounding structures, building techniques, and schemes of decoration: all these are synchronic material which enable the building to be given a secure anchorage in time. The festival itself, however, has a long history, and it is on this basis that the archaeologists are drawing a diachronic connection with Romulus; Livy tells us that the Lupercalia was a festival that existed even before the foundation of the city. The synchronic/diachronic distinction does not enable us to decide whether the archaeologists are correct or not. It is, however, useful as a tool for understanding what is at stake. They are deliberately overlooking the synchronic in the search for a particular kind of appeal which can only be achieved through reference to the diachronic interpretation of this monument. An Augustan Lupercalian chamber makes a much smaller impression than one that claims its origins with Romulus.

The aetiological character of most of the sources gives a heavy diachronic emphasis to Roman mythical material. Numa's books are a good example. Even though we can date their discovery to 181 BC, we cannot disconnect the story either from the subsequent reworking of the material in the sources (Valerius Antias and Livy), nor from whatever other traditions pre-dated the story. This is diachronic myth at its most challenging: it is impossible to pin down the creation of any part of it, or the intellectual issues it raises concerning philosophical insight and religion, to one particular time. Where diachrony is so pervasive, scholars are faced with a number of alternatives; the work of two leaders in the field is worth discussion in this light.

Georges Dumézil (1898–1986) was a prolific proponent of theories of Indo-European anthropology (his work is discussed in detail in CH. 18). Dumézil locates figures from Roman mythology within an Indo-European mythical culture, and he uses literary sources to provide clues to the original myths that they conceal. Working in the same traditions that influenced Lévi-Strauss (but with rather different results), Dumézil approaches diachronic sources for myth as expressions of an original network of mythical stories. Although he accepts that such a network would have its own history and evolution, it is the aim of his work to reveal the entire network in a synchronic manner. Such a procedure uses synchronic presentation as an aid to better understanding. We accept, for the purposes of analysis, that there was a pan-Indo-European proto-culture, and once we have explored the relationships between different myths in terms of their significance (a significance based largely upon natural phenomena and astronomy), then we can move on to distinguish between those parts of the system that come earlier, those which emerged later. Dumézil takes it for granted (like most working in this particular scholarly tradition) that genuine myths are the product of a preliterate consciousness. The diachronic nature of the sources for the myth, therefore, presents no particular obstacle: elements of myth will persist in the different retellings of the story over time, while other elements will be added as a result of different processes: the rationalizations of the author or his sources or literary traditions. The central task is to distinguish between the two, to recover the original myth, and to decipher the cluttered and confusing sources (such as the texts of Livy or Ovid) in order to reach back to their mythical core.

One noteworthy feature of Dumézil's work is his approach to his literary sources. In his *Camillus* (1980), for example, he sifts the different accounts of the battles led by the hero of Rome's fourth century BC campaigns against Italian cities, all of them written several centuries later than the events they describe. Rather than focus upon the context in which the different accounts were written (a synchronic approach to the sources),

Dumézil's concern is the underlying mythic structure, elements of which can be expressed in any of the accounts. Small details present in one author but absent in others (for example, the fact that a particular battle is mentioned as beginning at dawn) provide him with clues to an original religious, or mythical, significance. They are to be explained diachronically, in terms of the persistence of mythical traditions, rather than synchronically, in terms of the preoccupations of the particular source. Camillus, in his analysis, is a primitive dawn deity, transmuted into a historical figure by the rationalizing processes of literature.

The British historian T. P. Wiseman occupies a unique place in the study of Roman mythology. Representing a tradition of scholarship entirely different from the systematizing one that produced Dumézil, Wiseman's work derives some of its impetus from the German tradition of *Quellenkritik*, but is characterized by a historian's interest in locating particular sources in particular places and times – in other words, another combination of the synchronic and diachronic. His more recent work lays greater stress upon the diachronic character of mythology and has moved away from pinning mythical narrative down to a particular point of origin. In some of his earlier studies, though, he argues that individual myths had their origins in specific political situations in the mid-Republic. His approach was fuelled by the account given by Cicero (in his *Brutus*, a rather unconventional history of oratory of Rome) of the preservation of collections of myths relating to individual families by those families themselves, an idea that is also central to my reading of the traditions upon which Vergil drew. One recurrent feature of Wiseman's work is his interest in the earliest form of artistic expression: he examines, for example, the small collection of Etruscan engraved mirrors. These provide pictorial depictions of mythical scenes that predate any of the literary sources, and thereby escape some of the problems presented by them. By virtue of their diachronic evolution, the literary sources do not present us so easily with a single point of origin, nor even with just one version of a myth. A picture, however, can do that, although it too will have its own interpretative difficulties.

Roman mythology thus continues to play an important role in testing different kinds of historical method, as it has done since Niebuhr, or, indeed, Livy himself. And, as the excavators in Rome continue to prove, there is a fascination and challenge presented by the stories concerning Rome's origins that gives the field of Roman mythology a unique character. Roman myths demand a better understanding of the differences between history and myth, and of the role that such distinctions played in defining Roman culture. In turn, such a demand extends to the disciplines of history, archaeology, and literary criticism, and to any techniques that we develop to pursue our encounter with this very persistent collection of myths.

FURTHER READING

In one of the largest dedicated Classics libraries in the United Kingdom (the Joint Library of the Hellenic and Roman societies) there is no classification for Roman Mythology. The bibliography reflects this conceptual problem. The number of books in English is small, while much of the important work is contained in discussions of religion, or, indeed, history. Ando 2003 is an edited collection of important papers on religion from the last century; many of them contain useful observations on the function of myth, both for the Romans and for scholars of religion. Beard, North, and Price 1998 is a history and a sourcebook, and explores much mythical material. Feeney 1999 explores with concision and elegance the two poles between which Roman myth necessarily hovers. Dumézil's works have been translated in rather a piecemeal fashion (see the further reading for CH. 18), but *Camillus* is available (1980). Wiseman's *The Myths of Rome* (2004) represents something of a departure from his previous work, which is better exemplified in *Remus* (1995) or the essays collected in *Roman Drama and Roman History* (1998). *The Myths of Rome* is a rich collection of studies of a range of different sources, both ancient and modern, and includes, almost incidentally, a brilliant account of the history of the late Republic. My own heavily synchronic study, *Roman Historical Myths* (Fox 1996), examines the regal period in a range of Augustan authors, and contains a useful appendix on Varro (on whom there is still little general work in English). On Ovid's *Fasti*, see J. F. Miller 1991, Herbert-Brown 1994, and Newlands 1995. Two introductory volumes which have much to recommend them are Gardner 1993 and Warrior 2006. To explore the archaeological evidence for Romulus, those with Italian can consult Carandini and Capelli 2000, those without can read Wiseman's review article 'Reading Carandini' 2001. The *USA Today* article can be found on the Web at http://www.usatoday.com/tech/science/discoveries/2008–02–06-romulus-remus-lupercale_N.htm (accessed 13 July 2010).

NOTES

1. I cannot point readers towards a substantial discussion in English of *Quellenkritik* (or *Quellenforschung*, as it is sometimes known). Chaplin and Kraus (2009: 2–5) give a concise treatment. Howell and Prevenier (2001: 60–8) do so for modern historiography. For more detail, but without explicit theoretical context, see the introduction to Oakley (1997, especially 72–89).
2. Schiller's essay can be found online in a translation of a collection of his aesthetic writings at http://www.gutenberg.org/etext/6798 (accessed 8 November 2010). The edited translation of Helen Watanabe-O'Kelly (Schiller 1981) is

better but less easily accessible. On Schiller's formulation of these ideas, see Sharpe (1991: 170–97).

3. Wiseman (1995: 151–4) refers to the need to uncover 'the other Rome' if we are to understand Roman mythology: the other Rome refers to the period before Rome had acquired an empire, and before literature, with its centralizing effect on mythology, had taken hold.

4. On Niebuhr, the classic point of departure for ancient historians has been Momigliano (1957).

5. See Yavetz (1976).

6. Compare the (first) three functions of Indo-European ideology according to Dumézil (cf. CH. 18). Dumézil's ideas are discussed further below.

7. *Moral Essays* 263d–291d.

8. Hardie (1998) gives a thorough introduction to all aspects of the poet, with copious suggestions for further reading; pp. 63–83 are particularly useful from mythological perspectives.

9. Ovid's better-known *Metamorphoses*, is, of course, an epic mythological compendium. I have chosen to discuss *Fasti* because the mythical narratives of *Metamorphoses* do not have the same degree of engagement with Roman mythological tradition.

10. On the aetiologies of the *Aitia* see further Fantuzzi and Hunter (2004: 42–88).

CHAPTER FOURTEEN

Displaying Myth for Roman Eyes

Zahra Newby

Greek Myth in a Roman World

Everywhere one looked in the Roman world there were images of Greek myths: in the sculptures decorating baths, temples, and fora; on paintings and mosaics in private houses; and on small portable objects such as lamps, silverware, and seals. The aim of this chapter is to look at how myths were displayed in Roman art and what meanings they held for Roman eyes. I will suggest that mythological images provoked a range of readings depending on the contexts of display and reception: they might act as paradigms for human life, offering examples to imitate or avoid; provoke displays of high culture and learning; or serve as access points to a world of Greek culture in which one could find an escape from everyday life. From the second century AD, they also found a further role in funerary art as metaphors for the hopes and virtues of those whose tombs they decorated.

Defining mythological images is not as simple as it might at first appear. Myths are defined partly by what they are not – depictions of historical events such as battles or triumphs. They are also defined by the figures who feature in them – gods and heroes rather than 'real' historical men and women. Yet there are a number of areas where myth and history overlap, as with the figure of Aeneas, the legendary founder of the Roman race. Images of what we would call 'historical' and 'mythological' events could also be depicted side-by-side, implicitly awarding both the same truth value as depictions of past events, as in the scenes of the Gauls and Niobids shown on the doors of the

A Companion to Greek Mythology, First Edition. Edited by Ken Dowden and Niall Livingstone.
© 2014 John Wiley & Sons Ltd. Published 2014 by John Wiley & Sons Ltd.

Temple of Apollo Palatinus, on which more below. As stories which recount the deeds of gods and heroes, myths are intrinsically linked to religion. While cult statues of individual gods could appear alone, as objects of worship, they were often complemented by the display of narrative images featuring the god's involvement in a particular mythological act. Yet the meanings of these images might also extend beyond a religious reading into art historical or intellectual appreciation.

One aspect of Roman art which is particularly striking is the dominance of stories which first appeared in Greek myth. While a few representations of Roman stories such as the birth and rearing of Romulus and Remus do appear, the majority of images show figures and events which were already long known in Greek art and literature: the deeds of heroes such as Perseus, Hercules[1] and Theseus; the loves of the gods; and epic sagas such as the Trojan War or the voyage of the Argonauts. These stories entered Rome along with Greek philosophy, literature, and theatre, and became embedded into Roman thought. In art, the mythological representations form a subset of the larger category of ideal Greek art, which also encompassed images of victorious athletes, kings, and gods. This art had first arrived in Rome as the result of Rome's expansion and military conquests into the eastern Mediterranean between the third and first centuries BC.[2] Sculptures, painting, and precious metalware were all brought back to Rome as plunder. Initially these artworks were displayed in public spaces, dedicated in sanctuaries in thanks for the military victories which had secured them. Gradually, however, the taste for Greek art spread into the private sphere. The great villa-owners of the Republic filled their lavish homes with statues and paintings, while artists such as Pasiteles soon created a market in copies of Greek masterpieces as well creating new works which echoed classical forms.

Many of the original Greek masterpieces which were taken to Rome are now lost, destroyed over the course of the centuries. What we possess instead are the numerous new works which were created in the Roman period: these were either direct copies of Greek works or new creations that adapted classical styles and themes, often with a remarkable degree of flexibility and originality. Since the 1970s work on Roman marble copies has stressed this originality, as well as the ways that classicizing sculptures were used in their Roman contexts. While some were displayed purely for their artistic merit, reflecting the culture of connoisseurship which had developed alongside the importing of Greek masterpieces, others were chosen for their decorative merits, to create the right sort of atmosphere in a particular space.[3] In wall paintings too we find a great deal of innovation: groups of figures could be taken over from earlier models, but the backgrounds into which they were now placed and the addition of new supplementary figures often helped to change the tone and focus of the painting.[4]

Myths in the Public Sphere:
Temples and Baths

The first areas in which Greek art was displayed in Roman were public: statues and paintings were set up in religious sanctuaries and porticoes as offerings to the gods in thanks for military victories.[5] They also provided a way for victorious generals to share the proceeds of plunder through making these artworks accessible to public view. These statues and paintings included representations of individual gods, heroes, athletes, and historical figures as well as mythological tales. Statues of the gods could be reused as cult statues in new or restored Roman temples, as we see in Augustus's use of a statue of Apollo by Scopas in his new Temple of Apollo on the Palatine.[6] Paintings and statues were displayed in the porticoes or precincts around temples. We even find one example of a Greek temple pediment being transferred wholesale to Rome for use in a temple there, as in the temple of Apollo Sosianus in Rome which reused a pediment showing the Amazonomachy.[7] The same temple was also decorated with a sculptural group showing the deaths of the Niobids, probably displayed in the precinct.[8]

Augustus' Temple of Apollo on the Palatine, dedicated in 28 BC, featured a number of myths in its decoration and is a good example of the ways that they could be used for political messages.[9] From Propertius' description of the new temple in *Elegy* 2.31, we learn that the ivory doors of the temple showed the expulsion of the Gauls from Mount Parnassus and the deaths of the Niobids. These two examples, one historical, the other mythological, celebrated Apollo's punishment of mortals who stepped out of line and offered a potent warning. The nearby portico showed statues of the Danaids, the daughters of Danaus who killed their cousins, the sons of Danaus's brother Aegyptus, on their wedding night. Different versions of the myth existed, and it is very possible that the depiction here followed a version favourable to the Danaids in which the Egyptians were shown as the aggressors.[10] The myth offered a parallel to Augustus' own situation, evoking the war against Antony and his Egyptian consort, Cleopatra. The fratricidal strife between Danaus and Aegyptus echoed the sorrows of civil war, but also showed that war to be a necessary act. A further veiled reference to Antony might be seen in the terracotta plaques which decorated the precinct. Some of these show Hercules and Apollo competing for control of the Delphic tripod (fig. 14.1). Antony had adopted Hercules as his patron god, while Augustus linked himself to Apollo. We could see the plaques as alluding to the rivalry between the gods and their human protégés – a rivalry which had by now already been settled in Augustus' favour.[11] Yet the balanced representation of the two gods on the plaque also implies accommodation, suggesting that there was a place even for Hercules in the new Augustan religious sphere.[12]

Figure 14.1 Terracotta plaque showing the contest between Apollo and Hercules, from the Temple of Apollo on the Palatine.

This study of the myths displayed in the Temple of Apollo suggests a range of readings and significances. Myths could celebrate the actions of the patron deity, as on the doors with their images of the Gauls and Niobids, or on the plaques showing the struggle over the tripod. Yet at the same time they could also work allegorically, offering allusions to recent political events, or serve as moral warnings. While historical friezes could be used to celebrate particular military victories, for events which were rather more contentious, such as the victory over Antony, myth offered a way of exploring ideas of victory, vengeance, and rehabilitation in a sensitive and nuanced way.

Mythological sculptural groups formed part of the display of masterpieces of Greek art in Rome, appearing in a range of public contexts as well as in private villas and gardens. The art collection of the late Republican figure Asinius Pollio, consul in 40 BC, included a number of mythological pieces amongst its images of gods, heroes, and Muses, most notably a statue showing the punishment of Dirce by the sculptors Apollonios and Tauriskos.[13] Opinions differ as to whether this statue is identical with or the model for the statue group now know as the Farnese Bull (fig. 14.2) which was displayed in the Baths of Caracalla in Rome in the third century AD. The placement of Asinius

Figure 14.2 Farnese Bull, from the Baths of Caracalla, Rome.

Pollio's collection is unknown, though it was clearly on public display since Pliny tells us that Pollio was keen for it to be seen.[14] Many believe that it was displayed in the Atrium Libertatis ('Hall of Freedom') which Pollio built, though a placement in his lavish gardens is also highly possible.[15]

The public display of artworks was continued in the imperial period particularly in the adornment of lavish public baths. In addition to the Farnese Bull, which decorated the centre of a *palaestra* (exercise ground) in the Baths of Caracalla and was used as a fountain, this set of baths also featured two images of the weary Hercules holding the Apples of the Hesperides (the most famous is the Farnese Hercules in Naples) in addition to images of gods, heroes, and athletes.[16] These ideal statues helped to elevate the experience of bathing by their display of famous *opera nobilia* (famous works of art) while the naked bodies of athletes and heroes offered models for the bathers to aspire to.

The mythological pieces also offered refined entertainment. Both the Farnese Bull and the Farnese Hercules invite the viewer to walk round them to fully appreciate the scene represented: it is only when one looks at the back of the Hercules figure that one sees the apples in his hand, and appreciates that this weary figure has at last reached the end of his labours. Similarly, from the front view of the Farnese Bull we see only the figure of Dirce and her tormentors, the brothers Amphion and Zethus (fig. 14.2). On walking round, however, the figure of Antiope appears, revealing the motivation for this act: Dirce's cruelty towards their mother, Antiope, had driven the brothers to this act of revenge. Another piece discovered in the Baths of Caracalla, a figure of a naked man holding the body of a male child slung over his shoulder, suspended by his foot, has provoked much modern interpretation. Scholars have debated the identities of the two figures – is this Neoptolemus flinging the child Astyanax from the walls of Troy – or Achilles with the body of the dead Troilus? Ancient viewers too could have taken delight in discussing the identities of those portrayed, and also in seeing the links between the sculptural themes displayed in various parts of the baths.[17]

This brief overview of the display of mythological themes in public spaces in Rome suggests two important themes. The first is connoisseurship. Many of these artworks were Greek masterpieces of painting or sculpture which had been brought to Rome in the course of military victories. Their display in public sanctuaries, porticoes, and baths was influenced as much by their artistic status as works by famous Greek masters as by their mythological content, and they were often shown side-by-side with non-mythological images, such as portraits of famous individuals or statues of athletes. However, analysis of some particular complexes suggests that the display of certain specific mythological scenes could also evoke responses which went beyond pure aesthetic appreciation. The decorative programme of the Temple of Apollo on the Palatine uses myth as a metaphor for the events of the civil war, and shows Augustus as the protégé of a god who punished overweening mortal presumption but was also (through the provision of libraries in the precinct and the cult statue of Apollo Citharoedus) a god of the arts of peace and the intellect. In the baths, mythological sculptural groups were used for their artistic impact, to heighten the experience of bathing in a palatial ambience, and as manifest proof of the emperor's generosity towards his subjects. Yet in the daily experience of moving through the baths they could also provoke discussion and debate, providing a talking point for the bathers as well as opening up the fantasy that they were mingling with the figures of heroes and gods.

Fantasy and *Paideia*:
Myths in Villas and Gardens

In this next section I explore the display of mythological themes in the lavish settings of villas. Here they provoked, in various ways, the display of education and aesthetic appreciation and, over and above that, offered access to a fantasy world of myth and Greek culture. Once Greek artworks began flooding into Rome they soon began to enter the opulent villas of the Republican

Figure 14.3   Garden painting of Orpheus. House of Orpheus, Pompeii VI.14.20.

aristocracy in addition to being displayed in public settings. First-century BC figures like Hortensius (114–49 BC) and Lucullus (c. 110–57/6 BC) were renowned for the lavishness of their villa estates, filled with famous statues and paintings. Hortensius is said to have paid the huge sum of 144,000 sesterces for a painting of the Argonauts by the fourth-century BC artist Kydias which he displayed in a shrine in his villa at Tusculum.[18] It suggests his desire to show off his superb artistic taste and his possession of an Old Master painting.

Men like Hortensius also delighted in using their villas to escape from the world of business (*negotium*) into leisure (*otium*) and often staged elaborate dinner parties for their friends. These dinners could be immensely theatrical, and myth played a key role in this. Hortensius himself is said to have staged a dinner party in the game reserve of his villa in which he ordered that Orpheus be called. A man dressed as Orpheus, with a robe and harp, then began to sing. As soon as he blew a horn a throng of boars and deer gathered around the diners.[19] The effect was to transport the diners into the Thracian wilderness and the world of myth. A visual equivalent to this conceit can be seen in the painting which dominates the garden wall of the House of Orpheus in Pompeii (VI.14.20), showing Orpheus seated with his lyre amid a host of wild beasts (fig. 14.3).

Other mythological re-enactments at élite dinner parties include the famous Dinner of the Twelve Gods, when Augustus appeared dressed as the god Apollo (Suetonius, *Augustus* 70) and a dinner party in which Munatius Plancus is said to have played the role of the sea god Glaucus, performing a dance in which his naked body was painted blue, his head was encircled with reeds, and he wore a fish's tail![20] Even allowing for some exaggeration, these stories suggest the desire of the aristocracy to escape from the duties of everyday life into a fantasy world of mythological play-acting and grandiosity. These mythological masques continued into the imperial period, when we find the emperors themselves taking on the roles of heroes or gods, often in a manner which underlined their supreme power and authority. Statius (*Silvae* 4.2.10–11) records a public banquet hosted by the emperor Domitian which he likens to dining with Jupiter in heaven. While this might be poetic hyberbole, the emperor Commodus directly associated himself with the god Hercules: he added the god's name to his official titles and had a lion skin and club carried in front of him when he processed through the streets of Rome.[21] Dio's statement that he was even depicted in the guise of Hercules finds visual proof in a statue found in the Horti Lamiani, one of several vast villa parks on the outskirts of Rome which all gradually came under imperial ownership. This depicts the emperor Commodus with the lion skin and club of Hercules, holding the Apples of the Hesperides and originally flanked by two Tritons (fig. 14.4).

Slaves, too, could enhance the experience of mythological play-acting. The youths who acted as wine waiters were often compared to the mythical Ganymede, cupbearer to Jupiter, and found their sculptural equivalent in the numerous statues of 'sexy boys' that adorned lamp stands and decorated Roman villas.[22] The decoration of villas and gardens with satyrs, maenads, centaurs, and erotes, all of which appear in multiple versions from the excavations of Roman villas, created a conducive atmosphere for this play-acting, acting as a conduit into the world of myth.[23] The same sense of theatricality that emerges from élite dinners and recreation can also be seen in Roman public life, where executions sometimes took the form of mythological re-enactments. There, however, the figure of Orpheus met a grisly death at the claws of a wild bear rather than taming the beasts by his songs.[24]

Back in the villa, dinners were also the occasion for educated conversation and displays of competitive *paideia* (education, cultivation). This sort of display is amusingly satirized in Petronius' account of the dinner party given by Trimalchio in his *Satyricon*. The host's attempts to show off his education through discussion of the mythological scenes engraved on his silverware famously backfire when he refers, with stunning inaccuracy, to Cassandra killing her children and Daedalus shutting Niobe into the Trojan Horse (*Satyricon* 52). The *Saturnalia* of the second-century AD Greek satirist Lucian also gives a glimpse of the ways such silver vessels might have been viewed: diners are

Figure 14.4 Portrait of the emperor Commodus as Hercules.

imagined examining silver cups to determine their weight and discussing the accuracy of the stories depicted (*Saturnalia* 33). Some of the silver cups found in the House of the Menander at Pompeii were decorated with mythological scenes showing Venus and Mars and the Labours of Hercules and were probably designed to invite just such a response, indicating the host's wealth and education and prompting educated discussion.[25]

Visual cues for debate abounded in Roman *triclinia* (dining rooms), from the scenes on tableware to the mosaics on the floor, paintings on walls and sculptural decoration. The cave at Sperlonga is one of the best-known examples of a lavish villa *triclinium* and provides a good example of the ways that mythological representations could both provoke educated discussion and create an atmosphere of drama and excitement (fig. 14.5).[26] Excavations in the cave found the remains of four main sculptural groups probably dating from c. 30 BC as well as a number of other pieces from a variety of dates.[27] The main groups showed the Blinding of Polyphemus, placed in a recess at the back right of the cave; the figure of Scylla attacking Ulysses' (Odysseus') ship in the centre of the pool; and two groups placed either side of the entrance to the cave showing a warrior rescuing the body of a dead companion and

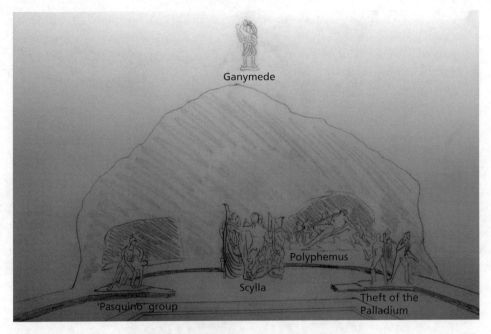

Figure 14.5   Reconstruction of the sculptural decoration of the cave at Sperlonga.

Diomedes and Ulysses stealing the statue of the Palladium from Troy. The choice of themes provokes discussion. Modern scholars have debated the literary models which lie behind the sculptures. The figures of Scylla and Polyphemus are a clear reference to Homer's *Odyssey* but others have suggested the influence of Ovid's *Metamorphoses* and Vergil's *Aeneid*.[28] Ancient viewers may also have discussed the appearance of these themes in literary works – a later ecphrastic (descriptive) inscription set up at the site specifically relates the sculptures to Vergil's epic.[29] Like later scholars they may also have discussed the moral messages and overall programme of the ensemble: Is the Ulysses represented here a figure to respect or a warning to avoid? How should we identify the two warriors in the rescue group? How did these statues link up to the rest of the sculptural display, such as the figure of Ganymede found outside the cave? Is there a punning warning about hospitality and the perils of drunkenness in the representation of the blinding of Polyphemus?

Rather than seeking to tie down the Sperlonga sculptures to one dominant programme or message we should admit that they seem to invite a multitude of readings depending on where one focuses one's attention. They were ideally placed to provoke the sorts of erudite discussions of which the Roman emperors and other members of the Roman élite seem so fond, as, for instance, at the dinner parties of the emperor Tiberius.[30] Yet as well as provoking intellectual discussion, the sculptures also facilitate an active immersion in a mythological realm. If we picture the figures lit up by lamps and flickering in the reflections in the water, we can imagine how the lines between sculpture and reality could have been blurred, enhancing the effect of transporting the guests back into the mythological past.

Programmatic Viewing in Domestic Wall-Painting

One of the major areas where we see an explosion of mythological images is in the painted decoration of houses. The vast majority of our evidence comes from the sites of Pompeii and Herculaneum, preserved by the eruption of Vesuvius in AD 79, though enough remains from houses at Rome and Ostia to suggest that Campania was fairly typical of its time. Pompeian wall painting is usually divided chronologically according to the Four Pompeian Styles first outlined by Mau.[31] Panels depicting figures ('figural panels') first appear in the late second style, at first in friezes along the top of the wall, such as the *Odyssey* landscapes from the Esquiline, and the *Iliad* frieze in the House of the Cryptoporticus at Pompeii. Later, central panels in the wall could be filled with large-scale figural images, such as the scenes of Polyphemus and Galatea and Argus and Io which decorated the central *tablinum* (office) in the House of Livia on the Palatine, dating from around 30 BC.

The real flowering of mythological painting, however, comes in the Third and Fourth styles, from the Augustan through to the Vespasianic periods. Mythological panels were placed at the centre of elaborate painted schemes in an effect reminiscent of public picture galleries (*pinacothecae*).[32] Whereas public porticoes were often hung with the paintings of Old Masters taken from the cities of Greece, private houses conveyed this sort of effect through the use of painted frescoes. The houses of Pompeii and Herculaneum abound with rooms where every wall is focused around a mythological panel. In some cases, as with third-style mythological landscapes, such as those in the House of the Orchard at Pompeii, the effect was to open the room out onto an imagined exterior world. In other cases, however, there seems to be an allusion to the display of famous Greek paintings, such as those which decorated public buildings, as well as the villas of the aristocracy.[33]

In the past these mythological panels were often interrogated for what they could tell us about the masterpieces of Greek painting, which have been almost entirely destroyed. Yet a closer look shows that even if models from pattern books were used to give a basic composition this was often altered by making changes to the setting and through the introduction of extra figures. Indeed, rather than being a series of individual copies of famous works from the past, the paintings in Pompeian houses often seem to have been deliberately combined as collections. We can look, then, at the motives lying behind these collections, and at the sorts of discussion and interpretation they could provoke.

Sometimes there is an evident thematic connection between a group of images. Three paintings in the *ala* (wing) off the *atrium* of the House of the Menander in Pompeii show different events from the story of the Fall of Troy – the arrival of the wooden horse before Troy, the priest Laocoön encircled by snakes, and Ajax's abduction of the priestess Cassandra as she clings to a statue of her patron goddess Athene.[34] A room in the so-called Villa Imperiale, just outside the walls of Pompeii, showed instead three events connected with the island of Crete. On the end wall the hero Theseus is shown victorious over the dead Minotaur, while on the left he is shown at a point later in the story as he abandons the sleeping Ariadne on the shores of Naxos after she had fled Crete with him. On the right wall another myth attached to Crete is shown: the body of the dead Icarus who fell to his death while escaping Crete on the wings constructed by his father Daedalus.[35]

In some cases thematic and compositional links could be combined, as in the *atrium* of the House of the Tragic Poet at Pompeii. A reconstruction of the original display (most of the panels are now in Naples or lost) shows that six figural panels decorated the room.[36] A number of these can be linked with the Trojan War – the wrath of Achilles, the taking of Briseis from Achilles, and Helen embarking on the ship that will take her to Troy. A fragment showing the naked Venus (Aphrodite) could have formed part of the scene of the Judgement of Paris, the ultimate cause of the war. The other two images, a scene of the goddess Juno (Hera) dressed as a bride and standing before Jupiter (Zeus) and a scene of Neptune's (Poseidon's) abduction of Amphitrite broaden the picture by introducing new themes. Some of the paintings are linked through compositional means, all three paintings on the eastern side of the *atrium* show standing draped women, two of them in front of seated male figures, respectively the figures of Juno and Jupiter, Briseis and Achilles, and Helen (probably with a seated figure of Paris, now lost). In addition to the thematic connections between the scenes, these compositional parallels also invite us to think about the images as contrasting examples of womanhood – a goddess, a concubine, and an adulterous queen.[37] The theme is continued in the rest of the decoration of the house – an image of the pious wife Alcestis appeared in the tablinum, while the decoration of the peristyle returned to the theme of the Trojan War in its representation of the sacrifice of Iphigenia.

The paintings in the House of the Tragic Poet are monumental and dramatic and combine thematic unity with compositional links. Elsewhere a house owner might combine drama in some rooms with lighter tones in other rooms. The House of the Vettii (Pompeii VI.15.1) is well known for the two

Figure 14.6   Wall paintings in room n in the House of the Vettii, Pompeii VI.15.1.

rooms opening off the peristyle with their collection of mythological paintings (rooms n and p). One shows on the end wall the death of Pentheus at
the hands of his maddened relatives, and on the right the punishment of
Dirce. These two scenes of violent death are accompanied on the left wall by
the image of the baby Hercules, who escapes death by strangling the snakes
which have been sent to kill him (fig. 14.6). In the companion room two
scenes of impiety are combined. We see Pasiphaë inspecting the wooden cow
which Daedalus has constructed to enable her to consummate her illicit love
for the bull and the punishment of Ixion for having attempted to rape Juno
(Hera). They are complemented by a third image showing a scene of salvation, the discovery of the sleeping Ariadne by the god Bacchus (Dionysus).
No one programme links these images and they have in the past been seen as
proof of the lack of education of the freedmen Vettii, who crammed in as
many references to myth as they possibly could, in a manner which some have
compared to that of Petronius' Trimalchio. Yet this is perhaps rather unfair on
the Vettii. Interpretations by scholars have seen a number of possible links
between the various paintings; it seems likely that they could have been specifically designed to provoke discussion of the contrasts and comparisons
between different situations.[38]

   These two rooms are focused around the display of the mythological panels. In their placement off the peristyle they were probably designed to be

lingered in by guests to the house who were here presented with miniature versions of public *pinacothecae*. The tone is one of grandeur and expense, designed to impress. Elsewhere in the house we find a lighter tone, as in the Cupid frieze which decorated a nearby reception room (oecus q). Elsewhere, mythological scenes reappear in smaller panels and seem designed for a more intimate viewing. In the small cubiculum d to the left of the entrance the abandoned Ariadne appears again. While the image in room p is full of antici-pation at the god's discovery of Ariadne here there is a more elegiac tone. Ariadne awakes to find herself alone while Theseus steals away in his ship at the top left. The scene is dominated by cool blues which reappear in the neighbouring wall, a scene of the love affair between Hero and Leander; Leander is shown swimming the Hellespont to reach his lover, locked up in her tower on the other side of the water. Both images show fishermen, quietly getting on with their daily lives as these tragic love affairs are in course. The painting that would have adorned the back wall of the room is now lost, but it may also have picked up the watery theme, perhaps showing Venus fishing, a scene popular in other Pompeian houses.

The quiet tone of these two panels, and their concentration on the love affairs of mythological figures is echoed in numerous other rooms in Pompeian houses. Narcissus is the most popular figure, usually shown sitting in an idyllic pastoral landscape either alone, or accompanied by the nymph Echo. Pendants to Narcissus include Endymion and Selene, Ganymede, Apollo with various lovers, Ariadne and satyrs and maenads, as well as other mythological lovers such as Pyramus and Thisbe.[39] These representations of famous love stories, occasionally happy (as with Perseus and Andromeda) but more often tragic, seem to have been immensely popular in Campania. They may have prompted debate and discussion, but they also served to set a tone for the rooms they decorated, elevating the experiences of daily life through the allusion to a world of intense eroticism, where love is celebrated but often brings destruc-tion in its wake. As we saw with mythological displays in villas, domestic paint-ings could be used to create a particular sort of atmosphere in the house, to provoke displays of learned erudition and to meditate upon the nature of human lives.

Displaying Myths in the Roman Empire

So far this account has been limited to the display of mythological images in Rome and Italy. However, the same range of mythological themes can be seen in the art of the Roman provinces; in mosaics, sculpture, and wall painting as well as silverware, glassware, and pottery. We often find mythological scenes used to reveal the education and status of the owner of the villa or house, tying him or her into the broader imperial elite which was partly defined by a thorough education in Greek and Latin literature.[40] This can be seen especially in mosaics. In the Villa at Lullingstone in Kent a mosaic image of the Rape of Europa is accompanied by an inscription alluding to Juno's enmity towards Aeneas, showing the owner's knowledge of Vergil's *Aeneid* and his flexible command of Greek mythology. Knowledge of the *Aeneid* is also asserted in the mosaic at Low Ham in Somerset with its scenes of Dido and Aeneas.[41]

Such references to specific literary texts are in fact fairly unusual. More commonly we find scenes of mythological episodes which were known through various sources.[42] These include the loves of gods and heroes as well as famous episodes from epic sages, such as the wrath of Achilles, the Judgement of Paris, or the Sacrifice of Iphigenia. Like the displays of paintings and sculpture already discussed, these made reference to the cultural knowledge of the host and helped to promote debate and discussion amongst guests. They also helped to provide models for human lives and interactions. In particular the concentration on erotic myths provide a number of paradigms for the relationship between the sexes, while the deeds of gods, heroes, and heroines also provided points of reference for particular virtues and vices.[43]

In other areas, particularly in the East where many of the myths were believed to have originally taken place, mythological representations could help to assert local senses of identity and individuality.[44] A corridor in the House of Menander at Daphne, a suburb of Antioch, was decorated with a mosaic showing the transformation of Daphne into a laurel tree. As well as being a pun on the house's location, this can also be seen as a proud assertion of the city's belief that the encounter between Apollo and Daphne had taken place there, rather than in Arkadia in Greece.[45]

Conclusions

From their display in houses, temples, baths, and public spaces we can see that myths fulfilled a variety of roles and offered different possibilities for interpretation in the Roman world. They opened up access to a wider realm of the imagination, helped to bond communities together in a show of shared culture, and also offered models for human lives and behaviour. As we will see in CH. 16, they were also displayed in funerary contexts, particularly on the marble sarcophagi which became popular in the second century AD. Here too we see the flexibility of myth to offer *exempla* and models, commenting on human life and also revealing the interests, values, and beliefs of those who chose this form of decoration to commemorate their lives and deaths.

FURTHER READING

On the introduction of Greek art to Rome see Pollitt 1978; P. Zanker 1979. On Roman copies (including, but not limited to mythological images) see Gazda (2002) and Perry (2005). The central study of Augustus' use of art remains P. Zanker 1988, but see also Galinsky 1996. On the Palatine Temple of Apollo see Kellum 1985 and Lefèvre 1989. For statues in baths and villas see respectively Manderscheid 1981 and Neudecker 1988, both in German but with useful catalogues. The sculptural display of the Baths of Caracalla is discussed by Marvin 1983 and DeLaine 1997, Appendix 4. The literature on Sperlonga is extensive, but Ridgway 2000; Weis 2000; and Beard and Henderson 2001 (74–82) provide good introductions in English. Early work on programmes of mythological paintings was done by Schefold (1952; 1962) and Thompson (1960; 1960–1). More recently see Brilliant 1984 (ch. 2); Bergmann 1994, 1995, 1996, 1999; and Lorenz 2008. Clarke 1991 and Leach 2004 also discuss mythological paintings in their examination of domestic decoration. The decoration of individual houses is Pompeii is catalogued in detail in Baldassare 1990–2003. On mythological mosaics see Lancha 1997; Muth 1998 (with English summary at 346–50); and Bowersock 2006 (ch. 2). For more general accounts of paintings and mosaics see Ling 1991 and Dunbabin 1999. For the iconography of different myths see *LIMC*.

NOTES

A British Academy Small Research Grant funded my initial research in Rome while the University of Warwick and the Arts and Humanities Research Council funded the leave during which the two chapters published here were written. I am grateful to all institutions for their support.

1. The Latin, of course, for Herakles. As this chapter is told from a Roman perspective, the Latin forms of *mythical* proper names are used, in contrast to most other chapters. (KD)
2. Pollitt (1978).
3. On connoisseurship see Pollitt (1978); on decoration (with discussion of Cicero's collection of statues) see Marvin (1993), and Neudecker (1988); a good overview is given by Koortbojian (2002).
4. B. Bergmann (1995: esp. 94–8).
5. P. Zanker (1979).
6. Pliny, *Natural History* 36.25.
7. La Rocca (1985).
8. Pliny, *Natural History* 36.28.
9. Kellum (1985); P. Zanker (1988: 85–7).

10. For discussion see Lefèvre (1989: 12–16); Galinsky (1996: 220–2); differently, Kellum (1985: 174–5).
11. Kellum (1985: 170–1); Favro (1996: 100).
12. Galinsky (1996: 222–4).
13. Pliny, *Natural History* 36.33–4.
14. Pliny, *Natural History* 36.33.
15. Coarelli (1993); Grimal (1984: 157, n. 6); La Rocca (1998: 229–39).
16. Marvin (1983); Gasparri (1983–4); DeLaine (1997: 265–7).
17. See most recently von den Hoff (2004: 108–11), who suggests that images of Skylla and Medea were also displayed here.
18. Pliny, *Natural History* 35.130.
19. Varro, *de re rustica (On countryside management)* 3.13
20. Velleius Paterculus 2.83.2.
21. Cassius Dio 73.15–17.
22. Bartman (2002).
23. See Tacitus, *Annals* 11.31 on the Bacchic grape harvest celebrated by the empress Messalina.
24. Martial, *Book of Spectacles* 21; Coleman (1990: esp. 62–3).
25. Painter (2001).
26. Amongst the extensive literature see A. Stewart (1977); Kuttner (2003: 117–35).
27. Dating: Kunze (1996: 175–83); accepted by A. Stewart (2000: 100); rejected by Weis (2000: 137–9).
28. Weis (2000) gives a brief review.
29. Squire (2007).
30. Suetonius, *Tiberius* 70.
31. Mau (1882); the best overview in English is Ling (1991).
32. Leach (2004: 132–52).
33. The Elder Philostratos' *Imagines* (Paintings) is set in one such villa, in a portico inset with panel paintings by a number of different artists; pref. 5.
34. Ling and Ling (2005: pls 6–10).
35. Leach (1988: 381–5).
36. See B. Bergmann (1994) for reconstruction.
37. B. Bergmann (1994: 245–6). For a comparison with the programme formed by a set of mythological reliefs, the Spada reliefs, see Newby (2002).
38. See esp. Clarke (1991: 222–7, fig. 131).
39. For a list of combinations see Thompson (1960: 151–60).
40. On myths on silverware as a sign of *paideia* in Late Antiquity, see Leader-Newby (2004: 123–71).
41. On mythological mosaics in Britain see Scott (2000: 113–30).
42. Lancha (1997) collects mosaics which make reference to literary *paideia*.
43. See especially Muth (1998).
44. On myths on public architecture in Asia Minor see Newby (2003).
45. Pausanias 8.20.1–4; Philostratos, *Life of Apollonius* 1.16; Libanios, *Orations* 11.94–6; Levi (1947: 1.198–216, esp. 211–4); on expressions of local identity in the Antioch mosaics see Newby (2007).

CHAPTER FIFTEEN

The Myth that Saves: Mysteries and Mysteriosophies

Ken Dowden

As sin is the greatest evil, being the root and source of all evil, Sacred Scripture uses the word 'salvation' mainly in the sense of liberation of the human race or of individual man from sin and its consequences.

Maas, 1912

Preservation from destruction or failure; in eschatology, deliverance from sin and eternal damnation.

Borrmans, 2008

This chapter starts with a large word: *soteriological*. Soteriological myth is mythology connected with salvation: it is the myth that saves. The story of Christ, and in particular of his crucifixion and resurrection, viewed from the perspective of the mythologist, is a soteriological myth. Gnostic stories of the fall and return of the soul to its celestial origins are soteriological myths. If the Greco-Egyptian goddess Isis and the Romano-Persian god Mithras and the Greco-Phrygian dying god Attis offer you salvation, then they are in the business of soteriology and so is their mythology, where we know it. Salvation is so fundamental a concept today that it is interesting and useful to see how it emerged in the Greek and Roman worlds, and that is what this chapter does, following the path of mythology.

A Companion to Greek Mythology, First Edition. Edited by Ken Dowden and Niall Livingstone.
© 2014 John Wiley & Sons Ltd. Published 2014 by John Wiley & Sons Ltd.

The *Homeric Hymn to Demeter* and the Eleusinian Mysteries

The oldest Greek myth in this soteriological tradition is the story of Demeter and Persephone, and our oldest version of that myth is the one told in the *Homeric Hymn to Demeter*. It is Homeric because Greeks thought it was by Homer, the author of the *Iliad* and *Odyssey*. In fact it cannot be, and neither can any of the other 'Homeric' hymns. But this hymn appears to be fairly old all the same, possibly a little earlier than 600 BC. Demeter is the goddess responsible for the fertile land – for instance, her civilized gift of wheat – and for the fertility, and more generally lives, of women. Her name was taken to mean 'Earth-Mother', though it is somewhat dubious how *De-* can mean 'earth'. The Homeric hymn is firmly focused on events at Eleusis, a cult site of Demeter on the coast around fifteen kilometres north-west of Athens. It was clearly composed for that cult.

The hymn tells how Demeter's daughter, here 'Kore' (the 'Daughter, Girl', i.e., of Demeter) but known to us by the name Persephone, is, with the connivance of her father Zeus, abducted by her uncle Hades, lord of the Underworld, and becomes his wife.

The abduction is only the prelude. What follows is the iconic search of Demeter for her daughter. The rites at Eleusis were known as the (Eleusinian, of course) Mysteries, a word used quite differently from the sense in which we use it: a *Mystery* is, and means, a 'secret rite', for which you require a special initiation and become a *mystes* (plural *mystai*). And when now the goddess Hekate appears, torch in hand, to help Demeter in her search, this is because in the blackness of night the *mystai* search, torch in hand, too. In her search, Demeter arrives at the palace of Keleos, king of Eleusis, and takes on the job of nurse to Demophon, the son of Keleos and his wife Metaneira. By night she burns off his mortality in the fire, but Metaneira pries on this secret and the result is that Demophon's prospects of immortality are lost. Demeter insists on the building of a temple at Eleusis and she retires there. Meanwhile, thanks to Demeter, the crops do not grow, and Zeus sends Hermes to her. She shall have Persephone back, but only for two-thirds of the year, as Persephone has consumed a pomegranate seed offered to her by Hades. And the hymn, a few lines before the end, turns to consider the Mysteries of Eleusis that Demeter hands down to Keleos and the other leaders at Eleusis:

> Venerable rites which there is no way one may transgress or discover
> Or utter, for a great reverence for the gods checks the voice.
> Blessed he who of men on the earth has seen these things,
> But he who is uninitiated in the rites, who has no share, never has the like
> For his portion when he is dead and gone beneath the squalid dark.

Homeric Hymn to Demeter, 478–82[1]

This is a remarkable religious development which has involved shifting the meaning of a key myth. The myth of Persephone's abduction, Demeter's search, and the marriage (on terms) to Hades has its home otherwise in the Thesmophoria, the very widespread festival that was celebrated by citizen women and their daughters in various Greek cities. Indeed, the purpose of Demeter and Kore in this myth, so far as one can tell, seems to be to mirror the role of woman and daughter and to work out the anxieties underlying the institution of marriage. At the same time, these issues are related to the particular nature of agricultural fertility and growth cycles. There is a dead period in the year when crops do not grow, and that is juxtaposed to Persephone's being in Hades' house while Demeter searches for her and lets crops die. But Persephone will be recovered for a while, just as crops will grow again. Extended then to the human race as a whole, the myth depicts the special nature of human immortality, that we are (as a Roman author was later to say) 'individually mortal, but in our collectivity as a whole species we go on for ever, undergoing the change of substituting one generation for another'.[2]

The Eleusinian myth too insists on the mortality of the human race through the figure of Demophon. It is no longer the myth of women, however, but rather one which has somehow been developed to address mankind as a whole, male and female alike. This is a change which was assisted by two key developments in the sixth century BC. First, was the regulation, organization, and systematization of the religion of Athens and its outlying villages (Eleusis maybe relatively newly amongst them). Second, was the impact of new thinking about souls and death, characteristic of Pythagoreans and pseudonymous literature (by 'Mousaios' or 'Orpheus', cf. CH. 4). Now the myth had taken on something of the quality of a *katabasis*, a descent to and return from the Underworld, and it became more explicitly about the conquest of death and the achievement of a future for men that had hitherto been terminally mortal. No longer would it be enough for men's souls to linger on in the Underworld of Homer, 'powerless skulls' who screeched like bats (*Odyssey* 11.49, 24.5–6). Nor would it be enough for them to conduct a pale image of their life on earth, fighting each other in law courts presided over by Minos (*Odyssey* 11.568–71). Yes, man will never be immortal like a god – it is not in his nature and that is why Metaneira *looked*. But under the protection of Demeter, and with restraint of human curiosity and strict observance of the ritual, something special awaits humans after death: something that mystics in classical Athens represented as a banquet of the blessed, and that Plato condemned wryly as eternal drunkenness (*Republic* 363c). But whatever the secret promise amounted to, soteriological myth had been born.

Visiting the Underworld

Just as the myth of Persephone could be converted to serve soteriological purposes, so in principle could any myth that involved the confrontation with death and in particular a descent to the Underworld, a *katabasis*. The oldest *katabasis* known to us is, of course, that in the Mesopotamian traditions of Gilgamesh (see CH. 19). It may be under the influence of this type of tradition that Greek epic tradition had developed, before the time of Homer, a *katabasis* for Herakles in which, with the help of Athene and Hermes, he retrieved the hound of Hades (Kerberos; *Odyssey* 11.623–6). Some tradition of *katabasis* must also underlie the colouring of Priam's journey to Achilles' tent, guided through the dark across the river by Hermes, to retrieve the body of Hektor in *Iliad* 24. Odysseus' own descent to the Underworld is rather disappointing as he does not really descend there – he crosses the River Okeanos and digs a trench for the dead to come up to him (for the most part). Theseus, like his model Herakles, would have the labour of a *katabasis* when he assisted his comrade Peirithoös in the latter's foolhardy descent to abduct Persephone herself. Various versions of this story apparently circulated, but the usual one has Herakles go down (again!) to rescue Theseus. Theseus seems to have been so tightly trapped in a 'Chair of Forgetfulness' that part of him was left behind, and that is why Athenians to this day have small bottoms.[3]

In later tradition, and particularly today, we know the tradition that Orpheus made a *katabasis* to fetch his wife Eurydike back from the Underworld (and failed by *looking* at the last moment: cf. Metaneira in the *Homeric Hymn*). This would seem an ideal myth to provide a grounding for the mystic philosophy of thinkers peddling 'Orphic' texts, but it would appear that this was not its early use (see Radcliffe Edmonds in CH. 4). This is in spite of the fact that Plato knew the story in the earlier fourth century BC (*Symposium* 179b–d), that Euripides probably did in the later fifth century (*Alcestis* 357–62), and that Aeschylus quite possibly did in his *Bassarids* in the earlier fifth century.[4] We should therefore hesitate to construct any pairing of this myth with soteriological hopes, and the myth of Eleusis thus turns out to be quite distinctive.

Resurrections: Dionysos and the Titans

Other myths too deal with the confrontation with death and survival or rebirth. Pelops – whose name survives in the 'Island of Pelops', the Peloponnese, and who stands at the beginnings of Argive genealogy as the ancestor of Agamemnon – is butchered by his own father Tantalos and served, repulsively, to the gods. But the gods bring him back to life, replacing his original shoulder (which had been eaten) with a distinctive ivory one. Pelops may thus be special, but again the myth is not used for soteriological purposes.

More promising is another cannibal crime, that of the Titans, who according to an 'Orphic' myth (see CH. 4) tore the baby Dionysos limb from limb, in a bizarre transposition of the dismemberment, *sparagmos*, of wild animals by his worshippers, the Bacchae. They tore him, then, into seven pieces, boiled him, roasted him, and (at least according to later authors) ate some of him.[5] Like Pelops, and maybe in imitation of him, Dionysos had to be recreated by the gods – and the Titans were blasted into soot by Zeus's thunderbolt. Thus, Dionysos dies and is reborn in this deviant myth, perhaps put together by Onomakritos at the end of the sixth century BC: at any rate, Pausanias (second century AD) claimed that 'Onomakritos, taking over the name of the Titans from Homer, put together rites (*orgia*) for Dionysos and in his poetry said the Titans were responsible for Dionysos' sufferings'.

Pindar (fifth century BC) speaks of 'those (souls) from whom Persephone will accept the penalty for (the) ancient Grief' (F 133). This slain Dionysos seems to be her son, and well might she grieve in that case. Some of this scenario may also underlie some comments of Plato in the mid-fourth century BC. People who overdo freedom eventually show 'disregard for oaths and assurances and overall for gods, as these people display and imitate the "ancient Titanic nature", arriving at that same situation all over again' (*Laws* 701c); and if you rob a temple it is 'as a result of ancient crimes unpurgeable by men' (*Laws* 854b). It is not, however, until much later, in a more mystic and soteriologically inclined age, that we discover unambiguous interpretations of this myth. Then we find the Middle-Platonic philosopher Plutarch (first century AD) telling us that 'the irrational, undisciplined and violent in us is not divine, but daimonic and the ancients called it Titans' (*On Eating Meat* 996c). And we will find this fully internalized in the Neoplatonists: Iamblichos (third–fourth century AD) reveals how, he says, the early Pythagoreans 'frequently used to encourage each other not to tear apart the god within them';[6] and Damaskios (fifth–sixth century AD), authoritative amongst late Neoplatonic commentators, explains the impact of the ancient Titanic nature on man:

> The Titanic life is an irrational one which tears apart our reason.
>
> It is better to consider it as existing everywhere, given that it begins with gods, namely the Titans. And as a result the appearance of independent reasoning and, as it were, being exclusively under one's own control, not under that of better or worse is generated in us by the Titans, inasmuch as we are tearing apart the Dionysos within us, smashing our uniform nature, the nature that is in a way in partnership with the better or worse. In this condition we are Titans, but when we agree on the alternative (the uniform nature), we become absolutely complete Dionysoses.[7]

This may not be a descent and a return, but this philosophical ethical direction is based on a myth almost of 'original sin', of a sin that must be purged before the soul may achieve its objective of what a Christian would call salvation. This material is very fragmentary, and there is always a danger of importing what seem from our perspective satisfactorily religious ideas too early. But whatever the precise case here, in the centuries of the Common Era it became possible to build clearly soteriological pictures on these archaic foundations, and even in classical Athens 'purifications' had been hawked round Athens by door-to-door salesmen. What, after all, did you need to be purified from?

Retreading Old Mythology: Odysseus and Salvation

Readers of mythology became more receptive to soteriological ideas during the Hellenistic period (324–31 BC), for two reasons (which both had their seeds in the classical period). The first was a response to the objections which philosophers had raised to myth: in defence, interpreters of Homer denied that these myths were literally true and turned instead to *allegorical* interpretations of mythology. If Homer had the gods fight each other in his presentation of mythology, this was not acceptable because gods, from a philosophical point of view, just could not be believed to indulge in the brutality of war with each other. The divine was not at war with itself – how could it be? On the other hand, if you interpreted the conflict of Hephaistos with the River Xanthos as being a way of talking about the contrast between the elements of fire and water in nature, then some insight into physical philosophy was provided by the poet and his mythology.

The second change was the increasing interest of thinkers in the individual, in the moral quality of the life they led, and in the prospects of their soul in an afterlife. The Hellenistic period saw a boom in ethical philosophy. Literature had always provided examples for discussing ethics and this leads in the end to the deliberate creation of literature in the light of ethical and then soteriological concerns. Thus the voyages of Odysseus could be interpreted allegorically as an image of the soul amid danger in this life struggling for a way to reach its true home. So 'in moral exegesis, the Sirens represent flattery, or pleasure, or poetry, or study, or contemplation … In mystic exegesis they are the music of the spheres whose charm influences the souls of the dead who wander in space' (Buffière).[8] Both these new directions invited the ingenuity of interpreters – and many Greek thinkers and performers had a weakness for the exploitation of ingenuity, in a way that can surprise modern readers who hold a more puritanical view of the role of truth, accuracy, and sheer evidence in research.

Thus over time a mythic vision developed that looked for ulterior signifi-cance in the mythology, and the *Odyssey* in particular became viewed as a myth developed by the most canonical of all Greek poets, Homer, to show the nature of man's life and the choices he must make in order to reach his true home. How this came about is a hard story to tell, as we lack evidence at the beginning of this trend of interpretation and only pick up hints. It is later, in the hands of the Neoplatonist philosophers (third–sixth centuries AD), that the picture emerges clearly.[9] So, for clarity, however odd it may seem, I am going to tell this story backwards, starting in the third century AD and rolling back to the first century BC.

Plotinos (AD 205–70), the single most outstanding Neoplatonic philoso-pher, sees the destination of the soul as the world Beyond, somewhere clear of the shifting uncertainties of this world that is characterized by *genesis*, the proc-ess of things coming into existence and passing out of existence, by instability and uncertainty, and by the lack of any real knowledge. The Beyond is where we belong. 'The soul wishes to escape evil: it must flee from here' (Plotinos, *Enneads* 1.2.1, paraphrasing Plato, *Theaitetos* 176a). 'So', he asks, 'what is the nature of the flight'? Haunted by this thought, Plotinos returns to it at 1.6.8 but now in a mythic environment, where the fate of Narkissos, swept into the depths by an illusory image, shifts kaleidoscopically to an Odyssean Hades:

> So too, one that is held by material beauty and will not break free shall be pre-cipitated, not in body but in Soul, down to the dark depths loathed of the Intellective-Being, where, blind even in the Lower-World, he shall have com-merce only with shadows, there as here.
>
> 'Let us flee then to the beloved Fatherland': this is the soundest counsel. But what is this flight? How are we to gain the open sea? For Odysseus is surely a parable to us when he commands the flight from the sorceries of Circe or Calypso – not content to linger for all the pleasure offered to his eyes and all the delight of sense filling his days. (Plotinos, *Enneads* 1.6.8, tr. MacKenna)

The quotation, 'Let us flee then to the beloved Fatherland' may verbally come from *Iliad* 2.140, but the formula of return 'to the fatherland' is the-matic to the *Odyssey* and appears no less than thirteen times there.[10] In differ-ent, and sometimes inconsistent ways, as M. J. Edwards (1988) has shown, Platonists turn to the experience of Odysseus to depict the striving of the Platonic soul immersed in the world of *genesis*. Thus Porphyry (c. 234–c. 310) depicts his master and mentor Plotinos himself as metaphorically swimming through a churning sea to a shore where he will fall asleep (like Odysseus on Scheria, *Odyssey* 5.399–493).[11]

This sort of view seems to find a literary reflection when, sometime in the third–fourth century AD, Heliodoros of Emesa wrote the greatest of the ancient Greek novels. His heroine Charikleia, to all appearances a Greek, must *return to her real homeland*, Ethiopia, and must at one stage dress, with her mentor, Kalasiris, in a disguise of rags (*Aithiopika* 6.10–11; cf. *Odyssey* 13.434–8). The novel even opens (1.1) with an enigmatic scene of slaughter at a banquet to awaken the reader's Odyssean range of reference (cf. *Odyssey* 22). The person who understands soteriological myth will benefit from this novel: 'This book, my friends, is like the *kykeon* (porridge-mix) of Circe: it turns those who read it profanely towards the lewd behaviour of pigs; but those who are philosophers like Odysseus it leads mystically to a higher truth. The book is educational and teaches philosophy.' This is a reported account of a Byzantine guru known as 'Philip the Philosopher', who may possibly date to the twelfth century AD.[12] But his era is practically irrelevant: with our classical tools we can see how the soteriological myth of the *Odyssey* had become so well established that its new 'meaning' might well be reflected by an author of Heliodoros' time.

But we do not have to wait this long for the myth to become established. Winding the clock back to the late second century AD, the Middle-Platonist Maximus of Tyre had recalled the very same passage of the *Odyssey* that Porphyry had conjured up.[13] Maximus sees the key moment in it as being where the sea goddess Leukothea presents Odysseus with her veil (*Odyssey* 5.333–53): 'When the soul falls into this turmoil and gives herself up to be carried on the unmanageable waves, she swims a sea that is hard to swim out of – until Philosophy herself receives her, supplying the reasoning that is hers just as Leukothea supplied the veil to Odysseus' (Maximus of Tyre, *Discourses* 11.10h). The mysterious veil has now become an image of salvation. And Porphyry also refers to another influential older contemporary of Maximus, Numenios of Apameia (mid-second century AD), as already thinking along similar lines:

> I do not think people like Numenios were off-target when they took Homer's Odysseus in the *Odyssey* as an image for someone making their way through successive births (*geneseis*, i.e., into the world) and so finally reaching those outside with no experience of any huge waves or the sea:
>
> > *till you reach those men who do not know the sea*
> > *nor eat food mixed with salt*
> > (*Odyssey* 11.122–3)
>
> The ocean and the sea and the huge wave, in Plato too, is what the material world is. (Numenios, F 33 (in Porphyry, *Cave of the Nymphs* Section 34))

When, then, was this 'meaning' of the *Odyssey* first known? Around AD 100, the Platonic philosopher Plutarch, if the fragment is correctly attributed,[14] was arguing as follows in a lost work about Circe's transmutation of Odysseus' companions into pigs:

> The myth presents an allegory (*ainigma*, literally 'riddle') of the doctrines of Pythagoras and Plato about the soul, to the effect that the soul is indestructible by nature and eternal, but not free from suffering or change. In the supposed moments of dissolution and death it undergoes change and refit into other types of body and in the case of pleasure it pursues that type which is applicable and appropriate to the similarity and practice of that lifestyle. (Plutarch, F 200 Sandbach)

By following education and philosophy, Plutarch continues, the soul can escape slipping into a bestial condition. Hermes, with his golden wand, represents the *logos* (reason) that keeps you from Circe's brew, the *kykeon*, that mixes everything in a swirl that can only lead back to *genesis* (rebirth into the world).

Somewhere about here, maybe, belongs the *Homeric Problems* of a certain Herakleitos (on whom see also CH. 6 in this volume). The text probably belongs to the first century AD, but could be a century earlier. What it presents is a defence of Homer's apparent impiety towards the gods – against notably Plato (Section 76) – by the demonstration that his account is at every turn allegorical. Most of his energy is expended on the *Iliad*, but elements of the *Odyssey* receive some attention: Athene is sent to Telemachos because he has now reached the age of reason (Section 61). Proteus, the shape-shifter whom Menelaos had to capture in order to discover how to return home (4.351–425), turns out (Section 65) to represent the beginnings of the world (*prōtos* = 'first'), when things had not yet assumed their final shape – that moment at the beginning of the universe so memorably captured by Ovid (*Metamorphoses* 1.5–20).[15] The Phaiakes on Scheria (e.g., *Odyssey* 8 with its games and entertainments), somewhat surprisingly, are men 'possessed by pleasure' (Section 69.7). And the whole wandering of Odysseus you will find (he says) is allegorical (Section 70). Even the bag of winds given to Odysseus by Aiolos (10.19–20) simply denotes that the man who has in his wisdom mastered astronomy knows how to make nature work with him (Section 70). This is a virtuoso display of allegory, and though it starts from a shared groundwork (*Odyssey* allegory of life, Kirke a threat to the wise man), there is a fantastic amount of improvisation that does not repeat common views and is indeed designed to impress us by its novelty. This has something in common with authors of the late first century AD, but it would take us too far beyond our scope to go further into this now.[16] What matters for us here is the impression we gain of a shared understanding that the *Odyssey* is about the individual's life and ethical choices.

Though it does not deal with the *Odyssey*, something of this climate of ideas is illuminated by an underground building at Rome of perhaps rather earlier in the century (the 40s AD are suggested).[17] This is the so-called Basilica (or Hypogaeum) at the Porta Maggiore, in Rome, which was discovered when foundations for the Ostia railway line were being dug, in April 1917.[18] These days you fight your way through trams and other traffic to find it has been closed since the late 1980s. Inside, there are stucco decorations depicting mythology with what appears to be a very soteriological tint. On the roof of the nave is a Ganymede being carried off to Olympos, an image of the rise of the soul to heaven with divine assistance and love. On the apse appears a figure leaping down from a rock to her death, her robes billowing. This appears to be the poet Sappho as she leapt, lovelorn, from the rock at Leukas. This story could, on the one hand, be immortalized as a story of unhappy love, as Ovid treated it in *Heroides* 15. On the other, it could be read as the soul committing itself to god, as a 'Pythagorean symbol of salvation' (as Carcopino once expressed it) amid other depictions of Eros catching butterflies (*psychai*, also 'souls'). Sappho's leap thus becomes the moment at which worldly love is transmuted into love for the divine.[19] It is much the same moment as Psyche's exposure on the rock to be wafted down by the Zephyrs to Cupid (her source of salvation). The interpretations are not universally accepted, but the mythological images are certainly suggestive, leading naturally to the view of Cumont and Carcopino that this was a 'Neopythagorean' meeting place. (Numenios, too, is frequently called 'Pythagorean'.)

At much the same time as this building was constructed, we find the Jewish tradition affected by this type of interpretation. In Alexandria, Philo, who we know went on an embassy to the emperor Gaius (Caligula, AD 37–41), wrote a massive commentary (in Greek) on the Pentateuch (the first five books of the Old Testament) allegorizing every last detail, and evidently following the manner of interpreters of Homer. So, when in Genesis (12.1–3) God instructs Abraham to leave his land, his kin and his father's home and move to the land that he shall show him, this is an allegory of salvation (*soteria*).[20] His 'land' represents the body (which all good Platonic philosophers wish to escape); his 'kin' are the senses (and we wish to leave the world of sense-perception, too); and the father's home represents the power of speech in which our higher intelligence (*nous*) resides in this world, but which in itself is a distraction from the spiritual realities that we should be contemplating. This may seem far-fetched, but Philo's writing is imbued with a passion and genuine religious devotion that is animated by this way of reading the text, and as a result the sacred scripture gains a soteriological depth even more appropriate to it than, perhaps, to Homer. But the quests are constantly the same, quests for salvation and the true home. Abraham must leave his world and seek a new home. Odysseus must leave Troy and find his true home, Ithaca. A particular story-type haunts the cultural imagination of these times and myth gains in meaning and resonance as a result. Philo was by no means inventing this sort of approach for himself when discussing Abraham. The Platonic approach must already exist in the interpretation of Homer for him to deploy it on the Old Testament.[21] Thus this method of interpretation is present from the beginnings of Middle Platonic philosophy and is

likely to have formed a significant current in the discussion of Homer significantly before Philo, which drives it back to at least the first century BC.

One Roman author writing an epic in the 30s and 20s BC is worth consideration in this light. Vergil, in his *Aeneid*, may indeed depict the effective
foundation of Rome and the Roman character, and he may indeed promote a
political mission partly relating to Augustus' regime and its moral and political
vision of itself. The *Aeneid* is also, however, rather philosophical and we know
that Vergil mixed in philosophical circles. The journey of Aeneas carries with
it the associations of the journey of Odysseus as it was perceived in Vergil's
time. So we should perhaps pause when Mercury descends to advise Aeneas to
leave Dido: this is, in its way, the Greek Hermes, the allegorized *logos*
('Reason'), descending from heaven to renew his awareness of his purpose in
life, like Hermes saving Odysseus from the *kykeon*, or like the 'divine *logos*'
that benefits Jacob in the world of sense-perception, which is what the place
Haran means (so Philo, *On Dreams* 1.68–70, interpreting Genesis 11–12).
The larger forces of reason and the irrational that prompt Aeneas' mission and
interrupt it are echoed in the divine apparatus by Jupiter and Juno. Of course,
we need to be careful not to be too wooden about such interpretation: it is
one dimension of a profoundly rich text, not a magic key.

Vergil's contemporary Horace seems also to be affected by this type of
philosophical discussion in his *Epistles*, where his comments seem too sustained to be merely the whimsical finding of a message in a famous text:

> Then again, for the power of virtue and wisdom,
> (Homer) set forth a useful example for us in Odysseus
> … unsinkable in the waves of adversity.
> You knew the songs of the Sirens and the cups of Circe
> – if he had foolishly and greedily drunk them with his companions,
> he would have been disgusting and demented under a whore of a mistress,
> he would have had the life of a filthy dog or a filth-loving pig.
> (Horace, *Epistles* 1.2.17–18, 22–6)

So the re-reading of Homer's *Odyssey* not only as profound or philosophical but
as a guide to life and salvation, as soteriological myth, is an increasingly significant factor in Greek and Roman culture. And it shows how mythology could be
accorded a new significance and live up to new demands on text and narrative.

New Mythologies: Gnostics and Others

There is no reason to suppose that what Philo did would have seemed a stunt
or an oddity: he does seem known and absorbed to some extent by certain
(later) Christians, for instance, Origen, and he did give a learned account of

the scriptures that served to put them on a par with Greek philosophers. From this point on, the role of (largely Platonic) philosophy would grow in Christian and other religious traditions. So, the myth of the Good Samaritan depicts a man going down from Jerusalem to Jericho who falls amongst brigands and is left for dead but for the intervention of a passing Samaritan (Luke 10.30–3). At least by the second century AD this was being read as a tale of the Fall of Man from heaven (Jerusalem) to this world (Jericho), where he is attacked by the powers and temptations of this world (brigands) but is saved by Jesus (the Samaritan).[22] And on the larger scale, the Christian story of Jesus' birth, life, crucifixion, resurrection, and ascension is an important portrayal of the figure of the suffering god that recurs in soteriological religions, starting in the case of our Greek world with the myth of Demeter at Eleusis. These myths stand in some relation to the life of devotees as they understand that life. They pattern their life as one of suffering sustained by the hope of a better afterlife and maybe even, in some cases, a kind of immortality. It then becomes important, as this vision develops, to adopt a belief that this world is not our true home. The religion of Demeter at Eleusis had not yet reached this stage, but Plato already had in the fourth century BC, as had the Pythagoreans before him. So, too, did the reinterpreted Homer of the last century BC.

An immediate offshoot of the Judaeo-Christian and Platonic traditions in the second century AD was what we refer to as 'Gnosticism'. This group of thinkers and cults, who privileged *gnosis* (special, indeed arcane, 'knowledge') was often in the penumbra of Christianity and hard to distinguish from it at the time: Valentinus (active in Rome, AD 140–60), one of the first Gnostics with whom we are concerned, is sometimes said to have been in the running for Bishop of Rome (i.e., pope). His younger contemporary Irenaeus, Bishop of Lyon (c. 130–c. 200), took the trouble to write *Against the Heresies* specifically to distance Gnostics from what he claimed was the authentic Christian Church. What is typical of these thinkers is the construction of very elaborate and complicated hierarchies of divine beings to form the set for a drama of the soul falling into this life. There is a figure, *Sophia* ('Wisdom'), who through some initial sin, such as a premature and unauthorized desire to know God, falls into this world (or calls into being a duplicate of herself to do so); there, beset by emotions, she suffers and wanders until she can be recovered from it by a redeemer (the Christos – the 'anointed', Christ).[23] Finally, all is put right and the Christos and Sophia, now back in the *Pleroma* ('Fullness', i.e., heaven), are married, as are other spirits, and the *Pleroma* is restored thereby to its original unity. But in the meantime the world has been created.

What I have presented here is a considerable simplification of a mythology that includes a whole strange new theogony and rationale for the universe, and which also has considerable variants between different systems as they seek to improve on earlier models, particularly that of Valentinus. But it serves to show recurrent features of soteriological myth. The duplication of the feminine and its suffering, with two Sophias, in its way recalls the fragmentation of the feminine in the division between Demeter and her daughter Persephone. It is the role of the daughter to undergo the principal suffering. But the story of a fallen daughter and her recovery by a redeemer appears again in the celebrated story of Cupid and Psyche in the Roman novel of Apuleius, the *Golden Ass* (c. 150/170 AD). There it forms the centrepiece of a novel that at least raises philosophical and religious issues, though scholars vary in their opinion of how seriously they are meant to be taken. Psyche (like Cinderella) is the youngest of three daughters. She is exposed on a rock, supposedly for a monster to take her (like Andromeda). But the Zephyrs waft her down to the palace of Cupid (Eros), god of love, and there she cohabits with him at night in a golden palace under the sole condition that she may not look upon him (like Sophia's offence of wanting to know God). But her sisters (Philo would tell us her kin represent sense-perception) egg her on to look upon Cupid, and she does so – at which point she is abandoned and must wander and suffer (like Sophia). She searches for him (inverting Demeter's search for Persephone or the search of the Christos for Sophia), undergoes trials, but eventually fails in her tasks and falls into a sleep like death. Then Cupid (like the Christos) appears and rescues her, and they are married on Olympos. It is a pretty story, told in what we perceive as a fairy-tale register, but it is pretty clearly also a soteriological myth, and no less a person than Plotinos refers to 'myths of Eros and Psyche'. *Psyche* of course means 'soul'.

Isis and Osiris

At the end of his novel, Apuleius presents us with a picture of the religion of the Egyptian goddess Isis. The narrator, Lucius, had been turned into an ass through magic in Book 3. Now, in Book 11, he tells us, he is converted back to human shape thanks to Isis. She has appeared to him in a dream, and provided him with the occasion, a festival of hers launching a new sailing season, to achieve the transformation. She has taken pity on his suffering and determined to save him from his travails. Half a century earlier, the Greek Platonist philosopher Plutarch had written his *Isis and Osiris* and told us the myth of Isis (Sections 13–16). Osiris had civilized the Egyptians and others, but his enemy Typhon (the Egyptian Seth, sometimes depicted as an ass) killed Osiris and cast the body in a coffin into the Nile. Isis now searches for Osiris (as Demeter had searched for Persephone) and at Byblos in Phoenicia stays with the queen and burns off the mortal parts of the body of her child, but is seen so doing by the queen (this is the story of Demeter with Metaneira and

Demophon). The message of secrecy and restraint is then doubly driven home when the boy sees Isis looking at the body of Osiris in the coffin and her glance kills him (Section 17). But now Typhon divides the body into fourteen parts. Isis finds them and assigns each one to a separate burial spot (so that there may be a ritual there). The one she does not find is the sexual organ, and as a result she makes a phallus (which is the reason the Egyptians do so for religious ceremonies).

The relationship between the suffering god of myth (Isis, note, rather than Osiris) and the initiate in her cult is then overtly stated by Plutarch:

> [Isis] did not overlook the trials and contests which she had endured, or her wanderings, or the many deeds of wisdom and of bravery, or let forgetfulness and silence absorb them. Rather, she included into her most holy rites images and allegories and icons of her sufferings of that time and sanctified them as a lesson in piety and a comfort for men and women gripped by similar circumstances (Plutarch, *Isis and Osiris*, Section 27)

This is more than aetiology (a story giving an account of why a practice happens): the mythology has become pervasive and more of a subject for contemplation and understanding than earlier centuries had known. It is part of what we require today of a sacred text, something which classical Greek culture did not really have, though Homer, a window on the mythology and an expression of it, gradually *became* a sacred text in some hands.

Cybele and Attis

Other cults too had their mythologies, of which I will mention briefly the cult of Cybele (the Magna Mater, 'Great Mother') and Attis, which eventually became incorporated in the Roman official calendar as known to us from the fourth century AD. One of the days of their festival, 25 March, was known as the *Hilaria* ('festival of rejoicing'), and it is to this day that a piece of liturgy preserved by a Christian polemicist of c. AD 350 seems to relate:

> Be of good cheer, initiates of the god that has been saved.
> You too will have salvation from labours.
> (Firmicus Maternus, *Error of the Profane Religions* 22)

Attis, the young male beloved of Agdistis (a form of the Great Mother) was driven to madness by her when he fell in love with a nymph. In his madness he castrated himself and died of his wounds.[24] From his blood, however, violets grow (and initiates will wreath trees with them). He is not quite 'saved' in a sense we would recognize, but he has given rise to new life, and that is the symbol. Just as the rebirth of the corn was associated with the Persephone myth, so there seems to be a connection to nature here from which initiates draw comfort and the hope of salvation at the time of the spring equinox. And fourth-century AD authors, though maybe on the basis of their own mystic interpretations, saw in the myth the fall of the soul into this world, exhibited by the sexual appetite for the nymph; in the castration (and the chopping down of a ritual tree), a rejection of the process of coming-into-being that characterizes this unstable world of ours; and finally, in the 'rejoicing', a depiction of 'the ascent back to the gods'.[25]

Mithras

Finally in this discussion we reach the cult of Mithras, which draws together myth and soteriology in a unique way. It is enigmatic as we have illustrations of the mythology but no written account of it. The poet Claudian, in AD 400, refers to Mithras as 'rotating the straying stars' (*et vaga … volventem sidera Mithram*).[26] This seems to be the central point of the Mithraic mythology and religion. Many sculptures show Mithras, in his Persian cap, slaying 'the' bull (this is a *tauroctony*, 'bull-slaying') and this somehow seems to be an image of the creation of the world and world order with which we live. The bull is in fact the constellation of Taurus, and what is depicted is now generally thought to be the shift in the path of the sun (actually a progressive movement of the earth's axis) that causes the sun to rise at the spring equinox against the background of a new constellation about every 2,160 years. This is the precession of the equinoxes. The Mithraic myth commemorated the end of the age in which the sun had risen against Taurus. Other animals and objects which represent constellations are part of this story, such as a dog (Canis Major), a lion (Leo), a crab (Cancer), a mixing bowl (Krater, the ancient name of the mini-constellation between Hydra and Leo). So the myth and depiction of the tauroctony is a sort of star map.

But the heavens are where our soul comes from and returns to and the rocky cave in which Mithras slays the bull is a model of our world, with a rocky 'firmament' that we know best from Genesis 1.7. At either side of this scene stand two twins, also in Persian hat and costume, one with a torch pointing upwards (Cautes, 'Burner' in Greek) and one with a torch pointing down (Cautopates, 'Burn-trampler'). These are symbols of life and death and, according to philosophical interpreters, represent the path of the soul down into the world (death) and the path of the soul back to the heavens (life). Frequently, around this main scene, there are panels giving us snapshots of other scenes in the mythology, for instance: Mithras is born from rock, whence the recognition-sign '*god from rock!*'; he produces water from a rock; the bull grazes, Mithras chases the bull, and rustles it;[27] a figure sleeps, perhaps Kronos (the Roman Saturn), who ruled the age before ours and whose name reflects time itself (*chronos*); Mithras stretches out his hand and greets the sun god (with whom he is sometimes identified).

This is a mythology that is at once a theogony (birth of Mithras), an astral cosmogony (changes in the constellations), and a soteriology (the descent of the soul into the body and its return). It may have been invented in first-century AD Rome, presumably on the basis of some earlier materials, though it is hard to trace any of them to Persia whence they were once thought to have come. It has captured the soteriological trend in myth and combined it with various forms of philosophy and science. It is not typical of myth in the Roman Empire, but it could not have arisen in any other environment.

Horizons of Another World

Thus pictorial art too had acquired new significance in the creation of myth and in challenging the viewer to understand, just as it had earlier in the Basilica at the Porta Maggiore. Somewhere here too belong the half-formed myths of the ecstatic religion of Dionysos, whose processions display generic satyrs and mainads swept up in the train of the god. The story of these maenads may be little more than that they accompanied Dionysos to India and back. India, constellations, the Gnostic *pleroma*, Cupid's palace, the Phrygia of Cybele, and the Egypt of Isis – all have in common that this world here is not the only place and maybe not a happy place: for our salvation we need to be put in contact with a different world, where the divine itself belongs. This too might be expected to be the thought-world of sarcophagi, that meeting-place of the two worlds. But perhaps we need to retain a little balance and the next chapter will explore that theme.

FURTHER READING

H. P. Foley (1993) offers a generous range of materials for the understanding of the *Homeric Hymn to Demeter*; for the cult at Eleusis, we go back to Mylonas 1961, and for its interpretation, Mystery cults as a whole have been very accessibly presented and beautifully illustrated by Bowden (2010); Burkert (1987) conducts a particularly searching analysis of the field. Isis, Mithras, and similar cults were dealt with lovingly by the classic and warmly imaginative Cumont 1911, but its view of Mithraism was founded on false premises and he does tend to impose the ideas of his time; today, if rather more clinically, we read Turcan 1996 (and for Cybele and Attis, Vermaseren

1977). On 'Orphism', the wary reader will take to heart the scepticism of Radcliffe Edmonds in CH. 4.

The Basilica at the Porta Maggiore is impossible to visit, difficult to understand, and there is little on it in English (indeed it is hard to find any reference to it), but there is some usefulness in material from shortly after the discovery – Strong and Jolliffe 1924, Bagnani 1919 – and briefly Beard, North, and Price 1998: i.273–4 and Vermaseren 1977: 55–7. The major study (in French) is Carcopino 1926. Internet searches for the terms *Basilica Porta Maggiore* will turn it up, with some illustrations.

Allegorical methods of reading are, ironically, best understood by reading Philo, whose works are accessible in English translation, notably the Loeb Classical Library edition in twelve volumes (Cambridge, MA 1929–53). Herakleitos is now available – introduction, text, translation, and notes – in Russell and Konstan 2005. The 1969 translation of Plotinus by Stephen MacKenna is a work of literature in its own right (see Guide to Fragmentary Texts, in the bibliography). For discussion of the method, see Dowden 1992: 24–5, Graf 1993a: 194–8, and the index to this volume.

NOTES

1. All translations in this chapter are my own, except for the inimitable translation of Plotinos by Stephen MacKenna.
2. Apuleius, *On the Divine Spirit of Socrates* Section 4 (*singillatim mortales, cunctim tamen uniuerso genere perpetui, uicissim sufficienda prole mutabiles*).
3. Apollodoros, *Epitome* 1.23; Scholiast on Aristophanes, *Knights* 1368a ('Tugged by Herakles, he left his bottom behind on the rock').
4. Gantz (1993: 722–3).
5. This account largely follows M. L. West 1983a: for example, 69, 74, and ch. 5. The older account of I. M. Linforth, a model of critical acumen in its time, now seems hypersceptical: Linforth (1941, ch. 5).
6. Iamblichos, *On the Pythagorean Life*, ch. 33, Section 240.
7. This text is found in W. Norvin (ed.), *Olympiodori Philosophi in Platonis Phaedonem Commentaria* (Lepizig 1913) 86–7, as Text B Section 9, but the anonymous commentary to which it belongs was identified as notes from a lecture of Damaskios by L. G. Westerink (Westerink 1977: 15–17). Westerink prints the text as Damascius, *In Phaedonem* I Section 9 (on p. 33) with facing translation.
8. Buffière 1962: 127 n. 9 (my translation from the French).
9. 'Ces pensées et leurs illustrations sont beaucoup plus anciennes que le néoplatonisme' ('These thoughts and their illustration are a good deal older than Neoplatonism'), Carcopino (1956: 199), and see his whole discussion of Odysseus (Ulysse) on pp. 199–202.
10 See M. J. Edwards (1988: 509) for some of these details and an article arising from them.

11. *Life of Plotinos* 22.25–44, supposedly an oracle from Delphi.
12. On Philip the Philosopher and Heliodoros, see Hunter (2005a). For a translation of the text from which Philip is known to us, see Lamberton (1986: 306–11).
13. *Discourses* 11.10h, with M. J. Edwards (1988: 509).
14. Our source for this fragment, John Stobaios (*Anthologies* 1.49.60), attributes it to Porphyry, but Sandbach's authoritative view is that either he is wrong (on linguistic grounds) or Porphyry was actually reproducing Plutarch at this point (Sandbach 1967: 125).
15. For the record, Proteus himself appears at *Metamorphoses* 8.725–37.
16. The authors in question are Ptolemy Chennos and Diktys of Crete. See my entries in *BNJ*, authors 49, 54, 56, and Dowden (forthcoming a).
17. Beard, North, and Price (1998: i.273), but cf. Vermaseren (1977: 55) for the reasoning (Carcopino's).
18. For this Basilica, see Further Reading in this chapter.
19. Carcopino (1956: 59).
20. Philo, *On the Migration of Abraham*, 1–3.
21. See Lamberton (1986: 44–54).
22. For example, Clement, *Rich Man's Salvation* 29. And see Dowden (forthcoming b).
23. For example, Sophia Achamoth in Irenaeus, *Against the Heresies*, 1.1.16–17. For an account of this type of myth, see Jonas (1963: 176–99).
24. The story is in, for example, Arnobius, *Against the Pagans* 5.6. There are variants.
25. Sallustius, *On Gods and the World* 10–11, cf. Julian, *Speech* 5.
26. *On the Consulate of Stilicho*, 1.63.
27. Recognition phrase: Firmicus Maternus, *Error of the Profane Religions*, 20.1. Rustling: Commodian, *Instructions*, 1.13.5 (mid-third century AD); Firmicus Maternus, *Error of the Profane Religions*, 5.2.

CHAPTER SIXTEEN

Myth and Death: Roman Mythological Sarcophagi

Zahra Newby

Myth and the Sarcophagus: The Question of Interpretation

The sudden emergence in the second century AD of marble sarcophagi decorated with stories from Greek mythology has been a cause of wonder and debate for over a century.[1] Leaving aside the question of the reasons behind the change from cremation to inhumation, great debate has also ensued over why particular myths were chosen and what messages they were supposed to convey.[2] In this chapter I will discuss the range of myths shown on Roman sarcophagi and suggest some ways forward in our understanding of their significance in a funerary context.

My main focus is on sarcophagi produced by workshops in the city of Rome, where sarcophagi with mythological themes were especially popular and can help to illuminate the ways in which Romans appropriated and adapted Greek myth for their own purposes. Two other major centres of sarcophagi production were located in Attica in mainland Greece and at Dokimeion in Asia Minor. Attic sarcophagi also feature mythological imagery, though the range of myths is more restricted than in Rome: scenes of the heroes Achilles, Hippolytos, and Meleager and the battles of the Trojan War are most popular.[3] In Asia Minor frieze sarcophagi (for which see below) are less popular than garland or columnar sarcophagi, and there are few examples of unified mythological narratives. However, individual mythological figures do appear in the niches of columnar sarcophagi. These imitated the statuary types that adorned contemporary buildings and contributed to the architectonic form of

A Companion to Greek Mythology, First Edition. Edited by Ken Dowden and Niall Livingstone.
© 2014 John Wiley & Sons Ltd. Published 2014 by John Wiley & Sons Ltd.

Table 16.1 Periodization of the second–third centuries AD.

period	dates	principal emperors
Hadrianic	117–138	Hadrian
Antonine	138–161	Antoninus Pius
	161–180	Marcus Aurelius
	180–192	Commodus
	192–193	Pertinax
Severan	193–211	Septimius Severus
	211–217	Caracalla
	218–222	Elagabalus
	222–235	Alexander Severus

these sarcophagi, but the figures chosen may also have provided analogies to the life and virtues of the deceased buried within.[4] The choices and presentation of mythological figures on sarcophagi differ in the east and west of the empire, and while some Roman sarcophagi added portrait features to mythological figures (discussed below), this is not found in the east. It seems likely that the ways myth was understood in the funerary sphere varied across the empire, with myths in the east probably much more tightly bound up with communal senses of Greek identity.[5]

The debate over the symbolism of mythological sarcophagi has largely focused around the large number of sarcophagi produced in Rome, and is still most clearly expressed by the polarized views of the French scholar Franz Cumont and the American Arthur Darby Nock in the 1940s.[6] While Cumont argued for complex allegorical symbolism concerning the fate of the soul after death, Nock expressed scepticism, stressing instead the link with representations of myth in other areas of Roman art and their association with classicism and education. Cumont's elaborate readings of mythology, which relied on the interpretations given in Neopythagorean texts, often in contrast to the features stressed by the reliefs themselves, have now largely fallen out of favour. Yet scholars are equally reluctant to accept Nock's minimalism, arguing that the selectivity with which certain myths and not others were depicted on sarcophagi suggests deliberate choice and, therefore, a particular significance for these myths in the funerary context.[7]

The opposition between Cumont and Nock was not only between seeing myth as either allegory or decor, but also between a view of funerary imagery as either expressing hopes and beliefs about the afterlife or as asserting messages about the past life of the deceased. It is this dichotomy between prospective and retrospective messages that has framed the debate since the 1970s. Those who see mythological scenes as prospective suggest that they assert a belief or hope in the afterlife; the assimilation of the deceased to gods and heroes suggests their apotheosis or heroization and images of Dionysiac revelry, or of Nereids and Tritons, show the souls of the dead in the Elysian fields or on their way to the Isles of the Blest.[8] Sceptics protest that earlier funerary imagery is primarily concerned with representing the deceased as they were during life, asserting their achievements and status, and they note that a widespread belief in the afterlife is not suggested by the evidence of funerary inscriptions, many of which assert that death is the end of everything.[9] Most recently Paul Zanker and Björn Ewald have widened the debate to suggest that myths can be read as consolations to the bereaved. Scenes of violent death could express the pain of the loss of a loved one, while scenes of feasting and revelry evoked the festivals and banquets which took place at the tomb.[10]

The primary way in which these myths are now thought to work is through analogy.[11] Rather than the complex allegories perceived by Cumont, more recent scholars have suggested instead that myths on sarcophagi work in a similar way to mythological *exempla* in poetry or oratory. So, for instance, just like Herakles, the deceased showed great courage and virtue during life, and just like Adonis or Achilles, he was doomed to an early death despite his heroism.[12] Yet the precise messages that could be drawn from these *exempla* still depended on individual beliefs. Herakles could be seen as an emblem of strength and virtue during life, or as the example of someone who gained immortality because of his labours. The choice of an analogical method of interpretation does not help in deciding whether Herakles offered a prospective or retrospective message.

There is also more room for nuance in the interpretation of scenes of revelry or the depiction of sleeping figures such as Ariadne and Endymion. While these may well be read as positive statements, consoling the bereaved with the thought that the deceased is now at rest, free from the cares of life, they do not necessarily express a firmly held belief in the afterlife. In contemporary society bereaved relatives can talk about their departed loved ones as watching over them, or put up images of angels on tombstones; however, not all would express a strong belief in the existence of heaven or an afterlife. In antiquity too, some symbols should perhaps be read euphemistically; representations of sleep might act as ciphers or metaphors for death rather than as assertions that the dead are really only asleep, waiting to be woken up. Studies of Roman funerary epigraphy suggest a wide range of attitudes to death, ranging from those that see death as the end of everything to those imagining the deceased as residing in the company of the gods. A similar range of ideas is to be expected from funerary art.[13] The beauty of myth was its flexibility: it offered models of heroism in life as well as hopes of rebirth, depending on the beliefs and needs of those who commissioned the tombs. In what follows, therefore, we will look at a number of sarcophagi and observe how the multivalency of myth suited it to the

Figure 16.1   Garland sarcophagus showing Theseus and Ariadne.

depiction of human lives and hopes. In this way we will move from a position of dogmatic interpretation to an awareness of the various needs that funerary imagery fulfilled.

The Earliest Myths on Sarcophagi: Garland Sarcophagi

The beginnings of the depiction of Greek myths in Roman funerary art seem to fall early in the Hadrianic period. The depiction of mythological scenes on cinerary urns and altars is very rare, and when it does appear seems to be influenced by their appearance on sarcophagi. Thus, it was on Hadrianic sarcophagi that mythological scenes start to appear.[14] The first sarcophagi are decorated with garlands of fruit and flowers held by Erotes or Victories and sometimes show small mythological vignettes in the lunettes above the garlands. Some of these formed a coherent mythological narrative, as we see on the sarcophagus with the myth of Theseus and Ariadne in New York (fig. 16.1) or that with the myth of Aktaion in the Louvre.[15] Often, though, vignettes from different myths are put together, or scenes of Dionysiac revelry or a sea thiasos are chosen.[16]

Interpreting the funerary significance of these themes is not always easy. While we might say that Aktaion's fate serves as an example of a tragic and untimely death, the focus of the scenes is actually on presenting the course of the narrative and the depiction of Aktaion's corpse is relegated to a side panel. Similarly, the depiction of the story of Ariadne and Theseus focuses on telling us the story, from Ariadne giving Theseus the thread which will lead him safely out of the labyrinth to the killing of the Minotaur and Ariadne's abandonment by Theseus. In the scenes that are chosen for depiction, and in the ways they are shown, there are some striking parallels with domestic paintings. The depiction of Polyphemos gazing at Galateia in a pastoral setting on the

Palazzo Mattei casket evokes the mythological landscapes we find in the third and fourth Pompeian styles, and the myths of Aktaion, Theseus, and Marsyas all reappear in domestic decoration.

These earliest mythological scenes are marked by their great variety. While a couple of themes shown here carry on into later mythological frieze sarcophagi, many simply drop out of the repertoire.[17] The earliest frieze sarcophagi appear around the same time and are also marked by the appearance of some unusual depictions which do not reappear later, as on the Velletri sarcophagus with its series of myths relating to the Underworld, and the so-called Peleus and Thetis sarcophagus in the Villa Albani.[18] The overlap between the garland sarcophagi and domestic decoration suggests that one factor behind the introduction of mythological imagery might have been to equate the tomb with the house. In his consolation to the freedman of Domitian, Abascantus, on the death of his wife, Statius equated the tomb of the dead woman to a house: 'domus ista, domus!' – 'It is a house, yes, a house!' (*Silvae* 5.1.237). At the same time Domitian himself constructed the Temple of the Flavian Family (*Templum Gentis Flaviae*) out of the house where he was born and used it as the family mausoleum.[19] Tomb architecture from the late first century also echoed that of houses with simple brick façades housing lavishly decorated interiors.[20] The same desire to evoke the atmosphere of the house may have influenced the decoration of marble sarcophagi with scenes taken from the repertoire of domestic decoration.[21]

Mythological Frieze Sarcophagi

Death and destruction

After this start, mythological sarcophagi soon settle down into the depiction of a set number of themes. Frieze sarcophagi now take over from garland sarcophagi as the primary carriers of myth. They start to appear during the Hadrianic period and mythological scenes continue until the middle of the third century, with a few examples continuing into the later third century. The depiction of myths seems to have been at its height in the Antonine and Severan periods, but with changes and developments evident over the course of time.

The sarcophagi of the second half of the second century feature around a dozen different myths, some of which die out at the end of the century and are replaced by new scenes. They can be broadly grouped into scenes of violent death or abduction and scenes of heroism. In the first group we find scenes such as the Rape of Persephone, an enduringly popular theme in funerary art and one which appears on grave altars and urns, tomb paintings, and mosaics as well as on sarcophagi.[22] This scene of a youthful maiden being dragged down to the Underworld by Hades and her mother's frantic searching

Figure 16.2   Niobids sarcophagus.

for her was the perfect analogy for the pain and grief of bereavement. While the myth may have had a particular resonance when commemorating the death of a young woman, inscriptions on cinerary urns and altars show that it could also be used to commemorate men or couples; the sudden violence of Persephone's abduction seems to have offered parallels for the loss of any loved one, regardless of age or gender.[23] The rape of the daughters of Leukippos by the Dioskouroi is also represented on around ten sarcophagi from 150–80. It too provided a mythological *exemplum* for sudden loss.

Other scenes of violence focus on death itself rather than abduction. Around ten sarcophagi show the deaths of the Niobids, as on one in the Vatican Galleria degli Candelabri (fig. 16.2).[24] The whole of the sarcophagus front is littered with dead and dying bodies, which extend also onto the front of the lid. To either side stand the vengeful gods Artemis and Apollo shooting arrows as the children attempt to flee. This scene of horrific destruction seems to emphasize the wastefulness of death. Niobe was the epitome of the grieving parent and could be used as a consolation to the bereaved.[25] Here, however, the stress of the sarcophagus is less on her grief than the terrible violence which produced it; these sarcophagi stress the horror of death rather than offering any form of consolation.

Figure 16.3 Orestes sarcophagus.

Other scenes of violent death appear in the myths of Orestes and Medea, focusing respectively on the destruction of Klytaimestra and Aigisthos and the death of Kreousa. We can read these scenes visually in a similar way to the deaths of the Niobids, as scenes of violent death which evoke horror and pathos. Yet the myths which lie behind these scenes complicate our understanding of them. A sarcophagus with the myth of Orestes in the Vatican was found in the same tomb as one showing the deaths of the Niobids, both examples of violent death (fig. 16.3). The centre of the sarcophagus is dominated by the carnage caused by Orestes; the dead bodies of Aigisthos and Klytaimestra lie on the floor while an old nurse recoils in horror and a slave picks up a plinth in self-defence. By analogy with the Niobids sarcophagus, the scene evokes horror and pathos at this scene of destruction. But whereas there our sympathies lie firmly with the innocent children, here the emotional response is more complex. To the left of the scene a draped male figure represents the ghost of Agamemnon, reminding us of Orestes' motivation for the murders, while the Furies rushing in from the right also point towards his guilt as a matricide. Orestes' dominance at the centre of the scene in heroic nudity and with sword in hand, accompanied by his friend Pylades, also draws our attention to him as a symbol of heroism. While the main chest of the sarcophagus draws from the Orestes story as retold in Aeschylus' *Oresteia*, the lid adds scenes from Euripides' *Iphigeneia among the Taurians*, visually retelling the story of how Orestes and Pylades were brought to be sacrificed to Artemis, recognized by Iphigeneia, and finally escaped taking the cult statue of the

Figure 16.4 Medea sarcophagus.

goddess away with them. The funerary implications of this myth are obscure; while it could be read as an example of escape from death, the reliefs concentrate on retelling the narrative rather than drawing any particular message. Instead, its depiction seems to have been prompted by the desire to add narrative context.

Similar motivations can be perceived in sarcophagi retelling the Medea myth, which also appear in the second half of the second century AD. These sarcophagi used to be a byword for the difficulties of interpreting mythological sarcophagi. Why on earth, it was asked, would Roman citizens want to present the infanticidal Medea on their sarcophagi? One answer was given by Margot Schmidt in her analysis of the Basel Medea sarcophagus who suggested that the apotheosis of the deceased was symbolized by the figure of Medea at the far right escaping in the chariot of the sun (fig. 16.4).[26] Klaus Fittschen later proposed a solution which gained wider acceptance, that the sarcophagus depicted the violent death of Kreousa and that she is the real focus of this group of sarcophagi.[27] Kreousa's preparations as a bride add pathos to her death in the centre of the scene and the impact of that death is shown by the reactions of those around her. Fittschen's reading is a persuasive one and does, I think, explain why this myth was chosen for depiction on sarcophagi. Yet, as he himself admits, it does not explain all the features of the sarcophagi. Thus, in addition to the death of Kreousa we are also shown Medea pondering the murder of her children and her escape. These might have been included to clarify the myth and make the identity of those involved clear. Yet the lid of the Basel sarcophagus and the short sides of some other sarcophagi also depict the events in Kolchis which form the backstory to Euripides' tragedy and were told in Apollonios' *Argonautika* – Jason's arrival in Kolchis, his mastery of the fire-breathing bulls, and his gaining possession of the Golden Fleece with Medea's help. If the sarcophagus was meant to commemorate the sudden death of a young woman, as the analogy to Kreousa might suggest, what significance did these scenes have? We could see an allusion to a couple, the man's heroism reflected in Jason's deeds and the woman's death in that of Kreousa, but even so the presence of Medea complicates the picture. While an analogy between the sudden death of Kreousa and the loss of a loved one may well have promoted the choice of this particular myth, the retelling of the myth does not confine itself to this one message but expands into the full narrative of the story.

Nock's explanation of myths on sarcophagi as being the result of 'classicism' has rather gone out of fashion, and rightly so, at least as a single explanatory factor. Yet these sarcophagi do suggest that knowledge of the mythological narratives as retold in particular literary accounts lay behind some of the myths on sarcophagi. Perhaps literary *paideia* played a role after all.[28] If not, why include those scenes that did not have a particular funerary significance? This is not to deny the importance of the myths as presenting analogies for the untimely death of a young bride, or the destruction of death. The myths could be used and read in many different ways simultaneously without the apparent contradictions in these messages, so apparent to the modern viewer, seeming to cause a problem for the ancient viewer. This filling out of the full context of myth may have been a natural impulse for artists and purchasers immersed in a culture of the visualization of myth, and influenced by the ways these myths had already been depicted in domestic decoration in paintings and in the minor arts such as silverware.

Mythological Frieze Sarcophagi

Heroism and virtue

In addition to those myths that focus on violent death or loss, a second group of second-century sarcophagi may have offered a more consolatory message. They focus on the lives, and sometimes deaths, of young heroes. Scenes of Achilles on Skyros concentrate on the heroism of the youth as he accepts his destiny as a warrior, though his early death may well have been in the back of the minds of those choosing these sarcophagi. The deeds of Herakles could also be viewed as providing an analogy to the virtues of the dead, and in a couple of late, third-century, examples the hero was actually given the portrait features of the man buried within.[29]

Other popular heroes are the hunters Adonis, Hippolytos, and Meleager. These three heroes were linked by their love of hunting, which often finds a prominent place on the sarcophagi. Both Adonis and Meleager sarcophagi begin in the middle of the second century. The Adonis sarcophagi show the hero taking his leave from his lover Aphrodite before entering the boar hunt in which he will receive a fatal wound. In some sarcophagi he is also shown later lying wounded in the goddess's arms. Adonis' story is a tragic one, stressing his heroism as well as his inability to avoid death, despite being loved by a goddess.[30] The Meleager sarcophagi divide into three groups. One, which continued well into the third century, concentrates on Meleager's heroism in the hunting of the Kalydonian boar; the other two are both confined to the second century and show the bringing home of his body and, less frequently, the events surrounding his death.[31] Sarcophagi showing Hippolytos begin around AD 180 and show parallels with the Adonis sarcophagi. Here Hippolytos is shown leaving Phaidra's presence in the left half of the relief and hunting on horseback at the right. This iconography of a mounted hunter was later taken over in the hunt sarcophagi of the third century, though with the prey changed from a boar to a lion.[32]

The story of Hippolytos had been famously retold by Euripides, whose tragedies were well-known in the Roman period, cited in literary works as well as being used as school texts.[33] Enough elements remain to identify the text of Euripides' *Hippolytos* here: the figure of the old nurse who seeks to persuade Hippolytos or his rejection of Phaidra. Yet the narrative of the Greek tragedy is much more muted here than it is in the scenes of Medea and Orestes and Iphigeneia. Instead, Hippolytos' rejection of Phaidra resembles a departure scene, designed to evoke the pain of loss without stressing the incestuous nature of Phaidra's love in the myth itself. In some sarcophagi Hippolytos is shown holding a diptych in his hand in the departure scene, an object that could be read at Phaidra's letter declaring her love, but which in fact seems to draw our attention to the youth's *paideia* more than it alludes to the mythological narrative.[34]

We can view the depiction of myths on Roman sarcophagi as balanced on a tightrope strung between the two poles of retelling the Greek mythological narrative (often with allusions to a particularly influential literary or theatrical text) and using the myth as an emblem for Roman values and beliefs. While the Orestes sarcophagi move towards the former, the Hippolytos sarcophagi lean closer towards the latter, stressing Hippolytos' heroism in the hunting scene and Phaidra's sense of loss at his departure.

The depiction of these myths stresses the virtues of the heroes, the love they inspire, and, often, the grief evoked at their deaths. An equivalent presentation of female virtues can be seen in the sarcophagi showing the myth of Alkestis. Again we have a myth which was the subject of an Euripidean tragedy turned to the purpose of expressing Roman values. Some imperial grave inscriptions compare the deceased woman to Alkestis – the model of a virtuous and loyal wife, who opted to die herself to save her husband from death.[35]

On the sarcophagi she is shown lying on her deathbed and surrounded by grieving relatives. On one particularly well-known example in the Vatican she, Admetos, and members of the family are all given portrait features.[36] An inscription on the lid identifies the sarcophagus as a dedication by an Ostian freedman, Gaius Junius Euhodus for himself and his wife Metilia Acte. The addition of portrait features equates the couple to Admetos and Alkestis, celebrating their great love and Metilia's wifely virtues. However, not all these sarcophagi were set up by bereaved husbands. A chest in France has a Greek inscription telling us that it was dedicated by a mother to her daughter; in these cases the depiction of a woman on her deathbed might have been enough to make it a suitable image for a grieving relative.[37]

Third-Century Trends: Consolation or Salvation?

Sarcophagi stressing the violence of death seem to be a particular feature of the second century AD and die out around 200. Depictions of myths which link closely to literary works, such as those of Medea, Hippolytos, Alkestis, and Orestes also decline in favour of images stressing the implications of these myths for Roman patrons. Some new myths were added to the repertoire while others which had begun in the second century continued to thrive in the third century. One such group is made up by sarcophagi showing the sleeping figures of Endymion and Ariadne.

The Endymion myth is the second most popular individual myth on sarcophagi after Meleager, running from the late Hadrianic period well into the third century AD.[38] Representations of the sleeping Ariadne are less common but should be seen as a subset of the large group of Dionysiac sarcophagi which were popular in both the second and the third century.[39] The two myths share a common iconography, showing a sleeping figure approached by a god or goddess. The beauty of the sleepers is often stressed through their nudity or the attendant figures who point them out to the deities. In the later examples the figures are set into backgrounds packed with figures, representing the Dionysiac thiasos or evoking pastoral joys.

From around AD 200, the figures of Ariadne and Endymion were increasingly given portrait features, or their faces left roughed out as if to receive them.[40] This identification between the hero or heroine and the deceased has often been used to support the idea that these myths are examples of the apotheosis or deification of the dead, showing their rebirth in the afterlife and their union with the divine, here embodied in the figures of Dionysos and Selene.[41] Yet other interpretations of the scene were also available to ancient viewers. Sleep and death were often equated: the representation of sleeping

Figure 16.5   Mars and Rhea Silvia, Endymion and Selene sarcophagus.

figures on sarcophagi might be read euphemistically, sleep being a less harsh way of representing death. There could also be a consolatory message here, envisaging the dead as merely asleep in an idyllic realm without necessarily implying belief in full-blown rebirth.

The union of the deceased, in the guise of Endymion or Ariadne, with a god has in the past been seen as a sign of immortality, the unity of the soul with the divine after death. However, on those sarcophagi where Endymion has portrait features Selene usually does too, and in most cases these are presumably the faces of a married couple. They assert that the couple's love would survive death, the hope that they would see the deceased in their dreams and later be reunited in death – ideas and hopes which also reappear in contemporary grave inscriptions.[42] While some purchasers may indeed have wished to assert a strong belief in immortality through their use of this myth, the imagery opens up a range of different options for interpretation. The myth could provide an analogy that offered hope and consolation to the bereaved, and those sarcophagi which were commissioned before death could have been a statement of faith that the love between husband and wife would continue after death.

One sarcophagus in the Vatican combines the scene of Selene approaching the sleeping Endymion with Mars approaching the sleeping Rhea Silvia (fig. 16.5).[43] The two myths clearly have visual similarities, and a few sarcophagi centred on Mars and Rhea Silvia group alone were produced in following decades. On this sarcophagus the original heads of Endymion and Selene are lost and have been restored, but both Mars and Rhea Silvia feature portrait faces. However, the styles of hair and beard shown seem to date from different periods. While Rhea Silvia wears a hairstyle of the early Severan period, the face of Mars is reminiscent of the period of Caracalla, some ten to fifteen years later.[44] The female portrait is marked by its youthfulness, while that of Mars is older, with lines across the forehead. It is possible that this

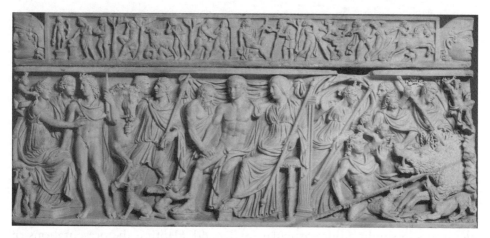

Figure 16.6   Adonis sarcophagus.

sarcophagus was commissioned by a man while still alive to commemorate himself and a wife who had died some ten years earlier. Her portrait may have been completed from a death mask, and her remains transferred to the new coffin. The man's devotion to his wife even after years without her is expressed by his decision to commission a sarcophagus commemorating them both, and perhaps expresses his hope for their reunion in death.

The addition of portraits on these sarcophagi helps to elucidate the meaning of the myths intended by those who commissioned them. Portraits have often been seen as simply intensifying the normal message presented by the mythological imagery, but many myths opened up a range of possible interpretations, as consolations to the bereaved, retrospective allusions to the virtues of the deceased and, sometimes, hopes and aspirations for a life after death. And on two sarcophagi from the late Severan period the addition of portrait features asserts a very positive message about the fate of the deceased which does, indeed, seem to support a belief in an afterlife.[45]

The first is a sarcophagus in the Vatican which shows the myth of Adonis (fig. 16.6). While other sarcophagi on this theme stress Adonis' departure from Aphrodite and his wounding in the hunt, here the hero and goddess are prominently positioned at the very centre of the relief and are both given portrait features. Their erect poses deny the fact of Adonis' impending death and instead stress the couple's eternal unity. Here, indeed, we find a sarcophagus which seems to declare that death is not the end, and that the love of such a couple will survive for ever. The second sarcophagus is one in the Capitoline Museum in Rome.[46] This shows the Rape of Persephone but again manipulates the usual iconography to show the figure of Persephone sitting erect, going willingly with the god, rather than lying slumped, prone, in his arms. She also wears portrait features – the clear message is of a welcoming of death, in contrast to the pain of bereavement which was stressed on the earlier sarcophagi.

Studies of mythological sarcophagi have often started with those featuring portrait heads and moved on to argue that the same meanings and symbolism must have held true for other examples showing the same myths. However, on these two examples the addition of portraits is accompanied by changes to the usual iconography to present different nuances of the myth. On other sarcophagi too, we sometimes find small changes to the usual iconography which redirect our focus or add extra information. Any approach to the symbolism of sarcophagi needs to look across the breadth of representations and to acknowledge that myths could mean a multitude of things to different people; it was in singling out particular myths and adapting the presentations of them that the buyer of a sarcophagi, whether commissioning his or her own tomb before death or acting on the death of a relative, could personalize the messages it presented.

Conclusions

During the century or so in which mythological sarcophagi were made in Rome we can see a number of changes, with an increasing desire to relate the myths explicitly to the lives of those they commemorated. Mythological scenes were only one of a range of options for sarcophagi which could also include scenes of marriage, magistracies, and warfare. In some cases the same underlying virtues seem to have been expressed by both mythological and 'human life' scenes, or images could be drawn from both realms to express the defining virtues of the deceased, as on a sarcophagi in Berlin which combines non-mythological scenes of marriage and sacrifice with a scene of Adonis in the hunt.[47]

The mythological scenes move gradually from a stress on the narratives of the myth to their relevance in the funerary context; though neither is entirely excluded in any representation. The very earliest scenes took myths from the domestic sphere and used them primarily as decoration, with less stress on a particular relevance for the funerary context. From around 150 until the late Antonine period a range of myths was used; they did have particular resonance in a funerary context, but also maintained their narrative focus even when this might have seemed inappropriate. Themes such as those of Medea, Orestes, and Meleager show the opportunities myth opened up for a range of interpretations, and the desire to fill in the narrative background, making links to domestic decoration as well as to literary education.

From the Severan period onwards we see a number of changes. Rather the space on sarcophagi being filled with extra details from the narrative of the

Figure 16.7 Achilles and Penthesileia sarcophagus.

myth, they are often occupied with symbolic figures and personifications of places or seasons, which serve to situate the message of the sarcophagus in a wider cosmic setting. At the same time, the central figures are often exaggerated and made larger in relationship to those around them and may be given portrait features to emphasize the relevance of the parallel drawn between the myth and the life and death of the person or persons buried within. Sometimes this concentration on central groups can lead to excerption, almost as if the background details cease to be important. The group of Achilles and Penthesileia sarcophagi, which emerged in the early third century, helps to illustrate this (fig. 16.7).[48] They grow out of a class of sarcophagi showing the battles between the Greeks and the Amazons. Here, however, the scene of battle is simply the backdrop to the couple presented at the centre – Achilles with the dying Penthesileia in his arms. The narrative details of the myth (especially the fact that Achilles himself has killed Penthesileia) are subsumed in the face of this visual illustration of devotion to a fallen partner and turned into a message of conjugal love by the frequent addition of portrait features.

Other sarcophagi could excerpt a central figure and depict it alone, outside the narrative context, as on some sarcophagi showing Ariadne and Endymion.[49] Here the sleeping figure seems to be a symbol sufficient in itself: the extent to which it carried with it the associations of the original narrative context remains a matter for debate. Scholars have often seen these excerpted figures as a sign of the demythologizing of sarcophagi which was to come in the later third century. The move away from mythological narratives leads either to the depiction of purely symbolic figures such as the Muses and the Seasons or to scenes of 'real life' such as magistrates or hunts. Thus we find two separate phenomena – a shift in the mode of representation, from narrative to symbolic, and a shift in subject matter, from the actions of heroes and gods to those of ordinary human beings. Yet there is no clear-cut division in either of these areas, rather a gradual shifting of balance.

One example of the demythologizing of sarcophagi is the move in the third century from depicting the mythological boar hunts of Adonis, Meleager, and Hippolytos to scenes of men on horseback in contemporary costume hunting lions. Here we can see a move from mythological to human protagonists. Yet at many levels the scene is no more 'realistic'. As Bernard Andreae noted, actual hunting of lions was restricted to emperors and the arena; if a true depiction of contemporary hunting was required then the prey ought to be hares, deer, or boars rather than lions. Instead the mode is idealizing and symbolic.[50] Andreae sees a soteriological (cf. CH. 15) message of victory over death, while I prefer to see an allusion to the virtue or courage of the deceased; but in both cases the mode remains idealizing rather than realistic. This is just as 'mythologizing' as depicting the deceased in the guise of a Greek hero. Here, however, the prototype is the emperor, or the heroes of the arena, rather than figures from Greek myth.

The narrative images of the second century could accommodate symbolism, allowing individual figures to be read as embodiments of heroism, beauty, education, or eternal repose. The same qualities were expressed in the sarcophagi of the third century, but through different means – the Muses acted as symbols of education, the hunter of lions as a symbol of virtue and courage. What changed was rather the way in which these aspirational statements about the dead were conveyed, a turning away from the complexities of mythological narrative in the desire to present a precise and easily intelligible message. The complex nuances of myth, with its possibilities for multiple interpretations, seem to have lost favour in the face of a desire to narrow down and control the messages of funerary symbolism.

FURTHER READING

Zanker and Ewald 2004 is now the crucial work, combining interpretation of the meanings of different myths with an overview of the ways they were represented. Those who do not read German can still benefit from the lavish illustrations; for reviews in English see Wood 2004 and Hallett 2005: 157–61.

For a handbook of all Roman sarcophagi Koch and Sichtermann 1982 is still a useful reference point. German scholarship also provides us with catalogues of the sarcophagi according to myth. Robert 1897–1919 is partly updated in the volumes by Grassinger 1999 (Achilles–Amazons), Sichtermann 1992 (Apollo–Graces), Koch 1975 (Meleager), and Rogge 1995 (Attic Achilles and Hippolytus sarcophagi). See also Jongste 1992 on Herakles and Gaggadis-Robin 1994 on Medea. In English, Koortbojian 1995 is an analysis of the Adonis and Endymion sarcophagi with implications for other myths. F. G. J. M. Müller 1994 gives an excellent account of the cultural context in which mythological sarcophagi appear in his Appendix 4; see also Brilliant 1984: ch. 4. On the symbolism of myths Cumont 1942 and Nock 1946 provide the starting points. Turcan 1978, North 1983, Grassinger 1998, Ewald 1999, and G. Davies 2003 review the various approaches. On the addition of portrait features to mythological figures see Newby (2011). For an overview of funerary art and architecture in general, Toynbee 1971 (new edition 1996), is still useful, though some of the interpretations are now dated. Von Hesberg 1992 provides a more detailed account of tomb architecture.

NOTES

1. F. G. J. M. Müller (1994: (139–70), Ewald (1999).
2. Toynbee (1971: 33–42).
3. Koch and Sichtermann (1982: 378–410); Rogge (1995).
4. Strocka (1984) discusses symbolism. A number show the deeds of Herakles, on which see Jongste (1992).
5. Ewald (2004).
6. Cumont (1942), Nock (1946).
7. For discussion see Turcan (1978), G. Davies (2003).
8. Engemann (1973), Wrede (1981).
9. North (1983); see Lattimore (1942) on funerary inscriptions.
10. Zanker and Ewald (2004).
11. Koortbojian (1995: 5–9).
12. F. G. J. M. Müller (1994: 87–100, 144–5).
13. For discussion, see Lattimore (1942, esp. 39–40 and 78–86 for contrasting statements).
14. There are also a few mythological paintings in tombs from the Augustan period (31 BC–AD 14), see Feraudi-Gruénais (2001: 164). For myths on urns and altars see Sinn (1987: 80–1), Boschung (1987: 51–2).
15. Herdejürgen (1996: 90–2, no. 23; 93–5, no. 26).
16. For example, Herdejürgen (1996: 97–8), no. 31 shows Oedipus and Polyphemos.
17. Two themes which reappear later are the Rape of Persephone and Medea on her chariot, shown on fragmentary sarcophagi: Herdejürgen (1996: 99–100, no. 35; 103, no. 40).
18. F. G. J. M. Müller (1994).

19. D'Ambra (1993: 39–41) with references.
20. Von Hesberg (1992).
21. Herdejürgen (1996: 34) notes the link with marble relief panels.
22. Lindner (1984).
23. Lindner (1984: nos 59, 60, 61, 65).
24. Robert (1897–1919: 3.378–80, no. 313). See now Zanker and Ewald (2004: 76–80, 355–9).
25. *Iliad* 24.601–2; Peek (1955: 461, no. 1545).
26. Schmidt (1969).
27. Fittschen (1992); now Zanker and Ewald (2004: 82–4).
28. See also F. G. J. M. Müller (1994: 166–9).
29. Robert (1897–1919: 1.126–7, no. 103; 130–2, no. 107). On portraits see further below.
30. Grassinger (1999: 70–90).
31. Koch (1975).
32. Andreae (1980).
33. See Pausanias 1.22.1 on knowledge of the myth; also Morgan (1998: 321–2, tables 22 and 23).
34. Zanker and Ewald (2004: 48, fig. 33).
35. Peek (1955: 636–40, no. 2005, l. 26–27).
36. Zanker and Ewald (2004: 202, fig. 182).
37. Grassinger (1999: nos 75, 79).
38. Rough figures are 200 Meleager sarcophagi, 110 Endymion, 90 Persephone.
39. Around 30 Ariadne sarcophagi of around 400 with Dionysiac scenes.
40. On unfinished heads see Andreae (1984b), Huskinson (1998). Note that portraits on mythological figures do not appear on sarcophagi produced in Attic and Asia Minor workshops.
41. Engemann (1973: 28–31); Wrede (1981: 168–75).
42. *CIL* 6.18817, discussed and translated by Koortbojian (1995: 108).
43. As a result of this, Rhea Silvia will give birth to the twins Romulus and Remus.
44. Fittschen (1984: 160, n. 47a). He suggests that the sarcophagus style also dates to the period of Caracalla.
45. Further on portrait heads, see Newby (2011: 189–227).
46. Zanker and Ewald (2004: 93–4, fig. 77; 370–2).
47. Brilliant (1992); Blome (1992).
48. Grassinger (1999: 179–87); Zanker and Ewald (2004: 52–4, fig. 36; 285–8).
49. Koortbojian (1995: (135–41).
50. Andreae (1980: 134–6).

CHAPTER SEVENTEEN

Myth in Christian Authors

Fritz Graf

Introduction

Greek mythology was the principal content of ancient poetry. As such, it had become a mainstay of the Greek educational system long before the Christianization of the Ancient World. From the beginnings of Greek literature, divine myths had been at the core of Greek thought and imagination about their city gods and, through their systematization in Hesiod's *Theogony*, at the core of a more uniform Greek discourse about the gods. Likewise, heroic myths defined the early history of the Greek states: the one epic narration of a common undertaking by heroes from all over Greece, Homer's *Iliad* and its sequel, the *Odyssey*, soon became the centre of a curriculum that defined well-educated Greeks wherever they came from, while local heroic mythology entered Greek historiography and its narration of the distant past. Refined theology and ethics, however, took exception to many of the divine myths as early as the late Archaic Age. Because of their double relevance, for theology and for education, these stories and the poems that narrated them could not altogether be jettisoned or replaced by more satisfactory ones, as Plato had wished; rather, Greek intellectuals developed several hermeneutical techniques to deal with them without rejecting them altogether. It is the intellectual toolkit that we subsume under the terms of *allegory* and, as a special form of allegorization in the divine sphere, *Euhemerism*.

It was not long before Christianity found it necessary to deal with mythology: once it left the narrow confines of Palestinian Judaism, it confronted, and was embedded in, a culture in which mythical discourse about the gods in words and images was omnipresent. Peter's Jerusalem was already a vastly multilingual city: 'And there were dwelling at Jerusalem Jews, devout men,

A Companion to Greek Mythology, First Edition. Edited by Ken Dowden and Niall Livingstone.
© 2014 John Wiley & Sons Ltd. Published 2014 by John Wiley & Sons Ltd.

out of every nation under heaven' (Acts 2.5 (King James Version)). Similarly, a growing number of members of well-educated men was amongst those who converted to Christianity: these converts – Hellenized Jews or pagans – had grown up with Homer, Hesiod, and the tragedians, or with Vergil and Ovid, and they were thus intimately familiar with the Greek mythological tradition. As part of their missionary expansion, Christian theological thinkers wanted to refute Greek and Roman religious traditions, and in so doing they placed much more emphasis on mythology, as the ancient discourse on the divine, than on ritual. The only exceptions were the mystery cults, and, later, animal sacrifice, something which was made easier as a result of the growth during the first centuries of the Imperial Age of pagan criticism, and sometimes even rejection, of these sacrifices.[1]

There has been a rapidly growing number of studies on the reception of the Greek and Roman cultural heritage in later literature and art. But the way in which ancient Christian culture dealt with Greek and Roman myth still lacks accounts that focus on the reaction to myth by Christian theologians, or that try to understand the broader picture. In 1957, the German patristic scholar Hugo Rahner explored the use of myth by the Church fathers; the book still remains fundamental.[2] There are some studies on myth in late antique poetry that implicitly concern Christian authors and their audiences, and the same is true for the visual arts;[3] and there is work on handbooks such as that of Fulgentius, or on the history of allegory.[4] But we lack an overall synthesis or detailed study of the way Christian orators such as Ambrose used mythology. As a result, this chapter represents a first step and cannot claim exhaustive coverage.[5]

The overall picture, however, is clear. Christian contact with Greek mythology went through two very different phases. In the beginning, Christian authors on some occasions use parallels from Greek myths to make the Christian core doctrines more comprehensible to a non-Christian Greek or Roman audience. Much, much more often, however, these early Christians reject the pagan mythological tradition, especially its divine myths. Myths deal with the gods of the Greeks and Romans, whom the Christians understand as demons, taking Paul's lead: 'But I say, that the things which the Gentiles sacrifice, they sacrifice to devils, and not to God: and I would not that ye should have fellowship with devils' (1 Corinthians 10.20 (King James Version)). Here the 'devils' of the King James Version represent *daimonia*, 'demons' in the Greek original, and the myths serve to show their absurd and immoral character. As a result, myths serve as a powerful tool to undermine Greek and Roman religion and thus to explain its rejection. In a somewhat different approach that nevertheless led to the same rejection, the Euhemerist reading of divine mythology proves that Greek and Roman gods are nothing but humans, worshipped because of their benefactions to humanity in its early days.

Soon, however, educated Christians realized that it was impossible to reject mythological poetry altogether; one had to accommodate it, again using the tools of allegorical interpretation and Euhemerism.[6] This became even more important once post-Constantinian Christianity moved from being a marginal religious group that fought with non-Christian religious traditions to a position at the centre of society. Quite apart from epic poetry or tragedies whose principal content consisted in bringing the mythical tradition to life, mythical examples and images had always been important in rhetoric and many other poetical genres. The rhetorical handbooks all talk about myth, and although μῦθος (*mythos*) or *fabula* was the least reliable and most fictional of the three standard modes of narration in their overall classification, it lived on. It was hard to create a purely Christian poetic tradition, which meant changing the educational curriculum. Such attempts only really succeeded when the new texts were used in liturgy, as happened in the West with the poems of Ambrose and Prudentius, and in the East with those of Ephraim the Syrian. Julian may have forced the transformation of the traditional literary genres into purely Christian ones upon reluctant Christian intellectuals, as a result of his anti-Christian reforms and his prohibition on Christians teaching the traditional texts, but it remained a transitory enterprise. This does not mean that we would not possess Christian tragedies or epic poems; but they never made a deep impact on the traditional curricula, neither in the Byzantine East nor in the Latin West.[7]

The Apologists' Use of Mythology

Neither the Gospels nor the Acts and Apostolic Letters deal with Greek mythology. Their authors, even Paul, were too much absorbed with the task of shaping the characteristics of Christianity within the Jewish tradition. As for pagan tradition, Paul's declaration (above) that all pagan gods were demons and should not receive worship, became the key argument for not even dealing with their stories. This changed in the early second century when a group of well-educated converts, the so-called apologists, begin to argue in favour of Christianity to a pagan audience. Their various writings have most often the form of an address to an emperor (or, once, to the Roman Senate) in which these men defend their fellow Christians against what they see as unjustified accusation due to a lack of understanding and knowledge of what Christianity professes, and why Christians reject the pagan traditions.[8] A considerable quantity of their writings is lost or preserved only through short citations, mainly in Eusebios' *Church History*. Most of the apologists wrote in Greek (some of their treatises have been preserved only in translation); the Latin tradition begins only towards the end of the second century.

The preserved writings begin with the fragmentary address of one Aristeides, addressed to Hadrian when the emperor visited Athens in 125 or 129. After that we encounter the influential Justin Martyr (executed c. 167 in Rome), his student Tatian whose *Apology* was addressed to Antoninus Verus, c. 156/7), Meliton the bishop of Sardis (*Apology* to Antoninus Pius in 196), and his otherwise unknown contemporary Athenagoras of Athens. These are all steeped in Homer, Hesiod, and the tragedians. Athenagoras also cites Herodotos *verbatim* and refers extensively to the theogonical writings of 'Orpheus' (for which see CH. 4).

The Latin tradition is somewhat less relevant, at least in its beginnings with Tertullian and Minucius Felix, contemporaries whose relationship and primacy is unclear but whose two apologetic works resonate closely with each other. Tertullian's, *Apologeticum*, addressed to the rulers (*antistites*) of the Roman Empire, is dated to AD 195; the *Octavius* of Minucius Felix, dating from about the same time, has the rather untypical form of a Christian dialogue, in which the author recalls a discussion with his close friend Octavius on true religion. In both works, myths are just one amongst many more arguments.

The apologists respond to mythology in three particular ways, which we can capture as follows:

1. Myths make Christ' story understandable

The main aim of the apologists is to prove the rationality and correctness of the Christian faith to an addressee to whom the Christian tenets were unknown. One way of doing so is to point to parallels between the story of Christ and the stories of the Greek gods, as Justin does: 'When we say also that the Word, who is the first-born of God, was produced without sexual union, and that he, Jesus Christ, our teacher, was crucified and died, and rose again, and ascended into heaven, we propound nothing different from what you believe regarding those whom you esteem sons of Zeus (Justin, *1 Apology* 21 (tr. after A. Roberts)). Hermes is the son of Zeus and is his word, Justin explains. Asklepios was born the son of a god and later slain, as were Dionysos and Herakles – not to mention the emperors who become gods after their death, or that 'all writers' call Zeus 'the father of men and gods'. And as to Jesus' birth from a virgin: well, did this not happen also to Perseus?

To insist on these parallels is perhaps the safest way to try to make Christianity understood to a non-Christian, but it is also the most reprehensible in the eyes of a Christian radical, since it accepts the pagan gods on the same level as the Christian god. Justin, who is the only apologist systematically to exploit such parallels, counteracts this later on with the demonstration that pagan myths are in reality distortions of the biblical truth, contrived by the machinations of demons 'in order to lead humanity astray'.[9] This radically devaluates the pagan stories, and with it the principal content of pagan education.[10] Other apologists use these parallels rather sparingly, comparing, for example, Jesus son of God to Herakles son of Zeus.[11]

2. *Myths are immoral and absurd*

It is much more common amongst apologists to take the mythical stories seriously and use them to undermine pagan gods and pagan religion. Worship practice is used rarely to do the same, and only in the case of spectacular rites, such as the child sacrifice to Kronos (Saturn), the Carthaginian Moloch.[12] It will be up to Clement of Alexandria, in the late second century, to do so more systematically, at least for the pagan mystery rites that he summarizes in a brutal sentence: 'In short, these are their mysteries: murder and burials.'[13] Worship as a human activity does not shed light directly on the nature of the gods; myths, when taken as seriously as the Gospels, do.

The apologists insist on two features of traditional myths: their immorality and their absurdity. Neither fits the nature of the divine as defined by Christian theology – or, for that matter, by pagan philosophical theology: the reproach of immorality is as old as Xenophanes of Colophon in the sixth century BC. The problem that Xenophanes attacked was the overdeveloped anthropomorphism of Greek gods. Aristeides, the first preserved apologist, stresses the same feature: the gods of the Greeks are fictitious, male or female, crippled, they work, use magic, play instruments, even die. But more important, 'some of their gods were found who were adulterers, and did murder, and were deluded, and envious, and wrathful and passionate, and parricides, and thieves, and robbers'; as such, they legitimized bad behaviour amongst men.[14] These accusations become fairly constant with many Christian authors well into the fourth century: Arnobius of Sicca, for example, repeats the same accusations, but with many more details, in Books 3–5 of his *Against the Pagans*, as does Lactantius (who was perhaps his student) in his *Divine Institutes*; their *Epitome*, an abbreviated version of the greater work, gives even disproportionally more space to this sort of demythologizing.

But the myths are not only immoral, they are also absurd and do not fit our expectations of the divine. Aristeides gives a catalogue that is often repeated and expanded: gods such as Zeus, driven by lust, change into animals and even into objects; Hermes is an avaricious thief and a sorcerer; Asklepios claimed to be a doctor but could not help himself being struck by lightning; Ares is not only an adulterer but was also fettered; Dionysos went mad and ate snakes – the list goes on for some time like this.[15] Athenagoras focuses on the stories that gods have been born, 'just like ourselves'. He does not stop at this criticism of anthropomorphism, but follows it up philosophically: the birth stories refute immortality, since what has been born must also die, an ontology worthy of Parmenides (fifth century BC) – and he introduces the philosophers who in turn had had their problems with these stories. In the introductory chapter to his *Oration to the Greeks*, Justin dwells on some absurdities of the Homeric poems – inconsistencies and moral flaws in the characters of Agamemnon, Achilles, and Odysseus. This prepares his audience for the later rejection of divine mythology as narrated, for example, in Hesiod's *Theogony*, and it confirms his rejection of the poetic (and educational) tradition: these poems are 'monuments of madness and intemperance'.

At the same time, the apologists insist that these myths have to be taken literally. Allegory is no solution – not because it would save the gods, in the way Greek allegorists wanted to save them, but because it leads to other absurdities. Athenagoras develops this approach: if Kronos is time and Hera air, this introduces change into the divine that cannot change, since time and air are changeable. But there is a more fundamental objection as well, once again based on the characteristics of the divine: though the divine rules and guides the world, physical allegorizing takes away this central task of the gods by making them into elements; simultaneously it then makes apparent the necessary assumption of a creator god behind them: 'The elements without their framer will not move'.[16]

3. The Euhemerist reading of myth

In this way, the principal pagan tool for saving the myths, physical allegory, has been rejected. But another tool was often eagerly embraced instead: this was the so-called Euhemerist reduction of the gods to early human rulers, who were, on this view, worshipped as gods because of their benefactions to humanity. In fact, this interpretative model goes back well before Euhemeros of Messene, after whom Euhemerism is named; it is as old as the Sophistic movement of the fifth century BC, first being attested in Prodikos.[17] Amongst the first Christians to exploit it is Meliton, the bishop of Sardis, in his address of AD c. 176 to Marcus Aurelius, where he explicitly parallels the Euhemerist elevation of ruler to god with the apotheosis of the deceased emperor: 'Even now they worship and honour the images of those of Caesarean rank' (Meliton, *Apology* 1 (tr. A. Roberts)).

In the Syriac version of his address, the only one preserved, he does not dwell very long on the topic: it must have seemed obvious to him. At about the same time, the Roman Minucius Felix stresses the importance of 'the writings of the historians', amongst them Prodikos of Keos and especially Euhemeros of Messene, who related the human careers of those who later became the gods.[18] Though Prodikos must have formulated his view as a serious theory to explain divine worship, Euhemeros' book, the *Hiera Anagraphe* ('Sacred

History') written under the first Ptolemy (ruled 323–282 BC), had a novelistic setting: the narrator reports what he had read on an inscription in the ruins of a temple on the fictitious island of Panchaia somewhere in the Indian Ocean. It was a popular book, translated by the poet Ennius (239–169 BC) into Latin, and copied wholesale by the historian Diodoros for part of his huge universal history, the *Library* (finished c. 30 BC). But it is mostly Christian writers who cite him, often through the intermediary of Diodoros, namely Arnobius and Augustine, Clement and Theodoret, and above all Eusebios and Lactantius in their systematic works on Christian teaching – Eusebios' *Preparation for the Gospel* and Lactantius' *Divine Institutes*, the latter using Ennius' translations, the former Diodoros' excerpts. To them he is, as he had already been to Minucius Felix, a serious historian and 'ancient authority' (*auctor antiquus*, according to Lactantius). This allowed them to cite him as a serious debunker of Greek and Roman gods, and they include long citations and paraphrases of his book in their various chapters where they attack and reject the pagan mythological traditions.[19]

Myth and the Rejection of Greek and Roman Religion

The third century and early fourth centuries witnessed the hardening of the frontline between Christians and the Roman state, partly driven by the political and economic crises that plagued a large part of this period. Under Decius (AD 249–51) and Diocletian (AD 284–305), Christian persecutions grew from local affairs to empire-wide oppression. The short apologetic defence, addressed to an emperor whose benevolence or sense of justice the orator and writer hoped to sway in favour of Christianity, ceded its place to several large-scale works that either addressed the pagan world in its entirety, such as Arnobius' *Against the Pagans* (*Adversus nationes*), Lactantius *Divine Institutes* (*Divinae institutiones*), and, after Constantine's radical change, Eusebios' *Preparation for the Gospel* (*Praeparatio evangelica*). These major treatises were still written to refute the pagans, but they also served progressively to explain Christian theology to possible converts. The rejection of pagan religion still remains a major goal of these writings, and myth plays an all-important role in the discrediting of pagan beliefs. This was based on the erroneous assumption that myths were comparable in their role in pagan religion to that of belief (*pistis, fides*) in Christianity. Pagan mythology is thus transformed into a body of theological teaching about the gods, and Christian writers such as Arnobius do not hesitate to designate the poets, from Homer to the tragedians, as *theologi*. The one pagan to continue this equivalence will be the emperor Julian; at his request his friend Sallustius wrote a treatise on pagan theology

(*On the Gods*), and two of his own speeches (*To the Mother of the Gods, To Helios the King*) were written in the same vein.[20]

Amongst the three Christian treatises I have mentioned, Arnobius' *Against the Pagans* is the one that most explicitly continues the apologetic aim, though on a much larger scale: the work addresses and tries to refute the global accusation that the rise of Christianity was the cause of all the catastrophes of the last decades, and that the gods had in anger stopped caring for humans. A key part in this argument is the demonstration that, far from professing a reprehensible and dangerous religion, the Christians alone have true religion, whereas pagan religion was entirely wrong. Out of his seven books Arnobius did this in the three (Books 3–5) in which myth plays a key role. He continued one of the several lines of arguments already found in the second century apologists, exposing, with a wealth of minute and learned detail, the immoral and unworthy nature of the pagan gods as expressed in Greek and Roman mythology. But, in contrast to the earlier apologists, he turned the tables: he now challenged the pagans to prove that 'there are other gods in nature, power, name' (*Against the Pagans* 3.3), and to do so in the face of an overwhelming array of myths that all seems to argue to the contrary. As already with the earlier apologists, worship played only a small part: Arnobius stressed the fact Christians too pray to, and honour, the divine, and that they could even be persuaded to pray to the pagan gods, if they only could be convinced that they were gods at all (3.6). But the fact that pagan gods all exhibit human characteristics and are embroiled in human activities, that they sometimes even have deformed bodies, that they make love and beget offspring, fight wars, and experience lust and hatred: all of this makes them unsuitable for worship and unworthy of the very name of divine. The argument that all this might be, and presumably is, nothing but licentious fiction (*fictio voluptuosa*) does not help either: these myths are all that we publicly know about the pagan gods, and if their nature were different, they should have been able to make sure that the truth reached the minds of pagan poets (*theologi*) (*Against the Pagans* 4.18). The assumption that the myths would contain a hidden truth needing to be teased out through allegorical explanation cannot convince Arnobius (here too, he follows earlier arguments): allegorical explanations are too clever by far to convince, the various interpreters contradict each other (5.32), they never interpret all the details of a given myth allegorically but select some items only (5.35), and there are plenty of myths where no allegorical interpretation seems to work at all (5.44). As a result, he views it merely as an artificial way 'to make disgraceful things decent' (*cohonestare res turpes*, 5.43). Metonymic use of divine names – such as Venus for 'love' or Mars for 'war' – is no less reprehensible: it is a disrespectful and sacrilegious use of divine names that should be holy (a Christian assumption based on the Old Testament that no pagan ever would have understood).

This rejection of allegorical explanations lived on well beyond Arnobius.[21] Lactantius followed him in rejecting Stoic allegorical explanations, very efficiently basing his rejection on Cicero's.[22] Augustine, being the austere philosopher he was, had more fundamental problems with pagan allegorizing (and, given this rejection, he also tried to put Christian allegorizing on a safe theoretical basis). There are those pagans, he said – including, presumably, members of his congregation with fuzzy allegiances – who justify the worship of their gods with an allegorical explanation and interpret Neptune as the sea or Sol as the sun; they claim: 'I do not worship an image, I worship what the images means'. This is a strategy recommended by Augustine's bête noire, the Neoplatonist philosopher Porphyry, but it cannot convince the bishop of Hippo. Maybe these half-Christians are not idolaters in the most technical sense, since they do not directly worship a divine image, but they still commit one of the gravest theological errors that Augustine castigated the fallible for over and over again, worshipping creation instead of its creator.[23]

In Lactantius and Eusebios, the refutation of pagan religion was merely the first step in a larger exposition of the Christian faith; as in Arnobius, pagan religion was seen as mainly expressed in the myths that were narrated in Greek and Roman poetry. In Book 1 of the *Institutes*, Lactantius starts from his own theological assumptions, which are, at least in part, informed by the pagan philosophical tradition: there is only one god who created and rules the universe (1.3), and god is without body and does not need sex for procreation (1.8). He measures the pagan myths against these standards and, not surprisingly, finds that pagan myths do not live up to them. Nor is it possible to defend them, either as poetic fictions that contain a hidden truth to be teased out by allegorical interpretation or as histories of benefactors of early humanity who were elevated to divine rank.

Eusebios' rejection ranges much wider. He looks not only at the Greek and Roman mythical traditions, but also at Phoenician and Egyptian ones. But the result is as bleak as it was for his predecessors: no story can be taken seriously as theology, and allegorical explanation falls short as ever. As he shows through a long quotation from a lost theological treatise of Plutarch,[24] 'even the wonderful and secret physiology of the Greek theology conveyed nothing divine, nor anything great and worthy of deity' (Eusebios, *Preparation for the Gospel* 3.2.1).[25]

The Persistence of Mythology

When, at the end of the fourth century AD, the emperor Theodosios I prohibited pagan worship, the recipients of this worship, the gods and heroes, did not go away, nor did their myths. But unlike the ritual survival and slow fading of these gods and heroes into the murky twilight of demonology, the myths remained what they had always been: stories told by poets, orators, or artists. They did not just survive in the texts of the pagan writers, beginning with Homer, that were still read and interpreted in schools or enjoyed by any new reader (provided they had survived the transition in book production from scroll to codex): as in the centuries before, they were retold or alluded to by the now Christian poets, used as examples by Christian orators, or depicted by Christian artists. The literary culture of the imperial age, nurtured and kept alive by a strong educational system and maintained as an expression of status pride and of identity by the elites, survived the political change of religions – its change and demise had other reasons than the rise of Christianity.[26]

Poetry

Of course, some of the poets of this Christian age wrote only on Christian topics, such as the Latin poet Prudentius or the Greek empress Eudokia, the wife of Theodosios I (ruled 378–95), even though they continued pagan forms or even used Homer's verses to tell the biblical creation story, as Eudokia did in her *Homerocento*. Others wrote both pagan and Christian poetry. They must have been educated both in the new faith and the traditional Greek and Roman literature. Earlier scholars were sometimes puzzled and felt tempted to either postulate two homonymous poets, one pagan and one Christian, or to postulate a conversion; but contemporary scholarship has correctly become sceptical of such easy solutions. The fifth-century poet Dracontius of Carthage wrote Christian poems such as the popular *De laudibus Dei* (dating from between 486 and 496), but also hexameter poems on *Medea, Helen, Hylas*, and an *Orestis tragoedia*, a long hexameter work on the Orestes myth.[27] Nonnos of Panopolis (before the mid-fifth century) wrote both a hexameter paraphrase of the Gospel of John and the huge and well-known epic in forty-eight books on Dionysos, the *Dionysiaka*. In neither case are speculations about a change of religious allegiance warranted: even if the authors did not grow up as Christians, there is no reason to assume that their mythical works were written before a (hypothetical) conversion.[28]

Other writers do not make our decision about their religious allegiance very easy; but maybe they would have regarded such a decision as irrelevant for their poetry anyway. Claudian (died before 404) wrote praise poems and other occasional poetry for Roman senators, and especially on the exploits of his patron, the Vandal Stilicho; but he also wrote the unfinished poem *De raptu Proserpinae* ('On the abduction of Proserpina (Persephone)'). Stilicho served Christian emperors and was presumably Christian himself; Claudian's religion remains unknown. But the point here, as with Nonnos, is not the personal religious allegiance of an author but his expectation that a poem on Proserpina or Dionysos would have an audience in a Christian world. There is not even the need to read these myths in an allegorical way, although similar themes in mosaic art (such as the stories of Dionysos or of the singer Orpheus amongst the animals) are open to a Christian reading: Orpheus singing amongst the animals shades into David the psalmist, and Dionysos the Saviour might well become an image for Christ.[29]

In some poetical genres, mythology was almost de rigueur; the generic tradition demanded it, and its omission needs explanation. In a detailed investigation published in the late 1980s, Michael Roberts studied the Latin *epithalamium*, a poetical genre with roots in early Greek poetry and ritual that in its Latin form is mainly attested in late antiquity. Mythology, especially the mythology of Venus, is important, and few of the existing poems leave it out, even if written by a Christian poet – though the two poems without myth, one by Paulinus the bishop of Nola, another by an anonymous poet, were both written for a Christian couple. Other Christian poets such as Sidonius Apollinaris, Dracontius, or Ennodius (who also wrote liturgical hymns) exhibit all the mythical ornamentation the rhetorical handbooks were demanding, as does Claudian's epithalamium: the use of myth has become a conventional feature for both poet and addressees.[30] Claudian's epic *De bello Gildonico* ('On the war with Gildo', written around 394–8) opens with the goddess Roma pleading with Jupiter and Jupiter's prophesies of the victories of Honorius (ruled 395–423): these are staple scenes of epic poetry in the wake of Vergil's *Aeneid* (19 BC); religion does not enter into it. The same holds true in the East, as shown, for example, by the works of Dioskoros of Aphrodito in Upper Egypt (died 585): an orator, lawyer, and writer, he left a body of occasional poems – encomia, panegyrics, epithalamia – that are full of mythological images.[31] In an encomion for a local aristocrat that is at the same time a petition, he can compare him to Homer, Ares, and Eros (4.4), or to 'Orpheus son of Calliope' (4.7); another nobleman, Kallinikos, is fittingly compared to Herakles who had the epithet Kallinikos (him of 'fine victory', 4.18). In an epithalamion, the love of the marrying couple is compared with several mythical love affairs whose success (Zeus and Leda, Zeus and Europa) or misfortune (Apollo and Daphne) the couple easily will outdo (4.33).

Prose orations

The use of myth in prose orations is even more interesting. Again, the use of myth as argument and *exemplum* (stereotyped example) belongs to the rhetorical tradition. Only radical Christian orators such as John Chrysostom in the East or Augustine in the West would abstain entirely from pagan imagery. Others used it freely, especially after the fourth century, continuing the pagan tradition. The speeches of an Eastern orator such as Choricius of Gaza (sixth century) are not only reminiscent of those of Libanios of Antioch, the pagan friend of Julian; they cite the classical authors from Homer onwards, and they are filled with allusions to traditional mythology.[32] It goes almost without saying that Choricius' wedding speeches – prose epithalamia – refer to Eros and Aphrodite in the same way the poetic epithalamia do; it is more telling for his culture that he does not hesitate to introduce a speech that praises a new church built by the archbishop of Gaza by comparing his own task to Herodotos' description of the city of Babylon, and the local festival to the gathering of the Ionians on Delos (*Oration* 2). Choricius, like his contemporary Dioskoros in Egypt, testifies to the unhesitating reception of Hellenic *paideia* amongst the Eastern elite. Had we the orations of their contemporaries in the West, we would doubtless see the same.[33]

A more surprising instance – because early, and because there can be no doubt about his religious adherence – is Ambrose in the Latin West. A well-educated administrator before being raised to the see of Milan in 374, he saw no reason not to use myth as a tool of persuasion. He can do so, in the way of the apologists, to elucidate for a pagan audience an aspect of Christian doctrine: 'Pagans should please compare with the benefits of Christ not their own gods' deeds but their fictions (*non facta sed ficta*)', he admonishes his audience, and then he proceeds to use Ovid's story of King Midas who turned to gold whatever he touched, with the most dire results: 'Such are the benefits of the idols that do damage even when they seem advantageous; but Christ's gifts seem tiny but are in reality huge.'[34] More often, however, pagan stories have a more direct moral that can be applied to human life. The fall of Ikaros from the sky because he was flying too close to the sun teaches us about the difference between the wise restraint of older age and the recklessness of the young: wise old men fly safely through life, but young people too easily yield to the lures of the world, forgetting the truths they were taught, and take a hard fall (he states this once as a general maxim, a second time applied to virginity).[35] Odysseus' many distractions on the way home, and especially the adventures with the Sirens, serve to explain why a religious man can be distracted in the course of his life from the thought of celestial things. Odysseus' travails can also stand for the dangers of avarice: whoever is too much dedicated to money is threatened by the noise of Charybdis and the sweet songs of the Sirens who again stand for the lure of desire.[36]

The Siren episode can be put to other uses as well: Odysseus stopped his ears in order not to yield to their erotic temptations, but a Christian opens his ears to the voice of Christ who brings salvation. And in the same way that Odysseus was tied to the wooden mast of his ship the Christian is tied to the wooden cross of Christ. In this very context, Ambrose gives a detailed exposition of the way poetic fiction elaborates this myth through the use of images – the sea, the female bodies of the Sirens, their rocky island – and implicitly rejects Arnobius' objection that allegorical readings rely on select detail only:

> What sea is more precipitous than secular life, so unreliable, so fickle, so deep, and so stormy thanks to the winds of foul spirits? What does the female shape mean other but the lures of debilitating desire that effeminates the self-restraint of a mind in their thrall? What do those shallows mean but the rocks that threaten our salvation? Nothing is as blind as the danger of worldly attractions: while it caresses the soul, it destroys your life and shatters the mind's perception on cliffs of the body. (tr. after H. De Romestin)[37]

As Rahner has shown, both Odysseus and the Sirens are images that Christian orators and writers used often. Ambrose fits into a much wider Greek tradition. The Sirens, legitimated, as Christian writers were quick to notice, by their presence in the Septuagint as creatures of the wilderness,[38] take on their own life as Christian symbols of all that is both highly attractive but also dangerous and destructive – from Greek literature, philosophy, and science to the many heresies. They can stand alone, but more often are combined with Odysseus, who in turn has become an image for the wise and ascetic Christian able to escape the snares of temptation, especially when bound to the cross-like mast of his ship that protects the faithful Christian against the dangers of this world, from lust to heresy.[39]

Education and the Survival of Myth

Ambrose was not the first Christian writer to exploit Odysseus' story in this way, and he was far from the last. Although the apologists initially rejected Homer as the arch-inventor of mythical fiction (sometimes backed by Plato's condemnation of the poet), already at the end of the second century Clement used the story of the Sirens, ironically enough, to attack Christian rejection of pagan storytelling:

> It seems to me that the majority of those who are Christians approach literature in a crude way, as so many companions of Odysseus evading not the Sirens but rhythms and melody, stopping their ears in a rejection of education, as if they would know that once they would succumb to Greek learning they would never return home again. But who selects the useful to help the catechumens, especially when they are Greek – 'the earth is the LORD's, and the fullness thereof' [Psalms 24:1] – should not let go of his love for culture like a brute animal: it is possible to harvest many helpful things for one's audience. Only one should not remain there as if it alone were useful, but once one has used it one should return home to the true philosophy. (Clement, *Stromateis* 6.11.89.1)

Clement points to the main reason that mythology survived: the literary works that told these stories were the mainstay of ancient education. Christians should not exclude themselves from this, and the catechumens might well have had a thorough pagan education before their conversion. Clement follows pagan educational tradition: the image of Odysseus's companions who have their ears stopped against the songs of the Sirens had appeared already in Plutarch's *On Reading Poets* where the philosophers refused to have young peoples' ears blocked against the beauty of Greek poetry but offered instead the tool of allegorical explanation to sanitize these beautiful but dangerous stories.[40] The Siren image lived on well after Clement, in this same educational context: in the later fourth century another Christian educator, Basil of Caesarea, gave it an interesting twist in his *To the Young, How One Can Profit From Greek Literature*.[41] This seminal treatise of Basil's, a short essay addressed to his nephews, insists on the value and usefulness of pagan literature for young Christians. One should not read everything, according to Basil, only those texts that talk about good people: 'But when the teacher addresses bad people as examples, one should turn away from them and cover one's ears not unlike Odysseus, as they tell us, eluded the songs of the Sirens' (Basil, *To the young* 4).

It deserves to be stressed that in education, with the exception of the catechumens, no real distinction was ever made between pagans and Christians. The most outstanding fourth-century scholar and teacher of literature, Aelius Donatus, taught both Servius, the pagan commentator on Vergil, and Jerome, the Christian translator of the Bible. We are left in the dark about Donatus' religious beliefs, but he might well have been a pagan, as was the orator Themistios who taught the then Christian prince Julian, the future emperor. In the same way, Christian teachers must have taught pagan students. The only person of consequence to object to this was, once again, the now converted emperor Julian. In a letter on teaching, he objected to Christians teaching pagan canonical texts:

> To Homer, Hesiod, Demosthenes, Lysias, Herodotos and Thucydides, the gods were the leaders of all education; did not some claim to be sacred to Hermes, others to the Muses? Thus, I think it to be absurd that the persons who explain their works would dishonour the gods they themselves had honoured. But although I deem this absurd, I do not demand that they should convert before teaching the young. I give them a choice: they should either not teach what they do not take seriously, or if they want to teach, they should first convince their students by their own attitude and show that neither Homer nor Hesiod nor anyone else was as stupid as <they think> and condemn them of irreligiosity, stupidity and error towards the gods. (Julian, *Letters* 61c Bidez)

The implication of this statement is not fully clear: whereas some scholars read it as prohibiting Christian teachers from teaching at all, it could also exhort

Christian teachers to employ the sort of allegorical reading of mythology the emperor applied himself in his theological speeches.

Commentaries were an important tool for teaching mythology. Teaching the poets had already created a need for commentaries in Hellenistic times, and this became more urgent during the imperial era, both to elucidate the many mythological allusions in poems such as the *Odyssey* or the *Aeneid* and to explain the stories they told in a way that was acceptable for young readers. There was a *Mythographus Homericus* as early as the first century AD, and Servius' commentary on Vergil conserves much of a similar *Mythographus Vergilianus*: these narrate the myths to which the poet alludes, without any allegorical explanations.[42] Plutarch's older contemporary, the Stoic philosopher Cornutus, wrote a Greek *Survey of the Content of Greek Theology*, a short narration of Greek mythology with ample physical allegories, obviously destined for the schools, that begins:

> Sky, my child, surrounds in a cycle earth and sea and whatever is on earth and in the sea: it got its name [*ouranós*] from this, since fair wind [*ouros*] is above and limits everything.
>
> Some poets say his son was Akmon, referring as in a riddle to his unceasing [*akmētos*] movement.

This is not the only place where physical explanation is intertwined with etymology to provide a key to Greek mythology in this obviously pedagogical way.

Allegorical or moralizing explanation remained vital throughout antiquity, and beyond. Cornutus' book is cited by Theodoret, the fifth-century bishop of Kurrhos in Syria (now in Turkey); and the 1881 edition of Cornutus' *Survey* gives a list of thirty-five Byzantine manuscripts from the twelfth century and later: although they testify first and foremost to the 'twelfth-century Renaissance', the survival of the treatise at all would have been impossible but for its appreciation by earlier generations of teachers. At about the time Theodoret was ordained bishop (423), the learned Roman aristocrat Ambrosius Theodosius Macrobius began his commentary on Cicero's *Dream of Scipio* – addressed, like Cornutus' booklet, to his son – with a classification of *fabulae*, non-factual narrations.[43] *Fabulae* either entertain or educate; comedies and novels only entertain, but all the others educate, either overtly as in the animal fables of Aesop, or covertly, concealing the truth under a narrative surface, as in the theological poetry of Hesiod or Orpheus or the philosophical myths of Plato or Cicero. Far from rejecting the traditional myths, even if their surface seems as unfitting for them as it is in the stories of the castration of Ouranos or the deposing of Kronos by Zeus, Macrobius postulates that the gods themselves prefer to be presented to the many in this traditional guise, and he cites

the case of Numenius who explained the Eleusinian mythology and was visited in a dream by the two goddesses who accused him of prostituting them.[44]
This is not only a defence of traditional mythology against Plato's rejection
but an implicit plea for reading them allegorically, to be viewed in the context
of the use of commentary as an educational tool for explaining classical texts
in the late antique school (that is why it is addressed to his son). It seems irrelevant whether Macrobius was still a pagan or more plausibly, given that he
most likely held a high administrative position, a Christian: Christian education continued pagan practice in the same way that the allegorical *Wedding of
Mercury and Philology* by Martianus Cappella did half a century later.[45]

Two centuries later, in the Latin West, allegorical interpretation of pagan
mythology found definitive literary expression for the centuries that followed:
this was the three books of *Mitologiae* ('Mythologies') by Fulgentius, who
describes his project in its prologue as follows:

> So what I wish to do is to expose the vacuity [of myth], not to make cosmetic
> improvements by making changes to what is already exposed … and so I watch
> out for the real impact of the material, so that I can recognize what secret
> knowledge my brain ought to know, once the mythical words of lying Greece
> have been buried.[46]

This constitutes a clear allegorical programme, and Fulgentius would keep to
it – but not before he has explained (1.1) how the first idol resulted from the
grief of a man (one 'Syrophanes of Egypt') for his son, and how it gave a focus
to the fears of that household, so proving that pagan idols are in reality dead
humans, and that it was fear that created the first gods.

Despite the developed sense of methodology expressed in his introduction,
in the fifty mythological chapters that Fulgentius wrote, he does not follow a
single consistent method of allegorical explanation. Most often, he explains
mythical figures as elements and natural phenomena: Jupiter/Zeus is fire,
Juno/Hera is air (1.3); Ceres is the full harvest, Proserpina the sowing (1.10);
Apollo is the sun (1.13). Other myths have a moral meaning: not surprisingly,
the story of Tantalus signifies the fate of the greedy rich (2.15); Paris judges
between the three basic forms of life, theoretical and contemplative (Minerva),
practical (Juno), and hedonistic (Venus), with Paris signifying human free will
(2.1); the three Furies represent the three stages of anger – quiet fury, angry
talk, aggression (1.7). Others again are historical: Endymion means the first
human who figured out the lunar month of thirty days ('therefore they say he
slept thirty years', 2.16). Etymology is often used, mostly in the fanciful way
of ancient etymologists, from Plato's *Kratylos* to Macrobius' *Saturnalia*: 'Zeus
in Greek means either life or heat' (1.3), connecting the name either with
some forms of *zoō* 'to live' (an etymology as old as Pherekydes of Syrus) or

with *zeō* "to boil, seethe"; the fury Megaira means *megalē eris*, 'great strife' (1.7); Bellerophon is *boulēphoros*, 'who relies on his wisdom', which Fulgentius confirms with a line from Homer, 'the *boulēphoros* man should not sleep all night long' (*Iliad* 2.24, *Mythologies* 3.1). Already from this small sample it becomes clear how much the learned Fulgentius relies on Greek and, more generally, pagan lore, whatever his direct sources were.

Scholars have discussed whether this Fulgentius, with the full name Fabius Planciades Fulgentius, who must have been writing in North Africa around AD 500, was the same Fulgentius who died in about 532 as bishop of Ruspe in North Africa and was famous as an outspoken anti-Arrianist monk and cleric. Whatever the answer to this question is, religion is irrelevant for the *Mythologies*. Although its author must be a Christian, nothing in his interpretations is manifestly Christian, except the introductory chapter against idolatry. Indeed, the organization of his first book is, if anything, clearly reminiscent of Ovid's *Metamorphoses*.

Conclusions

Looking back from the sixth century AD, the rejection of mythology by the apologists and their followers would seem almost to be an episode that had no long-term consequences, were it not for the role of their arguments in the final prohibition of pagan worship at the end of the fourth century. The Christianization of the imperial world left educational and literary traditions more or less intact: generic conventions of poetry and prose that called for the use of mythological narratives remained valid well after Theodosios. One is tempted to assert that this also testifies to the fact that myth had become more and more a matter of literature – Theodosios' prohibition of pagan worship concerned politics and religion, not literature and art. But this is an oversimplification. Even in the imperial epoch, narration of, and innovation in, mythology was also driven by local identities that focused on local worship, local shrines, and local families with their genealogies. The Christianization of the administration, and especially the prohibition of pagan worship, put an end to this. From then on, it was the works of literature alone (and the handbooks that condensed the literary traditions into convenient morsels) that dominated the use of myth in Christian poetry and prose. It is no coincidence that the allusions in Ambrose or Choricius are to the stories known from Homer, Herodotos, or Vergil and Ovid, namely to what was taught in schools. The only space left for mythical innovation was in the allegorical creation of myth: Martianus Capella used it in his immense *Wedding of Mercury and Philology*, and so did Boëthius in the impressive and highly influential *Consolation of Philosophy* (AD 523/4) with its splendid picture of a goddess

Philosophia and her struggle with the Muses. The future of myth would belong to allegory, both passive allegorical explanation in the spirit of Fulgentius, and active allegorical creation in the manner of Boëthius.

FURTHER READING

See the notes to this chapter for a guide to the bibliography of the various authors and periods covered in this chapter. For the subject overall, the Anglophone reader should first consult Rahner 1963 and Liebeschuetz 1995.

NOTES

1. See Petropoulou (2009).
2. Rahner (1963). For a survey article, see also Liebeschuetz (1995); von Haehling (2005), a collection of essays, is interesting, but lacks the unity and breadth of Rahner's book.
3. For the visual arts, see especially the seminal work Weitzmann (1952), and Weitzmann (1960).
4. Fulgentius: Hays (2004).
5. I thank my colleague Anthony Kaldellis for his help with the bibliography.
6. On the history of allegorical interpretation in Greece, see Pépin (1976 and 1987); on the Alexandrian roots of Christian allegory, Dawson (1992).
7. Julian's law (*codex Theodosianus* 13.3.5, dated 17 June 362; repealed 11 January 364, *codex Theodosianus* 13.3.6) and Julian, *Letters* 61c was read as a *de facto* prohibition on Christians teaching, see Marrou (1956: 323–4).
8. For an overview over this group see Norris (2004).
9. *1 Apology* 54–5.
10. *1 Apology* 54: the poets teach these stories 'to the youth who learn them'.
11. Tatian, *Oration* 21.
12. Aristeides, *Apology* 9 (*Barlaam and Joasaph* 27.244); Tertullian, *Apologeticus* 9.
13. φόνοι καὶ τάφοι, Clement, *Protreptikos* 2 (16 P.).
14. Aristeides *Apology* 8 in the Syriac version; cf. Ps.-John Damascene, *Barlaam and Joasaph* 27.244: 'so that, having these gods as advocates for bad behavior, they could commit adultery, robbery and murder'.
15. Aristeides, *Apology* 9–11; the parallel list in *Barlaam and Joasaph* is at 27.244–8. See also Minucius Felix, *Octavius* 22.1–7 and Tertullian, *Apologeticus* 14.
16. Athenagoras, *Embassy* 22, tr. B.P. Plummer.
17. DK 82 B 5.
18. *Octavius* 20.5–21.2 (Euhemeros, F 9 Winiarczyk, partly included in *FGrH* 63 F 4f).
19. See especially Lactantius, *Divine Institutes* 1.11 and Epitome 13;
20. For Julian, see Fontaine, Prato, and Marcone (1987) for an edition with commentary.

21. On the problem the Christians created for themselves and their allegorical reading of the Bible see Pépin (1987: 167–86).
22. Lactantius, *Divine Institutes* 1.12–13, after Cicero, *Nature of the Gods* bk. 3.
23. Augustine, *Sermo* 26.17–24, 34–5 Dolbeau; Porphyry, F 354–60 Smith.
24. Plutarch, *On the Daidala in Plataia* (F 157 Sandbach).
25. Translations not otherwise marked are my own.
26. See Bowersock (1990) and, for the later centuries, Kaldellis (2007); see also some of the essays in Johnson (2006). For the West, Curtius (1948) still remains fundamental.
27. See Kaufmann (2006).
28. See Willers (1992), citing a contemporary Egyptian tapestry that shows Christian and Dionysiac iconography.
29. On Orpheus see Irwin (1982); on Dionysus, Daszewski (1985).
30. Roberts (1989).
31. Commented edition: Fournet (1999); see also MacCoull (1988).
32. Webb (2006).
33. In the fragmentary *Oration* 2, Cassiodorus (consul in 514) uses the story of Achilles hidden amongst the daughters of Lykomedes.
34. Ambrose, *Exposition of the Gospel according to Luke* 6.88.
35. Ambrose, *Commentary on the Song of Songs* 16.
36. Ambrose, *On [the book of] Tobit* 1.5; *Exposition of the Christian Faith* 3.1.
37. *Exposition of the Gospel according to Luke* 4.1–2: *Quod autem mare abruptius quam saeculum, tam infidum, tam mobile, tam profundum, tam immundorum spirituum flatibus procellosum? quid sibi vult puellarum figura, nisi eviratae voluptatis illecebra, quae constantiam captae mentis effeminet? quae autem illa vada, nisi nostrae scopuli sunt salutis? nihil enim tam caecum, quam saecularis suavitatis periculum: quae dum mulcet animum, vitam obruit, et corporeis quibusdam scopulis sensum mentis illidit.*
38. Job 30.29; Isaiah 32.21–2; Jeremiah 50 (27).39; Micah 1.8.
39. Rahner (1963).
40. See the commented edition, Hillyard (1981).
41. See the commented edition, Wilson (1975).
42. On the *Mythographus Homericus*, absorbed in the D-Scholia to Homer but attested by several papyri, see Alan Cameron (2004: 27–8), and van Rossum-Steenbeek (1998: ch. 3); on the *Mythographus Vergilianus* see Cameron (2004: 184–216).
43. His classification is unusual; Isidore, *Etymologies* 1.44.5 gives a definition that continues traditions of rhetorical teaching that goes back to Hellenistic times, see Cicero, *On Invention* 1.27 and *Rhetorica to Herennius* 1.12.
44. Macrobius, *Scipio's Dream* 1.7–21.
45. Shanzer (1986) understands the work as pro-pagan propaganda; but this remains controversial.
46. *Mutatas itaque uanitates manifestare cupimus, non manifesta mutando fuscamus … certos itaque nos rerum praestolamur effectus, quo sepulto mendacis Greciae fabuloso commento quid misticum in his sapere debeat cerebrum agnoscamus.*

PART IV

OLDER TRADITIONS

CHAPTER EIGHTEEN

The Indo-European Background to Greek Mythology

Nicholas J. Allen

An Indo-European Mythology?

Most of the languages of Europe, some languages in ancient Asia Minor, the Iranian languages, and many of the Indian languages (amongst others) – all these have been shown to derive broadly from a single original language for which there is no direct evidence, an unattested 'protolanguage'. This language is called 'Indo-European' (IE), or, with emphasis on its hypothetical status, 'Proto-Indo-European'. This chapter takes for granted the family tree model: the attested IE languages derive branch by branch from the 'protolanguage', features of which can be reconstructed by comparative philology, the study of the shared features of the descendant languages. A common view is that the protolanguage was spoken north of the Caspian or Black Sea in the first half of the fourth millennium BC and then dispersed from there, diversifying as it did so.[1] However, the location and date of the protolanguage are less important here than the stories and particularly the myths that were surely told in it. Does comparison between attested IE mythologies enable us to envisage or even reconstruct an unattested IE *protomythology*?

The answer is not obvious. The protomythology might have changed so much faster than the protolanguage that comparison would prove fruitless; or traces of protomyths might have survived only in branches of IE other than Greek and Italic. Perhaps, in Greece, any such survivals were submerged by

---

A Companion to Greek Mythology, First Edition. Edited by Ken Dowden and Niall Livingstone.
© 2014 John Wiley & Sons Ltd. Published 2014 by John Wiley & Sons Ltd.

the culture of a pre-IE *substratum* (the people who were in Greece before the Greeks), by an *adstratum* (influence from West Asia and/or Egypt), by the innovatory character of Greek culture, or by a combination of these. As for Italy, some suppose that, apart from its borrowings from Greece, it possessed little mythology of any kind. But we shall argue that, as it happens, such pessimism is not justified.

'Mythology' will be taken broadly to cover narratives expressed in various genres (epic, mythography, pseudohistory, catalogues, iconography), but also to cover non-narrative beliefs about supernaturals and non-historical humans. Myths about creation, cosmology, and eschatology come close to philosophy, and the hypothesis of an IE protophilosophy is not impossible. To separate myths about gods from legends about humans is unhelpful where gods and humans interact and interbreed; also, as we shall see, cognate narratives may apply to the one sort of being in one region, to the other in another. Proto-IE myths must have been transmitted orally (perhaps alongside images) until they were written down, but I focus here on the content of the tradition rather than on the contexts of transmission (e.g., rituals or performances).

IE is of course only one amongst dozens of language families across the world, each potentially having its own mythology. Some linguists attempt to situate IE within an even larger and deeper super-family which they call 'Nostratic', and certainly, far from being some sort of Big Bang, proto-IE is merely the limit beyond which most linguists think their mode of comparativism ceases to work. Ultimately, IE myths will go back to those of our Palaeolithic ancestors who emerged from Africa.[2] Within IE, distinctions may be made between proto-IE proper (which includes the Anatolian branch), mature IE (which does not), and the even later Greco-Aryan, common ancestor of Greek and Indo-Iranian (c. 2500 BC);[3] but the early branching and early interactions within the language family remain controversial. Unfortunately, archaeology can here give only limited help.

Relative to its linguistic counterpart, IE comparative mythology is at present a somewhat marginal endeavour within academe, enjoying little institutional support. Its new recruits are mostly individuals trained and employed in some other field, often Classics, who sense the excitement of comparativism and accept the risks. The risks are not inconsiderable, for comparativists engage with cultures that they cannot hope to know as well as those who specialize in them: they face a vast literature, primary, commentarial, and comparative; they must choose amongst contesting views on priorities and methods; if they go astray, they waste everybody's time on fanciful structures and rapprochements, and even if they do not, they may well encounter neglect, even hostility, from those committed to traditional disciplinary boundaries. Small wonder that the status of the undertaking is controversial.

Three Approaches to the IE Heritage

Though a proper history is needed, many have claimed that nineteenth-century comparative mythology achieved little of lasting value. Nowadays, the two main divides are between (i) those who reject or ignore the theories of Georges Dumézil (1898–1986), and (ii) those who try to use them; and amongst the latter, between (a) those who accept Dumézil's 'trifunctional' schema as it stands, and (b) those who think it needs expansion. The writer belongs firmly in the final category (b) – a minority within a minority (the reader is warned!). Category (i) is well represented by the magisterial M. L. West (2007).

Dumézil was extremely prolific: a valuable bibliography lists 73 books, 246 articles, 540 items in all.[4] However, his IE work is essentially summarized in some fifteen books from the period he labelled his *phase du bilan* ('the stage of taking stock', 1966–2000, two titles being posthumous). Ranging well beyond myth, he focuses on IE ideology, expressed as much in ritual, law and social structure as in narratives. 'Ideology' here refers to a more or less unified body of ideas, and is studied comparatively by materials taken mainly from the Celtic, Germanic, Italic, Greek, and Indo-Iranian branches, with little use of Anatolian. Dumézil repudiated his early work, which relied heavily on Greek material, and he later rather avoided Greece.

Dumézil envisaged IE ideology (the IE conceptual world/worldview) as articulated into a small number of contrasting 'functions'. This term comes from the functions attributed to the estates from which, according to the texts, early Indian and Iranian society was constituted. However, it was soon extended to the specializations of deities and other agents, and by now it has come to mean a bundle of ideas, coordinate with other such bundles and, together with them, forming an ideology. One can think of the ideology as presenting a classification of the forces governing the world.

Naturally, the texts do not explicitly expound the ideology. What one finds, in different IE societies, is manifestations of the ancient ideology in particular contexts. The components of a society, the specialities of a set of heroes or priests, the procedures recognized in a law or ritual, correspond to each other in the sense that component A, speciality A and procedure A all relate to the same bundle of ideas, that is, to the same function, and similarly for B and C – till you arrive at a 'trifunctional schema', a system of three functions. There is nothing anthropologically odd about ideologies of this general type (which I call 'partitional'), nor about the fact that, over the long term, they tend to lose their pervasiveness and clear articulation, and thus become unrecognizable, in one context after another. The classical civilizations are situated typologically between an earlier period, when (presumably) the ideology was clearer and more pervasive, and the modern world, where ideologies are differently organized. The manifestation of the ideology in a classical text does not mean that the writer of the text adhered to it. Most manifestations will have had a long prehistory, mostly oral, which the writers were following without being fully aware of it.

I will not, however, start with Dumézil's schema, but with the less familiar pentadic (fivefold) schema, first adumbrated by the Rees brothers using Irish texts.[5] This schema is a hierarchy consisting of a triadic core and two extremities. The three core functions have numerical labels indicating both their ranking and the order in which their representatives typically occur in texts:

F1   the first function pertains to wisdom and knowledge, whether exercised in relation to gods (religion and ritual) or men (law);
F2   the second to dynamism, physical force, and war;
F3   the third to abundance and fecundity, together with their conditions and consequences (such as health, wealth, sexuality).

The two extremities are then grouped together under the fourth function, which pertains to what, relative to the core functions, is other, outside or beyond:

F4+   its positive aspect pertains to what is valued and transcendent;
F4−   its negative aspect to what is devalued (hated, feared, excluded).

Reasons for preferring a split fourth function to a fifth function have been advanced elsewhere, but include cyclical contexts where the extremes are juxtaposed (the Old Year, often devalued, adjoins a valued New Beginning). A simple manifestation of the pentadic ideology would be a social structure consisting of king, priests, warriors, producers, slaves/enemies. Such a structure might be realized only in ritual contexts – one need not envisage five lifestyles that would be archaeologically distinguishable.

Dumézil's schema has problems with both extremities. Representatives of the devalued half-function tend to be ignored or treated as later accretions, while the top of the hierarchy is coped with in various ways. Sometimes the first function is defined as covering sovereignty in addition to sacred knowledge, or it may be split into two aspects, which he names after Vedic gods – Varuṇa the remote and Mitra the close; sometimes kingship is treated as 'transfunctional', or characters are allocated to the shadowy category of 'framework hero' (*héros cadre*). Pentadic theory accepts that in contexts where only the core functions are represented a Dumézilian analysis is sufficient, and that in other contexts it may appear so: thus a tradition that loses a representative of the first function (F1) may present the sequence F4+, F2, F3.

In general, the pentadic theory subsumes the triadic one, offering greater specificity, scope, and versatility.[6]

Both these approaches emphasize structures – totalities characterized by the relations between their components as much as by the components in themselves. Those who reject the Dumézilian approach tend to be more aware of individual entities. Thus, faced with a sequence of gods in a particular context, Dumézilians will note the gods' number, order, and ranking, and the contrasts between them, and then look elsewhere in the IE world for lists of similar structure, while non-Dumézilians will focus on the name and attributes of the individual gods; and in the absence of etymological links the structural similarities will seem to them unpersuasive. If they recognize the similarities, they may attribute them either to chance or to universals: everyone thinks, exerts bodily strength, has appetites for food and sex – they will say – so the core functions must be found everywhere and tell us nothing significant about Indo-Europeans. Much safer to concentrate on language – for instance, on poetic figures and locutions – where the IE specificity of the comparisons is unquestionable. The sceptic's position may be supported by appeal to authority ('Most scholars ignore Dumézil', or 'The great so-and-so explicitly attacked him') or, as Dumézil himself did, by pointing to individual weaknesses here and there in his vast *oeuvre*, or to unacceptable 'analyses' by some of his would-be followers. In fact, few critics apart from Schlerath have seriously engaged with the facts.[7] Of Schlerath's objections some are valid and still unresolved, some are answered by pentadic theory, and some result from 'blindness to structure' or misunderstanding.

Case Studies

Rather than multiplying references to the vast comparativist literature I shall now present four case studies. This will allow slightly greater depth, though naturally the presentation is compressed. My main aim is to foster interest in the approach.

Theoretically, a distinction exists between identifying manifestations of IE ideology and identifying cognate narratives but, as will be seen, the two are in practice often interlinked.

1. A warrior king

The biography of Tullus Hostilius, the third of the four pre-Etruscan kings of Rome (supposedly ruled 672–641 BC), was compared by Dumézil with that of the Hindu king-and-warrior god Indra.[8] The following summaries come mostly from Livy and the *Mahābhārata*.[9] Since the Sanskrit epics reached their current form at least a millennium later than the Vedas, IE linguists prefer to use the earlier texts, but for mythologists the epic often proves more useful: much IE heritage bypassed the Vedas.

The asura demons are rivals of the gods.	Alba becomes a rival of Rome.
The god Tvaṣṭṛ fathers a demon-monster called Triśiras ('Three-headed').	Its leader Mettius has as champions the triplets called Curiatii.
Indra, king of the gods, defeats Triśiras and orders his triple decapitation.	At Rome, Tullus has as champions the triplets called Horatii; One Horatius kills all the Curiatii.
Furious, Tvaṣṭṛ produces the monstrous Vṛtra to continue the feud. Indra and Vṛtra make a pact, but by casuistry Indra kills Vṛtra.	Angered, Mettius incites the Fidenates to attack Rome. Tullus and Mettius make a treaty. Mettius breaks it; Tullus defeats the Fidenates, and by a trick kills Mettius.
Indra's killings produce a female spirit called Brahmahatyā ('Brahman-killing' – a terrible sin).	One of the Curiatii was the fiancé of Horatia, who reproaches her brother Horatius for the killings.
Because of his guilt, Indra goes into secret exile. He is eventually located and purified by a horse sacrifice. Brahmahatyā is dissipated into the environment.	Judging her unpatriotic, Horatius kills her and is tried for murder. Though eventually acquitted, Horatius receives ritual purification. Horatia is buried where she fell.
During his exile Indra's throne is occupied by the arrogant Nahuṣa. Exalted by his position, Nahuṣa attempts to seduce Indra's faithful wife Śacī, who communicates secretly with Indra.	The behaviour of Horatius was hasty and arrogant: exalted by his victory, he killed the faithful Horatia, whose engagement had been kept secret.
In sum, Indra defeated Triśiras and Vṛtra (both of them pro-Tvaṣṭṛ), and overcame associated problems which involved two females.	In sum, Tullus defeated the triplets and Fidenates (both pro-Mettius) and survived associated problems which involved a female.

As in all comparisons, similarities must be balanced against differences. The Sanskrit agents are frankly mythic – gods operating outside human space and time, and the story is self-contained. Livy's agents are humans living in Latium at a certain date, and the story is part of the continuous annalistic narrative. Within the stories the order of events differs: having placed the Sanskrit summary on the left, I have adjusted the Roman summary to fit it, *as if* Horatia's story came after the death of Mettius. Moreover, in that section, where the Sanskrit has two females, Livy has only Horatia.

Nevertheless, the scheme implies more than a dozen independent similarities, selected from well over sixty that have been noted.[10] Some of the sixty concern precise details of, for example, rituals. Some short passages, for instance, speeches, may reflect the three functions, but the story as a whole seems pentadic. The three heads of Triśiras probably reflect the core functions, and are bracketed between their divine father Tvaṣṭṛ and their successor, the monstrous Vṛtra. At Rome the 1–3–1 pattern is clear, but the Curiatii, scarcely differentiated, cannot be linked to individual functions.

The similarities are too many and too detailed to be explained other than by a common origin (a 'proto-narrative'); direct influence, either east–west or west–east, is extremely unlikely. One can wonder whether one of the stories is closer to the proto-narrative, that is, more conservative. The long-term decline of the functional ideology suggests that the Sanskrit tradition, which retains it better, is more conservative – which is why I have placed it on the left. If so, Roman tradition has probably fused two females who were originally distinct. However, such diachronic suggestions are less solid than the argument for cognacy.

2. A sequence of leaders

Dumézil analysed the sequence of Roman kings thus:

Romulus	F1 (Varuṇa aspect)
Numa	F1 (Mitra aspect)
Tullus	F2
Ancus	F3

The Etruscan kings (Tarquin I, Servius, Tarquin II) are in this context left unanalysed.[11] Pentadic analysis construes the first four as F4+, F1, F2, F3, and adds the final triad as F4–. The reinterpretation of Romulus as a transcendent divinized founder is unproblematic, as is the inclusion of the triad: Servius is a slave (which embarrasses Livy), and he is flanked by two foreigners, sometimes confused. The representation of a single half-function by a triad is no more problematic than the frequent inclusion of third-functional twins in trifunctional analyses. 'One function – one representative' is only the simplest case.

The Roman kings can be compared, in the *Mahābhārata*, with the five marshals of the Kauravas, the enemies of its heroes the Pāṇḍavas.[12] In the Sanskrit, the descending hierarchy is indicated by the decreasing tenures of the marshals, and the 1–3–1 structure by the fact that all, and only, the core marshals die in battle. The *personae* of the marshals accord with the functions: for instance, the second marshal, Droṇa, corresponding to the pious Numa, is himself a brahman and incarnates Bṛhaspati, the priest of the gods. The representatives of the two half-functions are particularly interesting. Like Romulus, Bhīṣma (F4+) has a very complex career (probably itself pentadic): it includes the forcible abduction of brides for others (cf. Rape of the Sabines) and the sharing of royal power with a clear representative of F3 (Vicitravīrya/Titus Tatius). Moreover, despite the respect they both enjoy, Bhīṣma leads the Kauravas and, by some accounts, Romulus is killed as a tyrant. As for Aśvatthāman (F4-), albeit no slave (cf. Servius), he incarnates and is possessed by Śiva, the Hindu outsider-deity par excellence,[13] and his 'army' is reduced to two soldiers (cf. the two Tarquins).

The Kaurava marshals each dominate different books of the epic, thereby dividing the war into five phases. This structure recalls the Trojan War as presented in sources such as the cyclic epics (see CH. 2) or Quintus of Smyrna:[14]

- In phase I the Trojans (the enemy, in a sense) are led by Hector, and their allies by Sarpedon.
- Thereafter (phases II–IV) three further leaders arrive from outside – Penthesileia with her Amazons, Memnon, and Eurypylos. All die in battle.
- In phase V, the Sack of Troy, the city is apparently leaderless.

The Greek story shows only hints of hierarchy or functionality, but the 1–3–1 pattern of phases is clear, and interesting parallels can be found at both extremes. If Bhīṣma is an incarnation of Dyaus, Sarpedon is the son of Zeus – the two theonyms being cognate (<*Dyēus, like the first syllable of Jupiter); and in both epics phase V is a nocturnal massacre of sleepers[15] within a walled and gated enclosure, the attackers being divided into two groups. Although the phase V victims are the heroes' side in the Sanskrit and the enemy in the Greek, the overall structural similarity again implies common origin.

Introducing a hypothetical proto-narrative into the comparison of two narratives complicates the analysis, and adding a third narrative multiplies the difficulties. Each two-way comparison suggests a different proto-narrative, and the three proto-narratives themselves need comparison; moreover, this *need* not point to a single original – oral traditions often have variants. The following remarks, necessarily superficial, minimize reference to proto-narratives.

Table 18.1 Pentadic analysis of four contexts.

Context	F4+	F1	F2	F3	F4–
Roman kings	Romulus	Numa	Tullus	Ancus	Etruscan triad
Roman ordo	rex sacrorum	flamen dialis	flamen martialis	flamen quirinalis	pontifex
Trojan leaders	Sarpedon	(Penthesilea)	(Memnon)	Eurypylus	—?
Kaurava leaders	Bhīṣma	Droṇa	Karṇa	Śalya	Aśvatthāman

All our three cases concern a sequence of leaders – military leaders of the enemy in the epics, kings at Rome. If this is paradoxical (early Rome's prime enemy being the neighbouring peoples it fights and incorporates), an explanation may lie in the Republic's hostility to monarchy in general. The F4+ leader is closely linked to the etymological descendent of *Dyēus, for Romulus directs most of his piety to Jupiter. Since Sarpedon is so much less elaborated and salient than Romulus and Bhīṣma, he may have lost narrative weight to his fellow commander Hektor, and conversely, the revered Romulus may have accumulated narrative weight (for instance, birth from Mars and post-mortem identification with Quirinus). Certainly, mythic beings can, over time, exchange attributes, sometimes gaining overall, sometimes losing.

Within the core triad the F1 slot is occupied by Penthesileia, who is not intrinsically first-functional (priestlike, etc.), and by Numa and Droṇa, who are. Numa is in fact devoted to the goddess Fides ('Trust'),[16] whose male counterpart Dius Fidius gives his name to the highest ranking amongst the *flamines maiores*. But these three priests (the *flamen dialis*, *flamen martialis* and *flamen quirinalis*) form the core of the *ordo sacerdotum* (the 'Class of Priests'), being bracketed by the *rex sacrorum* ('king for rites') above and the *pontifex* below.[17] The *ordo* also has its heterogeneous extremes: it has the 'king' above; and it has the specialist in funerals, and in placating the *manes* (spirits of the dead), below.[18] Thus, in its own right, the *ordo* expresses the pentadic ideology, providing a worthwhile Rome–Rome comparison with the kinglist and exemplifying the 'interweaving' of contexts. However, whereas Numa and the first flamen are linked via Fides, Tullus the warlike and Ancus (interpreted as the promoter of economic and demographic growth) are only linked with Mars and Quirinus respectively via the abstract notion of functions.

The results of pentadic analyses can be presented in matrix diagrams such as Table 18.1, which merits some comment.

1 In the cases tabulated the internal order of a row follows the text, but when the text order departs from the standard order of the functions, it can be adjusted.
2 Most entries earn their place by conforming to the definition of their function but bracketed entries, such as Penthesilea, do not.
3 Just here and there column entries are interlinked in suggestive ways, either within cultures (Numa and *flamen dialis*, as above) or between them (Numa and Droṇa, both emphatically aged).
4 An entry can appear in different columns in different contexts. Thus, viewed as marshal, Karṇa represents F2, but viewed as rejected half-brother of the Pāṇḍavas (the 'goodies'), he represents F4–.
5 The query for the Trojan leader under F4– leaves open the idea of inserting Aeneas, who leaves Troy somewhat as Tarquin II leaves Rome, or as Aśvatthāman leaves human society.

3. The succession myth

Hesiod's *Theogony* finds its best Indian parallel early in the *Mahābhārata* where, after substantial introductory material, the genealogies of heroes and gods appear in close proximity, starting at 1.57.[19] Tellings of the epic sometimes began here, with the words 'There was once a king named Uparicara' – a typical IE story opening. Uparicara ('Above-goer'), great-great-grandfather to Arjuna and the other major heroes, is in various ways primordial. The text gives him no parents, and his Iranian homologue is linked in complex ways to other primordial Indo-Iranian figures.[20] But above all, he resembles Ouranos in the way he begets his daughter. Briefly, both of them are interrupted while making amorous advances to their wives – respectively Girikā, daughter of a mountain (*giri*), and Gaia. Uparicara ejaculates elsewhere and entrusts his semen to a bird, but it is dropped in a river and there generates Satyavatī. Compare Kronos throwing his father's severed member into the sea, whence the white foam and Aphrodite.

Ouranos also parallels Satyavatī's stepson Bhīṣma. Both Ouranos and the Dyaus incarnated in Bhīṣma are names meaning 'heaven'. Both Ouranos and Bhīṣma lose kingship and virility on a single occasion. Both are followed in the next generation by a male who violently interrupts sexual activity, Ouranos by Kronos, the son who castrates him, Bhīṣma by Pāṇḍu, a stepson who shoots two copulating deer, with disastrous consequences for his own sexuality.

Bhīṣma, the avatar after all of Dyaus, not unnaturally finds points of comparison with the Greek Zeus. At their birth, Bhīṣma's mother, the Ganges, drowns his seven older brothers in her waters, just as Kronos swallows Zeus's five older siblings. Moreover, after being disabled on the battlefield,

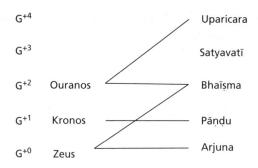

G⁺⁴		Uparicara
G⁺³		Satyavatī
G⁺²	Ouranos	Bhaīṣma
G⁺¹	Kronos	Pāṇḍu
G⁺⁰	Zeus	Arjuna

Figure 18.1 The succession myth in the *Theogony* and part of Arjuna's family tree: a diagrammatic comparison. The line of filiation in fact bypasses Bhīṣma, though he is regularly referred to as Arjuna's grandfather. For simplicity, the diagram omits Aphrodite, comparable to Satyavatī, in the first ascending generation (G+1).

Bhīṣma spends his final months nearby, out of doors, recumbent on a bed of arrows (like a *fakir* on a bed of nails). With this we should maybe compare the remarkable and unparalleled scene in which Zeus, sleeping with Hera on Mount Ida, is raised from the earth by upward-growing plants (*Iliad* 14.349).

Finally, Zeus, king of the gods, parallels Arjuna, begotten by the king of the gods. The contrast between Zeus's protracted war with the Titans and his rapid defeat of Typhōaeus matches the contrast between Arjuna defeating the Kauravas in a set-piece battle and his final duel with Aśvatthāman (similar in rhythm to the contrast between the Romans defeating the Curiatii and defeating Mettius).

The above comparison (independent of the functions) can be represented diagrammatically as in fig. 18.1. The three Greek males spread over three generations, while the four in the Sanskrit spread over five generations. The key figure is Bhīṣma, who corresponds semantically to Ouranos, etymologically to Zeus. Probably the Sanskrit again resembles the proto-narrative, which Greek tradition has compressed.

According to other lines of argument, Aphrodite has borrowed features from the IE Dawn Goddess *h₂éusōs (Latin *Aurōr-a*, Greek *Eōs*, Sanskrit *Uṣas*), and basically derives from the Semitic Ištar–Astarte.[21] No doubt she does synthesize different traditions. But we can go further. The IE Dawn Goddess is daughter of the primordial *Dyēus, and Sanskrit Uṣas is often the daughter of the Creator Prajāpati (later of Brahmā): when he embraces her, he is shot by Rudra. Thus Hesiod's Ouranos–Aphrodite pair bears comparison with the divine pair Prajāpati–Uṣas as well as with the human Uparicara–Satyavatī. Many further questions ensue within the IE tradition.

But Aphrodite also raises the question of how to balance the debt of Greek myth to IE heritage and West Asian influence. Similarities between Greek and

West Asian myths may be the result not of influence of the Near East on Greece, but of very old common origin (Nostratic or earlier), or of interaction at an early IE period – an IE substratum to Sumerian has even been proposed.[22] A millennium is not a long time in comparative mythology, and the greater age of West Asian sources must not be overemphasized. Another problem for the theory of direct borrowing is its implication that beforehand the Greeks had little to say about Zeus's biography. The greater the number and quality of Greco-Aryan rapprochements the more the balance tilts away from West-Asian influence.

4. An IE cycle about gods and men

The Greek Epic Cycle, which told both of gods and heroes, is only attested explicitly by texts that are post-Homeric and fragmentary (see CH. 2), and it is debated how far, in earlier oral forms, some such cycle pre-existed Homer and constituted the background against which the monumental epics arose. IE comparativism has much to contribute here. We have already suggested that Zeus's victories in the *Theogony*, and hence in the Cyclic *Titanomachia*, are related to Arjuna's against the Kauravas.

The first *Kypria* fragment tells how Earth (Ge), overloaded with humans, complains to Zeus and thereby brings about the Trojan War. The comparison has long been made with India (e.g., *Mahābhārata* 1.58) where Earth addresses the same complaint to Brahmā and brings about the Great War. The *Kypria* also recounts the Judgement of Paris, in which Dumézil analysed the three goddesses in terms of the three functions: Hera F1, Athene F2, Aphrodite F3.[23] A pentadic analysis is wider and more nuanced, putting Zeus under F4+ and Eris (not invited to the feast) under F4-, and locating Hera in the F1 slot but not accepting her as intrinsically F1.

On the vast question of an IE background to the *Iliad*, only the sparsest indications are possible here. The *Mahābhārata* includes (3.257–75) a resumé of the *Rāmāyaṇa*, the shorter Sanskrit epic in which a large expedition rescues the abducted queen Sītā from a distant city. Probably Greek tradition has combined proto-narrative versions of two stories: a *Rāmāyaṇa*-style expedition[24] and a *Mahābhārata*-style great war (recall the enemy leaders and the Bhīṣma-Sarpedon rapprochement above). One thing is certain: good comparisons between individual figures in the two traditions will prove very complicated – correspondences will regularly be multiple and overlapping. Thus, if Helen parallels Sītā in some respects, in others she parallels Draupadī, the Pāṇḍava queen; and she can be related to Uṣas and her cognates in yet others.[25] The complexities even embrace material culture: the shield of Achilles both reflects the pentadic ideology and is cognate with oral traditions about the Buddhist

Wheel of Life.[26] The night attack in Book 9, like the Sack of Troy, parallels the phase V massacre in the *Mahābhārata*.[27]

The Cycle's coverage of the rest of the Trojan War helped us above to recognize its five-phase structure. As for the *Odyssey*, again book-length treatment is needed, but in general Odysseus corresponds to Arjuna (occasionally to his elder brother Bhīma). The second half of Odysseus' *nostos*, from the Circe episode onwards, parallels the journey around India made by Arjuna in Book 1, during which he encounters females at each of the cardinal points. Up to a point, individual encounters in the two traditions can be matched. Notably, the Straits Monsters (Sirens, Skylla, and Charybdis) correspond in the Sanskrit to five crocodiles (nymphs metamorphosed by a curse), which suggests that Homer has reduced to two the *three* Sirens who appear in later sources. This encounter comes second in Odysseus' journey, third in Arjuna's, but a more interesting complication is that the Greek has fused proto-narrative versions of Arjuna's first solo journey with that of his second, which takes him to visit his divine father: Scheria, *as it were*, fuses Dvārakā, home of Krishna, with Indra's Heaven.[28] When Arjuna rejoins his four brothers, the Pāṇḍavas proceed in disguise to the palace of Virāṭa – compare the disguised Odysseus rejoining his associates in Ithaka and proceeding to his own palace. His multiple lying tales recall those told by each of the Pāṇḍavas, and both stories lead up to massacres of unwanted suitors.[29] However, a comparative analysis of the Greek massacre needs to take account of much more than events at Virāṭa's court.[30] For instance, the post-massacre conflict at Laertes' retreat parallels the second part of *Mahābhārata* 10.

Neither the *Telegony*, the concluding cyclic epic, nor the conclusion of Apollodoros' *Epitome* mention a curious tradition that appears in three very late sources.[31] Thus, Servius (on *Aeneid* 2.44) records that, after Odysseus returned, when he set off on other journeys he was turned into a horse. The comparison is with the close association of Arjuna and the animal victim in the Horse Sacrifice of *Mahābhārata* 15 (very close to the end of the epic). The same book has parallels for both of the sacrifices prescribed by Teiresias (*Odyssey* 11.130–4), and also for the father–son duel in the *Telegony*. Like Odysseus, Arjuna is killed by his son, but unlike him, he is resuscitated by magic. Father–son duels occur in several other IE traditions, and the Irish one is particularly comparable.[32]

Unless this section is sadly astray, comparativism can already say a certain amount about the content of the oral cycle that pre-existed the Homeric epics. Much of it found its way into the written Cycle, but not all – for instance, not the connection between one of the major heroes and a horse. The omission may have to do with the position of the episode in the cycle, for in the Sanskrit too, the end of the epic gives the impression of being less elaborated than the start. In general, of the two epics, the Sanskrit has been presented here as the more conservative, but this is only a hypothesis and one that is most unlikely to apply to all contexts. If one thinks of the Greek as deriving from the Sanskrit, this a potentially dangerous short cut: both derive from the proto-narrative. But to fill out our picture of the latter an immense amount of work is still needed.

Conclusion

The four case studies have mostly drawn on a single source from outside the classical world. However, we cannot yet be sure that the *Mahābhārata* will prove the most useful single text for comparativists, or pentadic theory the most useful theoretical approach, and other lines of work must be mentioned, however briefly. Thus, for Greek–Irish comparison, bearing especially on Apollo, we can turn to the work of Sergent. Dumézil's work on Germanic narrative relates particularly to the reign of Romulus (Sabine War), to the heroes Scaevola and Cocles (though his Cocles–Odin comparison can be doubted), to Camillus and to Herakles. An interesting comparison of Roman and Vedic ritual rightly casts doubt on Dumézil's category 'Minor Sovereigns'. The Greek contrast of praise and blame has IE roots. Greek, Indian, and Ossetic materials suggest a distinction within the cycle between an earlier generation of IE heroes and a later one.[33] Indo-Iranian evidence, including an oral tradition from Nuristan, suggests that Deukalion's flood belongs in an IE category of catastrophe myth.[34]

IE comparative mythology is an active field which will one day need a Companion all of its own. The ideas covered here may seem alien, perhaps bizarre, to some readers, but I hope that others will be stimulated to examine the materials and decide for themselves on the quality of the arguments. Judgements of similarity between structures and narratives constantly risk becoming tendentious or circular, and may contain an irreducible quantum of subjectivity; but for the analyst who is aware of them the difficulties are not prohibitive, and for the reader a good deal of verification is possible via translations. Contrary to a common prejudice, language-family based comparative mythology is not intrinsically 'speculative'. In favourable cases, lists of similarities between two stories will scarcely be contentious, and the level of confidence only declines if or when one attempts to imagine or reconstruct a proto-narrative. Tempting it may be, but this is in fact seldom necessary.

As yet satisfactory collaboration between comparativists and specialists is not well developed. However, there seems to be no good reason why specialists should not become attuned to assessing and looking out for ideological structures, and to welcoming the answers comparativism can give to certain questions about history and origins. Surprising findings are on the horizon.

FURTHER READING

The best surveys of the background to IE are Mallory and Adams 1997 and 2006. Non-Dumézilian approaches to IE comparative mythology can be found in the indispensable and quasi-encyclopaedic M. L. West 2007, and the enjoyable Watkins 1995.

The best introductions to Dumézil are in French: Dumézil 1987, and Desbordes *et al.* 1981 (with a good theoretical chapter by Desbordes herself and others by regional specialists). Eribon's biography (1992) answers ill-based accusations starting in the mid-1980s (e.g., Ginzburg 1985) that Dumézil's work was vitiated by right-wing political sentiments. In English one can still use Littleton 1982; and Puhvel 1987 is very much based on Dumézil's work. N. J. Allen 2000a contains relevant essays, for example, ch. 2, on the background to Dumézil's concept of ideology. For a critique of Dumézil one may turn to Belier 1991, but Schlerath's articles (1995–6) are better.

Dumézil's writings are very numerous and relatively few have been translated into English. The key studies to begin with are his trilogy *Mythe et épopée* (1968–73, some parts available in English); thereafter, perhaps *Dieux souverains* (1977, not available in English). The internet site www.georgesdumezil.org advertises a CD-ROM produced by A. Duroy (*Georges Dumézil: In memoriam*), which contains many Duméziliana, including texts and multimedia interviews.

For the study of the Mahābhārata, see Brockington 1998. For advice on translations, see Guide to Fragmentary and Less Easily Found Texts in the bibliography of this volume.

Relevant journals include *JIES, RHR, Ollodagos* (Brussels), *Studia Indo-Europaea* (Bucharest).

NOTES

1. Mallory and Adams (2006).
2. Witzel (2001).
3. M. L. West (2007: 19–20).
4. Coutau-Bégarie (1998).
5. Rees and Rees (1961: 95–139, esp. 132–3).
6. One discussion, while accepting the need to expand Dumézil's scheme, postulates an *undivided* fourth function, which pertains to disorder and stands outside the orderly trifunctional hierarchy: see Sauzeau and Sauzeau (2004).
7. Schlerath (1995–6).
8. Dumézil (1985a : Part 1); cf. Briquel (2006).
9. Livy 1.22–9; *Mahābhārata* 5.9.3–5.18.9.
10. N. J. Allen (2000b).

11. Dumézil (1968–73 : 1.268–84); (1969: 193–207).
12. N. J. Allen (2005).
13. N. J. Allen (2007a).
14. N. J. Allen (2004a).
15. Cf. Dowden (2010).
16. Dumézil (1977: 167–8).
17. Festus 299f L2.
18. Livy 1.20.7.
19. I use the Critical Edition; see N. J. Allen (2004b).
20. Dumézil (1968–73: vol. 2, parts 2–3).
21. Dunkel (1988–90); M. L. West (2007: 217–27).
22. Whittaker (2004).
23. Dumézil (1968–73: 1.580–6; 1985b: 15–3).
24. Lillie (1912), the rapprochements are better than the subtitle (*'An Argument that in the Indian Epics Homer Found the Theme of his Two Great Epics'*).
25. Jamison (1994); M. L. West (2007: 229–32, 438).
26. N. J. Allen (2006, 2007b).
27. Garbutt (2006).
28. N. J. Allen (1996). Cf. also E. B. West (2009).
29. N. J. Allen (2001); Sergent (2008).
30. Germain (1954); N. J. Allen (2002).
31. N. J. Allen (1995).
32. N. J. Allen (2000c); M. L. West (2007: 440).
33. Sergent (1999–2004); on Rome see Briquel (2007 and 2008); Woodard (2006); Nagy (1979); Vielle (1996).
34. N. J. Allen (2000d).

CHAPTER NINETEEN

Near Eastern Mythologies

Alasdair Livingstone and Birgit Haskamp

Belief in diverse gods who controlled nature and had the power to influence
humans and human affairs was deeply entrenched in the cultures of the ancient
Near East. Over a vast geographical spread including Anatolia and the Arabian
Peninsula a multiplicity of pantheons were believed to exist. Although in many
areas there are hints of mythology in proper names and in ritual and religious
texts, only in the case of three particular regions did a complex written mythology develop: the first is Mesopotamia, beginning approximately in the middle
of the third millennium BC; the second and third come about a thousand years
later, in Anatolia and on the Syrian littoral.[1] Of these three corpora, that of
Mesopotamia is by far the largest. Before proceeding we should make clear
that a discussion of the mythological elements in the Bible, and of their position in Near Eastern mythology in general, is beyond the scope of this article
(for some material of this type see CH. 20).

Mesopotamia

The nature of the sources

The most ancient Mesopotamian mythology was primarily that of the
Sumerians and in the Sumerian language, but almost from the outset it
included a leavening of Akkadian elements reflecting the mixed Sumerian and
Akkadian demographic of the region in the third millennium BC and stretching back into prehistory.[2] The term 'Akkadian' refers to the group of closely
related Semitic dialects that included Old Akkadian (third millennium BC),
Babylonian, and Assyrian (both second and first millennia BC) or to the Akkadian

Table 19.1 A chronological chart of Mesopotamia

Period	Historical overview	Literature
Jemdet Nasr Period	c. 3100–2900 BC	Invention of writing Earliest cuneiform tablets
Early Dynastic Period	c. 2900–2334 BC c. 2800 BC: Gilgameš, king of Uruk	Early Sumerian literature Earliest historical documents
Old Akkadian Period	2334–2113 BC 2334–2279 BC: Sargon of Akkad	Akkadian as language of empire Akkadian royal inscriptions
Ur III Period	2112–2004 BC	Sumerian revival
Old Babylonian Period	2003–1595 BC 1792–1750 BC: Hammurabi, king of Babylon	Sumerian dying out as a spoken language Scribal schools Abundant literature in Akkadian and Sumerian
Middle Babylonian Period	c. 1595–1000 BC c. 1595–1158 BC: Kassite dynasty	Redaction of cuneiform literature Formation of a canon
Neo-Assyrian Empire	c. 900–612 BC 668–631 BC: Aššurbanipal, king of Assyria	Further redaction of Babylonian literature in Assyria Aššurbanipal's libraries at Nineveh
Neo-Babylonian Empire	625–539 BC 604–562 BC: Nebuchadnezzar II, king of Babylon	Late Babylonian libraries
Persian Period	538–331 BC Achaemenid dynasty 331 BC: Battle of Gaugamela	Babylonian substantially replaced by Aramaic as the spoken language
Hellenistic Period	330–164 BC 330–323 BC: Alexander the Great, king of Babylon 305–164 BC: Seleucid dynasty	Berossos, author of the *Babyloniaka*
Parthian Period	c. 160 BC–AD 224	Last cuneiform tablets

people as such, whose mother tongue was Old Akkadian, and who were, in spite of the intermingling, distinguishable from Sumerians. Manuscripts, most commonly clay tablets, bearing text of mythological content and physically dating from the third millennium BC exist but are comparatively rare. Sumerian mythology is known principally from manuscripts deriving from Babylonian schools and temples that flourished during the Old Babylonian Period (2003–1595 BC) as Sumerian was gradually replaced by Babylonian but remained a language of learning and scholarship. Sumerian mythological texts survive because they were part of the corpus used to teach the Sumerian language in Babylonian schools. They were rapidly joined by a fast evolving body of literary and mythological texts in Babylonian that incorporated Sumerian elements, even verbatim borrowings from Sumerian, but had their own distinctively Babylonian character. The language of the new mythological texts and related literature in the Old Babylonian Period differs profoundly from the idiom found in the letters and documents of the period and reflects an urge to create a new poetic medium.

The volume of the Sumerian and Babylonian corpus of mythological texts is substantial, and its contents will be outlined below. All these texts were copied and recopied in scribal schools and temple libraries, resulting in what has been called the 'stream of tradition'. Their textual history can in many cases be followed over centuries through the Middle Babylonian Period (c. 1500–1000 BC) and into the first millennium BC. Many texts from later periods can be traced back to Old Babylonian originals or forerunners. There were times when a clear attempt to control the redaction of the literature was made. By far the most important of these was in the late Kassite period at the close of the second millennium BC when a process that has been referred to as canonization took place. Texts were divided into 'tablets' in a standardized manner with each tablet beginning and ending with the same lines, much as the epics of Homer came to be divided into 'books'. The *Epic of Gilgameš*, for example, was, after the process of canonization, normally written on eleven tablets and each tablet would begin and end at exactly the same place in the text and story – whether one had an exemplar from one of the southern cities of Babylonia, from any of the scribal centres in Assyria, or from elsewhere. Another feature of this canonization was that individual tablets were regularly equipped with colophons. A typical colophon would give the name of the text, usually its first line, the tablet number, and the incipit (start line) of the next tablet. This was often accompanied by the name, ancestry, and professional standing of the scribe or owner of the tablet, and sometimes a date.

As far as literature and mythology are concerned Assyria in the north was a slow awakener, but from the late Middle Assyrian period (towards the end of the second millennium BC) Assyria adopted Babylonian literature as its own. The greatest single source of modern knowledge of ancient

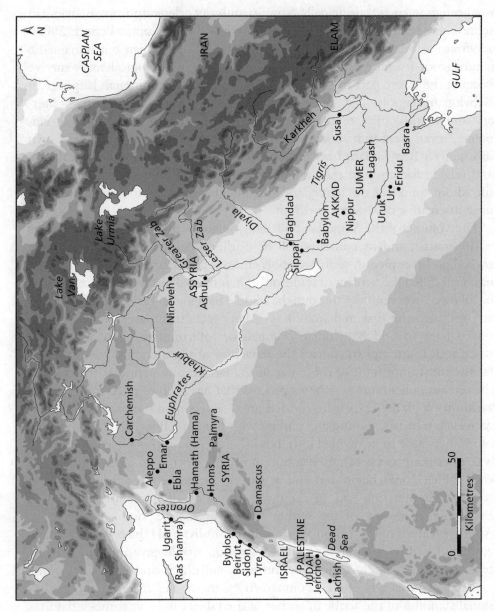

Map 1 Map of the Ancient Near East.

Mesopotamian culture is what remains of the complex of libraries founded, expanded, and nurtured by the Assyrian king Aššurbanipal at Nineveh in the seventh century BC. Estimated to have once contained some twenty thousand tablets (including official documents and royal correspondence as well as regular library texts) and ten thousand wax writing boards, these libraries represent by far the largest accumulation of written material that has come down to us from the ancient world. Aššurbanipal and his library agents strived for comprehensiveness, and there is hardly a text or genre that is not represented even amongst the 29,000 mainly broken pieces that are what remains of the library today in the British Museum. As important as the size of the library was its quality. The scribes and scholars employed by the king in his libraries were the best that could be found in Assyria and Babylonia. They not only collected and accumulated texts but edited them, copying them out in a standard library hand, in fixed formats and with informative colophons. The contents of the Aššurbanipal libraries provide a touchstone against which most of the other mythological material from Mesopotamia that has come down to us can be measured.

The complexity of the redaction of Mesopotamian literature in general and the richness of the sources available for its study provide ample material for a depth of textual criticism and history that has to date barely been attempted. Such work might clarify the vexed question of genre: some compositions deal mainly with heroes and their deeds and can be classified as legends while others are mainly mythological in a strict sense, but the boundaries are blurred. Modern convention has with some justification used the word 'epic', for example, to refer to, and indeed to name, the *Epic of Gilgameš* and the *Epic of Creation*; but in reality the former is a cycle of stories about a legendary king and hero, whereas the latter is an elaborately constructed myth accounting for the supremacy of Babylon and its city god. There is evidence in some cases that the Babylonians regarded a particular text as what we would call a song, or a ballad, but here also a strict definition remains elusive. Many texts begin with an encomium, somewhat in the manner of the openings of the Homeric epics, but the incitement in the opening lines to sing of a particular hero or god gives way to standard poetic narrative.

Metre seems to be lacking from Sumerian poetry, although the problem may be the inexactness of our reconstruction of the phonology of the Sumerian language. Dead by 1800 BC, we hear it through the voices of Babylonian scholars, themselves speakers of a long dead language. Babylonian, however, has a clear metric structure usually resembling a Greek iambic metron, but not consistently. In both Sumerian and Babylonian poetry much of the artifice lies in expression, the arrangement of ideas, and common devices such as metaphor and simile.

The mythological corpus is however much larger than what is represented by the purely mythological texts, since actual myths appear in a wide variety of contexts. While some myths were written down in their own right, more commonly mythological material was embedded in another context, such as within a hymn, prayer, ritual, or incantation. Royal inscriptions, sometimes poetic in nature, can also be a rich source of mythological material.

There are various circumstances unique to Mesopotamia that make Mesopotamian literature what it is and so constitute defining factors for the nature of the region's mythology. The material that it was written on, clay tablets, is of fundamental importance. Amongst fully elaborated literary compositions containing significant mythological material, the *Epic of Gilgameš* is the longest – extending, in its canonical form to eleven tablets, as we have seen above, and of which some three thousand lines survive. The authors, mostly anonymous, of Mesopotamian literature were therefore faced with the task of reducing their prose or poetry into a form that could feasibly be written within the context of the tablet as its medium. If one were to think of the work of Milman Parry (see, e.g., Parry 1971) and Albert Lord (e.g., Lord 1960. Parry 1971 and the huge collection Parry & Lord 195–80) and the sheer volume of oral literature that they recorded on tape, in comparison it would be quite impossible to transcribe the same amount of text onto clay tablets. More concretely, one can compare the lengths of the Homeric epics: the *Iliad* clocks in at 15,693 lines, while the *Odyssey* has 12,110. Given that the *Epic of Gilgameš* covers a wide range of themes – civilizing of a wild man, sex, friendship amongst heroes, a journey to the Mediterranean to slay a monster, interaction with the gods, death, a search for everlasting life, the primeval flood, advice from an alewife, conclusions about the good life, and much more – it needs a robust structure to cover this ground in a compass of only three thousand lines.

The gods of Mesopotamian myth

The cast of divine characters in Mesopotamian mythology is drawn selectively from the pantheon. It is unnecessary here to give a full account of Mesopotamian religion; it will suffice to single out those deities that play a role in the actual myths outlined below. Most gods had both Sumerian and Babylonian names, and in the following discussion the Babylonian names are given in parentheses after the Sumerian.

For much of Mesopotamian history the triumvirate of supreme deities was formed by the male deities An (Anu(m)), sky god, Enlil, god of the regions immediately above the earth disc's surface, and Enki (Ea), god of wisdom and the sweet water aquifers below the earth. They were closely followed in importance by the mother goddess Ninḫursag (with variant manifestations as Mami, Nintur, Bēlet-ilī, Ninmaḫ and Aruru). Inanna (Ištar), a capricious goddess of sex and war, was according to the most important traditions the daughter of An. Her long-suffering spouse was Dumuzi (Tammuz), god of shepherds and pastoral life. Ninurta, son of Enlil, was a god of war and agriculture while Ereškigal, sister of Inanna, and her spouse Nergal presided over the Underworld of the dead. The detailed affiliations of these deities could vary in different traditions. An important feature of the pantheon was that each of the principle deities had their own cult centre in their own city that they shared with their family. So, for example, An was god of Uruk, Enlil of Nippur, and Enki of Eridu, and these affiliations could play a significant role in the mythology. The mythology also played on the perceived or imagined characters of the gods. An and Enlil were usually august and remote; Enki was wise and a philanthropic magician but also one who enjoyed a tipple. The role of the hero Ninurta was often to avenge his father Enlil. Two further important deities should be mentioned, namely the moon god Nanna (Su'en), with his cult centre at Ur, and Marduk. Marduk emerges as city god of Babylon in the early second millennium BC and with the passing centuries takes on many but not all of the characteristics of the other great gods.

As far as the setting of the action is concerned, many myths reflect Mesopotamian cosmographical ideas, dividing the world into the earth disc (the world of humans with the Twin Rivers at its centre), a heavenly realm (the home of celestial deities), and the Underworld (the abode of chthonic deities, demons, and the dead). The boundaries between these three regions were, of course, also the stuff of mythology. To enter the Underworld one might simply descend into it, follow the road of no return, or cross a river, the Ḫubur, in a boat operated by a ferryman with various names according to different traditions.

The contents of Mesopotamian mythology cluster around a number of general themes. First, there are creation myths supported by mythological theogonies and related closely to myths that deal with cosmic events that threatened the created order, such as the flood, and how and in what circumstances order was restored and the cosmos saved. Also related to this mythological material are aetiological myths (those that give causes for things in the everyday world), including geographical and geological aetiology. There is a large group of mythological material preoccupied with love, sex, and fertility, the last of which connects to cycles involving dying gods. Other significant mythological genres involve journeys of the gods between each other's cult centres and the so-called adamindugga texts – mythological debates between two protagonists with a declared victor. An attempt will be made to provide a guide to how these themes were realized, selecting examples ranging over Sumerian, Babylonian, and Assyrian mythology.

Creation, theogony, and the cosmic order

Unsurprisingly, a whole range of myths commence with accounts of creation, and there is a considerable variety of length and detail of the information given in each case. The Sumerian myths that deal entirely or mainly with creation feature the wisdom god Enki and one or other of the manifestations of the mother goddess. In the composition known as *Enki and the World Order* the god creates various aspects of the world and determines the fate of each; in the myth *Enki and Ninḫursag* he also appears as a creator god, though in different circumstances. Key concepts include Enki filling the rivers Euphrates and Tigris with his life-giving and fertilizing semen, but the heavens and firmament are already in existence. Enki essentially arranges humanity and its key exigencies around the Twin Rivers. The myth of *Inanna and Enki* explains these exigencies in detail, revealing basic Sumerian conceptions about the world and its functioning. Inanna visits Enki, they banquet, and in an intoxicated state he gives her the principles of civilization, referred to by the Sumerian word 'me', a noun derived from the verb 'to be'. The 'me' are the things that were important to the Sumerians: wisdom, attentiveness, righteousness, various priestly offices, triumph, strife, lamentation, rejoicing, respect, awe, the assembled family, the plundering of cities, deceit, the crafts, kindling fire, and much more, with substantial text still lost in lacunae. Sobering up, Enki sends his vizier after Inanna to retrieve the 'me', which, although abstracts, were somehow also conceived of as physical objects that she, as Lady of Heaven, is carrying away in her transport option of choice, the Boat of Heaven.

Some Mesopotamian creation mythology does not feature a creator god. In the myth known as the *Theogony of Dunnu* (also known as the *Ḥarab* or *Plough Myth*) the cosmos begins with Plough mating with Earth thus creating Sea. Over a succession of seven generations of incest sons kill their fathers and entomb them in the primeval city Dunnu ('Fortress') in order to be able to marry their sisters. This text has been compared to Hesiod's *Theogony* (Lambert and Walcot 1965) but has many obscurities and, at least in Mesopotamia, few parallels. Amongst a number of other more succinct creation stories is one that has become known to scholarship as the *Legend of the Worm*. Here, Anu stands at the beginning causing a chain reaction of creation resulting in heaven, earth, rivers, canals, morass, and the Worm. The Worm complains to Ea that the fig and apricot are insufficient sources of nutriment, whereupon Ea places him in the jaws of mankind thus providing an aetiology for toothache. This is an example of embedded mythology since the whole text bears the rubric 'incantation' and is accompanied by a ritual and instructions to a dentist.

The mythology of the creation of man is known from various Sumerian and Babylonian sources and regularly includes the idea that mankind was created at the instigation of Enki with the specific intention of ridding the gods of toil, including agriculture and keeping the shrines, which would in the future be done by humans. In the Sumerian tale *Enki and Ninmaḫ* man is created in these circumstances from clay with Ninmaḫ as midwife. To celebrate the achievement the two deities arrange a banquet at which they become drunk and in this state also create the various classes of disabled people, for most of whom they create roles in society: the blind are to be musicians, infertile women to be weavers, the individual with no sexual parts a courtier, and so on. In the Babylonian myth of *Atraḫasīs* the creation story is given new twists: the mother goddess creates man not only from clay but from clay mixed with the blood of a slain god to give him intelligence. As the humans multiply, Enlil is bothered by their noise and the gods decide to wipe out the human race, first by starvation and illness, then by sending a cosmic flood. Ea, who is keen to protect his creation, advises the flood hero Atraḫasīs to build a huge boat and thus saves mankind, which had soon been sorely missed by the gods who were no longer receiving offerings. The gods then put other measures in place to control the population. The theme of the cosmic flood as a punishment for humankind's exuberant noisiness is ubiquitous in Near Eastern mythological material, but apart from *Atraḫasīs* is best known from the eleventh tablet of the *Epic of Gilgameš* where it forms a story within a story.

Creation was also under threat from other enemies, as appears most clearly in a group of myths in which the hero warrior god Ninurta was pitched against various forces perceived as being hostile to Mesopotamian civilization. In the Sumerian myth known to both ancient and modern scholarship as *Lugal-e* or *Lugal ud melambi nirgal* ('King, Storm Whose Splendour is Majestic') after its incipit, Ninurta battles against the demon Azag, who sends various rocks to assault the god. Ninurta defeats the rocks along with their demon master and then assigns them names and functions, so the myth is also aetiological. In the Akkadian Anzu myth *Bin šar dadmē* ('Son of the King of Creation'), while Ninurta's father Enlil is bathing he is robbed of the tablet of destinies by the monster bird Anzu, chaos ensues, but all is saved when Ninurta defeats Anzu and rescues the tablet. In *Ninurta's Return to Nippur*, also known as *Angimdimma* ('Fashioned like An'), Ninurta returns triumphantly to Enlil in Nippur after his many exploits with a whole array of spoils slung onto his chariot. The Ninurta mythology provides a marked contrast to the theogonic myths in which a father is not avenged but threatened by his son.

The mythological text known as the Babylonian *Epic of Creation* or *Enūma eliš* (after its *incipit*, 'When on High') incorporates elements from various other mythological material outlined above. Its purpose is to establish the supremacy of Marduk and his city and cult centre Babylon. The myth begins when neither heaven nor firmament existed but when the sweet waters (Apsû) mingled with the bitter (Tiāmat). This resulted in acts of creation leading to a theogony in which the fifth-generation god Ea, kills the first generation god

Apsû and takes over his domain. Tiāmat, however, remains a threat to order and it is only Ea's son, Marduk, who can and does vanquish her. Marduk creates the cosmos in its present form out of Tiāmat's body with Babylon occupying a central position. In a final act of creation Marduk and Ea create primeval man from clay mixed with the blood of Tiāmat's lover, Qingu. As in *Atraḫasīs* and other Mesopotamian myths, man is to serve the gods in cult and save them from toil. The cultic aspect had a practical counterpart in the recitation of the text of *Enūma eliš* in the first (New Year's festival) and ninth months of the annual cultic calendar at Babylon. While *Enūma eliš* portrays Marduk as a triumphant and benevolent deity, another myth known as the *Epic of Erra*, which is both much longer and also more enigmatic, paints a much bleaker picture of the god. In this myth, Erra, god of pestilence and violence, suffering from boredom, determines with his band of seven demons to upset the mechanisms that underpin cosmic order. The opportunity arises when Marduk steps down from his throne for statue refurbishment. Erra allows himself to be sweet-talked by the other gods, however, so that the chance for chaos is missed. When Marduk returns to his cult centre Erra regrets the missed opportunity and consoles himself by provoking a human war in Babylonia with its attendant murderous mass misery and destruction of cult centres as well as human cities and abodes. *Erra* appears to be a first millennium BC product and it has been argued that it is a mythological tractate with specific historical contexts.

Aetiology

While aetiological references abound in Mesopotamian mythology, some myths are first and foremost aetiological. In *Inanna and Ebiḫ* the violent nature of the goddess comes to the fore. She is clad in terror and roars like a lion. Since the mountains did not 'put their noses to the ground' in humility toward her she solicited the support of her father An with the result that Mount Ebiḫ was destroyed and took on the strange geological features that were familiar to the Babylonians. Another myth, very recently published (George 2009: 1–15), gives an aetiological explanation for a geological feature in the mountains of eastern Syria: it was created as a sanctuary for Ea's son Bazi, a ram god associated with herding and transhumance in that region. Aetiological mythology spans much of the world and culture of the ancient Mesopotamians. The story of Enmerkar, king of Uruk, and the Lord of Aratta, warlord in an uncivilized region in the mountains to the east of Sumer, signals the superiority of literate Mesopotamia. To avoid messengers garbling messages, Enmerkar invented cuneiform. But when the Lord of Aratta received a written message he was not pleased, his brow furrowed and he declared the cuneiform writing to be but nails. A detail in the *Epic of Gilgameš* is an example of the minor points of aetiology that abound. The *kappi* bird is so called because it cries *kappi, kappi*, 'my wing, my wing' ever since Ištar in a fit of pique destroyed its wing.

Myths of the pantheon

A large and important part of Mesopotamian mythology concerns itself with the relationships between deities, taking the family structure of the pantheon outlined above as a basis. In the Sumerian myth *Enlil and Ninlil* the hapless Ninlil is seduced by Enlil while she is bathing in the river despite her insistence that she is unready for sex: her vagina is too small for intercourse and her lips unready for kissing. Unperturbed, Enlil impregnates her with various great gods including the moon god Su'en and the Underworld god Nergal. Enlil's behaviour is noticed by the 'fifty great gods' and the 'seven great gods who decide destinies'. He is declared impure and told to leave Nippur, but all turns out well and Ninlil becomes Enlil's consort as she is indeed to remain for many centuries. The Akkadian myth *Nergal and Ereškigal* tells the story behind the liaison of this chthonic couple while the Sumerian myth known as the *Marriage of Martu* reflects the derisive attitude of Sumerian city folk towards the nomadic Amorites.

There are various versions and cycles of myths connecting different aspects of love, fertility, and death, but central to these themes are the deities Dumuzi, shepherd and pastoral god, and Inanna. In the text known as *Inanna's/Ištar's Descent*, extant in both Sumerian and Akkadian versions, Dumuzi's lover Ištar descends to the Underworld, the abode of her sister Queen Ereškigal whose reign she wishes to usurp. The end of the myth is badly damaged but it is clear that the final outcome involves Dumuzi having to spend half the year in the Underworld, resulting in the withering of vegetation, in order to atone for Ištar's behaviour and secure her release. This myth is pivotal to the cult of Dumuzi copiously documented in incantations, love lyrics, and laments.

Another well-attested theme with cultic connections involves the journeys of the gods within Sumer. A text conventionally known as *Enki's Journey to Nippur* is in fact mainly a glorification of Enki's city Eridu and the building activities he instigated there but it concludes with Enki visiting his father Enlil in Nippur, where the son arranges a sumptuous banquet for father. A comparable text, *Nanna-Su'en's Journey* from Ur to Nippur describes every aspect of this journey in exquisite detail, beginning even with the assembly from foreign lands of the materials needed to build the boat. The procession of ritual and cargo boats sails along the canals and rivers and as it passes the towns and villages there is singing and music as well as feasting and rejoicing. These and other myths mediate between the city gods and the hub of the pantheon at Nippur.

Contest literature

The Sumerian 'adamindugga' contest literature[3] consists of organized confrontation between mythologized manifestations of two related or competitive features of the world of the Sumerians. Examples are *Grain and Sheep*, *Bird and Fish*, and *Winter and Summer*. In each case the contestants are placed in a cosmological setting and a debate ensues with adjudication and the declaration of the winner. In the case of *Winter and Summer* a narrator defends the qualities of each season in turn before declaring Winter to be the winner. *Grain and Sheep* is more typical with each being its own advocate. With a total length of 193 lines the text begins with a cosmology in which An spawns the great gods but not sheep or grain. The deficiencies of this situation are elaborated in poetic manner. Yarn is lacking for the loom of Uttu, goddess of weaving and herself a spider. Various types of grain are enumerated and their non-existence deplored. That there was no cloth to wear nor royal turban leads to the punch line: the people of those days had no bread to eat and went about naked. Enki then spoke to Enlil, leading to sheep and grain being created on the Holy Mound. After creating wealth and sustenance in the land, Sheep and Grain enjoy a banquet with sweet wine and beer in a dining hall and start a point-by-point quarrel about their relative merits and contributions to civilization. Enki and Enlil hear the debate and Enlil declares the winner: 'People should submit to the yoke of Grain. Whoever has silver, whoever has jewels, whoever has cattle, whoever has sheep shall take a seat at the gate of whoever has grain, and pass his time there.' The text ends with the statement: 'Dispute between Sheep and Grain. Sheep is left behind and Grain comes forward – praise be to father Enki!'

Heroes and wise kings

Some texts that fall into the category of epic literature need to be considered here because they have significant mythological components. These are comparable to the Homeric epics in that the worlds of gods and men interact freely with one another. Mesopotamian epic is dominated by stories about the exploits of three legendary Early Dynastic kings of Uruk, namely the aforementioned Enmerkar, Lugalbanda, and his son Gilgameš by the cow goddess, Ninsun. The Lugalbanda material which features the hero's exploits in the mountains to the east of Mesopotamia is known primarily from copies of texts from the early second millennium BC and did not enjoy wide currency later. Unlike the stories about his father, the Sumerian Gilgameš material caught the imagination of the Babylonians and spouted a new literature in their own language. The most substantial Gilgameš text from the Old Babylonian period was known as *Surpassing All Other Kings* and consisted of a series of at least three tablets. During the Kassite period many of the Gilgameš tales were forged into a single long epic story in eleven tablets, the standard or canonical *Epic of Gilgameš*. Babylonian literary tradition ascribes this achievement to one man, a certain Sîn-leqe-unnīni about whom nothing else is known. His version of the epic was to remain standard for the rest of Mesopotamian history in a manuscript tradition rich in both Assyria and Babylonia. Sîn-leqe-unnīni began his version with an encomium to Gilgameš as a wise man and traveller, moving on to his royal role as builder of his city. There is an invitation to walk up upon the walls of Uruk and admire their artifice: did not the seven sages lay their foundations? This provides a literary frame since the story ends with Gilgameš' final companion, the boatman Uršanabi, walking on the walls and admiring the city. Between these two episodes is an exploration of the human condition as Gilgameš is transformed from a ruthless dictator exercising the *ius primae noctis* in his city to a wise and sagacious ruler. A final development in the epic's textual history occurred in the first millennium when the Sumerian Gilgameš story *Gilgameš, Enkidu, and the Netherworld* was translated into Babylonian and added to canonical *Gilgameš* as a twelfth tablet, regardless of the fact that it made nonsense out of the original plot. In this story Gilgameš' friend and companion Enkidu, whose death provided the crisis of the epic, is still alive and descends to the Underworld to retrieve two items of sports equipment that Gilgameš had lost. Having failed to disguise himself after intruding into the world of the dead he is held back there, and Gilgameš can only conjure up his spirit to question it on conditions in the Underworld, a scene reminiscent of Book 11 of Homer's *Odyssey*.

Two other stories are those of the wise kings Adapa and Etana who flew into the heavens on birds and hobnobbed with the gods. There was a continuing tradition of tales about rulers who are known to have been historical figures, such as the Old Akkadian king Sargon in the late third millennium BC, but the mythological content is negligible and so they do not need to be treated here.

Anatolia

Through its geographical position Anatolia has always acted as a link between East and West. It is therefore particularly fortunate that the cuneiform archives at Ḫattuša, first unearthed at the beginning of the twentieth century AD, open a unique window on this meeting of cultures during the latter half of the second millennium BC. Ḫattuša (modern Boğazköy) was the capital of the Hittite kingdom that flourished between about 1600 and 1200 BC.

The people known to modern scholarship as Hittites were speakers of an Indo-European language that they recorded in Babylonian cuneiform on clay

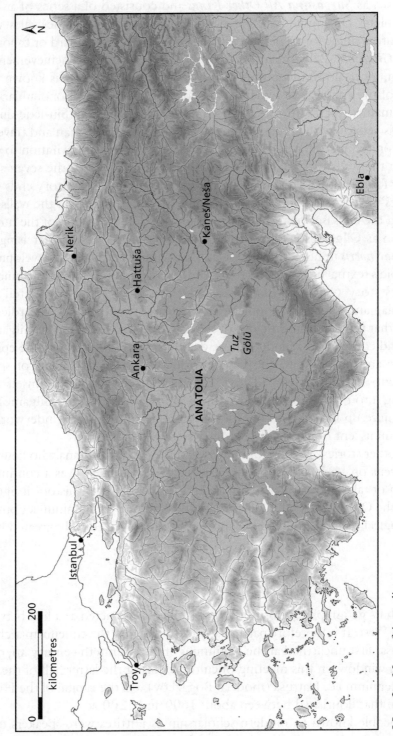

Map 2 Map of Anatolia.

tablets; but theirs is not the only language represented in the archives of Ḫattuša. Two other languages, Luvian and Palaic, belong to the same Anatolian branch of Indo-European as Hittite while the attestation of Indo-Iranian is limited to a few technical terms in a text on horse training. Unrelated and still insufficiently understood, Hattic (also known as Proto-Hattic) was the language of the indigenous population of the 'Land of Ḫatti' and appears in cultic contexts. As the Hittite kingdom gradually expanded and became an empire, it entered the sphere of cultural influence of the – again unrelated – Hurrian language that dominated the lands of Upper Syria, and the cuneiform libraries at Ḫattuša reflect the interest of the Hittite elite in all matters Hurrian from the fourteenth century BC onwards. Equally the corpus of Akkadian texts, to Hittite scribes the language of learning and the *lingua franca* of their day, shows the Mesopotamian influence on Hittite culture and contains some of the Mesopotamian mythological material outlined above, including legends woven around the Old Akkadian kings, the myth concerning the flood hero Atraḫasīs, and the *Epic of Gilgameš*. These stories borrowed from Mesopotamia were not only copied out at Ḫattuša, but also translated and adapted for a Hittite audience, although this material is quite fragmentary. The popularity of the *Epic of Gilgameš* outside Mesopotamia is borne witness to by the existence of a Hurrian version that might throw more light on the epic's textual history were it not for our imperfect understanding of the language. The practice of constantly copying older library texts was similar at Ḫattuša to practice in Mesopotamia though, there is less tangible evidence for the involvement of scribal schools in the process than was the case in Mesopotamia. As a result, many texts are only available to us in copies of the fourteenth–thirteenth centuries BC, although linguistic or palaeographical features in them point to greater antiquity.

Since Hittite, Luvian, and Palaic constitute the oldest recorded Indo-European languages, one might have entertained the hope that the cuneiform texts from Ḫattuša could give us a glimpse into early Indo-European culture and mythology. Sadly, this is not the case. From the cuneiform documents dating to the time of the Old Assyrian trading colonies in Anatolia it is clear that the three dialects of the Anatolian branch of Indo-European languages had already developed their distinctive characteristics by the early second millennium BC. Based on an estimate of how long this process would have taken, most scholars place the arrival of the ancestors of the Hittites and related peoples in Anatolia in the third millennium BC. The fact that members of this Anatolian group display certain archaic linguistic traits not otherwise found in Indo-European languages makes the theory that Indo-European had its origin in Anatolia itself unlikely; the existence of these features rather bespeaks a scenario in which the Anatolian group broke off from the Proto-Indo-European complex at a comparatively early stage, thus retaining more archaic characteristics.

That Anatolia was not the Indo-European homeland can also be deduced from the surprisingly low profile of Indo-European deities in Hittite religion and mythology.

There is no evidence that the collective memory of the Hittites stretched back to a time before they settled in Anatolia. The legends mentioned above of the kings of Akkad doing battle in Anatolia in the latter half of the third millennium BC may well contain some real historical elements, but they do not tell us anything about the history of the Hittites. The earliest historical text found in the archives at Ḫattuša, the *Anitta Chronicle*, describes events that date to the time of the Old Assyrian trading colonies in the early second millennium BC, when Anatolia was divided into a number of principalities. This document, the *res gestae* of one Anitta of Kuššar[4] (whose palace has been excavated at the site of Kaneš, modern Kültepe, in Cappadocia), and of his father, interestingly mentions a number of deities, amongst them the Indo-European sky god Siu(n) (cf. Greek Zeus). There is, however, no evidence that Anitta had any connection with the later Hittite kings at Ḫattuša, a place where he sowed cress to prevent future settlement. But the Hittites regarded Anitta's princely seat Kaneš (Neša in Hittite sources) as their ancestral city and even referred to their own language as 'Nesite'; only their king Ḫattušili (meaning 'the man of Ḫattuša') in the sixteenth century BC decided to defy the curse and move his capital to Ḫattuša. An early Hittite narrative tells of the queen of Kaneš and how she gave birth to thirty sons in one year, but, realizing they were quite a handful, placed them in reed baskets and put them into the river. The river then carried them to the city of Zalpa on the coast of the Black Sea where the gods raised them; after some time she gave birth to thirty daughters whom she brought up herself. This is not only one of the earliest attested variations on the theme of the royal child/hero exposed at birth and of the fairy-tale motif of siblings miraculously finding each other, but also a quasi-historical text detailing the relationship between the two cities.[5]

Hittite religion is a complex affair and a demonstration of how language, culture, and ethnicity are independent variables. The Hittite king and queen had to give attention to a plethora of local cults to fulfil their religious duties. In a process that has been described as 'an extreme form of polytheism', new deities encountered during the expansion of the Hittite sphere of influence were incorporated into the ever growing pantheon summed up by the Hittites themselves as 'the thousand gods of Ḫatti', a rather accurate estimate (van Gessel 1998–2001). The storm god of Ḫatti, one of the many storm gods venerated in different cult centres in Anatolia, was regarded as the head of this unruly pantheon; and as the Hittites forgot about their Indo-European heritage, the god Siu(n) was sidelined by the storm god and his consort, the sun goddess of Arinna. She was one of the most prominent deities in the local Hattic religion that formed the backbone of Hittite cult practice. Some myths, although only recorded in Hittite, are thought to be of Old Anatolian and so mostly Hattic origin. They are easily distinguished, not only by their cast of Old Anatolian deities and their recognizably Anatolian geographical setting: they are also deeply embedded in the cultic calendar and have various ritual functions. So, for instance, we may look at the story of the storm god's confrontation with the serpent Illuyanka (cf. CH. 27, pp. 511–12). This comes in two versions, both claiming to record the account given by a certain Kella, priest of the storm god of Nerik (modern Oymaağaç Höyük), an important cult centre north of Ḫattuša. One of these versions was said to be the core text of the *Purulli* festival, reminding us of how *Enūma eliš* was recited during the Babylonian New Year's festival (cf. above).[6] Both the Mesopotamian and the Anatolian myth present a conflict between a god and a dragon-like monster; but this is where the similarities end, as the storm god, weakened by an earlier defeat to such an extent that he needs the help of a mortal, cuts a rather pitiful figure and only succeeds through deceit. *Illuyanka* bears an uncanny resemblance to the story of Zeus' fight against Typhon, particularly in the version found in Apollodoros (1.6.3), where the removal of Zeus' tendons is matched by the storm god's loss of his heart and eyes in the Hittite myth.

The cult context of Hattic mythology is even more obvious in a number of (sometimes very fragmentary) myths that deal with the disappearance of a deity and contain the ritual that needs to be performed to placate the angry god or goddess and bring them back. The best known and most complete version of this vanishing-god type of myth concerns the storm god's son, Telipinu, though all of them follow substantially the same pattern. For unknown reasons Telipinu becomes agitated and storms off in a huff, taking fertility and abundance with him. The effect of the disappearance of the god is felt throughout the world as famine breaks out. Even the gods are affected and send out search parties for Telipinu; the sun god sends the sharp-eyed eagle, but even he cannot find the missing god. Finally the mother goddess Ḫannaḫanna sends out the little bee, although the other gods think that such a small insect will not succeed where they have failed. It locates the sulking god in the meadow and stings his hands and feet to wake him up, but instead of coming quietly Telipinu grows even angrier. This is when the ritual section of the text sets in: the healing goddess Kamrušepa performs various acts of sympathetic magic to appease the god and finally succeeds in calming him down. Fertility is finally restored, and blessings are handed out. Other subjects of this seasonal myth are the storm god himself, the sun god (whose disappearance results in the land being paralysed by frost), and the mother goddess.

Much of the Old Anatolian mythological material with its integration of ritual elements is difficult to understand, and comprehension is not helped by the frequently fragmentary state of the texts. This is the case with a short narrative known after its incipit as *When the Storm God Thunders Frightfully*, or also in modern scholarship as *The Moon that Fell from Heaven*, which is preserved on a tablet that has the Hattic version in the left-hand column while the right-hand column contains the Hittite translation. The title of the composition essentially sums up the plot: having been terrified by the storm god's loud thundering the moon god falls out of the sky to earth, where he lies paralysed with fear, and only Kamrušepa, looking down from her heavenly vantage point, notices his disappearance.[7]

While it is difficult to separate mythological material with an Old Anatolian background from its cult context, the textual classification is much more straightforward when it comes to a number of important myths that are associated with the process of Hurrianization of Hittite religion. The reasons for this phenomenon are still unclear; some scholars believe that at the time of the Empire Period the Hittite royal family itself was of Hurrian origin, but took on traditional Hittite throne names. The clearest expression of this trend can be found on the walls of the rock sanctuary Yazılıkaya outside Ḫattuša, where the well-ordered, hierarchical pantheon depicted in the form of a procession stands in stark contrast to the earlier anarchic idea of the 'thousand gods' that happily accommodated several sun deities and a couple of moon gods at the same time. This reorganization could only be achieved through radical syncretism, and so the august divine couple at the centre of the parade where the male and female deities come together are identified as the Hurrian storm god Teššub and the Syrian goddess Ḫebat, an unlikely substitute for the sun goddess of Arinna.

Teššub and an all-Hurrian cast of deities feature in a number of myths, known principally from tablets in Hittite, that form part of one great mythological composition which we call the 'Kumarbi Cycle'. All of these, texts, which are unfortunately sometimes quite fragmentary, have certain characteristics in common: where a colophon survives they are described as the 'song' of one of the protagonists or else the text contains the phrase 'I sing of ...'. They can also be recognized by their content, the struggle of Kumarbi, 'Father of all the gods' (originally a grain god based at the city of Urkeš, modern Tell Mozan), against the storm god Teššub. They are set in the Syro-Mesopotamian realm rather than Anatolia. The story starts with a particularly intriguing text that bears the original title *The Song of Kumarbi* but has entered modern scholarly consciousness under the name *Kumarbi and the Kingship of Heaven*. It begins with an encomium directed to the 'primeval gods' and then invites these deities to listen to the tale; this request is followed by a short succession myth. First the god Alalu reigns in heaven, but after nine years his servant Anu (one of several Mesopotamian deities to have entered the Hurrian pantheon) usurps his throne, driving him into the earth. After another nine years Alalu's son Kumarbi, who has become Anu's cupbearer, avenges his father and topples

Anu, who tries to make a swift exit skywards. Pulling Anu down by his feet Kumarbi bites off his genitals and swallows them. As Kumarbi lets out a triumphant laugh Anu tells him that he has now become pregnant with three terrible gods, namely the storm god Teššub, the river Tigris, and the god Tašmišu. Kumarbi spits out whatever he can of the semen; the next passage is unfortunately very fragmentary, but it seems that the spat out semen creates some awful being when it hits a mountain. Meanwhile Kumarbi after a gestation period gives birth to several mighty gods, including the storm god Teššub, who, after a discussion of possible exit points, chooses what is referred to as 'the good place' in the Hittite text. One god emerges from Kumarbi's skull. In another broken passage Kumarbi threatens to eat Teššub but is given a block of basalt instead that injures his teeth. The rest of the story is very fragmentary so that it is difficult to follow the plot, but Kumarbi and his followers are planning to get rid of Teššub. The god Ea plays an important role, apparently independent of both parties, and Teššub's bull Šeri warns Teššub not to curse Ea. Finally, the earth gives birth to two children. The close connections of this myth with Hesiod's *Theogony* (especially 154–82, 453–506) are obvious and were recognized instantly after its decipherment (Güterbock 1948).

The next episodes of the Kumarbi Cycle deal with Kumarbi's various and increasingly sophisticated attempts to get rid of Teššub and regain the kingship. In the *Song of the God LAMMA*, LAMMA (the correct reading of the name is uncertain) battles Teššub and becomes king, but is later apparently deposed. The last three stories of the cycle describe how Kumarbi tries to gain victory with the help of different sons he fathered, the first one being a boy called Silver; the text is very fragmentary and the end of the myth is not preserved. The second son, by the sea god's daughter, is Ḫedammu, a sea serpent, who is apparently defeated after being seduced by Teššub's sister, the beautiful Šauška (the Hurrian Ištar). Last in the series is the *Song of Ullikummi* in which the main character is the love child of Kumarbi and a rock; the little stone monster Ullikummi is placed on the shoulder of Upelluri, who, like Atlas in Greek mythology, stands in the sea and bears on himself heaven and earth. Ullikummi grows at an alarming rate out of the sea and begins to threaten the heavens when he is spotted by the sun god, who alerts Teššub and his followers. Šauška attempts the same strategy as against Ḫedammu but ends up crying tears of frustration as she realizes that the unfeeling, deaf, and blind stone monster is impervious to her feminine charms. A battle begins, but Ullikummi seems invincible. Finally Teššub enlists the help of wise Ea who discovers Ullikummi's base when he visits Upelluri. Ea asks the primeval gods for the copper-cutting instrument that was used to separate heaven and earth at the beginning of time; the ending is again lost but probably the tool is used successfully on Ullikummi and he is defeated. The gaps in the narrative and the overall incomplete state of the material make it difficult to establish the correct order of the episodes, particularly of the *Song of LAMMA* and the *Song of Silver*. The reconstruction followed here is the one suggested by Hoffner (1998), but others might equally be possible. So far only a small fragment of a Hurrian language manuscript of the Kumarbi Cycle has been securely identified (Giorgieri 2001), although another fragment that describes a fight between Teššub and the sea god could be part of the *Song of Ḫedammu* (Rutherford 2001b). Whatever cult context the composition originally had[8] has been mainly lost in the Hittite version to its entertainment value, ranging from accounts of exciting cosmic battles to low comedy.

Human beings are almost completely absent from the narratives of the Kumarbi Cycle known to date, even if their existence is obviously being taken for granted. This is different in another, earlier, text that predates the Hurrianization of Hittite religion and, like the Hattic–Hittite tale of *The Moon That Fell from Heaven*, exists in large parts as a true Hurrian–Hittite bilingual, in which Syro-Hurrian deities in the Hurrian text have been replaced by their Anatolian counterparts in the Hittite translation, the *Song of Release*. It demonstrates the problems of classification of ancient texts that do not fit any modern definition of genre; although, like the stories that make up the Kumarbi Cycle, it is labelled as a 'song' and has a short proem, it is made up of seemingly disjoined sections of varying nature. It could be described as a morality tale, since the underlying theme of the text appears to be justice. Thus, the 'release' of the title refers to release from debt, an act of establishing justice by any ruler craving popularity. The composition starts off with a number of parables in which objects or animals that act in an ungrateful manner towards their maker or benefactor or are greedy and discontented with their lot are likened to human beings. This is followed by the description of a feast prepared by the Underworld goddess Allani in her palace for Teššub, his brother Tašmišu, and the primeval deities. Unfortunately the text breaks off, leaving the development of the plot open to speculation, but in the next preserved section the action switches to earth, where, in the city of Ebla (modern Tell Mardikh) in Syria, the just ruler of the city is at loggerheads with a mass orator who seems to have convinced the council of the city to refuse the king's wish for granting the release from debt. Teššub becomes involved in the proceedings and vows to destroy the city if the ruler fails to remit debts; the end of the story is again lost, but might have contained an explanation for the (historical) destruction of Ebla.

The mingling of gods and mortals found in the *Song of Release* is even more pronounced in a number of myths of a fairy-tale nature. Two of them, the *Tale of Appu* and the story of *The Sun God, the Cow, and the Fisherman* explore the theme of childlessness, while the *Tale of Hunter Kešši*, which contains an account of a number of dreams, tells the story of a man so obsessed with his beautiful wife that he neglects his duty towards the gods as well as his elderly mother.

Finally, it needs to be pointed out that the world of the Hittites has also been recognized in the setting of Homer's Trojan War, as can be seen, for example, from the similarities between the funerary ritual for the Hittite king and the description of Patroklos' funeral in Book 23 of the *Iliad*. Since the 1960s more and more scholars have shared the opinion that the city Wiluša that appears in Hittite documents is to be identified with the Troy of classical Greek sources (see CH. 22 for a different view). Watkins (1995: 146–9) has made a particularly intriguing suggestion: in a Hittite text that lists various Luvian songs to be sung on a number on occasions there is an incipit of an otherwise unknown composition called *When They Came from Steep Wiluša*; could this be a Anatolian precursor of the *Iliad*? The numerous links between Anatolian and Greek mythology have been touched upon, but closer investigation is beyond the scope of this contribution; Anatolia is also the bridge to Mesopotamia. Similarly, the next area to be discussed has various links with Mesopotamia, Anatolia, and the world of the Aegean.

Ugarit

Ugarit (modern Ras Shamra, cf. CH. 20) was an important maritime city occupying a key position on the Syrian littoral with trade links in every direction. Unlike in Mesopotamia, where there is a well-documented mythology spanning many centuries, what we have at Ugarit is a snapshot: literary texts from scribal libraries and schools written down in the earlier half of the fourteenth century BC before the city was subject to violent destruction and abandonment. At this period the local dynasty of the city loosely recognized the sovereignty of the Hittite Great King at Ḫattuša, and this is reflected in the existence of Hittite, Hurrian, and Akkadian texts in the city's scribal libraries. The concern here, however, will be with the mythological texts in Ugaritic itself, a West Semitic language closer to Hebrew than to the East Semitic Akkadian. It would be easier to study Ugaritic mythology if we knew more about the Ugaritic language, but we have only a tiny volume of material in comparison with Akkadian and there is no significant native tradition of lexicography. Elucidation of the Ugaritic language is largely contingent on comparative etymology, with the result that the basic meaning of a line can rest on whether the cognate has been found in Hebrew, Arabic, or another language. Commentaries on Ugaritic texts ring the changes on the comparative lexical possibilities and their implications.

The philological problems are compounded by the fact that Ugaritic mythology has its own identity independent of that of Mesopotamia or Anatolia so that there are very few mythological parallels that can be used to throw constructive light on it. It is customary to distinguish between those myths that have mainly divine focus and those that focus on kings and their deeds. The important myths in the former group are the Baal ('Lord') myth and the *Myth of Dawn and Dusk* (Šaḥr and Šalim). The *Baal Myth* (see also CH. 20) is known from six tablets, and despite some controversy these tablets are generally regarded as being capable of sequential arrangement resulting in a text of 2,350 lines telling a coherent story. Arranged thus, the *Baal Myth*, sometimes referred to as the 'Baal Cycle', is by far the most substantial Ugaritic mythological text. The head of the pantheon is El ('The God'), who favours a watery deity called Yamm ('Sea'). Baal challenges Yamm, defeats and kills him, an event that leads in some way to the building of his own royal palace. Mōt ('Death') then challenges Baal and kills him, but after a period in the Underworld Baal returns. Although there are echoes of *Enūma eliš* and *Ištar's Descent* here they are not close or substantial enough to elucidate the many problematic passages and puzzling episodes. One of the most lucid of the Ugaritic myths centres on the triad Baal, Ašertu (Ugaritic Aṭirat), and her husband Elkunirsa, and it owes its clarity to the fact that it has come down to us in Hittite translation on a tablet excavated at Ḫattuša. That this myth is Ugaritic is clear not only from the protagonists but also from elements of Ugaritic poetic structure that come through in the ancient translation. The beginning of the myth involves Ašertu's attempted infidelity with Baal, but later on she is sleeping with her husband before flying off like a bird to look for Baal and warn him of Elkunirsa's planned revenge.

Dawn and Dusk is known from a single well-preserved tablet from Ugarit that is believed to contain the complete text. It is a myth of engenderment in which the two eponymous protagonists result from the liaison of El with two human females. The text is complex and does not flow freely as one expects in the Mesopotamian mythological narratives. Of its seventy-six lines approximately the first third deals with diverse and partly unclear motifs in small units. The next third deals with the births, while in the rest 'The Gracious Gods', apparently Dawn and Dusk, are banished to the desert and then invent agriculture.

The two principal myths with royal focus are those of *Kirta* and *Aqhat*. Kirta, a just king, loses his seven wives through death and pestilence before obtaining an heir. In a dream El appears to him and tempts him with gifts but he refuses them and insists that what he needs is a son. El vouchsafes to him the appropriate measure: he is to gather together a vast army to besiege the city of Udm whose king, Pabil, will also tempt him with gifts which he is to refuse, insisting on the hand of Pabil's beautiful daughter Ḥurraya. He does this, pausing in his campaign to offer gold and silver to Aṭirat of Tyre. He duly wins Hurraya, but she will be missed by the folk of Udm as a cow lows for her calf and a soldier longs for his mother. Baal rises in the assembly and causes El to bless Kirta and promise him eight sons, one of whom – probably the first born and heir, Yaṣṣub – will be suckled by Aṯirat and the virgin Anat, wet nurses of the gods. Kirta then becomes ill but is cured. Yaṣṣub, unaware of events since the sickness of the king has been hushed up, accuses his father of neglecting his duties and vows to take over the throne. Kirta curses him and calls on an Underworld deity to break his skull. The *Aqhat* myth also recounts how a father (Danil) obtained a son (Aqhat), but it is the son who is at the centre of the story. He is cajoled by the goddess Anat to hand over to her his favourite bow but he refuses. She curses him, and on his death his sister Puǵat vows to avenge him – but here the tablet becomes fragmentary and broken.

One last Ugaritic myth, *Nikkal and Kōṯarat*, has clear Mesopotamian affinities. This takes the form of a hymn to Nikkal and an otherwise unknown deity. The hymn sings of the productive marriage of Nikkal to Yariḫ ('Moon'); Nikkal is without doubt the Ugaritic reflex of the originally Sumerian goddess Ningal, consort of the moon god Nanna (Su'en). The main part of the hymn deals with the betrothal and this leads on to a further hymn within a hymn, this time to the Kōṯarat, the daughters of the new moon.

Theories Relating to Mesopotamian Mythology

The Babylonians had their own school of myth and ritual that resulted in a corpus of texts dubbed by modern scholarship 'mythological explanatory texts'. These texts have in the past been regarded as esoteric, but the occurrence of the lines of thought that underpins them in a growing variety of sources shows that this type of thinking was more widespread than has previously been supposed. Characteristic is a reading into temple rituals of mythology where the rituals and mythology do not strictly speaking belong together. This apparent incongruity can become easier to understand when placed in the context of Babylonian thinking. There are other areas of Babylonian speculation where patterns that we recognize as coincidental are sought between words and numbers in order to yield certain types of information or supposedly prove theological assertions. The significance of the mythological explanatory texts is that certain types of mythology are being used to explain certain types of rituals. An example can be given: 'They carry the Woman of the City on their heads and necks and go to a field and scatter grain: that is Marduk because he trampled on the necks of those disobedient [to him].' It is quite certain that this fertility ritual had nothing whatsoever to do with Marduk's defeat of his mythological opponents. The point is that the author is using techniques of abstract association to link a ritual of fertility with a cosmic myth in which fertility and the seasons and agricultural cycle were created and established.[9]

More information on the interpretation of Babylonian mythology is available from the early Hellenistic period when Berossos, a priest of Bel in Babylon, wrote a book in Greek called the *Babyloniaka* (*BNJ* 680) with the aim of explaining Babylonian culture, including mythology, to a Greek audience. Although our understanding of Berossos' work is bedevilled not only by the fragmentary and second-hand nature of the material we are obliged to work with, and by his own conciseness, much can be learned from it. Whether writing about Mesopotamian mythology or history, he gives a blow-by-blow narrative, essentially a catalogue of facts. There are, however, a few instances where he gives away what may be elements of interpretation that existed in the thinking and teaching of Babylonian priests that did not find their way into the ancient learned commentaries and explanatory texts that we possess. For example, in describing the myth of the creation of man from clay and the blood of a slain demon, as referred to above, Berossos provides the rider that this explains why men are intelligent and have a share of divine wisdom. In another example, describing a version of the creation best known to us from the *Epic of Creation*, also outlined above, he explains that this is to talk about nature allegorically. In principle this could refer to the reception of troubling myths as *allegory* in the Greek tradition (see INDEX s.v.), but this seems unlikely, since, although he wrote Greek, Berossos had clearly only been educated in the Babylonian tradition. The use of the word allegory by a Babylonian priest is striking but recalls a common feature of ancient commentaries on Babylonian religious and literary texts where not only a primary but also secondary and tertiary meanings are established.[10]

Such general interpretation of Mesopotamian mythology as there is in modern scholarship has tended to have been achieved by those who have contributed most to the identification and publication of the tablets. First to be mentioned must be Kramer who copied thousands of Sumerian mythological texts mainly from Nippur and Ur in Istanbul, London, and Philadelphia and was responsible for the earliest coherent translations of much of the Sumerian mythology that has been outlined above. Straightforward in his approach to the Sumerian mythology S. N. Kramer tended to regard it as being of the nature of folklore. As well as his industry in making so much Sumerian mythology available for the first time, Kramer was one of the first to write popular books on the Sumerians that brought them and their mythology to the public. Jacobsen, in contrast, searched for core meanings in the mythology and drew on anthropology and comparative mythology in his interpretation. In his *Treasures of Darkness* (1976) Jacobsen offers a history and social interpretation of Mesopotamian mythology across the three millennia. This is further expounded in his essay 'Toward the Image of Tammuz' (Jacobsen 1970), which provides an interpretation of individual Sumerian deities and mythological motifs, taking close account of Sumerian society, the Sumerian economy, and the ancient life of the land. Thus he strives usually successfully to distinguish between beliefs and mythology of the agriculturalists, pastoralists, and other groups, also taking into account divergences within Sumer. Bottéro, in his many *oeuvres* on Babylonian mythological themes, offers a close analysis of the mythology coupled with highly intuitive study of the religious beliefs and the thinking implicit in the texts. Von Soden (1984) has proposed a framework within which Mesopotamian mythology may be analysed involving a distinction between reflected and constructed mythology, where, essentially, the reflected mythology evolves while the constructed mythology is consciously constructed. Little attention has been given to this theory, but von Soden acknowledges the complexity of the matter in that even according to his scheme reflected mythology may contain constructed elements and constructed mythology draw on tradition. This approach may yet prove to be productive of understanding. The wider context of Mesopotamian mythology, including its impact on Hebrew traditions, has been explored by Lambert, who notes that it was short units of information or mythology that most easily crossed script and language boundaries. Kirk (1970) takes as his starting point the theoretical approaches to myth achieved by scholars such as Malinowski, Eliade, and Lévi-Strauss and includes Near Eastern mythology within a compass that ranges across several continents. To date this work remains the only serious attempt to study some of the material outlined above from anthropological perspectives.

The study of ancient Near Eastern mythology reflects the relative youth of Assyriology and the related disciplines. A start has been made but there is still much work to do both in the task of recovering the actual mythology and in its interpretation.

FURTHER READING

For Mesopotamian religion in general see Bottéro 2001. Jacobsen 1987 and Black, *et al.* 2004 are anthologies of Sumerian mythology. Foster 2005 gives a broad compendium of Akkadian literature, while Dalley 1989 offers annotated translations of the principal Babylonian myths; Foster 2007 is a concise history of Akkadian literature. For Hittite religion in general consult Haas 1994 and Popko 1995. Translations of Hittite myths can be found in Hoffner 1998, where additional material has been incorporated into first edition (1990). Ugaritic mythology is treated comprehensively in Gibson 1978 and, more recently, S. B. Parker 1997. Near Eastern compositions of epic nature are dealt with in J. M. Foley 2005. Sasson 1995 contains articles on almost every conceivable ancient Near Eastern topic, including religion, mythology, and literature.

Since the study by Lambert and Walcot 1965 was provoked by the discovery of the *Ḫarab Myth*, other scholars have engaged in comparisons between Near Eastern and Greek mythology. Walcot 1966 followed up this article with a broader study in monograph form. M. L. West 1971 went so far as suggesting oriental influences on early

Greek philosophy. Duchemin 1995, a posthumous anthology, includes a perceptive treatment of the orientalizing influences on Hesiod and a highly original comparative study of the personification of abstracts and natural elements in Hesiod and ancient Near Eastern texts. Burkert 1992 takes the view that not only Greek literature, but also Greek religion was significantly influenced by Near Eastern models. While Penglase 1994 has given particular attention to the Homeric *Hymns*, M. L. West 1999 has taken a much broader view and amassed a large and varied corpus of parallels and proposed borrowings into Greek literature from the Near East.

NOTES

1. For a mythological dictionary and work of reference covering Mesopotamia, Anatolia, and the Levant consult Haussig (1965). A large selection of mythological texts in translation from all three of these areas is provided by Hallo and Younger (2003a, b, and c), which now replaces Pritchard (1969).
2. The bilingual character of Mesopotamian society can be demonstrated by reference to the interaction between the two languages, Sumerian and Akkadian, themselves. For example, in Akkadian, unlike in any other Semitic language, the main verb stands at the end of a sentence, a feature emulating Sumerian sentence structure.
3. Written – visually suggesting contest – with two crossed 'person' signs.
4. Neu (1974); Carruba (2003).
5. For a translation of this 'tale of two cities' and the other Hittite myths discussed here, see the authoritative work by Hoffner (1998).
6. For the implications of this performance context, in terms of 'pragmatics', see ch. 27. (KD)
7. It seems likely, although not stated expressly in the text, that there is a connection between this myth and one of the many festivals that Hittite sources describe in minute detail (cf. Haas 1994: 375, 377).
8. It has, for example, been interpreted as a seasonal myth; cf. Haas (1994: 82–99).
9. For an edition and discussion of texts of this type see A. Livingstone (1986).
10. These commentaries deal with philological as well as cultural problems from an ancient Babylonian point of view. They were compiled for a wide variety of compositions, but unfortunately a modern edition of them has yet to be published.

CHAPTER TWENTY

Levantine, Egyptian, and Greek Mythological Conceptions of the Beyond

Nanno Marinatos and Nicolas Wyatt

Introduction: A Common Market in Beyonds

Many concepts about the Beyond are common to Greece, the Levant, and Egypt in the period between c. 2000 and 600 BC. In this chapter we look at beliefs current in these different societies to come to some understanding and appreciation of their cultural overlap in this area. We present, first, our joint introduction to the subject, and then Wyatt explores the Levantine concept of the Beyond while Marinatos goes on to provide a separate discussion of Greek and Egyptian ideas.

Common Beyond

The similarities in the concepts of the Beyond to be found in Greece, the Near East and Egypt are so many that mere coincidence is not possible The similarities are so many that mere coincidence is not possible. We may safely postulate multiple points of contact over a long period of time.

One constant motif is that the Beyond is completely separated from the world of the living. The barriers are imaginary gates, mountains, a deep river, 'waters of death', or the Red Sea (see Wyatt's discussion, 'The Beyond in the Levant', below). The territory of the dead is situated across a river, on a horizontal plane, or beneath the earth, as an Underworld, or even in the sky,

A Companion to Greek Mythology, First Edition. Edited by Ken Dowden and Niall Livingstone. © 2014 John Wiley & Sons Ltd. Published 2014 by John Wiley & Sons Ltd.

amongst the stars. These alternative locations are attested even for the same culture. For example, Odysseus crosses the Okeanos to go to Hades, but Persephone goes under the earth (Homeric *Hymn to Demeter* 335, 349, 409). In Sophocles' *Antigone*, Erebos is referred to as being under the sea (587), but in Euripides's *Orestes*, divinized Helen is in heaven together, with the stars (1683–5). Going back to the third millennium, in Egypt of the Old Kingdom, the dead king becomes one of the stars, but in the second millennium, in the New Kingdom, the dead may descend into deep caverns or sail in a boat to Elysium. In the *Epic of Gilgameš* (third–first millennium; see CH. 19), the hero must cross the waters of death to reach the island of the immortal Utnapištim (*Gilgameš* x ii, tr. Dalley 1989: 102). Yet, in the Sumerian version, where the hero is called Bilgameš, his friend Enkidu has to go to the depths of the earth to recover for him what he has dropped in the Underworld (*Bilgameš* l. 175, tr. George 1999: 184). Thus, the location of the world of the dead varied, the common feature being its inaccessibility to humans of this earth. And the variations are attested for the entire East Mediterranean, which shows that ideas mutated and spread from one place to the next.

Another idea common to Greece and the Orient is the specific barrier of waters. The boat which transfers the dead sails by itself one way or has a special ferryman who refuses to return the dead to the other bank from which he has collected them. The Greek Charon sails one way; Ur-šanabi, the ferryman in the Babylonian *Epic of Gilgameš*, does not return the hero to the same bank from which the latter has embarked but takes him through another path back to Uruk (*Gilgameš* xi. v). In Egyptian spells it is stated: 'To be said to the Ferryman of the Field of Reeds, so his face (will be) toward the gods who are on the other side of the river' (Mueller 1972: 104). Circe tells Odysseus that he will sail to Hades on a boat that needs no pilot and will sail of its own accord (*Odyssey* 10. 505).

Another recurring feature that characterizes the Beyond is darkness, although there is one immediate exception: the heavenly Jerusalem flooded with pure light (Revelation 21.22). Odysseus enters a dark world when he sails to Hades (see 'The Beyond in the Odyssey and Egypt', below); and Babylonian Ištar goes to the 'dark House'. 'Broad Tartaros is deep', says Zeus to Hera in the *Iliad* (8. 477–81). It is also dark.

Immortality is an issue addressed by many of the ancient traditions, but it is not always solved in the same way, even within the same culture. In Archaic Greek thought, the feature which distinguishes heroes from ordinary dead is not the imperishability of their soul (*psyche*) – for it is imperishable anyway – but of individual memory. The dead in the Hades of the *Odyssey* exist and will exist in perpetuity; what matters is that they have forgotten who they are. To remedy this situation, some Greeks were willing to purchase gold leaves (the so-called Orphic leaves or *lamellae*, cf. pp. 90, 106) giving instructions on the geography of the beyond. Many of them have been found in various graves, ranging from southern Italy to Pelina in Thessaly and to Crete (late fifth century–third century BC). Some of the instructions specify that the dead ought to drink only from the fountain of Memory, which shows this preoccupation with the loss of individual personality at death.

Hesiod and Homer distinguished heroes from the ordinary dead by placing them in a location distinct from Hades, across from it on the banks of Okeanos. They live on the Isles of the *Makares* (Blest) and unlike the other dead never go to Hades (Hesiod, *Works and Days* 167–72). Menelaos, according to Homer, goes to the Elysian Fields, at 'the ends of the earth' where Rhadamanthys ensures the best possible lives for people (*Odyssey* 4.565–8). The Isles of the Makares and the Elysian Fields are similar places, both located by the river Okeanos. What is more, there is beauty in both, a good climate and an abundance of food. We hear nothing that leads to the conclusion that the heroes there have lost their memory, and in any case they live in a place which is distinct from Hades and is never confused with it.

In Ugaritic literature we also find distinctions between the ordinary dead and the kings, heroes, or saviours. And Ugaritic literature also presents us with the idea that the ends of the earth are full of beauty and constitute an entrance to the Beyond (Wyatt considers this later in the chapter at 'The Beyond in the Levant').

Rewards, and punishments for sins were introduced in later times and do not feature in the period under consideration. The few exceptions in the *Odyssey* are discussed separately by Marinatos below in 'The Beyond in the Odyssey and Egypt'.

The common traits of Mediterranean and Near Eastern traditions may be better understood by reference to a visual map of the Beyond. We are lucky that such a document exists in the form of a clay tablet from Babylon (now in the British Museum),[1] dating to the seventh–fifth century BC. Fortunately, the design is accompanied by inscriptions, and the back of the tablet has a commentary. An adaptation of this Babylonian map is presented in Figure 20.1.

The world is a circle with an outer rim and triangular projections which represent the Beyond. The outer rim is a river and the mass of water constitutes a clear boundary between the human sphere and the Beyond. The most important feature of the cosmic river is that it is not crossable by humans. It matches the shield of Achilles as described in the *Iliad* (18.478–608), the latter being a veritable model of the universe surrounded by river Okeanos.

Homer does not mention Hades in his description of the shield of Achilles; but, on the basis of what has been said here, we may place it on the far side of Okeanos (figs 20.2 and 20.4 below)

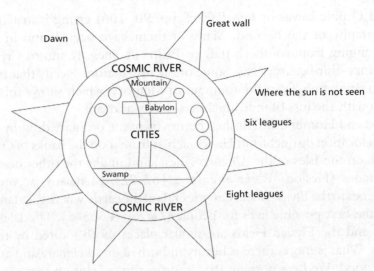

Figure 20.1 Reconstruction of the Babylonian World Map (British Museum 92687).

The Infrastructure for a Common Beyond

One important question is how the *koine* (common market) of motifs spread in the Near East, Egypt, and Greece and, given the fact that we are covering a very long period, from the Bronze to the Iron Age, the answer is by no means simple. Trade is an insufficient answer because it is not self-evident why motifs should be picked up and transmitted, nor why they should be received at the other end. We also need to confront the problem of language barriers from one cultural area to the next. The factor of time needs to be taken into consideration too. How and why did the ideas survive in Greek literature over a period of many generations? Oral tradition, which is often invoked, is doubtful because oral memory dies out. How many people remember who their great-grandfather was? Without written documents, genealogy scarcely survives. Herodotos, for example, knows next to nothing about the eighth century BC and earlier.

Walter Burkert and Martin West have given ingenious historical answers to explain the similarities between Greece and the Near East in the seventh to sixth century, but Egypt must also be added to the areas with which Greeks had close contacts.

The following factors, then, contributed to the forging of a *koine*:

1 Multilingualism;
2 The existence of world-dominions and multi-ethnic empires, such as the ninth–sixth century Assyrian and Persian empires, which surely facilitated

and encouraged trade contacts but also meetings between professional artists in foreign courts (e.g., the Ionian sculptors who worked in Achaemenid Pasargadae);

3 The existence of multilingual libraries, such as that of Ashurbanibal in Nineveh;
4 Bilingual schools;
5 Greek mercenaries in the service of Assyrian, Egyptian, and Persian kings.

Herodotos testifies that the Egyptian pharaoh Psammetichos (seventh century BC) 'even went so far as to put some Egyptian boys ... to be taught Greek' (Herodotos 2.154, tr. de Sélincourt). Evidently, Psammetichos's reliance on Greek mercenaries and his gratitude to them led him to promote bilingual schools in his country. Most interesting is the story of a certain Pedon who was in the service of Psammetichos II (595–89). He was a Greek from Priene who had earned special merit and received 'a golden bracelet and a city' for his 'manliness'. To commemorate this glory, he set up a basalt monument of typical Egyptian style. The inscription is written in Greek but echoes Egyptian practice and values. This testimony gives an idea of how cosmopolitan some Greeks were. They were not only merchants; they were mercenaries and sometimes trusted personal aids of kings.

A possible scenario may be envisaged given the five factors listed above: professional bards and poets travelled together with Greek mercenaries and officials of their country from one court and city to the next. Their principal service may have been to entertain Greeks abroad but they made it their job to learn new stories from their foreign counterparts. In short, the profession of the itinerant poet may have been favoured by the global circumstances of war and flourishing economic enterprises. Itinerant poets would have brought the new motifs back to Greece, integrating them into Hellenized narratives.

A similar scenario may be postulated for the Bronze Age, except that the contacts at that time would have been organized mainly through the initiatives of royal courtiers and kings. Nevertheless, bilingualism may be postulated for this period as well.

In conclusion, the *koine* may be explained through the opportunities given to polyglot poets both during the Bronze Age and the historical period. What is less plausible is the traditional view that Elysium and other concepts were transmitted automatically through the Minoans and Mycenaeans via oral tradition and memory. This explanation is inadequate because it is not self-evident: who transmits what and why during long periods of economic recession? We need to visualize a concrete social and historical context which would have made transmission rewarding to the transmitter, in this case the itinerant multilingual poet.

The Beyond in the Levant

'Levant', Ugarit

By the Levant we refer to the Near Eastern countries on the Mediterranean. Today these are Syria, the Lebanon, and Israel. In ancient Greek times these regions were Phoenicia and Palestine. The principal religious texts we have from this region are, of course, the contents of the (Hebrew and Greek) Old Testament. The Phoenicians, by contrast, despite their huge importance for the cultural contact of Greece with the Near East, doubtless in mythological respects as in others (most notably the alphabet), have left us no mythological texts.[2] Thus, when Philo of Byblos (first–second century AD) reported in Greek the mythology of a Phoenician, Sanchuniathon,[3] it was generally believed by modern scholars that he had invented the material, as we had no Phoenician texts with which to compare his colourful mythology. That situation changed drastically when the site of Ras Shamra (ten kilometres north of Latakia, the main Mediterranean port of modern Syria) was excavated following its discovery in 1928. This turned out to be the site of the ancient Ugarit, a major port flourishing from around 1450 to 1200 BC. And, more important, amongst its tablets was a substantial number of religious and mythological texts that gave us the insight into this part of the world that we had hitherto been lacking and which notably confirmed aspects of the material of Philo's Sanchuniathon. The resulting situation is that for religion and mythology of the Levant it is these Ugaritic texts and the biblical texts that constitute our principal information. And that is the material of this contribution.

The civilizations of the Near East were not, however, hermetically sealed from each other: quite the opposite. Consequently, we will find that the Hebrew texts reflect, and even transmit, mythological ideas that we find in Ugarit and that both are part of a family that stretches to the Mesopotamian cultures that are dealt with in the previous chapter (CH. 19). Ugaritic and Hebrew as languages are West Semitic; Akkadian is East Semitic. Only Sumerian was of a different family altogether, and its mythology was fully embraced by the Akkadian-speaking peoples.

Location and character of the Beyond

It is a natural and widely-evidenced tendency to link experience of the real world to the imagined universe of the Beyond, identifying well-known landmarks such as rivers and caves as cosmic boundaries, entrances to it, and so on, as well as using the familiar trappings of civilization in this world (for example, the metaphor of the city), presumably as a means of coming to terms with the inevitability of death and the other issues noted above. This 'geographicaliza-tion' also allowed the Beyond to play a formative, contrapuntal role in the construction of the world of the living.

Approaching the topic in a comparative manner, we see two main tenden-cies in the description of the Beyond. On the one hand, it could be seen negatively (that is, with a measure of protest and rejection), as a place of hor-ror, sometimes personified to express an element of malignity and terror reflecting the fear people must have felt in contemplating it. But it could also be seen more positively (that is, with greater acceptance). These sequential stages represent the psychological process of coming to terms with the death of loved ones and then oneself.

With regard to location, the common Semitic term (Ugaritic *arṣ(u)*, Hebrew *'ereṣ*, Akkadian *erṣetu*, Old Akkadian *arṣatu*) denoted 'earth, ground, Underworld, land'. There is an ambivalence in the term, denoting both the earth which humans inhabit, namely the ground on which they stand, and the abode of the dead below. We may sense this ambivalence in Genesis 1.1, which reads something like 'In the beginning of God's making of heaven and earth', but carries primordial overtones of 'God's separating of heaven/ sky and Underworld'. Experience *on* the earth gives rise, after all, to the metaphorical use of earth matters to describe what was supposed to happen *under* the earth, and this serves to emphasize the continuity between living and dead.

The Ugaritic Underworld[4] is not just dark, but specifically *dusty* and indeed is known as the 'house of dust' (*bt ḫptt*),[5] something we find in this couplet:

> and go down into the house of dust;
> > be numbered among those descending into the Underworld.
> > > (*KTU* 1.4 viii 7)

This is reflected in the language of several passages of the Old Testament, for instance, the following:

> By the sweat of your brow you shall eat food,
> > until you return to the ground;
> > for from it you were taken.
> Dust indeed you are,
> > and to dust you will return,
> > > (Genesis 3.19)[6]

> His bones were filled with the vigour of youth;
> > but (now) it lies in the dust with him
> > > (Job 20.11)

> Together in the dust they lie,
> and worms cover them.
> (Job 21.26)

A similar idea is found in Egypt, for in the *Pyramid Texts*, the king was empowered to 'clear away the dust' from about him.[7] And in turn, we find the same conception, of a house of dust, in the Akkadian *bīt epri*, and can imagine that the mythology of Ugarit would have had no problem with an Akkadian passage that combines this motif with other similar ones (the dark, the place of no return, and so on):[8]

> To Kurnugi, land of [no return],
>   Ishtar, daughter of sin was [determined] to go;
> the daughter of Sin was determined to go
>   to the dark house, dwelling of Erkalla's god,
> to the house which those who enter cannot leave,
>   on the road where travelling is one-way only,
> to the house where those who enter are deprived of light,
>   where dust is their food, clay their bread.
> They see no light, they dwell in darkness,
>   they are clothed like birds, with feathers.
> Over the door and the bolt, dust has settled.
> (*Descent of Ištar* 1–11)

This sort of motif makes an appearance in the couplet at Job 10.21 too:

> Before I go and do not return,
>   to a land of darkness and deep gloom.[9]

Another metaphor involves the idea of a *devouring mouth*. We find this idea in Ugarit's most famous text, the *Baal* poem (see also CH. 19), where a warning is given to two messenger gods about to go on an embassy to the fearsome Mot, personification of death and lord of the Underworld:

> But take care, attendants of the god,
>   do not draw near divine Mot,
> lest he offer you up like a lamb in his mouth,
>   like a kid in the opening of his maw!
> (*KTU* 1.4 viii 15–20)

Mot's reply intensifies the metaphor:

> 'My appetite is the appetite of the monster of the deep,
>   the desire of the shark in the sea ...

Look, in truth does my throat devour clay,
  and with both my hands I devour them …

[the heavens] will be hot, [they will shine]
  [when I tear you in pieces],
[I shall devour (you),]
  [thighs, blood and forearms;]
[you will indeed go down into the throat of divine Mot,]
  [into the maw of the Beloved of El, the hero.]...'
                            (*KTU* 1.5 i 15–35, excerpts)

His gaping maw is all-devouring:

[He extends a lip to the ea]rth,
  a lip to the heavens,
[he extends] a tongue to the stars…
            (*KTU* 1.5 ii 2–3)

And he even threatens Baal with the destruction of humanity itself:

If the first of you brothers you do not give,
  then I shall seize [ ]
(it will be) time that I ate [mankind],
  that I ate the multitud[es of the earth]!'
            (*KTU* 1.6 v 21–5)

Being devoured is perhaps one of the most terrifying images of death, allowing no possibility of individual survival. It is not absent, either, from the Old Testament, where an earthquake is described as divine punishment:

Then the ground beneath them split open; and the Underworld (*hā'āreṣ*) opened its mouth and swallowed them and their families … And they and all who were with them went down alive into Sheol, and the earth (*hā'āreṣ*) closed over them, and they perished from the midst of the community. And at their cries all the Israelites around them fled, shouting, 'We do not want the Underworld to swallow us!' (Numbers 16.31b–32a, 33–4)

This passage plays on the similarity of the verb, *bālaʿ*, 'swallow', to the name Belial (*bᶜlí yaʿal*, 'Worthless'), a soubriquet of Death. He is seen here as the 'Swallower'.

Biblical imagery, however, could also see the Beyond in *maritime* terms, with overtones of shipwreck and drowning.[10] Thus in the psalm in Jonah, the anti-hero of the composition laments,

> You cast me into the depths,
>   into the heart of Sea,
>   and River encircled me.
> All your breakers and your waves passed over me ...
>
> Waters washed round me up to my throat;
>   Deep encircled me.
> Extinction was wound round my head
>   at the roots of the mountains.
> I went down into the Underworld;
>   its coils were about me for ever.
>
> (Jonah 2.4–7)

The Hebrew term *yam sûp*, sometimes understood as the Red Sea, or the 'Sea of Reeds' (in the eastern Nile Delta), strictly denoted the 'the sea of the end', that is, at the end of the world,[11] the Greek *Okeanos*. I have proposed that in the story of the exodus, it indicated 'the sea of extinction', marking off Egypt as a symbolic Beyond from the land of the living, Palestine.[12] In crossing the *yam sûp* in the exodus, the Israelites passed from one to the other, bounded by the borderlands of the wilderness. The common Hebrew term Sheol (*šeʾôl*) is opaque, but was linked by Albright with the notion of a *post mortem* trial of the dead, or may have had the sense of 'asking' (*šāʾal*, 'ask'), pointing to the consultation of the dead (on which see further below). It is perhaps, however, safest to accept the opacity of the term.[13] It functioned as a synonym for *hāʾāreṣ*, meaning the place to which the dead descended, as in Jonah 2.7 above. It is noteworthy that travelling to Egypt was always expressed in terms of 'going downwards', as into the Underworld (e.g. Genesis 12.10, Numbers 20.15).

There is sometimes a more positive approach, however, and here perhaps the most basic metaphor, suggesting a reversion to a pre-birth security, occurs in the biblical image of the earth as the *mother's womb*:

> Naked I came forth from my mother's womb,
>   and naked I shall return thither.
>
> (Job 1.21)

This motif recurs in Genesis 2–3, with the motherhood of the earth (*ʾadāmâ*), echoed in the Man's name (*ʾādām*) in 2.7, an indication of his autochthonous nature; and Job 1.21 and Genesis 3.19 (cited above) find a late echo in *Ben Sira* (Ecclesiasticus) 40.1:

> A great hardship has (God) apportioned to all men,
>   and a heavy yoke on the sons of Adam:
> from the day on which they come forth from the womb of their mother,
>   until the day when they return to the mother of all.

Many of the Near Eastern images of the Underworld were direct transfers of upper-world social phenomena, such as the city, of which the god of death was king or queen. These seem to be metaphors designed to instil acceptance of death: 'life' in the hereafter – for annihilation could scarcely be conceived, even when it was feared – would be qualitatively different, but still familiar terrain. Thus, the Akkadian Nergal (god of the Underworld) may have been viewed as meaning 'Lord of the Great City (Sumerian EN.URU.GAL).[14]

The Ugaritic Mot was king of this subterranean city:

> Then they set their faces towards divine Mot,
>   towards his city Muddy,
>   a pit the seat of his enthronement,
>   a crevice the land of his inheritance.
>   (*KTU* 1.5 ii 13–16)

This 'concave kingdom' is described in words which parodied the mountain dwelling of Baal, king of the gods. A biblical counterpart, with a frisson of fear, is hinted at in Job 18.13–14, inasmuch as it describes Death as 'the *king* of terrors'.

The broader *cosmological setting* of the Ugaritian city of Death is described in lines including those on the House of Dust that we saw earlier:

> 'So set your faces towards the mountain of Trġzz,
>   towards the mountain of T̲rmg,
>   towards the twin (peaks) of the boundary of the Underworld.
>   Raise the mountain on your hands,
>   the hill on top of your hands,
>   and go down into the house of dust;
>   be numbered among those descending into the Underworld'
>   (*KTU* 1.4 viii 1–9)

The *twin peaks* which mark the entrance to the Underworld are a classic trope: the source of the idea cannot be traced with certainty, but it occurs throughout the ancient Near East. The Babylonian world map, dating from c. 700 BC (fig. 20.1) shows the world as a disc surrounded by the Okeanos; beyond are eight triangles, which may be interpreted as four pairs of mountains controlling each of the cardinal points.[15] The mountain to the East and West was called 'Mount Twin' (*mašu*), and represented in double form on cylinder seals.[16] It can be the same mountain with eastern and western peaks, as apparently in *Gilgameš* IX ii 1–9.[17] The eastern and western horizons in Egypt, too, were represented in iconography and writing as each of twin peaks, through which the sun rose and set; and the Egyptian term for horizon, *akhet*,[18] was written with a rising sun between two peaks. Cosmic mountains in general may have been selected because of their physical shape as much as locality. Thus Mount Zaphon on the Syrian coast featured in Hittite, Syrian, and Greek cosmology,[19] and had two peaks (Kasion and Anti-Kasion), as did the Lebanon (Lebanon and Anti-Lebanon = Hermon).

The mountains identified above, Trġzz and Ṯrmg, appear from their form to be Hurrian names[20] for Mount Zaphon, which must have boasted an entrance to the Underworld: when Baal's corpse was recovered by Anat and Shapsh, it was buried on Mount Zaphon in 'a grave of the gods of the Underworld' (*KTU* 1.6 i 17–18). Hans Güterbock went so far as to see there an analogue of the Korykian Cave of Mount Parnassos at Delphi.[21] And J. B. Curtis (1957) claimed to have discovered a cult of a local form of Nergal surviving down into the Christian era on the Mount of Olives, which itself has two summits.

The people

The people of the Beyond are named from a variety of points of view. They are

- the 'dead' – *mtm* in Ugaritic, *mētîm* in Hebrew (and Akkadian *mītû*);
- the Ugaritic *rpum* (i.e., *Rapiuma*) 'healers', Hebrew *rᵉpā'îm*, 'saviours', 'heroes' – these *Rapiuma* may even have left their trace in a puzzling epithet, *meropes*, applied in Greek epic to men (μέροπες ἄνθρωποι), supposedly meaning 'mortal';[22]
- the Ugaritic *mlkm*, '(dead) kings' (like *malkû*, Underworld gods at Mari, or Akkadian *mālikû*, 'counsellors', of worshipped ancestors);
- the *inš ilm*, 'divine people', *ġṯrm*, 'powerful ones', *ṯᶜm*, 'heroes', *ṯrmnm*, 'lords', *ilhm*, 'gods', *ilm*, 'gods', *ẓlm*, 'protective spirits', and *ilnym*, 'divinities, chthonian gods', are all designations specific to dead kings.[23]

We gain an interesting insight from the hymn to Baal at the end of the *Baal* poem from Ugarit. This presents Shapsh, the sun goddess (on whom see further below) as the deity who sends the dead down to Baal, in his presumptive role as lord of the Underworld over against Mot:

> Shapsh sends the *Rapiuma* down to you;
>   Shapsh sends down to you the chthonian gods (*ilnym*).
> Your company are the gods (*ilm*);
>   lo, the dead (*mtm*) are your company.
>   (*KTU* 1.6 vi 45–8 (following Husser 1997))

The diversity of vocabulary in the list above and partly reflected in this passage indicates a division, which may be summarized in the following manner.

Ordinary people are 'dead' (*mtm*) in the Underworld, though that description may require qualification, since they are apparently not simply annihilated – some elemental part lives on, and can even be conscious. The other Ugaritic terms above all appear to denote dead kings, and to indicate that somehow they survived death and continued to function; and the Hebrew and Akkadian situations are analogous. It is increasingly becoming recognized, for example, that in Judah dead kings continued to perform a role as spirits affirming the nation's right to its territory, and that they required nurturing after death both for their own and for the nation's benefit. This is why proper burial and care for the dead was so important, as it was in Greece.[24]

There is also reason to believe that in both Ugarit and Israel–Judah, there was a form of divine kingship;[25] evidence from Mesopotamia is only sporadic.[26] We have several surviving texts from Ugarit, liturgies[27] concerning the celebration of the dead (a *kispum* rite, perhaps indicated by *KTU* 1.39, 1.113, and parts of 1.161), the burial of a dead king Niqmaddu III or IV (the number is uncertain), and invocation of the ancestors (parts of *KTU* 1.161), which has analogues in biblical thought and indicates that dead kings were divine and joined a body of ancient kings called the *Rapiuma* (*rpum* above). They might thenceforth be invoked on behalf of the living. Whether the Ugaritic terms had precisely the same reference, or pointed to gradations of divinity, function, or rank, remains uncertain. Various of these terms appear in pantheon lists or as the recipients of offerings.

Tombs at Ugarit were constructed within the walls of individual houses or the royal palaces at Ugarit and Ras Ibn Hani (and cf. the royal tombs at Ebla), indicating the continuing mutual involvement of the living and the dead (for recent discussion see Niehr in Cornelius and Niehr (2004: 79–86), Niehr (2007)). The royal tomb in the palace in Ugarit had peculiar features. Adjacent to the *dromos* (approach way) was a pit: it was in this, which incorporated an entrance to the Underworld, that Niehr (2007: 227–30) surmised that puppies were abandoned on the occasion of royal interments, a rite with Hittite associations and echoed in the story of *Kirta*:

> Like dogs shall we howl at your tomb,
>> like whelps in the pit of your funerary shrine?
>>> (*KTU* 1.16 i 2–3)

and it may be the implicit locus of the seven sacrifices to the Underworld powers at the burial of a king (*KTU* 1.161.27–30). This text was concerned with both the funeral of the penultimate king of Ugarit (Niqmaddu III–IV) and the invocation of earlier kings, including the *Rapiuma*, who were summoned into the *dromos* of the tomb to greet their new fellow chthonian god. It must have been an Israelite funerary rite analogous to this that lies behind Isaiah

14.9–10, where the prophet subversively envisages the reception of a Babylonian king by his ancestors, including the *rʿpāʾim*, as he descends into the Underworld.

Brichto (1973) demonstrated the importance of the appropriate burial rites in early Israelite society, where the continual management of the plot by his descendants guaranteed the continual well-being of the dead in the family plot, which in turn guaranteed the continued proprietorship and management of the plot by the family, showing the symbiotic relationship of living and dead. An episode in Genesis makes interesting reading in this context. Here the childless Abra(ha)m laments, 'What can you give me, since I am childless, and the one who will pour libations on my tomb … is Eliezer?' (Genesis 15.2).

If the patriarch does not have a legitimate son of his own, his line will die out. He envisages a member of his household, a servant, not a son, performing the rites. The problem is, of course, resolved in the sequel, which serves precisely to show how divine favour will grant Abraham a son. One of the most important roles of a son is the performance of his father's funeral rites. A graphic account of this whole nexus of thought occurs in the *Aqhat* narrative from Ugarit, where the childless Danel yearns for a son, and sets about performing the appropriate rites:

> so that he may beget a son in his house,
>   a scion in the midst of his palace.
> He shall set up the *stela* of his ancestral god (*ilib*),[28]
>   in the sanctuary the *cippus* of his kinsman;
>   into the earth sending forth his dying breath,
>   into the dust protecting his progress
>   (*KTU* 1.17 i 25–8)

The penultimate line in this passage, 'into the earth sending forth his dying breath', illustrates a further aspect of the appropriate burial procedures. It is a matter not of bringing his spirit up from the earth (as in earlier translations), but of keeping it firmly down there.[29] The conception of the surviving 'soul' and its subsequent experience was expressed in similar terms in the various cultures.[30]

There is an implied threat in this provision: it was important precisely to put and to keep the dead in their place. Hence the serious threat to the entire cosmic order implied in Ištar's threat, when slighted by the hero, to bring up the dead to outnumber the living in *Gilgameš*:

> I shall smash *underworld* together with its dwelling-place,
>   I shall *raze* the nether regions *to the ground*,
> I shall bring up the dead to consume the living,
>   I shall make the dead outnumber the living!
>   (*Gilgameš* VI III 97–100 (George 2003: 625))

The same formula also occurs in *Ištar's Descent* and in *Nergal and Ereškigal.*

Even kings, implicitly divine, could seek rest, and curse those who disturbed it,[31] though the Phoenician inscription of Pyrgi explicitly envisaged him as divine.[32]

One interesting area of speculation concerns the sun's nocturnal activity. Does he pass through the Underworld? The model for this lies in Egyptian thought, where it appears that the sun must cross the infernal Nile from west to east in order to re-emerge the following morning. But even the Egyptian evidence is ambiguous: if the image of the sun as devoured at dusk by Nut to be reborn the following morning is taken seriously it implies a celestial nocturnal journey of the sun through the goddess's body, namely the sky.[33] All the same, the nightly conflict in which the serpent Apepi (Apophis) attacks the barque of Ra does presuppose a subterranean location.

The Ugaritic evidence is tantalizing. Perhaps, as many have thought, the sun-goddess Shapsh accompanied the dead into the Underworld, and also travelled on a night-barque like the Egyptian Ra. But this is not as straightforward as it looks. She may assist Anat in the recovery of Baal's corpse (*KTU* 1.6 i 11–15), but this was not yet *in* the Underworld. In a different mythical scenario, Baal has conquered Mot and become lord of the Underworld; now, according to the closing hymn to Baal (*KTU* 1.6 vi 35–52), Shapsh directs the various divine and human denizens of the Underworld down to him:

> Shapsh sends the Rapiuma down to you;
>   Shapsh sends down to you the chthonian gods.
> Your company are the gods;
>   lo, the dead are your company.
> As for Kothar, he is your magician,
>   and Hasis is your enchanter.
> Against Yam, Arsh and the Dragon is Kothar-and-Hasis;
>   (with his) hand he banishes (them), does Kothar-and-Hasis.
>   (*KTU* 1.6 vi 46–52 (following Husser (1997),
>   cited in part above))

The last four lines have normally been understood as an address to a Shapsh riding in the night-barque on the analogy of Ra; but on Husser's understanding of the text, her supervision of events from above gives the better sense.[34]

A word of caution is required, however. This evidence may appear to present us with a Shapsh who does not go *into* the Underworld. This view may also be supported by the formula, borrowed from Egyptian usage, of the solar assimilation of the king's death:

> To the going in of the sun Kirta will indeed come,
>   To the setting of the sun our master.
>   (*KTU* 1.15 v 18–20)

The 'going in' (*ʿrb*, the technical term for the setting of the sun) is neutral with regard to the issue of *where* the Sun goes at night, and may simply refer to its horizontal journey back to the east, on the Greek analogy. But this still remains in tension with the burial rite of King Niqmaddu (*KTU* 1.161) discussed above, which clearly envisages an Underworld. The relevant passage here reads:

> Go down, Shapsh,
> yea, go down, Great Luminary!
> May Shapsh shine upon him.
> (*KTU* 1.161 R 18–19)

This appears to mean that the goddess shines on the deceased king *in* the Underworld, perhaps indicating that she is there too.

We have noted the connection the dead have with the living at funerals. There is evidence of further continuing or sporadic communication – or even, something quite different, communion. *Communication* allows for the alien nature of the dead, who must be approached with great caution; *communion* suggests a continuing rapport between the generations, those past continuing to assist their descendants through their lives.

A passage in 1 Samuel tells how, by seeking help from the medium at Endor (the so-called Witch of Endor), King Saul of Israel flouted the proscription of necromancy he had himself enforced:

> Saul consulted Yahweh, but Yahweh did not answer him, either in dreams, or oracles or by prophets. So Saul said to his servants, 'Seek for me a woman who is a medium, so that I may go and consult her.' And his servants replied, 'There is a medium at Endor.' So Saul disguised himself, changing his clothes, and went off with two men and came to the woman by night. He said, 'Reveal the future to me by means of a ghost, and conjure up for me the person whose name I shall give you ...' Then the woman asked, 'Whom shall I conjure up for you?' He replied, 'Conjure up Samuel for me.'
>
> The woman saw Samuel and gave a great cry, saying to Saul, 'Why have you deceived me? You are Saul!' The king said to her, 'Do not be frightened. What can you see?' The woman said to Saul, 'I see a spirit coming up from the Underworld.' He said to her, 'What does he look like?' And she replied, 'It is an old man coming up, and he is wrapped in a cloak.' Then Saul knew that it was Samuel, and he bowed his face to the ground and paid him homage. And Samuel said to Saul, 'Why have you disturbed me by conjuring me up?' And Saul said, 'I am very distressed. The Philistines have declared war on me, and God has abandoned me, and no longer answers me through the prophets or dreams; so I have invoked you to tell me what to do.' (1 Samuel 28.6–15)

This is certainly a Deuteronomistic text, perhaps of the sixth century BC, much later, of course, than the narrated event (supposedly eleventh century). The picture it presents parallels the tradition of *Odyssey* 11 (and cf. Vergil, *Aeneid* 6), and well echoes the danger and solemnity of the process. The 'spirit' emerging, and perhaps visible to the medium, but not to Saul, is called *ˀlōhîm*, 'a god'. Whether this is because Samuel, as a judge (*šōpēt* = 'ruler') in Israel, was quasi-royal, and therefore part of a belief system like the Ugaritian or later Israelite royal ideology, or was simply a general term for the dead as supernatural, is an imponderable. The oldest version of this motif is the invocation of Enkidu by Gilgameš.[35] In addition to this oracular function of the dead is the communion implied in the regular system of communal meals hinted at in both Ugaritic and biblical sources (and probably partly suppressed in the case of the biblical record), and more fully exemplified in the considerable body of Mesopotamian materials.[36]

Other biblical diatribes against necromancy indicate that it was prevalent in Israel, though again we cannot discern the circumstances of its observance.[37] The prohibition, presented in terms of its vacuity, is rather evidence that it was popular precisely because it was regarded as effective, but rivalled the exclusive oracular claims of Yahweh.

Conclusion

We have seen that the Levantine evidence points to a conception of the Underworld and human involvement with it that is not dissimilar to Greek views. It could be conceptualized on the basis of experience as an extension, a mirror-image, of the world of the living, a place on the one hand to be feared (as of an all-devouring maw and a land of no return, a place of drowning), and on the other, tamed by the use of homelier metaphors (as a city, with dwellings and a king, or as a mother to whom her children return). Terms for the dead frequently reflect a theological dimension: kings in particular seem to have been seen as in some way divine. All the dead continued to have a relationship with the living, and the ritualization of death provided for their enduring involvement with the living, both in oracular contexts and also in communal meals which pacified them, emphasized their solidarity with the living, and provided a legal basis for the inheritance of property. The matter of the precise involvement of the sun in the Underworld is uncertain. But it appears that in some Ugaritic texts the sun goddess (Shapsh) does not actually enter the Underworld herself, though (presumably from above) she oversees some infernal events. In others, a descent does seem to be envisaged.

The Beyond in the *Odyssey* and Egypt

The routes of Odysseus to the world of the dead are clearly described in *Odyssey* 10 and 11. The narrative is precise enough to enable a reconstruction of a map, and once such a map is drawn, it will be made clear that the designation of Hades as an Underworld in the *Odyssey* may need to serious re-thinking. *Beyond* is a better term.

Putting the Beyond on the map

Odysseus receives unpleasant news from Circe already during his stay on her island: he cannot return home unless first he visits the House of Hades (10.490–515). He is highly distressed: how will he be able to sail to Hades without a guide (10.501)? Circe then gives him instructions about what to do, and obligingly provides a description of the topography. As we shall see, this description may be used to reconstruct a landscape, even a map (fig. 20.4).

First, he must cross the River Okeanos by ship and leave the world of the living behind. Then, he will come to the opposite bank, at the grove of Persephone, where he will leave his ship. Next, he will proceed on foot to Hades until he reaches a spot where two rivers, Kokytos ('Wailing') and Pyriphlegethon ('Blazing Fire'), meet and flow into Acheron. The confluence of the two rivers is marked by a stone, and at this spot he will dig a pit and invoke the dead from under the earth.

We get a second description of this journey from Odysseus himself (*Odyssey* 11.1–22). He and his men sail to the end of the Okeanos (11.13) and arrive at the *demos* of the Kimmerians, a community enveloped in a cloud of perpetual mist that is never penetrated by the sun's rays. According to this description, the Kimmerians are not located in the north, as some later ancient authors seem to have thought (cf. Herodotos 4. 11), but *on the other side* of the cosmic river.[38] It is important to note that the sun has been left behind.[39] Finally, the party proceeds along the banks of the river; the men reach the spot where they are to sacrifice and invoke the shades.

The journey takes place on a *horizontal* level rather than a vertical one. And yet, in other places of the *Odyssey* a descent is implied (cf. 11.65, 'and his soul went down to Hades'). It has been mentioned, in the introduction to this chapter, however that the two are not incompatible even within the same tradition (and see fig. 20.2). If one takes the horizontal journey, the crossing of Okeanos, the boundary between the living and the dead, is the most crucial step. As for the pit where he meets the shades, Odysseus never goes down: he stays where he is and interviews the ghosts.

Another description of the journey is furnished in the last book of the *Odyssey* (24.10–14) when the souls of the murdered suitors are led by Hermes to Hades. They too walk along the bank of the River Okeanos; then they pass by the White Rock (*Leukas*), the Gates of the Sun, the Demos of Dreams, until they finally reach the Meadow of Asphodels. This series of landmarks differs from those described by Circe, and yet they do not contradict her narrative; they simply add to the complexity of the topography of the Beyond.

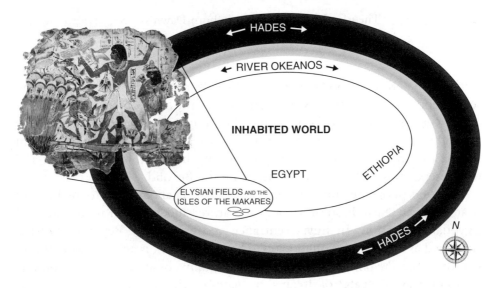

Figure 20.2 The Homeric Beyond reconstructed with a possible portrayal of the Egyptian Field of Reeds (see pp. 384, 406; fresco from the tomb of Nabamun, Eighteenth Dynasty before 1350 BC; British Museum BM 37977).

Circe's island as gate to another world

We now turn to the cosmology of the *Odyssey*, which will be elucidated through a discussion of Circe's island. Odysseus must reach this island *before* he crosses the Okeanos to the Underworld but, for reasons that are never explicitly stated in the text, he *must return* there before he can go on with his journey. This detail shows that the island of Circe is an *interface between the two worlds*. For this reason, we may envisage the island as a gate, metaphorically speaking.

It is further clear from the text that the island is not located within the normal space of the inhabited world. Odysseus is disorientated when he is there because he cannot discern where the sun rises and where it sets. 'My friends', he says, 'we do not know where East is, nor where the bright sun goes down under the earth' (10.190–2, tr. E. V. Rieu). It follows from this passage that east and west are very close together; so close, in fact, that Odysseus cannot tell them apart. We shall see later that this puzzle is solved if we envisage Circe's isle as equivalent to the Egyptian gates of the sun. Another point of relevance is that when the men sail away from the island the sun sets and does not rise again until the return of the company from the Beyond (12.8). Thus, Odysseus seems to have moved *beyond* the realm of the sun's orbit.[40]

There is good evidence too that Circe is related to the sun. This is her island:

> The island Aiaia, where early-born Dawn's
> house and dances are and the risings of the Sun.
>   (*Odyssey* 12.3–4, tr. KD)

Both Circe and her brother Aietes are the offspring of the sun (10.138; and see Hesiod, *Theogony* 1011: 'Circe, daughter of the Sun'). All this information about Circe's kinship to the sun, and the designation of her habitat as the ground of dawn, reveals that the she has a connection with the solar path from sunrise to sunset. To use our metaphor again, the island is a gate – east and west – separating the inhabited world from the Beyond.

The concept of gate, functioning as both a barrier and passage to the Beyond is at home in Near Eastern art and literature, and it is almost certainly of Egyptian derivation. In Egypt, entrance and exit to the Beyond (*duat*) is envisaged as a passage through gates. The 'sky's door', is an expression found already in the *Pyramid Texts* of the Old Kingdom; compare with the Homeric 'gates of heaven', 'gates of dreams' or 'gates of Hades' (*Iliad* 8.393, *Odyssey* 4.809, *Iliad* 5.646).[41] Passage to the Beyond in the form of a gate is visually attested also in Egyptian funerary papyri and tomb paintings.[42] A text from the times of Nebuchadnezzar I (1125–1104 BC) explicitly mentions the great gate of heaven; it is also mentioned in Genesis in connection with Jacob's dream:

> And he was afraid and said, How dreadful *is* this place! this is none other but
> the house of God, and this *is* the gate of heaven.
>   (Genesis 28.17 (King James Version))

But another question now arises. If we may confidently state that the sun does not cross the river, and does not reach the Beyond[43] – where then *does* he go at night?[44]

A fragment of the mid- to late seventh-century BC poet Mimnermos supplies us with the answer: the sun sleeps in a golden chamber by the banks of the Okeanos:

> the city of Aietes, where the swift Sun's
> rays lie in a golden chamber
> by the lips of the Okeanos, where divine Jason went.
>   (Mimnermos F 11a West, tr. KD)

Then in F 12 we are further told that the sun sleeps at night in a winged barque made by Hephaistos himself. He travels, Mimnermos imagines, along the Okeanos from the west (the land of Hesperides), to the east (the land of the Aithiopes). In short, the sun travels along the river from west to east and then climbs upwards. It is important to stress that in no case

A COSMOLOGICAL MAP

BASED ON MIMNERMUS' FRAGMENT 12

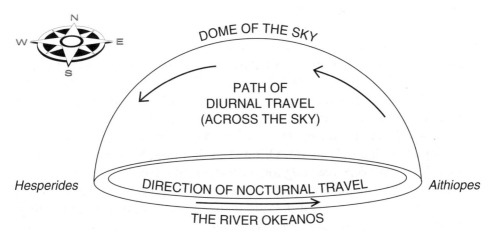

Figure 20.3 The World of Mimnermos.

does he cross the Okeanos and that he travels on both the horizontal and vertical plane (fig. 20.3).

So, by combining the narrative of the *Odyssey* with the fragments of Mimnermos, we arrive at three important conclusions:

1 the Beyond which Odysseus visits lies on a horizontal plane;
2 the sun travels along the Okeanos but not across it – he never reaches the other side;
3 because the sun does not cross this river, the Beyond is a sunless universe and hence a *nocturnal* universe.

Yet we must not make the mistake of identifying the nocturnal world of the Beyond with Tartaros, the location of which is *under* the earth, 'as far below earth as the sky is above earth' (Hesiod, *Theogony* 720).[45] Tartaros is thus a separate region, a pit in the depths of the cosmos, a prison for unruly gods – which Odysseus certainly does not visit!

Odyssey 11 and its problematic geography

We move now from the subject of cosmic geography to certain problematic passages in Book 11 which concern the encounters between Odysseus and the dead. Odysseus has two types of meetings in the Beyond. He either has visions of heroes, some of whom are said to be in the Meadow of Asphodels, or converses with ghosts that have risen from the Underworld and by drinking the blood he has offered them regain the power of speech. (*Odyssey* 11.539, 573).

Odysseus never talks to these figures. More importantly, he never descends himself into the lower world. The question, then, is, where are these heroes located? And, where is the Meadow of Asphodels? And, how can Odysseus see the heroes if he has not moved?

Four points merit attention. First, the word used by Homer is *ideein*, 'to see/gaze'. Odysseus sees the heroes but he does not talk to them. Second, the figures, Minos, Tityos, Tantalos, and Sisyphos, belong to the remote mythical past rather than Odysseus' own generation (11.568, 576–600). Third, the hunter Orion is described as a giant (*pelōrios*, 11.572–3); and he is, of course, another transgressor, along with Sisyphos and Tantalos, since he consorted with the goddess Eos (Dawn, *Odyssey* 5.121–4). Fourth and last, all the heroes are engaged in repetitive action: Orion keeps hunting, Sisyphos keeps rolling a stone, Tantalos keeps reaching for the water in the lake.

Stanford, in his commentary of the *Odyssey*, was very aware that there is a problem here, in the sense that the visions entail a different model of metaphysics than the one hitherto described about the ghosts: 'The activities of Minos, Orion and Heracles, contrast strongly with the ineffectiveness of the previous wraiths and imply conditions more like the Elysian Fields. Up to now O[dysseus] has been sitting near the shore of the dark land of ghosts; here we suddenly find him viewing inner regions and varied scenes' (Stanford 1965: 401).

Stanford's conclusion was that the passage was an interpolation from an 'Orphic' source (cf. CH. 4). But a clue to the mystery may be supplied by the fact that Orion is already a constellation in the Homeric texts (*Odyssey* 5.274; *Iliad* 18.488). Moreover, Plutarch associates Orion with the Egyptian constellations Horos and Seth (*Isis and Osiris* 21–2), whereas other sources identify Orion with Osiris.[46] These identifications open up a new perspective. They show not only that Orion is a cluster of stars but also point to a connection with Egypt. We begin to suspect that the other figures as well were translated from Egyptian constellations in the nocturnal sky. This would explain why Orion is huge: Odysseus now sees him in *his true form*, not as a set of stars but a gigantic figure. This theory of constellations also explains why he and the others are engaged in repetitive motion in perpetuity: they are like the stars when they rise and set. Finally, we understand why Odysseus does not talk to the figures: he sees them at a distance, not in the Underworld, but in the nocturnal sky. And, if this is correct, the Meadow of Asphodels is located in the nocturnal sky beyond Hades. In other words, the asphodels are stars (fig. 20.4).

This theory may go against the accepted opinion that the dead heroes are trapped in the hell of the Underworld, yet there is much to recommend it. There is substantial (if sporadic) evidence to the effect that Elysium (reserved for heroes or and not for ordinary dead) could be envisaged in the sky. For example, as early as Euripides, Helen was thought to have become a star

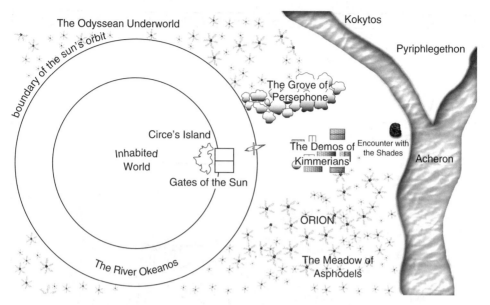

Figure 20.4 The Homeric Beyond situated in the sky.

(Euripides, *Orestes* 1631). An alleged Pythagorean fragment testifies that the Isles of the Makares are the sun and the moon.[47]

Evidence inscribed on the 'Orphic' gold *lamellae* (see CH. 4)[48] also refers to the stars. These gold tablets were full of instructions of how the dead (with whom they were buried) ought to behave in the Beyond. The dead were also told what to say to the guards in Hades. On one specimen from Pharsalos, Thessaly, dated to c.350–300 BC, the deceased is instructed to tell 'the whole entire truth' that 'I am a child of earth and starry sky. My name is Starry (*asterios*).'[49] Similar expressions, 'I am the son of earth and starry sky,' are found many times.[50] Last but not least, Plutarch clearly states that the constellations in the sky are souls, *psychai* (*Isis and Osiris* 21). All this shows that Hades is distinct from nocturnal sky and that the latter is also the Beyond.

The Egyptian night sky

In the last section of this essay we shall turn to Egypt, which is the source of the nocturnal cosmology. But Egyptian cosmological models were diverse, and because various ones existed even during the same time period it is essential that the sources of the parallels be dated if the possibility of transmission from one culture to another is to be made plausible.

In the Egyptian language, the other world was called *duat*. This is not strictly an *Under*world but rather the place where gods and dead alike lived,

Figure 20.5 The Heavenly Cow (Nut) from Tutankhamun's tomb.

the location of which varied depending on which cosmological model was followed. The dead were conceived as stars already during the Old Kingdom. At that time, however, the privilege of becoming a circumpolar star was allotted only to kings, although later it was extended to common people.[51] Because of this belief, the starry nocturnal sky was considered a primary source of afterworld topography, or cosmography. The Field of Reeds (*Aaru*) and the celestial Nile were located in the sky.[52]

This tradition continues in the New Kingdom.[53] According to the celestial model, the *Book of Night* and *Book of Sky*, the *duat* was envisaged in the sky.[54] And in this model, the sun travels inside the body of the sky goddess Nut at night (see p. 397 above). Sometimes this goddess is envisaged as a celestial cow, and in this form she is represented in Tutankhamun's tomb (fig. 20.5).[55] The implication is that the sun does not leave the sky at night but is hidden from view because he is inside her. In the ceilings of Ramses IV and VI, the sky is divided in two halves, the nocturnal and diurnal.[56]

The sun's entry and exit from the body of Nut may easily be likened, metaphorically speaking, to the double gate of Circe's island. Circe is like Nut since she controls the entry and exit of the sun.[57] One difference is that the sun travels *along* the Okeanos according to Mimnermos F 12 and this seems to work well with the *Odyssey*, as we have seen above. The sun's journey is thus different in the Egyptian *Book of Night*, according to which the goddess swallows the sun. Thus, the Homeric metaphysics are not identical the Egyptian *Book of Night*, but they share some basic concepts.

One more question may be answered by reference to Egyptian sky cosmology. We might ask why Odysseus sees Orion, Sisyphos, and Tantalos, the transgressors, along with Minos in the Meadow of Asphodels (i.e., the stars). Why are beneficent and malevolent figures mixed together? It is clear that this cannot be 'hell'. Once more Egyptian beliefs supply a key to the riddle. According to the *Book of Night* successive figures appear in the ceilings of royal tombs because the sky moves and the nocturnal landscape changes. In the ninth hour of the *Book of Night*, Osiris and the other gods are present; the blessed appear in the tenth hour. Odysseus then sees the equivalent of the ninth hour of the night. He sees the judge Minos first:

> Then it was that I saw Minos, the splendid son of Zeus,
> with a golden sceptre dispensing justice to the dead
> (*Odyssey* 11.568–9)

Only then does he see the transgressors.

Conclusion

So, the geography of the *Odyssey* is comprehensible if we take into account that the Beyond is not just Hades but also the sky – the Meadow of Asphodels (fig. 20.4). That the metaphysics of the *Odyssey* have been influenced by a *koine* of concepts current the East Mediterranean around the eighth–seventh century BC is a plausible hypothesis. The reconstructed map makes many details clear and illustrates how vertical and horizontal dimensions must be taken into account to understand the Beyond. And once again we see that the world of Greek mythology does not live quarantined from other major civilizations, be they in the Levant or in Egypt.

FURTHER READING

See especially J. P. Allen 1988 on Egyptian creation stories; Burkert 1992 and 2004 on Greek interactions with the Near East; Dalley 1989 for accessible versions of Mesopotamian mythic texts; Hornung 1999 for Egyptian texts concerning the afterlife; Marinatos 2000 on the *Odyssey*; Marinatos and Anderson 2010 on Elysium and Egypt; and Simpson (ed.) 2003 for an anthology of relevant Egyptian texts.

NOTES

1. BM 92687, maybe from Sippar (southern Iraq).
2. So we are left to draw what conclusions we can from scattered inscriptions, for example, the Pyrgi inscription: Knoppers (1992).
3. *BNJ* 790, with the commentary of Anthony Kaldellis and Carolina López Ruiz. For those without access to *BNJ*, a significant proportion of the remains of Philo of Byblos is preserved in Eusebios, *Ecclesiastical History* 1.9. (KD)
4. For the Ugaritic and related expressions see Tromp (1969); M. L. West (1997, 151–67), Horowitz (1998: 268–95, 348–62).
5. Watson (2008).
6. For the ideological content of this verse see Wyatt (forthcoming).
7. *PT*, for example, 419, 535.
8. Cf. *Nergal and Ereshkigal* ii–iii, Dalley (1989: 155, 168, *CS* i 381, 386).
9. Translations, where not otherwise attributed, are by the author.
10. Tromp (1969: 59–66); Wyatt (1996: 102–5).
11. Montgomery (1938); Snaith (1965).
12. Wyatt (1996: 84–9; 2005, 38–54).
13. Albright (1956: 257). See Wyatt (1996: 111).
14. Horowitz (1998: 293).
15. Horowitz (1998: 20–42); Wyatt (2001: 81–2).
16. Horowitz (1998: 97 n. 3); Dijkstra (1991).
17. Cited by Horowitz (1998: 97–8).
18. On its cosmological nuances see Wyatt (2001: 184–5) and J. P. Allen (2005: 425).
19. Wyatt (2005b: 102–24); Dijkstra (1991).
20. Tsevat (1974).
21. Hoffner (1997: 41), cf. Nonnos, *Dionysiaka* i 140, 258–60, ii 3–5.
22. Discussed by Annus (1999), and continued discussion in Wyatt (2007b).
23. See del Olmo (1999) *passim*.
24. See Brichto (1973), Wyatt (2010: 73–5), Stavrakopoulou 2010.
25. See Wyatt (2005a: 191–220, 2010: 72–3, 75–6).
26. Frankfort (1948: 224–6).
27. See generally del Olmo (1999: 213–53) and, for individual texts, Pardee (2000).
28. The term *ilib* (cognate with Hebrew '*ōb*, a term used in necromancy and with various nuances), is conventionally understood as 'ancestral god', mentioned here and appearing *before* the high god El in the pantheon list (KTU 1.47.2, etc), its sense being fixed by the Akkadian term dingir *abi* occurring in an Akkadian list RS 20.24.1 ('the god of the ancestor' (Wyatt 2002: 360)). Whether this has any bearing on the fate of individuals, or relates strictly to a remote clan ancestor, or even a personal daemon, remains an unknown.
29. See Husser (1995).
30. Onians (1951: 93–174), M. L. West (1997: 151–5).
31. See the sarcophagus inscriptions of Ahiram and Eshmunazar of Byblos and Tabnit of Sidon: McCarter (2003: 181–3).

32. McCarter (2003: 184). See also Knoppers (1992).
33. See J. P. Allen (2005: 9).
34. Husser (1997), though he did not recognize that the goddess did *not* herself descend. B. B. Schmidt (1994: 85–8) also argues persuasively in favour of this view.
35. *Gilgamesh* XII (George 2003: 729–35); see J. B. Curtis (1957: 165).
36. In general see Bayliss (1973) and Tsukimoto (1985), and for the Ugaritic and biblical material T. H. Lewis (1989), B. B. Schmidt (1994), Niehr (2006, 2007). Evidence from Ebla and Qatna further indicates the pan-Syrian dimension to these beliefs and practices.
37. 2 Kings 21.6, Isaiah 8.19, Deuteronomy 18.11, Leviticus 19.31, 20.6, 27.
38. Cf. Stanford (1965) on this passage, Strasburger (1998), Marinatos (2000), and most recently Alexiou (2008).
39. The words used are *erebos, zophos* (e.g., 11.37, 57).
40. Marinatos (2000: 383–416).
41. J. P. Allen (2005: 122, no. 307; cf. 121, no. 313); For gates in Egyptian eschatology see Mueller (1972: 111), Hornung (1999: 55–76).
42. Keel (1978: 14, figs 10–13); Shedid (1994: fig. 20).
43. In one amusing passage of the *Odyssey*, the sun expresses his displeasure with the gods and threatens to go on strike and shine amongst the dead. Zeus is worried and sees to it that the order of the universe is maintained immediately granting the sun his wishes (*Odyssey* 12.377–88).
44. In the *Odyssey* we are told that the sun leaves the waters and climbs up in the sky (3.1–3) or that he rises from the deep ocean (19.434).
45. See the whole of 720–5; and cf. *Iliad* 8.13, 481.
46. Hornung (1982b: 80).
47. Riedweg (2002: 100).
48. Ch. 4 n. 96 above.
49. Graf and Johnston (2007: nos. 25, 34–5).
50. Graf and Johnston (2007: nos. 8, 10–14, 16, 18, 25). On the Pelinna tablets (Graf and Johnston no. 26 a–b), the deceased is a bull or ram which falls into milk. This would make sense if the milk refers to the milky way, namely the celestial Nile.
51. J. P. Allen 1988 and 2005.
52. *PT* 422 (Simpson 2003: 257).
53. There existed diverse and complementary models about the *duat* in the New Kingdom. According to the so-called *Book of the Earth* and *Book of Caverns*, the Underworld was located under the earth Hornung (1999: 95–103).
54. Note also the existence of astronomical ceilings of the eighteenth and nineteenth dynasties, a tradition that continues into the Ptolemaic period in the temple of Hathor at Denderah. We thus have a continuity of the celestial Beyond that spans some thousand years and which makes transmission to the Archaic Greek world plausible. See Wilkinson 1991.
55. Hornung (1999: 148–52, fig. 93).
56. Hornung (1999: 112–35); J. P. Allen (1988: 5).

57. Marinatos (2000). The theory that the sun traveled through the body of Nut
     entailed a problem for Egyptian philosophers. How could there be two skies, a
     bright one with the sun, and a dark one studded with stars? To solve it, and to
     explain how night and day could coexist in the sky, the Egyptians envisaged two
     skies. On the ceiling of the tomb of Ramses IV and IV we find two goddesses,
     or rather a double Nut, arranged back to back

PART V

INTERPRETATION

CHAPTER TWENTY-ONE

Interpreting Images: Mysteries, Mistakes, and Misunderstandings

Susan Woodford

The images of myths that have come down to us from antiquity are often both beautiful and evocative, but interpreting them is sometimes less straightforward than it might seem. Occasionally we can actually be misled, deceived, or confused by an ancient inscription or description or by a seemingly plausible or long-accepted post-antique interpretation. Here are six examples of the sorts of mysteries, mistakes, and misunderstandings one may encounter.

A Missing Myth?

Around 540 BC the Greek artist Exekias decorated a handsome vase with a scene of Ajax and Achilles playing a game (fig. 21.1). One of the most beautiful vases surviving from antiquity, and probably one of the most beautiful ever made, it combines a design of powerful simplicity and elegance with the most exquisite and delicate detail.

The two heroes have rested their shields behind them. They hold their spears loosely as they bend in toward the game with intense concentration. The composition is carefully designed to fit with the shape of the vase; the discarded shields lead the eye up to the bottom of the handles, while the spears point up to the top of the handles and – another subtle touch – the curved backs of the heroes echo the curve of the vase itself. Incisions of great refinement define the elaborate embroidery on the cloaks, the curls of the hair, and

A Companion to Greek Mythology, First Edition. Edited by Ken Dowden and Niall Livingstone.
© 2014 John Wiley & Sons Ltd. Published 2014 by John Wiley & Sons Ltd.

Figure 21.1 Ajax and Achilles playing a game. Attic black-figure amphora 540–530 BC, by Exekias.

the meticulously combed beards. We know who the two heroes are because Exekias has written their names beside them: Achilles to the left, Ajax to the right. We even know what numbers each hero has thrown, for Achilles calls out 'four' but Ajax only 'three'.

Depicting Achilles and Ajax together in this way evoked many associations in a Greek audience. The two heroes had been related to each other on various levels from the time of Homer on. In the *Iliad* Ajax and Achilles were portrayed as equal and opposite in the way their camps were placed each at one end of the Greek line at Troy. The symmetrical placement of the two heroes on either side of the gaming board gives visible shape within a compact image to the placement of their camps, recalling Homer's words: 'These two heroes had drawn up their shapely ships at the furthermost ends, trusting to their valour and the strength of their hands'.[1]

Homer often describes Ajax as 'second only to Achilles'.[2] On the vase Achilles, wearing his helmet, gives the appearance of being the greater hero and seems to dominate the scene, even though his head is no higher than that of Ajax. The relative importance of the two heroes is also delicately indicated by the fact that Ajax's throw is lower than Achilles'.

In other matters too the heroes are related. Ajax is the one to fight Hektor in the seventh book of the *Iliad*, prefiguring Achilles' later decisive single combat with the Trojan hero in Book 22. He it is who speaks most persuasively to Achilles when an embassy is sent to try to convince Achilles to rejoin the battle.[3] Even after Achilles' death a bond persists between the two, as it was generally accepted that Ajax carried the body of Achilles out of the battle.[4] Eventually there arose a tradition that Ajax and Achilles were actually cousins, a familial link invented to bind them still more closely together.[5]

Such associations may well have contributed to the power of the image for the ancient Greeks. But what was the story portrayed on the vase? Here we are at a loss. There is no preserved literary source that tells of Ajax and Achilles playing a game, nor any reference to such a source. Did the vase painter know something that we don't?

Very likely. Artists depicting myths in antiquity did not depend on texts for their stories in the way we are dependent on texts for decoding images. Greek artists' lives were pervaded by myths. They first became acquainted with myths in early childhood, listening at their mother's knee. Later they heard more from teachers and public recitations at religious festivals, or saw them enacted in the theatre, but only rarely (if ever) would any artist turn to books to read about myths, and certainly not much before the end of the fifth century BC. Storytelling was largely an oral affair, and each teller was free to vary and embellish the basic story as he or she saw fit. Myths were wonderfully flexible, constantly told and retold. The available store of myths was far richer and more varied than we can possibly know.

Translating a story from a flowing narrative into a static visual image is an awkward and complicated procedure. Most artists probably thought through to the gist of the myth and then found some way to convey that.[6] If we also know the myth, this will be enough for us. But *knowing* the myth is crucial: you cannot recognize the image of a myth unless you already know it.

Identifying the story behind this vase painting of Ajax and Achilles has tantalized and frustrated scholars for generations. Vase painters working later than Exekias liked to depict two heroes engrossed in their game, often with Athene inserted between them and occasionally with a battle shown raging on either side of them. This has encouraged some scholars to suggest that there once was a story (now lost) that told of the two warriors being so distracted by their game that they missed the call to battle and needed to be roused by the goddess. Perhaps so – but perhaps not. Making up a story to fit the image is both seductive and fun, but not the same as actually identifying the story that inspired the artist.

Although we can often grasp the general sense of the myth being depicted, sometimes we cannot. In truth we really do not know exactly what story Exekias was illustrating in this beautiful vase or whether he was just depicting a slice of heroic life: warriors at play when not warring.[7] Confessing our ignorance is painful, but necessary: the myth behind this haunting image remains elusive.

A Mistaken Inscription?

We might think that a name inscribed on a Greek vase or a description in an ancient text ought to provide a definitive identification. But this is not always so. For instance, there are many representations of Achilles' mother, Thetis, presenting his armour to him. When the name of Thetis is actually written beside the goddess as she gives armour to a warrior, it would seem that there could be no doubt which scene is depicted. But on a vase in Leipzig, Thetis (her name inscribed) is handing the armour over not to Achilles, but, unexpectedly, to *Menelaos* (his name also inscribed).[8] What does this mean?

No surviving written source suggests any occasion when Thetis is in any way concerned with the arming of Menelaos. Either we are dealing here with a highly irregular (and very obscure) version of the Trojan myth, or the artist simply made a mistake and mixed the names up. Could the moral of the story be that you can't always trust an inscription?

Perhaps so. People today (even scholars) can confuse the names of mythological personages, so this would not be surprising. What is more surprising is *how seldom* this actually seems to have happened in antiquity.

A Muddled Guidebook?

We are lucky to have large sections of the pedimental sculptures from the Temple of Zeus at Olympia still preserved,[9] as well as Pausanias' eye-witness description of what the sculptures looked like when the building was intact. Pausanias says:

> those in the back pediment are by Alkamenes, a contemporary of Pheidias, ranking next after him for skill as a sculptor. What he carved on the pediment is the fight between the Lapiths and the Centaurs at the marriage of Peirithoös. In the centre of the pediment is *Peirithoös* [my italics]. On one side of him is Eurytion, who has seized the wife of Peirithoös, with Kaineus bringing help to Peirithoös, and on the other side is Theseus defending himself against the centaurs with an axe. One centaur has seized a maid, another a boy in the prime of youth. Alkamenes, I think, carved this scene because he had learned from Homer that Peirithoös was a son of Zeus and because he knew that Theseus was a great-grandson of Pelops.[10]

Pausanias' identification of the subject certainly seems correct, to judge from the extant fragments (fig. 8.8, p. 165).[11] One centaur has indeed seized a maid and another a youth. However, of the over-large figure in the centre clearly is not an image of the mortal Peirithoös but of a powerful and imposing god, most probably Apollo. Peirithoös and his long-standing friend Theseus are surely the two male figures on a human scale flanking the central god.

Where did Pausanias' error come from? Presumably, like many tourists today, he used a local guide, and as is also true nowadays, not all guides are to be trusted!

A Misidentified Myth?

The two instances above suggest that even people living in antiquity could have trouble identifying myths and mythological figures. For people living in the twenty-first century the difficulties are even greater, as so many works both of art and of literature have been lost.

Not surprisingly, errors have been made. Occasionally they have been recognized and corrected. One example comes from a vase drawn and commented on in the eighteenth century (fig. 21.2), though now preserved only in some small fragments. The drawing shows (from left to right) a man with a spear moving to the left but looking toward the centre, while a woman rushes toward him, arms outstretched. Towards the centre a man kneels on a wide, low structure holding a sword threateningly against the unprotected stomach

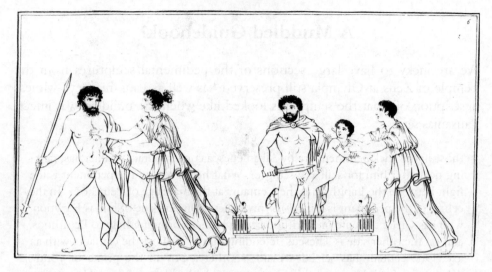

Figure 21.2   J. H. W. Tischbein, engraving of an 'ancient vase'.

of a young boy. The child reaches out to the right towards a woman who hurries to him with arms extended.

What does this assemblage of figures mean? An eighteenth-century scholar thought he recognized the subject. He drew his ideas from Servius, a fourth-century AD commentator on the *Aeneid* of Vergil.[12] He explained the scene as follows:

> The life of Astyanax [the infant son of the Trojan hero Hektor] gave uneasiness to the Greeks; they were apprehensive lest he should one day become the avenger of his father Hector and be the restorer of Troy. The winds being unfavourable for the return to Greece, Calchas declared that to satisfy the gods it was necessary that Astyanax should be thrown from the top of the walls; in vain had Andromache [the child's mother] concealed her son, Ulysses discovered him and caused the cruel sentence to be executed.
>
> … [the drawing] represents the moment which preceded this barbarous execution. A young girl, perhaps Polyxena, aunt to the young prince, intercedes with Ulysses on his behalf. This fierce king had given his orders and pays no attention to the supplication which is addressed to him. A soldier placed on top of a turret holds Astyanax on one of his knees, he threatens him with his sword and turns his eyes towards Ulysses to be ready to obey his commands on the first signal. A slight uneasiness is expressed in the child's countenance, he stretches out his arms towards his nurse, who trembling and in despair tries to retard the final moment in hopes that Ulysses might be brought to relent.[13]

The story appears to fit the image well. But it is wrong.

The problem does not arise from the fact that the author is using as the basis of his description a literary source written some eight hundred years after the vase was painted in the fourth century BC. Often very late writers can preserve information from much earlier sources. The problem is: it is not the right story.

By the middle of the nineteenth century the correct myth had been identified – and it concerned neither Odysseus (Ulysses) nor Astyanax.[14] The image is in fact drawn from a once popular, but now lost, tragedy by Euripides composed in the fifth century BC. The tragedy dealt with the hero Telephos. Telephos was the king of Mysia, a country near Troy on the coast of Asia Minor. When the Greeks first set out to fight the Trojans in order to recapture Helen, they did not know exactly where Troy was and landed by accident in Mysia. Mistaking the Mysians for Trojans, the Greeks attacked them and wounded their king, Telephos. Once they realized their mistake, the Greeks went home to obtain more accurate geographical information before setting out again.

Time passed, but Telephos' wound did not heal. He was advised by an oracle to go to the Greeks and ask for help from the one who had wounded him. In desperation, Telephos went to the palace of Agamemnon, the leader of the Greek forces. This was a daring thing to do, for having fought against the Greeks, he was suspect amongst them. Once Telephos arrived, frightened and alone, he rushed to seek sanctuary on an altar. To ensure that he would be safe there and to get a fair hearing, he snatched up Agamemnon's infant son, Orestes, and held the child as a hostage. The idea of threatening the baby was an innovation introduced into the traditional story by Euripides.

The situation was fraught. Touchy Agamemnon in hot temper might be ready to endanger his son rather than have his authority challenged by Telephos, but his wife, Klytaimestra, was not of the same mind. She was concerned, above all, to protect the baby. The rich irony here is that Klytaimestra's mother-love was not to be reciprocated by her son when he grew up. This very Orestes, saved by his mother's intervention when he was an infant, ultimately murdered her, a grisly matricide often dramatized in the fifth century BC (as in the surviving *Libation Bearers* of Aeschylus and *Electra* plays of Sophocles and Euripides). The Greeks watching the performance of Euripides' tragedy knew the gory end of the story, and must have been thrilled by the invention of such a poignant early episode.

With this tragedy in mind, one reads the drawing rather differently. The man at the far left is Agamemnon, menacing spear in hand, angry to be placed in a difficult situation by Telephos. The woman with arms extended is Klytaimestra, entreating him to put the safety of the child before his vanity. Telephos kneels on the altar (the low structure with small sphinxes at each corner) and threatens Orestes with his sword. The woman at the far right with the cropped hair of a slave may be the child's anxious nurse.

Why does this story fit the image better than the one about Astyanax? It is not only that the low structure in the centre looks more like an altar than a turret but also that in this reading four of the five figures are major players in the drama (only the nurse is a supernumerary). Furthermore, Euripides' tragedy was well known and much appreciated in antiquity. It captured the imagination of both artists and writers. Aristophanes enjoyed parodying this tense encounter, and vase painters in southern Italy illustrated the dramatic episode over and over in a variety of images, especially during the fourth century BC when this vase was made. Finally, many vase paintings still exist showing the imminent death of Astyanax, but they never show him being threatened in this way and none, so far as we know, shows the child about to be hurled from the walls of Troy, though this event was often described in literature.

If, indeed, the drawing refers to Telephos – and no better suggestion has been made – we can see that though literary sources can sometimes illuminate images (as in the case of Euripides' *Telephos*) at other times the pictorial tradition and the literary tradition go their separate ways (as in the matter of the death of Astyanax).

A Misidentified Figure?

A large portion of the east pediment of the Siphnian Treasury at Delphi has been preserved, with only a few heads of the figures missing (fig. 8.7, p. 165). The central part clearly shows a well-known myth: Herakles stealing the tripod of Apollo. Herakles had asked for an oracle from Apollo, and when Apollo refused to oblige him, the outraged Herakles picked up Apollo's mantic tripod and tried to carry it off, intending to set up his own oracle. Needless to say, Apollo clung on to this treasured piece of cult furniture.

This childish tug-of-war over the tripod was an extremely popular subject, particularly amongst Athenian vase painters from the middle of the sixth century BC through the first quarter of the fifth century BC. Dozens of vases illustrating it survive. The most popular scheme showed four figures: Herakles grasping the tripod while Apollo clings on to it, flanked by Artemis standing behind her brother and Athene behind her protégé, Herakles. The symmetrical opposition of the two contestants dominates this standard composition, and usually no central figure intervenes: the emphasis is on the conflict of the two principals.

Occasionally, however, a figure is introduced as a central feature, most conspicuously on the pediment of the Siphnian Treasury, where the triangular design of the pediment demands it. This headless, heavily draped personage, considerably larger than both Herakles and Apollo, was long believed to be

Athene. Apollo (to the left) has his supporter Artemis holding on to him (further left), while no one stands to the right of Herakles to encourage the hero. Furthermore, the central figure is clearly grasping Apollo's wrist as if to force him to release the coveted object.

The idea that Athene should be so very large, overtopping the two male figures, puzzled one imaginative twentieth-century scholar.[15] Could the assumption that this central figure was Athene be the consequence of an Athenian bias amongst modern scholars? Would the goddess be so overwhelmingly important in Delphi or for the Aegean island of Siphnos, whose city paid for this Treasury?

The two literary sources that tell the story in most detail are both much later than the Siphnian Treasury, which was built shortly before 525 BC, but they rely on earlier traditions.[16] Both related that Zeus intervened to settle the dispute. Could the central figure, then, be Zeus? He would be expected to be taller than his two less magnificent sons and the most appropriate person to mediate between them.

Once this inspired idea was suggested, more and more details became apparent which confirmed it. The dignified long garment worn by the central figure would have been suitable for either Zeus or Athene, but if Athene had been intended, some hint of her characteristic snake-fringed aegis should have been given. There was no such hint. Furthermore, the long garment only reaches to the ankles of the central figure, while the robes of the indisputably female figures in the pediment trail on the ground. Finally, the trace of a beard, very similar to Herakles' well-preserved beard, can be detected just to the left of the locks falling on that side. The new identification of the central figure was thus convincingly confirmed.

A Real Girl in a Mythical Context?

Beautiful Helen's life of adventure began long before she met the charming Trojan prince Paris. When she was still quite a young girl, she was abducted by the Athenian hero Theseus. This thoroughly naughty act by their local hero did not go unnoticed by Athenian vase painters.

One vase shows Theseus at the far right, walking to the right with an elegant woman caught up in his arms.[17] He looks back at another woman who is eagerly pursuing him, perhaps attempting to stop him. Theseus' friend, Peirithoös, brings up the rear, sword in hand, anxiously looking behind him. The names of Theseus and Peirithoös appear to be correctly inscribed, but the woman being carried off is labelled Korone, not Helen, as might be expected, and the woman pursuing is called Helen. Why has Theseus got hold of the wrong girl?

Perhaps the painter just mixed up the names, as on the vase where Thetis gives armour to the incorrect hero. But there might be more to it than that. No personage called Korone has any place in the myth of Theseus' rape of Helen, though Peirithoös does belong there. However, Korone was the name of a celebrated woman actually living at the time the vase was painted (about 515–510 BC). She was praised for her beauty on another vase, and her name was attached to the image of a hetaira (courtesan) on a third vase.

So Korone may have been a real person, not a mythological character at all. This seems all the more likely because the artist who painted the vase (and others in his group) appears to have felt free to introduce the names of real people into their images, not only the one discussed here, but also those of a famous musician and an impressive athlete of the time.[18]

Whether the painter wanted just to represent two female figures famous for their beauty or whether he wanted to suggest that the mortal Korone was even more desirable than the legendary Helen is impossible to decide. But one can argue convincingly that he did intend *something*, and that what appears at first glance to be a mere confusion of names may actually have had a subtle intended meaning.

Conclusion

So, fitting the right story to an image, and identifying the characters represented, is a delightful but exacting task. Deciding just how tight the fit should be requires delicacy and rigour, and it is not made easier by the fact that both ancient artists and writers and modern scholars can sometimes lead one astray.

FURTHER READING

In addition to the footnotes to this chapter, please see Further Reading at the end of CH. 8.

NOTES

1. *Iliad* 11.7–9, tr. A. T. Murray.
2. *Iliad* 2.768–9; *Odyssey* 11.469, 24.17.
3. *Iliad* 9.622–55.
4. See Apollodoros *Epitome* 5.4 (cf. Proklos, *Chrestomathia* 193–4).

5. Pindar *Isthmian* 6.19–30; Gantz 814.
6. See Small (2003).
7. See Woodford (1982).
8. Leipzig, Archaeological Institute T 3327, dated around 540 bc. For an illustration, see Woodford (2003: 203, fig. 165).
9. West Pediment of the Temple of Zeus, Olympia, Olympia Museum.
10. Pausanias 5.10.8 (tr. W. H. S. Jones and H. A. Ormerod), orthography modified.
11. An ingenious (and probably correct) new interpretation of the centaur battle on the west pediment of the Temple of Zeus at Olympia has been offered by Westervelt (2009). She also offers a plausible explanation of why Pausanias' guide got so much wrong.
12. Servius on Vergil, *Aeneid* 3.489.
13. Count Italinsky, in Hamilton (1795: 24).
14. Jahn (1841: 44–6).
15. Ridgway (1965).
16. Diodoros 4.31.4–5 and Apollodoros 2.6.2; see further Gantz 437–9.
17. Munich, Museum Antiker Kleinkunst (Staatliche Antikensammlungen) 2309.
18. Williams (2005: 271–83); for an illustration, see Boardman (1975: fig. 34, 1).

CHAPTER TWENTY-TWO

The Myth of History: The Case of Troy

Dieter Hertel

The complex relationship between 'myth' and 'history' has been explored in CH. 10. As was seen there, one perennially tempting way of simplifying this relationship is to claim that myth *is* a kind of history. According to this view, myth comes into being when real past events are embellished, embroidered, and endowed with fantastical elements through being told and re-told, while at the same time their exact location in past time grows hazy or is forgotten.

Few scholars today would favour the widespread application of such an approach, which is necessarily very speculative and which may falsify the nature of myth altogether.[1] At the same time, we cannot discount the possibility that some myths do have some kind of historical core. After all, as was seen in CH. 10, history itself, both ancient and modern, is very capable indeed of generating myths, and historiography of assimilating itself to mythic patterns. In this chapter, the story of the Trojan War is used as a test case for the idea of a true story behind myth.[2] Troy is an interesting example because the war marks both the end of myth, in the sense that no major mythic stories are presented as taking place after its heroes' homeward journeys (the *nostoi*),[3] and the threshold of history, in that it is seen as an essential reference point by both Herodotos and Thucydides when beginning their hugely influential accounts of recent or contemporary wars.

The War at Troy

The outline story of the Trojan War is retold here, familiar as it is, because some of its patterns will be unpicked in detail in the discussion which follows

A Companion to Greek Mythology, First Edition. Edited by Ken Dowden and Niall Livingstone.
© 2014 John Wiley & Sons Ltd. Published 2014 by John Wiley & Sons Ltd.

and because its historicity cannot be determined without knowing what it is that might be claimed to be historical.

Paris

Paris, second son of Priam, King of Troy (the land is Troy, the city Ilios or Ilion), watches his father's flocks on Mount Ida in the southern Troad. He is required to judge which of the three goddesses Hera, Athene, and Aphrodite is the most beautiful. Aphrodite successfully persuades him to choose her by promising him the most beautiful woman in the world.

The Greek heroes

Some time later, Paris sails to Sparta and carries off the wife of King Menelaos: Helen, famous as the most beautiful woman in the world. He also carries off some of Menelaos' treasure. With the support of his brother Agamemnon, king of Mycenae and mightiest of the Greek rulers, Menelaos calls together all the Greek kings and their followers to wage war on Troy. Agamemnon is the overall leader. Other heroes include Achilles, from Phthia and Hellas in the east and north-east of mainland Greece, Ajax son of Telamon from Salamis, Ajax son of Oileus from East Lokris, Diomedes from Argos, Nestor and his son Antilochos from Pylos, and Odysseus from Ithaca. The Greek army sails to the Trojan coast and sets up camp along the Hellespont.

The Trojan heroes

On the Trojan side, too, there is a coalition, comprised of rulers and their followers from kingdoms in Asia Minor and the Balkans. This is led by Hektor, eldest son of King Priam. Hektor's brave cousin Aeneas, ruler of the Dardanians of the southern Troad, is a more junior Trojan commander. The greatest heroes of all are Achilles amongst the Greeks and Hektor amongst the Trojans.

The gods

During the war, some of the Olympian gods (such as Athene, Hera, and Poseidon) support the Greeks, while others (such as Aphrodite, Apollo, and Artemis) support the Trojans. All assaults on Troy are unsuccessful, both because of the city's mighty walls, built by divine hands, and because of the defenders' valour.

Iliad: the Wrath of Achilles

The Greeks besiege Troy for ten years. The *Iliad* deals only with an episode it alleges took place in year nine of the war. Its subject is declared in the opening line: 'Sing, goddess, the wrath of Achilles, son of Peleus'. Achilles' honour is offended when Agamemnon unjustly takes from him his prize of war, the slave girl Briseis. Filled with wrath against Agamemnon, he withdraws both himself and his followers, the Myrmidons, from the fighting. As he remains obdurate in spite of heavy losses suffered by the Greek army in his absence, Agamemnon now sends Odysseus, Ajax, and Phoinix, a father-figure and companion of Achilles, on an embassy to promise him gifts. Achilles rejects the approach. At last, as the Trojans break through the freshly built fortifications of the Greek camp, Achilles permits his closest friend Patroklos to enter the fight, wearing Achilles' own armour and leading the Myrmidons. Patroklos drives back the Trojans, but he is slain by Hektor, with Apollo's help, before the Skaian Gates of Troy. Hektor strips Achilles' armour from Patroklos' body.

Iliad: revenge for Patroklos

Patroklos' death brings Achilles back into the fighting to avenge his friend. Reconciled with Agamemnon and equipped with new armour made by Hephaistos, he kills many Trojans in the waters of the River Skamandros. Hektor awaits Achilles in front of the Skaian Gates, but takes flight at his approach. Three times Hektor and Achilles run round the walls of Troy. At last they stop by the springs outside the walls, where Achilles, aided by Athene, kills Hektor with the great spear which only he (and his father) can wield. Achilles ties Hektor's corpse to his chariot and drags it through the dust, then leaves it unburied. After Patroklos has been honoured with funeral games, Priam, guided by Hermes, comes secretly to the Greek camp to plead in person with Achilles for the ransom of his son's body. Achilles agrees, and Hektor is buried by the Trojans. So ends the *Iliad*.

The end of the war

Achilles goes on to defeat newly arrived allies of the Trojans – the Amazon queen Penthesileia, and Memnon, king of the Ethiopians – before himself being killed, by an arrow shot by Paris and guided by Apollo. After Achilles' burial, there is a dispute over his armour between Ajax (son of Telamon) and Odysseus, who together had rescued his body from the Trojans. The Greeks decide in favour of Odysseus; Ajax, affronted, commits suicide.

Paris is now killed, shot with an arrow by the newly arrived Greek warrior Philoktetes. Having continued to attack Troy in vain, the Greek fleet sails away, but hides at the nearby island of Tenedos. In their abandoned camp the Greeks leave a great wooden horse as a votive offering to Athene; but hidden in the horse are the bravest Greek heroes. In spite of warnings, the jubilant Trojans pull the horse into the city. As the Trojans sleep off their victory celebrations, the Greek heroes leave the horse, signal to the fleet, and open the gates. The outcome is that the Trojan men are slaughtered and the women and children taken into slavery. The Greeks have varied fortunes on their homeward journeys (*nostoi*). Agamemnon arrives home only to be killed by his wife Klytaimestra; Ajax son of Oileus is killed at sea; Odysseus reaches Ithaca only after long and perilous wanderings.

The question, then, is, What history, if any, underlies these events?

The Homeric Epics and the Epic Cycle

Our oldest sources for the myth of the Trojan War are the Homeric poems (see CH. 2), the *Iliad* and the *Odyssey*, composed around 700–650 BC.[4] Other epic poems written down in the seventh–sixth centuries BC relate traditions of events situated before or after the plot of the *Iliad*, but these survive only in fragments or plot summaries: the *Kypria*, the *Aithiopis*, the *Iliou Persis* (*Sack of Troy*), the *Little Iliad*, and the *Nostoi* or *Returns* of the Greek heroes, collectively making up the 'Epic Cycle' (again, see CH.2).

Since the eighteenth century AD the nature and origins of the Homeric epics as we have them have been a subject of vigorous debate. Some scholars argued, on the basis of inconsistencies and contradictions within the poems, that they were assembled from pieces of pre-existing shorter poems of varied antiquity, pieces which can in principle be identified and separated. These were the *Analysts*. Other scholars emphasized the uniformity of the *Iliad* and of the *Odyssey* and their coherence of poetic vision, pointing to a single creative intelligence: these were the *Unitarians*. A final approach is *Neo-analysis*, a term coined by J. T. Kakridis in the mid-twentieth century AD. Neo-analysis is simultaneously a reaction against traditional Analyst scholarship and a kind of synthesis of Unitarian and Analyst positions. Neo-analysts see the *Iliad* and *Odyssey* as the work of creative poets who adopted and adapted material from pre-existing Greek (and perhaps other) poetic traditions, often leaving seams or traces which can still be detected.

Another important strand of Homeric scholarship is the *Oral Poetry* School, following the pioneering work of Milman Parry. Such scholarship emphasizes the extent to which the Homeric epics share characteristics with orally transmitted bardic poetry which has been observed as a living oral tradition in other times and cultures, for instance in Bosnia in the twentieth century. Such poetry makes much use of established, recurrent formulae and type-scenes, but it is also highly improvisatory, with familiar stories being created anew for each performance. Insofar as the Homeric poems are the products of such an oral tradition, then, to record them in writing was not just to commit them to a new storage medium but to effect a fundamental change in the kind of thing they were. The oral poetry perspective also has important, and much debated, implications both for the Unitarian emphasis on a coherent large-scale poetic vision and for the Analyst project of teasing apart different elements or layers within the epics.[5]

The Antiquity of the Hexameter

The epics are composed in a dactylic hexameter verse form. How far does this verse form go back? Some scholars maintain that it may have developed as early as the sixteenth century BC – in which case, there is a chance that the fixed verse form may have captured snapshots of an early historical reality and preserved them from distortion or change, like insects preserved in amber. If so, this might encourage us to look for signs in the poems of an actual conflict which took place centuries before they were written down, in, say, 1300 or 1190/1180 BC (1183, according to the third-century BC scholar Eratosthenes of Kyrene). Others, however, believe that hexameter poetry arose much later, after the decline of the Mycenaean palace civilization (in other words, after about 1190 BC).

Two interesting linguistic examples will help illustrate the lines of the debate:

1 The standard Classical Greek word for 'and' is *kai* (καί). This word occurs very often in the Homeric epics, *but it does not occur* in Mycenaean Greek, in second-millennium BC Greek as we see it in the Linear B tablets: here the word is *kʷe*, ancestor of later Greek *te* (τε) and the same word ultimately as the Latin *-que*. It is very hard to 'translate' Homeric verses back into Mycenaean Greek without *kai*. This would suggest that Homer's verse is predominantly 'modern'.

2 On the other hand, many Homeric formulae depend on a very ancient linguistic feature known as *tmesis* ('chopping'). This is the separation of a prefix from its verb by putting other words between them, a practice that seems already to have disappeared from Greek by the date of the Linear B tablets. This is a hard effect to describe in English, but, for example, at *Iliad* 3.142 we see Helen *teren kata dakru cheousa* – '"*downpouring*" a soft tear', except that by *tmesis*, in the word order of the Greek, the *down* is separated from the *pouring* and we get: 'soft *down* tear *pouring*'.[6] This is already impossible, as far as we can tell, in Mycenaean Greek.

So there is some reason to believe that the epics do contain at least some material which goes back to a very early date indeed – and there are other arguments that point the same way. But the evidence is not all one way, and, in any case, will we believe that the fact that some features of language are preserved in formulae makes it any more likely that Homer preserves some record of real events?

The Shaping of the Story

If we approach the story of Troy as found in the epics with a view to analysing its sources we find that the picture is very complex indeed, and that any fundamental historical core is likely to be very slight. The work of the poet or poets in shaping and developing the plot has been deep and pervasive. This is demonstrated, in spite of many inconsistencies and contradictions, by the *Iliad*'s consistent focus on the master-theme of the wrath of Achilles and its effects, as will be seen in more detail below. The *Iliad* sports a large cast of characters: on the Trojan side, not only Hektor and Paris but Aeneas, Antenor, Glaukos, and Sarpedon; and, on the Greek side, Diomedes, Sthenelos, Odysseus, Patroklos, Antilochos, Idomeneus, Tlepolemos, and others supporting Achilles, Menelaos, and Agamemnon. This is another clue that what we have here is a number of different traditions which have been worked together into a single poetic vision.

It is worth looking briefly at just one of these figures: Hektor. Here is a defender of his home town, selfless and always ready to fight for his city. His character is profoundly shaped by a way of thinking which already foreshadows the *polis* ideology of the Classical Greek world.[7] This is not, then, a figure belonging to a much older tradition going back to the world of the Mycenaean palaces. 'Hektor' does appear in the Mycenaean Linear B tablets, but not as a name for members of the elite.[8] And he has remarkably little presence in the Trojan War outside the *Iliad* – it is as though he had been invented for it, as some neo-analysts thought (cf. CH. 2).[9] There are other heroes who appear to be derived from legends which have nothing to do with the story of Troy but, rather, from local conflicts. The Cretan King Idomeneus, for example, defeats an enemy, Phaistos (*Iliad* 5.43–7), who bears the name of a well-known city in Idomeneus' Crete. The Lykian ruler Sarpedon kills Tlepolemos, king of Rhodes, a story that could have it origins in the defeat of Rhodian Greeks trying to occupy Lykian territory in the Dark Ages. In both cases we detect older local legends which have been found a place in the story of Troy. Other protagonists, such as Helen, Menelaos, Agamemnon, and Odysseus, have their roots in religion and cult, but have come down to Homer as human characters.

The *Iliad* also has many elements which are recognizable as standard building blocks of folk tale. The abduction of a woman leads to war. Two brothers attempt a rescue and gather other men to support them. In hard fighting, a hero's best friend is killed. The hero takes revenge. A leading attacker is killed by a defender (Achilles by Paris). The defender is killed in turn by a leader of the attackers (Paris by Philoktetes). The attacking army is victorious, the abducted woman is recovered, and there is a journey home. Other familiar motifs are the warrior who falls first (Protesilaos, whose name means 'First of the army') and the great hero destined to die young (Achilles). In the Wooden Horse, too, we recognize an ancient and widespread story pattern, which appeared much earlier in Egypt in the story of the Taking of Joppa (modern Jaffa). In that story, soldiers were smuggled into the town in sacks supposedly containing offerings. Why do we now have a horse in place of the sacks? The horse is an animal associated with Athene, one of the goddesses supporting the Greeks in their efforts to sack Troy. Perhaps this goddess in some guise actually had a shrine in the historical city of Ilion; perhaps a figure of a horse was a notable votive offering in that shrine. In any case, it is easy enough to imagine how the motif of the trick to resolve the stalemate might have entered the story, and how it might then have developed and taken distinctive shape within it.

Core Personnel

It has been suggested above that the figure of the principal Trojan hero, Hektor, is a recent arrival in the myth. Narrative logic, then, requires his place to be filled by someone else in earlier stages of the legend. This earlier protagonist would seem to be Paris. The reasons are as follows. As an archer, he represents a more ancient type of warrior figure. As the man who went on the expedition to Greece to abduct Helen, he is the leader figure, a man of courage, and the initiator of the war that determines the destiny of Troy. He is the one who kills the strongest of the attackers, Achilles, and then in turn falls (bravely?) in an archery duel with Philoktetes. According to an oracle, his death is a precondition for the fall of Troy. He was once, then, the principal defender and hero of his home town. His alternative name, 'Alexandros', means 'defender against, or warder-off of, men', and provides an indication of what his original heroic qualities may have been. The features of a valiant warrior can perhaps still be discerned underneath his rather unfavourable characterization in the *Iliad*. Perhaps, as social values changed, it was only when abducting a woman came to be seen as a mark not of warlike bravado but of susceptibility to seductive charms that Paris acquired a negative image. Is there a real historical personage (or more than one, as the two names might suggest) behind the character of Paris in the story?[10] We cannot tell.

In the beginning, the single main hero on the Greek side was Achilles. Next comes Philoktetes, whose presence with his bow is required if the Greeks are to take Troy. These two heroes (and Protesilaos too, the first warrior to fall) belong to an older stage of the legend.[11] A clue to this is the fact that they were not amongst the suitors of Helen and that strictly speaking her abduction thus has nothing to do with them; it is the other Greek heroes who courted her and swore the oath to assist her chosen husband. It is also significant that Achilles is killed by Paris and Paris by Philoktetes. There is no version of the legend in which the role of killing Paris is assigned to another Greek hero such as Ajax son of Telamon, Ajax son of Oileus, Diomedes, or Menelaos. This last has a particularly strong claim according to the principles of folk tale: as the victim of theft and initiator of the revenge expedition, he should be the one to slay the thief.

We can go further and say that the figure of Achilles reveals itself as older than any of the other Greek heroes, including Philoktetes. Achilles alone makes conquests on the way to Troy: the islands of Skyros, Lesbos, and Tenedos.[12] Achilles alone makes conquests in the Troad: the towns of Lyrnessos, Pedasos, and Thebe in the southern part of the region,[13] as well as twenty-three other unnamed cities. And Achilles is the Greek warrior who dies the paradigmatic hero's death during the assault on Troy. The deaths of other heroes such as Patroklos and Antilochos echo or prefigure his. Thus, the ancient core of the myth consists of Achilles fighting in the Troad and against Troy, and of his death at the hands of Paris.

The Character of Achilles

Great heroism is certainly Achilles' essential trait. Examining this figure in the *Iliad* and in other legends, however, we find that he is associated not just with the doing of heroic deeds, but with folklore and cult motifs that suggest more primitive origins. His father is a hunter, a participant in the famous hunt for the Kalydonian Boar; his mother, Thetis, is a mermaid or sea goddess. Thetis holds the baby Achilles over or in the fire in order to ensure, or possibly to test, his immortality: his uncomprehending mortal father intervenes. Achilles grows up without his mother, who has returned to join her father Nereus in the sea; he lives alone in the wilds of Mount Pelion, where he is educated by a centaur, the peaceable and wise Cheiron. He becomes a swift runner and potent warrior who wields a mighty spear, made of the wood of a tree from Pelion and handled only by himself and his father. He wears armour made by the god Hephaistos. There is an oracle that, if he leads a warrior life, he will die young but die a hero.

Thus we find the characteristics of an evidently mythical personage associated with the name of Achilles. It of course remains possible that a fabulous biography which originally belonged to someone else has been transferred, in the course of the tradition, to an Achilles who was originally a real person. But the name 'Achilles', like the name 'Hektor' (cf. above), is attested in the Linear B tablets for ordinary people, not the elite.[14]

An Historical Core? When and Where?

If, in our quest for a possible historical core of the legend, we remove fantastical and folkloric motifs, what do we have left? Not very much. In fact, we have a speculative story which has been told by historians and philologists since the nineteenth century AD: perhaps some Greeks tried in vain to penetrate the Skamandros valley at some time in deep antiquity, perhaps under the leadership of a man called Achilles. Maybe there were several such assaults, which in oral poetry were rolled together into one. Sometime later, Greek colonists settle peacefully at Troy, as the archaeological record shows (though the myth does not reflect this). Or there is an alternative scenario worth considering: perhaps in reality peaceful colonization of the Troad by Greeks came first, and the legend of a violent assault only developed afterwards. This possibility will be discussed further below.

If we accept the hypothesis of some such historical core to the myth, the next question is *when* the events in question might have taken place. We must start by returning to the sheer exceptionality of Achilles. Unlike him, the Greeks in the *Iliad* who come to Troy from centres of Mycenaean civilization such as Mycenae itself, Tiryns, Pylos, Athens, Thebes, and Knossos make no conquests on the way to Troy or in the Troad itself. Their commanders are linked to the myth only by the motif of Helen's abduction and the oath sworn by her suitors. None of them is killed by Paris; in no version is Paris killed by any of them. This suggests that these places and their kings are not integral to older forms of the legend. If we look toward the homelands of Achilles and Philoktetes, on the other hand, and of Protesilaos too, we notice something significant. They come from the east or north-east of mainland Greece: Achilles from Phthia/Hellas, Protesilaos from Phthia, Philoktetes from the Magnesian peninsula. This region is the base from which Aiolian Greeks began to colonize the islands of Skyros, Lesbos, and Tenedos as well as the mainland north-west Anatolia. Thus it makes sense for these Greeks in particular to be the enemies of the ancient defender of Troy, Paris, and his followers. This in turn suggests that the myth of Troy did not emerge in the Mycenaean world or in the Mycenaean centres of the thirteenth or twelfth century BC, but rather in connection with what has traditionally been known as the 'Aiolian colonization', a sequence of events from the end of the Mycenaean period or the beginning of the Early Iron Age, around 1020 BC or a bit earlier.[15]

... and which Troy?

This would lead us to the conclusion that the object of any imagined Greek assault or assaults on Troy was the city represented by the layer known to archaeologists today as Troy VIIb2. Peaceful Greek colonization of the site of Troy would then have taken place after the end of that settlement.

The most important settlement of Bronze Age Troy was the one now represented by the layer known as Troy VI. It existed c. 1700–1300 BC and consisted of a citadel (figs 21.1 and 21.2) and a lower city of scattered houses which was unfortified. It was probably the main power base in the Troad, or at least in the northern Troad. A very strong fortification wall, with towers and bastions, surrounded the acropolis; it was approximately 550 metres in length, and its stone base was 4–5 metres thick.[16] In the citadel some very big houses, but smaller ones as well, stood on terraces. This settlement was inhabited by a non-Greek population whose language was related to Luvian and Lydian. Troy VI can scarcely be identified, though, with the *Wilusa* mentioned in Hittite sources. What is there to be said against the identification of *Wilusa* and Ilios/ Ilion?

1 No one has satisfactorily explained the change in the name ending from *-usa* to *–ios* (or *–ion*).
2 The geographical hints in the Hittite sources more likely point to a location in the south-western part of Asia Minor.
3 In the early Byzantine bishopric lists, a place called Ilousa (sometimes also called Elousa) appears as the residence of a bishop in the region of Beycesultan on the upper Maiandros river, while Ilion in the Troad is named as a different bishophric. (So Beycesultan, itself an important Middle and Late Bronze Age site, *could* be the ancient Wilusa).

Troy VI was destroyed by earthquake and by fire. Survivors then rebuilt the city, repaired the defensive wall, and built houses, mostly smaller than before, densely concentrated within the citadel: this was the city now known as Troy VIIa. It in turn was destroyed by intense fire around 1190 BC. Recent discoveries suggest that this could have resulted from hostilities, but if so it must have been a surprise attack: scanty remains of weapons and human bone point to little fighting in the lower city or acropolis, and it seems likely that many of the inhabitants fled.

In the next layer, Troy VIIb1, we find houses built using an unusual method, the 'standing-stone technique', and a new form of ceramics, Coarse Ware made without the use of the potter's wheel. These cultural features, characteristic of Macedonia and Thrace, suggest invaders from the Balkans – the 'Dardanians'? We should also, however, consider the possibility that the mysterious marauding 'Sea Peoples', known from Egyptian accounts, destroyed Troy VIIa and left it in ruins, a situation which was then exploited by incomers from the Balkans. In either case, some at least of the earlier population must have survived because building methods and types of pottery characteristic of Troy VIIa persist in Troy VIIb1. Troy VIIb1 was destroyed around 1100 BC, possibly by fire.

The conclusion is, then, that neither Troy VI nor Troy VIIa was destroyed by a Mycenaean army. In the case of Troy VIIa, this is corroborated by the fact that Mycenaean citadels and settlements on the Greek mainland themselves suffered catastrophes at the time of its destruction. In the last decades of the thirteenth century BC, reinforcement of defensive structures indicates that Mycenaean rulers were on the defensive, anticipating invasion.

The last Bronze Age layer at the site of Troy is Troy VIIb2. It is marked by an increased use of the standing-stone building technique and by the introduction of another form of pottery not made on a wheel, the 'Knobbed Ware' originating in what is now east Romania and south-east Bulgaria, though the Coarse Ware of Troy VIIb1 and the wheel-made ware of Troy VIIa continue to appear alongside it. Around 1020 BC, Troy VIIb2 was destroyed in its turn by earthquake and by fire.

Soon after this we find Greek building forms, and Greek-style ceramics: imported Protogeometric pottery from eastern mainland Greece; locally produced Protogeometric pots imitating mainland Greek models; other forms of Greek painted pottery; and the Aeolic Grey Ware, typical of Aiolian colonies from about 1020 BC. This all points to settlement by Greeks, Aiolians in particular, apparently taking advantage of the disaster which had destroyed Troy VIIb2 and weakened its population. Once again, though, the continued appearance of Coarse Ware and Knobbed Ware into the ninth century BC shows that the culture of the pre-Greek population continued to be represented on the site for some time.

As we go into the ninth century BC, these forms of pottery eventually disappear; in their place we find a new style of high-quality painted pottery known as G 2/3 Ware. Distinctively Greek mortuary sites develop, as does a new cult site for the goddess Athene in the upper reaches of the settlement. All this suggests increasing, if not complete, Greek domination of Troy at this period, a supposition which is supported by the fact that a number of Trojan locations in the *Iliad* have Greek names. In short, from around 900 BC Greek settlers seem to be in control of Troy, with the pre-Greek population subordinated and to a greater or lesser extent assimilated.

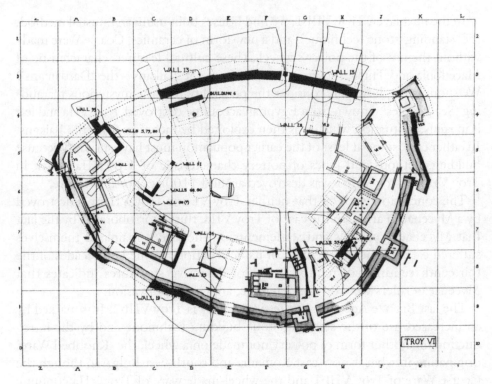

Figure 22.1   Plan of the citadel of Troy VI (1700–1300 BC) with its mighty fortification wall and the so-called north-west bastion in squares J/K/L3/4 (the huge bastion encloses a large quadratic well). The wall was damaged in parts by an earthquake accompanied by conflagrations around 1300 BC, repaired during Troy VIIa (1300–1190 BC), damaged in places once more about 1190 BC, reinforced during Troy VIIb1 (1190–1100 BC – compare fig. 22.3) and presumably repaired during Troy VIIb2. After Easton (1990: 8).

The defensive wall which surrounded Troy VI and VIIa (figs 22.1, 22.2) was repaired, and in places massively reinforced, during Troy VIIb1, giving the stone base a thickness of five to eight metres (fig. 22.3). The upper part of the wall was built up with mud brick, and crowned with a walkway along the battlements.[17] The wall was probably repaired from time to time. In the early years of Troy VIII, most houses were inside the walls, so what had previously been a citadel wall was now in effect a city wall. It must have struck both inhabitants and visitors as a mighty bulwark, matched only in Greece by the fortification walls of Mycenaean citadels (which came to be known as 'Cyclopean'). Fortifications built for Greek cities in the first millennium BC, such as the ninth–eighth century BC walls of Smyrna, must have seemed slight by comparison. Thus it is easy to understand how the wall of Troy VIII, enduring and rebuilt from the city's earlier phases, appeared impregnable,

Figure 22.2 The northern corner of the stone base of the so-called north-west bastion of Troy. This still stands up to a height of 7 metres. At the time of Troy VI the bastion reached a height of at least 12 metres, the upper part being made of mud brick. This part was reinforced during Troy VIIa, VIIb, and perhaps Troy VIII too (from 1020 BC onwards) with stone walls outside and inside; the portion above these walls was erected in mud brick. The height of the bastion grew more and more, up to at least 14 or 15 metres during Troy VIII. In front of the base you can see the remains of a structure of c. 400 BC with a well; to the left of the base, a part of the mighty 'wall IX N', added in the third century BC.

heroic, to its inhabitants. This helps us to understand the story of Greek poets, especially Homer, that the walls of Troy were built by divine hands in the mythic past (*Iliad* 21.441–60).

Our analysis of the structure and probable sources of the Trojan War narrative and of the archaeological evidence leave us with two alternative scenarios:

1   Greeks repeatedly tried to conquer Troy. They were prevented by a combination of the city's strong fortifications, the courage of its defenders, and their own small numbers and limited strength of arms. Some attackers were slain and others withdrew, possibly to the southern coast of the Troad or to

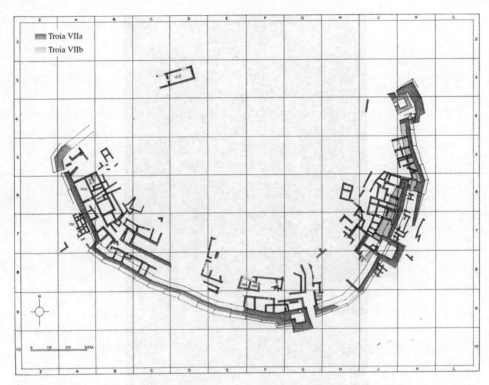

Figure 22.3 Plan of the citadel of Troy VIIa and VIIb (1190–1020 BC), with the reinforcements of the fortification wall in the E and SE region from the time of Troy VIIb1. Above the renovated stone base of the wall there was a structure of mud brick. This was Troy VIII's city wall at an early date, later repeatedly repaired.

Tenedos. Then Troy was struck by a natural disaster and its population weakened. The Greeks could now occupy the city with little resistance.

2   Greeks established themselves on the southern shore of the Troad or in Tenedos. Some of them were looking for a new place to settle, and set their eyes on Troy. It was strongly defended, so they did not attack but reconnoitred the site. Later, they observed that the city had been struck by a natural disaster and its population weakened. They could thus settle in Troy without a fight. Later, as memory of these events faded, stories of failed but heroic attacks began to be told. People could see the apparently impregnable walls; tradition maintained that the city was once 'Trojan', but it was now Greek; they were raised in a warrior culture; the logic of the story was irresistible.

Take Scenario 1. It is possible that the attackers were indeed led by a man called Achilles, and that he fell in the struggle. Later, attributes of a much older mythical figure, who need not have been called Achilles, were transferred to him. In Scenario 2, a legendary figure called Achilles equipped with fabulous attributes came to establish himself as the mythic protagonist, the Davy Crockett, of Aiolian colonization. When the stories of unsuccessful attacks on Troy began to be told, this hero figure naturally took pride of place. His noble death at the hands of a god, doubtless part of a much early tradition, fitted the idea of heroic but doomed assaults on Troy perfectly.

In either case, the disaster that ended Troy VIIb2 and let the Greeks into the city was ultimately explained as the work of a deity, Athene. Perhaps it was the introduction of this divine agency and the correspondingly diminished role of the human protagonist that led to the introduction of the character of Philoktetes, to re-energize the drama. He kills Paris with an arrow, possibly just at the moment when the Trojan heroes are taking refuge in the city through the Skaian gates. The city then falls to the Greeks, again, of course, with Athene's help.

Each of these scenarios connects the myth with Greek colonization of the Troad as we have reconstructed it, and provides a satisfactory foundation myth for the descendants of the early Greek colonists. In each version, the wall of Troy plays a crucial role. In the first, it motivates the length of the siege, the many unsuccessful assaults, and the death of Achilles (and of his Johnny-come-lately adversary, Hektor) outside the walls. In the second, the wall itself is the very reason for postulating futile attacks, whose story is then developed in line with other legends. Either way, the historical story at the root of the legend (if there was one) soon becomes more-or-less irrelevant as poetic priorities take control, and as the Siren power of folkloric story patterns makes itself felt. If there was a memory of an ancient surprise attack, for example, it is easy to see how this story might have come to incorporate, and give specific local colour to, the widespread story pattern that is represented by the stratagem of the Wooden Horse.

The Ethos of the *Iliad*

This was all transformed, however, and given a completely new direction, by the *Iliad*'s focus on the wrath of Achilles and its effects. The poet initially presents Achilles' refusal to compromise as understandable in the light of Agamemnon's insult to his honour. As the suffering of the Greeks in his absence becomes more intense, however, the poet's presentation of Achilles' conduct develops. His intractable insistence on avenging his own honour leads to the death of many other Greek warriors, to the death of his friend Patroklos, and ultimately to his own death. Recognition of the overriding importance of the community is crucial, but it is something which Achilles, for all his pre-eminence and power as a character, does not achieve: he is a hero unable to discipline himself. The *Iliad* presents Achilles as a great hero guilty of excessive individualism. His qualified, but extraordinary, reconciliation with Priam in Book 24 is an episode of exceptional and enduring power, the most powerful moment of the *Iliad*; but here too he acts as an individual (with thoughts of his own father), not as a representative of collective values.

Thus Homer's reinterpretation of the story of the Trojan War clearly represents a criticism of a certain version of traditional values, and articulates a new vision of heroism. The *Iliad* asserts that a great warrior hero must take responsibility for the community that has nurtured him, and support his people through whatever affliction may befall them, even if his own pride is afflicted. This is a far cry from any possible events involving real people, Greek and Trojan, in the Troad in deep antiquity. That said, it is plainly rooted in real human experience, and the possibility that it has some roots (however remote and obscure) in real events should not be discounted.

FURTHER READING

On the character of the settlements Troy VI and VIIa: Hertel and Kolb 2003. Defending the hypothesis that the myth has a historical core: Korfmann 2005; Korfmann, Latacz, and Hawkins 2004; Latacz 2005/ 2004; M. L. West 2004. Criticizing the hypothesis that the myth has a historical core, arguing for a late development of the hexameter, and dealing with the problem of translating Homeric verses back into Mycenaean Greek: Kullmann 2002. Criticizing the hypothesis that the myth has a historical core on archaeological and historical grounds: Hertel 1982, 2001, 2003, 2004 (see p. 86 nn.4 and 5 for references to earlier scholarship on this subject), 2008a, 2008b. Discussion of recent discoveries which could hint that Troy VIIa fell by conquest: Becks, Rigter, and Hnila 2006: 46 f., but cf. Koppenhöfer 1997: 312–14 and figure 6.2–6 (with some different suggestions about the find locations of the weapon remains referred to by Becks) and Hertel 2004. On the Early Greek Pottery from Troy: Hertel 2008b. On folk-tale/fairy-tale motifs: Lesky 1966; Hölscher 1988; Hertel 2008a, 106–10; Hertel 2008b. 'The New Quarrel over Troy', Ulf 2004: articles on archaeological, philological (development of heroic verse and epic poetry), linguistic (development of the hexameter), and historical aspects of the debate by scholars critical of the idea that the myth has a historical core. Companion volumes: Morris and Powell 1997; Fowler 2004a; J. M. Foley 2005.

NOTES

1. A remarkable exception to this, and well worth considering, is Finkelberg (2005) (KD). On falsification, see Dowden (1992: 62, and, on Troy, 65–8).
2. For a comparative overview of the relationship between epic poetry and history see Raaflaub (2005).
3. This proposition (cf. Dowden 1992: 20–1) constitutes a generalization which is broadly true but requires some special pleading. For example, the fortunes of

Agamemnon's children, Orestes, Elektra, and (in versions where she survives the sacrifice at Aulis) Iphigeneia, must be treated as an extension of their father's *nostos*, as must those of Achilles' son Neoptolemos and the shadowy half-brothers assigned to Telemachos by Hesiod, *Theogony* 1011–14. Another special case is the anti-*nostos* of Aeneas, a journey away from his old home towards the distant prospect of a new one, providing the springboard for the foundation myths of Rome: see Chapter 13.

4. For an introduction to the complex question of the circumstances in which the epics were composed and committed to writing, see, for example, Turner (1997), Fowler (2004b).

5. On neo-analysis see further Willcock (1997); on the significance of oral tradition, Foley (1997); also Foley (2005) for a handy introduction to modern oral epics.

6. For a survey of the issues see Horrocks (1997: 195–203 (201–3 on *tmesis*)). See also M. L. West (1988) on specific early Mycenaean and even earlier elements in Homeric epic, including some examples of Homeric lines 'translated' into Mycenaean Greek (and dealing with the problem of *kai*: 158 on *Iliad* 16.857 = 22.363); critical observations in Chadwick (1990); further discussion and examples in Bennet (1997: 523–31). For an attempt to trace the roots of early Greek (and other) poetry still further back, into Indo-European, see M. L. West (2007).

7. For a cautious discussion of the early roots of the idea of the *polis* in Archaic Greece, see Hall (2007a). 'Hektor is a positive model precisely because he understands his leadership in terms of saving his polis': Raaflaub (1997: 632).

8. See *e-ko-to* in the Index of Personal Names, Ventris and Chadwick (1956: 417).

9. See, for example, Scheliha (1943: ch. 6 'Die von Homer erfundenen Gestalten' ('Characters invented by Homer') 221, and especially Kullmann 1960: 182–5). Hektor is, of course, like Patroklos, expendable in a non-traditional timeframe (sometime in the last year of the war, cf. CH. 2 p. 29, but before the significant moments when Achilles dies and Troy falls) (KD).

10. The two names have, of course, been supposed to mark initiatory name change (Achilles and his son Neoptolemos also had other names), cf. Gartziou-Tatti (1992) (KD).

11. For another reconstruction of the 'organic' personnel of the Trojan War story see M. L. West (1988: 161–2).

12. *Iliad* 9.668; 9.129, 271; 11.625.

13. 2.690–1, 19.60, 20.92, 191; 20.92; 1.366–7, 2.691, 6.414–16.

14. See *a-ki-re-u* in the Index of Personal Names, Ventris and Chadwick (1956: 417).

15. This is the view taken by Dowden (1992: 67–8). For a critical, and sceptical, overview of the evidence concerning this 'Aiolian colonization', see C. B. Rose (2008). H. N. Parker (2008) also questions the validity of 'Aiolian' as a linguistic category.

16. See the reconstruction of Troy VIIa in Connolly (1986: 49) with figure. In Troy VI the level behind the stone wall base stood deeper, no houses stood on the stone base, the gate to the right was in a different place, and the wall further to the right had not yet been built. The towers in the background to the right are fictitious.

17. See Hertel (2003: 47–53, figs 8–15 and fig. HVa at the back of the book).

CHAPTER TWENTY-THREE

Women and Myth

Sian Lewis

The Case of Danaos' Daughters

Aigyptos and Danaos, so the story goes, were brothers and rulers of Egypt and Libya respectively, and each had fifty children, Aigyptos fifty sons and Danaos fifty daughters. Aigyptos wished to marry his sons to his brother's children, but the Danaid sisters had no desire to marry, so they fled for sanctuary to Argos with their father. The Aigyptioi followed them to Greece and persuaded the Argive king Pelasgos to agree to the marriages. Each Danaid was thus assigned to one of her cousins and the fifty marriages were celebrated, but on the wedding night all but one of the brides killed her new husband. Hypermestra was the only one to save her husband, Lynkeus, and her motives are variously given: either she fell in love with him, or, respecting her wish not to marry, he refused to take her virginity, and so she spared him. In some accounts Lynkeus then killed Danaos in revenge for his brothers, and sometimes killed the other sisters too, becoming king himself, though in most versions the Danaids were purified of their crime and remarried, their new suitors competing in a footrace for the right to have first choice of the brides. An alternative tradition became popular in Roman times which saw the Danaids punished for their crime in the afterlife by being forced to spend eternity filling a vat of water using leaking jars.[1]

The myth of the Danaids resists obvious interpretation. Is it a myth about women and marriage, or a tale of conflict between brothers? Are the Danaids absolved of their murders or subject to an eternity of punishment? Is Hypermestra or Lynkeus the hero of the story, and should we see Hypermestra as a brave individualist or as a disobedient daughter? Possibly for this reason it is not a myth which is commonly told or performed today, yet it clearly offered

A Companion to Greek Mythology, First Edition. Edited by Ken Dowden and Niall Livingstone.
© 2014 John Wiley & Sons Ltd. Published 2014 by John Wiley & Sons Ltd.

much to the Greeks and Romans, since it figured in more versions than any other story, the subject of epic poetry, drama, and art.[2] It is a useful place from which to begin a consideration of women in mythology, both for the story itself with its unusual perspectives, and for the contrast between its ancient and modern popularity. The women of Greek and Roman myth have attracted a great deal of attention, both scholarly and artistic, yet our efforts to extract from myth a coherent story about gender have led to a kind of modern myth-making, in which some stories are over emphasized while others are neglected. This chapter aims to examine the orthodoxies which have arisen about 'women in myth' and to suggests some approaches by which we might broaden the current critical perspective.

Gender and Myth in Modern Scholarship

In studies of gender relations in antiquity, mythology has always played a large role. When feminist scholarship emerged in Classics in the 1970s, scholars trying to write a history of women found mythology a resource much richer than historical or legal accounts. This was both because of the sheer amount of material it contained and because poetry and drama offered not just female figures in abundance, but powerful and active ones. Given the dearth of evidence about the lives of women to be found in historical sources, the existence of interesting and influential mythological women offered a way to affirm the social importance of women.[3] So studies such as Pomeroy's *Goddesses, Whores, Wives and Slaves* (1975) and Lefkowitz's *Women in Greek Myth* (1986) turned very readily to myth for an exploration of ancient ideas about women, and most subsequent works have followed their lead.[4]

Furthermore, classical scholarship was strongly influenced by the early phase of Western feminism, in which a particular relationship with modern fairy tales grew up. From the 1970s and 1980s, feminist thinkers began to identify and discuss the sexism which underlay many familiar stories and the way that this influenced their listeners' outlook on the world – the princess waiting to be rescued by the prince, the aged witches who terrorized children, the wicked stepmother and the heroic woodcutter. Once this was recognized, there developed a very strong interest in the rewriting of fairy tales from a feminist perspective, of which Angela Carter became the most famous exponent.[5] The mythologies of classical Greece and Rome came to be presented by feminist writers as a similarly entrenched sexist system, in need of reappropriation or revision by female readers. The most influential study was the French feminist writer Hélène Cixous' reappropriation of Medusa. Cixous suggested that Medusa might be reclaimed as a positive and subversive female figure, her power lying in beauty rather than horror. Similar treatments have been afforded to Helen, transforming her from powerless object to desiring woman, and to Psyche and Penelope.[6] The fundamental principle – that the stories told by a culture can by their nature validate a particular ideology, and that those who oppose that ideology can resist it through a process of reappropriation of the tales – has had a profound effect on gender scholars' approach to myth in Britain and North America.

Women in Myth as 'Role Models'

Such scholarship interprets classical myth as a system which justified male control of women, by providing on the one hand examples of dutiful and self-sacrificing women who subordinate themselves to male concerns and on the other 'negative role models' such as Klytaimestra and the Amazons who show the destructive potential of female power should it be allowed free rein. Particularly influential have been the psychoanalytic approaches which detect a male fear of women (specifically of the mother) and a consequent wish to limit female power, and interpretations of myth in terms of ritual or structure have tended to adopt the same fundamental approach.[7] The women of classical myth are, thus, either victims or monsters, the stories serving to model appropriate and inappropriate female behaviour. This view can easily be supported from a reading of the most familiar ancient myths: stories interpreted as encapsulating gender hostility include the wives and mothers in tragedy who kill their husbands (Klytaimestra, Deianeira) or their children (Medea, Prokne), the female monsters combated by heroes (the Gorgons, Harpies, and Amazons), the many accounts of young women or nymphs abducted by gods (Korone, Semele, Oreithyia, and Persephone), and the tale of the first woman of all, Pandora. Construed in this way, the myths do indeed seem to have a single message to impart about the roles suitable for women, and the consequences for society should that order be overthrown.

Powerful though this orthodoxy is, it gains its power from partiality. All these stories can be paralleled by similar myths in which the gender of the participants is different. Wives kill husbands and children, certainly, but Herakles too murders his children, as do Agamemnon and Tantalus, while both Herakles and Kephalos were supposed to have killed their wives. Heroes kill male monsters as well as female, such as the Python fought by Apollo, or Geryon and Antaios who were defeated by Herakles. Eos carries off both Tithonos and Kephalos, as Aphrodite does Anchises, while Kalypso imprisons Odysseus as her lover on the island of Ogygia. To some extent the partial view is the result of differential survival: the tales in extant Greek tragedy tend to receive most attention (although Euripides' *Herakles*, which shows the murder of his children, is surprisingly marginalized compared to the tale of Medea).

But it is also the result of scholarly choice, and the treatment of the Pandora story is a particularly interesting example of the eclipse of one myth by another which better matches our expectations.

The Case of Pandora

The creation of Pandora was related by Hesiod in two versions, one in the *Theogony* and one in the *Works and Days*, where it appears as part of the story of the Five Ages of Man. Pandora, a creature 'like a lovely woman', was made by the gods and presented to Epimetheus as a punishment for mankind's theft of fire from Olympos, and the story, suggesting as it does that women were a separate race from men, has taken pride of place in explanations of the Greek attitude towards women since the 1970s.[8] But the creation of Pandora was not the end of the story – in the next generation Prometheus and Epimetheus each had a child, Pyrrha and Deukalion, who married and who were the sole survivors of a great flood that wiped out the rest of humanity. As they contemplated the empty world that was left they were told by Hermes to create a new human race by casting stones behind them. The stones cast by Pyrrha became women and those by Deukalion men, and so the world was repopulated. In this story, Deucalion and Pyrrha are the first man and first woman, and share equally in the recreation of the earth: the story formed the opening of the *Ehoiai* (or *Catalogue of Women*), the poem which carries on where Hesiod's *Theogony* leaves off (see CH. 3), and appears in Pindar and Ovid.[9] Yet it has been largely eclipsed from studies of women and myth because it does not tell the same story as Pandora.

The orthodoxy that myth demonstrates and justifies male control of women has become very powerful in studies of gender, yet it is necessarily one-sided. It is perfectly possible to construct a system of classical myth which is 'about' men and women, and equally possible to construct one which is not; myth could as well be held to explore the nature of mortality or the problem of obedience to the gods. Indeed it would be foolish to expect myths to tell a single story, since their very nature is to be malleable and polysemic. But an investigation of women and gender in myth which takes the orthodoxy as its starting point thereby limits its conclusion: one can demonstrate that the interpretation of myth is in accordance with the orthodoxy, or one can look for 'alternative readings' of well-known myths, speculating on ways in which ancient women might have reappropriated them, despite the lack of evidence for such activity.[10] It is more productive to consider the extant myths in their variety of surviving forms, since looking more widely at the whole complex of surviving mythological representations enables us to see what is really there.

The Pliability of Myth: The Danaids Again

In antiquity, the tales we encounter were not primarily written; they circulated as stories, and the written versions we have today, far from being canonical, are occasional crystallizations of a particular myth in one or another form. Ancient myths were perfectly subject to recasting by any teller who cared to change them, because there was no authoritative version for a speaker to challenge. What we have today is therefore not a canonical set of stories, but a series of versions from different periods and places. In fact, because many of the media which have survived from antiquity were competitive, we may have preserved for us versions of myths which were deliberately composed in order to be strikingly new and different. Athenian tragic playwrights, for example, could recast their mythological material into new and shocking forms to give their work novelty (as with both Medea and Prokne, for instance), or could compose versions of the same story with markedly different characterizations (such as Euripides' treatments of the Hippolytos myth).[11] We also have to recognize that the mythological stories we find in literature and art may not be representative of the whole corpus, because of the vagaries of survival: Aeschylus wrote a Danaid trilogy which has not come down to us, and similarly figures such as Hypsipyle, Eos, and Prokne all suffer diminished importance through the loss of literary sources.

The story of the Danaids also illustrates how myths could develop over time. In its archaic and classical form the myth focuses on the forced marriage and husband murders, with subsequent purification for the sisters followed by remarriage. In the fourth and third centuries BC, however, it became a very popular topic in southern Italian pot painting, in scenes illustrating the punishment of the Danaids in Hades. From Hellenistic times onwards the myth became an exemplary tale of crime and punishment, as two previously unrelated myths, one figuring the murderous daughters of Danaos and the other the leaky jar-fillers, were conflated. The myth continued to be popular in Roman art in this form, and appeared both in the *Aeneid* and in a remarkable statue-group outside Augustus' Temple of Palatine Apollo.[12] There is thus no single version of the story, nor a single meaning, but instead a series of meanings expressed at different times and in different ways.

Myth in Visual Art

The history of the Danaid myth sketched above includes within it an artistic tradition as well as a literary one, and this indicates an approach which may offer a partial solution: to consider the evidence of art in comparison with literary sources. It is valuable because the stories which were told in poetry and drama are not usually those which are prominent in art, and where the same story is told there are often some very significant shifts of emphasis. A well-known example of this is Medea: our extant literary sources are dominated by Medea's relations with Jason and her murder of their children, but Attic pot painters chose to focus instead on the tale of her deceit of the daughters of Pelias, whose attempts to rejuvenate their father according to her instructions brought about his death, a story much neglected in modern accounts.[13]

Patterns of representation in art can be revealing, even within a small historical period: in a study of the representation of the gods on Attic pottery, for instance, Scheffer identified a pattern which was distinct from both literary accounts and from archaeological evidence.[14] In the sixth–fifth century BC Dionysos is by far the most popular figure, and in the fourth–third century Nike and Eros. Athene, Hermes, and Apollo are also very popular, while Zeus is relatively uncommon, as are Hera, Aphrodite, and Demeter. This pattern of representation is not what one would expect either from our knowledge of state cult or from the evidence of poetry and drama. Of course, the reason for this is that painters chose to focus on particular types of story suited to their purpose: Dionysos takes centre stage on pottery with his retinue of satyrs and mainads because of his links with both banqueting and the afterlife, while Hermes appears as guide and protector to the heroes whose exploits are depicted; Hera and Aphrodite, in contrast, tend to appear only in the Judgement of Paris, and in general scenes of the gods on Olympos. The analysis indicates that the different uses of the gods – by painters, poets, and in cult – are entirely distinct, with no one taking precedence over the others.

Female Deities on Attic Pots

Representations of mythological stories in Greek and Roman art, discussed in detail in CHs 8, 14, 16, and 21 of this volume, are, of course, both numerous and varied – in reliefs and wall-paintings, statues, ceramics, mirrors, and sarcophagi – and I will necessarily limit discussion here to a small but indicative study of one particular area. A brief comparison of the frequency of depictions of mythological women (immortal and mortal) on Attic pots likewise offers a fresh perspective on the popularity of certain myths.[15] Given the provenance of these pots from Athens it is not surprising that the most commonly depicted female figure should be Athene, with 3,441 images, but the pattern of representation of other goddesses is less predictable. Nike appears 1,795 times (largely as a personification of athletic success) and Artemis 639; next in frequency are Thetis, mother of Achilles (398) and Eos, goddess of the dawn (289).

Thetis is familiar from epic poetry, figuring in the *Iliad* where she offers divine assistance and comfort to her son. She is depicted both in this role, and in her courtship with Peleus, specifically the wrestling match by which he won her as his bride. Eos is less well known to modern audiences, again as a result of a fragmentary literary tradition: like Thetis, she figured in epic poetry, but this time in a cyclic epic of which only fragments survive, the *Aithiopis*. Her role there was as the mother of the Ethiopian warrior Memnon (the most handsome man who went to Troy), and she is depicted in this role on pots, especially mourning her son's death, although the majority of depictions focus on the stories of her abductions of the handsome youths Tithonos and Kephalos. Next in popularity was Leto, mother of Apollo and Artemis, with 225 depictions, followed by Demeter (193, of which 122 are with Persephone), and Oreithyia (68).

The first thing to emerge from this comparison is a surprisingly large role for mothers in the images on the pots. The archetypal mother of classical mythology appears to us to be Demeter, who by her withdrawal from the earth when her daughter Persephone was abducted by Hades forced Zeus to intervene to restore her. Yet myth has far more to say about the relationship between mothers and sons. Thetis and Eos, as we have seen, both appear frequently in Attic vase-painting as mothers to their heroic sons Achilles and Memnon. Thetis of course plays a significant role in the *Iliad*: Achilles calls on her for assistance in his anger, she persuades Zeus to turn the battle against the Greeks, and she provides divine armour for him when he returns to the fight.[16] The story of Eos and Memnon in the *Aithiopis* was similar: Eos too lent aid to her son in battle, and she asked Zeus to grant him immortality after his death.[17] Both Thetis and Eos lend aid to their sons at Troy, intervene in their conflicts, and mourn their deaths. They even come together in the episode of the *psychostasia* ('soul-weighing'): towards the end of the Trojan War Achilles and Memnon met in single combat, and in order to decide their fate Zeus weighed the souls of the two combatants against each other in the scale of destiny. Both divine mothers were present, each attempting to influence Zeus to protect her child. Images of the *psychostasia* appear on several vases, with Eos and Thetis always present, and it also formed the subject of another lost trilogy of plays by Aeschylus.[18]

Mothers and Sons: Mythic Perspectives

The significant factor here is that of the continuing role of the mother: we tend to focus on the many stories of the birth of heroes or gods found in myth, but both Eos and Thetis preserve a relationship with their adult sons, who continue to turn to their mothers for assistance and comfort throughout life. A similar relationship informs the many representations of Leto, mother of Apollo and Artemis. In literature Leto has been seen as a rather dull figure whose role begins and ends with the bearing of her children, and her appearances on pottery, where she forms part of the 'Delphic Triad' of Leto, Artemis, and Apollo, are often labelled 'Apollo with Artemis and Leto', but this fails to do justice to her role in cult and in art.[19] Leto was not an adjunct to Apolline cult, but part of a distinct family group, and her role as a mother in cult can be paralleled by several other examples.

According to Larsen, mothers and sons were worshipped together in heroic cult more often than fathers and sons (or fathers and daughters), and mother–son cult is found throughout Greece, with pairs such as Auge and Telephos, Elara and Tityos, Alkmene and Herakles, and even Homer and his mother Klymene.[20] Alkmene in particular had one of the most widespread of heroic tomb cults, and she was worshipped in Athens alongside her son, also appearing in his imagery: on a black-figure hydria in London she stands beside his *kline* (couch) as he dines in the presence of the gods.[21] As well as the many images of the Delphic Triad, Leto figures in two myths on Attic pottery, both with her children: the death of Tityos and the slaughter of the Niobids. Again, these are often interpreted as stories belonging to Apollo or Artemis in which Leto is present only as a bystander, but in fact she was the motivator of events in each case. Attacked by Tityos, she summoned Apollo to kill him; angered by Niobe's claim to more successful motherhood, she prevailed on her children to destroy Niobe's offspring. Like Eos and Thetis, Leto does not fade from significance once her childbearing is done: because of their divine nature, her relationship with her children is unending, and it also remains close, particularly with her son.

More than Marriage?

Such a depiction is the more remarkable because it has often been said that classical myth encapsulates a particular social view of women: that myth is interested in women only at the moment of marriageability.[22] On this view, in broad terms, myths concern virgins who are raped by gods and heroes and married (or destroyed), or competed for and married, or else who sacrifice themselves and fail to achieve marriage. Even those myths which present married women dramatize the failure of marriage through violent action, the saving of it through self-sacrifice. This, it is argued, reflects the value given to women within classical society: their importance lay in their ability to marry successfully and to produce children, hence the concentration on this vital period. Other female life stages – childhood, motherhood, old age – receive little attention. But this, as suggested above, is a partial view of a partial survival.

Mothers and Sons: Social Perspectives

Our understanding of the role of motherhood is affected by our own perspective. The neglect of the mother's role beyond early childhood reflects modern Western (or perhaps northern European) expectations about the family, assuming that a mother would normally fade from a child's life once that child reached adulthood. This may have been the case with daughters (and myths of mother and daughter are few, beyond Demeter's loss and recovery of Persephone), but Greece and Rome, as traditional societies, offered a continuing role for the mother of a son. As a wife was usually considerably younger than her husband, she would obviously tend to live much longer (assuming that she survived childbearing) and would remain in the household of her son once her husband was dead. Speeches from the law courts of Athens show us examples of widowed mothers who continue to live in the house with an adult son, and these are active and competent women who play a part in the son's affairs.[23] The role of mother was not one which ended upon a son's marriage, and pots draw attention to this aspect of the myths which has been lost or forgotten in the literary tradition.

Pursued – and Pursuing

Apart from their role as mothers, the primary area of interest in female figures amongst pot painters was 'pursuit' scenes involving Eos, Thetis, and also Helen. Helen is most often shown being abducted by Theseus; Thetis, wrestling with Peleus, who managed to win her hand by this means; and Eos, abducting her mortal lovers Tithonos or Kephalos.[24] The theme is one which has been discussed extensively elsewhere, but we should note both the dissonance with literature – Eos and Thetis' pursuits scarcely feature in poetry – and the challenge they pose to orthodox interpretations.[25]

The pursuit of women by gods or heroes, itself a very frequent theme in art, is often linked to ideas of marriageability, where the unmarried *parthenos* needs to be 'caught' by her suitor and tamed into marriage. But neither the pursuits of Eos nor Thetis wrestling fit easily with this interpretation. Eos' scenes are evidently a counterpart to the pursuits of women by male gods, and the theme has been convincingly associated with funerary ritual, but they also foreground a tale of female desire which is neither threatening nor adversarial. Similarly, in the images of Peleus and Thetis wrestling the scene is not one of a frightened woman being claimed by a superior man but a contest in which the combatants hold equal power. Thetis is supposed to have used her shape-shifting ability to deter Peleus, turning into a snake, a lion, and a fish, and the images depict the moment of balanced competition between the pair. Peleus cannot simply come down like Zeus or Poseidon, but must prove himself the equal of his future wife. The scenes of Eos and Thetis, then, are evocative of female power, but not female power beyond bounds or requiring mastery: the status of the pursuer and pursued varies in each case, and the myth provides the space for several different scenarios to be played out within the same theme.

The Danaids (Again) and Other Sisters

The most serious criticism of the use of myth in gender studies is that it serves only to exemplify what we already know – that we can identify patterns in myth which illustrate social norms, but we cannot use myth alone as evidence for those norms.[26] Implicit in this, however, is the assumption that one would only interrogate myth on those areas already identified in historical sources. Is it in fact possible to exploit myth to explore areas about which we know little?

The myth of the Danaids is unusual to a modern eye because of the large number of daughters within the tale – fifty, every one of whom is named in Apollodoros. It is one of many classical myths which include large families of sisters: the fifty daughters of Thespios, each of whom bore a child to Herakles, the fifty Nereids, the fourteen daughters of Priam, and the seven Pleiades. Many more myths focus on groups of three sisters, mortal (the Minyads, the Proitids, the daughters of Kekrops and of Erechtheus) and immortal (the Gorgons, Graiai, Harpies, and Erinyes). This is in itself noteworthy, since the social valuing of sons over daughters in Greek and Roman society meant that groups of brothers were far more common in real life than groups of sisters: we see few but the wealthiest families in our sources with more than one daughter.[27] From a historical point of view the attention paid to sister relationships is fascinating, because it is something unlikely to surface in historical sources; although relations between brother and sister are surprisingly well documented, no source which might record ideas about sisterhood survives.

It might be objected that the existence of large families of mythological sisters is simply a mythographer's convenience: if one aimed to trace the lineage of heroes back to a small group of progenitors it was necessary for the originating ancestors to have numerous daughters in order to create each family line. This is certainly the case with some groups, such as the daughters of Asopos or of Pelops, where the women are no more than cyphers with no story of their own, but most sisters are the centre of their own myth and their descendants (if they have any) are secondary.[28] Although there are some similarly large groups of brothers to be found (the fifty sons of Priam or the fifty Aigyptioi) there are significant differences in the way that brother and sister relationships are treated: conflict is far more common amongst brothers than sisters, and brothers each tend to have their own story rather than sharing a single fate.

Why, then, are sisters significant in myth? We are familiar with the pairs of sisters in extant Attic tragedy – Antigone and Ismene in *Antigone*, for example, or Elektra and Chrysothemis in Sophocles' *Electra*, who dramatize debates about women's obedience to authority and loyalty to their family.[29] But sister relationships in myth go well beyond this. The stories told about groups of sisters fall into several patterns – self-sacrifice (such as the daughters of Erechtheus), punishment by a god for wrong-doing (the daughters of Kekrops), transformation (the sisters of Meleager) – but some underlying themes stand out.

The first is solidarity and loyalty. Myths of mothers and daughters supposedly foreshadow the inevitable breaking of familial bonds when a daughter leaves her parents to marry, yet the sister relationship in myth remains paramount even when one or more sisters are married. A clear example is the story of Prokne and Philomela. Central to the story is the relationship between the two sisters – Philomela is brought by Prokne's husband, Tereus, to visit her, suffering his brutality along the way, and Prokne, when she learns what Tereus has done, kills their son in revenge for his treatment of her sister.[30] The bond between the sisters has not been broken by Prokne's marriage and removal to Thrace, and her actions demonstrate that loyalty towards Philomela overrides the marital relationship.

A similar theme, though in less grisly form, can be found in the tale of the daughters of Minyas: the three sisters, Leukippe, Arsippe, and Alkathoē, refuse to take part in the worship of Dionysos with the other women of Thebes, preferring to stay at home and work at their looms. Dionysos, angry at their rejection of his rites, causes the looms to burst into life with vines and ivy, and manifests himself in animal form. The sisters go into a frenzy and sacrifice Leukippe's son to the god; they are then transformed into bats.[31] In this case we see a group of sisters who, though all married, are still defined by their relationship to each other and meet a common fate. Even families of monstrous or supernatural sisters show the same close relationship: the Graiai, the Harpies, and the Hesperides (all explicitly said to be sisters) live together forever at the margins of the earth, and only the three Gorgons undergo separation when Medusa (the mortal sister) is killed by Perseus, leaving her two immortal sisters to pursue him fruitlessly. The contrast with the brothers of myth, so often antagonistic, could not be greater: we find no myths of sisterly conflict or competitiveness, as is common in European folk tale.

Of course, mythological sisters do not always share the same fate. Hypermestra, the Danaid who saves her husband, stands out from her sisters, although the myth is not really presented as a morality story in this way. Of the daughters of Proitos, who are driven mad by Hera after committing sacrilege in her temple, one dies while her sisters are healed, and in some versions one or more of Kekrops' daughters survives while her sisters are killed by Athene.[32] But even when their fates differ, sisters do not win at each other's expense: we have no tales of family rivalry sparked by sisterly dispute, even given the potential for such conflict between, for example, the sisters Helen and Klytaimestra. Indeed, the sister relationship seems to take the place of friendship between women.

Friendship is not often found in classical myth, Theseus and Peirithoös being the only genuine example. The best-known stories of friendship, such as that of Damon and Pythias, tend to be historical, invented under the influence of philosophical thought.[33] But friendship amongst women is entirely absent. Goddesses such as Artemis and Thetis surround themselves with bands of nymphs or Nereids, but these are not personal friends as the nymphs could not be on a level of equality with the deity. The closest approach to a friend is the figure of Pallas, found in a variant story of the childhood of Athene – Athene unfortunately killed her girlhood companion in mock battle and adopted her name in remembrance – but even here Pallas is sometimes said to have been Athene's sister.[34] The sister relationship, more complex and richer than that of brothers, and lasting throughout life, substitutes for friendship.

Myth in Gender Studies, Gender in Myth Studies

Seeking ways in which myth spoke about women's experience is well and good, but we should not, as already stated, mistake the part for the whole. Myth is always polysemic, and it is possible to interpret these same stories in ways to which gender is incidental: the myths of sisterhood discussed above, for instance, as well as depicting female solidarity, often concern the divide between human and divine – how do humans react to the revelation of the divine? how does one breach the border between mortal and immortal? This latter theme is also taken up by many male-centred myths, primarily those of the Dioskouroi and of Herakles, who breaches the boundary between death and life successfully on several occasions. Is the importance given to myth by feminist scholars simply a reflection of their own concerns? Certainly the centrality of mythology in gender scholarship has never been matched by a strong interest in gender amongst those who study mythology. Gender is one aspect of the interpretation of myth, certainly, but it has not been a major one; scholarship on mythology has tended to focus on the structures of myth and the influence of ritual. So the role of mythology in gender studies has become much greater than the role of gender in mythological studies, and the role of myth in validating and indoctrinating ideas about relations between the sexes is seen as very large from one perspective, but very small from the other.

The Myth of Mythic Norms

Indeed, one might wonder whether myth is a sensible place to look for normative conclusions about gender, given the very fluid and fantastical world it depicts. The world of myth is one where gender is presented as less important than in reality: women could be warriors, men could live as women, and even physical sex could change; is this the kind of place that we should look for norms and certitudes?

The handful of stories which treat changes of gender depict it as surprisingly undisruptive. The seer Teiresias, for instance, finds himself transformed from male to female after encountering two serpents in the forest, and simply resigns herself to life as a woman; seven years later she seizes the opportunity to return to being male, but looks on the changes philosophically.[35] The nymph Kainis chose to change from female to male (becoming Kaineus), either to avoid rape by Poseidon or because she was not permitted to have children. Iphis, too, changes from female to male in an act of divine wish-fulfilment: brought up as a boy, she fears exposure on her wedding night, but her mother prays to Isis who turns Iphis into a man and enables her to marry the next day. The story of Iphis closely reflects other myths of 'wishes granted', such as Herodotos' story of the ugly Spartan baby who was made beautiful through the intervention of Helen.[36] Change of gender is thus not treated as a cause for alarm or as an upsetting of the order of things, nor does it bring disaster in its wake. Given this attitude it is all the more surprising that the myth of the Amazons as masculinized women should be credited with as much shock value in the ancient world as it has been.

Viewed in this way, myth loses its familiar role of exemplifying ideas and norms which we have already deduced, but offers instead a prospect of new avenues to explore. The desire to use mythology as evidence for ancient attitudes towards gender has led us to focus on those stories which treat (or appear to treat) male–female relationships, and to interpret them in terms of gender opposition, but we should not assume that myth had a single story to tell, or that its sole purpose was to justify ancient gender relations. The challenge is to use the less familiar myths as well as the familiar and to become aware of the differing purposes of each tale when presented in different media. It should not surprise us that classical myth treated many different themes, so that women (and men) of all ages could find their own life experience reflected in them. The breadth of representations offers us the scope to consider not only roles such as mother or sister but many others too, such as sisters in

relation to brothers, or old women.[37] The topic of 'women in mythology'
deserves to be more than a single well-trodden path, and in turn an appreciation of the richness and complexity of classical myth will bring a fuller understanding of the relevance of gender in its interpretation.

FURTHER READING

There are many useful collections of Greek myths, such as Morford and Lenardon 2007
or Hard 2004, presenting the traditions as a coherent and chronological set of stories,
but more valuable to the scholar is Gantz's *Early Greek Myth* (Gantz: see Abbreviations),
an invaluable compendium of the variant forms of each myth found in both literature
and art. For Roman myths, Wiseman 2004 is both full and thought provoking.

Representations of myths in ancient visual media are catalogued in the *LIMC* with
excellent and full illustration. The many mythological images on Attic pottery are
gathered in the vast and searchable Beazley Archive Database (http://www.beazley.
ox.ac.uk/databases/pottery.htm).

Studies of individual mythological women are numerous: for Medea, see Clauss and
Johnston 1997 and Gentili and Perusino 2000; for Medusa, Zajko and Leonard 2006;
for Thetis, Slatkin 1991. The Routledge *Gods and Heroes of the Ancient World* series
includes studies of Athene (Deacy 2008), Diana (Glinister forthcoming), Aphrodite
(Cyrino 2010), and Medea (E. Griffiths 2006). Reeder 1995 gives an accessible presentation of the art of the major figures, with a rather conventional commentary.
Heroines have been studied by Jennifer Larson (1995) and Deborah Lyons (1997),
and nymphs by Larson (2001).

Good surveys of the development of scholarship on the topic of gender and myth
can be found in Zajko 2007 and Doherty 2001. Sister relationships, in both myth and
life, are surprisingly little studied; the best starting point is still Golden 1990. Other
interesting perspectives on myth can be found in Thomas Van Nortwick 2008 (on the
depiction of old men), and in Luc Brisson 2002.

NOTES

1. Pindar, *Pythian* 9.120–6, *Nemean* 10.1–6, Ovid, *Heroides* 14, Apollodoros 2.1.5;
    Gantz 203–8, Keuls (1974).
2. Keuls (1974: 4).
3. Zajko (2007: 397–8).
4. For example, Blundell (1995), Fantham *et al.* (1994), Reeder (1995), Just
    (1989). A notable exception is Dowden (1995), see below.
5. Best known is Carter's collection *The Bloody Chamber* (1979); see Sellers (2001).
6. Zajko and Leonard (2006): see Zajko (2007). This continues with works like
    Atwood's *Penelopiad* (2005), an interpretation of Penelope's story from the
    Odyssey, and Duffy's *The World's Wife* (1999).

7. Most influential have been the psychoanalytic approaches: see Slater (1968) and Loraux (1995, 1998). Doherty (2001) offers a good summary of the scholarship.
8. Hesiod, *Theogony* 570–616, *Works and Days* 53–105; Zeitlin (1995 and 1996, with bibliography).
9. Pindar, *Olympian* 9.42–6, 49–53, Ovid, *Metamorphoses* 1.163–312, Apollodoros 1.7.2; Gantz 164–5. On the *Ehoiai* see CH. 3 in this volume.
10. Dowden (1995), Zajko (2007: 390–1).
11. Sourvinou-Inwood (1997), March (2000), Barrett (1964: 10–15).
12. Vergil, *Aeneid* 10.495–505; see S. J. Harrison (1998) and Keuls (1974).
13. E. Griffiths (2006: 14–26); Isler-Kerényi (2000).
14. Scheffer (2001).
15. All the figures are taken from the Beazley Archive Database; the numbers are necessarily approximate, but large enough to be representative.
16. Slatkin (1991) sees the *menis* (wrath) of Thetis as the great unspoken force in the *Iliad*; see also Loraux (1998).
17. C. Weiss, 'Eos', *LIMC* 3.1 (1986: 747–89).
18. Woodford (1993: 92–3); A. Kossatz-Dreissmann, 'Memnon', *LIMC* 6.1 (1992: 448–71).
19. Shapiro (1989: 56–8); L. Kahil, 'Leto', *LIMC* 6.1 (1992: 256–64). It is note-worthy that *LIMC* catalogues the Delphic Triad scenes, and indeed all scenes of Leto and Apollo together, under 'Apollo'.
20. Larson (1995: 89–96).
21. Black-figure hydria, London British Museum B301 (from Vulci; Alcmene Painter, c. 530 BC). Even the Gorgon Medusa makes an unlikely mother on the west pediment of the Temple of Artemis at Corcyra.
22. Dowden (1989).
23. Foxhall (1989), V. J. Hunter (1989), Demand (1994: 15–17).
24. C. Weiss, 'Eos', *LIMC* 3.1 (1986: 747–89), R. Volkommer, 'Thetis', *LIMC* 8.1 (1997: 6–14), L. Kahil, 'Helene', *LIMC* 6.1 (1992: 498–563, nos 27–67).
25. Kaempf-Dimitriadou (1969); S. Lewis (2002: 199–205).
26. Dowden (1995: 53).
27. Golden (1990: 135–6), Cox (1998: ch. 4).
28. M. L. West (1985: 155–64). It has also been suggested (Hadzisteliou-Price 1971) that multiple sisters in myth are the result of a pattern of reduplication attaching particularly to female deities, but this seems to apply more to cult, where we find undifferentiated female groups such as Nymphs, Horai, or Charites; the sisters of myth tend to be differentiated by name and role. See also Larson (2001: 259–60).
29. Goldhill (1986: ch.4).
30. Ovid, *Metamorphoses* 6.424–674, Apollodoros 3.14.8; Gantz 239–41.
31. Ovid, *Metamorphoses* 4.1–42, 389–415; Aelian, *Varia Historia* 3.42, Antoninus Liberalis 10 'Minyads'. In some versions the sisters are transformed into owls.
32. Daughters of Proitos: Apollodoros 2.2.2, Bakchylides 11; see Calame (2001: 117–18); daughters of Kekrops: Euripides, *Ion* 9–26, 260–82, Ovid, *Metamorphoses* 2.552–61, Apollodoros 3.14.6; Gantz 235–8.

33. See Konstan (1997). Of other well-known pairs, Orestes and Pylades are cousins and Herakles and Iolaos, uncle and nephew; the relationship between Achilles and Patroklos is both eroticized and unequal.
34. Apollodoros 3.12.3.
35. Hesiod F 275 MW (F 211a Most, Apollodoros, *Library* 3.6.7), Ovid, *Metamorphoses* 3.322–38; Brisson (2002).
36. Kainis: Ovid, *Metamorphoses* 12.189–535; Iphis: *Met.* 9.666–797, Antoninus Liberalis 17 'Leukippos'; Helen and the Spartan baby: Herodotos 6.61; see Austin (1994: 32).
37. Van Nortwick (2008: ch. 6) offers an excellent study of old men in myth.

CHAPTER TWENTY-FOUR

Mythology of the Black Land: Greek Myths and Egyptian Origins

Ian Rutherford

Egypt in Greek Myth

Greek myths about Egypt have elicited great interest in recently, particularly in response to the 'Afro-centrist' reading of them set out in Martin Bernal's *Black Athena* (1987–2006), which sees in them the 'Ancient Model' for Bernal's theory of the origins of Greek culture from Egypt. An opposing view, in vogue since the publication of Edith Hall's book *Inventing the Barbarian* in 1989, is that Greek traditions about Egypt have nothing to do with ancient events and everything to do with Greek self-definition. There is, I believe, another view between these which sees Greek myths about Egypt neither as a record of historical events nor wholly as a Greek construction but as at least to some extent indebted to contemporary Egyptian mythological and historical traditions.

The people of Greek mythology with the best claim to be 'black' are, of course, not the Egyptians, but the Aithiopes (Ethiopians): the Greek name *Aithiopes* (*Aithiops* in the singular) may be translated 'with burned face'. They are located south of Egypt in Nubia in historical sources, but for Homer in either the distant east or the distant west, close to the sun at its rising or setting.[1] Homer tells us that the gods feast with the Aithiopes, clearly a Golden Age motif – just as Apollo is elsewhere said to feast with the Hyperboreans of the far North. In general they were considered the paradigm of piety.[2]

A Companion to Greek Mythology, First Edition. Edited by Ken Dowden and Niall Livingstone.
© 2014 John Wiley & Sons Ltd. Published 2014 by John Wiley & Sons Ltd.

An early attempt to incorporate the Aithiopes into a Greek mythological framework is made in the Hesiodic *Catalogue of Women* F 150 MW (98 Most) (for this work see CH. 3). Here we are presented with a list of miscellaneous races mothered by Gaia, including the Skythians, whose father was Zeus, the 'Blacks' (Greek *Melanes*), the Aithiopes, the Subterraneans (Gk *Katoudaioi*: perhaps the same people as the Trogodytai, later to become Troglodytai/ Troglodytes),[3] and the Pygmies, whose father was Poseidon. All seem to be imagined as living in the south.[4] These groups are not related to the main families of Greek genealogy except through their descent from Gaia and, in some cases, from other important gods.

The most famous Ethiopian in Greek mythology is Memnon, son of Tithonos and Dawn (Eos) and focal figure of the cyclic epic *Aithiopis*, where he appears as a champion on the Trojan side (see CH. 2). The fact that Memnon's mother is Dawn points to origins in the extreme east, and Memnon is often associated with the Persian city of Sousa.[5] On the other hand, from the Hellenistic period Greeks connected him with area of Egyptian Thebes, particularly the two statues of the New Kingdom pharaoh Amenhotep III and with the mortuary temple of another New Kingdom pharaoh, Seti I, at Abydos.[6] Some modern scholars believe that the name might be a distant memory of either Amenemhet of the Twelfth Dynasty (Bernal) or Amenhotep III (Griffith).[7]

By the classical period, the Aithiopes in general (though not Memnon himself) are represented in art as having Black-African physical features of the sort that the Egyptians themselves had long associated with Nubia (Snowden 1996). Egyptians did not represent themselves in the same way, and the Greeks followed their example, though it is worth noting that Herodotos (2.104) identifies the inhabitants of Kolchis as descendants of the Egyptian soldiers who accompanied Sesostris on his campaigns on the grounds of their appearance: ὅτι μελάγχροές εἰσι καὶ οὐλότριχες ('because they are black-skinned and woolly haired').

Greek Myth and Egyptian Myth

Compared with the land of the Aithiopes, Egypt is much more accessible in Greek mythology. Menelaos and Helen have gifts from the Egyptian queen (*Odyssey* 4.125–35, 227–30). Odysseus claims, in one of his lying tales, to have stayed there seven years (*Odyssey* 14.285–6), an episode that sounds like a distant reflection of the attacks of the Sea Peoples recorded in New Kingdom temples. We know that in the Bronze Age people from the Aegean did actually visit Egypt. These links are reinforced by genealogical connections: one Egyptian royal family, that of Aigyptos and Danaos, is drawn from one of the

Greek mythological families, the Inachidai of Argos, and even the all-important Egyptian deity Isis is given a Greek origin.

Like all ancient cultures, Egypt had a rich tradition of culturally central narratives of the sort we would call 'myths', and such narratives were probably in existence from the earliest period.[8] On the face of it, the chief Egyptian myths that survive are focused on early traditions about the gods. Examples include several spectacular theogonies; the myth of Osiris and the subsequent conflicts of Horus and Seth; the myth of the Heavenly Cow, concerning the origin of mankind; and the myth of the anger of the goddess Tefnut, the 'Sun's Eye', who leaves Egypt and has to be brought back by the god Thoth.[9] That may be partly because the sources are official religious texts. Although we know quite a lot about the exploits of human beings (particularly pharaohs) in early Egypt, these traditions are not normally thought of as 'myth' by modern scholars because they come to us as the official records, often self-authored, of historical figures who really existed. Alongside these there may have existed popular traditions about great men of the past, such as Sesostris, but our evidence for these is greatly inferior, often dependent on late Egyptian or even Greek sources. There are traces of local mythological traditions as well.[10]

Egyptian myth has more in common with Greek myth than is often realized. While explicit awareness of Egyptian mythology does not show up in Greek sources until the fifth century BC,[11] and we find clear signs of influence in cosmogonic texts from the period of the Roman Empire,[12] there may have been diffusion earlier on. It has been suggested that the motif of one primeval deity castrating another (conventionally regarded as Greek, with probable Near Eastern background) occurs in Egyptian texts, and that the Orphic myth of a cosmic egg is Egyptian.[13] The idea of a Golden Age when men and gods consorted is attested in Egyptian sources, as is the idea that in this period Justice (Ma'at) descended to earth.[14] The idea of a judicial council of gods is common to Greek and Egyptian mythology.[15] The idea and name of the Sphinx could be Egyptian.[16] Other influences have been detected in the Hellenistic period.[17] Some have suggested that major aspects of Greek religion, such as Dionysos or the Underworld, were influenced by Egypt.[18] Martin Bernal has detected many further mythological parallels. For example, the motif that 'a cow determines where to found a city' appears in Greek myth in the foundation story of the city of Thebes, where it is connected with the Theban goddess Athene Onga or Onka.[19] It appears also in an Egyptian text of the Roman period from the town of Esna, in which Neith (the Egyptian goddess conventionally identified with Athene by the Greeks), in the form of a cow, founds Sais.[20]

Individual cases of borrowing are not provable, but it is probably right to think of Egyptian mythology as part of the general myth-ritual *koine* (shared language) of the eastern Mediterranean and western Asia. The direction of borrowing is not necessarily always from Egypt. It has been argued, for example, that the Greek mytheme of the dismemberment of Dionysos might have influenced Egyptian narratives about Osiris, and even that late Egyptian representations of divine conflict might reflect Homer.[21]

Egyptian Tales in Greece

We have an initial problem of definition. The simplest course would be to class as myth stories that ended up being considered part of myth by Apollodoros and other Greek mythographers. On this principle the story of the Danaids would be in, but other stories about Egyptians colonizing Greece (such as the story of Sais and Athens: see below) would be out. Equally, Herodotos' story about the world-conquering Sesostris would be out, because the father of history regarded it as historical. This is a little arbitrary, and in practice it makes more sense to include both types of story in the manner outlined below.

Stories of the Egyptian colonization of Greece

The myth-complex of the Danaids,
The Danaid myth-complex was attested from the time of the Hesiodic *Catalogue* (F 127–128 MW, 75 and 76a Most) and the epic *Danais* (Gantz 203), probably developed by the historian Hekataios of Miletos (Burstein 2009), and given canonical form in Aeschylus' *Suppliants*. Danaos flees from Egypt to Argos with his daughters, pursued by his brother Aigyptos and his sons, who are intent on forcing the daughters into marriage. In the Hellenistic period, the Hellenized Egyptian writer Manetho[22] identified Aigyptos and Danaos with figures of Egyptian history: Aigyptos with Sethos-Ramesses (the name sounds like a pharaoh of the Nineteenth Dynasty) and Danaos with his brother Harmais. In Manetho's version it is Harmais-Danaos, left in Egypt when Sethos-Ramesses-Aigyptos is campaigning abroad, who engages in sexual aggression: was Manetho altering Greek myth to create a version less offensive to Egyptian sensibilities?

The brothers are descended from the line of Inachos of Argos, via Io, who wandered in the form of a cow to Egypt. Danaos' descendants in Greece included Danae and Perseus. The names Danaos/Danae suggest the Homeric term for the Greeks, *Danaoi*, which may well have a Bronze Age origin.[23] Io gives birth to Epaphos, touched by the hand of Zeus,[24] and Epaphos' daughter Libya is the matriarch of all the eastern family lines. One of her sons, Belos (whose name obviously comes from the Semitic divine name Ba'al) is father of Aigyptos, Danaos, and Thronie, mother of Arabos. Her other son, Agenor, is father of Phoenix, Kadmos, and Kepheus, father of Andromeda. Zeus Ammon is another son of Libya in later tradition (Colin 1997).

The bovine figure of Io suggests the bovine Egyptian goddess Hathor, often identified with Isis, who is thus given a Greek origin; centuries later, Plutarch asserts that 'Isis' is a Greek name.[25] Epaphos was identified with the Apis bull (who is not the child of Isis or any other goddess in the Egyptian version). The name 'Apis' also seems to have been an eponymous hero in the Peloponnese (an alternative name for which was the 'Apian land': e.g., Aeschylus, *Agamemnon* 256–7), who may at an early date have been identified with the Egyptian bull deity; Aeschylus' assertion that the Peloponnesian Apis is a Greek (from Naupaktos: *Suppliants* 262) seems to be a calculated revision of that tradition.[26]

The story of the Danaids is not the only myth of Egyptian colonization:

Athens and Sais

The idea that Athens was founded in the tenth millennium BC from Sais in Egypt (home of the goddess Neith, in Greek eyes the Egyptian equivalent of Athene) is first related in Plato's *Timaios* in the context of the Atlantis myth, attributed to an Egyptian source of the sixth century BC. This was in fact a refoundation after Athens was destroyed by an earthquake, and some time after Athens and Egypt had defeated the empire of Atlantis. Athens in its earlier incarnation was actually older than Sais, which could therefore itself be the colony (though Plato does not say this). Whether or not the Atlantis myth predates Plato, the link between Athens and Sais is likely to be much older.[27]

Sesostris and Kolchis

In his account of Egyptian history, Herodotos tells the story of Sesostris, who undertook campaigns throughout Western Asia (2.104). It was troops left behind from his army who colonized Kolchis (on the Black Sea, roughly modern Abkhazia), which explains, Herodotos tells us, the characteristic skin and hair of the Kolchians. Fragments of the story of Sesostris survive in both Greek and Demotic Egyptian versions in the Hellenistic period.[28]

A general colonization

This is more what we find in the fourth-century BC philosopher and historian Hekataios of Abdera, as summarized by Diodoros, 1.28:[29]

> Now the Egyptians say that also after these events a great number of colonies were spread from Egypt over all the inhabited world. To Babylon, for instance, colonists were led by Belus, who was held to be the son of Poseidon and Libya; and after establishing himself on the Euphrates river he appointed priests, called Chaldaeans by the Babylonians, who were exempt from taxation and free from

every kind of service to the state, as are the priests of Egypt; and they also make observations of the stars, following the example of the Egyptian priests, physicists, and astrologers. They say also that those who set forth with Danaus, likewise from Egypt, settled what is practically the oldest city in Greece, Argos, and that the nation of the Colchi in Pontus and that of the Jews, which lies between Arabia and Syria, were founded as colonies by certain emigrants from their country; and this is the reason why it is a long-established institution amongst these two peoples to circumcise their male children, the custom having been brought over from Egypt. Even the Athenians, they say, are colonists from Saïs in Egypt, and they undertake to offer proofs of such a relationship; for the Athenians are the only Greeks who call their city 'Asty,' a name brought over from the city Asty in Egypt. Furthermore, their body politic... (tr. Oldfather)

So we have five acts of colonization: in addition to Kolchis, Argos, and Athens, we now have Belos going to Babylon and the Jewish migration. The latter is clearly motivated by the Exodus narrative, which must have become known to Greek historians around this time; Manetho attempted[30] to fit both Exodus and the Danaids into the matrix of Egyptian history. The figure of Belos seems to come from the genealogy of the Inachids, which implies that, as the son of Epaphos, he was born in Egypt; we might have expected Agenor to be mentioned as well, perhaps as the colonizer of Phoenicia. No Egyptian colonist founds Macedon in this text, but Macedon is one of the children of the Egyptian culture hero Osiris in Hekataios/ Diodoros' rationalizing narrative (Diodoros 1.18). Hekataios' colonization narrative is a Ptolemaic rewriting of Mediterranean history, with Egypt as its point of origin (Hekataios was probably employed as an official by Ptolemy I Soter, founder of the Ptolemaic dynasty in Egypt).[31] The third-century BC scholar Istros, known as 'the Callimachean', later wrote a work called *Aigyptiōn Apoikiai* (*Colonies of the Egyptians*) which dealt with Danaos and other matters (*FGrH* 334 F 43–46).[32]

Egyptian violence

The chief example here is Bousiris, the violent king of Egypt, who attempts to sacrifice Herakles. Bousiris's name goes back to the name of an Egyptian town sacred to Osiris (*Pr-Wsjrj* = 'House of Osiris'), but the figure cannot be traced back to an Egyptian original, although his Osirian associations suggest the conflict between Osiris/Horus as the forces of order and Seth. This tradition is first attested in the genealogical writer Pherekydes of Athens and the epic poet Panyassis of Halikarnassos (both early fifth century BC).[33] Panyassis' younger relative Herodotos is disbelieving of it (2.45), but later Greek historians, such as Manetho and Diodoros, are more willing to accept it.[34] Even Egyptologists who doubt whether human sacrifice was practiced in Egypt, at least since pre-dynastic times, concede that the language official texts use to describe the punishment of enemies sometimes suggests human sacrifice.[35] The French Egyptologist Yoyotte has shown that human sacrifice is consistent with the language of Egyptian religious texts, such as the 'Ritual for Repelling Evil'.[36]

Note that Herakles' other African adversary, Antaios, seems to be imagined as located in Libya or Mauritania, even though in the Hellenistic period the name Antaios came to be used for the Egyptian deity 'ntywy of the tenth Nome of Upper Egypt.[37]

Other myths

According to an aetiology promulgated by Pindar (F 58), the oracles of Zeus Ammon at Siwa and of Zeus at Dodona were both founded either by two doves who flew from Thebes in Egypt (seat of Amun-Re, often identified with Zeus-Ammon) or (in the Greek version) by two priestesses abducted by Phoenicians from the same place. The two most important oracles in the Greek world at this time apart from Delphi are thus linked by a common Egyptian aetiology. It makes perfect sense for the oracle of Ammon, situated in an oasis half way between Kyrene and the Nile, to be a foundation from Egyptian Thebes, but the claim that the Greek oracle at Dodona is Egyptian in origin is much more surprising.[38]

Plato, on the other hand, presents two significant Egyptian myths: one is the myth of Atlantis, which is attributed to Egyptian sources (see above); the second, in the *Phaedrus*, is that of the god Thoth's invention of writing and its rejection by king Thamous (a rationalized version of Ammon-Re?), on the grounds that it is not after all a 'drug for memory', but 'drug for forgetfulness'.[39] The idea that writing damages civilization seems less at home in Egypt than in Greece, where oral traditions were more recent.[40] And Thoth is not said to have invented writing in any Egyptian source, though he was associated with perception (*sia*) and knowledge (*rekh*), and is regularly said to have distinguished the different languages.[41] An Egyptian model of some kind for the story of Thoth and Thamous cannot, therefore, be ruled out.[42]

Interpretations

Most scholars today are inclined to hold that these myths are historical only insofar as they reflect the ideology of the period they come from, not because they transmit authentic traditions from the distant past. In other words, Greek myths dealing with Egypt are no more historical than Greek myths about the fantastical Aithiopes. Ideological positions that Greek myths of Egypt seem to encapsulate include:

1   Egyptians are not like us Greeks, they are barbarian. Specifically, they are aggressive, and in particular sexually aggressive: one of the main themes of the Danaid myth is that forced marriage is wrong (cf. Zeitlin 1992). They sacrifice strangers. They are 'dark', an association which to the Greeks might suggest the chthonic sphere.[43] They are also renowned for mysterious drugs, such as those which Helen is said to have acquired in Egypt at *Odyssey* 4.227–32, and for strange wisdom, such as that of Thoth in the story in Plato's *Phaedrus*.

2   Because our ancestors came from a distant, ancient, and prestigious culture, we are superior to other Greeks whose ancestors came from less ancient and prestigious places or were indigenous. Paradoxically, that does not make us foreign, because our ancestors' ancestors were themselves from Greece – a genealogical space-time loop. Views about origins are subject to negotiation, though, and we seem to see signs even in Greek sources of dialogue between different such views: the 'Egyptomanic' view that the eponym of the 'Apian' Peloponnese is the Apis bull is answered by Aeschylus' claim that it was in fact a home-grown Apis from Naupaktos. The 'Egyptomanic' view that Athens was founded from Sais found in Plato's Atlantis story and in Hekataios is perhaps answered by the Atthidographers (local historians of Athens and Attica), who assert the autochthonous origin of Athens.[44]

Martin Bernal's position is that Greek myths about Egyptian colonization preserve a record of historical events. This is what he calls the 'Ancient Model' of the origins of Greece, which was later replaced by the modern model of Indo-European origins. Specifically, Bernal believes that the Egyptians established a colony at Greek Thebes in the Twelfth Dynasty in the time of Senwosret II ('Sesostris'), that is, in the nineteenth century BC, and that the Herakles myth preserves the memory of an Egyptian ruler there. The Hyksos rulers who were expelled from Egypt at the end of the Second Intermediate Period and the start of the New Kingdom (sixteenth century BC) then also migrated to Greece, giving rise to the myth of the Danaids. In Bernal's view, Greek ideas about Minoan Crete also have their origins in the cultural matrix of Hyksos-Egyptian culture. Thus, the myth of Minos and the Minotaur have Egyptian origins, Minos himself being a form of the Egyptian deity Min.

It must be admitted that classicists have traditionally been readier to dismiss any historical basis myths about Egyptian origin than for myths about early migrations from the north or across the Aegean, or migration from the Orient (Kadmos), or indeed for the story of the Trojan War, on which see CH. 22 in this volume (although, of course, plenty of people have dismissed all these as well). We should at least be consistent in our approach. And, it can be argued, the tendency to rule out the possibility that myths encode historical events can be taken too far: Jan Vansina's work on oral tradition provides at least a basic justification for the thesis that this is possible (Vansina 1965, 1985). So why not take the Danaids at face value?

The answer must be that the sensible way of dealing with the issue of the historicity of myths is to give them credence if and only if there is external evidence that supports it. In the case of the myth of Egyptian colonization of Greece, we have remarkably little corroborative evidence from Greece: very little archaeology or material culture, no undisputed evidence of significance influence on the language, religion, or society. Furthermore, Egyptian documentary records from the second millennium BC provide no certain evidence for Egyptian interventions in the Aegean. The best evidence is a list of apparently Aegean place names from statue bases at Egyptian Thebes, which show that Egyptians either visited these places or received tribute from them, but cannot prove that they established colonies there. One might contrast the case of the tradition of Trojan War, which has found a limited but significant degree of corroboration in archaeology and in Hittite historical documents (see CH. 22 in this volume). Considering its evident power, it is remarkable how little evidence there is for expansion by Egypt in the Mediterranean, with the exception of the southern Levantine coast.[45] (To that extent, the Jewish tradition of an early connection with Egypt is slightly more defensible than the Greek one).

A third position, somewhere between simply accepting or denying their historical basis, is that Greek myths and traditions about Egypt to some extent continue hypothetical Egyptian traditions which Greeks may have encountered in Egypt in the seventh to fifth century BC, and indeed which might have arisen precisely in the context of contact between Egyptians and foreigners in this period. Such traditions were probably at least partly orally transmitted, though they may also have been written down in new demotic script; at any rate, the media would have to have been distinct from the official documents that survive. As Loprieno has shown, this was a period when Egyptians' views about their past may have been going through a radical transformation: on the one hand a sense may have been developing that they are cut off from the past glories of the Bronze Age, and on the other hand, in compensation for that traditions develop which emphasize the power of Egypt. The key example of this is the Sesostris story, which seems to have already been known to Herodotos in the fifth century BC,[46] and may have arisen in Egypt in response to foreign domination. As we have seen, the Sesostris story included the establishment of one colony in Kolchis; for all we know, other Egyptian oral traditions were already experimenting with the idea that Egypt founded colonies in Greece. The tradition about the link between Sais and Athens could conceivably have been promulgated from the Egyptian side.

FURTHER READING

The best guide in English is Vasunia 2001. For Egyptian mythology, see Lichtheim 1973–80 and Simpson 2003. Martin Bernal's historicizing use of Greek mythology relating to Egypt is set out in Bernal 1987–2006: vol. 2 (1991). For the idea of Egyptian influence on Greek mythology, see Burkert 2004. For Egyptian influence on Greek mythology in the Hellenistic period, see Noegel 2004.

NOTES

1. See, for example, Ballabriga (1986), Romm (1992).
2. Snowden (1970 at 150) suggests that the eponymous founder of Delphi, Delphos, who in some versions had a mother whose name meant 'black', may have been imagined as of Ethiopian origin.
3. See Herodotos 4.183.
4. Hirschberger (2004 *ad loc.*).
5. Snowden (1970: 151 with n. 48). He is buried at Paltos in Syria according to Simonides, *PMG* 539, cf. Gantz 622–4; this points to the later geographical confusion between Ethiopia and India.
6. See Bataille (1952); add Demetrios 643 *FGrH* (and *BNJ* with English translation and commentary) F 1 = Athenaios 15.680ab.
7. For the Memnonion and Memnon, see Rutherford (2003). Bernal (1987–2006: 2.257–69); Griffith (1998).
8. Definition of Egyptian myth: Baines (1996a); early existence: Baines (1991); *contra*, Assmann (1977), who thinks they started in the New Kingdom; a good survey of motifs in Sternberg-El Hotabi (1985).
9. Theogonies: Van Dijk (1995: 1699–1702); J. P. Allen (1988); Horus and Seth: Lichtheim (1973–80: 2.214–23); Simpson (2003: 93–103); the myth of the 'Heavenly Cow': Lichtheim (1973–80: 2.197–9); Simpson (2003: 289–98); the 'Sun's Eye': Lichtheim (1973–80: 3.156–9 (excerpt)), S. West (1969).
10. Examples include the Papyrus Jumilhac, which relates to the seventeenth Nome of Upper Egypt (Vandier 1962; Derchain 1990) and P. Brooklyn 47.218.84, which relates to the Delta (Meeks 2006).
11. Pindar F 91 refers to the gods turning into animals, which looks Egyptian (J. Gwyn Griffiths 1960; see Rutherford, CH. 5 in this volume); Hellanikos *FGrH* 4 F 54 (on which see Derchain 1956) refers to the gathering of the gods at the city of Tindion; both incidents are connected with the story of Typhon.
12. Bergman (1982); Broze (2003); Sauneron (1961).
13. Castration: Meltzer (1974); egg: Morenz (1950). On the category of 'Orphic' myth see CH. 4 in this volume.
14. Otto (1969), Hornung (1982a). On Ma'at, see also Faraone and Teeter (2004).
15. Greek: Long (1987: 75–7); Egyptian: Meeks and Favard-Meeks (1996, 40–6).

16. E. L. Brown (1974), with Goedicke (1970); cf. Bernal (1987–2006: 3.465) with McGready (1968: 250); for an alternative view, J. Katz (2006).

17. See, for example, Noegel (2004) on Egyptian solar mythology and Apollonios' *Argonautika*, and Stephens (2003 *passim*). On Delos and Egyptian myth, see Selden (1998: 388–405).

18. Burkert (2004) on Dionysos and Osiris; R. D. Griffith (1997c) on the Underworld.

19. Hellanikos *FGrH* 4 F 51; Pausanias 9.12.2–3.

20. Bernal 2.101–2; El-Sayed (1982, n.1024 2.634–5); Sauneron (1962: 270) (not identified as the source in Bernal): when she reached Sais, on the evening of the thirteenth of Epiphi, this was a great and grand festival in the sky, on the earth, and in every land. She then took the form of the goddess Wreret; she took her bow in her fist, bent it in her hand, and fixed herself at the castle of Neith, with her son Re.

21. Casadio (1996), Derchain (1974); cf. Walcot (1962) on the relationship between Hesiod's *Works and Days* and the Egyptian *Instructions of 'Onchsheshonqy*.

22. *FGrH* 609 F 9a and 10a: see Verbrugghe and Wickersham (1996) for translation.

23. It is also interested that in some Bronze Age Egyptian sources the term 'Tanaya' (Tnyw) seems to refer to Greece (Latacz 2004: 130, Edel 1966).

24. The name Epaphos suggests the Greek verb *ephaptō* meaning, amongst other things, 'lay hands on'. In Sophocles' *Inachos*, Io may have been impregnated by a 'sooty' (Greek *aithos*) Zeus: see Seaford (1980), S. West (1984).

25. Richter (2001).

26. Froidefond (1971: 108).

27. Vasunia (2001, esp. 229–36); J. Gwyn Griffiths (1983).

28. On Sesostris, see Malaise (1966). Kolchis plays a role in Bernal's modern mythopoesis (1987–2006: 2. 245–57).

29. O. Murray (1970).

30. In a somewhat confused manner to judge from Josephus' summary in *Against Apion* 1.93–105 (*FGrH* 609 F 9a).

31. Quack (2005: 24) claims to have found evidence for Osiris as a culture hero in demotic texts.

32. See Fraser (1972: 512, 738); S. Jackson (2000).

33. *FGrH* 3 F 17; F 12 *PEG*.

34. See J. Gwyn Griffiths (1948). Manetho *FGrH* 609 F 22 (Plutarch, *On Isis and Osiris* 73, 380c–d) mentions 'Typhonian men' burnt alive at Eileithyiapolis, and F 14 (Porphyry *On Abstinence* 2.55) mentions human sacrifice to Hera at Heliopolis, which the pharaoh 'Amosis' replaced with the offering of wax dummies. Diodoros tells of 'red men' being sacrificed near the grave of Osiris (1.88).

35. Lloyd (1975–88: 2.213–15) cites Caminos (1958: 48) but argues that this is about punishment, not sacrifice.

36. Yoyotte (1980–1).

37. See BNP s.v. 'Antaeus' (Graf).

38. Bernal (1987–2006: 3.187) claims that Dodona is equivalent to a cult name *Ddwn* under which Zeus-Ammon was worshipped at Siwa, referring to English (1959), but that article refers to 'the name Dedun of the great god of Cush on the Nile' (51). Kuhlmann (1988: 53–7) sees the myth as part of the Osiris myth.

39. On Plato's use of myth see CH. 9 in this volume.

40. The thought had been expressed a few decades earlier in Euripides' *Palamedes* F 578.

41. Perception and wisdom: Meeks and Favard-Meeks (1996: 101); languages: Meeks and Favard-Meeks (1996: 103), Cerny (1948), Sauneron (1960).

42. Meeks and Favard-Meeks (1996: 100–2).

43. Notice that 'sooty Zeus' in Sophocles' *Inachos* (see S. West 1984) may have a chthonic aspect, just as the list of peoples in Hesiod F 150 MW (98 Most) seems to suggest peoples of the earth.

44. Thus, for Phanodemos Athens founded Sais: *FGrH* 325 F 25 and see Jacoby at *FGrH* IIIB, 193–4; also Jacoby on Philochoros *FGrH* 328 F 93 IIIB 389–90.

45. A good guide is Redford (1992).

46. The name Sesostris is also restored as a conjecture by Bergk, on the basis of a comparison with Herodotos, in a fragment of the late sixth-century BC iambic poet Hipponax (F 42.3 West).

CHAPTER TWENTY-FIVE

Psychoanalysis:
The Wellspring of Myth?

Richard H. Armstrong

Myth and the Beginnings of Psychoanalysis

We cannot begin this discussion of psychoanalytical approaches to myth without first recognizing how much psychoanalysis itself has relied upon myth from its inception in the early work of Sigmund Freud (1856–1939). For Freud, the recourse to myth illustrated the disciplinary power of psychoanalysis to elucidate the evolution and workings of the human mind across history, even from remotest antiquity. Freud approached myth as the product of the 'childhood' of the human species, built upon analogy with the childhood of the individual. This approach exemplifies the pervasive influence on thinkers of his era of the view that the development of the individual replays the development of the whole species, encapsulated in 'Haeckel's Law': 'ontogeny recapitulates phylogeny'.[1]

Though originally a clinical technique devised by Vienna neurologists, psychoanalysis quickly developed into an all-encompassing 'science of the mind', or more specifically, a science of decoding the meaning of such disparate phenomena as hysterical symptoms, dreams, parapraxes (what are colloquially known as 'Freudian slips'), literature, art, religion, and myth. As a traditional narrative form embodying enigmatic but supposedly universal truths, myth represented to Freud and his followers a treasure trove of collective unconscious thinking akin to dreams. Freud even referred to myth as 'the age-old dreams of youthful humanity'.[2]

Since myth appears like the anonymous product of a collective process, it seems to form a bridge between the radically personal and hermetic content

---

of dreams – an area of great concern in psychoanalytic therapy – and the world of public meaning. Unlike the work of art or literature, myth is not usually seen as forged by the individual creative mind alone, and so it cannot be dismissed as a whim or individual fancy. Thus myth is a fact of collective experience – even if that experience is merely the common one of anxiety or desire, as psychoanalysis so often insists. To speak of myth psychoanalytically is to use it as a universal transcript of the human mind.

Why Apply Psychoanalysis to Myth?

Psychoanalysis developed a systematic approach to myth in the early twentieth century. At this time, Freud's burgeoning psychoanalytic movement began to attract followers who were either lay persons, such as Otto Rank (1884–1939) and Theodor Reik (1888–1969), or medical men like Freud with a humanistic education and broad cultural interests, such as Karl Abraham (1877–1925), Fritz Wittels (1880–1950), Ernest Jones (1879–1958), and Carl Gustav Jung (1875–1961).[3] While Freud expressed in broad outline the relevance of myth to psychoanalysis, he left the detailed analysis to students of culture such as Rank.[4]

As happens in many intellectual revolutions, a tendency to work quickly and eclectically in making new claims based on a compelling theory sometimes discredited psychoanalytic interpretation of myth in the eyes of professional classicists and other scholars.[5] In-fighting amongst members of the movement itself often took on quasi-mythic proportions, as Freud's heirs sought to challenge his work by reinterpreting key myths, particularly that of Oedipus (of which more below).

It is certainly possible to object that psychoanalytic interpretations lurch toward reductiveness, or tend to generate systematic interpretations that translate the narrative into a set of pre-established truths. Such objections, however, are not unique to the case of psychoanalysis; in fact, they can be made of many other schools of myth interpretation, going back to the Stoics and Neoplatonists in antiquity (for discussion of some Neoplatonist uses of myth, see Dowden in CH. 15).

The psychological approach should remain a voice in the choir of myth interpretation. One cannot delve into the regions of religious and political thought without awareness of psychological issues, particularly in reference to the nature of collective memory or how religion functions to address human anxieties and aspirations. Psychoanalysis becomes especially relevant when myth is centred on intergenerational strife, for instance in the context of theogonies, or when dreams are integral to a mythic narrative.

In addition, the history of psychoanalytic reading of myth is also an essential part of twentieth-century culture, part of the modern 'work on myth' which the German thinker Hans Blumenberg identified as characteristic of post-Enlightenment thought.[6] If we retain the view that myth is still an important part of the story of humanity, psychoanalysis remains 'good to think with' as we come to grips with mythic narrative.

The contention of the approach is that myth performs – amongst other things – vital psychological functions. As Caldwell formulates them, they are

1 to 'allow the expression of unconscious, usually repressed, ideas in a conventional and socially sanctioned form';
2 to 'use the emotional content attached to these ideas to energize other, nonemotional functions of myth'; and
3 to 'provide a societal response to psychological needs, whether universal or culture-specific'.[7]

Case Study: Freud's Oedipal Insights

We can see the early investment of psychoanalysis in myth in Freud's letter to his friend and confidant, Wilhelm Fliess. This contains the first mention of what would later be termed the 'Oedipus complex'. Here Freud reflects upon a major shift in his thinking: what he previously thought were memories of sexual abuse in his patients are actually instances of childhood fantasy. Suddenly Freud realizes why Sophocles' drama *Oedipus Tyrannus* could have such success upon the modern stage, in spite of the fact that its ostensible themes are so remote from the modern audience: 'The Greek legend seizes upon a compulsion which everyone recognizes because he senses its existence within himself. Everyone in the audience was once a budding Oedipus in fantasy and each recoils in horror from the dream fulfillment here transplanted into reality, with the full quantity of repression which separates his infantile state from his present one.'[8]

In essence, Freud's claim is that an unconscious content of the myth is still very much available to the modern audience since we all undergo the 'reality' of fantasizing about these Oedipal crimes during a stage of our early development. This experience is later repressed, but not erased. It lingers in the unconscious as a repressed desire and can be reawakened by the subtle manipulation of narrative (as in Sophocles' play) or the process of dreaming. In both cases, there is a disjunction between what is 'manifest' – the action of Sophocles' play as we see it or the dream as we dream it – and what is 'latent' – the experiential truth of 'Oedipal' desire. The powerful emotional impact of the Oedipus myth is proof, Freud contends, of the quantity of repression needed to bury this desire within us as civilized moderns. The audience's intense reaction comes about through the release of tensions in our minds, which we experience consciously as aesthetic pleasure, though its roots lie deep in our life histories.

It is useful to trace Freud's continuing interpretation of the Oedipus myth, since the complex which takes its name from it would become a cornerstone of Freudian developmental and cultural theory, and it remains the prime example of the psychoanalytic approach to myth. As Freud developed his interpretation a few years later in his seminal work, *The Interpretation of Dreams* (1900), he began to tie the universal nature of the psychological complex to the universal appeal of the myth:

> This discovery [i.e., of the existence of oedipal feelings in all people] is confirmed by a legend that has come down to us from classical antiquity: a legend whose profound and *universal power to move* can only be understood if the hypothesis I have put forward in regard to the psychology of children *has an equally universal validity*. What I have in mind is the legend of King Oedipus and Sophocles' drama which bears his name.[9]

The circularity of reasoning here has troubled many people, but it stems from Freud's desire to see in the inalterable workings of fate that plague Oedipus a symbolic expression of a universal human situation:

> His destiny moves us only because it might have been ours – because the oracle laid the same curse upon us before our birth as upon him. It is the fate of all of us, perhaps, to direct our first sexual impulse towards our mother and our first hatred and our first murderous wish against our father. Our dreams convince us that that is so.[10]

Here we see how Freud detects direct evidence of a correlation between the 'oedipal' content in common dreams and the ancient myth of Oedipus. The discovery of powerfully ambivalent feelings in his patients towards their parents – feelings typified by the extremes of incestuous lust and homicidal rage – led him to hypothesize a stage of psycho-sexual development at which one undergoes, almost as a natural law, a dire mental conflict. We must face this conflict through no fault of our own, like Oedipus. But unlike Oedipus, most healthy people forego bringing these desires for sexual possession or murder into reality and pass through this crisis by renouncing and repressing them. But the conflict, though consciously overcome, is merely relegated to the unconscious, and the divided mind works imperfectly to keep it under house arrest. Any relaxation of repression can lead to its reawakening and re-expression, as occurs in dreaming. When an audience member innocently goes to see Sophocles' tragedy, he is lulled into a state of passive enjoyment; but through a process of identification with Oedipus, he comes to experience powerful emotions: in sum, he *re*-experiences the 'Oedipal' feelings he once knew and to an extent will always retain in the unconscious. The uncanny relationship between childhood experience and archaic narratives thus explains the compelling interest of myth long after its original social and religious context has disappeared.

Freud's *modus operandi* requires us to look at myth as a set of conflicts, symptoms, and compromises. For example, in order to make his case, Freud turned the myth of Oedipus into a riddle from the start: why can a story so caught up in the archaic notion of 'fate' and the will of the gods still appeal to people today, who eschew such fatalism? We might reply that it remains a serious philosophical or theological problem, or alternatively, that our interest is in fact aesthetic and thus independent of this moral, philosophical or theological apparatus. His answer, however, is that the story is actually about something other than the tragic failure of a man to avoid his fate, which in itself would not make a very compelling story. In Freud's analysis, Sophocles seems to have succeeded with *Oedipus* almost in spite of his conscious intentions as a playwright, since the myth was saying more through him than he could possibly have intended.

> It is a surprising thing that the tragedy of Sophocles does not call up indignant repudiation in his audience … For fundamentally it is an amoral work: it absolves men from moral responsibility, exhibits the gods as promoters of crime and shows the impotence of the moral impulses of men which struggle against crime. It might easily be supposed that the material of the legend had in view an indictment of the gods and of fate; and in the hands of Euripides, the critic and enemy of the gods, it would probably have become such an indictment. But with the devout Sophocles there is no question of an application of that kind. The difficulty is overcome by the *pious sophistry* that to bow to the will of the gods is the highest morality even when it promotes crime. I cannot think that this morality is a strong point of the play, but it has *no influence on its effect*. It is not to it that the auditor reacts but to the *secret sense and content* of the legend.[11]

To understand the story, then, one must penetrate beyond its narrative surface and plumb the depths of its psychic content. This is something only psychoanalysis is able to do for us, Freud claims, as it possesses the most thoroughly tested means of decoding deep psychological messages, as a result of long clinical practice. Myths, religions, and great artists are able to *send* such messages, but only a psychoanalytic understanding will enable one to ferret out their psychic truth.

Freudian psychoanalysis grew to ensconce the Oedipus complex as central to both its individual and social psychology, and as such, the myth of Oedipus is literally emblematic of the psychoanalytic movement. Later developments in psychoanalytic theory have led to different emphases, but a common pattern remains. Myth is understood as the encoded expression not just of childhood experience, but also of a kind of forgotten folklore of childhood, a belief system we find hard to recognize as conscious adults.

Psychoanalytic interpretation finds behind, say, theogonic myth the childhood residue of birth trauma, longing for symbiotic bondedness, sexual curiosity and its attendant anxiety, the pains and joys of individuation, or the gothic drama of Oedipal revolt and castration anxiety. A first step in interpretation is therefore often a simple synopsis of human development as currently understood by psychoanalytic theory, followed by a checklist of the common modes of encryption that take unconscious fantasies or memories and turn them into mythic narratives.[12]

Unconscious thinking is known as the 'primary process', and it uses modes different from our conscious thinking but commonly found in dreaming or poetry. So to understand a myth, one must look for the processes of 'condensation' (one element may represent numerous things) and 'displacement' (emotional energy associated with one element may be displaced onto a similar but different element). These processes transform the latent content inherent in the narrative situation (e.g., the deep psychological concerns surrounding intergenerational strife and individual development) into the manifest content of the myth (e.g., Hesiod's *Theogony*).

Central to these processes are the common psychoanalytic ideas of 'overdetermination' and 'defence mechanism'. Condensation causes meaning often to be 'overdetermined' or derived from many psychic sources; as Caldwell aptly says, condensation 'is the psychological equivalent of the literary term *ambiguity*'.[13] If we play by the rules of the unconscious, an element can mean contradictory things and remain perfectly valid as a psychic expression, just as a poem can thrive on its ambiguity. Defence mechanisms are psychical operations that allow the conscious mind to 'defend' itself from the unthinkable relegated to the unconscious. Common mechanisms relevant to myth are symbolism, splitting, and projection.

In the case of symbolism, the mind is distanced from the painful truth by displacing it onto an abstract entity or object, as in the case of the 'triple road' in *Oedipus the King* (*triplês … keleuthou*, 800–1), scene of Oedipus' murder of Laios. While we might see the three fates of Jocasta, Laios, and Oedipus symbolized here in the place where three roads meet, one can also see – through overdetermination – the Y shape suggestive of the vulva.[14] This pits Jocasta as the site of the conflict between father and son for 'access', whereby the son then shows his phallic mastery by bludgeoning his father to death with a walking stick (*skeptron*, *Oedipus the King* 811). As well as an aid to walking, a *skeptron* can be a staff of office, hence the English word 'sceptre'. The stick itself is thus a symbol that condenses his phallic crime both with royal authority (commonly symbolized in Greek iconography by possession of a long *skeptron*, as in depictions of Zeus) and with blindness, since by the end of the play it guides him down the road, as Teiresias prophesies (456). So the walking stick is a contradictory symbol both of Oedipus' triumph over his father and of his punishment.[15]

Splitting (also known as decomposition) is a way of dealing with the inherent ambivalence of feelings toward loved ones, which can seem bewildering, especially to a child. A figure towards whom one has both intense love and hatred splits into two figures: a very good and a very bad one. Oedipus' two fathers – the imperious, infanticidal Laios and the kind King Polybos of Corinth who actually raised him – are a good example of this mechanism.[16] Thus, Laios is a haughty stranger whom Oedipus kills in open conflict, while Polybos is the good father Oedipus goes far out of his way to avoid killing. He even oddly rationalizes the oracle's meaning by thinking Polybos died out of longing for him, a clear fantasy of a doting father (969–70). Similarly, Oedipus has two mothers, Jocasta, who conspired to do away with him as an infant and with whom he incestuously begets children, and Meropē, whom again he flees so as not to harm (he exaggeratedly dreads returning to her in Corinth after Polybos' death lest he fulfill the oracle: 988–99).[17] Oedipus' intentional actions against his Corinthian parents are scrupulous and sound, but he does great harm unconsciously to his Theban parents, who in turn have acted hostilely towards him as an infant. The contrivance of the mythic narrative thus masks – and yet expresses – the psychic reality of deep ambivalence within family relations.

Lastly, projection is a means of externalizing an internal desire or conflict that is worrisome by displacing it onto another person or entity. As in Freud's reading, we could see that the 'fate of Oedipus' as expressed by the Delphic Oracle is in fact a way of concealing our inner psychological turmoil by turning it outward into the metaphysical worst-case scenario of a particular Theban individual. He becomes a unique example (*paradeigma*, 1193) of human misery as the chorus states, but in reality he is a kind of projective scapegoat for our collective Oedipal guilt. In fact, much of Freud's theory of religion assumes that religious systems are basically systematic projections of psychic conflict onto the world; this was an early conviction of his, again going back to his correspondence with Fliess: 'The dim inner perception of one's own psychic apparatus stimulates thought illusions, which of course are projected onto the outside and, characteristically, into the future and the beyond. Immortality, retribution, the entire beyond are all reflections of our psychic internal [world]. *Meschugge* ('crazy', in Yiddish)? Psycho-mythology.'[18] Unfortunately, this makes the religious point of view fundamentally neurotic or at best childish in Freud's thought (see *The Future of An Illusion*, 1927). Even some of his followers found this attitude disappointing, considering the massive influence of religion on human life.

Analysing Myth, Analysing Patients:
Controlling Interpretation

Given the complexity and subtlety of these hermeneutical tools, it is easy to see how 'overdetermination' may quickly lead to 'over-interpretation'. There are fewer grounds to exclude a possible meaning once considerations like contradiction, inconsistency, and disproportion have been jettisoned or defined as unimportant. It is clear, then, why psychoanalytic interpretation can provoke a certain hermeneutical anxiety: there is seemingly no end to it.

Take for example, a splendid interpretation by Richard Caldwell of Theseus in the labyrinth of Minos. Freud himself saw the labyrinth as a symbol of the 'anal birth' theory of young children, who know a baby is inside their mother but do not know how else it could possibly come out unless by defecation.[19] This is one of those childhood theories that remain alive in the Tartaros of our unconscious, waiting to manifest themselves again. Caldwell concurs with Freud's view, but further enriches his exegesis of the myth:

> When the Athenian prince Theseus kills the Minotaur (the 'Minos-Bull') in the center of this labyrinth, then emerges with the help of an umbilical thread to escape with the Cretan princess Ariadne, the fantasy of anal birth is combined with oedipal rivalry and triumph. In the center of the mother's body, the hero meets and overcomes the representation of paternal sexuality (the Minotaur) and thus takes for himself, immediately after birth, the desired and forbidden female.[20]

Such hermeneutical finesse can be quite disarming, and it is easy to see why followers of Freud felt they possessed a magic key with which to unlock millennial mysteries. But as Karl Popper argued, one must be careful not to confuse explanatory power with scientific verifiability.[21]

Freud himself was aware of the problem that a daring new way to interrogate texts could quickly fall into rote-work analysis. In therapy, interpretations are crosschecked with patient reactions and are thus given a degree of verification or critical reaction. How one is to crosscheck cultural interpretations is less clear, though sensitivity to context (an essential requirement of clinical dream interpretation) and comparative study of myth often strengthen a case. But the overall directive psychoanalysis extends to us is to 'listen with the third ear' to such narratives, putting our own unconscious mind in contact with the unconscious or latent content of the myth.[22] And the cultural knowledge of such things is essential to being a good analyst. In his later formulation for the education of an analyst, Freud listed 'the history of civilization, mythology, the psychology of religion and the science of literature' as the most important components, while claiming that 'the great mass of what is taught in medical schools is of no use' to the would-be analyst.[23]

Freud's Heirs and Critics

Psychoanalysis has a complicated history of descendants encompassing a number of subsequent schools of thought and clinical practice: Will Therapy, Individual Psychology, Analytic Psychology, Object-Relations Psychology, Self-psychology, Lacanian Psychoanalysis. Freud's interest in myth is quite often encoded in these offspring, where he himself comes to stand as a theogonic figure more like Ouranos or Kronos than Zeus. The central role Freud created for the Oedipus complex has often been the cause of dynamic ruptures within psychoanalysis. Freud came to see this complex not just as developmentally central to all human children (regardless of culture, class, or era), but also as historically central on account of a prehistoric enactment of a primal patricide that became an unconscious memory for the whole species (see *Totem and Taboo*, 1913). The paradigm he thus created for human culture is tragic and dire, sometimes seen as viewing it only in terms of 'Guilty Man'.[24] The complaint is that Freud's view tends to force one into a mode of resignation in the face of civilization's demands upon the psyche (see *Civilization and Its Discontents*, 1929), instead of allowing for creative, dynamic, and purposeful alternatives.

Not surprisingly, attempts to get beyond Freud have often involved reinterpreting the Oedipus myth as a way of pointing out a fatal blindness to some basic truth. Otto Rank, for example, did extensive study and investigation of mythology while a member of the Freudian circle. He later came to reinterpret the Oedipus myth after undergoing a painful rupture with Freud, who had practically adopted him as a son. Rank's struggle for intellectual autonomy seems patent in his desire to remove the conflictual paradigm of the Oedipus complex:

> For as little as the father wants to continue to exist only in his sons, just as little has the son an inclination to play only the part of a successor to the father. In this sense Oedipus rebels likewise against the role of son as against that of father and not as son against his father. This double conflict in the individual himself who wants to be neither father nor son, but simply Self, is portrayed in the myth in all its features.[25]

Much later, the influential Self-psychologist Heinz Kohut (1913–81) came to reassess the role of Oedipus in psychoanalytic theory, which he blamed for being entirely too focused on conflict and not on more positive and nurturing relationships. He thus proposed a counter-myth centred on the relationship between Odysseus and Telemachos that could engineer an escape from the dead end of Freud's tragic paradigm. Kohut recounts the myth of Odysseus' attempt to evade service in the Trojan War by feigning insanity. He pretends not to recognize the emissaries. He yokes an ox and ass together, and ploughs his field tossing salt over his shoulders into the furrows instead of seed. But Palamedes, suspecting a ruse, seizes the infant Telemachos and flings him in front of Odysseus' plough; Odysseus ploughs in a semi-circle to avoid his son, giving the lie to his deception. Kohut seizes on this small detail to refute the Freudian idea of endless patricide.

> it is a fitting symbol of that joyful awareness of the human self of being tempo-
> ral, of having an unrolling destiny: a preparatory beginning, a flourishing mid-
> dle, and a retrospective end; a fitting symbol of the fact that healthy man
> experiences, and with deepest joy, the next generation as an extension of his own
> self. It is the primacy of the support for the succeeding generation, therefore,
> which is normal and human, not intergenerational strife and mutual wishes to
> kill and to destroy.[26]

Such revisionist interpretations in turn sparked defences of Freud's more tragic views, most notably in the work of Jacques Lacan.[27] Indeed, the debate surrounding Freud's debt to tragedy makes a useful focal point for assessing the conflicting claims of post-Freudian psychologies.

Perhaps the best known amongst Freud's dissenters is Carl Gustav Jung and his school of Analytic Psychology, which has influenced prolific writers on myth such as the classical scholar Carl Kerényi (1897–1973), the comparatist Joseph Campbell (1904–87), and the psychologist James Hillman (1926–). The rift between Freud and Jung originated as the two were writing seminal works in 1911–13; Freud was delving deeply into Frazer's *Golden Bough* while writing *Totem and Taboo* and Jung was completing *Wandlungen und Symbole der Libido* ('Transformations and Symbols of the Libido').[28] Both are works deeply engaged in the psychological investigation of mythology and primitive cultures. Both posit the unconscious as the real key to what primitive culture is up to and how it relates to modern man. But they move toward two different destinations.

Freud posited that the unconscious mind contains memory traces of a primordial event, the murder of the 'primal father', which was constitutive of human culture. In other words, this theory assumes that we all share unconsciously in a collective trauma and guilt over violent origins that continuously manifests itself through a process known as 'the return of the repressed'. Jung, on the other hand, began to elaborate a more complex view of a collective unconscious, the contents of which he came to call 'archetypes'.[29] Some discussion of Jung's approach is warranted here, since Jungians remain the most committed to the idea that 'mythological knowledge' is an essential adjunct to therapeutic work and psychological insight. In some Jungian training institutes, mythological study remains an important part of clinical training to this day.

In Jung's view, all humans share in a collective unconscious that is mytho-poeic (mythmaking) in nature; thus myth never loses its essential relevance to us, but remains a powerful source of insight into our unconscious minds and motivations. The archetypes that constitute the collective unconscious are not like innate ideas or memories so much as inherited schemata that organize experience; in fact, Jung likened the archetype to an organ (see further below). An archetype informs experience, but it has no experiential content of its own. Hence, it can be a slippery object of analysis.

> No archetype can be reduced to a simple formula. It is a vessel which we can never empty, never fill. It has a potential existence only, and when it takes shape in matter it is no longer what it was. It persists throughout the ages and requires interpreting ever anew. The archetypes are the imperishable elements of the unconscious, but they change their shape continually.[30]

Freud's discovery of the Oedipus complex, Jung felt, was really the discovery of just one archetype amongst many; indeed, their full number is unknown. They manifest or instantiate themselves as 'archetypal images' in dreams and creative works, but also in the products of psychosis, in scientific and philo-sophical ideas, and in the myths and symbols of world religions. A list of some Jungian archetypes begins to resemble the ingredients of a complex fantasy novel more than a pantheon: the god, the goddess, the trickster, the child, the father, the mother, the scapegoat, the beast, the hero, the self, the shadow, the anima, the animus, the sage, the fool, the wizard, the tree, water, etc. Like the Platonic theory of forms, the theory of archetypes might be said to have a 'population problem' – there is no limit to the number of forms, or arche-types, that may be required or postulated.

There is also a significant difference between Freudians and Jungians in their hermeneutical approaches. Jung objected to the way Freudian analysis relies heavily on the distinction between manifest (or 'merely apparent') con-tent and latent (or 'real' or 'root') content, which too often reduces the former to the latter. He preferred to stress the inherent integrity of the symbol and the image, and jettisoned the notion that the mind is largely deceptive in its symbol-creation because of the machinations of an internal censor. He also objected to Freud's characterization of fantasy generally and religion in par-ticular. He professed a greater faith and interest in what is healthy and creative in the human psyche, and what is prospective (forward looking), not just ret-rospective.[31]

Jung's style of interpretation is more focused on what for a Freudian would be the 'surface narrative', but it remains a depth psychology. Unlike the subtle and ingenious tricks of the Freudian toolkit, the main concepts in Jungian exegesis boil down to the following: explication, amplification, and active imagination. Whereas a Freudian might chop up and decode a mythic narrative, a Jungian tries to adhere more to the more obvious message the myth (or dream) and its symbols seek to convey. Explication involves expounding the *manifest* content. Amplification is the subsequent investigation of what the relevant symbols, motifs, or images – say, questing, serpents, sphinxes, or Great Mother figures – have embodied historically in human culture. This is wide-ranging comparative work, creating a parallel discourse between world cultural history and the particular myth (or in clinical practice, the patient's own situation).

Active imagination, on the other hand, is a meditative technique that seeks to bridge the conscious and unconscious through some deployment of imagination or fantasy, such as visualization, automatic writing, or a creative artwork of some kind.[32] This technique presupposes that one will 'run with' the unconscious elements that are manifesting themselves and trying to speak, rather than using the conscious mind to dissect, translate, and dispose of them in the Freudian manner. This is again because Jung conceives of the archetype more as a function than a discrete expression of the psyche:

> Not for a moment dare we succumb to the illusion that an archetype can be finally explained and disposed of. Even the best attempts at explanation are only more or less successful translations into another metaphorical language. (Indeed, language itself is only an image.) The most we can do is to *dream the myth onwards* and give it a modern dress. And whatever explanation or interpretation does to it, we do to our own souls as well, with corresponding results for our own well-being. The archetype – let us never forget this – is a psychic organ present in all of us. A bad explanation means a correspondingly bad attitude to this organ, which may thus be injured.[33]

The Jungian approach, then, can be seen as deeply committed to the autonomy and priority of myth, a psychological attempt to co-opt mythic discourse while at the same time allowing it to retain its otherness. Myth does not just represent the residue of our primitive past; its archetypal nature means it exists very much in the here and now, since 'it is not just a *vestige*, but a system functioning in the present'.[34] The principle of radical autonomy has been a mainstay in other approaches to myth, and is clearly echoed in Kerényi's statement that a 'mythologem [mythic motif] speaks for itself, acts for itself, and is true of itself just like any other lofty scientific theory or musical creation, or indeed any true work of art'.[35] But the injunction to think *prospectively* through myth, to 'dream the myth onward' as one forges one's selfhood, is a distinctive contribution of Jungian psychology to the modern deployment of myth.

Conclusions

One might be tempted to conclude that all these psychological approaches have accomplished is to fall into scientific mythologies of their own while trying to co-opt, contain, or commandeer the mystique of myth. That allegation would hardly be shocking to psychoanalysis. Such a conclusion was actually reached by both Freud and Jung, for whom the scientific worldview inevitably creates or retains its own myths. Indeed, even the committed rationalist Karl Popper freely acknowledged the mythopoeic element in scientific theories.[36] But the difference lies in the fact that the psychoanalytic view assumes that what we are doing is reappropriating and reintegrating myth into modernity through psychological insight, not just replacing one set of myths with another. This cultural reintegration is clearly tied to the need for the psychologist herself or himself to become whole, or fully individuated. As Jung puts it:

> Psychology, as one of the many expressions of psychic life, operates with ideas which in their turn are derived from archetypal structures and thus generate a somewhat more abstract kind of myth. Psychology therefore translates the archaic speech of myth into a modern mythologem – not yet, of course, recognized as such – which constitutes one element of the myth 'science'. This seemingly hopeless undertaking is a *living and lived myth*, satisfying to persons of a corresponding temperament, indeed beneficial in so far as they have been cut off from their psychic origins by neurotic dissociation.[37]

Thus, no matter what we make of psychoanalytic interpretations, we must at least pay attention to this project of human reintegration with myth through the discursive vector of psychoanalysis. As a paradoxical 'rational theory of the irrational', psychoanalysis becomes the space where myth re-enters modern culture, and where tragedy returns as a paradigm of human subjectivity. Luigi Zoja has gone so far as to say that the invention of psychoanalysis made way for a return to obscurity and profundity in a hyper-rational age: 'Psychoanalysis had to be invented in order to reconstruct a place where mystery might again be a sacred guest rather than always an enemy, always to be slain.'[38] Perhaps psychoanalysis itself should be read as a symptom of secular individualism's continued yearning for the sacred.

FURTHER READING

The *locus classicus* of Freud's Oedipal interpretation of Sophocles' play occurs in his seminal work, *The Interpretation of Dreams* (Freud 1999: 201–5). For a sympathetic and comprehensive treatment, see Rudnytsky 1987. The particular importance of drama in Freud's understanding of myth is explored in Armstrong (forthcoming). For a discussion of the Oedipal paradigm more widely connected to Freud's general deployment of antiquity, see Armstrong 2005: ch. 3. Some spirited refutations of Freud by classicists include Vernant 1988, Kirk 1970: 273–80, and Eisner 1987: ch. 1.

Since Freud's followers did much of the heavy lifting in the application of psychoanalysis to myth, it is important to take note of their work. An early programmatic statement is Rank and Sachs 1916. Otto Rank's work is especially important, though it gradually drifts from the Freudian mainstream: see Rank 1919, 1991, 2004, and 1929. Géza Róheim was the first psychoanalytic anthropologist, and relevant works include Róheim 2005 and 1992. Lastly, the lay analyst Reik presents (1957) a late reverberation of Freud's myth of the primal horde. Caldwell 1989 is a clear application of Freudian theory to Greek theogonic myth, and a good place to start for beginners.

The standard place for a look at Jungian theory is Jung and Kerényi 1973, though Jung 1959 is also useful. For a deeper look, see Jung 1953–92: vol. 9.1 *The Archetypes and the Collective Unconscious* (1959). Michael Vannoy Adams continues a spirited defence of the Jungian approach in Adams 2001 and 2004. Perhaps the most popular avenue to Jungian ideas in America has been through the work of Joseph Campbell, particularly his *The Hero with a Thousand Faces* (2008), though Campbell was not a strict Jungian. The work has been popular with Hollywood directors such as Stanley Kubrick and George Lucas. Lastly, classicist Norman Austin (1990) attempts an eclectic approach with Lacanian elements.

NOTES

1. Named after the German evolutionary biologist Ernst Haeckel (1834–1919). For a brief discussion of the role of evolutionary theory in the study of myth see Csapo (2005: 46–7). For an extensive study of Haeckel's life, work, and influence, see Richards (2008).
2. Freud (1953–74: 9.152).
3. For an overview of the movement's cultural development, see Makari (2008) and L. Rose (1998). For antiquity's role in its development, see especially Armstrong (2005).
4. See for example Rank (1919, 1929, 1992).
5. A classic attack upon the psychoanalytic approach to myth is Vernant (1988).
6. Blumenberg (1985).
7. Caldwell (1990: 346).
8. Letter to Fliess, October 15, 1897, in J. M. Masson (1985: 272).
9. Freud (1953–74: 4.261, my emphasis).
10. Freud (1953–74: 4.262).
11. Freud (1953–74: 16.331, my emphasis).
12. A good example is Caldwell (1989).
13. Caldwell (1989: 59).
14. Abraham (1955).

15. It is also commonly assumed in the psychoanalytic reading that blinding is the equivalent of castration (i.e., the symbolic substitution of two eyes for two testicles), the archetypal paternal punishment of the son.

16. This detail of the psychoanalytic reading is missed by Vernant, who argues that the hero of *Oedipus* 'has no trace of an Oedipus complex' since he was not raised by Laiòs and Jocasta (1988: 108). On the contrary, the myth expresses the complex *by the fact* that splitting is so clearly present; Oedipus' 'good' set of parents have no connection to the 'bad' parents.

17. Another instance of splitting mentioned in psychoanalytic interpretations of the myth is that between Jocasta and the Sphinx, both of whom 'commit suicide after a riddle, the question of identity, has been solved' (Caldwell 1990: 372). But Freud himself chose to interpret the Sphinx as a figure of the father, not of the mother (Freud 1953–74, vol. 21: 188); see Armstrong (2005: 82 f.).

18. Letter to Fliess, December 12, 1897, in J. M. Masson (1985: 286).

19. Freud (1953–74: 22.25).

20. Caldwell (1989: 31).

21. Popper (2002: 44–6).

22. See Reik (1948).

23. Freud (1953–74: 20.246).

24. See Kohut (1982), for example.

25. Rank (1932: 193–4).

26. Kohut (1982: 404).

27. See especially 'The Essence of Tragedy' and 'The Tragic Dimension of Analytical Experience', in J.-A. Miller (1992: 243–325). Also helpful are P. A. Miller (2007: ch. 3) and Leonard (2005: 101–30).

28. Originally published in German in 1911–12, this was later republished with considerable changes in 1956 as *Symbols of Transformation*; see Jung (1953–92: vol. 5).

29. Jung's key writings on the archetype and the collective unconscious are collected in Jung (1953–92: vol. 9, part 1).

30. Jung and Kerényi (1969: 98).

31. See Jung (1953–92: vol. 4) for his collected writings on Freud and psychoanalysis.

32. See Chodorow (ed.) (1997) for a convenient anthology of his scattered discussions of this technique.

33. Jung and Kerényi (1969: 79, original emphasis).

34. Jung and Kerényi (1969: 81, original emphasis).

35. Jung and Kerényi (1969: 46).

36. Popper (2002: ch. 4).

37. Jung and Kerényi (1969: 98–9, original emphasis).

38. Zoja (1998: 37).

CHAPTER TWENTY-SIX

Initiation: The Key to Myth?

Ken Dowden

Rites of Passage

If mythology was not in some sense puzzling, we would be wasting our time explaining and exploring it. Myth plays a vital part in a society's picture of itself, in defining what sort of society it is and what are the roles of its various peoples and places. It reflects a shared experience which is meaningful to individuals. It also sets a society in history as it is perceived and 'remembered': cultural memory, and shared history, is in the last resort a division of mythmaking. But Greek mythology is also a very particular organism that has grown out of a specific society at a specific stage, or series of stages, in its development. Even if myth is continually added to and renewed, we can still take the view that the basic stock of Greek myths had been formed by the time of Homer and Hesiod, or at least Pseudo-Hesiod (see CH. 3). The formative age for that mythology is in all probability the Mycenaean Age, say 1500–1100 BC; and the codifying age is the Dark Age, which brings us down to the 700s (this chronology will be discussed further in 'Qualification 1' below). Thus, the societies in which Greek myth played a role as it was formed were not as close to today as they were to Indo-European times (see CH. 18), when the linguistic ancestors of Greeks, Sanskrit-writing Indians, and modern English-speakers were still talking in dialects that could be understood by each other. Their society too was radically different not only from our modern post-industrial, high-technology age, but also from the world of the Greek city-state, the *polis*, where we picture philosophers, poets, and politicians mingling on the streets of democratic Athens.

A Companion to Greek Mythology, First Edition. Edited by Ken Dowden and Niall Livingstone.
© 2014 John Wiley & Sons Ltd. Published 2014 by John Wiley & Sons Ltd.

We have no direct written evidence of these societies, except for the Linear B account tablets which give us some idea of central palace economies in the Mycenaean Age; even archaeology perhaps reveals more about those palaces than it does about the Dark Age or about the population at large. Thus, our picture of these societies has to be deduced from the treacherous mythological representations, or traced back from the later archaic and classical societies where some elements are visibly survivals from older structures, or approached typologically from unrelated societies at what we guess may be a similar stage of development. There is no single developmental path of societies and that does make the typological approach rather fragile, but similar circumstances may generate comparable societies and *initiation* is a remarkable case in point.

Initiation in English is the formal introduction of someone to a new status or to new competences. Loosely, we can say that this book serves to initiate some of its readers into the study of classical mythology. But in the study of peoples across the world (anthropology, or ethnology) initiation is something more specific. It is the ritual (ceremony, rite), or sequence of rituals, that is used to give a person, or more commonly a group of persons, a new social status. The most common, and the one we are concerned with here, is the marking of the transfer from being a youth to being an adult – from boy to man, or from girl to woman, rites which are undergone by an age-group.

Initiation rituals belong to a larger class of rites that was defined in 1909 by Arnold van Gennep (van Gennep 1960). These are what he called *rites de passage*, the rites that achieve the transition from one condition to another and which are now, following him, called 'rites of passage' or 'passage rites'. These rites, on van Gennep's analysis, fall into a sequence of three subcategories: rites of separation, which end your attachment to the previous condition; *rites de marge*, transition rites (they take place on the 'margins'), those which put you in no man's land, and which mark you as neither what you were nor what you will become; and finally *rites d'agrégation*, rites of incorporation, that enrol you in your new society.[1] From the perspective of entering a house, where the key location is the threshold, *limen* in Latin, these stages are successively 'pre-liminal', 'liminal', and 'post-liminal'. 'Liminal' has on the whole proved a more useful piece of jargon than 'transition (rites)'.

The theory, in the case of Greek mythology, is that the societies that existed in the times when Greek mythology was formed did indeed have initiation rites rather resembling those found ethnographically, and that quite a number of myths reflect these rites both in their general shape and in particular details. But it should be noted at the outset that it is the rites of separation, characteristically dramatic and maybe psychologically difficult for participants, that dominate the relevant myths.

Iphigeneia and Girls as Animals

Greek mythology is concerned, inter alia, with the virtue, or otherwise, of wives (see CH. 23). But a remarkable number of girls ('maidens') have trouble reaching that stage at all.[2] They may be turned into animals, plants, or even finally constellations (the Proitids, Daphne, Kallisto); they may need to murder their prospective husbands (the Danaids); they may need to give their lives for the community (the Erechtheids); they may die in the course of a pursuit (Iphinoe); or be slaughtered or sacrificed, preferably by their father (the returning Idomeneus). The most famous example of the last category is Iphigeneia, the daughter of Agamemnon.

Her story, as we know it, is part of the saga of the Trojan War, and its focus falls on her father Agamemnon. Helen, the wife of his brother, Menelaos, has been stolen by Paris, the son of the Trojan king Priam; Agamemnon has assembled the Greek forces that will head to Troy to avenge his brother. Their ships are now at Aulis, on the coast of Boiotia facing the long island of Euboia; but Agamemnon cannot gain favourable winds. This is because he has offended the goddess Artemis by shooting a deer. It is not wholly clear why this action has offended Artemis, but one version goes that he boasted as he shot the deer that 'not even Artemis' could have shot like that. The prophet Kalchas now pronounces that Agamemnon must sacrifice his daughter if he is to sail to Troy, and Iphigeneia is sent for, ostensibly in order that she may be married to Achilles. Some authors give the impression she is sacrificed; others report that a deer is substituted by Artemis at the last moment and Iphigeneia herself is whisked off to serve Artemis at her shrine amongst the 'Tauroi', a Thracian tribe with a name conveniently similar to Artemis' epithet Tauropolos (she of the 'bulls', *tauroi*).

If this were all, we would probably be none the wiser. But there are also related myths told in the next land south of Boiotia, namely Attica (the territory of Athens). On the East coast, at Brauron (near Athens airport), a maiden plays with a wild bear but it scratches her and her brothers shoot it. A plague now descends on the Athenians and an oracle pronounces that their maidens must in future *arkteuein* ('do the bear (rite)') before they can marry. On the West coast, at Mounychia (near the old port of Athens), again a bear is killed by the Athenians and again a plague results. The oracle prescribes the sacrifice of his daughter by someone who is willing. At this point, Embaros (who is a byword for ingenuity ever after) agrees, provided he gains the priesthood for his clan. But he hides his daughter in the inner room of the temple and proceeds to sacrifice a goat which he has dressed in his daughter's clothes.

The common structure of these myths is as follows:

an animal is killed	Artemis is angry	an oracle prescribes a remedy	a girl is to be sacrificed by her father	but she is not and an animal is substituted	the prospect of marriage
			the *Arkteia* is to take place		

The account in which the *Arkteia* becomes a necessity veers from myth to what myth signifies. But in all cases we are at a shrine of Artemis and in two (Aulis, Brauron) the question of marriage arises. The *Arkteia* was indeed a ritual which select Athenian maidens performed prior to marriage. And all versions show an oscillation of identity between girl and animal, emphasizing that one may under special conditions substitute for the other. In two versions (Aulis, Mounychia) the slayer is the father.

An initiatory interpretation works as follows. The sacrifice expresses the dynamics of the key moment of separation in the initiation ceremony. To become marriageable, a girl must leave the control of her father and enter the control of her husband. In the Greek context this happens within the ritual embrace of the relevant goddess, Artemis. This is dramatically, but logically, represented by father and daughter engaging in a ceremony in the Artemis shrine in which the father symbolically kills the daughter. Mock-death and mock-killing are staples of the phase of separation in initiation ceremonies. They are the necessary preliminary to rebirth and are also reflected in the change of names and change of appearance which can occur at this stage. But the girl is not really dead: she has become something outside the human category altogether, namely an animal, if a vulnerable one specially loved by the goddess. The goddess has helped her to survive the transition by adopting the girl into her service for a period, and indeed the example of the *arktoi* shows that girls *did* spend a period in the goddess's service. It is only after this that marriage becomes available, the marriage to which Athenian girls looked forward and the marriage which was offered (albeit deceitfully) to Iphigeneia.

The myth of Iphigeneia would on this view find its formative context in a regional family of rituals. I have argued elsewhere that this includes some traces of a deer-ritual prior to marriage in Thessaly, and maybe also aspects of the Dionysos cult in Boiotia, in particular the ritual garb of the maenads (raving matrons), the deer-dress (*nebris*). It is possible that there is also an outlier in Arkadia, where the nymph Kallisto ('Prettiest') is also turned into a bear and shot, this time maybe by Artemis.[3]

A different region is constituted by the Argolid, Sikyon, and neighbouring areas. There we find a mythology of the daughters of Proitos, King of Tiryns, who offend Hera,[4] perhaps by deriding the appearance of her statue. The result is that they suffer from a whitening disease (leprosy, perhaps), and in their madness become convinced that they are cows, then start roaming over the wilds of the Peloponnese. They must eventually find a place to be cured. According to Bakchylides (*Epinician Ode* 11), it is by their father in the waters of Lousoi (north Arcadia). In the most colourful version of the story, though, it is in a ritual chase by the young men, led by the prophet Melampous ('Blackfoot'), a chase of such vigour that one of them, Iphinoē, dies at Sikyon – and you can see her tomb.[5] This ritual chase of the not-quite married is reflected again in the myth of the Danaids (honoured at Argos), who must escape their would-be husbands, who are the sons of Egypt (and therefore black).

Thus, once again, on an initiatory view, there is a parade of appropriate motifs. The subjects are those on the verge of marriage. The Proitids, in a ritual environment (the temple of Hera), lose their human identity and become confused with animals. Their whitening may reflect the use of white daubs in initiation rituals (part of the scenery of changing identity). They also leave their home and have no bearings. Meanwhile there is a clear hint of a ritual chase of the sexes (one which we also know happened in Boiotia in the Dionysos cult), looking as though the normal paleness of women and tanned skins of men is exaggerated through black and white daubings, maybe washed off at the end. If one of the girls dies, that may indicate that in a sense they all die and that the transition is a difficult one. Are the Proitids attractive enough to marry? No longer. And the Danaids' slaughter of their husbands is as clear a rejection of marriage as you will find in any myth. In this liminal period they are unmarried and unmarriageable.[6]

Somewhere in the background of all this seem to lie organized rites, repeated from year to year (or sometimes maybe at gaps of more than a year). Their function seems to be to take the available girls and convert them psychologically and ritually so that they are ready for marriage. The evidence for the ritual, however, is very thin and this evidence comes from well after the time of formation of these myths (cf. on 'Qualification 1', below); thus, it is possible that the ritual alongside which the myth originally made sense has decayed. We might well ask now whether the *Arkteia* for which we have evidence had not changed significantly over the centuries. Presumably, it had originally not been a ceremony for the Athenian state but for the people of the village of Brauron, where in later years it had come to seem like a colourful local part of the Athenian heritage, with its saffron-dyed robes and running races. In fact, however, it was a survival of rites that had once been held in most places, of which Brauron and (on the other side of Attica) Mounychia were only survivals. The whole of the eligible maidenhood of Attica was scarcely going to assemble at Brauron for the *Arkteia*: thus, by its nature in an amalgamated ('syncretized') Attica, it would be available only to *select* girls. We cannot know whether in origin the ceremony had been restricted to the daughters of leading folk; but it seems unlikely that they would be sufficiently numerous. We do not have evidence for non-mythical girls masquerading as cows at Tiryns, though as Argos destroyed the city and much of its culture in the 470s BC, this is not surprising. But as Spartan boys were dragooned in *agelai* (herds) and led by *bouagoi* (ox-leaders), there is nothing implausible about the young girls of Tiryns and its region practising being cows in the same way that Brauronian girls practised being bears. Given that Hera is standardly 'cow-faced' (*boöpis*) in Homer, usually translated 'ox-eyed', it would seem appropriate.[7]

The Destiny of the Warrior

Boys' myths do not map so easily onto rites and their patterns. But there exists, all the same, a range of myths addressing the key point at which the boy becomes the warrior. Phaistos is in south-central Crete, a bus ride from Heraklion. Today we visit it for its magnificent Minoan palace. But it was a living community in classical times too, and there we hear of a myth associated with a ritual, which the Hellenistic poet Nicander (third–second century BC) had told in Book 2 of his now lost *Metamorphoses* (we have the story as reported by Antoninus Liberalis (second–third century AD?) in his *Metamorphoses* (17), a prose work which draws extensively on Nicander's poem.[8] A woman called Galateia is pregnant with the child of her husband Lampros ('brilliant') and he prays it will be a boy. But it isn't. So she pretends it is and calls it Leukippos ('white-horse', strangely often the name of the king's son in mythology).[9] Leukippos grows up and her beauty is such that Galateia fears she cannot any longer fool Lampros. So she goes to the temple of Leto and implores her to make Leukippos a boy, which indeed Leto does.

> The people of Phaistos even today commemorate this sex-change and sacrifice to Leto of Growth (*Phytia*), who caused the girl to grow male organs; and they call the festival the *Ekdysia* [the (festival of the) Casting Off (of clothes)], since the girl cast off her *peplos* [robe]. And it is the custom that those who are getting married must first lie beside the statue of Leukippos.

This strange myth concerns the 'coming-out' of a male under the auspices of a goddess at maturity, and it is associated with the boundary you must cross to reach marriage and with a specific festival, apparently celebrating male 'maturation'. The myth is presented as aetiological, that is, as giving the reason why a ceremony is held. But in myth-analysis we regard the chain of causation as being rather in the opposite direction, from ritual to myth: the myth exists because the ritual did, and it serves to explain the dynamics of the ritual.

The ritual seems to be in initiatory territory, and the myth exists to explore the dynamics of this moment in human ritual life.

So far this is to interpret a single myth rather heavily. But there are a number of comparable myths. One that is important for us was also mentioned by Nicander and appears in the same chapter of Antoninus' *Metamorphoses* (Galateia's prayer was clearly a fine set-piece in which she cited others who had undergone sex-change in order to support her request). This is the myth of Kaineus, situated in Thessaly in mainland Greece. This character is originally a girl, Kainis, and Poseidon is enamoured of her and agrees to grant her a wish. She wishes to become a man and invincible.[10] The story goes on to tell how Kaineus caused people to swear by his spear, and defeated the Centaurs until they took whole fir trees and pounded him into the ground. The latter part is something of a cautionary story, but the sex-change at adolescence (she is not yet married) – granted by Poseidon, a god sometimes elsewhere associated with youths – seems to be from a similar stable to the story of Leukippos.

We then turn to a more famous story, that of Achilles. This greatest of warriors in the Trojan War was not originally going to join the expedition. Indeed, his mother Thetis, knowing he would die if he went, had 'disguised him in women's dress and left him with Lykomedes as a maiden'.[11] Achilles comes from Phthia, a region of Thessaly, and Lykomedes is the ruler of the island of Skyros, around 150 kilometres away, on the other side of Euboia. This ruse does not escape the attention of the Greek forces assembling for Troy. An embassy is sent, and Odysseus cunningly lays out a selection of women's goods and weaponry before the royal girls on Skyros, whereupon Achilles' interest in the weaponry gives him away. Achilles has been sent to what is effectively a margin, something that matters for the liminal stage of initiation, as we have seen above in van Gennep's analysis.[12] It is at this point that his gender role is defined and he is no longer counted amongst the females: he can now go to war. So it is that once again, as in the case of Iphigeneia, a story leading up to the Trojan War seems to belong with a family of myths, sometimes local ones not particularly well known, and to concern issues of how you cross the threshold to adulthood – whether to marriage or to war. These are issues that also attract rituals, and the Leukippos case is specifically connected to a ritual, though we know nothing else about it. And just as Artemis holds the ring in the case of several girls' myths and rituals, so we find in these cases too that the crucial act must be performed by a god – Poseidon or Leto, though obviously this may also be a narrative necessity.

Another myth which seems to belong in this area, though it takes rather a different direction, is that of Zeus and Ganymede. The myth is simple: Ganymede is the most beautiful adolescent and Zeus is enamoured of him; so his eagle carries Ganymede to Olympus where he will be Zeus's cup-bearer.[13] This then matches a bizarre ritual in Crete, reported by Ephoros in his lost *History* (*FGrH* 70 F 149). It is the custom for a specially attractive youth, who is called the *kleinos* ('famous') to be ritually abducted by a lover, with the agreement of the friends and family of the *kleinos*, and to be taken into the wilds (with the friends and family) to hunt and feast with the lover for two months. At the end they return to the city (it is not stated which one) and the *kleinos* receives a warrior's outfit, an ox, and a cup. The ox is sacrificed to Zeus; the cup recalls the role of Ganymede, as does the sexuality of this abduction and further details regarding intercourse during the period in the wilds. The warrior's outfit links visibly with the weaponry selected by Achilles to end his own period at a margin as a girl. Thus this ritual is part of a family of myths and rituals which deal with the emerging warrior and more generally the emerging male.

The Theory in a Nutshell

At this point I am going to draw out a possible, if rather extreme, version of the thinking behind the initiatory theory of myth. It will be extreme so that it may be as clear as possible and so that we may see where it could be exaggerating and where it needs to be pruned back.

On this theory, the Greeks who generated this mythology used to hold initiation rites both for boys and, separately, for girls. These effected their transition to their adult roles, as warriors and as wives or, rather, mothers. Every year, or maybe every two or four years, the next cohort of boys/girls would go through the rites in honour of a god such as Poseidon, Leto, Hera, or Artemis – whichever was the local guardian of youth or controller of the portal to adulthood. These rites would be characterized by a van Gennep structure: separation, time at a margin or a shrine in a margin, return (or, rather, entry) to the adult community. Girls would tend to be considered as animals or nymphs in the marginal period, boys as wolves or even as feminized. We cannot know whether 'training' as we would envisage it was part of these ceremonies, but it is not unlikely that it was – perhaps weaving for girls and the manipulation of weapons, especially in hunting, for boys. Because these rites existed, myths also existed in a sort of dialogue with the rites. The moment of separation above all was dramatized, and we catch some sight of the period in the margins. Return to the 'city' is not generally visible. It would be crude to say that myths were invented to explain pre-existing rites, as though the rites had no voice before that, and it would be much preferable to view myth and rite as a counterpoint to each other, each describing in their own language the issues in question. But the fact remains that this view, if accepted, explains why some myths existed and why they existed in the form that they did. It is a historical explanation of Greek mythology. There are many myths that should be explained in this way and if we knew more about rituals it would be easier to identify them. But this is not a universal theory of myth: it explains one class, if an important one, of Greek mythology.

Qualifying the Conclusions

That would be a very comfortable point at which to end this chapter, but it leaves too many loose ends and we need to enter a number of qualifications to this theory before we can rest content.

Qualification 1: the date of the rites

There are a number of rituals and customs across ancient Greece that bear comparison with the format of initiation ceremonies known from anthropology. In Sparta and on Crete we hear of boys being gathered into *agelai* ('herds', though the technical term according to the lexicographer Hesychios was a *boua*, denoting a collection of oxen) and being led by *bouagoi* ('ox-drivers'). The concept of age-classes is most fully developed at Sparta, where boys between the ages of seven and seventeen were gathered into named groups: we hear (successively) of *mikichiddomenoi* or *mikichizomenoi* (apparently the term for a boy in year three), *pratopampaides* ('first all-the-boys'), *hatropampaides* ('grown? all-the-boys'), *melleirenes* ('about-to-be *eirenes*) and *eirenes* (applied to twenty-year-olds).[14] We also see in Sparta an emphasis on communal eating in *syssitia* ('joint-eatings' – 'messes' in the army sense), which brings back memories of the social organization of peoples studied by anthropologists. Cretans and Spartans, however, belong to the Dorian tribe of Greeks, the one which had least impact on the corpus of mythology and was least influenced by the palace cultures and organization of the Mycenaean Age. It may be, therefore, that they present a window onto a common culture of the earliest Greek peoples, perhaps around 2000 BC, but they are not available to be used to explain the myths we have.

Table 26.1 Initiation theory and periods of Greek culture.

Hypothetical timeline	
c.2000 or earlier	shared Greek culture, including organization by age-groups and initiation of final age-group into adulthood
c.1600–1100	'Late Helladic' – Mycenaean palaces, creation of the mythology *as we know it*
c.1100–900	population movements in Greece, arrival of the Spartans as we know them
c.750–600	Homer, Hesiod, and Pseudo-Hesiod standardize the mythology
480–323	Classical period of Greece

In fact we have no evidence of the full-scale implementation of initiation by age-cohort amongst the Greek peoples and cities that did bear the mythology. What we have instead are isolated and largely unique practices, supplemented with a lot of guesswork, which is always in danger of the fallacy of circular argument (*petitio principii*) – namely to argue that such-and-such rite, for example the *Arkteia* at Brauron, must be understood as a relic of standard initiations which we speculate existed, and then to use it to demonstrate the existence of those initiations. However, supposing that the *Arkteia* is a relic of an initiation rite, and so is a *Nebeia* ('deer-rite') apparently preliminary to marriage, known from a few inscriptions in Thessaly, and if Kaineus implies some lost rite of Poseidon, and if Achilles on Skyros gives us an insight into other Thessalians (the Dolopes) – if all of this is correct, it still remains clear that initiation was not all that widespread in the classical and post-classical societies that we know about. The mythology is more widespread and must therefore go back to a much earlier period if it was originally underpinning initiation practices. We should think of how Martin Nilsson once demonstrated that the places of interest in Greek mythology as a whole mainly reflect the places of significance *in Mycenaean times*. He concluded from this that the mythology itself originated in Mycenaean times.[15] This was before the population movements that brought about Doric-speaking Sparta and Crete, and at this time cultural continuities might well explain the extension of the Artemis bear-based and deer-based mythologies stretching from Thessaly through Aulis in Boiotia to Attica and onwards maybe to Arcadia (Kallisto). On this view, what we have is the wreckage, the cultural archaeology, of the ritual and mythological systems of the Mycenaean age, except that the myth, when sufficiently highly coloured, survived longer.

Qualification 2: the development of the mythology

The mythology we have looked at displays its own pattern of preservation and transformation. At Phaistos, the myth was still felt to be linked to the *Ekdysia* in the cult of Leto. At Brauron or Mounychia in Attica, myths of locals, maiden, bear, cunning priest, and sacrifice were still the currency of local traditions and local religious sites. From our perspective these are unreformed, still in something like their pristine condition, except that the Brauron myth has become so functional that it has lost the mythologems of sacrifice and substitution.

But it is not through the ritual at Aulis that the myth of Agamemnon and the sacrifice of Iphigeneia circulated; indeed, we have no direct evidence at all for such a ritual. Instead, the drama of the myth has found a new home in the context of the Trojan saga. Now it can talk about the pressures of leadership, the pollution of the expedition from the start, state the price for this pollution, and introduce (or replay) the motif of the anger of the gods under which we all labour; it also serves as another nail in the coffin of the House of Atreus and will provide good copy for tragedians. Poor Iphigeneia, and the important stage in women's life that she might once have represented, pass into oblivion. Achilles and his hiding amongst the girls on Skyros cease to be a representation of a stage in self-definition, and become something slightly, but meaningfully, different: now Achilles takes his fate on his shoulders and heads towards the death Thetis had sought to avoid, recognizing that his nature allows no other course. And a paradoxical story of a transvestite Achilles is available for the joy of the readers of cyclic epic (see CH. 2; it is not so much as mentioned by Homer),[16] for spectators of Euripides lost youthful tragedy the *Skyrians*, and for the classical painter Polygnotos (*fl.* 480–440 BC) and his Roman imitators.[17]

Myths are very capable of redeployment, and in classical times have become a systematic body of stories (see CH. 3) shared amongst others by creative artists and used as part of the evocative range of interlocking texts that give life and meaning to artistic production, in short 'intertextuality'. Thus, whatever the origins, from a *diachronic* (long march of time) point of view, the use of myth in the times for which we have direct evidence depends on the precise point in history at which they are uttered or alluded to and on that basis undergo *synchronic* (snapshot of a system at a given time) analysis. Initiation is a diachronic tool.

Qualification 3: selectivity and plurality

The story of Iphigeneia, at the level of myth, is about what happens to one girl. It is not a story of how a whole age-group was sacrificed, or about how that group had a herd of deer substituted for it. This then raises the question of whether Greeks really did have rites designed to deal with the totality of girls of that age-group, which is the pattern for the rites discussed by ethnologists.

The first possible solution to this problem is that myth is by its nature selective. This is evidently true in some sense of most narrative, in that the plurality of readers becomes associated with events that generally happen to individuals, and in myth it is individuals of high status. For our myths, it becomes the function of customs to associate the plurality of those affected with the singular character on whom the story is focused. So, apparently all those intending marriage at Phaistos will lie beside the tomb of Leukippos, who somehow through his story captures the dynamics of this transitional moment in their lives. And apparently girls at Sikyon intending marriage will pour a libation and offer a lock of their hair to the dead Iphinoë at her tomb.[18] Indeed, the Brauron version of the girl's myth, at the point where it fails to tell the story of sacrifice and substitution, states that the consequence was that all Athenian girls had to undergo the *Arkteia* before marriage (though we know this was not true in classical times).

A second observation is that myths argued to be of the initiatory type do from time to time present groups rather than individuals. Thus at Tiryns, the tale is that the *three* daughters of the king, Proitos, are afflicted with madness and roam thinking they are cows. They become singular at Sikyon, where *one* of them dies, Iphinoë, much as across some parts of the Greek landscape you might find a tomb not of 'the Amazons', but of *one particular* Amazon, whichever one it is in that instance.[19] Amazons are an interesting group: they are girls of military age, that is, girls who exist to be the inverse of the trainee warrior and who fail to follow the required track to marriage. This is why Theseus, an embodiment of Athenian youth, must defeat them. Likewise, the *Nymphs* by their name denote girls just before 'marriage' (it is the same root that gives us the word 'nuptial', through Latin). These girls in myth are clearly distinctly plural and often found in the company of Artemis. But if there is to be death or metamorphosis, that is for an individual: so, Kallisto in Arkadia, made pregnant by Zeus, must be transformed into a bear (and later set amongst the constellations). Finally, the Danaids at Argos, who reject marriage in the splendidly exaggerated way that is characteristic of myth, by *killing* their would-be husbands (but they will be married in the end anyway) number fifty. Fifty is a fascinating number in Greek culture. It is also the number of the daughters of Thespios (the eponym of Thespiai in Boiotia), all of whom are bedded by Herakles. And more broadly it is the number of the Argonauts, and of the number of dancers in the chorus for the dithyramb. There are some signs that as a number for a group this goes back even to Indo-European times. In effect the number fifty is shorthand for the totality of the relevant age-group.[20] So at least in the case of the Danaids, there is a sense in which the whole age-group *does* appear in the myth.

Thirdly, however, the few rituals we know seem to be selective. The chorus leader in Aristophanes' *Lysistrata* reels off a list of distinguished religious positions she has held and this is where being a Bear at Brauron figures:

At the age of seven I was immediately an *Arrhēphoros*;
And then at ten I was an *Aletris* for the *Archēgetis* (Athene);
And then, with my *Krokōtos* (saffron robe) I was an *Arktos* (bear) at the Brauronia;
And at one stage I was a *Kanēphoros*, as a beautiful girl with my necklace of figs.
(Aristophanes, *Lysistrata* 641–6)

This is obviously not something that just anyone could do. The Cretan abductee, the *Kleinos*, is special because of this distinction, and the name *Kallisto* ('Most Beautiful') in mythology points to beauty competitions that we can dimly perceive as existing, for instance on the island of Lesbos, to distinguish one girl from all the others. Perhaps it is like a folk tale when we read what happened to the three daughters, princesses then, of King Proitos of Tiryns, but of course kings' daughters also existed in real life and had ritual counterparts, such as the *Arrhēphoroi* (the girls who 'carry that which cannot be spoken') at Athens (and the Vestal Virgins at Rome). Indeed the dividing line between ritual representatives of the community and boy priests and virgin priestesses is hard to make out.

Moreover, if we simply stuck to 'initiation' as our tool for interpretation, we would ride roughshod over the complex place of youth and virginity in Greek religion. The story of Io, for instance, the unfortunate recipient of Zeus's affections at the Argive Heraion who must be rejected by Hera and driven across the earth in cow-form (and is thus rather like her neighbours the Proitids), is much more than a generic story of adolescent girls. In fact, Io stands in some contrapuntal relationship to the lifelong virgin priestess of Hera at the Argive Heraion, a figure so well established and so long lasting that Hellanikos (fifth century BC) could draw up a chronology, in at least three books, of these priestesses,[21] and they could be used to date events, as indeed they were by Thucydides on one occasion (Thucydides 2.2, 'in the 48th year of the priesthood of Chrysis at Argos'). So selectivity is a genuine feature of Greek ritual as well as of Greek mythology, but the more the rituals are selective, the more we need to be careful about their function within their societies and not to imagine, at least when we are discussing historical times, that initiation actually unlocks these issues.

Qualification 4: myths invented on the pattern of old myths

Thus we are driven back to the position that the real virtue of the initiatory method is that it uncovers the prehistory of Greek social customs and establishes the primary grounds for the creation of a range of myths. Obviously we will feel surer about this in some cases than in others. But there is a final logical difficulty. Granted that such myths may have existed, it remains true that Greek mythology is an intertextual system, where each part of the system (each myth) is capable of being influenced by the typical features of the rest of the system. So, if we have a myth in front of us that seems to be of initiatory format, there remains the problem that it may be so constructed in imitation of other myths and not as a result of a 'genuine' background in the ritual of some specific place.

Geography is an important tool for determining how specific the connection of a given myth may be with the real life of a given region. If a myth is told at Brauron about events at Brauron, then a link with ritual at Brauron may reasonably be made. And the same applies to Mounychia. The next gradation takes us to Aulis. Aulis is a specific place, standing in a similar relation to Tanagra (Boiotia) as perhaps Mounychia (or Brauron) does to Athens. It is the sea-margin relative to the large settlement of Tanagra. The mythology operates on the basis that there is a cult of Artemis at Aulis, and its sacred landscape is outlined at *Iliad* 2.303–5, with the specific sacral combination of spring and trees and altar.[22] It is of this cult-place that the myth of Iphigeneia is told. It is therefore speculative but not unreasonable to suppose that this myth has originated from the cult of Aulis, a Boiotian Brauron. Aulis may indeed have been a good place to muster ships for the Trojan War (one thinks of the role of nearby Thermopylai and Artemision in the Persian Wars), but I think that it is this local myth that has actually attracted Agamemnon's story to this location.

Achilles at Skyros is a more difficult case. Skyros is a real enough island. Viewed from most places in Greece, it looks pretty isolated and marginal. If Achilles belongs in Thessaly, then Skyros looks as though it could be a sort of Brauron/Aulis-plus (and the Dolopes who lived in south-west Thessaly were also the inhabitants of Skyros). The tale went that Skyros used to be inhabited by pre-Greek peoples, and its soil was clay, poor for agriculture, good for goats – and it also had marble quarries, later much prized by the Romans.[23] It had been inhabited since early Helladic times but, despite Mycenaean remains, it is hard to see it as an independent economy and political power. It might well therefore be a cult-place whose significance could be as a margin, the Aulis of the Dolopes (though long ago Ludwig Preller thought of these stories as the local tales of Dolopians on Skyros, and that is not impossible).[24] Thus it seems to offer a comparable rhythm to other geographies we have looked at, and the theme of feminization is handled in a distinctive way. This myth could well go back to an initiatory ritual context.

Achilles' son Neoptolemos has a similar story too, that he is placed with Lykomedes on Skyros and must be brought from there to the Trojan War. In some way Neoptolemos' story fits better: Lykomedes is his mother's father ('maternal grandfather') and the maternal grandfather or uncle appears to have been an important person for initiation, all the way back to Indo-European times.[25] It is notable, for instance, that Odysseus acquires his (initiatory?) wound in a boar hunt when called to his maternal grandfather Autolykos at adolescence. Neoptolemos also exhibits name-change, receiving that name from Phoinix to replace his childhood name Pyrrhos ('Redhead'). Name-change in initiations can be a mark of adopting a new identity: 'Among the Sara the returning novices had to be introduced to their parents after having received a new name since their parents were supposed not to know them anymore.'[26] Achilles had originally been called Pyrrha (amongst the girls) or Ligyron; Herakles was originally called something like Alkides; and Alexandros the boy becomes the man Paris, a figure who in a sense fails the transition to warriorhood. But these names are not mere wilful alternatives.

But though initiatory characteristics can be found in the case of Paris,[27] it is hard to see where we would place any corresponding ritual. Not, surely, amongst Trojans. This is a story now running loose from ritual but bearing 'initiatory' hallmarks, created and elaborated when the dynamics that we find in initiation were understood, but maybe no more than that.

The case of Philoktetes on Lemnos is similar, maybe. On the way to Troy (a formula for incorporation of a story belonging elsewhere, if ever there was one), the Greek fleet is at Lemnos and Philoktetes is bitten on the foot by a snake. The smell from his suppurating wound is terrible and so are his cries. The Greeks therefore leave him on Lemnos until they find out that they need him and the bow of Herakles, which is his now, in order to capture Troy – and, it turns out, he will be the one to kill Paris (on the shape of the story see further CH. 22). Another embassy – like the one that fetched Achilles or Neoptolemos – is now needed to bring him to Troy. He is wounded, he bears a bow, and lives in the wild, hunting, but he has a mission to accomplish at the end. The initiatory overtones are strong, and so is the educational dimension when Sophocles in his tragedy the *Philoktetes* presents us with a Neoptolemos learning the real values of a civilized warrior.[28] But the geography does not seem to present a solution. Lemnos is a margin maybe for warriors in Troy, but Troy is an imaginary setting for foreigners, not a centre of Greek culture. It remains possible that Philoktetes is a genuine hero of myth on Lemnos, but if so his story has been altered beyond recognition in its adaptation to the Trojan War. My view is that, whatever old elements this contains, the appearance of initiation explains the flavour of the myth but probably not its origin.

Finally, let us look at Odysseus. Here is a man named by his maternal grandfather, Autolykos, and later sent to him, at which time he acquires a leg wound. His story is of wandering and performing feats in deeply uncivilized places. He can be seen as losing his identity while in the cave with Polyphemos – is he not 'No-one' (*Odyssey* 9.366)? He undergoes a confrontation with death and return. And finally he must assume (or resume) his identity as Odysseus, king of Ithaka. In the process he must go through a sort of marriage ritual: as happens for the heroine Draupadī in the ancient Indian *Mahābhārata* (1.174–88),[29] Penelope chooses a husband (the Indian ritual is a *svayamvara*, a 'self-choose'), and that must be done through an elaborate shooting feat. He is, thus, finally established as an accomplished warrior and is married.

There is no doubt that the *Odyssey* is an elaborate construction from very diverse elements, which convincingly dismantles and assembles a real hero and in the process interrogates many of the major values by which Greeks live. But it is not the 'sacred story' (*hieros logos*) of any ritual and is visibly in very large part a literary and intertextual production. Again, the geography helps. Can the kernel really be some story from the island of Ithaka? Penelope's father Ikar(i)os actually belongs in Sparta, and it was there that he set up a foot race for his daughter's hand, which was won by Odysseus. That tradition does not sit well with the main story of Odysseus. If he won such a race, he should have somehow won a kingdom there in the process – those are the rules of mythology, where property not infrequently passes via the female line (why else did the suitors beset Penelope?).[30] And one can see the awkwardness of location displayed in the story that Ikaros tried to persuade Odysseus to stay at Sparta (he declined to do so).[31]

So, even on an optimistic view of what can be recovered, or implied, about initiation in much earlier times, there are quite a number of mantraps.

Conclusions

Initiation has seemed important because features from initiation rites worldwide recur in Greek mythology, and because there are at least some facts of social organization and ritual that tempt us to assume a fully fledged system of age cohorts at an earlier stage. There is, however, a question one stage further back: why is initiation so widespread in societies studied by ethnologists? This seems more to be a matter of how the human animal characteristically behaves and views itself. Adulthood is not an arbitrary notion but one that is present in all human societies. It is a condition that, one way or another, must be entered. Physiology is not enough. Around that transition there arise issues of how an adult is to behave and what their respective functions are. What is it to be a warrior, or a graduate? What anxieties result for those about to face this transition and how may they be expressed and resolved? These fundamental concerns do drive initiation rituals, and personally I think that these rituals have specifically driven some of the Greek mythology. But the underlying concerns also drive many forms of narrative – novels in our time, and myths in ancient times – and thus Greek mythology is independently driven to replay the issues that were also present in some rituals.[32] The Telemachos of the *Odyssey* is recognizably a character undergoing that transition: he goes wandering in search of his father and in a way in search of his own role and identity; he is under the protection of a goddess as he does so; and he will return and perform the feat of a warrior. The study of initiation helps us to recognize these dynamics. But in this case it does state the origin of the myth. Homer has made it up, with his usual sureness of touch.

FURTHER READING

For a quick guide to initiation theory see Dowden 1992: ch. 7. This rested on Dowden 1989, a fairly full exploration of the theory as an explanation for the role of maidens in myth. Almost simultaneously, Brulé (1987, in French) had delivered closely comparable results, mainly focusing on girls at Athens. The theory became the subject of conferences whose papers were later amplified and published: Moreau 1992 (in French) and Padilla 1999, both basically in favour of using the theory, where Dowden 1999 raises a number of the 'qualifications' discussed above; Dodd and Faraone 2003, generally more sceptical (note Graf 2003), but not always, as in the creative chapter of Marinatos (2003). See, in response to this criticism, Dowden 2011 (in French).

Reading matter relevant to initiation stretches far beyond this, however. The study of the initiation of the male warrior first emerged in the hands of scholars sympathetic to the comparison of Greek practices with those of less developed societies, such as ethnographers had studied in Africa and Australia. So in some ways the theory begins with the work of Jane Harrison, who, though still living in the intellectual world of Sir James Frazer (see CH. 28), laid great stress on the significance of initiation customs for the interpretation of Greek, or at least some Cretan, material (J. E. Harrison 1912: ch.1). A much more thoroughgoing analysis of initiation in Greek society, with ample ethnographic parallels, and a particular focus on Sparta, was then presented by Jeanmaire (1939, in French) and in some ways later by Louis Gernet (see CH. 28). The 1960s marked a turning point: Brelich 1969 was a landmark: now there was, if in Italian, a thorough study of initiation, putting together festival and mythology, even if reviewers did not unanimously welcome it. Burkert (1966b, in German) deployed elements of initiation theory to work with the mythology and rituals affecting girls on the acropolis of Athens and their relationship to the great festival of Athens, the Panathenaia. And most important of all, Vidal-Naquet's 1986b (1968) searching and sensitive analysis of Athenian mythology, imagination, and landscape, unravelled the initiatory ideology behind the *ephebeia* (period of military service of Athenian youths). He later (Vidal-Naquet 1992 (1971)) conducted a similar analysis of the hero Philoktetes in Sophocles' play of that name (see also Lada-Richards 1997), though with more troubling theoretical implications (see Dowden 1999: 227–8). A further tantalizing piece of detective work on an individual ritual (and myth) is Graf's essay (2000 (1978)) on the case of the Lokrian maidens. For a more systematic view of the anthropology and semiotics of girls' rituals and their mythology, deriving from 1977, and now acknowledged as far ahead of its time, see Calame 1997 and especially 2001.

NOTES

1. Van Gennep (1960: 21).
2. See Dowden (1989).
3. Dowden (1992: 106–7).
4. Hesiod, *Catalogue of Women* F 130–133 MW (78–83 Most).
5. Apollodoros 2.2; Pausanias 1.43.4 mentions the tomb.
6. On the Proitids, see Dowden (1989: ch. 4, 1992: 108–9), Brulé (1987: 219–21).

7. Interestingly *boöpis* is also used as an epithet for Proitos' wife Stheneboia in Hesiod, *Catalogue of Women* F 129 MW (77 Most).

8. On Leukippos at Phaistos, see Dowden (1989: 65–7, 1992: 118).

9. See Dowden (1989: 62–7).

10. See, for example, Apollodoros, *Epitome* 1.22.

11. See, for example, Apollodoros, *Epitome* 1.8.

12. The theme of margin is explored by Vidal-Naquet in his discussions of the Black Hunter (1986) and of Philoktetes (1992); the margin dominates van Gennep's book (index s.v. 'Transition, Rites of', or in the French original 'Marge (périodes de)'). Achilles' Skyros is the equivalent of Philoktetes' Lemnos.

13. See, for example, *Homeric Hymn* 5 to *Aphrodite* 206–17; Apollodoros 3.13 for the role of the eagle.

14. For the Spartan system in an initiatory context, see above all Jeanmaire (1939). These terms are known from inscriptions: for example, IG V.1 256 (first century BC: *mikichiddomenos* and *pratopampais*), IG V,1 279 (first–second century AD: *pratopampaides*, *hatropampaides*, and *eirenes*), IG V.1 296 (second century AD: *mikichizomenoi* and *melleironeia*, the condition of being a *melleiren*). The fairly late date of these inscriptions is not surprising in itself, since Spartans of the classical period were much less inclined to commit matters to writing than were their rivals in Athens; the antiquity of the system has, however, been questioned: see for example, Kennell (1995). The *eirenes* figure in Xenophon's account of Spartan education (*Constitution of the Spartans* 2.5, 2.11) and are probably mentioned by Herodotos (9.85: the text is in doubt), while both *eirenes* and *melleirenes* appear in Plutarch's account in his *Life of Lycurgus* 17.

15. Nilsson (1932).

16. *Kypria* F 19 West (= Scholiast D on *Iliad* 19.326). Pausanias 1.22.6 may even be right that Homer is distancing himself from such a tradition by having Achilles capture Skyros.

17. Polygnotos: Pausanias 1.22.6. The best account of this myth is given (in German) by Robert (1920–6: 3.2.1 1106–10); see also Gantz (1993: 581).

18. Pausanias 1.43.4.

19. On Amazons see Blok (1994) and especially Dowden (1997).

20. On the number fifty see, for example, Dowden (1989: 157–8; 1992: 116).

21. *Priestesses of Hera at Argos*, in *FGrH* (and soon *BNJ* with English translation and commentary) 4 F 74–84. For Hellanikos, see CH. 3.

22. Spring, tree, and stone (here replaced by altar) are the standard set of markers for a pagan religious site: see Dowden (2000: 35–8).

23. Nikolaos of Damascus *FGrH* 90 F 41; Byzantine dictionaries, for example the *Etymologicum Genuinum*, s.v. *Arginousai*; Strabo 9.5.16.

24. L. Preller, *Griechische Mythologie* 2 'Die Heroen' (Berlin 1861²), 418: 'wo thessalische Doloper von Achill und seinem Sohne Pyrrhos oder Neoptolemos erzählten' ('where Thessalian Dolopes told stories about Achilles and his son Pyrrhos or Neoptolemos'). For the local significance of myth, see Graf, CH. 11.

25. On these issues see especially Bremmer (1983).

26. Bremmer (1978: 8).
27. See Gartziou-Tatti (1992).
28. We also know how Aeschylus and Euripides handled the story of Philoktetes: see Dio of Chrysostom, *Oration* 52.
29. For the *Mahābhārata* see CH. 18.
30. See the fascinating analysis of Finkelberg (2005: esp. 69–70).
31. Pausanias 3.12.1, 3.20.10–11; rather rationalized version in Apollodoros, *Library* 3.10.8. Material about Ikar(i)os was probably circulating in archaic epic poems outside the Homeric mainstream, cf. *GEF*: Asios F 10 and *Alkmaionis* F 5.
32. See Dowden (1999).

CHAPTER TWENTY-SEVEN

The Semiotics and Pragmatics of Myth

Claude Calame, translated by Ken Dowden

'*A science that studies the life of signs within society* is conceivable; it would be a part of social psychology and consequently of general psychology; I shall call it *semiology* (from Greek *sēmeîon* 'sign').'[1] These reflections of Ferdinand de Saussure (1857–1913) on language as a system of signs marked a decisive break from all those evolutionist perspectives, from Giambattista Vico (1668–1744) to Ernst Cassirer (1874–1945), that had associated myth as an entity with the first stages in the development of human thought. That had constantly led to a failure to distinguish between, on the one hand, a variety of forms of narrative and of language in various different social contexts, and, on the other, some primitive mode of reasoning.

Greek Myth and the Logic of Narrative

Saussure laid down two linguistic principles that are indispensable for a rigorous analysis of the narratives that we lump together under the modern, partly metaphorical, category of 'myth' – in contrast to the Greek word *mythos*, which denotes any form of discourse that is argued and thought out effectively:

1 In a system of signs such as language, each item is defined by its value relative to neighbouring elements – and this applies just as much to the phonetic perspective (dealing with the 'signifier') as it does to the perspective of meaning ('the signified').
2 No language as a linguistic system (*langue*) has any existence except when it is made present by speech (*parole*) – through utterances whose elements

A Companion to Greek Mythology, First Edition. Edited by Ken Dowden and Niall Livingstone.
© 2014 John Wiley & Sons Ltd. Published 2014 by John Wiley & Sons Ltd.

require examination for their syntax (the syntagmatic dimension) just as much as they do at the level of possible substitutes (the paradigmatic dimension).

When these two principles are applied to the study of mythology, they underpin various narratological analyses that focus on the unfolding of the narrative action of the myth in accordance with a particular logic; and on the other hand they give rise to structural analyses that are sensitive to the values embodied by the logic of the narrative, and to their organization into a certain number of binary oppositions. This, then, is how the great comparativist venture of Claude Lévi-Strauss – significantly entitled 'Mythologiques' (*Mythologica*, or maybe Mytho-*logics*) – came into existence. In the system of mythology, on his view, an individual myth can only achieve its meaning through the position it occupies relative to other versions and other myths (the principle of 'value'), and through the impact of logical permutations and transformations (the principle of the paradigmatic dimension) which in the end result from the structures of the human mind. Furthermore, within the individual myth and because of the mediating influence of the narrative sequence, the narration is organized on several levels (e.g., geographical, economical, and technical, sociological, cosmological, alimentary) that are considered to be 'codes'. Here, the semantic material is arranged, on the model provided by phonology, into great binary oppositions – such as the famous contrasts between nature and culture, male and female, raw and cooked.[2] These binary oppositions belong to the category of invariants and underpin the fundamental structures of meaning: they are the operators used in what has become the structural analysis of myth.

Syntax: 'narrative functions'/'motifemes'

Borrowing the concept of 'narrative function' from the Russian folklorist and formalist, Vladimir Propp, Lévi-Strauss turned himself into a mythographer and attempted to reduce the legend of the family of Oedipus to a single version. Next, he broke it down into a sequence of 'mythemes', which he then reorganized on the paradigmatic level into a series of oppositions based on the overvaluing of parental relationships and the lame gait associated with human autochthony (the quality of being born from the earth itself). So he dealt with the attachment felt by Kadmos to his sister Europa, the marriage of Oedipus to his mother, the love of Antigone for her brother Polyneikes, and the lameness implicit in the names Labdakos, Laios, and Oedipus ('Swollen-foot'). This was a contradictory logic through which an attempt was made to solve definitively the question of the origin and birth of mankind – from a single beginning or from two!

However, in the attempt to create a structural system, theorists have built on Propp's 'morphology of the folktale' (Propp 1968). This entails consideration of the *sequence of 'narrative functions'* (which sometimes become 'motifemes') and all their variants (e.g., a wrong committed, a lack identified, reaction of the hero, acquisition of a magical agent, trials), as well as the concept of *character type* (e.g., hero, dispatcher, opponent, helper). The aim is then to identify the standard structure of a narrative, with its sequence determined by the logic of the narrative (lack, manipulation, competence, performance, sanction),[3] and its protagonists, who are termed 'actants' in recognition of their functional roles: sender and receiver; subject (hero) and anti-subject; helper and opponent. As this logic is based on the transformation of states, it provokes a reversal of the content when thought of in terms of contraries and contradictions, for example, from nature to culture. This is how narratology – the science of narration – was born, with the help in particular of Algirdas Greimas.[4]

From the structuralist point of view, which closes the text in on itself, myth is immediately reduced to a narration by a mythographer, and it is the shape of the narration that becomes the operator in the reading of its plot. In this way, narratives as diverse as the madness that seizes the daughters of King Proitos (founder of Tiryns), the suicide of the three daughters of Kekrops (the autochthonous first king of Athens), or the Bacchic frenzy that condemns to an act of cannibalism the daughters of Minyas (founder of Orchomenos and ancestor of the Minyans) – all these can be reduced not only to the same plot but also compared one with another. In each case, the onset of madness is caused by an offended god: Hera, because of the arrogance of the three Proitids; Athene, because two of the Kekropids had broken her ban; and Dionysos, in the case of the three Minyads, as they refused to take part in his orgiastic cult.[5]

It is this practice of mythographical narratology that, for example, Walter Burkert follows when he reduces the birth story of several founding heroes to a single sequence of five narrative acts, approaching them from the perspective of their mother: Kallisto, mother of Arkas founder of Arkadia; Danae, mother of Perseus, founder of Mycenae; Io, mother of Epaphos, ancestor of the Danaans; Tyro, mother of Pelias and Neleus, future kings of Iolkos and Pylos respectively.[6] In the first stage (entitled 'leaving home' by Burkert) the young girl abandons childhood and family. Next ('the idyll of seclusion'), the adolescent goes through a period at the margins: Kallisto becomes Artemis' companion, hunting in the forest; Danae is imprisoned in an underground chamber of bronze; Io is condemned to virginity, becoming the priestess of Hera; Tyro, after being educated by her paternal uncle, goes to a river-god with whom she is in love. The young girl is next seduced, violated, made pregnant by a god ('rape'): Kallisto, Danae, and Io are seduced by Zeus, whose generative power can take the form of rain or a simple touch – he does not take on the appearance of an adolescent god like Apollo; Tyro unites with Poseidon, who has taken the form of the river. The young girl is then severely punished ('tribulation') – whether she is transformed into a bear like Kallisto, into a heifer like Io, shut up in a chest and cast upon the sea, as Danae is, or persecuted and made into a martyr by her stepmother as happens to Tyro. Lastly, the mother is rehabilitated ('rescue') after giving birth to a future founding hero: hunted as a bear by her own son, Kallisto is saved by Zeus himself and changed into a constellation; facing the advances of the king of Seriphos (who has given her hospitality), Danae is saved by her son Perseus, who turns the would-be suitor into stone by showing him the head of Medusa; Tyro is equally saved by her children, who kill the cruel stepmother; and as for Io she marries one Telegonos, a king of Egypt, or she introduces the cult of a Demeter that Egyptians assimilate to that of Isis.

As Burkert recognizes himself, this type of exercise in structural narratology can only be pulled off at the cost of extreme simplifications that reduce narratives, in their different versions and values, to a learned mythographic compendium. Even if we look no further than settings in tragedy, we are struck by the variations: according to Euripides' *Helen*, Zeus unites with Kallisto when she has already been transformed into a bear; the wanderings of Io, transformed into a heifer, to the ends of the earth – a matter of 'tribulation' rather than 'seclusion' – take place, according to the *Prometheus* of Aeschylus, *before* her congress with Zeus and therefore before the birth of the founding hero; in the *Diktyoulkoi* ('Net-fishers'), a satyr-play by Aeschylus, Danae is saved on the island of Seriphos by a band of satyrs; and the maltreatment of Tyro by her cruel stepmother Sidero is not just (apparently) an invention of Sophocles – who devoted two tragedies to these two female characters – but actually begins *before* the birth of the two children from the union with Poseidon.[7]

In Burkert's ethological and evolutionist approach, the narrative format is adapted from the functions defined by Propp (for a morphology based on a substantial corpus of folk tales) and then placed side by side with the ritual format found in rites of passage, and more precisely in tribal rites of initiation with their three standard phases: *separation* (from the world of childhood); *marginal period* (marked by a symbolic death); *incorporation* in the adult community with a new status, as described in CH. 26 of this volume. In turn this ritualized cultural behaviour can be traced back to the fundamental 'functions' of biological development: puberty, defloration, pregnancy, giving birth.

The practice of comparative narratology

We cannot be sure of an increase in understanding as an outcome of this type of formalism. Nevertheless, the narrative format can prove a useful tool for comparison when we are comparing two mythical narrations belonging to different cultures.

This is what happens, for instance, when we compare the Hittite myth of the struggle of the storm god against the dragon Illuyanka (see CH. 19) with the Greek myth of the battle of Zeus against the snakey, hundred-headed monster Typhon. The old version and the more recent version of the Hittite narrative can be reduced to a sequence of eight 'motifemes' (a term which can keep track of the semantic value of the function and of the action in question) that make up the 'combat-tale':

1 combat between hero ('champion', the storm god) and his opponent (the dragon);
2 defeat of the hero – the dragon has torn out his heart and eyes;
3 despair of the hero;
4 aid from a mortal helper – the god's son, born from the affair of the storm god with the daughter of the dragon;
5 the helper tricks the opponent – the dragon's wife returns the vital organs of the god;
6 the opponent loses his advantage – in a new combat against the storm god;
7 the hero defeats his enemy;
8 and the mortal helper dies – the storm god kills the dragon and his own son.

All this follows a scenario found in action films and cartoons, quite apart from bearing the traces of a programme inscribed in the biological nature of mankind.[8] Above all, this scenario would enable us to compare the Greek narrative with the twin Hittite versions and to take stock, from the angle of narrative logic, of the meaning of the two acts that make up these foundation narratives: (i) in his preliminary victory over Zeus, Typhon gains the sickle that Zeus was using to try and cut off the vipers attached to the monster's body and removes the tendons from the hands and feet of Zeus; (ii) Hermes and Aigipan steal the tendons from the dragon Delphyne, who has been hiding them in a cave, and this allows the final victory of Zeus over the monster Typhon, using his mighty thunder. However, this comparison cannot be productive unless it makes distinctions. Burkert tries to explain the disappearance in Greece of the motifeme of the death of the helper through the genealogy of the narrative itself – at the point where the later version of the Hittite narrative was rehandled and hellenized, probably in Cilicia.

Burkert next proceeds to identify the form and function of the inscription through which the two Hittite versions are known to us, basing himself for the Greek version on the mythographic narrative in the *Library* attributed to Apollodoros; that is, the liturgical character of the inscription which has the old and the new versions of the Hittite narrative is bracketed off by the narratological analysis. As it happens, the epigraphical text opens with an invocation calling for the prosperity and fertility of the Hittite land. And the enunciative character of these opening lines places the narration in the context of the cult of the storm god, particularly in the town of Nerik (one of the major religious centres in the Hittite empire) and its celebration of the *Purulli* festival (see CH. 19, p. 373). The recital of both versions formed an integral part of the ritual, as also in other places in the country, going through the aetiology of the ritual devoted to the 'the Storm-God of Heaven' worshipped at Nerik, and it was performed by the priest of the god.[9] For us, this text ends with details of a ritual procession and the means envisaged for welcoming in an exact order the gods who will take part in it.

The hymnic character of this double narrative, just as much as its actual inclusion in a ritual, make it a ritual act itself; and these different pragmatic processes endow the plot of the narrative, and the primordial figures that it brings to life, with an impact that is at once political and religious, within a particular institutional and cultural mix. It is within this cultic and cultural framework that it is able to acquire its whole meaning.

On the other hand, for his narratological comparison, Burkert selects the mythographic version presented by the late manual attributed to Apollodoros; and by this reduction of the narrative to a sequence of motifemes the historian of Greek religion increases the mythographic aspect of a narrative that remains, in this particular case, exceptionally rich in cosmic colouring and in references to mountain geography. Possibly the bardic version incorporated in Hesiod's *Theogony* might allow us to restore its agenda as a narration focused on the primordial combat that unleashes the forces of the cosmos and radically changes its constituent elements.[10] However, the logic of the theogonic narrative, being targeted as it is on the assertion of the rule of Zeus, doubtless ruled out the preliminary defeat of the master of Olympos and the intervention of a divine helper: as ruler of gods and men, Zeus evidently could only be the sole and undisputed protagonist of a cosmic duel complementary to the battle against the Titans. In any case, this narrative, with its simplified narratological sequence, takes on the same aetiological value as the Hittite narrative: the fact is that unforeseeable storms and gales, the ones that in the present capsize ships and ruin harvests, are traceable to the action of Typhoeus, who in the past was hurled into Tartaros by Zeus.

Semantics: codes and binary oppositions

We move on now from the *syntagmatic* logic of 'mythic' narratives to their semantic organization, which is a matter of *paradigm*. This is where Marcel Detienne has entirely justifiably borrowed from Lévi-Strauss the concept of semantic material organized as a set of codes to leaf through. The master-concept, or organizing principle, of a structural analysis that moves on from narrative logic to the architecture of meaning is once more the *binary opposition*. That is what drives us to make explicit in narrative and ritual the metaphorical values attributed in Greek culture to plants and animals in a meaningful ecology. That is what allows us to organize these values into contrasting features: the world of text becomes no longer a matter of linear development; it is, rather, one of deep structures which relate to the surrounding world like a huge interactive collection of representations – anticipating a concept that postmodern cultural relativism has ended up privileging.

Thanks to the skill of Detienne, one of the best known structural analyses is the one that contrasts the culture of the gardens of Adonis, whose blossoming is ephemeral and futile, with agricultural practices that form part of the long process of production in cereal agriculture. On the one hand we have Aphrodite and the flitting powers of erotic seduction, on the other, Demeter supporting legitimate and fertile marriage and the production of cereals which assure the survival of mankind. The ambivalence of mint, fragrant and aphrodisiac, but also moist and abortive, is illuminated by the story of Mintha, the concubine of Hades in his Underworld; it is implicitly contrasted with the complex ripening of the crops of Demeter, supported by the legitimate marriage of Persephone to the same Hades and by the rediscovery of mother and daughter.[11]

These initial oppositions, through the values placed on gods and plants, now enable us, for example, to compare the Adonia ritual with the Thesmophoria festival in this binary way. First, divinities: Adonis and his mistress Aphrodite contrast with Demeter Thesmophoros and her daughter Persephone. Next, the sociological code: courtesans and concubines are contrasted with legitimate wives. Sexual behaviour: sexual relations are contrasted with continence. Plants: we have incense and myrrh on the one hand and *agnus castus* on the other. Perfumes are exploited to excess at the Adonia, but the 'Bees' (the married women) hate seductive perfumes at the Thesmophoria. Such are the codes that articulate the semantic material of Greek mythology – attested in texts that range from the *Homeric Hymns* to Oppian's *Halieutika* via such works as Ovid's *Metamorphoses* or Ps.-Aristotle, *Problems*.

According to Detienne, such organization and manipulation of the semantic material in Greek myth is only made possible by viewing the totality of these narratives as tying into a 'mythology-framework of thought', in which, through different types of discourse, a 'mythology-knowledge' unfolds.[12]

Since this there have been, in the semiotic study of Greek myth, numerous attempts to combine the paradigmatic dimension with the syntagmatic dimension – often reducing one to the other. So, on the Anglo-Saxon front, thanks to Geoffrey Kirk, Homer's narrative of Odysseus' encounter with Polyphemos has been viewed from a Lévi-Straussian perspective and has become 'the myth of the Kyklopes'. Through the reduction of narrative functions into permanent distinctive traits, the Polyphemos of the *Odyssey* oscillates between the poles of 'super-uncivilized' (or 'barbaric') and 'relatively civilized': on one side we have the monstrous creature who is ignorant of cereal food and instead feeds on raw human flesh, recognizing neither gods nor the laws of men; on the other, the shepherd who loves his sheep and feeds on produce from their milk, recognizing the power of Poseidon. And as for the Kyklopes who live in the caves around the home of Polyphemos, their character is then divided between the (super-)civilized and the uncivilized: close to the gods, they enjoy a sort of Golden Age where neither agriculture nor viticulture are needed; however, neither do they have assemblies or customary law or any respect for Zeus. So it is that the narrative combines 'contradictory elements into a fantastic amalgam', in a series of poetic ambiguities based on the opposition of *nomos* to *physis* (convention to nature). To this extent, the Odyssean Kyklopes and Polyphemos may be compared with Gilgameš, the protagonist of the Akkadian epic (CH. 19), or with Cheiron and his Centaur brothers who distribute their half-animal nature and their sometimes violent acts between nature and culture.[13]

However, when we turn to the narrative weaving of codes and the structural articulation of cultural categories which are often thought universal, we have to take into account the role of the logic implied by the narrative 'grammar' – not so much a logic resting on the avoidance of contradiction, as a 'logic of the ambiguous, of the equivocal, of polarity'. As a result, Jean-Pierre Vernant suggested interpreting the two Hesiodic versions of the creation of Pandora, for Greeks the first mortal woman, in the light of the logic implied by the narrative of Prometheus' division of the sacrificial animal between men and gods. Through the various contrasts and homologies that articulate the semantic content in relation to the cultural context, the logic of ambivalence that pervades Hesiod's double narrative allows us to follow a series of inverse homologies between the figure of Pandora (the incarnation of the cereals that Zeus hides from men to punish them) and that of Prometheus (who hides the meat from the gods to keep it for men). There is also an inverted homology between the female womb where man lays down his seed in order to beget his progeny and guarantee his survival, and the belly which hides from view the sacrificial meat that ought to be consumed, thus consecrating the separation of gods and mortals. Thenceforth ambiguity and ambivalence characterize the relations between mortal men and gods to the extent that the gift of sacrifice is also a sort of concealment. So it is that the hallmark of the human condition is the ambivalent mixture of good and bad, of life and death.[14]

When they are set in motion by the narrative logic, homologies and reversals may, as they alternate between the categories of 'same' and 'other', organize myths as different as those of Narcissus and Herakles. On the one hand, we are led to perceive a young man refusing to yield to the sexual advances that tender beauty arouses and provoking the death of his lover before, in mirror fashion, he becomes the victim of his own beauty in an illusion that reduces 'other' to 'same'. On the other hand, we are presented with a civilizing hero who mediates between different sociological classes, whose life story (if we limit it to the labours) is written with an aristocratic-inspired logic, founded on contradictory motifs and registers (achievement and failure, necessity and free will). It also merges, in the Greek value system, the two categories of work for oneself and work for others and oscillates between profit and glory, payment and gratitude, slavery and freedom – and so on.[15]

Pragmatics: Performed Narratives

As we have already observed, any analysis that starts from semiotics – whatever the particular type of narratology or structural semantics involved – tends to reduce narrations which we judge belong to a culture's 'mythology' to simple mythographic narratives. It regularly cuts them off from their context and 'co-text'.

Lévi-Strauss himself, in an exemplary study, recognizes that certain codes that serve to organize the semantic context depend on, and make reference to, the reality of the culture in question. This is what happens with the geographic, techno-economic, and sociological 'levels' which determine the operation, over and above the cosmological code, of the four different versions of the 'Story of Asdiwal'. This story presents us with the nomadic itinerary that underpins the co-ordinates of the tribe, economy, and culture of the Tsimshian territory.[16] The surface sequences, which make up the lengthy narrative action of the founding hero, are organized less in virtue of codes than in accordance with deeper-seated 'schemas' that are interwoven in a melodic counterpoint of binary oppositions. This counterpoint recalls musical composition as it leads to the transformation of the feminine, expressed through the east–west axis and characterized by famine and movement, into the masculine, ordered on the high–low axis and marked by satiety and immobility. Now, it turns out that if the 'structure of the message' takes us to the meaning of a myth, then the myth must stand in a dialectical type of relationship to reality. So, for example, the mythic narrative inverts the institutions that in other ways it recognizes. So, if, when it is put side by side with a 'weakened' version, the narrative transformation brought about at several levels by the schemas makes reference to history (as known to the narrative) and its cultural payload, the question raised by Lévi-Strauss's analysis boils down to that of what it is that narratives we consider mythic actually refer to.

Myth, fiction, and reference

If we are inclined to stand by an analysis of discourse that is faithful to Saussurian principles, the reference of myth raises the issues of (i) the entirety of external signifiers from which it draws its symbolic universe, and (ii) the narrative and discursive forms that apply it to a precise social and institutional environment. This discursive realization is often a matter of ritual, and the resultant linguistic productions – which is what myths are – direct us to the ecology of that culture as well as to the universe of representations that constitute it and to the institutions that set their seal on its creation. The mythic narrative, let us not forget, is an object of belief, and in this respect it is endowed with discursive reference and a certain discursive impact. From his own perspective of functionalist anthropology, Bronisław Malinowski had already demonstrated on the one hand that meaning did not reside in the word or phrase alone but in its use in a context: 'The pragmatic relevance of words is greatest when those words are uttered actually within the situation to which they belong and uttered so that they achieve an immediate, practical effect.'[17]

And on the other hand, he had shown that traditional narratives, over and above their function of entertainment, assume the culturally essential function of perpetuating the social order.[18] Ahead of his time, he was thus, for the narratives that we label 'myth', laying down the foundations of what has since become the pragmatics of discourse. So we can see that well before the 'speech-acts' of John Searle, Malinowski was already aware of statements whose utterance contributes to the performance of an action, even if they do not wholly correspond to this act. In his anthropology of the Trobriand islanders, he observes that words pronounced, particularly in the case of religious utterances, function as acts: within the framework of pragmatics, he is in a way inventing the category of 'performative'. So, though they are often thought of as narrative fictions, stories that foreground heroes or gods turn out to present a strong pragmatic dimension. And this is by reason of their external reference as well as their circumstances of production and utterance.

Paradoxically, however, when we substitute appreciation of the pragmatics of discourse for structural approaches we find this presents a great deal of ambivalence as to the character and role of narrative fiction, particularly in the creation of mythic narrative. The point is that, in the perspective opened up by the philosophy of language, if you want to decide whether a narrative such as a myth has a factual or a fictional character, you can only turn to how it is produced and how it is received: everything depends on the author's intentions and on the associations which the narrative rouses at the point of its reception. So, narrative fiction on this view is a game of pretence (Searle 1979: 65–7).[19] In fact, if mythical discourse works, it is because of the strong relationship that narrative fiction and the world of text have with a world of cultural representations that corresponds to a universe of belief inscribed in space and time, and it is because of the poetic and practical, and usually ritualized, forms of communication that incorporate them in this universe.

Before they were transformed by a native literate culture into written *mythoi*, before they became 'fables' in the Enlightenment, and before they were established by the anthropological tradition first as 'Greek myths', then as 'Greek mythology', the Greek heroic narratives were active – in, and thanks to, their poetic form – within their particular ritual and cultural circumstances. So they passed through various poetic genres to us: Homeric narratives, lyric poetry, hymns, tragic settings, and so on. If we were to ignore that, we would be blunting most aspects of their meaning; and in the process we would be wiping out the plurality of narrative versions demanded partly by generic rules with their strong practical and institutional component, and partly by the varying ritual circumstances for their utterance and the varying historical circumstances that have led to its production. That would mean forgetting pragmatics and the functions that give rise to meaning. So, for example, we would be forgetting that the dive of Theseus – the founding hero of modern Athens – into the Aegean and his visit to his mother-in-law Amphitrite, celebrated in the narrative paean of seven young girls and seven young boys that he would presently save from the clutches of the Minotaur, forms the subject of a pair of pragmatic displays. One is iconic because it is inscribed on one of the walls of the Theseion next to the Athenian *agora*, reconstructed after the Persian War. The other is poetic: the heroic narrative is sung in a dithyramb by Bakchylides in honour of Apollo of Delos; the poem is performed by a chorus on the occasion of the great festival that brings together on that island representatives of all the cities that belong to the Delian League under the control of the Athenians.[20]

What in fact matters is the complex relations established through verbal means by the poem itself and the 'myth' narrated in it, with their world of reference. These relationships are at once semantic and figurative, syntagmatic and logical, pragmatic and functional, ritual and institutional. This may be a world of words (or pictures) that is created, fabricated, and indeed fictional in the etymological sense of the word. But its semantic cohesiveness and its internal logic depend heavily, and paradoxically, on the coherence of the relationships established with the external natural and social world at the point first of creation, then of poetic and musical performance.

Thanks to the resources of creative and poetic imagination, the influence of the verbal and rhythmic expression, the facilities that all languages offer for *deixis* (demonstration) through utterance, Greek myth stands out as a powerful instrument for poetic, musical, and social action. It creates 'possible worlds' in rhythmic poetic forms and various ritualized performances (yes, with a 'ludic' dimension). By these means Greek heroic narrative is a key operator in the symbolic construction of social beings in the context of their cultural and religious identity, in 'anthropopoietics'.[21] This happens in common reception in institutional situations which vary according to the context supplied by political circumstances and the cultural constellation, which form the world of reference.

So, once we abandon the structural principal of text, the narratological and semiotic approach to (Greek) myth can only be pragmatic – that is, anthropological in the broad sense of the term.

Sappho: reference by 'here and now'

This proposition can be illustrated on a small scale by a lyric poem of Sappho's from the island of Lesbos at the beginning of the sixth century BC. Though very fragmentary, these few lines in Aeolic metre show the linguistic relationship woven by practically every lyric poem between the heroic past of the civic community (the 'myth') and the *here and now* of its performance (corresponding to a ritual'):

> Here, near me, [appear ...
> powerful Hera, your [beauty? ...
> whom the Atreidai invoked [...
> the (illustrious) kings.
>
> Having completed [...
> first around (Ilion) [...
> they left to come to this very place [...
> (but) they could not [...
>
> Before (invoking) you and Zeus the god of suppliants [...
> and the lovely (son) of Thyone [...
> But now [...
> as of old.
>
> Holy and beautiful [...
> ...] maiden[s ...

(Sappho, F17 Voigt)[22]

From the first line of the poem, the particle *dē* (approximately translated 'here', but really indicating immediacy) focuses the appeal to the goddess Hera on the 'here and now' in which the poem is performed: this verbal gesture amounts to a *demonstratio ad oculos* (a 'display before your very eyes').[23] Straightaway the 'speech act' implied by the direct appeal to hear in the vocative, is set in the time and space of the song that is being performed. Given the present state of the text, this time cannot be determined more precisely, but another lyric composition, of Sappho's contemporary Alkaios does enable us to define the space. Alkaios' poem addresses the three divinities mentioned in Sappho in a similar way, and shares the same place: Zeus as protector of suppliants, Aiolian Hera, mother of everything, and Dionysos Kemelios, the eater of raw meat.[24] In this poem, also in Aeolic metre, several indicators of a demonstrative type show not only that the *I/we* of the song is probably a choral group of young women, but also that this chorus is situated in the pan-Lesbian sanctuary to the three divinities invoked. This poem belongs to a particular point in history and reflects the preparations being made for the liberation of Mytilene, the city on Lesbos ruled by the tyrant Pittakos. Another of his poems informs us, *inter alia*, that this sanctuary, common to the various little *poleis* on the island, was the scene for the famous beauty contests for women. It is these women in particular that Sappho was preparing for an accomplished womanhood through their aesthetic attitudes and the erotic charm of the poetic word.[25] So this is the cult space in which the probable choral group sang Sappho's poem and invited the goddess Hera to join them. In order then to reinforce the cultural impact of their sung appeal, the choral voice evokes a 'mythic' event situated in the paradigmatic time of heroes, namely the visit to this same place that is sacred to Hera by the Atreidai on the occasion of their return from the battlefield of Troy. However, significantly, the version of the return of the Achaian heroes adopted by Sappho is different from the one told in the cyclic epic the *Nostoi* ('Returns'); and it diverges in particular from the epic version reflected in the *Odyssey* (which mentions how Nestor, Diomedes, and Menelaos returned home via Lesbos).[26] Sappho reformulates the brief narrative setting and focuses it on Lesbos. Not only does Agamemnon now honour the island with his presence but Hera, the goddess of the local triad including also Zeus of Suppliants and Dionysos son of Thyone, must be responsible for assuring the safe return of these Greek heroes.

Everything happens as though the poetic argument underlying the appeal for Hera's intervention rested on an early exercise of mythography. The poem only mentions certain elements in the plot and a few proper names borrowed from the great heroic cycle. But there remains a nuance, that in this apparently mythographic narrative of Sappho's, the time and space of the heroic action are tightly woven into the time and space of the 'song act' constituted by the performance of the poem: the category of 'myth' thus infiltrates the category of 'rite'. In fact, it is not only that the location of the past action is marked by the deictic adverb *tyide* ['to this very place'], in effect 'here before our eyes'. More than that, in the narrative evocation of the *nostos* of the Atreidai, Hera is always present as *you*. So, in this poem with its strong pragmatic dimension, the two levels of utterance carefully distinguished by Émile Benveniste interlock: the category of 'discourse' characterized by the indicators *I/you*, *here*, and *now* constituting 'the formal apparatus of utterance', overlay the category of 'history' or 'narrative', marked by the forms *he/she*, *there*, and *once upon a time*.[27]

Starting from this spatial identity, the temporal return of the heroic past towards the cultic execution of the poem in the present is guaranteed by the expression *nyn de* ('but now'), a frequent one in lyric poetry. Furthermore, the scraps of papyrus found at Oxyrhynchus allow us to suppose that one or more young girls ('maiden(s)') took part in the ceremony that constituted the *here and now* of the poem, and this is what invites us to envisage that the mythic narrative of the return of the Atreidai via Lesbos was sung by a choral group of young girls. The mythic narrative probably finds its final stage of confirmation (Propp's 'sanction', cf. p. 509 above and n. 3) in the choral performance of the poem *here and now*.

In any case, it is doubtless not a matter of chance if, in this context where heroic past and the present of the poem's cultic utterance coincide, the time of the return of the Atreidai seems to be marked as *palaion* ('of old'). This term takes us back to one of the native categories that we should substitute in the case of ancient Greece for the modern concept of 'myth' such as has entered our encyclopaedic knowledge through comparative cultural anthropology. Anthropological respect for native categories, those classified as 'emic', would lead us in this case to favour the first Greek historiographers. If we are to avoid all the misunderstandings that can arise from the prejudices raised by treatment of myth as 'fabulous' or 'fictive', we should only use the term 'myth' with reference to the *palaion*, the *archaion* (ancient), if not quite to a *logos* (account). These, in fact, are the terms which in classical Greece are used to mark a narrative action which relates to the age of heroes but is referred to the present from the angle of the discursive forms that shape its plasticity.[28]

Myth between Fiction and Performance

An approach to the semantic universes created by mythical poetics which is based on speech acts and the semantics of narration reminds us of a key fact: precisely because of its discursive form, Greek myth is also ritual – it is a *legomenon* (utterance) that is simultaneously a *drōmenon* (action), if not a *deiknymenon* (display),[29] to the extent that the heroic action evoked is carried by the voice in the act of singing the lyric poem, which then in turn corresponds to an act of cult. This relationship, which belongs to the pragmatic category but tends to the performative, is often reinforced when the poetic narrative tells the event from which the ritual providing setting for the poetic performance originated.[30] So what we are witnessing, through the devices of musical and choreographic poetry, is the setting in aesthetic discourse of a mythic narrative in action – which we will promptly label 'fictional'. Poetic pragmatics places the internal narrative and semantic coherence of this possible world in relation to the world of *here and now* at its particular historical, cultural, and religious moment.

Thus there is nothing more misleading than the evolutionist perspective that still haunts the conception of myth offered to us by an Ernst Cassirer, and nothing more artificial than the distinction between three supposed stages of *Sprache, Mythos,* and *Erkenntnis* – namely, *language* as the concrete expression of meaning, *myth* as a form of thought expressing the self and the soul, and *knowledge* as scientific and belonging to a conceptual category.[31] So it is that myth is ontologized for the benefit of a last avatar of German idealism: myth is given a substance that will help it defend progress towards a form of reason which is the prerogative of European thought, and Greek myth will once more guarantee the illusory passage from *mythos* to *logos*.[32]

This also means that, in contrast to any fiction in the normal sense of the term, the huge narrative domain now marked off as (Greek) 'mythology' deserves no charter of semantic independence or of structural closure. If it is true that one of the first actions in cultural anthropology is classification and also that religious phenomenology is based on establishing typologies, we will not be surprised at the success of structural analyses of myth. Reducing semantic universes with their plasticity and evolutions to a series of binary oppositions, as favoured by research into artificial intelligence, is doubtless intellectually as satisfying as it is reassuring. However, from the perspective of practical anthropology as much as that of pragmatic semiotics, such constructions are no longer defensible, and indeed through structural closure, the semiotic analysis of myth introduces the danger of a new Europo-centric idealism. When coupled with a perspective of anthropological relativism which is just as relevant to our readings of myth, a pragmatic opening-up to take in specific situations in space and time restores cultural and aesthetic creativity to these narratives with their poetic polysemy.

Myth is created when phonic and verbal material is endowed with rhythm, when the syntax of utterance mixes 'narrative' and 'discourse', and when poetic semantics are based on metaphor and on the deictic pragmatics of a poetry of action. Thus 'myth' collapses into its poetics – a poetics that is fundamentally referential and practical, at least as far as ancient Greece goes. And as a result, through the medium of poetic song, the temporal and spatial dimensions of heroic legend are related to the *here and now* of ritual celebration, in ritualized political and religious circumstances and at a historical and cultural point where this, coinciding with the present, finds its relevance and therefore its truth. As a verbal poetic creation, heroic narrative with its extraordinary plasticity therefore represents a form of knowledge, a form of practical knowledge. Its impact is of the 'anthropopoietic' category and may be realized by the collective practice of a body of people as well as by the symbolic speculation of collective memory, a collective memory that is subject to the vagaries of the creation and reformulation of cultures.

FURTHER READING

For an introduction to methods of reading and analysing Greek myth, one can start with the useful introductory works of Dowden (1992: 22–38), Graf (1993a: 35–56), Buxton (1994: 182–218), and especially Saïd (1993: 79–110). See also the various structural readings of Greek myths in Csapo 2005: 181–261, and the practical exercises usefully offered by Delattre 2005. Collections of readings of Greek myth influenced by the semio-narrative approach can be found in J. Bremmer 1987, Calame 1988, Edmunds 1990, and Woodard 2007. Interpretations in the areas of narratology and structural analysis have been proposed successively by Kirk 1970 and Burkert 1979. Calame 2003 presents different versions of a foundation myth in a reading that combines narrative analysis, semantic study, and attention to pragmatics (see also Calame 2009a and 2009c). For semio-narrative analysis of myth in general, the reader may refer to the classic studies now collected in del Ninno 2007. For the various versions and poetic forms of Greek myths, the manual of Gantz (1993) is indispensable. Finally, Greimas and Courtés 1983 is the best resource for understanding the technical terms of semiotics and language.

NOTES

1. Saussure (1915 [1974]: 16).
2. See the introductory pages of *Mythologiques* (Lévi-Strauss 1964: 17–22, 26–34; cf. Saïd 1993: 98–9), to which one may add the methodological comments that punctuate the work of 1973 (e.g., 82–4, 189–93, 244–5, 322–5).
3. In the form mentioned here, *lack* coincides with a rupture in the narrative equilibrium: it provokes the quest and the *manipulation* by the sender, who confirms – often in a contract – the *competences* of the hero; it then leads to the *performance* of the hero, which is acknowledged in the *sanction* (formal acknowledgement) by the sender, at the end of the narrative.
4. The canonical schema for narration has taken different forms, which are listed and commented by Adam (1991: 65–95).
5. See, on this point, the nuanced comparative analysis of Dowden (1989: 71–95).
6. Burkert (1979: ch. 1).
7. Cf. Burkert (1979: 7 and n. 20), Euripides, *Helen* 375–80 (Kallisto); Aeschylus, *Prometheus* 829–35, 846–51 (on the practical significance of the tribulations of Io, see Calame (2000a: 124–30); the Egyptian marriage of Io is not attested before Apollodoros, *Library* 2.1.3); *TGF* 3. 161–2 (editor's introductory note on *Diktyoulkoi*); *TGF* 4. 463–4 (editor's introductory note on *Tyro*) and F 648: cf. Gantz (1993: 198–204).
8. Hittite cuneiform inscription, translated in *ANET* 125–6; amongst the many discussions, see Burkert (1979: 7–10, 14–18).
9. Cf. Labat *et al.* (1970; 526–9, also 513, 519).
10. Hesiod, *Theogony* 820–60, with the comparative commentary of M. L. West (1966: 379–97), who notes that the nature and deeds of Typhoeus must also be

set alongside those of the monster Ullikumi in the Hurrian succession narrative (for which see 1966: 21).

11. Detienne (1994: 72–98).
12. Detienne (1988: 31–2).
13. According to the comparative analysis presented by Kirk (1970: 132–71, the quotation is from 168). See also, for example, the landscapes of Pan analysed by Borgeaud (1988: 73–114) as lying between hunting and stock-rearing, nature and culture.
14. According to the study of the 'myth of Prometheus in Hesiod' by Vernant (1974: 177–94), complemented by the methodological observations formulated at 244–50 (the quotation is at 250). There is an attempt to systematize on the basis of a 'semiotic square' in Csapo (2005: 247–61).
15. See, respectively, the narratological analysis of different versions of the Narcissus story presented by Pellizer (1991: 46–58), and the very much structurally inspired study that brings to a schematic end the review of historical methodology in Csapo (2005: 301–15).
16. Lévi-Strauss (1973: 175–233).
17. Malinowski (1935: 2.52, cf. 46; and see altogether vol. 2, part 4 'An Ethnographic Theory of Language', esp. divisions 3–5), and cf. the reflections of the linguist and semiotician Adam (1995: 234–43).
18. Malinowski (1935: 2.47).
19. Searle (1979: ch. 3, 'The logical status of fictional discourse'), for example (67): 'Telling stories really is a separate language game; to be played it requires a separate set of conventions, though these conventions are not meaning rules.' See also the useful commentary of Genette (2004: 143). For Greek myths, cf. Delattre (2005: 34–43).
20. Pausanias 1.17.3–6 and Bacchylides 17, cf. Calame (2009b: 143–94). On the different types of performance of Greek myth, see, for example, Graf (1993a: 142–68) and Buxton (1994: 18–52).
21. On the concept of 'anthropopoiesis', the (cultural) fabrication of man, see the studies in Affergan *et al.* (2003: esp. 17–74 (on the 'fictive' cf. 75–98)).
22. Also in English in D. A. Campbell, *Greek Lyric*, Loeb Classical Library, 1 (Cambridge MA, London 1990²) 68–9.
23. For commentary on Sappho F17 see especially Aloni (1997: 28–9), with bibliographic references for the various supplements proposed to fill in the gaps. The argument summarized here is developed at length in Calame (2009c: 3–7).
24. Alkaios F 129 Voigt; for the political role of this 'pan-Lesbian' sanctuary, see especially Burnett (1983: 157–63).
25. Alkaios F 130 B, 17–40 Voigt.
26. *Odyssey* 3.165–72; Page (1959: 59–62) notes the important variants in the Lesbian version of this 'return', especially the probable presence of Agamemnon.
27. See the classic chapters of Benveniste (1966: 237–50, 258–66); for the interaction of 'discourse' and 'story/narrative' with gestural verbal *deixis* as its starting point, see my argument in Calame (2004), and the other contributions to that special issue of the journal *Arethusa*.

28. For the two concepts of *palaion* and *arkhaion*, see Calame (2003: 22–7).
29. These are the traditional categories for describing the constituents of the ritual at the Eleusinian mysteries, cf. Mylonas (1961: 261–74).
30. The aetiological functions of mythic narratives in relation to ritual are explained by Graf (1993a: 101–20) and Delattre (2005: 185–222).
31. In addition to his masterwork, *The Philosophy of Symbolic Forms* (Cassirer 1955–7), see Cassirer (1973: 62–83).
32 Criticism of this ontological conception of myth in Detienne (1981: 87–123, 225–42), and Calame (2003: 3–8).

PART VI

CONSPECTUS

CHAPTER TWENTY-EIGHT

A Brief History of the Study of Greek Mythology

Jan N. Bremmer

The History of Mythology

The study of Greek mythology has a long history, of about 2,500 years. The first mythological 'handbooks' were already written around 500 BC (see CH. 3),[1] and interest has rarely ever disappeared. Yet each time has its own interests and approaches, depending on the social and cultural circumstances of the day. It is the function of this chapter briefly to present that history. Naturally, it is impossible to treat every period in detail, and I will strictly concentrate on the history of Greek myth rather than the study of mythology in general. This history has, of course, been described before, and I have gratefully profited from earlier histories.[2] Yet there is room for a new version, as our knowledge of the study and collecting of mythology in antiquity itself, which we usually call 'mythography', has recently been the subject of a fresh approach by Alan Cameron.[3] Moreover, as the scholars who dominated the study of mythology in the second half of the twentieth century are gradually passing away, it becomes easier to look back at what has been a fascinating era in the study of Greek mythology.

Antiquity

In the Golden Age of Roman poetry, Roman poets often took material from their learned Greek sources, such as Callimachus and Apollonios of Rhodes. Parthenios of Nikaia, a Greek poet who had been brought to Rome in the

---

A Companion to Greek Mythology, First Edition. Edited by Ken Dowden and Niall Livingstone.
© 2014 John Wiley & Sons Ltd. Published 2014 by John Wiley & Sons Ltd.

earlier first century BC, even dedicated a small book with mythological love stories, *Sufferings in Love*, to Cornelius Gallus (c. 70–26 BC), clearly anticipating that Gallus would use them 'for hexameters and elegiacs'.[4] In fact, there must have been many Hellenistic and Imperial mythographical handbooks, but they have virtually all been lost to us.[5] Even when we have surviving specimens from Hellenistic times, such as the rationalizing, probably late fourth-century BC, Palaiphatos' *On Unbelievable Tales*, which was an important source for Servius (below), and Eratosthenes' *Catasterisms*, our surviving texts are only strongly abridged versions of the originals.[6]

The same is true for the much longer *Genealogiae* of the mythographer Hyginus (who wrote under Augustus, 31 BC– AD 14), of which we also have only an abridged version, which modern editors commonly call *Fabulae*. It gives not only all kinds of potted mythological plots but also provides lists of all kinds of mythological subjects, such as 'Those who have become immortal from mortals' (224), 'Those who founded the first temples of the gods' (225) or 'Mothers who killed their sons' (239).[7] Such lists came in handy for a culture, the so-called Second Sophistic of the second–third century AD, that greatly appreciated mythological allusions in the novel, oratory, pantomimes, and the visual arts. A man or woman of culture was supposed to know Greek mythology just as in our times older generations were supposed to know the stories of the Bible. As it was part of the display of conspicuous education (*paideia*) to cite mythological details and their sources, we still have many references to obscure mythographers, so much so that many of these references may well be totally invented.[8] That is why we not only have such lists in Hyginus, but also on many papyri.[9] In fact, it is clear that even schoolchildren had to learn such lists, as school exercises on papyri demonstrate.[10] For example, a fairly recently published papyrus begins with the sons of the Seven against Thebes, continues with minor female goddesses, such as the Fates, Horai, Graces, Sirens, Gorgons, Titanesses, Eumenides, Harpies, Hesperides, and, if that is not enough, concludes with the Sentences (pithy sayings) of the Seven Wise Men.[11]

Another surviving Augustan collection with Hellenistic material, if again in slightly abridged form, is that of Konon (*BNJ* 26), whose collection of fifty narratives focuses on foundations of cities (*ktiseis*) and stories that give rise to cult practices (these stories are '*aitia*'). He also pays attention to homosexual and heterosexual love stories.[12] The second- or third-century author Antoninus Liberalis collected a series of forty-one *Transformations* taken from many Hellenistic authors who are often indicated by name, which displays a great interest in metamorphoses and local cult *aitia*.[13] Finally, in the later first century AD, some of the Hellenistic material was also collected in a kind of mythological guide to Homer, the so-called *Mythographus Homericus*, a lost handbook that contained at least 250 mythological stories, much of which survives only in bits and pieces in the scholia to Homer.[14]

Fortunately, we also have a somewhat more narrative source: the handbook of 'Apollodoros' that dates perhaps from the first century AD (see pp. 66–72). Apollodoros gives us many Greek myths, and in his genealogical sections he follows the Hesiodic *Catalogue* (CH. 3) extensively, although adapted to the contemporary *Orphic Rhapsodies* (CH. 4) in a number of details. Yet he was certainly not a first-hand reader of many of the works he cites. It has become increasingly clear that Apollodoros too is already dependent on other Hellenistic mythographical handbooks.[15] His main source may well be the erudite scholar Apollodoros of Athens (c. 180–120 BC). whose rationalizing work *On Gods* was clearly an important quarry for later authors on mythology. This Apollodoros was a real scholar whose main interest was the interpretation of the names and epithets of the gods, but who to that end also distinguished different versions and sources of myths.

It was, then, the need to possess cultural capital at the beginning of our era that has saved many details from ancient mythological sources for us.[16] Other sources were the handbooks written as companions for the leading Roman poets Ovid and Vergil. These became increasingly important by the fourth century AD when mythological poetry experienced a kind of revival. Especially Servius, the learned commentator on Vergil, has preserved an immense wealth of mythological data for us, and it has only very recently become clear that he derived much of what he records from a, or several, lost handbook(s) that was (were) probably written in the second century, which Alan Cameron calls the *Mythographus Vergilianus*. Its model was the already mentioned *Mythographus Homericus*.[17]

The Middle Ages

The growing apart of the Eastern and Western halves of the Roman Empire, and the eventual fall of the latter, made knowledge of Greek mythology an ever scarcer commodity in the West in the centuries between the fall of Rome to the Germanic peoples and the rise of Charlemagne (see CH. 17). In fact, those who had knowledge of Greek and Greek mythology were gradually reduced to an extremely small minority. The main sources available were the already mentioned Servius, astronomical works (and commentaries on them), such as the Latin translation of Aratos and Hyginus' *On Astronomy*, which contained much material to explain the mythological names of the constellations, the scholia on Statius' *Thebaid*, and the learned, probably mid-sixth-century Fulgentius, with his etymologizing and allegorizing style (CH. 17, pp. 334–5).[18] The available evidence, to which we of course have to add Ovid's *Metamorphoses*, which was the richest Latin text available for anybody interested in Greek myth during the Middle Ages, depreciated in quality through the earlier Middle Ages through the ongoing loss of manuscripts, but also developed, in particular into the allegorizing direction due to Fulgentius' influence. Yet the need for commentaries on the most popular school author, Vergil, and also for glosses on other popular authors, kept the interest in mythology alive, especially in French and Anglo-Saxon schools, as students had to know the stories behind all the strange names they met in their texts in order to understand what was going on.[19]

A pleasant surprise took place in 1831 when it was announced that at least three mythographers had been discovered in the Vatican, which subsequently became known as the First, Second, and Third Vatican Mythographer, even though the First is known only from one, the Second from more than ten and the Third from more than forty manuscripts. The First, and most important, Vatican Mythographer collected his myths, about 230 in number, from the Latin sources at his disposal, but especially from Servius and, if somewhat less, from the scholia on Statius. He no longer had access to Greek sources and therefore probably did not indicate his sources. Moreover, he does not use any systematic criteria in his enumeration. This is immediately clear at the beginning, as the first three entries deal with Prometheus, Neptunus and Minerva, and Scylla. His aim was to compose a mythological repertory for the schools – in which he must have succeeded, as his model was taken over by the other two Vatican Mythographers.[20] Unfortunately, his exact date, like those of the others, has not yet been established, but he must have lived between AD 875 and 1025, and possibly worked in France. Although, his work is rarely consulted any longer, he has been very successful in one aspect. He calls the Greek myths *fabulae*, and this term, instead of our modern 'myth', maintained itself as the most common one in Germany into the eighteenth century and in France well into the nineteenth century.[21]

The Renaissance and the Early Modern Period

Although the Mythographers were successful for a while, their dry style could no longer satisfy the Renaissance, and their latest manuscript predates the age of the printed book. The competition came from Italy,[22] where, in 1380, the famous author of the *Decamerone*, Boccaccio (1313–75), published *On the Genealogy of the Pagan Gods* (*De genealogia deorum gentilium*) in three books, which became the model for all Renaissance mythographies of Italy. The book was immediately highly popular and, after having been printed in Venice in 1472, reached ten editions in the next sixty years, not to mention the Italian, Spanish, and French versions. Like many medieval scholars, Boccaccio thought that great truths were hidden beneath the surface of the classical myths which he promised to unveil. He thus continued the allegorical approach but combined it with the medieval encyclopedic tradition. However, he followed a genealogical model of exposition, did not know Greek (although he did quote Arabic astrologers), did not distinguish between different versions, and did not manage to package his erudition in such a way that it was easy for poets or artists to consult. In fact, as is true of many classical handbooks – contemporary with him and indeed earlier – his knowledge is often indirect and frequently based on his predecessors.[23]

This all changed with the appearance of Natale Conti's *Mythologiae* in Venice in 1567,[24] the most lucid, learned, and accessible mythography of the Late Medieval and Renaissance period, which was often reprinted. Natale Conti or Natalis Comes (1520–?82) was a learned man, who not only knew Greek, but also translated Greek works, such as Athenaios, and even wrote Greek poetry.[25] It is therefore not surprising that his work contains about 3,000 references to Greek and Roman literature, although he did not shrink from cleverly faking a number of them. In his expositions, Conti weighed the potential value of each myth to the Renaissance Christian. His work is thus not only a mythological handbook but also a manual of behaviour. It is probably this combined quality that made his work the most popular handbook in the sixteenth and seventeenth centuries. It appeared early enough to be used in England by Spenser, but Milton and Robert Burton consulted him too. His influence would endure until the later seventeenth century, as his work was last reprinted in Hanover in 1669.[26]

Although the study of mythology did not make much progress in the seventeenth century and myth was still approached as part of erudition and etymologies,[27] the world did change. The great European discoveries brought an enormous mass of evidence about foreign peoples with religions the Europeans never had even dreamt of. This made the more perceptive intellectuals realize that the traditional stories from Greece and Rome perhaps were more than just 'stories' – *fabulae*, as they were still called in imitation of the First Vatican Mythographer – and did deserve serious attention.

The Enlightenment

The turning point in this development is a brief essay, *De l'origine des fables*, published in 1724, but probably written in the 1690s, by the Frenchman Bernard de Fontenelle (1657–1757). It still is a delight to read because of its light, rationalistic tone, which not only suggests a human origin for religion and a scepsis regarding miracles – in this respect Fontenelle is a forerunner of David Hume – but also imagines the birth of myth from simple accidents: 'A young man fell into the river and no one could recover the body. What happened? The philosophy of the time teaches that there are in the river young

girls who rule it. The girls have carried off the young man – as is very natural –
and one needs no proofs in order to believe it.'

From one such story 'primitive man' made many others by analogy, according to Fontenelle. But he did not stop at reflecting on the origin of myth.
He also inaugurated the comparative method by noting similarities 'between
the fables of the Americans and those of the Greeks', such as both sending
'the souls of those who have lived badly to certain muddy and disagreeable
lakes'. Even more astonishing is his comparison of the myth of Orpheus with
that of the Inca Manco Capac in that both were a kind of culture bringer.
Rather daringly, Fontenelle also concluded from this comparison that the
Greeks, like the Americans, had been 'savages'. Finally, he noted that writing
helped to disseminate myths but also fixed them in the state they were. This
interest in the effects of writing on myth is highly unusual and will not be
found again until contemporary analyses. At the end of his essay he strongly
rejected the idea that the Greek myths contained 'hidden secrets of the physical and moral world'. On the contrary, they revealed 'the history of the errors
of the human mind'. It is clear that Fontenelle was on the side of the moderns
in the famous 'Quarrel of the ancients and moderns'. His essay is perhaps one
of the most influential attempts at discrediting the ancient allegorical approach
of myth. It also shows that the medieval and Renaissance approach had come
to an end, without there yet being a new paradigm.[28]

Unlike Fontenelle, who paid little attention to any particular myth, his
learned compatriot Nicolas Fréret (1688–1749) added another, perhaps even
more important, aspect: mythology as expression of the culture, customs, and
social order of a specific community. He thus explained the three divine generations of Hesiod's *Theogony* – Ouranos and Gaia, Kronos and Rhea, and
Zeus – as the reflection of three theological systems. The myth of the Thracian
king Lykourgos' resistance against Dionysos and his mainads in *Iliad* 6
reflected the resistance of the northern Greeks against the introduction of the
god's cult; this interpretation was long accepted and disproved only by the
discovery of Dionysos' name in the Linear B tablets.[29]

These French views also received attention outside France.[30] Christian
Gottlob Heyne (1729–1812), Professor of Greek and University Librarian at
Göttingen,[31] almost certainly knew Fontenelle and certainly was acquainted
with Fréret. Heyne was deeply interested in Greek myth and often wrote
about it: he even edited the mythographer Apollodoros in an edition that long
remained authoritative (1782–3). In Heyne's opinion it was important to
have handbooks of Greek myth for artists and pupils, but he also considered
Greek myth important for the study of mankind, philosophy, and religion. Yet
in order to avoid the connotation 'false tale' of Greek *mythos* he came up with
a new term for these Greek traditions. Instead of the usual German *Fabel* and
Fabellehre ('mythology'), he introduced the term *mythus* in 1783,[32] and

posited that myth explained the admirable and frightening sides of nature. Moreover, like his friend Johann Gottfried Herder (1744–1803),[33] he departed from the presupposition that myth had a local origin and gave expression to the *Volksgeist*.[34] Unlike Fréret, Heyne was more interested in myth in general than in specific myths. He wrote much about the origin of mythic thought, but in the end he made not much progress with the interpretation of individual myths. In fact, towards the end of his life he wrote a kind of guide for the interpretation of Greek mythology in which he argued that the mythical language (*sermo mythicus*) should not be analysed according to modern criteria but according to the usage of ancient times. Moreover, myths that seem to defy interpretation can be interpreted by comparing them to those of the 'savages' or by applying what we know about the ancient culture. Finally, as there is no system in Greek mythology we always have to look first for the origin of the myths. In the end, Heyne was clearly rather sceptical about the possibility of our bringing some order to the 'chaos' of Greek mythology.[35]

Nineteenth-Century German Scholarship

Heyne was indebted to the Enlightenment, but also to the beginning of the Romantic movement. It was especially the latter that would be highly influential in Germany. It is probably no exaggeration to state that one of its consequences was a 'longing for myth' that would remain a feature of German culture well into the twentieth century.[36] Yet this fascination did not immediately promote a proper understanding of myth. At the beginning of the nineteenth century, the Heidelberg classicist Friedrich Creuzer (1771–1858) published a huge four-volume work, *The Symbolism and Mythology of Ancient Peoples, Especially the Greeks,* that attracted much attention and fierce discussion.[37] Creuzer, like other contemporaries such as Herder and Goethe, had been much impressed by the recent translations of Indian classics, such as the *Bhagavadgītā* (1785) and the *Upanishads* (1801) and thought that these contained a much older body of myth than the Greeks possessed. Consequently, Creuzer tried to interpret Greek mythology using an Indian key but also the help of the Neoplatonist tradition – and fertility symbols, which had more recently come to the fore in scholarly discourse.[38] Naturally this did not result in a clear method, quite the contrary, and his symbolic approach, though influential, was soon rejected.[39]

It is therefore not surprising that in 1825 one of Heyne's successors at Göttingen, Karl Otfried Müller (1797–1840), published a new study with the programmatic title *Prolegomena to a Scientific Mythology*.[40] With Müller we are well into the age of Romanticism, and this is clearly visible in his work.[41] Myth was for him 'Narratives of acts and fates of individuals', which belong to a time preceding the real history of Greece. It is highly interesting that Müller, a close friend of the Grimm brothers and familiar with their work on fairy tales, stresses that myth is a narrative, as this aspect has often been neglected in subsequent research. In fact, that myths could travel and incorporate elements from other cultures was not recognized by Müller either. But he stressed that myth did not, as many a forerunner and contemporary still thought, contain symbolic, allegorical, or philosophical wisdom. This was enormous progress – from which his most important successors could no longer retreat.

Following Herder, Müller stressed that myth was the reflection of the national (= tribal) identity ('Mythos als Stammsage') and of different historical periods. Thus the myths of Demeter belonged to the world of the prehistoric peasants, whereas those of Zeus and the Olympians were typical of the feudal, Homeric way of life. Müller's interest was mainly historical with little attention to the intellectual content of myth. For him, myth was primarily an important instrument to penetrate the darkness of Greek tribal prehistory, for which reason he focused not only on the myths of specific peoples but also of particular places, thus initiating an important strand in the study of mythology up to the present day. Müller even reflected on the relationship between myth and ritual by postulating, certainly partially rightly as we will see presently, that myth arose from cult.[42] His interest in the tribal nature of Greek mythology was shared by his contemporaries, and in Germany with its *Kleinstaaterei* Müller's influence would last well until the beginning of the twentieth century.[43]

It was one of the disastrous legacies of Romanticism that scholars now started to see Nature everywhere in Greek myth. This becomes very clear in the leading and often reprinted German handbook of Greek mythology of the second half of the nineteenth century by the Hellenist Ludwig Preller (1810–61).[44] Preller divided his *Griechische Mythologie* into two volumes, one on the gods and one on the heroes. We should not forget, though, that German scholars long used the term 'mythology' where modern scholars would use the term 'religion'.[45] In other words, his *Griechische Mythologie* still combined the study of Greek mythology and religion in a manner that later scholars would gradually abandon. While still using Heyne's term *mythus*, Preller had an open mind and, unlike later German scholars, still admitted influence from the Orient; in many ways his was the first modern systematic collection of the mythological evidence. The fascination with Nature is also very much apparent in the books and largest dictionary of Greek mythology ever, Wilhelm Heinrich Roscher's (1845–1923) *Ausführliches Lexikon der griechischen und römischen Mythologie* ('Detailed Dictionary of Greek and Roman Mythology', 1884–1937), which is still useful for its collection of material, though not for the interpretations that it makes. For example, Roscher interpreted Apollo as a solar god and the protector of colonies because sunny weather was required for the sending of colonists overseas, and the slaying of Python in Delphi symbolized the victory of the sun god over the power of winter.[46]

Nature still played a substantial role in the mythological interpretations of two great German scholars at the end of the nineteenth century and the beginning of the twentieth century. The most learned classical scholar of his day, Hermann Usener (1834–1905), turned to mythology on several occasions.[47] One of his memorable works deals with the myths of the Flood in Greece, in which he attempted to show that this myth had developed from the image of the *Lichtgott* ('god of light') landing on the shore. The importance attached to light already shows how much Usener was still indebted to the nature paradigm and its antiquated solar mythology. Yet the fact that he looked for a single underlying idea in the different myths of the Flood still strikes one as rather a modern thing to do and it does constitute a valuable insight into mythology.[48]

Towards the end of his life, in 1904, Usener also considered the relationship between myth and ritual. His starting point was a ritual at Delphi in which a tent is destroyed that the dragon Python supposedly lurked in.[49] The fact that the approach to the tent was called Doloneia and the month in which this ritual took place was called *Ilaios* led Usener to postulate that the myth of the capture of Troy (*Ilion*) originated from this ritual. This is obviously unconvincing, but his idea that ritual produced myth was also canvassed at the same time by English scholars (below) and has stood the test of time.[50] Finally, in the same year, 1904, he also published a programmatic essay on mythology, which in one point is still highly relevant. Usener rightly argued that mythology is a full part of the history of Greek religion.[51] This is an important insight, as mythology is strangely absent from the leading twentieth-century handbooks of Greek religion by Nilsson and Walter Burkert. Anyone who thinks of Hesiod's *Theogony*, the myths about the gods in the *Homeric Hymns*, or the many cult *aitia* in the mythographical handbooks can only be amazed by this absence.

At the end of the Great War the German philologist and archaeologist Carl Robert (1850–1922) issued an impressively learned update of Preller's long, influential study (above). Robert's formative period was still very much influenced by Karl Otfried Müller, and, following the original plan of Preller's handbook on Greek mythology, he ordered the myths of heroes in a strictly geographical manner, starting with Thessaly and Northern Boeotia. He saw this area as rich in myths at a very early period of time. It is indeed the case that Pelion, for instance, looks like an extremely old centre of Greek mythology, as Achilles was raised here by Cheiron and the Argonauts left here from Volos (ancient Iolkos). However, Robert starts with a discussion of the Centaurs and the Lapiths, figures that have attracted little attention recently.

He was not so much interested in their position between men and animals or in their social function as educators, as we would be today, but rather he focuses on their names, their origins, and their adoption by other cities, such as Athens and Corinth. In this manner he surveys all landscapes of ancient Greece and discusses their main heroes and heroines in a strictly positivist manner, which, much more than the work of his predecessors, also made use of the archaeological evidence. In a way, his impressive erudition could not be bettered, and for a long time his work marked the end of a serious engagement with mythology in Germany.[52]

Myth and the British

In Great Britain interest focused less on the prehistory of Greece and more on classical Greece itself as the cradle of civilization.[53] Increasing colonial expansion made the relationship between the white, 'civilized' race and the coloured 'savages', as they were called, more and more problematic; simultaneously, the Industrial Revolution had greatly enlarged the contrast between modern urban life and that of those dependent on the land and those in the Celtic periphery. Growing urbanization made the interpretation of ancient myths through the nature paradigm attractive, and this fascination with nature even led the leading historian of religion at the time, Friedrich Max Müller (1823–1900), to allegorize nature to such an extent that he explained Achilles (and Siegfried) as a representation of the sun. This absurdity made one of his more positivist critics, Lewis Richard Farnell (1856–1934), observe that mythology evidently was no more than 'highly figurative conversation about the weather'.[54]

As the interpretation of mythology through the nature paradigm imploded under the stresses of empirical work, notably in anthropology, all over Europe an interest in ritual came to prominence.[55] In Great Britain this especially manifested itself in the work of Jane Harrison, one of England's most original classicists at the turn of the nineteenth century.[56] Unlike many contemporaries, Harrison was very sensitive to new developments in German classics, French sociology, and British anthropology. But unlike many later classicists, she saw no problem in comparing Greek myths with those of the 'primitives'. Moreover, in contrast to most of her literary and philological colleagues, she was well trained in archaeology and always incorporated vases and sculptures in her analyses. It was in the preface to her 1890 study *Mythology & Monuments of Ancient Athens* that she first formulated her view on the relationship between myth and ritual: 'in the large majority of cases ritual practice misunderstood explains the elaboration of myth'. This was a completely new view at the time, as myth had dominated the scholars' agenda for most of the nineteenth century. But to whom do we owe this idea?

In the very first of the public lectures that had been published in 1889 as his *Lectures on the Religion of the Semites*, the extremely learned and imaginative William Robertson Smith (1846–94) had already noted, 'In all such cases it is probable, in most cases it is certain, that the myth is merely the explanation of a religious usage; and ordinarily it is such an explanation as could not have arisen till the original sense of the usage had more or less fallen into oblivion' (Smith 1889: 19). Even before that, in 1888, Paper 2 of the Cambridge Classical Tripos carried the title 'Mythology and Ritual' and asked 'How far is it possible to distinguish between the religious rituals of the Homeric poems, and those of historical Greece?'[57] Neither Harrison nor Smith was involved in the tripos, but the enormously erudite and industrious James George Frazer (1854–1941) belonged to the first examiners. Frazer was very much interested in ritual, as can be seen from his voluminous *The Golden Bough* (1890[1]) and his still valuable commentary on Pausanias (1898). But as he was also a close friend of Robertson Smith,[58] the final answer to the question of who first developed this perspective cannot be arrived at until and unless we find more documents.[59] This is even more the case, as Harrison was also acquainted with the work of Karl Otfried Müller, who, as we saw, had already reflected on the relation between myth and ritual. In any case, Harrison's stress on the importance of ritual for Greek religion was shared by only a small group of British scholars – people such as Gilbert Murray (1866–1956) and Francis Macdonald Cornford (1874–1943), who would soon be called the 'Cambridge School' or the 'Cambridge Ritualists'.[60]

Most of Harrison's views and ideas were rejected by her contemporaries. Yet in one respect she would be an important forerunner for late twentieth-century scholars of Greek mythology. In her second big book, *Themis* (1912), which carried the telling subtitle 'A Study in the Social Origins of Greek Religion', Harrison introduced the idea that ancient initiation rites lay in the background of the mythical traditions about the Kouretes, young men connected with the birth of Zeus.[61] In other words, it was no longer nature or ritual misunderstood that offered the key to the understanding of mythology, but a social institution. However, Harrison's highly fertile idea had little effect on the wider classical world. Her book appeared just before the First World War, which was a watershed in her own activities; moreover this period saw the rise of functionalism in anthropology, as personified by Bronisław Malinowski,[62] and functionalism had little interest in mythology. Meanwhile, in Germany interest in mythology died with Usener and Robert, and the scholar who came to dominate the classical world was Ulrich von Wilamowitz-Möllendorff (1848–1931), who loathed the idea of 'savages' in Greece, rejected the comparative approach, which indeed had over-extended itself, and had little interest in mythology. The replacement of myth by ritual had also been embraced by Martin P. Nilsson (1874–1967), a Swedish farmer's son, who had been strongly influenced by the books of Wilhelm Mannhardt (1831–80) on the peasant customs of Western Europe.[63] Mannhardt's investigations, which also included some Greek myths, had led to the widespread acceptance of agriculture as an important key to the interpretation of Greek religion, mythology included. Nilsson's erudition and longevity (an often neglected factor in the history of scholarship) canonized the agrarian interpretation of ritual; more than this, however, it ensured that myth, disregarded in his authoritative handbook, which dominated the study of Greek religion in the middle of the twentieth century, entered a long period of widespread neglect.[64]

Contemporary Approaches to Myth

This neglect lasted, broadly speaking, from the First World War until the middle of the 1960s. However, as often happens, a general neglect does not exclude the possibility of outsiders working against the grain of the times. This is what happened in the case of mythology: in Germany two scholars tried to break away from the Wilamowitz type of *Altertumswissenschaft* ('science of antiquity'): Walter F. Otto (1874–1958) and Karl Kerényi (1897–1973), who eventually applied Jung's idea of archetypes to Greek myth.[65] As their approaches proved to be untenable and led into cul-de-sacs, they need not bother us here, but it is different with another outsider.

One of the pupils of Durkheim was Louis Gernet (1882–1962), who spent much of his professional life in Algiers – literally and symbolically at the margin of the classical world. Gernet was particularly interested in myth.[66] He not only pursued the transformations of mythical images into other fields, such as utopias and the novel, he also looked at Greek myth in an attempt to recover social values and institutions from the times before our literary documentation. As his thought is perhaps not always expressed as clearly as it might be and often results in a somewhat vague and impressionistic vocabulary, it is worth spelling out some examples.[67] When Polyneikes bribed Eriphyle with a necklace to persuade her husband Amphiaraos to join the military expedition against Thebes, Gernet wonders why this obliged the husband to go. In the end, he sees here the obliging force of the gift – as is hardly surprising, given that his fellow Durkheimian Marcel Mauss had written specifically on gift-giving (*Essai sur le don*, 1925).[68] Gernet was especially fascinated by myths connected with divine kingship and accession to the throne, which he saw as deriving from a period that preceded Archaic Greece, surely under the influence of Frazer's *Golden Bough*.[69] Thus, he could rightly see the Golden Fleece as a talisman with connotations of royalty, wealth, and the sun,[70] although he could not yet suspect the connection with the Hittite *kurša*, a sheepskin or goatskin hunting bag which served as an important cult object, as has become clearer in recent times.[71] He also turned several times to myths connected with the youth of Theseus,[72] although this did not always result in publications;[73] these he saw as memories of feudal times in which initiation played a central role. Yet Gernet was careful not to reduce the various mythical themes to a single scheme, and he distinguished the earlier parts of Theseus' career, which he saw as connected with rites of investiture, from the later parts, in which he saw a case of tribal initiation. At the same time, he also noted that we cannot restore prehistory from Theseus' mythological exploits, as his traditions had been mediated by historical Athens and its *polis*-centred institutions.[74]

Gernet's most important pupil was Jean-Pierre Vernant (1914–2007),[75] who with Walter Burkert (b. 1931: below) dominated the world of Greek religion in the last decades of the twentieth century. These decades also saw a great revival of interest in Greek mythology, although in retrospect we can now see that its main period lasted from 1965 till about 1980, when Burkert's interests started to shift to the Ancient Near East, and Vernant's fruitful cooperation with fellow Parisians Marcel Detienne and Pierre Vidal-Naquet (1930–2006) disintegrated, and, as so often is the case with pop groups, their subsequent solo careers were less productive than their period of collaboration.[76] A second stream of publications – by their pupils and younger colleagues – took place in a short period from 1987 to 1994,[77] after which interest seems to have subsided somewhat. It is not so easy to analyse objectively a period in which one has oneself grown up and of which one has been part. It is therefore with some hesitation that I would like to note the following selection as important results since the middle of the 1960s.

1 'Myth' is a somewhat problematic term. The Greek word *mythos* basically started as meaning 'a speech-act indicating authority' but gradually evolved into 'imaginative tale' when Greek historians, philosophers, and mythographers started to contest the stories about the past and/or about gods. In the fifth century BC, *mythos* could still have both positive and negative connotations, but eventually the balance shifted so that *mythoi* were presumed to be false unless proved otherwise.[78] As already seen, that is why Heyne introduced the new term *mythus*, not *mythos*, for the type of tales we nowadays usually call 'myth'. Yet it took a long time before the term was generally accepted: even Gernet still normally uses *légende*, 'legend', where most of us would say 'myth'. It is perhaps true that 'myth is not susceptible to a catch-all definition',[79] yet a definition as 'traditional tales relevant to society' takes us some considerable way, as long as we realize that 'traditional' includes 'looking traditional'. Even though Greek myths were created well into Late Antiquity (third–fourth century AD), they were modelled on more traditional stories and thus could be recognized as 'myth'. At the same time, it is also true

that 'myth' is not a clear-cut category, as it sometimes shades into what we would call a fairy tale or a folk tale, tales that in general are not relevant for society at large. In other words, 'myth' is a modern category and its main value is heuristic.[80]

2   Myth is part of a cultural tradition, but many Greek myths are relatively late, since only a few can be proved to go back to Indo-European times (on which see CH. 18), such as the myth of the first horse, Arion; the abduction of Helen; Prometheus' theft of fire; and Herakles' cattle raiding. These myths focus on central concerns of society (horses, women, fire, cattle) on which depended their survival over several millennia.[81] Most Greek myths, by contrast, presuppose the political situation of Archaic and Classical Greece and are accordingly not very old. This is not surprising, as the public performance of myths determined their acceptability. In other words, myths had to be continuously adapted to new social and political circumstances. Basically, Greek mythology was an open-ended, ever changing system.

3   Myth is primarily a narrative that was told or sung in different communities or in front of varying audiences. This suggests that myth could cross national, social, and cultural borders. And indeed, the studies of Walter Burkert and Martin West have shown that from the eighth century BC onwards Greece acquired a number of myths and mythical themes from the Ancient Near East, the best known perhaps being the myth of Kronos and the Titans, and the myth of the Flood.[82] This may seem pretty obvious. Yet the nineteenth century so closely connected myths with specific cultures that Usener still denied that Greece had taken over the motif of Deukalion's Flood from the Ancient Near East.[83]

4   Myth not only relates the deeds of mortals and immortals, but it also makes reference to animals and landscapes. All these elements of myth are 'good to think with'. This means that through myth the Greeks could explore the limits of mortality by pitting divinities against humans, such as Athene against Ariadne in a spinning contest,[84] or by relating the sad fate of king Salmoneus, who had transgressed the boundaries of mortality by trying to imitate Zeus and therefore was struck down by the latter's thunderbolt. Greek myths also illustrate the limits of acceptable matrimonial behaviour, such as the disastrous consequences of Helen's leaving of her husband for Paris or the fatal outcomes of Herakles bringing a concubine into his and Deianeira's home. Oedipus' myth well illustrates what happens when one kills one's father, and how a family is torn apart when sons starts to quarrel.

Myth operates in a somewhat different manner with animals, plants, and landscapes. In myth, animals and plants often display symbolic traits that are ascribed to them by the Greeks, wolves, for instance, receive an equal share after a kill or are all alike, clearly reflections of Greek practices and ideals.[85] Pines are linked with wildness and aggressive violence, and these traits clearly cannot be separated from their mountainous existence.[86] Mountains in myth can reflect reality, so that we hear of herdsmen and hunters going to the mountains, but myths also 'refract, transforming the world by a process of selective emphasis and clarification and exaggeration'.[87] This means that the danger of the mountains can be stressed by locating monsters on mountains, such as the Sphinx or Centaurs. Or their wildness is 'clarified' by letting mortals and immortals, two incongruous categories in ancient Greece, make love on mountains, as do Anchises and Aphrodite in the *Homeric Hymn to Aphrodite*. So, understandably, trees growing on mountains can be symbolic of that wildness.

5   Myth is not a repository of long-term history,[88] as recent investigations have demonstrated that oral tradition remembers events only for a short period of time.[89] This does not mean that myth stood outside history. On the contrary, myth is initially the product of a specific person, time, and place, even though we often can no longer reconstruct the circumstances of its production, performance, and transmission. Yet this does not mean that myth is the one-to-one reflection of a certain community. Myth can present an idealized image, but it can also falsify reality. For example, cities schemed to make themselves more important by 'hijacking' Hellenic myths: both Athens and Megara claimed that the sacrifice of Iphigeneia had taken place in their area instead of in Aulis and thus tried to secure the fame of the Trojan War for themselves.[90] Especially in Hellenistic and Roman times myths were invented and manipulated to construct kinship relations between two cities, and in Late Antiquity poets still travelled the ancient world to relate foundation myths and sing the praises of local heroes.[91]

6   Our final point concerns a much more fiercely debated issue: the relation between myth and ritual, two modes of symbolic expression that have often been related to one another. The historiography of this century-long debate is relatively clear and needs no longer occupy us in detail.[92] After the love affair with myth of the nineteenth century the tide turned around 1900 when scholars started to claim the priority of ritual, which was indeed the prevailing view for most of the twentieth century. It was one of the imaginative ideas of Walter Burkert to reverse the tide once again and to claim that myth and ritual arose at the same time, *pari passu*.[93]

But is Burkert's suggestion helpful? Let us look at a strange Greek ritual that can help us to better see the problems at stake.

In 1970, Burkert published an innovative study of a ritual that was celebrated yearly on Lemnos and that clearly reflects a New Year festival.[94] On the level of ritual, every nine years the Lemnians extinguished their fires for a nine-day period.[95] During this period, they sacrificed to the chthonic gods, and women chewed garlic which drove their men away. After the fireless period, a ship from Delos brought new fire and thus helped to restore the normal social order. According to the corresponding myth, the Lemnian women had incurred the wrath of Aphrodite who penalized them with a foul smell. Understandably, their husbands consoled themselves with their Thracian slave girls instead. In reaction, the women murdered their husbands except for the king, who was able to escape with the help of his daughter Hypsipyle. This celibate period lasted until the Argonauts landed on Lemnos on their return from seizing the Golden Fleece. They were much welcomed by the women in a rather licentious festival, and thus the normal sexual (and social) order was once again restored.[96]

When we look at the myth and the corresponding ritual, it is clear that Burkert was right to stress that the structure and mood of myth often corresponds with that of the relevant ritual. At the same time we should also note that the myth does not wholly reflect the plot of the ritual as Burkert suggests. It is rather striking, but the extinction and the rekindling of fire, which seem to be amongst the most important acts of the ritual, are wholly absent from the myth. This shows that myth does not automatically reflect ritual. The myth, rather, concentrates on the role of the women. As a result we can consider myth as an 'emic' or insider's commentary on the ritual. Apparently, for the Greeks this was the most important and intriguing part of the complex of concerns reflected in myth and ritual. The myth also preserves an interesting piece of sociological history: the saving of the king's life. It seems that even in historical times myth could not easily relate the murder of a king without repercussions – it may even be that behind this detail there are those ancient ideas about sacred kingship that were so dear to the hearts of Frazer and Gernet. Finally, it is clear that the myth strongly exaggerates: in the ritual the women keep their males at a distance by their foul smell, but in the myth they murder them. Myth, in other words, can exaggerate and picture as permanent what is only symbolic and temporary in ritual.

The myth of the Lemnian women was highly popular and occurs in all kinds of genres: in epic and lyric, in tragedy, comedy, and even in Roman poetry.[97] Each genre had its own rules, and this meant that the myth could be related in many different ways and always without any reference to the ritual. In fact, if we did not have a late antique comment on the arrival of the ship we would never have known about an important part of the ancient ritual. Neither do we know anything about the performance of the myth during the ritual. This should make us beware of seeing in the interaction of myth and ritual *the* key to a better understanding of the relationship,[98] even if it is true that every new performance can introduce new accents and innovations both to the myth and, if to a lesser degree, to the ritual.

The relation between myth and ritual becomes even more complicated when we try to relate a myth not to a specific ritual but to a more general existing ritual scenario. Quite a few myths or details in myth have been related to rites of initiation. Now when we realize the great importance of youthful choruses in archaic Greece, it seems reasonable to accept that the process of maturation was of great importance to Greek society at the stage that many myths must have been 'invented'.[99] This means that we reasonably can compare the snatching of Ganymede to become Zeus' wine-pourer with the snatching of boys in Cretan initiation rituals, as wine pouring was a set task of boys during their process of coming of age.[100] Similarly, the feminization of gods and heroes before they become adults or warriors, such as Achilles' stay amongst the daughters of King Lykomedes of Skyros before going to Troy or Dionysos' appearance as a girl before emerging as a powerful god in the *Homeric Hymn to Dionysos* and Euripides' *Bacchae*,[101] can hardly be separated from rites of initiation – whether the Greeks once dressed up their initiates as girls or called them such. Yet these examples also demonstrate that we are already far removed from actual rites of transvestism in initiation and that what were once ritual acts have later have become literary motifs in non-ritual contexts.[102] In the end, the relationship between myth and ritual cannot be interpreted by a catch-all explanation. Every myth has to be looked at individually, and even then we often still look at a glass darkly. Greek mythology is not an easy subject.

FURTHER READING

Graf 1993a: chs. 1–2 provides a richly informative account of this area, as does his article on Myth in *BNP* (and Burkert 1980 and Jamme 1995 are useful for those with, respectively, German and French). Greek myth itself can most quickly be learned from Gantz (see Abbreviations) and from Buxton 2004, but note also Dowden 1992. The iconography is now available in the splendid *LIMC*. Good introductions to the varying approaches to myth are Bremmer 1987 and Graf 1993a. For the role of Greek myth in the Roman period, see Zanker and Ewald 2004. For the modern period Von Hendy 2002 and Williamson 2004 present intensive studies, whereas Doty 2000 will be more useful to those seeking guidance. Extracts from significant modern mythologists, in translation, are presented (in translation where necessary) by Feldman and Richardson 1972. Finally, for the fragments of the early mythographers and the development of mythography, see now Fowler 2000 and Cameron 2004, respectively.

NOTES

1. For the surviving fragments of the early mythographers see Fowler (2000).
2. See Burkert (1980); Graf (1993a: 9–56); Jamme (1995); F. Graf, *BNP* s.v. Myth Section V.

3. Cameron (2004); unfortunately, this important study contains neither an *index locorum* nor a bibliography, which does not make it easy to consult. Henrichs (1987) is still important.
4. Parthenios, *Preface*, cf. the excellent edition and commentary of Lightfoot (1999), with her study of 'Mythography' (224–40). Note now also the lightly corrected text and translation in Lightfoot (ed.) (2009: 467–647).
5. For a very full list see Cameron (2004: 27–32).
6. Palaiphatos: see now Stern (1996), Cameron (2004: 204–6). Eratosthenes: see now the new editions with commentary by J. Pàmias (2004) and Pàmias and Geus (2007).
7. Cameron (2004: 33–51). For the most recent text and translation see Marshall (1993) (edition of the Latin text) and Smith and Trzaskoma (2007: 95–182) (annotated English translation).
8. See the worrying analysis of Cameron (2004: 89–163).
9. See the excellent discussion by Cameron (2004: 217–52).
10. Clarysse and Wouters (1970).
11. van Rossum-Steenbeek (1997: 320–1) (= *POxy* 61.4099). Van Rossum usefully re-edits many mythological papyri but is not always fully used by Cameron (2004).
12. See now M. K. Brown (2002), to be read with the review of Lightfoot (2005).
13. The standard edition is that of Papathomopoulos (1968).
14. For the most recent bibliography see Cameron (2004: 28 n. 116); and Montanari (2002).
15. Huys (1997) to be added to Cameron (2004: 93–106); Huys and Colomo (2004). There is a good modern translation in Smith and Trzaskoma (2007: 1–93).
16. The display of cultural capital is also visible in the many surviving mythological wall paintings from Pompeii, see most recently Beard (2008: 141–52); Lorenz (2008); Muth (1998).
17. Cameron (2004: 184–216).
18. Whitbread (1971); Hays (2003); Wolff (2009).
19. Herren (1998 and 1998–9); Miles (2006).
20. For the Second see now Jakobi (2008).
21. France: Starobinski (1989: 233–62) ('Fable et mythologie au xviie et xviiie siècles'). Germany: see, for example, Schisling (1793); Damm (1797).
22. Guthmüller (1986); Gibellini (2005).
23. See Zaccaria (1998).
24. For the date of the *editio princeps* see P. Ford (1998).
25. This has escaped Cameron (2004: 251).
26. For useful introductions and bibliographical data see now Iglesias Montiel and Morán (1988); Mulryan and Brown (2006). Also note the reprint of the *editio princeps* (Conti 1976).
27. Faisant and Godard de Donville (1982).
28. Niderst (1989: 187–202). I quote from the English translation by Feldman and Richardson (1972: 7–18). For a good German translation and an important

study by W. Krauss, 'Fontenelle und die Aufklärung', see H. Bergmann (1989: 228–42, 371–439, respectively); Von Hendy (2002: 5–7) is brief but interesting; on the date, Marcone (2009).

29. Fréret (1756), apparently not reprinted in Fréret's collected works. For Fréret see R. Simon (1961); Barret-Kriegel (1988: 163–209, 277–82) (bibliography); Grell and Volpilhac-Auger (1994).

30. For the study of myth in the eighteenth century see Mockerl (1981); Grell and Michel (1988).

31. For Heyne see most recently Fornaro (2004); Heidenreich (2006). For his bibliography see Haase (2002).

32. Heyne (1783: xxix): *fabulas seu quo vocabulo lubentius utor, mythos* ('*fabulae* or the word I would sooner use, *mythi*').

33. For Herder and myth see Verra (1966); Faust (1977).

34. Horstmann (1972), Chiarini (1989), and, especially, Graf (1993b).

35. Heyne (1807).

36. Williamson (2004).

37. Creuzer (1810–12). The third edition contained about 3,000 pages, and the abridged edition (Darmstadt 1822) still numbered 940 pages.

38. For Creuzer see Fornaro (2001); Williamson (2004: 121–50); Humphreys (2004: 199–214) (good contextualization); Engehausen, Schlechter, and Schwindt (2008); Fornaro (2008).

39. See the documents in Howald (1926).

40. Carolus Otfried Müller (1825).

41. On Müller see most recently Unte and Rohlfing (1997); Calder and Schlesier (1998); Calder, Smith, and Vaio (2002).

42. C. O. Müller (1825: 108–9, 235, 257).

43. He was followed by another Müller, Heinrich Dietrich Müller (1823–93): see H. D. Müller (1857–69). For a critical discussion of the Müllers and others of their ilk see Gruppe (1887: 139–51).

44. Preller (1854). For Preller see Stichling (1863), Baumeister (1888).

45. For many examples, see Henrichs (1986: 187–90).

46. For Roscher see now Konaris (2010).

47. For Usener see Bremmer (1990b); Ehlers (ed.) (1992); Wessels (2003: 7–95); Kany (2004).

48. Usener (1899).

49. For this ritual, see Ephoros *FGrH* 70 F31b (Strabo 9.3.12).

50. Usener (1913: 447–67).

51. Usener (1907: 37–65).

52. Robert (1920–6). For Robert see Kern (1927).

53. Jenkyns (1980); Turner (1981).

54. Farnell (1896: 9).

55. Bremmer (1998: 14–24).

56. Schlesier (1994: 123–92) (the best study of her work); Demoor (1999); Beard (2000); A. Robinson (2002).

57. Beard (2000: 125–7).

58. Ackerman (1987: 53–94); Johnstone (1995: 331–50). For Frazer, see most recently Stocking (1995: 126–51); Bremmer (1996); Rosa (1997); Stocking (2001: 147–61).
59. It seems certain, though, that Smith had influenced Harrison, cf. Bremmer (1991: 238).
60. Calder (1991); Korom (2004).
61. J. E. Harrison (1912: 1–29), although she had not noticed that the thought had already occurred to Usener (see Usener 1913: 190).
62. On Malinowski (1884–1942) and his influence, see most recently Gellner (1998); M. W. Young (2004).
63. Mannhardt (1875–7), cf. Tybjerg (1993); Kippenberg (2002: 81–7).
64. Nilsson (1944). On Nilsson see Bierl and Calder (1991).
65. Stavru (2005) (with excellent bibliography); Graf (2006).
66. For Gernet see Humphreys (1978: 76–106, 283–7) ('The work of Louis Gernet') and, on a much better documentary basis, di Donato (1990: 1–130) ('L'antropologia storica di Louis Gernet'). For Gernet's views we now have an important publication of notes on Greek myth, mainly written in the 1940s: Gernet (2004 –*Polyvalence des images. Testi e frammenti sulla leggenda greca*). This 'new' book also shows Gernet's great indebtedness to Usener, which is still somewhat underestimated in di Donato: 233–44 ('Usener n'habite plus ici' – 'Usener doesn't live here anymore'). On the other hand, Gernet is much more reticent about Jane Harrison, cf. di Donato: 255–63.
67. This aspect of Gernet is rightly stressed by Humphreys (1978: 89).
68. Gernet (1968: 104–8), and Gernet (1983: 262–6).
69. Cf. Gernet and Boulanger (1932: 84 n. 402).
70. Gernet (1968: 119–23, 2004: 49–52, 123–55).
71. Bremmer (2008: 310–17).
72. For the older stages of this myth, see Calame (1996); Servadei (2005); and now *POxy* 68.4640.
73. See the observations of Soldani in Gernet (2004: 88–90).
74. Gernet (2004: 53–6, 102–22). Although Gernet had already connected Theseus with initiation in 1932, as appears from Gernet and Boulanger (1932: 78), the publication of Jeanmaire (1939) clearly was a great stimulus, even though Gernet's review was fairly critical, cf. Gernet (1983: 201–11).
75. On Vernant see di Donato (1990: 209–44); Laks (1998); Paradiso (2001).
76. Highlights of this period are: Vernant (1965); Burkert (1972b); Detienne (1972); Vidal-Naquet (1981a).
77. Cf. Bremmer (1987); Calame (1988); Edmunds (1990); Dowden (1992); Graf (1993a); Saïd (1993); Buxton (1994).
78. For the transition, see now the important study by R. L. Fowler (2009).
79. Lightfoot (1999: 231).
80. For full discussions, see Bremmer, 'What is a Greek Myth?', in Bremmer (1987: 1–9); Dowden (1992: 3–7).
81. Bremmer (1999a: 18 (Arion), 57); P. Jackson (2006); M. L. West (2007: 229–32 (Helen), 272–4 (Prometheus), 451 (Herakles)).

82. Burkert (1992, 2003, and 2004). M. L. West (1997), to be read with the observations of Dowden (2001) and Wasserman (2001). See now also Bremmer (2008), Bernabé (2008).

83. Usener (1899: 244–8); see now Bremmer (2008 101–16).

84. Contests between mortals and immortals: Weiler (1974: 37–128). Salmoneus: Mestuzini (1988); E. Simon (1994).

85. A very stimulating study: Buxton (1987).

86. A pioneer book on the symbolism of plants is Detienne (1972).

87. Buxton (1994: 87–8) gives many nice examples of this process.

88. For many interesting observations see Dowden (1992: 57–92).

89. For Greece, see Thomas (1989).

90. Cf. Bremmer (2001); for other such examples see Graf (1979); Lardinois (1992); Pariente (1992).

91. Curty (1995); C. P. Jones (1999); Cameron (2004: 224–8).

92. See the surveys by Versnel (1993: 15–88); Burkert (2002: 1–22); Bremmer (2005), which I have freely used in my discussion of modern ideas; Kowalzig (2007: 13–23).

93. Burkert (1979: 56–8), who is followed by Versnel (1993: 74–88). Neither Burkert's socio-biological explanation of the close relation between myth and ritual nor his interest in the theories of Vladimir Propp (Burkert1979: 14–18) are persuasive, cf. Bremmer (2005: 38–43); Kowalzig (2007: 19–21) (myth and ritual); Lightfoot (1999: 237–40 (Propp)); Bremmer (2010).

94. Burkert (1970).

95. Unfortunately, the manuscript reading of the Greek 'every nine years' is disputed, but see now Löschhorn (2007: 277–9) with important epigraphic evidence.

96. For such licentious festivals, see now Bremmer (2008: 261–5).

97. For a very full new study, see Masciadri (2008: 164–258).

98. Contra Kowalzig (2007).

99. Calame (1997); Dowden (1989).

100. Bremmer (1990a: 141); Dowden (1992: 112–15).

101. Dowden (1992: 118); Bremmer (1999a).

102. See, for example, Dowden (1999).

Bibliography

Guide to Fragmentary and Less Easily Found Texts

Akousilaos	Author 2 in *FGrH/BNJ*.
Apollodoros, *Library*	Greek text with parallel English translation and notes: Frazer (1921); English translation also in R. S. Smith and Trzaskoma (eds) (2007).
Hekataios	Author 1 in *FGrH/BNJ*.
Hellanikos	Author 4 in *FGrH/BNJ*.
Herakleitos, *Homeric Problems*	With English translation, introduction and notes in Russell and Konstan (eds) (2005).
Hesiod and Ps.-Hesiod, fragments:	For convenience we have given fragment numbers in two systems, those of MW and Most (see Abbreviations). MW references are widely found in the scholarly literature, but Most is easier to lay hands on and includes parallel English translation. Most's edition is the best place to get a sense of what remains of the *Catalogue of Women* and how it appears to have been organized.
Hyginus	English translation in R. S. Smith and Trzaskoma (eds) (2007).
Kallimachos	The standard edition of the Greek text of the surviving works and fragments is Pfeiffer's: R. Pfeiffer (ed.) (1949) *Callimachus I: Fragmenta*, Oxford (Pfeiffer i); R. Pfeiffer (ed.) (1953) *Callimachus II: Hymni et Epigrammata*, Oxford (Pfeiffer ii). See also *SH* and, for the *Hekale*, Hollis (1990). For English translations, see Nisetich (2001).

A Companion to Greek Mythology, First Edition. Edited by Ken Dowden and Niall Livingstone.
© 2014 John Wiley & Sons Ltd. Published 2014 by John Wiley & Sons Ltd.

Mahābhārata	Translations of the *Vulgate text*: K.M. Ganguli (Calcutta 1883–96, much reprinted; available 16.7.10 at http://www.sacred-texts.com/hin/maha); Clay Sanskrit Library (New York, in progress); of the *Critical Edition*: Chicago, in progress. Most useful now to the English reader is: J. D. Smith, *The Mahābhārata*, abridged and translated (London 2009).
Palaiphatos *On Unbelievable Tales (Peri Apistōn)*	Stern 1996 provides introduction, annotated English translation, and Greek text.
Parthenios	Text and English translation in Lightfoot (2009); for fuller discussion see Lightfoot (1999).
Pherekydes	Author 3 in *FGrH/BNJ*.
Pindar, fragments	our numbering follows H. Maehler (ed.) (1989) *Pindari Carmina cum Fragmentis*. Pars II: *Fragmenta, Indices* [Bibliotheca Teubneriana], Leipzig. A selection of fragments with parallel English translation may be found in W. J. Race (ed. and tr.) 1997 *Pindar: Nemean Odes, Isthmian Odes, Fragments* [Loeb Classical Library], Cambridge MA, London, who also follows Maehler's numbering.
Plotinos	See Stephen MacKenna (1969) *Plotinus: the Enneads*[4], London. There is also an abridged edition (Penguin Books: London 1991).

Additional guidance

1 See also Abbreviations for some collections of fragmentary material such as *FGrH*.
2 For more general guidance on ancient texts which present myth, see Hard 2004: 1–20 'Sources of Myth'.
3 The reader is reminded of some major collections of texts in translation:

The Loeb Classical Library (Harvard University Press: Cambridge, MA, London): see http://www.hup.harvard.edu/loeb/
Oxford World's Classics (Oxford University Press: Oxford, New York): see http://www.oup.com/worldsclassics/
Penguin Classics (Penguin Books: London, New York): see www.penguinclassics.com

General Bibliography

Abbreviations of the titles of journals/periodicals (e.g. *JHS* for *Journal of Hellenic Studies*) follow *L'Année philologique* (Paris 1928–date), whose list may be found at http://www.annee-philologique.com/aph/files/sigles_fr.pdf.
For other abbreviations, see the List of abbreviations on p. xxv.

Abraham, K. (1955) 'The "Trifurcation of the Road" in the Oedipus Myth', in *Clinical Papers and Essays on Psychoanalysis*, New York, 83–5.

Abry, C., F. Létoublon, and P. Hameau (eds) (2010) *Les Rites de passage 1909–2009: De la Grèce d'Homère à notre XXIe siècle*, Grenoble.

Ackermann, H. C., Jean-Robert Gisler, and Lilly Kahil (1981–97) *Lexicon Iconographicum Mythologiae Classicae*, 8 vols, Zurich.

Ackerman, R. (1987) *J. G. Frazer: His Life and Work*, Cambridge.

Adam, J.-M. (1991) *Le Récit*³, Paris.

Adam, J.-M. (1995) 'Aspects du récit en anthropologie', in J.-M. Adam, M.-J. Borel, C. Calame, and M. Kilani, *Le Discours anthropologique: Description, narration, savoir*², Lausanne [1990¹] 227–54.

Adams, M. V. (2001) *The Mythological Unconscious*, New York.

Adams, M. V. (2004) *The Fantasy Principle: Psychoanalysis of the Imagination*, Hove, New York.

Aélion, R. (1983) *Euripide héritier d'Eschyle*, 2 vols, Paris.

Aélion, R. (1986) *Quelques grands mythes héroïques dans l'œuvre d'Euripide*, Paris.

Affergan, F., S. Borutti, C. Calame, *et al.* (2003) *Figures de l'humain: les représentations de l'anthropologie*, Paris.

Ahl, F. and H. M. Roisman (1996) *The Odyssey Re-Formed*, Ithaca NY.

Ahrensdorf, P. J. (2004) 'The Limits of Political Rationalism: Enlightenment and Religion in *Oedipus the Tyrant*', *Journal of Politics* 66, 773–99.

Alaux, J. (2007) *Lectures tragiques d'Homère*, Paris.

Alaux, J. and F. Létoublon (2005) 'Mythes grecs de la terre', in *Les Représentations de la terre dans la littérature et l'art européens, imaginaire et idéologie*, Nouveaux cahiers polonais 4, 217–31.

Albright, W. F. (1956) Review of M. H. Pope 1955 *El in the Ugaritic Texts*, Leiden, *JBL* 75, 255–7.

Alexiou, S. (2008) Από τον κόσμο του Ομήρου. Θρύλος και Αλήθεια στην γεωγραφία της Οδύσσειας, *Nea Estia* 163, 64–76.

Allen, J. P. (1988) *Genesis in Egypt: The Philosophy of Ancient Egyptian Creation Accounts*, New Haven.

Allen, J. P. (2005) *The Ancient Egyptian Pyramid Texts*. Society of Biblical Literature Writings from the Ancient World 23, Atlanta.

Allen, N. J. (1995) 'Why did Odysseus become a Horse?' *Journal of the Anthropological Society of Oxford* 26, 143–54.

Allen, N. J. (1996) 'The Hero's Five Relationships: A Proto-Indo-European Story', in J. Leslie (ed.) *Myth and Myth-Making*, London, 1–20.

Allen, N. J. (2000a) *Categories and Classifications*, Oxford.

Allen, N. J. (2000b) 'The Indra-Tullus Comparison', *General Linguistics* 40, 149–71.

Allen, N. J. (2000c) 'Cúchulainn's Women and some Indo-European Comparisons', *Emania* 18, 57–64.

Allen, N. J. (2000d) 'Imra, Pentads and Catastrophes', *Ollodagos* 14, 278–308.

Allen, N. J. (2001) 'Athena and Durga: Warrior Goddesses in Greek and Sanskrit Epic', in S. Deacy and A. Villing (eds) *Athena in the Classical World*, Leiden: 367–82.

Allen, N. J. (2002) 'Pénélope et Draupadī: la validité de la comparaison', in Hurst and Létoublon (eds) 2002: 305–12.

Allen, N. J. (2004a) 'Dyaus and Bhīṣma, Zeus and Sarpedon: Towards a History of the Indo-European Sky God', *Gaia* 8, 29–36.

Allen, N. J. (2004b) 'Bhīṣma and Hesiod's Succession Myth', *International Journal of Hindu Studies* 8, 57–79.

Allen, N. J. (2005) 'Romulus et Bhīshma: structures entrecroisées', *Anthropologie et sociétés* 29, 21–44.

Allen, N. J. (2006) 'The Buddhist Wheel of Existence and Two Greek Comparisons', in M. V. García Quintela, F. J. González García, and F. Criado Boado (eds) *Anthropology of the Indo-European World and Material Culture*, Budapest, 219–28.

Allen, N. J. (2007a) 'Śiva and Indo-European Ideology: One Line of Thought', *International Journal of Hindu Studies* 11, 191–207.

Allen, N. J. (2007b) 'The Shield of Achilles and Indo-European Tradition', *CFC(G)* 17 (2007) 33–44.

Aloni, A. (1997) *Saffo: Frammenti*, Florence.

Alster, B. (ed.) (1980) *Death in Mesopotamia: papers read at the XXVIe Rencontre assyriologique international*. Mesopotamia 8, Copenhagen.

Andersen, Ø. (1990) 'The Making of the Past in the *Iliad*', *HSPh* 93, 25–45.

Ando, C. (ed.) (2003) *Roman Religion*, Edinburgh.

Andreae, B. (1980) *Die Antiken Sarkophagreliefs* 1 Die Sarkophage. Die Sarkophage mit Darstellungen aus dem Menschenleben, 2 Die Römischen Jagdsarkophage, Berlin.

Andreae, B. (ed.) (1984a) *Symposium über die antiken Sarkophage, Pisa 5.–12. September 1982*. Marburger Winckelmann-Programm 1984.

Andreae, B. (1984b) 'Bossierte Porträts auf römischen Sarkophagen – ein ungelöstes Problem', in Andreae (ed.) 1984a: 109–28.

Annas, J. (1982) 'Plato's Myths of Judgement', *Phronesis* 27, 119–43.

Annus, A. (1999) 'Are there Greek Rephaim? On the Etymology of Greek *Meropes* and *Titanes*', *UF* 31, 13–30.

Armstrong, R. (2005) *A Compulsion for Antiquity: Freud and the Ancient World*, Ithaca NY.

Armstrong, R. (forthcoming) 'Freud and the Drama of Oedipal Truth', in K. Ormand (ed.) *A Companion to Sophocles*, Malden MA, Oxford, Carlton.

Assmann, J. (1977) 'Die Verborgenheit des Mythos in Ägypten', *Göttinger Miszellen* 25, 7–43.

Assmann, J. (1992) *Das kulturelle Gedächtnis: Schrift, Erinnerung und politische Identität in frühen Hochkulturen*[1], Munich [2007[6]].

Astour, M. C. (1967) *Hellenosemitica: An Ethnic and Cultural Study in West Semitic Impact on Mycenaean Greece*[2], Leiden [1965[1]].

Atwood, M. (2005) *The Penelopiad*, Edinburgh, New York, Melbourne.

Aubriot-Sévin, D. (1992) *Prière et conceptions religieuses en Grèce ancienne*, Lyon, Paris.

Austin, N. (1990) *Meaning and Being in Myth*, University Park PA, London.

Austin, N. (1994) *Helen of Troy and Her Shameless Phantom*, Ithaca NY.

Bachofen, J. J. (1861) *Das Mutterrecht: eine Untersuchung über die Gynaikokratie der alten Welt nach ihrer religiösen und rechtlichen Natur*, Stuttgart [available at www. archive.org at 25/07/2010. *An English Translation of Bachofen's* Mutterrecht *(Mother Right) (1861): A Study of the Religious and Juridical Aspects of Gynecocracy in the Ancient World*, tr. D. Partenheimer, 5 vols, Lewiston NY, Lampeter 2003–7].

Bachofen, J. J. (1967) *Myth, Religion and Mother Right: Selected Writings of J. J. Bachofen*, tr. R. Manheim, Princeton.

Bagnani, G. (1919) 'The Subterranean Basilica at Porta Maggiore', *JRS* 9, 78–85.

Baines, J. (1991) 'Egyptian Myth and Discourse: Myth, Gods and the Early Written and Iconographical Record', *JNES* 50, 81–105.

Baines, J. (1996a) 'Myth and Literature', in Loprieno 1996a: 361–77.

Baines, J. (1996b) 'The Aims and Methods of Black Athena', in Lefkowitz and Maclean Rogers 1996: 27–48.

Bakker, E. (1997) 'The Study of Homeric Discourse', in Morris and Powell (eds) 1997: 284–304.

Baldassare, I. (ed.) (1990–2003) *Pompei: pitture e mosaici*, 11 vols, Rome.

Baldry, H. C. (1971) *The Greek Tragic Theatre*, London.

Ballabriga, A. (1986) *Le Soleil et Tartare*, Paris.

Barrett, W. S. (1964) *Euripides,* Hippolytus, *Edited With an Introduction and Commentary*, Oxford.

Barret-Kriegel, B. (1988) *Jean Mabillon*, Paris.

Barrigon, C. (2002) 'La 'Logique' du recit mythique dans l'ode rhodienne de Pindare (Pind. O. VII)', *Kernos* 15, 41–52.

Barthes, R. (1957) *Mythologies*, Paris [abridged: *Mythologies*, tr. A.Lavers, London, 1972].

Bartman, E. (2002) 'Eros's Flame: Images of Sexy Boys in Roman Ideal Sculpture', in Gazda (ed.) 2002: 249–71.

Bataille, A. (1952) *Les Memnonia: recherches de papyrologie et d'épigraphie grecques sur la nécropole de la Thèbes d'Égypte aux époques hellénistique et romaine*, Cairo.

Baumeister, A. (1888) 'Ludwig Preller', in *Allgemeine deutsche Biographie* 26, Leipzig, 561–6.

Bayliss, M. (1973) 'The Cult of Dead Kin in Assyria and Babylonia', *Iraq* 35, 115–25.

Beard, M. (2000) *The Invention of Jane Harrison*, Cambridge MA, London.

Beard, M. (2008) *Pompeii: The Life of a Roman Town*, London.

Beard, M. and J. Henderson (2001) *Classical Art from Greece to Rome*, Oxford.

Beard, M., J. North, and S. Price (1998) *Religions of Rome*, 2 vols, 1 A History, 2 A Sourcebook, Cambridge.

Beckerath, J. von (1994) 'Osorkon IV = Herakles', *Göttinger Miszellen* 139, 7–8.

Becks, R., W. Rigter, and P. Hnila (2006) 'Das Terrassenhaus im westlichen Unterstadtviertel von Troia', *Studia Troica* 16, 27–88.

Belier, W. W. (1991) *Decayed Gods*, Leiden.

Bennet, J. (1997) 'Homer and the Bronze Age', in Morris and Powell (eds) 1997: 511–59.

Benveniste, E. (1966) *Problèmes de linguistique générale*, Paris.

Bergman, J. (1982) 'Ancient Egyptian Theogony in a Greek Magical Papyrus (PGM VII, ll. 516–521)', in M. Heerma van Voss *et al.* (eds) *Studies in Egyptian Religion Dedicated to Professor Jan Zandee. Numen* Supplement 43, Leiden, 28–37.

Bergmann, B. (1994) 'The Roman House as Memory Theater: The House of the Tragic Poet in Pompeii', *ABull* 76, 225–56.

Bergmann, B. (1995) 'Greek Masterpieces and Roman Recreative Fictions', *HSPh* 97, 79–120.

Bergmann, B. (1996) 'The Pregnant Moment: Tragic Wives in the Roman Interior', in Kampen (ed.) 1996: 199–218.

Bergmann, B. (1999) 'Rhythms of Recognition: Mythological Encounters in Roman Landscape Painting', in de Angelis and Muth (eds) 1999: 81–107.

Bergmann, H. (ed.) (1989) *Bernard de Fontenelle: Philosophische Neuigkeiten für Leute von Welt und für Gelehrte*, Leipzig.

Bernabé, A. (ed.) (1987) *Poetae Epici Graeci I*, Leipzig.

Bernabé, A. (1997) 'Orfeotelestas, charlatanes, intérpretes: transmisores de la palabra órfica', in M. del C. Bosch and M. A. Fornes (eds), *Homenatge a Miquel Dolç*, Palma de Mallorca, 37–41.

Bernabé, A. (1998a) 'La palabra de orfeo: religión y magia', in A. Vega, Juan Antonio Rodríguez Tous, and Raquel Bouso (eds), *Estética y religión: El discurso del cuerpo y de los sentidos*, Barcelona, 157–72.

Bernabé, A. (1998b) 'Nacimientos y muertes de Dioniso en los mitos órficos', in C. Sánchez Fernández and P. Cabrera Bonet (eds), *En los límites de Dioniso*, Murcia, 29–40.

Bernabé, A. (2002a) 'La Toile de Pénélope: a-t-il existé un mythe orphique sur Dionysos et les Titans?' *RHR* 219, 401–33.

Bernabé, A. (2002b) 'Referencias a textos órficos en Diodoro', in L. Torraca (ed.), *Scritti in onore di Italo Gallo*, Naples, 67–96.

Bernabé, A. (2002c) 'La Théogonie orphique du papyrus de Derveni', *Kernos* 15, 91–129.

Bernabé, A. (2003) 'Autour du mythe orphique sur Dionysos et les Titans. Quelque notes critiques', in D. A. P. Chuvin (ed.), *Des Géants à Dionysos: Mélanges offerts à F. Vian*, Alessandria, 25–39.

Bernabé, A. (ed.) (2004, 2005, 2007) *Poetae Epici Graeci II: Orphicorum Graecorum testimonia et fragmenta*, 3 fascicles, Munich.

Bernabé, A. (2004b) 'Orphisme et présocratiques: bilan et prespectives d'un dialogue complexe', in A. Laks and C. Louguet (eds), *Qu'est-ce que la philosophie présocratique? What is Presocratic Philosophy?* Villeneuve-d'Ascq, 205–47.

Bernabé, A. (2008) *Dioses, héroes y orígenes del mundo: lecturas de mitología*, Madrid.

Bernabé, A. and F. Casadesús (eds) (2008) *Orfeo y la tradición órfica*, 2 vols, Madrid.

Bernal, M. (1987–2006) *Black Athena: The Afro-Asiatic Roots of Classical Civilization* 1 'The Fabrication of Ancient Greece, 1785–1985' (1987), 2 'The Archaeological and Documentary Evidence' (1991), 3 'The Linguistic Evidence' (2006), New Brunswick.

Bernal, M. (2001) *Black Athena Writes Back: Martin Bernal Responds to his Critics*, Durham NC, London.

Betegh, G. (2004) *The Derveni Papyrus: Cosmology, Theology and Interpretation*, Cambridge.

Bettelheim, B. (1976) *The Uses of Enchantment: The Meaning and Importance of Fairy Tales*, London.

Bianchi, U. (1965) 'Initiation, mystères, gnose: pour l'histoire de la mystique dans le paganisme gréco-oriental', in C. J. Bleeker (ed.), *Initiation: Contributions to the Theme of the Study Conference of the International Association for the History of Religions, Strasbourg, September 17th–22nd, 1964*, Leiden, 154–71.

Bickermann, E. J. (1952) 'Origines Gentium', *CPh* 47, 65–81 [repr. in Bickermann 1985: 399–417].

Bickermann, E. J. (1985) *Religions and Politics in the Hellenistic and Roman Periods*, ed. E. Gabba, M. Smith, Como.

Bierl, A. and W. M. Calder III (1991) 'Instinct against Proof. The Correspondence between Ulrich von Wilamowitz-Moellendorff and Martin P. Nilsson on *Religionsgeschichte* (1920–1930)', *Eranos* 89, 73–99 [repr. in W. M. Calder III (ed.) 1994 *Further Letters of Ulrich von Wilamowitz-Moellendorff*, Hildesheim, 151–78].

Bing, P. (1988) *The Well-Read Muse: Past and Present in Callimachus and the Hellenistic Poets*, Göttingen.

Black, J. A., G. Cunningham, E. Robson, and G. Zólyomi (2004) *The Literature of Ancient Sumer*, Oxford, New York.

Blok, J. H. (1994) *The Early Amazons: Modern and Ancient Perspectives on a Persistent Myth*, Leiden.

Blome, P. (1992) 'Funerärsymbolische Collagen auf mythologischen Sarkophagreliefs', *SIFC* 10.2, 1061–73.

Blum, R. (1991) *Kallimachos: The Alexandrian Library and the Origins of Bibliography*, tr. H. H Wellisch, Madison.

Blumenberg, H. (1985) *Work on Myth*, Cambridge MA.

Blundell, S. (1995) *Women in Ancient Greece*, London.

Boardman, J. (1975) *Athenian Red Figure Vases: The Archaic Period*, London, New York.

Boardman, J. and N. G. L. Hammond (1982) *Cambridge Ancient History* 3.3² 'The Expansion of the Greek World, Eighth to Sixth Centuries', Cambridge.

Bons J. (2007) 'Gorgias the Sophist and Early Rhetoric', in Worthington (ed.) 2007a: 37–46.

Borg, B. E. (ed.) (2004) *Paideia: The World of the Second Sophistic*, Millenium-Studien 2, Berlin, New York.

Borgeaud, P. (1988) *The Cult of Pan in Ancient Greece*, tr. K. Atlass, J. Redfield, Chicago [*Recherches sur le dieu Pan*, Geneva, Rome 1979].

Borrmans, M. (2008) 'Salvation', in J. D. McAuliffe (ed.), *Encyclopaedia of the Qur'ān*, http://www.brillonline.nl/subscriber/entry?entry=q3_SIM-00368) (accessed 16 December 2008)

Boschung, D. (1987) *Antike Grabaltäre aus den Nekropolen Roms*, Acta Bernensia 10, Bern.

Bosworth, A. B. (1993) *Conquest and Empire: The Reign of Alexander the Great*, Cambridge.

Bosworth, A. B. (2003) 'Arrian, Megasthenes, and the Making of Myth', in López Férez (ed.) 2003: 299–320.

Bothmer, D. von (1957) *Amazons in Greek Art*, Oxford.

Bottéro, J. (2001) *Religion in Ancient Mesopotamia* Chicago, London.

Bowden, H. (2010) *Mystery Cults in the Ancient World*, London.

Bowersock, G. W. (1990) *Hellenism in Late Antiquity*, Cambridge.

Bowersock, G. W. (2006) *Mosaics as History: The Near East from Late Antiquity to Islam*, Cambridge MA, London.

Bowersock, G. W., W. Burkert, and M. C. J. Putnam (eds) (1979) *Arktouros: Hellenic Studies Presented to Bernard M. W. Knox*, Berlin.

Bowman, A. K. (1986) *Egypt after the Pharaohs*, Berkeley.

Bowlby, R. (2007) *Freudian Mythologies: Greek Tragedy and Modern Identities*, Oxford.

Bowra, C. M. (1964) *Pindar*, Oxford.

Braun, F. R. G. (1982) 'The Greeks in Egypt', in Boardman and Hammon (eds) 1982: 32–56.

Brelich, A. (1969) *Paides e parthenoi*, Rome.

Bremer, J. M., I. J. F. De Jong, and J. Kalff (eds) 1987 *Homer: Beyond Oral Poetry. Recent Trends in Homeric Interpretation*, Amsterdam.

Bremmer, J. N. (1978) 'Heroes, Rituals and the Trojan War', *Studi Storico-religiosi* 2, 5–38.

Bremmer, J. N. (1983) 'The Importance of the Maternal Uncle and Grandfather in Archaic and Classical Greece and Early Byzantium', *ZPE* 50, 173–86.

Bremmer, J. N. (ed.) (1987) *Interpretations of Greek Mythology*, London, New York, Sydney.

Bremmer, J. N. (1990a) 'Adolescents, Symposium and Pederasty', in Murray (ed.) 1990: 135–48.

Bremmer, J. N. (1990b) 'Hermann Usener', in W. W. Briggs and W. M. Calder III (eds), *Classical Scholarship: A Biographical Encyclopedia*, New York, 462–78.

Bremmer, J. N. (1991) 'Gerardus van der Leeuw and Jane Ellen Harrison', in H. G. Kippenberg and B. Luchesi (eds) *Religionswissenschaft und Kulturkritik*, Marburg, 237–41.

Bremmer, J. N. (1996) 'James George Frazer en The Golden Bough', *Hermeneus* 68, 212–21.

Bremmer, J. N. (1998) '"Religion", "Ritual" and the Opposition "Sacred vs. Profane": Notes Towards a Terminological "Genealogy"', in F. Graf (ed.), *Ansichten griechischer Rituale: Festschrift für Walter Burkert*, Stuttgart, Leipzig, 9–32.

Bremmer, J. N. (1999a) *Greek Religion²*, Greece & Rome New Surveys in the Classics 24, Oxford [1994¹].

Bremmer, J. N. (1999b) 'Transvestite Dionysos' in Padilla 1999: 183–200.

Bremmer, J. N. (2001) 'Sacrificing a Child in Ancient Greece: The Case of Iphigeneia', in E. Noort and E. J. C. Tigchelaar (eds) *The Sacrifice of Isaac*, Leiden, 21–43.

Bremmer, J. N. (2005) 'Myth and Ritual in Ancient Greece: Observations on a Difficult Relationship', in von Haehling 2005: 21–43.

Bremmer, J. N. (2008) *Greek Religion and Culture, the Bible and the Ancient Near East*, Leiden.

Bremmer, J. N. (2009) 'Zeus' Own Country: Cult and Myth in the Pride of Halicarnassus', in Dill and Walde (eds) 2009: 292–312.

Bremmer, J. N. (2010) 'Walter Burkert on Ancient Myth and Ritual: Some Personal Observations', in A. Bierl and W. Braungart (eds) *Gewalt und Opfer: Im Dialog mit Walter Burkert*. MythosEikonPoiesis 2, Berlin, New York, 71–86.

Brichto, H. C. (1973) 'Kin, Cult, Land and Afterlife – A Biblical Complex', *HebrUCA* 44, 1–54.

Brilliant, R. (1984) *Visual Narratives: Storytelling in Etruscan and Roman Art*, Ithaca NY, London.

Brilliant, R. (1992) 'Roman Myth/Greek Myth: Reciprocity and Appropriation on a Roman Sarcophagus in Berlin', *SIFC* 10.2, 1030–45 [repr. in R. Brilliant 1994 *Commentaries on Roman Art: Selected Studies*, London, 423–38].

Briquel, D. (2006) 'Le Règne de Tullus Hostilius et l'idéologie indo-européenne des trois fonctions', *RHR* 221, 23–62.

Briquel, D. (2007) *Mythe et revolution: La fabrication d'un récit: la naissance de la république à Rome*, Brussels.

Briquel, D. (2008) *La Prise de Rome par les Gaulois: lecture mythique d'un événement historique*, Paris.

Brisson, L. (1995) *Orphée et l'Orphisme dans l'Antiquité gréco-romaine*, Aldershot.

Brisson, L. (1998) *Plato the Myth Maker*, tr. G. Naddaf, Chicago.

Brisson, L. (2002) *Sexual Ambivalence: Androgyny and Hermaphroditism in Graeco-Roman Antiquity*, tr. J. Lloyd, Berkeley.

Brisson, L. (2004) *How Philosophers Saved Myths: Allegorical Interpretation and Classical Mythology*, tr. C. Tihanyi, Chicago, London.

Brockington, J. (1998) *The Sanskrit Epics* (*Handbook of Oriental Studies*, Section 2 South Asia, 12), Leiden.

Brophy, J. (1991) 'Die Königsnovelle: An Egyptian Literary Form' *Bulletin of the Australian Centre for Egyptology* 2, 15–22.

Brown, E. L. (1974) 'Egyptian Pakht – Hellenic Sphinx', *Archaeological News* 3, 9–12.

Brown, J. P. (1995–2001) *Israel and Hellas*, 3 vols. Beihefte zur Zeitschrift für die Alttestamentliche Wissenschaft 231 (1995), 276 (2000), 299 (2001), Berlin.

Brown, J. P. (2003) *Ancient Israel and Ancient Greece: Religion, Politics and Culture*, Minneapolis [Selected papers from Brown 1995–2001].

Brown, M. K. (ed.) (2002) *The* Narratives *of Konon*, Beiträge zur Altertumskunde 163, Munich.

Broze, M. (2003) 'Le Rire et les larmes du démiurge. La cosmogonie de Neith à Esna et ses parallèlles grecs', *Égypte Afrique et Orient* 29, 5–10.

Brulé, P. (1987) *La Fille d'Athènes*, Paris.

Brunel, P. (1995) *Le Mythe d'Électre*³, Paris.

Budelmann, F. (ed.) (2009) *The Cambridge Companion to Greek Lyric*, Cambridge.

Buffière, F. (1962) *Héraclite: allégories d'Homère*, Collection Budé, Paris.

Buitenwerf, R. (2003) *Book III of the Sibylline Oracles and its Social Setting*, Leiden, Boston.

Bulloch, A. W., E. S. Gruen, A. A. Long, and A. Stewart (eds) (1993) *Images & Ideologies: Self-definition in the Hellenistic World*. Hellenistic Culture and Society 12, Berkeley, Los Angeles, London.

Burgess, J. (2001) *The Tradition of the Trojan War in Homer and the Epic Cycle*, Baltimore.

Burgess, J. (2005) 'The Death of Achilles by Rhapsodes', in R. Rabel (ed), *Approaches to Homer, Ancient and Modern*, Swansea, 119–34.

Burian, P. (1997) 'Myth into *muthos*: The Shaping of Tragic Plot', in Easterling (ed.) 1997: 178–208.

Burkert, W. (1965) 'Demaratos, Astrabakos und Herakles: Königsmythos und Politik zur Zeit der Perserkriege', *MH* 22, 166–77 [tr. as 'Demaratos, Astrabakos, and Herakles: Kingship, Myth, and Politics at the Time of the Persian Wars (Herodotus 6.67–69)' in Burkert 2001: 97–110].

Burkert, W. (1966a) 'Greek Tragedy and Sacrificial Ritual', *GRBS* 7, 87–121.

Burkert, W. (1966b) 'Kekropidensage und Arrhephoria: Vom Initiationsritus zum Panathenäenfest', *Hermes* 94 (1966) 1–25.

Burkert, W. (1970) 'Iason, Hypsipyle and New Fire at Lemnos: A Study in Myth and Ritual', *CQ* 20, 1–16 [repr. with a few addenda in Buxton 2000: 227–49].

Burkert, W. (1972a) *Lore and Science in Ancient Pythagoreanism*, tr. E. L. Minar Jr, Cambridge, MA.

Burkert, W. (1972b) *Homo necans: Interpretationen altgriechisher Opferriten und Mythen*[1], Berlin, New York [1997[2]; *Homo Necans: The Anthropology of Ancient Greek Sacrificial Ritual and Myth*, tr. P. Bing, Berkeley, Los Angeles, London 1983].

Burkert, W. (1979) *Structure and History in Greek Mythology and Ritual*, Berkeley, Los Angeles, London.

Burkert, W. (1980) 'Griechische Mythologie und die Geistesgeschichte der Moderne', in *Entretiens Hardt* 26, Geneva, 159–207.

Burkert, W. (1982) 'Craft Versus Sect: the Problem of Orphics and Pythagoreans', in B. Meyer and E. P. Sanders (eds), *Jewish and Christian Self-Definition* 3 'Self-Definition in the Greco-Roman World', Philadelphia, 1–22.

Burkert, W. (1987) *Ancient Mystery Cults*, Cambridge MA, London.

Burkert, W. (1992) *The Orientalizing Revolution: Near Eastern Revolution in the Early Archaic Age*, tr. M. E. Pinder, W. Burkert, Cambridge MA, London [*Die orientilisierende Epoche in der griechischen Religion und Literatur*, Heidelberg 1984].

Burkert, W. (2001) *Savage Energies: Lessons of Myth and Ritual in Ancient Greece*, tr. P. Bing, Chicago.

Burkert, W. (2002) 'Mythos and Ritual: im Wechselwind der Moderne', in H. F. J. Horstmanshoff, H. W. Singor, F. T. van Straten, and J. H. M. Strubbe (eds) *Kykeon: Studies in honor of H. S. Versnel*, Religions in the Graeco-Roman World 142, Leiden, 1–22.

Burkert, W. (2003) *Kleine Schriften* 2 Orientalia, Göttingen.

Burkert, W. (2004) *Babylon, Memphis, Persepolis: Eastern Contexts of Greek Culture*, Cambridge MA.

Burkert, W. (2006) *Kleine Schriften* 3 Mystica, Orphica, Pythagorica, Göttingen.

Burnett, A. P. (1983) *Three Archaic Poets: Archilochus, Alcaeus, Sappho*, London.

Burnett, A. P. (2005) *Pindar's Songs For Young Athletes of Aegina*, Oxford.

Burnyeat, M. (2009) '*Eikôs Muthos*', in Partenie (ed.) 2009: 167–86.

Burstein, S. M. (1985) (ed. and tr.) *Translated Documents of Greece and Rome* 3 The Hellenistic Age from the Battle of Ipsos to the Death of Kleopatra VII, Cambridge.

Burstein, S. M. (2009) 'Hecataeus of Miletus and the Greek Encounter with Egypt', *Ancient West and East* 8, 133–46

Burton, A. (1972) *Diodorus Siculus Book 1: A Commentary*, Leiden.

Buxton, R. (1987) 'Wolves and Werewolves in Greek Thought', in Bremmer (ed.) 1987, 60–79.

Buxton, R. (1994) *Imaginary Greece: The Contexts of Mythology*, Cambridge.

Buxton, R. (ed.) (1999) *From Myth to Reason? Studies in the Development of Greek Thought*, Oxford.

Buxton, R. (ed.) (2000) *Oxford Readings in Greek Religion*, Oxford.

Buxton, R. (2004) *The Complete World of Greek Mythology*, London.

Cairns, D. L. (2001) *Oxford Readings in the Iliad*[1], Oxford [2004[2]].

Calame, C. (ed.) (1988) *Métamorphoses du mythe dans la Grèce antique*, Geneva.

Calame, C. (1996) *Thésée et l'imaginaire athénien*[2], Lausanne [1990[1]].

Calame, C. (1997) *Choruses of Young Women in Ancient Greece*, Lanham [see also Calame 2001].

Calame, C. (2000a) *Poétique des mythes dans la Grèce antique*, Paris.

Calame, C. (2000b) *Le Récit en Grèce ancienne*, Paris.

Calame, C. (2001) *Choruses of Young Women in Ancient Greece: Their Morphology, Religious Role and Social Function*, tr. D. Collins, J. Orion, Lanham MD [new, revised ed. of Calame 1997].

Calame, C. (2003) *Myth and History in Ancient Greece: The Symbolic Creation of a Colony*, tr. D. W. Berman, Princeton [*Mythe et histoire dans l'antiquité grecque: La création symbolique d'une colonie*, Lausanne 1996].

Calame, C. (2004) 'Deictic Ambiguity and Auto-Referentiality: Some Examples from Greek Poetics', *Arethusa* 37, 415–43.

Calame, C. (2005) *The Craft of Poetic Speech in Ancient Greece*, tr. J. Orion, Ithaca NY.

Calame, C. (2009a) *Greek Mythology: Poetics, Pragmatics and Fiction*, tr. J. Lloyd, Cambridge [*Poétique des mythes dans la Grèce antique*, Paris 2000].

Calame, C. (2009b) *Poetic and Performative Memory in Ancient Greece: Heroic Reference and Ritual Gestures in Time and Space*, tr. H. Patton, Cambridge MA, London [*Pratiques poétiques de la mémoire: représentations de l'espace-temps en Grèce ancienne*, Paris 2006].

Calame, C. (2009c) 'Referential Fiction and Poetic Ritual: Towards a Pragmatics of Myth (Sappho 17 and Bacchylides 13)', *Trends in Classics* 1, 1–17.

Calder, W. M., III (ed.) (1991) *The Cambridge Ritualists Reconsidered*, Atlanta.

Calder, W. M., III and R. Schlesier (eds) (1998) *Zwischen Rationalismus und Romantik: Karl Otfried Müller und die antike Kultur*, Hildesheim.

Calder, W. M., III, R. S. Smith, and J. Vaio (eds) (2002) *Teaching the English Wissenschaft: The Letters of Sir George Cornewall Lewis to Karl Otfried Müller (1828–1839)*, Hildesheim.

Caldwell R. (1989) *The Origin of the Gods: A Psychoanalytic Study of Greek Theogonic Myth*, New York.

Caldwell R. (1990) 'The Psychoanalytic Interpretation of Greek Myth', in Edmunds (ed.) 1990: 344–89.

Cancik, H. and H. Schneider (eds) (2002) *Brill's New Pauly: Encyclopaedia of the Ancient World*, 22 vols, Leiden. www.brillonline.nl (accessed 4 August 2010).

Cameron, A. (1995) *Callimachus and his Critics*, Princeton.

Cameron, A. (2004) *Greek Mythography in the Roman World*, Oxford.

Caminos, R. A. (1958) *The Chronicle of Prince Osorkon*, Rome.

Campbell, D. A. (1990) *Greek Lyric* 1², Loeb Classical Library, Cambridge MA, London.

Campbell, J. (2008) *The Hero with a Thousand Faces³*, Novato CA [1949¹].

Campbell, W. J. (2000) 'Not Likely Sent: The Remington-Hearst "Telegrams"', *Journalism and Mass Communication Quarterly* 77, 405–22.

Capra, A. (2010) 'Plato's Hesiod and the Will of Zeus: Philosophical Rhapsody in the *Timaeus* and the *Critias*', in Haubold and Boys-Stones (eds) 2010: 200–18.

Carandini, A. and R. Capelli (eds) (2000) *Romolo, Remo e la fondazione della città*, Milan.

Carcopino, J. (1926) *La Basilique pythagoricienne de la Porte Majeure*¹, Paris.

Carcopino, J. (1956) *De Pythagore aux apôtres*, Paris.

Carey, C. (2007) 'Epideictic Oratory', in Worthington (ed.) 2007a: 236–52.

Carpenter, T. H. (1991) *Art and Myth in Ancient Greece*, London.

Carruba, O. (2003) *Anittae res gestae*, Studia Mediterranea 13/Series Hethaea 1, Pavia.

Carter, A. (1979) *The Bloody Chamber and Other Stories*, London.

Cartledge, P. (1997) '"Deep Plays": Theatre as Process in Greek Civic Life', in Easterling (ed.) 1997: 3–35.

Cartledge, P., P. Garnsey, and E. S. Gruen (eds) (1997) *Hellenistic Constructs: Essays in Culture, History, and Historiography*. Hellenistic Culture and Society 26, Berkeley, Los Angeles, London.

Casadio, G. (1996) 'Osiride in Grecia e Dioniso in Egitto', in I. Gallo (ed.), *Plutarco e la religione*, Naples 201–27.

Cassirer, E. (1925) *Sprache und Mythos: ein Beitrag zum Problem der Götternamen*, Berlin.

Cassirer, E. (1946) *Language and Myth*, tr. S. K. Langer, London, New York [tr. of Cassirer 1925].

Cassirer, E. (1955–7) *The Philosophy of Symbolic* Forms, 3 vols, tr. R. Manheim, New Haven, London.

Cassirer, E. (1973) *Langage et mythe: à propos du nom des dieux*, tr. O. Hansen Love, Paris [tr. of Cassirer 1925].

Cerny, J. (1948) 'Thoth as Creator of Language', *JEA* 34, 121–2.

Chadwick, J. (1990) 'The Descent of the Greek Epic', *JHS* 110 (1990) 174–7.

Chamoux, F. (2003) *Hellenistic Civilization*, Oxford.

Champlin, E. (2003) *Nero*, Cambridge MA.

Chaplin, J. D. and C. S. Kraus (eds) (2009) *Oxford Readings in Classical Studies: Livy*, Oxford.

Chiarini, G. (1989) 'Ch.G. Heyne e gli inizi dello studio scientifico della mythologia', *Lares* 55, 317–31.

Chlup, R. (2007) 'The Semantics of Fertility: Levels of Meaning in the Thesmophoria', *Kernos* 20, 69–96.

Chodorow, J. (ed.) (1997) *Jung on Active Imagination*, Princeton.

Clarysse, W. and A. Wouters (1970) 'A Schoolboy's Exercise in the Chester Beatty Library', *AncSoc* 1, 201–35.

Clarke, J. R. (1991) *The Houses of Roman Italy*, Berkeley, Los Angeles, London.

Clauss, J. J. and S. I. Johnston (eds) (1997) *Medea: Essays on Medea in Myth, Literature, Philosophy and Art*, Princeton.

Clay, D. (2007) 'Plato Philomythos', in Woodard (ed.) 2007: 210–36.

Clay, J. S. (1983) *The Wrath of Athena: Gods and Men in the 'Odyssey'*, Princeton.

Clay, J. S. (1997a) *The Politics of Olympus: Form and Meaning in the Major Homeric Hymns*, Princeton.

Clay, J. S. (1997b) 'The Homeric Hymns', in Morris and Powell (eds) 1997: 489–507.

Clay, J. S. (2003) *Hesiod's Cosmos*, Cambridge, New York.

Coarelli, F. (1993) 'Atrium Libertatis', *Lexicon Topographicum Urbis Romae* 1, Rome, 133–5.

Coleman, K. (1990) 'Fatal Charades: Roman Executions Staged as Mythological Enactments', *JRS* 80, 44–73.

Colin, F. (1997) 'Ammon, Parammon, Poséidon, Héra et Libye à Siwa', *BIAO* 97, 97–108.

Colson, F. H. and G. H. Whitaker (eds), *Philo with an English Translation*, Loeb Classical Library, 12 vols, London, Cambridge MA 1929–53.

Colvin, S. (2007) *A Historical Greek Reader: Mycenean to the Koiné*, Oxford.

Connolly, P. (1986) *The Legend of Odysseus*, Oxford.

Conti, N. (1976) *Natalis Comes: Mythologiae: Venice 1567*, New York [reprint of the edition published by Comin da Trino, Venice 1567].

Cornelius, I. and H. Niehr (2004) *Götter und Kulte in Ugarit: Kultur und Religion einer nordsyrischen Königstadt in der Spätbronzezeit*, Mainz.

Cornford, F. M. (1907) *Thucydides Mythistoricus*, London.

Coutau-Bégarie, H. (1998) *L'Oeuvre de Georges Dumézil: catalogue raisonné*, Paris.

Cox, C. A. (1998) *Household Interests: Property, Marriage Strategies and Family Dynamics in Ancient Athens*, Princeton.

Creuzer, F. (1810–12) *Symbolik und Mythologie der alten Völker, besonders der Griechen*[1], Darmstadt [1819–22[2]; 1836–43[3]].

Cribiore, R. (2001) *Gymnastics of the Mind: Greek Education in Hellenistic and Roman Egypt*, Princeton, Oxford.

Csapo, E. (2005) *Theories of Mythology*, Malden, Oxford, Carlton (Victoria).

Cumont, F. (1911) *Oriental Religions in Roman Paganism*, tr. G. Showerman, Chicago, London [tr. of *Les Religions orientales dans le paganisme romain*, Paris 1909[2]; 1929[4] is better].

Cumont, F. (1942) *Recherches sur le symbolisme funéraire des Romains*, Paris.

Curtis, J. B. (1957) 'An Investigation of the Mount of Olives in the Judaeo-Christian Tradition', *HebrUCA* 28, 137–80.

Curtius, E. R. (1948) *Europäische Literatur und lateinisches Mittelalter*, Bern [*European literature and the Latin Middle Ages*, tr. W. R. Trask, London, New York 1953].

Curty, O. (1995) *Les Parentés légendaires entre cités grecques: catalogue raisonnée des inscriptions contenant le terme* ΣΥΓΓΕΝΕΙΑ *et analyse critique*, Hautes études du monde gréco-romain 20, Geneva.

Cyrino, M. S. (2010) *Aphrodite*, London, New York.

D'Alessio, G. B. (2005a) 'The *Megalai Ehoiai*: a Survey of the Fragments', in Hunter (ed.) 2005: 176–216.

D'Alessio, G. B. (2005b) 'Ordered from the Catalogue: Pindar, Bacchylides and Hesiodic Genealogical Poetry', in Hunter (ed.) 2005: 217–38.

D'Alessio, G. B. (2009) 'Re-constructing Pindar's *First Hymn*: The Theban "Theogony" and the Birth of Apollo', in L. Athanassaki, R. P. Martin, and J. F. Miller (eds) *Apolline Politics and Poetics*, Athens, 129–48.

Dalley, S. (1989) *Myths from Mesopotamia: Creation, The Flood, Gilgamesh, and Others* [World's Classics], Oxford, New York.

D'Ambra, E. (1993) *Private Lives, Imperial Virtues: The Frieze of the Forum Transitorium in Rome*, Princeton.

D'Ambra, E. (ed.) (1993) *Roman Art in Context: An Anthology*, Englewood Cliffs NJ.

Damm, C. T. (1797) *Götter-Lehre und Fabel-Geschichte der alten griechischen und römischen Welt*, Berlin.

Danek, G. (1998) *Epos und Zitat: Studien zu den Quellen der Odyssee*, Vienna.

Daszewski, W. (1985) *Dionysos der Erlöser: Griechische Mythen im spätantiken Cypern*, Mainz.

Daumas, F. (1963) 'L'Origine égyptienne du jugement des âmes dans le *Gorgias* de Platon', in R. Godel, *De l'humanisme à l'humain* (Paris), 187–203.

Davies, G. (2003) 'Roman Funerary Symbolism in the Early Empire' in J. B. Wilkins, E. Herring (eds) 2003 *Inhabiting Symbols: Symbol and Image in the Ancient Mediterranean*. Accordia Specialist Studies on the Ancient Mediterranean 5, 211–27.

Davies, M. (2006) '"Self-Consolation" in the *Iliad*', *CQ* 56, 582–665.

Dawson, D. (1992) *Allegorical Readers and Cultural Revision in Ancient Alexandria*, Berkeley.

Deacy, S. (2008) *Athena*, Abingdon, New York.

de Angelis, F. and S. Muth (eds) (1999) *Im Spiegel des Mythos: Bilderwelt und Lebenswelt*, Wiesbaden.

Deforge, B. (1986) *Eschyle, poète cosmique*, Paris.

de Grummond, N. T. and B. S. Ridgway (eds) (2000) *From Pergamon to Sperlonga: Sculpture and Context*, Berkeley, Los Angeles, London.

Diels, H. and W. Kranz (eds) (1951–2) *Die Fragmente der Vorsokratiker*, Zurich.

de Jong, I. J. F. (2001) *A Narratological Commentary on the Odyssey*, Cambridge.

Delattre, C. (2005) *Manuel de mythologie grecque*, Paris.

DeLaine, J. (1997) *The Baths of Caracalla*, JRA Supplement 25, Portsmouth RI.

del Ninno, M. (ed.) (2007) *Etnosemiotica: Questioni di metodo*, Rome.

del Olmo Lete, G. (1999) *Canaanite Religion According to the Liturgical Texts of Ugarit*, Bethesda MD.

Demand, N. H. (1994) *Birth, Death and Motherhood in Classical Greece*, Baltimore.

Demont, P. and A. Lebeau (1996) *Introduction au théâtre grec antique*, Paris.

Demoor, M. (1999) 'Portret van de antropologe als een jonge vrouw: Jane Ellen Harrisons recensies voor The Athenaeum', *Tijdschrift voor geschiedenis* 112, 191–201.

Derchain, P. (1956) 'Un conte égyptien chez Hellanicos de Lesbos', *AC* 25, 408–11.

Derchain, P. (1970) 'Les Pleurs d'Isis et la crue du Nil', *Chroniques d'Égypte* 45, 282–4.

Derchain, P. (1974) 'Miettes §4. Homère à Edfu', *Revue d' Égyptologie* 26, 15–19.

Derchain, P. (1990) 'L'auteur du papyrus Jumilhac', *Revue d' Égyptologie* 41, 9–30.

Derrida, J. (1981) 'Plato's Pharmacy', in *Dissemination*, tr. B. Johnson, Chicago, 69–186 ['La Pharmacie de Platon', in *La Dissémination*, Paris 1972, 108–38].

Desbordes, F., *et al.* (1981) *Pour un temps: Georges Dumézil*, Paris, Aix-en-Provence.

Detienne, M. (1972) *Les Jardins d'Adonis*, with introduction by J.-P. Vernant, Paris [1989², with afterword by the author; 2007³, with preface by the author and contributions by J.-P. Vernant and C. Lévi-Strauss; for Eng. tr. see Detienne 1994].

Detienne, M. (1979) *Dionysos Slain*, Baltimore.

Detienne, M. (1981) *L'Invention de la mythologie*, Paris [1986, *The Creation of Mythology*, tr. M. Cook, Chicago].

Detienne, M. (1986) 'Dionysos dans ses parousies, un dieu épidémique', in *L'Association Dionysiaque dans les Sociétés Anciennes: actes de la table ronde organisée par l'École francaise de* Rome, Rome, 53–83.

Detienne, M. (1988) 'La Double écriture de la mythologie', in Calame (ed.). 1988: 17–33.

Detienne, M. (1994) *The Gardens of Adonis: Spices in Greek Mythology*, tr. J. Lloyd, with afterword tr. F. I. Zeitlin, Princeton [tr. of Detienne 1972¹/1989²].

Detienne, M. (1996) *The Masters of Truth in Archaic Greece*, tr. J. Lloyd, New York, Cambridge MA, London.

Devereux, G. (1966) 'The Exploitation of Ambiguity in Pindaros O.3.27', *RhM* 109, 289–98.

Dewald, C. and J. Marincola (eds) (2006) *The Cambridge Companion to Herodotus*, Cambridge.

Dickey, E. (2007) *Ancient Greek Scholarship*, Oxford, New York.

Dickson, K. (1995) *Nestor: Poetic Memory in Greek Epic*, London.

Dietrich, M., O. Loretz, and J. Sanmartin (eds) (1976) *Die keilalphabetische Texte aus Ugarit, einschließlich der keilalphabetischen Texte außerhalb Ugarits*. Alter Orient und Altes Testament 24, Neukirchen-Vluyn.

di Donato, R. (1990) *Per una antropologia storica del mondo antico*, Florence.

Dijkstra, M. (1991) 'The Weather-god on Two Mountains', *UF* 23, 127–40.

Dill, U. and C. Walde (eds) (2009) *Antike Mythen: Medien, Transformationen und Konstruktionen*, Berlin.

Dillery, J. (2005) 'Sacred History', *AJPh* 126, 505–26.

Dittenberger, W. (ed.) (1903) *Orientis Graeci Inscriptiones Selectae*, 4 vols, Leipzig.

Dodd, D. B. and C. A. Faraone (eds) (2003) *Initiation in Ancient Greek Rituals and Narratives: New critical perspectives*, London, New York.

Dodds, E. R. (1966) 'On Misunderstanding the *Oedipus Rex*', *G&R* 13, 37–49.

Doherty, L. E. (2001) *Gender and the Interpretation of Classical Myth*, London.

Doniger, W. (1998) *The Implied Spider: Politics & Theology in Myth*, New York, Chichester.

Doniger, W. (1999) *Splitting the Difference: Gender and Myth in Ancient Greece and India*, Chicago.

Doty, W. G. (2000) *Mythography: The Study of Myths and Rituals*², Tuscaloosa, London [1986¹].

Dougherty, C. (2001) *The Raft of Odysseus: The Ethnographic Imagination of Homer's Odyssey*, Oxford.

Dover, K. J. (1972) *Aristophanic Comedy*, London.

Dowden, K. (1989) *Death and the Maiden: Girls' Initiation Rites in Greek Mythology*, London, New York.

Dowden, K. (1992) *The Uses of Greek Mythology*, London, New York.

Dowden, K. (1995) 'Approaching Women through Myth: Vital Tool or Self-delusion?' in B. Levick and R. Hawley (eds) *Women in Antiquity: New Assessments*, London, 44–57.

Dowden, K. (1996) 'Homer's Sense of Text', *JHS* 116, 47–61.

Dowden, K. (1997) 'The Amazons: Development and Functions', *RhM* 140, 97–128.

Dowden, K. (1999) 'Fluctuating Meanings: "Passage Rites" in Ritual, Myth, *Odyssey*, and the Greek Romance', in Padilla (ed.) 1999: 221–46.

Dowden, K. (2000) *European Paganism: The Realities of Cult from Antiquity to the Middle Ages*, London, New York.

Dowden, K. (2001) 'West on the East: Martin West's *East Face of Helicon* and its forerunners', *JHS* 121, 167–75.

Dowden, K. (2004) 'The Epic Tradition in Greece', in Fowler (ed.) 2004a: 188–205.

Dowden, K. (2007) 'Olympian Gods, Olympian Pantheon', in Ogden (ed.) 2007: 41–55.

Dowden, K. (2010) 'Trojan Night', in M. Christopoulos, E. D. Karakantza, and O. Levaniouk (eds) *Light and Darkness in Ancient Greek Myth and Religion*, Lanham MD, 110–20.

Dowden, K. (2011) 'Van Gennep et l'initiation dans la mythologie grecque: mort prématurée d'un paradigme?' *Gaia* 14.

Dowden, K. (forthcoming a) 'Fact and Fiction in the New Mythology: 100 BC–AD 100', in J. R. Morgan, and I. Repath (eds), *'Where the Truth Lies': Lies and Metafiction in Ancient Literature*, Groningen.

Dowden, K. (forthcoming b) '"But There is a Difference in the Ends ...": Brigands and Teleology in the Ancient Novel', in M. Paschalis and S. Panayiotakis (eds), *The Construction of the Real and the Ideal in the Ancient Novel*, Groningen.

Dräger, P. (1997) 'Hatte Psaumis graue Haare? Pindar und der Mythos' *RhM* 140, 1–7.

Drews, R. (2005) 'The Laurion Mines and a Bronze Age Name for the Greek Mainland', *JIES* 33, 227–32.

Dubois, P. (2005) 'Oedipus as Detective: Sophocles, Simenon, Robbe-Grillet', *Yale French Studies* 108, 102–15.

Duffy, C. A. (1999) *The World's Wife*, London.

Duchemin, J. (1995) *Mythes grecs et sources orientales: Vérité des mythes*, Paris.

Dumézil, G. (1968–73) *Mythe et épopée*, 3 vols, Paris [3 vols in 1, Paris 1997].

Dumézil, G. (1969) *Idées romaines*, Paris.

Dumézil, G. (1977) *Les Dieux souverains des Indo-Européens*, Paris.

Dumézil, G. (1980) *Camillus: A Study of Indo-European Mythology as Roman History*, ed. U. Strutynski, tr. A. Aronowicz, J. Bryson, Berkeley, London.

Dumézil, G. (1985a) *Heur et malheur du guerrier²*, Paris [1969¹; *The Destiny of the Warrior*, tr. A. Hiltebeitel, Chicago 1970].

Dumézil, G. (1985b) *L'Oubli de l'homme et l'honneur des dieux*, Paris.

Dumézil, G. (1987) *Entretiens avec Didier Eribon*, Paris.

Dunbabin, K. M. D. (1999) *The Mosaics of the Greek and Roman World*, Cambridge.

Dunbar, N. (1995) *Aristophanes: Birds*, Oxford.

Dunkel, G. E. (1988–90) 'Vater Himmels Gattin', *Die Sprache* 34, 1–26.

Durand, G. (1992) *Les Structures anthropologiques de l'imaginaire¹¹*, Paris [1969¹].

Easterling, P. E. (ed.) (1997) *The Cambridge Companion to Greek Tragedy*, Cambridge.

Easton, D. F. (1990) 'Reconstructing Schliemann's Troy', in W. W. Calder III and J. Cobet (eds), *Heinrich Schliemann nach hundert Jahren*, Frankfurt.

Edel.,E. (1966) *Die Ortsnamenlisten aus dem Totentempel Amenophis III*, Bonn.

Edgar, C. C. (1906) 'Two Bronze Portraits from Egypt', *JHS* 26, 281–2.

Edmonds, R. (1999) 'Tearing Apart the Zagreus Myth: A Few Disparaging Remarks on Orphism and Original Sin', *ClAnt* 18, 1–24.

Edmonds, R. (2004) *Myths of the Underworld Journey: Plato, Aristophanes, and the 'Orphic' Gold Tablets*, Cambridge, New York.

Edmonds, R. (2006) 'To Sit in Solemn Silence? *Thronosis* in Ritual, Myth, and Iconography', *AJPh* 127, 347–66.

Edmonds, R. (2008a) 'Extra-ordinary People: Mystai and Magoi, Magicians and Orphics in the Derveni Papyrus', *CPh* 103, 16–39.

Edmonds, R. (2008b) 'Recycling Laertes' Shroud: More on Orphism and Original Sin', Center for Hellenic Studies Online Publications, chs.harvard.edu/chs/redmonds.

Edmonds, R. (2009) 'A Curious Concoction: Tradition and Innovation in Olympiodorus' "Orphic" Creation of Mankind', *AJPh* 130, 511–32.

Edmonds, R. (2010a) 'The Children of Earth and Starry Heaven: The Meaning and Function of the Formula in the "Orphic" Gold Tablets', in A. Bernabé Pajares, F. Casadesús Bordoy, and M. A. Santamaría Álvarez (eds), *Orfeo y el orfismo: nuevas perspectivas*, Alicante, 98–121.

Edmonds, R. (2010b) 'Sacred Scripture or Oracles for the Dead? The Semiotic Situation of the "Orphic" Gold Tablets', in R. Edmonds (ed.) 2010 *The Orphic Gold Tablets and Greek Religion: Further Along the Path*, Cambridge, New York.

Edmonds, R. (forthcoming) 'Persephone and ποινή: Recompense for the Powers of the Underworld in the "Orphic" Gold Tablets and Pindar fr., 133', in F. Graf (ed.), *Ritual Texts for the Afterlife*, Leiden.

Edmunds, L. (1990) 'Introduction: The Practice of Greek Mythology', in L. Edmunds (ed.) 1990.

Edmunds, L. (ed.) (1990) *Approaches to Greek Myth*, Baltimore, London.

Edmunds, L. (1993) *Myth in Homer: A Handbook²*, Highland Park.

Edmunds, L. (1997) 'Myth in Homer', in Morris and Powell (eds) 1997: 415–41.

Edwards, M. J. (1988) 'Scenes from the Later Wanderings of Odysseus', *CQ* 38, 509–21.

Edwards, M. W. (1987) *Homer Poet of the Iliad*, Baltimore.

Edwards, M. W. (1997) 'Homeric Style and Oral Poetics', in Morris and Powell (eds) 1997: 261–83.

Edwards, M. W. (2005) 'Homer's *Iliad*', in Foley (ed.) 2005: 302–14.

Ehlers, D. (ed.) (1992) *Hermann Diels, Hermann Usener, Eduard Zeller: Briefwechsel*, 2 vols, Berlin.

Eisner, R. (1987) *The Road to Daulis: Psychoanalysis, Psychology and Classical Mythology*, Syracuse NY.

Ekroth, G. (2007) 'What is a Hero?' in Ogden (ed.) 2007: 100–14.

Eliade, M. (1969) *Le Mythe de l'éternel retour: archétypes et répétition²*, Paris [1949¹; *The Myth of the Eternal Return*, tr. W. A. Trask, New York 1954, London 1955].

El Murr, D. (2010) 'Hesiod, Plato and the Golden Age: Hesiodic Motifs in the Myth of the *Politicus*', in Haubold and Boys-Stones (eds) 2010: 276–97.

El-Sayed, R. (1982) *La Déesse Neith de Sais*, 2 vols, Cairo.

Engehausen, F., A. Schlechter, and J. P. Schwindt (eds) (2008) *Friedrich Creuzer 1771–1858: Philologie und Mythologie im Zeitalter der Romantik*, Heidelberg, Weil am Rhein.

Engemann, J. (1973) *Untersuchungen zur Sepulkralsymbolik der späteren römischen Kaiserzeit*, Jahrbuch für Antike und Christentum Ergänzungsband 2, Münster.

Engelmann, H. (1976) *Die Inschriften von Kyme* [*Inschriften griechischer Städte aus Kleinasien* 5], Bonn.

English, P. (1959) 'Cushites, Colchians, and Khazars', *JNES* 18, 49–53.

Erbse, H. (1999) 'Über Pindars Umgang mit dem Mythos', *Hermes* 127, 13–32.

Eribon, D. (1992) *Faut-il brûler Dumézil?* Paris.

Errington, R. M. (2008) *A History of the Hellenistic World*, Malden MA, Oxford.

Erskine, A. (ed.) (2003) *A Companion to the Hellenistic World*, Malden MA, Oxford, Carlton.

Ewald, B. (1999) 'Death and Myth. New Books on Roman Sarcophagi', *AJA* 103, 344–8.

Ewald, B. (2004) 'Men, Muscle and Myth. Attic Sarcophagi in the Context of the Second Sophistic', in Borg (ed.) 2004: 229–67.

Faisant, C. and L. Godard de Donville (eds) (1982) *La Mythologie au xviiᵉ siècle*, Marseille.

Fantham, E., H. P. Foley, N. B. Kampen, *et al.* (1994) *Women in the Classical World: Image and Text*, Oxford.

Fantuzzi, M. (1995) 'Mythological Paradigms in the Bucolic Poetry of Theocritus', *PCPhS* 41, 16–29.

Fantuzzi, M. and R. Hunter (2004) *Tradition and Innovation in Hellenistic Poetry*, Cambridge.

Faraone, C. and E. Teeter (2004) 'Egyptian Maat and Hesiodic Metis', *Mnemosyne* 57, 177–208.

Farnell, L. R. (1896) *The Cults of the Greek States* 1, Oxford.

Faust, U. (1977) *Mythologien und Religionen des Ostens bei Johann Gottfried Herder*, Münster.

Favro, D. (1996) *The Urban Image of Augustan Rome*, Cambridge.

Feeney, D. (1999) *Literature and Religion at Rome*, Cambridge.

Feldman, B. and R. D. Richardson (1972) *The Rise of Modern Mythology (1680–1860)*, Bloomington, London.

Felson-Rubin, N. (1993) *Regarding Penelope: From Character to Poetics*, Princeton.

Felson-Rubin, N. and L. Slatkin (2004) 'Gender and Homeric Epic', in Fowler (ed.) 2004a: 91–114.

Feraudi-Gruénais, F. (2001) *Ubi diutius nobis habitandum est: die Innendekoration der kaiserzeitlichen Gräber Roms*, Wiesbaden.

Ferrari, G. R. F. (ed.) (2007) *The Cambridge Companion to Plato's Republic*, Cambridge.

Ferrari, G. R. F. (2009) 'Glaucon's Reward, Philosophy's Debt: the Myth of Er', in Partenie (ed.) 2009: 116–33.

Finglass, P. J. (2005) 'Is there a *Polis* in Sophocles' *Electra*?' *Phoenix* 59, 199–209.

Finkelberg, M. (2005) *Greeks and Pre-Greeks: Aegean Prehistory and Greek Heroic Tradition*, Cambridge.

Finley, J. H. Jr (1951) 'The Date of Paean 6 and Nemean 7', *HSPh* 60, 61–80.

Fittschen, K. (1984) 'Über Sarkophage mit Porträts verschiedener Personen', in Andreae (ed.) 1984: 129–61.

Fittschen, K. (1992) 'Der Tod des Kreusa und der Niobiden. Überlegungen zur Deutung griechischer Mythen auf römischen Sarkophagen', *SIFC* 10.2, 1046–60.

Foley, H. P. (1978) 'Reverse Similes and Sex Roles in the *Odyssey*', *Arethusa* 11, 7–26.

Foley, H. P. (1985) *Ritual Irony: Poetry and Sacrifice in Euripides*, Ithaca.

Foley, H. P. (ed.) (1993) *The Homeric Hymn to Demeter: Translation, Commentary and Interpretive Essays*, Princeton.

Foley, H. P. (2003) 'Choral Identity in Greek Tragedy', *CPh* 98, 1–30.

Foley, J. M. (1991) *Immanent Art: From Structure to Meaning in Traditional Oral Epic*, Bloomington.

Foley, J. M. (1997) 'Oral Tradition and its Implications', in Morris and Powell (eds) 1997: 146–73.

Foley, J. M. (ed.) (2005) *A Companion to Ancient Epic*, Malden MA, Oxford, Chichester.

Fontaine, J., C. Prato, and A. Marcone (eds) (1987) *Giuliano Imperatore: Alla Madre degli Dei ed Altri Discorsi*, Milan.

Fontenrose, J. (1978) *The Delphic Oracle*, Berkeley.

Ford, A. (1997) 'Epic as Genre', in Morris and Powell (eds) 1997: 396–414.

Ford, A. (2002) *The Origins of Criticism: Literary Culture and Poetic Theory in Classical Greece*, Princeton.

Ford, P. (1998) 'The Mythologiae of Natale Conti and the Pléiade', in J. F. Alcina *et al.* (eds) *Acta Conventus Neo-Latini Bariensis: Proceedings of the Ninth International Congress of Neo-Latin Studies, Bari 29 August to 3 September 1994.* Medieval & Renaissance Texts & Studies 184, Tempe AZ, 243–50.

Fornaro, S. (2001) 'Friedrich Creuzer und die Diskussion über Philologie und Mythologie zu Beginn des 19. Jhs.', in M. Korenjak and K. Töchterle (eds) *Pontes* 1, Innsbruck, 28–42.

Fornaro, S. (2004) *I Greci senza lumi: l'antropologia della Grecia antica in Christian Gottlob Heyne (1729–1812) e nel suo tempo*, Nachrichten von der Akademie der Wissenschaften zu Göttingen I, Philologisch–Historische Klasse, 5, Göttingen.

Fornaro, S. (2008) 'Friedrich Creuzers Mythologie', *Freiburger Universitätsblätter* 181, 59–68.

Foster, B. R. (2005) *Before the Muses: An Anthology of Akkadian Literature*[3], Bethesda MD.

Foster, B. R. (2007) *Akkadian Literature of the Late Period.* Guides to the Mesopotamian Textual Record 2, Münster.

Fournet, J.-L. (1999) *Hellénisme dans l'Égypte du VIe siècle: la bibliothèque et l'oeuvre de Dioscore d'Aphrodité*, Cairo.

Fowler, R. L. (1996) 'Herodotos and his Contemporaries', *JHS* 116, 62–87.

Fowler, R. L. (1998) 'Genealogical Thinking: Hesiod's *Catalogue*, and the creation of the Hellenes', *PCPhS* 44, 1–19.

Fowler, R. L. (2000) *Early Greek Mythography*, 1 Text and Introduction, Oxford.

Fowler, R. L. (ed.) (2004a) *The Cambridge Companion to Homer*, Cambridge.

Fowler, R. L. (2004b) 'The Homeric Question', in Fowler (ed.) 2004a: 220–32.

Fowler, R. L. (2009) 'Thoughts on Myth and Religion in Early Greek Historiography', *Minerva* 22, 21–39.

Fox, M. A. (1996) *Roman Historical Myths*, Oxford.

Fox, M. A. and N. R. Livingstone (2007) 'Rhetoric and Historiography', in Worthington (ed.) 2007a: 542–61.

Foxhall, L. (1989) 'Household, Gender and Property in Classical Athens', *CQ* 39, 22–44.

Frankfort, H. (1948) *Kingship and the Gods: A Study of Ancient Near Eastern Religion and the Integration of Society & Nature*, Chicago.

Fraser, P. M. (1972) *Ptolemaic Alexandria*, 3 vols, Oxford.

Fraser, P. M. (1996) *Cities of Alexander the Great*, Oxford.

Frazer, J. G. (ed. and tr.) (1921) *Apollodorus*, Loeb Classical Library, 2 vols, London, New York.

Fréret, N. (1756) 'Réflexions générales sur la nature de la religion des Grecs, et sur l'idée qu'on doit se former de leur mythologie', *Histoire de l'académie royale des inscriptions et belles-lettres* 23, 17–26.

Freud, S. (1953–74) *The Standard Edition of the Complete Psychological Works of Sigmund Freud*, ed. and tr. J. Strachey, London.

Freud, S. (1999) *The Interpretation of Dreams*, Oxford World's Classics, tr. J. Crick, Oxford.

Friis-Johansen, K. (1967) *The Iliad in Early Greek Art*, Copenhagen.

Froidefond, C. (1971) *Le Mirage égyptien dans la littérature grecque d'Homère à Aristote*, Aix-en-Provence.

Frye, N. (1957) *Anatomy of Criticism: Four Essays*, Princeton.

Frye, N. (1963) *Fables of Identity: Studies in Poetic Mythology*, New York, London.

Hiller von Gaertringen, F. (ed.) (1903–9) *Inscriptiones Graecae* XII, 5. *Inscriptiones Cycladum*, 2 vols, Berlin.

Gaggadis-Robin, V. (1994) *Jason et Médée sur les sarcophages d'époque Impériale*, Collection de l'école française de Rome 191, Rome.

Gagné, R. (2006) 'What is the Pride of Halicarnassus?' *ClassAnt* 25, 1–33.

Galinsky, K. (1972) *The Herakles Theme: The Adaptation of the Hero in Literature from Homer to the Twentieth Century*, Oxford.

Galinsky, K. (1996) *Augustan Culture: An Interpretive Introduction*, Princeton.

Gamel, M.-K. (2002) 'From *Thesmophoriazousai* to *The Julie Thesmo Show*: Adaptation, Performance, Reception', *AJPh* 123, 465–99.

Gantz, T. (1993) *Early Greek Myth: A Guide to Literary and Artistic Sources*, Baltimore, London.

Garbutt, K. (2006) 'An Indo-European Night Raid', *JIES* 34, 183–200.

Gardner, J. F. (1993) *Roman Myths*, London, Austin.

Gartziou-Tatti, A. (1992) 'Pâris-Alexandre dans l'*Iliade*', in Moreau (ed.) 1992, 73–92.

Gasparri, C. (1983–4) 'Sculture provenienti dalle Terme di Caracalla e di Diocleziano', *Rivista dell' Instituto Nazionale di Archeologia e Storia dell' Arte* 3.6–7, 133–150.

Gazda, E. K. (ed.) (2002) *The Ancient Art of Emulation: Studies in Artistic Originality and Tradition from the Present to Classical Antiquity*, Ann Arbor.

Gellner, E. (1998) *Language and Solitude: Wittgenstein, Malinowski, and the Habsburg Dilemma*, Cambridge.

Genette, G. (2004) *Fiction et diction*, précédé de *Introduction à l'architexte*[2] [1991[1]].

Gentili, B. and F. Perusino (eds) (2000) *Medea nella letteratura e nell'arte*, Venice.

George, A. R. (1999) *The Epic of Gilgamesh: A New Translation*, Penguin Classics, London.

George, A. R. (2003) *The Babylonian Gilgamesh Epic: Introduction, Critical Edition and Cuneiform Texts*, 2 vols, Oxford.

George, A. R. (2009) *Babylonian Literary Texts in the Schøyen Collection*, Cornell University Studies in Assyriology and Sumerology 10/ Manuscripts in the Schøyen Collection, Cuneiform Texts 4, Bethesda MD.

Gerber, D. E. (2002) *A Commentary on Pindar Olympian Nine*, Hermes Einzelschriften 87, Stuttgart.

Germain, G. (1954) *Genèse de l'Odyssée: le fantastique et le sacré*, Paris.

Gernet, L. (1968) *Anthropologie de la Grèce antique*[2], Paris [repr. 1982; 1948[1]].

Gernet, L. (1983) *Les Grecs sans miracle*, Paris [1936[1]].

Gernet, L. (2004) *Polyvalence des images: testi e frammenti sulla leggenda greca*, ed. A. Soldani, Pisa.

Gernet, L. and A. Boulanger (1932) *Le Génie grec dans la religion*, Paris.

P. Gibellini, P. (ed.) (2005) *Il mito nella letteratura italiana* 1 'dal Medioevo al Rinascimento', Brescia.

Gibson, J. C. L. (1978) *Canaanite Myths and Legends²*, Edinburgh.

Gill, C. (1977) 'The Genre of the Atlantis Story', *CPh* 72, 287–304.

Gill, C. (1979) 'Plato's Atlantis Story and the Birth of Fiction', *Philosophy and Literature* 3, 64–78.

Gill, C. (1993) 'Plato on Falsehood – Not Fiction', in Gill and Wiseman (eds) 1993: 38–87.

Gill, C. and P. Wiseman (eds) (1993) *Lies and Fiction in the Ancient World*, Exeter.

Ginzburg, C. (1985) 'Mythologie germanique et nazisme. Sur un livre ancien de Georges Dumézil', *Annales ESC* 40, 695–715 [available on 16.7.10 at: http://www.persee.fr/web/revues/home/prescript/article/ahess_0395-2649_1985_num_40_4_283199].

Giorgieri, M. (2001) 'Die hurritische Fassung des Ullikummi-Lieds und ihre hethitische Parallele', in G. Wilhelm (ed.) *Akten des IV: Internationales Kongresses für Hethitologie: Würzburg, 4.-8. Oktober 1999*, Studien zu den Boğazköy-Texten 45, Wiesbaden, 134–55.

Glinister, F. (forthcoming) *Diana*, London, New York.

Goedicke, H. (1970) 'The Story of a Herdsman', *Chroniques d'Égypte* 45, 244–66.

Götze, A. (1957) *Kleinasien: Kulturgeschichte des Alten Orients*, Munich.

Golden, M. (1990) *Children and Childhood in Classical Athens*, Baltimore.

Goldhill, S. (1986) *Reading Greek Tragedy*, Cambridge.

Goldhill, S. (1987) 'The Great Dionysia and Civic Ideology', *JHS* 107, 58–76.

Goldhill, S. (2000) 'Civic Ideology and the Problem of Difference: The Politics of Aeschylean Tragedy, Once Again', *JHS* 120, 34–56.

Goldhill, S. (2002) *The Invention of Prose*, Greece & Rome New Surveys in the Classics 32, Oxford.

Gordon, R. L. (ed.) (1981) *Myth, Society and Religion*, Cambridge.

Gould, J. (1973) 'Hiketeia', *JHS* 93, 74–103 [repr. with Addendum in J. Gould 2001 *Myth, Ritual Memory, and Exchange: Essays in Greek Literature and Culture*, Oxford, 22–77].

Graf, F. (1979) 'Das Götterbildnis aus dem Taurerland', *AW* 10, 33–41.

Graf, F. (ed.) (1993) *Mythos in mythenloser Gesellschaft: Das Paradigma Roms*, Stuttgart.

Graf, F. (1993a) *Greek Mythology: An Introduction*, tr. T. Marier, Baltimore, London [*Griechische Mythologie*, Munich, Zurich 1987].

Graf, F. (1993b) 'Die Entstehung des Mythosbegriffs bei Christian Gottlob Heyne', in Graf (ed.) 1993: 284–94.

Graf, F. (2000) 'The Locrian Maidens', in R. G. A. Buxton (ed.), *Oxford Readings in Greek Religion*, Oxford, ch. 11, Eng. tr. ['Die lokrischen Mädchen', *Studi Storico-Religiosi* 2 (1978) 61–79].

Graf, F. (2001) 'Mythos II', in *Der Neue Pauly* 15.1, Stuttgart, Weimar, 643–8.

Graf, F. (2003) 'Initiation: A Concept with a Troubled History', in Dodd and Faraone (eds) 2003: 3–24.

Graf, F. (2006) 'Griechische und römische Mythologie bei Karl Kerényi', in R. Schlesier and R. Sanchino Martínez (eds) *Neuhumanismus und Anthropologie des griechischen Mythos: Karl Kerényi im europäischen Kontext des 20. Jahrhunderts*, Locarno, 71–82.

Graf, F. (2009) 'Zeus and his Paredroi in Halikarnassos. A Study on Religion and Inscriptions,' in Á. Martínez Fernández (ed.), *Estudios de Epigrafía Griega*, La Laguna, 333–48.

Graf, F. and S. Iles Johnston (2007) *Ritual Texts for the Afterlife*, London, New York.

Graham, A. J. (1982) 'The Colonial Expansion of Greece', in Boardman and Hammond (eds) 1982: 83–162.

Granger, H. (2007) 'Poetry and Prose: Xenophanes of Colophon', *TAPhA* 137, 403–33.

Grassinger, D. (1998) 'Mythen auf römischen Sarkophagen', *JRA* 11, 554–6.

Grassinger, D. (1999) *Die antiken Sarkophagreliefs* 12 Die Mythologischen Sarkophage, 1 Achill, Adonis, Aeneas, Aktaion, Alkestis, Amazonen, Berlin.

Green, P. (1997) *The Argonautica of Apollonios Rhodios*, Berkeley.

Green, P. (1998) 'The Muses' Birdcage, Then and Now: Cameron on Apollonios Rhodios', *Arion* 6, 57–70.

Green, P. (ed.) (1993) *Hellenistic History and Culture*, Hellenistic Culture and Society 9, Berkeley, Los Angeles, London.

Greimas, A. J. and J. Courtés (1983) *Semiotics and Language: An Analytical Dictionary*, tr. Larry Christ, Daniel Patte, James Lee, Edward McMahon II, Gary Phillips, and Michael Rengstorf, Bloomington.

Grell, C. and C. Michel (eds) (1988) *Primitivisme et mythes des origines dans la France des Lumières, 1680–1820*, Paris.

Grell, C. and C. Volpilhac-Auger (eds) (1994) *Nicolas Fréret, légende et vérité*, Oxford.

Griffin, J. (1977a) 'The Epic Cycle and the Uniqueness of Homer', *JHS* 97, 39–53.

Griffin, J. (1977b) 'Homer and Excess', in Bremer, De Jong and Kalff (eds) 1981: 85–104.

Griffin, J. (1980) *Homer on Life and Death*, Oxford.

Griffin, J. (1998) 'The Social Function of Attic Tragedy', *JHS* 48, 39–61.

Griffith, R. D. (1989) 'Pelops and Sicily: The Myth of Pindar', *JHS* 109, 171–3.

Griffith, R. D. (1994) 'Nektar and nitron', *Glotta* 72, 20–3.

Griffith, R. D. (1996) 'Homer's Black Earth and the Land of Egypt', *Athenaeum* 84, 251–4.

Griffith, R. D. (1997a) 'Homeric ΔIΙΠΕΤΕΟΣ ΠΟΤΑΜΟΙΟ and the Celestial Nile', *AJPh* 118, 353–62.

Griffith, R. D. (1997b) 'Criteria for Evaluating Hypothetical Egyptian Loan-words in Greek', *ICS* 22, 1–6.

Griffith, R. D. (1997c) 'The Voice of the Dead in Homer's *Odyssey* and in Egyptian Funerary Texts', *SMEA* 39, 219–40.

Griffith, R. D. (1998) 'The Origin of Memnon', CA 17, 212–34.

Griffith, R. D. (2001) 'Sailing to Elysium: Menelaus' Afterlife and Egyptian Religion', *Phoenix* 55, 213–43.

Griffith, R. D. (2005) 'God's Blue Hair in Homer's *Odyssey* and in Eighteenth-Dynasty Egypt', *CQ* 44, 329–34.

Griffiths, A. (1989) 'Was Kleomenes mad?' in Powell (ed.) 1989: 51–78.

Griffiths, A. (2001) 'Kissing Cousins', in Luraghi (ed.) 2001: 161–78.

Griffiths, A. (2006) 'Stories and Storytelling in the *Histories*', in Dewald and Marincola (eds) 2006: 130–44.

Griffiths, E. (2006) *Medea*, London.

Griffiths, F. (1979) *Theocritus at Court*, Leiden.

Griffiths, J. Gwyn (1948) 'Human Sacrifice in Egypt: the Classical Evidence', *ASAE* 48, 409–23.

Griffiths, J. Gwyn (1960) 'The Flight of the Gods Before Typhon. An Unrecognised Myth', *Hermes* 88, 374–6.

Griffiths, J. Gwyn (1965) 'A Translation from the Egyptian by Eudoxus', *CQ* 15, 75–8.

Griffiths, J. Gwyn (1983) 'Atlantis and Egypt', *Historia* 34, 2–28.

Grimal, P. (1984) *Les Jardins Romains*[3], Paris.

Gruppe, O. (1887) *Die griechischen Culte und Mythen in ihren Beziehungen zu den orientalischen Religionen* 1, Leipzig [no further volumes appeared].

Güterbock, H. G. (1946) *Kumarbi*, Zurich, New York.

Güterbock, H. G. (1948) 'The Hittite Version of the Hurrian Kumarbi Myths: Oriental Forerunners of Hesiod', *AJA* 52, 123–134 [repr. in Hoffner 1997: 39–48].

Guthmüller, B. (1986) *Studien zur antiken Mythologie in der italienischen Renaissance*, Weinheim.

Guthrie, W. K. C. (1952) *Orpheus and Greek Religion: A Study of the Orphic Movement*[2], London.

Gutzwiller, K. J. (2007) *A Guide to Hellenistic Literature*, Malden MA, Oxford, Carlton.

Haas, V. (1994) *Geschichte der hethitischen Religion*. Handbuch der Orientalistik, Abt. 1, vol. 15, Leiden, New York, Cologne.

Haase, F.-A. (2002) *Christian Gottlob Heyne (1729–1812): Bibliographie zu Leben und Werk: Gedruckte Veröffentlichungen: Zeitgenössische Schriften zu seiner Rezeption. Forschungsliteratur*, Heidelberg.

Hadzisteliou-Price, T. (1971) 'Double and Multiple Representations in Greek Art and Religious Thought', *JHS* 91, 48–69.

Haehling, R. von (ed.) (2005) *Griechische Mythologie und frühes Christentum*, Darmstadt.

Halbwachs, M. (1992) *On Collective Memory*, tr. L. A. Coser, Chicago, London [*Les Cadres sociaux de la mémoire*, Paris 1925[1], 1935[2]].

Hall, E. (1996) 'When is a Myth Not a Myth? Bernal's "Ancient Model"', in Lefkowitz and Maclean Rogers 1996: 333–48.

Hall, J. M. (2002) *Hellenicity: Between Ethnicity and Culture*, Chicago.

Hall, J. M. (2007a) 'Polis, Community, and Ethnic Identity', in Shapiro (ed.) 2007: 40–60.

Hall, J. M. (2007b) 'Politics and Greek Myth', in Woodard (ed.) 2007: 331–54.

Hallett, C. H. (2005) review of Zanker and Ewald 2004, in *Art Bulletin* 87, 157–61.

Halleux, R. and J. Schamp (eds) (1985) *Les Lapidaires grecs: Lapidaire Orphique; Kérygmes lapidaires d'Orphée; Socrate et Denys; Lapidaire nautique; Damigéron-Evax*, Paris.

Halliwell, F. S. (1988) *Plato: Republic 10*, Warminster.

Halliwell, F. S. (2007) 'The Life-and-Death Journey of the Soul: Interpreting the Myth of Er', in Ferrari 2007: 445–73.

Hallo, W. W. and K. L. Younger Jr (eds) (2003a) *The Context of Scripture* 1 Canonical Compositions from the Biblical World, Leiden, Boston.

Hallo, W. W. and K. L. Younger Jr (eds) (2003b) *The Context of Scripture* 2 Monumental Inscriptions from the Biblical World, Leiden, Boston.

Hallo, W. W. and K. L. Younger Jr (eds) (2003c) *The Context of Scripture* 3 Archival Documents from the Biblical World, Leiden, Boston.

Hamilton, W. (1795) *Collection of Engravings from Ancient Vases mostly of pure Greek Workmanship discovered in Sepulchres in the Kingdom of the Two Sicilies but chiefly in the Neighbourhood of Naples during the course of the years MDCCLXXXIX and MDCCXXXX now in the possession of Sir Wm. Hamilton His Britannic Majestaty's* [sic] *Envoy Extry. and Plenipotentiary at the Court of Naples with remarks on each vase by the Collector* 2, Naples.

Hansen, W. (1997) 'Homer and the Folktale', in Morris and Powell (eds) 1997: 442–62.

Hansen, W. (2002) *Ariadne's Thread: A Guide to International Tales Found in Classical Literature*, Ithaca NY.

Hard, R. (2004) *The Routledge Handbook of Greek Mythology: Based on H. J. Rose's Handbook of Greek Mythology*, London, New York.

Hardie, P. (1998) *Virgil*, Greece & Rome New Surveys in the Classics 28, Oxford.

Harrison, J. E. (1912) *Themis: A Study of the Social Origins of Greek Religion*,[1] with an excursus on the ritual forms preserved in Greek tragedy, by Gilbert Murray, and a chapter on the origin of the olympic games, by F. M. Cornford, London [Cambridge 1926[2]].

Harrison, S. J. (1998) 'The Sword-belt of Pallas: Moral Symbolism and Political Ideology: Aeneid 10.495–505', in H.-P. Stahl (ed.), *Vergil's Aeneid: Augustan Epic and Political Context*, London, 223–42.

Haubold, J. (2002) 'Greek Epic: A Near Eastern Genre?' *PCPS* 48, 1–19.

Haubold, J. and G. Boys-Stones (eds) (2010) *Plato and Hesiod*, Oxford.

Haussig, H. W. (1965) *Wörterbuch der Mythologie* I Die Alten Kulturvölker, 1 Götter und Mythen im Vorderen Orient, Stuttgart.

Havelock, E. (1963) *Preface to Plato*, Oxford.

Hays, G. (2003) 'The Date and Identity of the Mythographer Fulgentius', *Journal of Medieval Latin* 13, 163–252.

Hays, G. (2004) 'Romuleis Libicisque Litteris: Fulgentius and the "Vandal Renaissance"', in A. H. Merrills (ed.) *Vandals, Romans and Berbers: New Perspectives on Late Antique North Africa*, Aldershot, 101–32.

Hazzard, R. A. (2000) *Imagination of a Monarchy: Studies in Ptolemaic Propaganda*, Toronto.

Heath, M. (1986) 'The Origins of Modern Pindaric Criticism', *JHS* 106, 85–98.

Heidenreich, M. (2006) *Christian Gottlob Heyne und die Alte Geschichte*, Munich, Leipzig.

Heinhold-Krahmer, S. (2004) 'Ist die Identität von Ilios und Wilusa endgültig bewiesen?' *SMEA* 46.1, 29–57.

Held, G. F. (1987) 'Phoinix, Agamemnon and Achilleus: Parables and Paradeigmata', *CQ* 37, 249–61.

Henrichs, A. (1986) 'Welckers Götterlehre', in W. M. Calder III, A. Köhnken, W. Kullmann, and G. Pflug (eds), *Friedrich Gottlieb Welcker: Werk und Wirkung*, Hermes Einzelschriften 49, Stuttgart, 179–229.

Henrichs, A. (1987) 'Three Approaches to Greek Mythography', in Bremmer (ed.) 1987: 242–77.

Herbert-Brown, G. (1994) *Ovid and the Fasti: An Historical Study*, Oxford.

Herdejürgen, H. (1996) *Die antiken Sarkophagreliefs* 6.2 Stadrömische und Italische Girlandensarkophage 1, Berlin.

Herington, C. J. (1985) *Poetry into Drama: Early Tragedy and the Greek Poetic Tradition*, Berkeley.

Herren, M. (1998) 'The Transmission and Reception of Graeco-Roman Mythology in Anglo-Saxon England, 670–800', *Anglo-Saxon England* 27, 87–103.

Herren, M. (1998–9) 'The Earliest European Study of Graeco-Roman Mythology (AD 600–900)', *ACD* 34–5, 25–49.

Hertel, D. (1982) 'Über die Vielschichtigkeit des Troianischen Krieges. Die Archäologie von Troia VI, VII und VIII', in J. Cobet and B. Patzek (eds), *Archäologie und historische Erinnerung: Nach 100 Jahren Heinrich Schliemann*, Essen, 73–104.

Hertel, D. (2001) 'Troia: Sage und Geschichte', *Mitteilungen aus dem Heinrich-Schliemann-Museum* 7, 19–40.

Hertel, D. (2003) *Die Mauern von Troia: Mythos und Geschichte im antiken Ilion*, Munich.

Hertel, D. (2004) 'Die Gleichsetzung einer archäologischen Schicht von Troia mit dem homerischen Ilios', in Ulf (ed.) 2004: 85–104.

Hertel, D. (2008a) *Troia: Archäologie, Geschichte, Mythos*³, Munich.

Hertel, D. (2008b) *Das frühe Ilion: Die Besiedlung Troias durch die Griechen (1020–650/25 v.Chr)*, Zetemeta 130, Munich.

Hertel, D. (2008c) 'Die frühe griechische Keramik der Schliemann-Sammlung in Berlin (1020–650/25 v. Chr.)', in M. Wemhoff, D. Hertel, and A. Hänsel (eds), *Heinrich Schliemanns Sammlung Trojanischer Altertümer – Neuvorlage* 1 Forschungsgeschichte, keramische Funde der Schichten VII bis IX, Nadeln, Gewichte und durchgelochte Tongeräte, Berlin, 93–173.

Hertel, D. and F. Kolb (2003) 'Troy in Clearer Perspective', *AS* 53, 71–88.

Hesberg, H., Von (1992) *Römische Grabbauten*, Darmstadt.

Heubeck, A. and S. West (1988) *A Commentary on Homer's Odyssey* 1, Oxford.

Hexter, R. and D. Selden (eds) (1992) *Innovations of Antiquity*, London.

Heyne, C. G. (ed.) (1783) *Apollodori bibliothecae libri tres et fragmenta*, Göttingen.

Heyne, C. G. (1807) 'Sermonis mythici sive symbolici interpretatio ad caussas et rationes ductasque inde regulas revocata', *Commentationes Societatis Regiae Scientiarum Gottingensis recentiores*, n.s. 16, 285–323.

Hicks, R. I. (1962) 'Egyptian Elements in Greek Mythology', *TAPA* 93, 90–108.

Higbie, C. (1995) *Heroes' Names, Homeric Identities*, Albert Bates Lord Series 10, New York, London.

Higbie, C. (2007) 'Hellenistic Mythographers', in Woodard (ed.) 2007: 237–54.

Hillyard, B. P. (1981) *Plutarch, De audiendo: A Text and Commentary*, New York.

Hirschberger, M. (2004) *Gynaikon Katalogos und Megalai Ehoiai: Ein Kommentar zu den Fragmenten zweier hesiodeischer Epen*, Munich.

Hoff, R. von den (2004) 'Horror and Amazement: Colossal Mythological Statue Groups and the New Rhetoric of Images in Late Second and Early Third Century Rome', in Borg (ed.) 2004: 105–29.

Hoffmann. F. (1994) 'Seilflechter in der Unterwelt', *ZPE* 100, 339–46.

Hoffner, H. A., Jr (1998) *Hittite Myths*², Society of Biblical Literature Writings from the Ancient World 2, Atlanta [1990¹].

Hoffner, H. A., Jr (ed.) (1997) *Perspectives on Hittite Civilization: Selected Writings of Hans Gustav Güterbock*, Assyriological Studies 26, Chicago.

Hölbl, G. (2001) *A History of the Ptolemaic Empire*, London.

Hölscher, T. (1999) 'Immagini mitologiche e valori sociali nella Grecia arcaica', in de Angelis and Muth (eds) 1999: 11–30.

Hölscher, U. (1988) *Die Odyssee: Märchen zwischen Epos und Roman*, Munich.

Holladay, C. (1996) *Fragments from Hellenistic Jewish Authors*, 4 Orphica, Chico CA.

Hollis, A. S. (1990) *Callimachus: Hecale*, Oxford.

Holzberg, N. (2002) *The Ancient Fable*, tr. C. Jackson-Holzberg, Bloomington IN.

Hordern, J. (2000) 'Notes on the Orphic Papyrus from Gurob', *ZPE* 129, 131–40.

Hornung, E. (1982a) *Der Ägyptische Mythos von der Himmelskuh: Eine Ätiologie des Unvollkommenen*, Göttingen.

Hornung, E. (1982b) *Conceptions of God in Ancient Egypt: The One and the Many*, tr. J. Baines, Ithaca NY.

Hornung, E. (1990a) *Das Totenbuch der Ägypter*, Zurich, Munich [1979¹].

Hornung, E. (1990b) *The Valley of the Kings: Horizon of Eternity*, tr. D. Warburton, New York.

Hornung, E. (1999) *The Ancient Egyptian Books of the Afterlife*, Ithaca.

Horowitz, W. (1998) *Mesopotamian Cosmic Geography*, Mesopotamian Civilizations 8, Winona Lake.

Horrocks, G. (1997) 'Homer's Dialect', in Morris and Powell (eds) 1997: 193–217.

E.-A. Horstmann (1972), 'Mythologie und Altertumswissenschaft: Der Mythosbegriff bei Christian Gottlob Heyne', *ABG* 16, 60–85.

Howald, E. (1926) *Der Kampf um Creuzers Symbolik: Eine Auswahl von Dokumenten*, Tübingen.

Howell, M. and W. Prevenier (2001) *From Reliable Sources*, Ithaca NY.

Hubbard, T. K. (1987a) 'Two Notes on the Myth of Aeacus in Pindar', *GRBS* 28, 5–22.

Hubbard, T. K. (1987b) 'The "Cooking" of Pelops. Pindar and the Process of Mythological Revisionism', *Helios* 14, 3–21.

Hubbard, T. K. (1989) '*Kukneia Makha*: Subtext and Allusion in *Olympian* 10.15–16', *MD* 23, 137–43.

Hubbard, T. K. (1992) 'Remaking Myth and Rewriting History: Cult Tradition in Pindar's Ninth *Nemean*', *HSPh* 94, 77–111.

Hubbard, T. K. (1993) 'The Theban Amphiaraion and Pindar's Vision on the Road to Delphi', *MH* 50, 193–203.

Humphreys, S. C. (1978) *Anthropology and the Greeks*, London.

Humphreys, S. C. (2004) *The Strangeness of Gods*, Oxford.

Hunger, H. (1959) *Lexikon der griechischen und römischen Mythologie: mit Hinweisen auf das Fortwirken antiker Stoffe und Motive in der bildenden Kunst, Literatur und Musik des Abendlandes bis zur Gegenwart*[5], Vienna.

Hunter, R. L. (2003) *Theocritus: Encomium of Ptolemy Philadelphus*, Cambridge.

Hunter, R. L. (2005a) '"Philip the Philosopher" on the *Aithiopika* of Heliodorus', in S. J. Harrison, M. Paschalis, and S. Frangoulidis (eds), *Metaphor and the Ancient Novel*, Ancient Narrative Supplement 4, Groningen, 123–38.

Hunter, R. L. (ed.) (2005b) *The Hesiodic Catalogue of Women. Constructions and Reconstructions*, Cambridge.

Hunter, V. J. (1989) 'The Athenian Widow and her Kin', *Journal of Family History* 14, 291–311.

Hurst, A. and F. Létoublon (eds) (2002) *La Mythologie et l'Odyssée: hommage à Gabriel Germain*, Geneva.

Huskinson, J. (1998) '"Unfinished Portrait Heads" on Later Roman Sarcophagi: Some New Perspectives', *PBSR* 76, 129–68.

Husser, J.-M. (1995) 'Culte des ancêtres ou rites funéraires? A propos du "catalogue" des devoirs du fils (KTU 1.17 i–ii)', *UF* 27, 115–27.

Husser, J.-M. (1997) 'Shapash psychopompe et le pseudo-hymne au soleil (KTU 1.6 vi 42–53)', *UF* 29, 227–44.

Hutchinson, G. O. (1988) *Hellenistic Poetry*, Oxford.

Huxley, G. L. (1973) 'The Date of Pherekydes of Athens' *GRBS* 14, 140–1.

Huxley, G. L. (1975) *Pindar's Vision of the Past*, Belfast.

Huys, M. (1997) '125 Years of Scholarship on Apollodorus the Mythographer: A Bibliographical Survey', *AC* 66, 319–51.

Huys, M. and D. Colomo (2004) 'Bibliographical Survey on Apollodorus the Mythographer: A Supplement', *AC* 73, 219–37.

Iglesias Montiel, R. M. and C. A. Morán (eds) (1988) *Natale Conti, Mitologia*, Murcia.

Irwin, E. (1982) 'The Songs of Orpheus and the New Song of Christ', in J. Warden (ed.), *Orpheus: The Metamorphoses of a Myth*, Toronto, 51–62.

Isager, S. (1998) 'The Pride of Halikarnassos: Editio princeps of an inscription from Salmakis', *ZPE* 123, 1–23 [repr. in Isager and Pedersen (eds) 2004: 217–37].

Isager, S. and P. Pedersen (eds) (2004) *The Salmakis Inscription and Hellenistic Halikarnassos*, Odense.

Isler-Kerényi, C. (2000) 'Immagini di Medea', in B. Gentili and F. Perusino (eds), *Medea nella letteratura e nell'arte*, Venice.

Isler-Kerényi, C. (2007) *Dionysos in Archaic Greece: An Understanding through Images*, tr. W. G. E. Watson, Leiden, Boston.

Jackson, P. (2006) *The Transformations of Helen: Indo-European Myth and the Roots of the Trojan Cycle*, Münchener Studien zur Sprachwissenschaft Beiheft 23, Dettelbach.

Jackson, S. (2000) *Istrus the Callimachean*, Amsterdam.

Jacobsen, T. (1970) 'Toward the Image of Tammuz', in W. L. Moran (ed.) *Toward the Image of Tammuz and Other Essays on Mesopotamian History and Culture*, Harvard Semitic Series 21, Cambridge MA, 73–101.

Jacobsen, T. (1976) *The Treasures of Darkness: A History of Mesopotamian Religion*, New Haven, London.

Jacobsen, T. (1987) *The Harps That Once … Sumerian Poetry in Translation*, New Haven, London.

Jacoby, F. (1923–30, 1940–58) *Die Fragmente der griechischen Historiker*, Berlin (1923–30); Leiden (1940–58).

Jahn, O. (1841) *Telephos und Troilos*, Kiel.

Jakobi, R. (2008) 'Zur Überlieferung des Zweiten Vatikanischen Mythographen', *RHT* 3, 283–6.

Jameson, M. (2004) 'Troizen and Halikarnassos in the Hellenistic Era,' in Isager and Pederson (eds) 2004: 93–107.

Jamison, S. W. (1994) 'Draupadī on the Walls of Troy: Iliad 3 from an Indic Perspective', *ClAnt* 13, 5–16.

Jamme, C. (1995) *Introduction à la philosophie du mythe*, 2 'Époque moderne et contemporaine', Paris.

Jaynes, J. (1982) *The Origin of Consciousness in the Breakdown of the Bicameral Mind*, Boston MA [1976[1]].

Jeanmaire, H. (1939) *Couroi et Courètes: essai sur l'éducation spartiate et sur les rites d'adolescence dans l'antiquité hellénique*, Lille.

Jenkyns, R. (1980) *The Victorians and Ancient Greece*, Oxford.

Johnson, S. F. (ed.) (2006) *Greek Literature in Late Antiquity: Dynamism, Didacticism, Classicism*, Aldershot.

Johnstone, W. (ed.) (1995) *William Robertson Smith*, Sheffield.

Jonas, H. (1963) *The Gnostic Religion*[2], Boston.

Jones, C. P. (1999) *Kinship Diplomacy in the Ancient World*, Cambridge MA.

Jones, P. V. (1995) 'Poetic Invention: The Fighting around Troy in the First Nine Years of the Trojan War', in Ø. Andersen and M. W. Dickie (eds), *Homer's World*, Bergen, 101–21.

Jongste, P. F. B. (1992) *The Twelve Labours of Hercules on Roman Sarcophagi*, Rome.

Jouan, F. (1966) *Euripide et la légende des chants Cypriens*, Paris.

Jouan, F. and H. Van Looy (eds) (1998–2003) *Euripide: Fragments*, 4 vols, Paris.

Jouanna, J. (2002) 'Mythe et rite: la fondation des jeux olympiques chez Pindare' *Ktema* 27, 105–18.

Jouanna, J. (2007) *Sophocle*, Paris.

Judet de La Combe, P. (2001) 'Remarks on Aeschylus' Homer' in N. Loraux, G. Nagy, L. Slatkin (eds) *Postwar French Thought* 3, New York, 384–94.

Jung, C. G. (1953–92) *The Collected Works of C. G. Jung*, ed. H. Herbert, M. Fordham, G. Adler, New York, Princeton.

Jung, C. G. (1959) *Four Archetypes: Mother, Rebirth, Spirit, Trickster*, tr. R. F. C. Hull, Princeton.

Jung, C. G. and C. Kerényi (1951) *Introduction to a Science of Mythology: The Myth of the Divine Child and the Mysteries of Eleusis*, tr. R. F. C. Hull, London.

Jung, C. G. and C. Kerényi (1969) *Essays on a Science of Mythology*, tr. R. F. C. Hull, Princeton.

Just, R. (1989) *Women in Athenian Law and Life*, London.

Kaempf-Dimitriadou, S. (1969) *Die Liebe der Gotter in der attischen Kunst des 5. Jahrhunderts v. Chr.*, Bern.

Kahn, C. (2009) 'The Myth of the *Statesman*', in Partenie (ed.) 2009: 148–66.

Kakridis, J. T. (1949) *Homeric Researches*, Lund.

Kakridis, J. T. (1971) *Homer Revisited*, Lund.

Kaldellis, A. (2007) *Hellenism in Byzantium: The Transformations of Greek Identity and the Reception of the Classical Tradition*, Cambridge.

Kampen, N. B. (ed.) (1996) *Sexuality in Ancient Art*, Cambridge.

Kannicht, R. (2004) *Tragicorum graecorum fragmenta* 5 Euripedes, Göttingen.

Kany, R. (2004) 'Hermann Usener as Historian of Religion', *ARG* 6, 159–76.

Kapuściński, R. (2007) *Travels With Herodotus*, tr. K. Glowczewska, London.

Kassel, R. and C. Austin (1983–98) *Poetae Comici Graeci*, Berlin, New York.

Katz, J. (2006) 'The Riddle of the *sp(h)ij-*: The Greek Sphinx and her Indic and Indo-European Background', in G.-J. Pinault and D. Petit (eds), *La Langue poétique Indo-Européenne*, Paris 157–94.

Katz, M. (1991) *Penelope's Renown: Meaning and Indeterminacy in the Odyssey*, Princeton.

Kaufmann, H. (2006) *Dracontius* Romul., *10 (Medea)*: *Einleitung, Text, Übersetzung und Kommentar*, Heidelberg.

Keel, O. (1978) *The Symbolism of the Biblical World: Ancient Near Eastern Iconography and the Book of Psalms*, tr. T. J. Hallett, New York.

Kellum, B. (1985) 'Sculptural Programs and Propaganda in Augustan Rome: The Temple of Apollo on the Palatine', in Winkes (ed.) 1985: 169–76.

Kennell, N. M. (1995) *The Gymnasium of Virtue: Education and Culture in Ancient Sparta*, Chapel Hill, London.

Kerényi, C. (or K.) (1976a) (marked 1975) *Zeus and Hera: Archetypal Image of Father, Husband and Wife*, Archetypal Images in Greek Religion 5, tr. C. Holme, London [*Zeus und Hera: Urbild des Vaters, des Gatten und der Frau*, Studies in the History of Religions 20, Leiden 1972].

Kerényi, C. (or K.) (1976b) *Dionysos: Archetypal Image of Indestructible Life*, Archetypal Images in Greek Religion 2, tr. (from the original ms) R. Manheim, London.

Kern, O. (1922) *Orphicorum Fragmenta*, Berlin.

Kern, O. (1927) *Hermann Diels und Carl Robert: Ein biographischer Versuch*, Leipzig.

Keuls, E. C. (1974) *The Water Carriers in Hades: A Study of Catharsis through Toil in Classical Antiquity*, Amsterdam.

Keuls, E. C. (1985) *The Reign of the Phallus: Sexual Politics in Ancient Athens*, New York.

Kippenberg, H. (2002) *Discovering Religious History in the Modern Age*, Princeton, Oxford.

Kirk, G. S. (1970) *Myth: Its Meaning and Functions in Ancient and Other Cultures*, Cambridge, Berkeley, Los Angeles.

Kirk, G. S. (1974) *The Nature of Greek Myths*, Harmondsworth.

Kirk, G. S., J. E. Raven, and M. Schofield (1983) *The Presocratic Philosophers: A Critical History with a Selection of Texts*[2], Cambridge [1960[1]].

Knoppers, G. N. (1992) '"The God in His Temple": The Phoenician Text from Pyrgi as a Funerary Inscription', *JNES* 51, 105–20.

Koch, G. (1975) *Die antiken Sarcophagreliefs*, 12 Die Mythologischen Sarkophage, 6 Meleager, Berlin.

Koch, G. and H. Sichtermann (1982) *Römische Sarkophage*, Handbuch der Archäologie, Munich.

Koenen, L. (1977) *Eine agonistische Inschrift aus Ägypten und frühptolemäische Königsfeste*, Beiträge zur klassischen Philologie 56, Meisenheim am Glan.

Köhnken, A. (1971) *Die Funktion des Mythos bei Pindar: Interpretationen zu sechs Pindargedichten*, Berlin.

Köhnken, A. (1974) 'Pindar as Innovator: Poseidon Hippios and the Relevance of the Pelops Story in *Olympian* 1', *CQ* 27, 199–206.

Kohut, H. (1982) 'Introspection, Empathy, and the Semi-Circle of Mental Health', *International Journal of Psycho-Analysis* 63, 395–407.

Konaris, M. (2010) 'The Greek Gods in Late Nineteenth- and Early Twentieth-Century German and British Scholarship', in J. N. Bremmer and A. Erskine (eds), *The Gods of Ancient Greece*, Edinburgh, 483–503.

Konstan, D. (1997) *Friendship in the Classical World*, Cambridge.

Koortbojian, M. (1995) *Myth, Meaning and Memory on Roman Sarcophagi*, Berkeley, Los Angeles, London.

Koortbojian, M. (2002) 'Forms of Attention: Four Notes on Replication and Variation', in Gazda (ed.) 2002: 173–204.

Koppenhöfer, D. (1997) 'Troia VII – Versuch einer Zusammenschau einschließlich der Ergebnisse des Jahres 1995', *Studia Troica* 7, 295–353.

Korfmann, M. (2005) 'Der wahre Kern des Mythos: Die moderne Troiaforschung geht über die Suche nach dem historischen Kern des homerischen Epos weit hinaus', *Antike Welt* 36, 59–65.

Korfmann, M., J. Latacz, and J. D. Hawkins (2004) 'Was there a Trojan War?' *Archaeology* 57.3, 36–41.

Korom, F. J. (2004) 'Ritualistische Theorie', in R. W. Brednich (ed.), *Enzyklopädie des Märchens* 11, Berlin, New York, 724–31.

Kouremenos, T., G. Parassoglou, and K. Tsantsanoglou (2006) *The Derveni Papyrus*, Florence.

Kowalzig, B. (2007) *Singing for the Gods: Performances of Myth and Ritual in Archaic and Classical Greece*, Oxford, New York.

Kraus, C. S. and A. J. Woodman (1997) *Latin Historians*, Greece & Rome New Surveys in the Classics 27, Oxford.

Krummen, E. (1990) *Pyrsos Hymnon: festliche Gegenwart und mythisch-rituelle Tradition als Voraussetzung einer Pindarinterpretation (Isthmie 4, Pythie 5, Olympie 1 und 3)*, Berlin.

Kuhlmann, K. P. (1988) *Das Ammoneion: Archäologie, Geschichte und Kulturpraxis des Orakels von Siwa*, Mainz.

Kuhn, T. S. (1996) *The Structure of Scientific Revolutions*[3], Chicago [1962[1]].

Kullmann, W. (1960) *Die Quellen der Ilias*, Wiesbaden.

Kullmann, W. (1981) 'Zur Methode der Neoanalyse in der Homerforschung', *WS* 15, 5–42.

Kullmann, W. (1992) *Homerische Motive*, Stuttgart.

Kullmann, W. (2002) 'Homer und das Troia der späten Bronzezeit', in A. Rengakos (ed.), *W. Kullmann, Realität, Imagination und Theorie: Kleine Schriften zu Epos und Tragödie in der Antike*, Stuttgart, 97–138.

Kunze, C. (1996) 'Zur Datierung des Laokoon und der Skyllagruppe aus Sperlonga', *JDAI* 111, 139–223.

Kuttner, A. (2003) 'Delight and Danger: Motion in the Roman Water Garden at Sperlonga and Tivoli', in M. Conan (ed.) 2003 *Landscape Design and the Experience of Motion*, Washington DC, 103–56.

Labat, R., *et al.* (1970) *Les Religions du Proche-Orient asiatique: textes babyloniens, ougaritiques, hittites*, Paris.

Lada-Richards, I. (1997) 'Neoptolemus and the Bow: Ritual *thea* and Theatrical Vision in Sophocles' *Philoctetes*', *JHS* 117, 179–83.

Laks, A. (1998) 'Les Origines de Jean-Pierre Vernant', *Critique* 612, 268–82.

Lambert, W. G. and P. Walcot (1965) 'A New Babylonian Theogony and Hesiod', *Kadmos* 4, 64–72.

Lamberton, R. (1986) *Homer the Theologian: Neoplatonist Allegorical Reading and the Growth of the Epic Tradition*, Berkeley, Los Angeles, London.

Lamberton, R. (1988) *Hesiod*, New Haven, London.

Lancha, J. (1997) *Mosaïque de culture dans l'occident Romain (Ie– IVe s.)*, Rome.

La Rocca, E. (1985) *Amazzonomachia*, Rome.

La Rocca, E. (1998) 'Artisti Rodii negli *Horti* Romani', in E. La Rocca and M. Cima (eds) 1998 *Horti Romani: Atti del convegno internazionale Roma 4–6 Maggio 1995*, Rome, 203–74.

Lardinois, A. (1992) 'Greek Myths for Athenian Rituals', *GRBS* 33, 313–27.

Larson, J. (1995) *Greek Heroine Cults*, Madison WI.

Larson, J. (2001) *Greek Nymphs: Myth, Cult, Lore*, Oxford.

Larson, J. (2007) 'A Land Full of Gods: Nature Deities in Greek Religion', in Ogden (ed.) 2007: 56–70.

Latacz, J. (2000) *Pindari Dithyramborum Fragmenta*, Rome, Pisa.

Latacz, J. (2003) *Troia und Homer: Der Weg zur Lösung eines alten Rätsels*, abridged and revised, Munich [Stuttgart 2001¹].

Latacz, J. (2004) *Troy and Homer: Towards a Solution of an Old Mystery*, tr. K. Windle, R. Ireland, Oxford [tr. of Latacz 2003: see also Latacz 2005].

Latacz, J. (2005) *Troia und Homer: Der Weg zur Lösung eines alten Rätsels⁵*, Leipzig 2005 [Stuttgart 2001¹].

Lattimore, R. (1942) *Themes in Greek and Latin Epitaphs*, Urbana.

Lavecchia, S. (1996) 'P. Oxy. 2622 e il 'Secondo Ditirambo' di Pindaro', *ZPE* 110, 1–26.

Leach, E. (1974) *Lévi-Strauss²*, London [1970¹].

Leach, E. W. (1988) *The Rhetoric of Space: Literary and Artistic Representations of Landscape in Republican and Augustan Rome*, Princeton.

Leach, E. W. (2004) *The Social Life of Painting in Ancient Rome and on the Bay of Naples*, Cambridge.

Leader-Newby, R. E. (2004) *Silver and Society in Late Antiquity: Functions and Meanings of Silver Plate in the Fourth to Seventh Centuries*, Aldershot.

Lefèvre, E. (1989) *Das Bild-Programm des Apollo-Tempels auf dem Palatin*, Konstanz.

Lefkowitz, M. (1980) 'The Quarrel between Callimachus and Apollonius', *ZPE* 40, 1–19.

Lefkowitz, M. (1986) *Women in Greek Myth*, London.

Lefkowitz, M. and G. MacLean Rogers (eds) (1996) *Black Athena Revisited*, Chapell Hill and London.

Leonard, M. (2005) *Athens in Paris*, Oxford.

Lesky, A. (1966) 'Peleus und Thetis im frühen Epos', in W. Kraus (ed.), *Albin Lesky, Gesammelte Schriften: Aufsätze und Reden zu antiker und deutscher Dichtung und Kultur*, Bern, Munich, 401–9.

Lesky, A. (1978) *Greek Tragedy³*, tr. H. A. Frankfort, London, New York.

Lesky, A. (1983) 'Decision and Responsibility in Aeschylus', in E. Segal (ed.) 1983: 13–23.

Létoublon, F. (1985) 'Les Dieux et les hommes. Le langage et sa référence dans l'antiquité grecque archaïque', in Γλώσσα και πραγματικότητα στην ελληνική φιλοσοφία – *Language and Reality in Greek Philosophy*, Athens, 92–9.

Létoublon, F. (1999) 'L'indescriptible bouclier', in J. N. Kazazis and A. Rengakos (eds), *Euphrosyne: Studies in Ancient Epic and Its Legacy in Honor of Dimitri N. Maronitis*, Stuttgart, 210–20.

Létoublon, F. (2001) 'Le Récit homérique, de la formule à l'image', *Europe* 865 Homère, 20–47.

Létoublon, F. (2002) 'L'Aventure et les scènes de tempête dans *l'Odyssée*', in M. Reichel and A. Rengakos (eds), *Epea pteroenta: Beiträge zur Homerforschung: Festschrift für Wolfgang Kullmann*, Stuttgart, 99–117.

Létoublon, F. (2003) 'Patience, mon coeur! *Geduld, mein Herze*', *Gaia* 7, 321–46.

Létoublon, F. (2004) 'Le Rossignol, l'hirondelle et l'araignée', *Europe* 904–5 Mythe et mythologie dans l'antiquité gréco-romaine, 73–102.

Létoublon, F. (2006) 'Ulysse, homme de la parole', in J. de Romilly, F. Létoublon, and P. Citati (eds), *Homère sur les traces d'Ulysse*, Paris, 53–63.

Létoublon, F. (2007) 'La Lance en frêne du Pélion et les armes d'Achille', in P. Sauzeau and T. Van Compernolle (eds), *Les Armes dans l'Antiquité: De la technique à l'imaginaire*, Montpellier, 215–29.

Levi, D, (1947) *Antioch Mosaic Pavements*, Princeton.

Lévi-Strauss, C. (1958) *Anthropologie structurale*, Paris [*Structural Anthoplogy* New York 1963].

Lévi-Strauss, C. (1964) *Mythologiques* 1 'Le Cru et le cuit', Paris.

Lévi-Strauss, C. (1966) *The Savage Mind*, Chicago [*La Pensée sauvage*, Paris 1962].

Lévi-Strauss, C. (1971) *Mythologiques* 4 'L'homme nu', Paris.

Lévi-Strauss, C. (1973) *Anthropologie structurale deux*, Paris.

Lévi-Strauss, C. and D. Eribon (1998) *De près et de loin*, Paris.

Lewis, N. (1978) *Naples '44*, London.

Lewis, S. (2002) *The Athenian Woman: An Iconographic Handbook*, London.

Lewis, T. H. (1989) *Cults of the Dead in Ancient Israel and Ugarit*, Harvard Semitic Monographs 39, Atlanta.

Lichtheim, M. (1973–80) *Ancient Egyptian Literature: A Book of Readings*, 3 vols, Berkeley, London.

Liebeschuetz, W. (1995) 'Pagan Mythology in the Christian Empire', *IJCT* 2, 193–208.

Lightfoot, J. (1999) *Parthenius of Nicaea: Extant Works Edited with an Introduction and Commentary*, Oxford.

Lightfoot, J. (2005) Review of M. K. Brown 2002, *Gnomon* 77, 299–304.

Lightfoot, J. (ed.) (2009) *Hellenistic Collection: Philitas, Alexander of Aetolia, Hermesianax, Euphorion, Parthenius*, Loeb Classical Library, Cambridge MA.

Lillie, A. (1912) *Rama and Homer: An Argument that in the Indian Epics Homer Found the Theme of his Two Great Epics*, with preface by Gilbert Murray, London.

Lindner, R. (1984) *Der Raub der Persephone in der antiken Kunst*, Würzburg.

Linforth, I. M. (1941) *The Arts of Orpheus*, Berkeley, Los Angeles.

Ling, R. (1991) *Roman Painting*, Cambridge.

Ling, R. and L. Ling (2005) *The Insula of the Menander at Pompeii* 2 The Decorations, Oxford.

Littleton, C. S. (1982) *The New Comparative Mythology*³, Berkeley.

Livingstone, A. (1986) *Mystical and Mythological Explanatory Works of Assyrian and Babylonian Scholars*, Oxford.

Livingstone, N. R. (1998) 'The Voice of Isocrates and the Dissemination of Cultural Power', in Y. L. Too and N. R. Livingstone (eds), *Pedagogy and Power: Rhetorics of Classical Learning*, Cambridge.

Livingstone, N. R. (2001) *A Commentary on Isocrates' Busiris*, Mnemosyne Suppl. 223, Leiden.

Lloyd, A. B. (1975–88) *Herodotus Book II*, 3 vols, Leiden.

Lloyd-Jones, H. (1999a) 'The Pride of Halicarnassus', *ZPE* 124, 1–14.

Lloyd-Jones, H. (1999b) 'The Pride of Halicarnassus (ZPE 124 [1999] 1–14): Corrigenda and Addenda', *ZPE* 127, 63–5.

Lloyd-Jones, H. and P. Parsons (eds) (1983) *Supplementum Hellenisticum*, Berlin.

Löschhorn, B. (2007) 'Weniger bekanntes aus Attika', in I. Hajnal (ed.), *Die altgrie-chischen Dialekte*, Innsbruck, 265–353.

Long, C. L. (1987) *The Twelve Gods of Greece and Rome*, Leiden.

López Férez, J. A. (ed.) (2003) *Mitos en la literatura griega helenística e imperial*, Estudios de Filología Griega 8, Madrid.

López-Ruiz, C. (2009) 'Mopsos and Cultural Exchange between Greeks and Locals in Cilicia', in Dill and Walde (eds) 2009: 382–96.

Loprieno, A. (ed.) (1996a) *Ancient Egyptian Literature: History and Forms*, Probleme der Ägyptologie 10, Leiden.

Loprieno, A. (1996b) 'The "King's Novel"', in Loprieno (ed.) 1996a: 277–95.

Loprieno, A. (2003) 'Views of the Past in Egypt During the First Millennium BC', in J. Tait (ed.), *Never Had the Like Occurred: Egypt's View of its Past*, London, 139–54.

Loraux, N. (1986) *The Invention of Athens: The Funeral Oration in the Classical City*, tr. A. Sheridan, Cambridge MA.

Loraux, N. (1987) *Tragic Ways of Killing a Woman*, tr. A. Forster, Cambridge MA.

Loraux, N. (1995) *The Experiences of Teiresias: The Feminine and the Greek Man*, tr. P. Wissing, Princeton.

Loraux, N. (1998) *Mothers in Mourning, with the Essay 'Of Amnesty and its Opposite'*, tr. C. Pache, Ithaca NY.

Loraux, N. (2002) *The Mourning Voice: an Essay on Greek Tragedy*, tr. E. Trapnell Rawlings, Ithaca NY.

Lord, A. B. (1960) *The Singer of Tales*[1], Cambridge MA [S. Mitchell, G. Nagy (eds), 2000[2]].

Lord, A. B. (1991) *Epic Singers and Oral Tradition*, Ithaca NY.

Lord, A. B. (1995) *The Singer Resumes the Tale*, ed. M. L. Lord, Ithaca NY.

Lorenz, K. (2008) *Bilder machen Räume: Mythenbilder in pompeianischen Häusern*, Berlin, New York.

Loscalzo, D. (2001) 'Pindaro tra μῦθος e λόγος', in M. Cannatà Fera and G. B. D'Alessio (eds) *I lirici greci: forme della comunicazione e storia del testo: atti dell' Incontro di Studi, Messina, 5–6 novembre 1999*, Pelorias 8, Messina, 165–81.

Lowe, N. J. (2000) 'Comic Plots and the Invention of Fiction', in D. Harvey and J. Wilkins (eds) *The Rivals of Aristophanes: Studies in Athenian Old Comedy*, London, 259–72.

Lübbert, E. (1881) *De Pindari carmine Olympico decimo*, Dissertation, Kiel.

Luraghi, N. (ed.) (2001) *The Historian's Craft in the Age of Herodotus*, Oxford.

Lyons, D. (1997) *Gender and Immortality: Heroines in Ancient Greek Myth and Cult*, Princeton.

McCarter, P. K. (2003) 'Phoenician Inscriptions', in Hallo and Younger (eds) 2003b: 181–4.

MacCoull, L. S. B. (1988) *Dioscorus of Aphrodito: His Work and His World*, Berkeley.

McGready, A. G. (1968) 'Egyptian Words in the Greek Vocabulary', *Glotta* 46, 247–54.

Makari, G. (2008) *Revolution in Mind: The Creation of Psychoanalysis*, New York.

Malaise, M. (1966) 'Sésostris, Pharaon de légende et d'histoire', *Chroniques d'Égypte* 41, 244–72.

Malinowski, B. (1935) *Coral Gardens and their Magic: A Study of the Methods of Tilling the Soil and of Agricultural Rites in the Trobriand Islands*, 2 vols, London.

Malinowski, B. (1948) *Magic, Science and Religion and Other Essays*, Boston MA, Glencoe IL.

Malkin, I. (1994) *Myth and Territory in the Spartan Mediterranean*, Cambridge.

Malkin, I. (1998) *The Returns of Odysseus: Colonization and Ethnicity*, Berkeley.

Mallory, J. P. and D. Q. Adams (1997) *Encyclopaedia of Indo-European Culture*, London.

Mallory, J. P. and D. Q. Adams (2006) *Oxford Introduction to Proto-Indo-European and the Proto-Indo-European World*, Oxford.

Manderscheid, H. (1981) *Die Skulpturenaustattung der kaiserzeitlichen Thermenanlagen*, Berlin.

Mann, R. (1994) 'Pindar's Homer and Pindar's Myths', *GRBS* 35, 313–37.

Mannhardt, W. (1875–7) *Wald- und Feldkult*, 2 vols, Berlin.

Manning, J. G. (2010) *The Last Pharaohs: Egypt under the Ptolemies 305–30 BC*, Princeton, Oxford.

March, J. (2000) 'Vases and Tragic Drama: Euripides' *Medea* and Sophocles' Lost *Tereus*', in N. K. Rutter and B. A. Sparkes (eds) *Word and Image in Ancient Greece*, Edinburgh, 119–39.

Marcone, A. (2009) 'L'*Origine des Fables* de Fontenelle', in *Sul mondo antico: scritti vari di storia della storiografia moderna*, Florence, 95–112 [= *RSI* 120 (2008) 1109–29].

Marinatos, N. (2000) 'The Cosmic Journey of Odysseus', *Numen* 48, 383–416.

Marinatos, N. (2003) 'Striding across Boundaries: Hermes and Aphrodite as Gods of Initiation', in Dodd and Faraone (eds) 2003: ch. 7.

Marinatos, N. (2009) 'The So-called Hell and Sinners in the Odyssey and Homeric Cosmology', *Numen* 56, 186–97.

Marinatos, N. (2010) *Minoan Kingship and the Solar Goddess: A Near Eastern Koine*. Urbana-Champaign.

Marinatos, N. and S. A. Anderson (2010) 'Elysium and Egypt', *Journal of Ancient Egyptian Interconnections*, 2.2, 13–24.

Marrou, H.-I. (1956) A *History of Education in Antiquity*, tr. G. Lamb, London, New York [*Histoire de l'éducation dans l'Antiquité*, Paris 1948[1], 1965[6]].

Marshall, P. K. (1993) *Hyginus, Fabulae*, Bibliotheca Teubneriana, Stuttgart, Leipzig [2002[2], Munich].

Martin, R. P. (1989) *The Language of Heroes: Speech and Performance in the Iliad*, Ithaca NY.

Marvin, M. (1983) 'Freestanding Sculpture from the Baths of Caracalla', *AJA* 87, 347–83.

Marvin, M. (1993) 'Copying in Roman Sculpture: The Replica Series', in D'Ambra (ed.) 1993: 161–88.

Masciadri, V. (2008) *Eine Insel im Meer der Geschichten: Untersuchungen zu Mythos aus Lemnos,* Potsdamer altertumswissenschaftliche Beiträge 18, Stuttgart.

Mass, A. (1912) 'Salvation', in *The Catholic Encyclopedia,* http://www.newadvent. org/cathen/13407a.htm (accessed 16 December 2008).

Masson, E. (1967) *Recherches sur les plus anciens emprunts sémitiques en grec,* Paris.

Masson, J. M. (ed.) (1985) *The Complete Letters of Sigmund Freud to Wilhelm Fliess, 1887–1904,* Cambridge MA.

Masson, O. (1950) 'A propos d'un rituel hittite pour la lustration d'une armée: le rite de purification par le passage entre les deux parties d'une victime', *RHR* 137, 5–25.

Mau, A. (1882) *Geschichte der decorativen Wandmalerei in Pompeji,* Berlin.

Meyer, C., *et al.* (2005) *Le Livre noir de la psychanalyse: vivre, penser et aller mieux sans Freud,* Paris.

Meeks, D. (2006) *Mythes et légendes du Delta: d'après le papyrus Brooklyn 47.218.84,* Cairo.

Meeks, D. and C. Favard-Meeks (1996) *Daily Life of the Egyptian Gods,* Ithaca NY.

Meltzer, E. S. (1974) 'Egyptian Parallels for an Incident in Hesiod's Theogony and an Episode in the Kumarbi Myth', *JNES* 33, 154–7.

Merkelbach, R. (1999) 'Die goldene Totenpässe: ägyptisch, orphisch, bakchisch', *ZPE* 128, 1–13.

Merkelbach, R. and M. L. West (1967) *Fragmenta Hesiodea,* Oxford.

Merkelbach, R., M. L. West, and F. Solmsen (eds) (1990) *Hesiodi Theogonia, Opera et Dies, Scutum, Fragmenta Selecta,*[3] Oxford Classical Texts, Oxford.

Mestuzini, A. (1988) 'Salmoneo', in *Enciclopedia Virgiliana* 4, 663–6.

Meulenaere, H. de (1953) 'La Légende de Phéros d'après Hérodote', *Chroniques d'Égypte* 28, 248–60.

Michaud, J.-M. (ed.) (2007) *Le Royaume d'Ougarit de la Crète à l'Euphrate: Nouveaux axes de recherche,* Sherbrooke Quebec, 219–42.

Miles, B. (2006) 'Irish Evidence for Shared Sources of Classical Mythology in Anglo-Saxon England and Medieval Ireland', in G. R. Wieland, C. Ruff, and R. G. Arthur (eds), *Insignis sophiae arcator: Essays in Honour of Michael W. Herren on his 65th Birthday.* Publications of the Journal of Medieval Latin 6, Turnhout, 124–48.

Miller, J.-A. (ed.) (1992) *The Seminar of Jacques Lacan,* 7 The Ethics of Psychoanalysis 1959–1960, tr. D. Porter, New York, London.

Miller, J. F. (1991) *Ovid's Elegiac Festivals,* Frankfurt.

Miller, P. A. (2007) *Postmodern Spiritual Practices,* Columbus OH.

Minchin, E. (2001) *Homer and the Resources of Memory: Some Applications of Cognitive Theory to the Iliad and the Odyssey,* Oxford.

Mockerl, H. (1981) *Poesie und Mythos,* Frankfurt.

Momigliano, A. (1957) 'Perizonius, Niebuhr and the Character of Early Roman Tradition', *JRS* 47, 104–14.

Montanari, F. (2002) 'Ancora sul Mythographus Homericus (e l'*Odissea*)', in Hurst and Létoublon (eds) 2002: 129–44.

Montgomery, J. A. (1938) '*Yām Sûf* ('the Red Sea') = *Ultimum Mare?*' *JAOS* 58, 131–2.

Morand, A.-F. (2001) *Études sur les hymnes orphiques*, Leiden, Boston.

Moreau, A. (ed.) (1992) *L'Initiation: les rites d'adolescence et les mystères*, 2 vols, Montpellier.

Morenz, S. (1950) 'Ägypten und die altorphische Kosmogonie', in S. Morenz (ed.), *Aus Antike und Orient: Festschrift Wilhelm Schubart zum 75. Geburtstage*, Leipzig, 64–111 [repr. in Morenz 1975: 452–95].

Morenz, S. (1975) *Religion und Geschichte des alten Ägypten: gesammelte Aufsätze*, ed. E. Blumenthal, S. Herrmann, Cologne.

Moretti, J -Ch. (2001) *Théâtre et société dans la Grèce antique: une archéologie des pratiques théâtrales*, Paris.

Morford, M. P. O. and R. J. Lenardon (2007) *Classical Mythology*⁸, Oxford.

Morgan, K. (1998) 'Designer History: Plato's Atlantis Story and Fourth-Century Ideology', *JHS* 118, 101–8.

Morgan, K. (2000) *Myth and Philosophy from the Presocratics to Plato*, Cambridge.

Morgan, T. (1998) *Literate Education in the Hellenistic and Roman Worlds*, Cambridge.

Mori, A. (2008) *The Politics of Apollonius Rhodius' Argonautica*, Cambridge, New York.

Morris, I. and B. Powell (eds) (1997) *A New Companion to Homer*, Leiden.

Most, G. W. (1997) 'Hesiod's Myth of the five (or three or four) races', *PCPS* 43, 104–27.

Most, G. W. (2006–7) *Hesiod*, 2 vols, Loeb Classical Library, Cambridge MA.

Moulton, C. (1981) *Aristophanic Poetry*, Göttingen.

Moyer, I. S. (2002) 'Herodotus and the Egyptian Mirage: The Genealogies of the Theban Priests', *JHS* 122, 70–90.

Mueller, D. (1972) 'An Early Egyptian Guide to the Hereafter', *JEA* 58, 99–126.

Muellner, L. (1996) *The Anger of Achilles: Mēnis in Greek Epic*, Ithaca NY, London.

Müller, C. O. (1825) *Prolegomena zu einer wissenschaftlichen Mythologie*, Göttingen [repr. with introduction by K. Kerényi, Darmstadt 1970; *Introduction to a Scientific System of Mythology*, tr. J. Leitch, London 1844, available on 16.7.10 at www.archive.org].

Müller, F. G. J. M. (1994) *Iconological Studies in Roman Art* 1 The So-Called Peleus and Thetis Sarcophagus in the Villa Albani, Amsterdam.

Müller, H. D. (1857–69) *Mythologie der griechischen Stämme*, 2 vols, Göttingen.

Mulryan, J. and S. Brown (eds) (2006) *Natale Conti's Mythologiae*, 2 vols, Tempe AZ.

Murnaghan, S. (1987) *Disguise and Recognition in the Odyssey*, Princeton.

Murray, O. (1970) 'Hecataeus of Abdera and Pharaonic Kingship', *JEA* 56, 141–71.

Murray, O. (ed.) (1990) *Sympotica*, Oxford.

Murray, P. (1999) 'What is a *Muthos* for Plato?' in Buxton (ed.) 1999: 251–62.

Muth, S. (1998) *Erleben von Raum – Leben im Raum: Zur Funktion mythologischer Mosaikbilder in der römisch-kaiserzeitlichen Wohnarchitektur*, Heidelberg.

Mylonas, G. E. (1961) *Eleusis and the Eleusinian Mysteries*, Princeton.

Nagy, G. (1979) *The Best of the Achaeans: Concepts of the Hero in Archaic Greek Poetry*, Baltimore.

Nagy, G. (1986) 'Pindar's *Olympian* 1 and the Aetiology of the Olympian Games', *TAPhA* 116, 71–88.

Nagy, G. (1990) *Pindar's Homer: The Lyric Possession of an Epic Past*, Baltimore.

Nagy, G. (1992) 'Mythologicum exemplum in Homer', in Hexter and Selden (eds) 1992: 311–31.

Nagy, G. (2007) 'Homer and Greek Myth', in Woodard (ed.) 2007: 52–82.

Neu, E. (1974) *Der Anitta-Text*, Studien zu den Boçazköy-Texten 18, Wiesbaden.

Neudecker, R. (1988) *Die Skulpturenausstattung römischer Villen in Italien*, Mainz.

Newby, Z. (2002) 'Reading Programs in Graeco-Roman Art: reflections on the Spada reliefs', in D. Fredrick (ed.) 2002 *The Roman Gaze: Vision, Power and the Body*, Baltimore, 110–48.

Newby, Z. (2003) 'Art and Identity in Asia Minor', in S. Scott and J. Webster (eds) 2003 *Roman Imperialism and Provincial Art*, Cambridge, 192–213.

Newby, Z. (2007) 'Landscape and Local Identity in the Mosaics of Antioch', in C. Adams and J. Roy (eds) 2007 *Travel, Geography and Culture in Ancient Greece, Egypt and the Near East*, Oxford, 185–205.

Newby, Z. (2011) 'In the Guise of Gods and Heroes: Portrait Heads on Roman Mythological Sarcophagi', in J. Elsner and J. Huskinson (eds) *Life, Death and Representation: New Work on Roman Sarcophagi*, Millenium Studies: Studies in the Culture and History of the First Millennium C.E. 29, Berlin, 189–227.

Newby, Z. and R. Leader-Newby (eds) (2007) *Art and Inscriptions in the Ancient World*, Cambridge.

Newlands, C. E. (1995) *Playing with Time*, Ithaca NY.

Nickel, R. (2003) 'The Wrath of Demeter: Story Pattern in the 'Hymn to Demeter', *QUCC* 73, 59–82

Niderst, A. (ed.) (1989) *B. de Fontenelle: oeuvres complètes* 3, Paris.

Niehr, H. (2006) 'The Royal Funeral in Ancient Syria: A Comparative View on the Tombs in the Palaces of Qatna, Kumidi and Ugarit', *Journal of Northwest Semitic Languages* 32, 1–24.

Niehr, H. (2007) 'The Topography of Death in the Royal Palace of Ugarit: Preliminary Thoughts on the Basis of Archaeological and Textual Data', in Michaud (ed.) 2007: 219–42.

Nilsson, M. P. (1927) *The Minoan-Mycenaean Religion and its Survival in Greek Religion*, Lund [1950²].

Nilsson, M. P. (1932) *The Mycenaean Origin of Greek Mythology*, Berkeley, Los Angeles.

Nilsson, M. P. (1944) *Geschichte der griechischen Religion* 1¹, Munich [1955², 1967³].

Nilsson, M. P. (1951) *Cults, Myths, Oracles, and Politics in Ancient Greece*, Lund.

Nisetich, F (ed. and tr.) (2001) *The Poems of Callimachus, with Introduction, Notes, and Glossary*, Oxford.

Nock, A. D. (1946) 'Sarcophagi and Symbolism', *AJA* 50, 140–70.

Noegel, S. B. (2004) 'Apollonius' *Argonautika* and Egyptian Solar Mythology', *CW* 97, 123–36.

Norris, R. A., Jr (2004) 'The Apologists', in F. Young, L. Ayres, and A. Louth (eds), *The Cambridge History of Early Christian Literature*, Cambridge, 36–44.

North, J. A. (1983) 'These he Cannot Take', *JRS* 73, 169–74.

Nutkowicz, H. (2006) *L'Homme face à la mort au royaume de Juda: rites, pratiques et représentations*, Paris.

Oakley, S. P. (1997) *A Commentary on Livy Books VI–X* 1 Introduction and Book VI, Oxford.

Oettinger, N. (2008) 'The Seer Mopsos as a Historical Figure', in B. J. Collins, M. R. Bachvarova, and I. Rutherford (eds) *Anatolian Interfaces: Hittites, Greeks, and Their Neighbors: Proceedings of an International Conference on Cross-cultural Interaction 2004*, Oxford, 63–6.

Ogden, D. (ed.) (2002) *The Hellenistic World: New Perspectives*, London.

Ogden, D. (ed.) (2007) *A Companion to Greek Religion*, Oxford, Malden.

Olson, S. Douglas (2007) *Broken Laughter: Select Fragments of Greek Comedy, Edited with Introduction, Commentary, and Translation*, Oxford.

Onians, R. B. (1951) *The Origins of European Thought about the Body, the Mind, the Soul, the World, Time, and Fate*, Cambridge.

Otto, E. (1969) 'Das "Goldene Zeitalter" in einem Ägyptischen Text', in P. Derchain (ed.), *Religions en Égypte Hellénistique et Romaine*, Paris, 93–108.

Padilla, M. (ed.) (1999) *Rites of Passage in Ancient Greece: Literature, Religion, Society*, Bucknell Review 43.1, Lewisburg, London, Toronto.

Page, D. L. (1959) *Sappho and Alcaeus: An Introduction to the Study of Ancient Lesbian Poetry*[2], Oxford.

Page, D. L. (ed.) (1962) *Poetae Melici Graeci*, Oxford.

Painter, K. S. (2001) *The Insula of the Menander at Pompeii* 4 The Silver Treasure, Oxford.

Pàmias, J. (ed.) (2004) *Eratòstenes de Cirene, Catasterismes: introducció, edició crítica, traducció i notes*, Barcelona.

Pàmias, J. and K. Geus (eds) (2007) *Sternsagen: Catasterismi, griechisch-deutsch: Text, übersetzung, kommentar*, Bibliotheca classicorum 2, Oberhaid.

Pantazis, V. D. (2009) 'Wilusa. Reconsidering the Evidence', *Klio* 91, 291–310.

Papathomopoulos, M. (ed.) (1968) *Antoninus Liberalis: les métamorphoses*, Collection Budé, Paris.

Papillon, T. L. (2007) 'Isocrates', in Worthington (ed.) 2007a: 58–74.

Paradiso, A. (2001) 'Jean-Pierre Vernant', *Belfagor* 56, 287–306

Pardee, D. (2000) *Les Textes rituels*, 2 vols, Ras-Shamra – Ougarit 12, Paris.

Pariente, A. (1992) 'Le Monument argien des "Sept contra Thèbes"', in M. Piérart (ed.), *Polydipsion Argos: Argos de la fin des palais mycéniens à la constitution de l'État classique*, Athens, Fribourg, Paris, 195–229.

Parke, H. W. (1933) 'The Bones of Pelops and the Siege of Troy', *Hermathena* 48, 153–62.

Parker, H. N. (2008) 'The Linguistic Case for the Aiolian Migration Reconsidered', *Hesperia* 77, 431–64.

Parker, R. (1995) 'Early Orphism', in A. Powell (ed.), *The Greek World*, London, 483–510.

Parker, R. (2005) *Polytheism and Society at Athens*, Oxford, New York.

Parker, S. B. (ed.) (1997) *Ugaritic Narrative Poetry*, Society of Biblical Literature Writings from the Ancient World 9, Atlanta.

Parry, M. (1971) *The Making of Homeric Verse: The Collected Papers of Milman Parry*, ed. A. Parry, Oxford.

Parry, M. (ed.) and A.B. Lord (tr.) (Vol 6, D. Bynum) (1953–80) *Serbocroatian Heroic Songs*, 6 vols, Cambridge, Harvard, Belgrade.

Partenie, C. (ed.) (2004) *Plato, Selected Myths*, Oxford.

Partenie, C. (ed.) (2009) *Plato's Myths*, Cambridge.

Pearson, L. (1939) *Early Ionian Historians*, Oxford.

Peek, W. (1955) *Griechische Vers-Inschriften*, Berlin.

Pellizer, E. (1991) *La peripezia dell'eletto: Racconti eroici della Grecia antica*, Palermo.

Pender, E. (2010) 'Chaos Corrected: Hesiod in Plato's Creation Myth', in Haubold and Boys-Stones (eds) 2010: 219–45.

Penglase, C. (1994) *Greek Myths and Mesopotamia: Parallels and Influence in the Homeric Hymns and Hesiod*, London.

Pépin, J. (1976) *Mythe et allégorie: les origines grecques et les contestations judéo-chrétiennes*[2], Paris [1958[1]].

Pépin, J. (1987) *La Tradition d'allégorie: de Philon d'Alexandrie à Dante*, Paris.

Peradotto, J. (1991) *Man in the Middle Voice: Name and Narration in the Odyssey*, Princeton.

Perceau, S. (2002) *La Parole vive: communiquer en catalogue dans l'épopée homérique*, Leuven.

Perlman, P. J. (1995) '*Invocatio* and *Imprecatio*: the Hymn to the Greatest Kouros from Palaikastro and the Oath in Ancient Crete', *JHS* 115, 161–7.

Perry, B. E. (2005) *Babrius and Phaedrus*, Loeb Classical Library, London.

Perry, E. (2005) *The Aesthetics of Emulation in the Visual Arts of Ancient Rome*, Cambridge.

Petropoulou, M.-Z. (2009) *Animal Sacrifice in Ancient Greek Religion, Judaism, and Christianity, 100) BC–AD 200*, Oxford.

Pfeiffer, R. (1968) *History of Classical Scholarship from the Beginning to the End of the Hellenistic Age*, Oxford.

Pickard-Cambridge, A. W. (1962) *Dithyramb, Tragedy and Comedy*[2], revised by T. B. L. Webster, Oxford.

Pickard-Cambridge, A. W. (1988) *The Dramatic Festivals of Athens*[2], revised by J. Gould and D. M. Lewis, reissued with a supplement and corrections, Oxford.

Pike, D. L. (1984) 'Pindar's Treatment of the Heracles Myths', *AClass* 27, 15–22.

Pirenne-Delforges, V. (2008) *Retour à la source: Pausanias et la religion grecque*, Kernos Supplement 20, Liège.

Plantikow, M., W. Helck, and W. Westendorf (1975–87) *Lexicon der Ägyptologie*, Wiesbaden.

Poduska, D. M. (1999) 'Classical Myth in Music: A Selective List', *Classical World* 92, 195–276.

Pollitt, J. J. (1978) 'The Impact of Greek Art on Rome', *TAPhA* 108, 155–74.

Pomeroy, S. B. (1975) *Goddesses, Whores, Wives and Slaves*, New York.

Popko, M. (1995) *Religions of Asia Minor*, Warsaw.

Popper, K. (2002) *Conjectures and Refutations*, London [1963[1]].

Powell, A. (ed.) (1989) *Classical Sparta: Techniques behind her Success*, London.

Preller, L. (1854) *Griechische Mythologie*[1], Berlin [1860–1[2]; 1872[3]].

Price, S. (1999) *Religions of the Ancient Greeks*, Cambridge.

Pritchard, J. B. (ed.) (1969) *Ancient Near Eastern Texts Relating to the Old Testament*[3], with supplement, Princeton.

Propp, V. I. (1968) *Morphology of the Folktale*[2], tr. L. Scott, Austin, London [Морфология сказки, Leningrad 1928].

Puhvel, J. (1987) *Comparative Mythology*, Baltimore.

Quack. J. F. (2005) *Einführung in die Altägyptische Literaturgeschichte III. Die demotische und gräko-ägyptische Literatur*. Einführungen und Quellentexte zur Ägyptologie 3, Münster.

Raaflaub, K. A. (1997) 'Homeric Society', in Morris and Powell (eds) 1997: 624–48.

Raaflaub, K. A. (2005) 'Epic and History', in J. M. Foley (ed.) 2005: 55–70.

Race, W. H. (1989) 'Elements of Style in Pindaric Break-Offs', *AJPh* 110, 189–209.

Radt, S. (1977) *Tragicorum graecorum fragmenta* 4 Sophocles, Göttingen.

Radt, S. (1985) *Tragicorum graecorum fragmenta* 3 Aeschylus, Göttingen.

Rahner, H. (1963) *Greek Myths and Christian Mystery*, tr. B. Battershaw, London [*Griechische Mythen in christlicher Deutung*, Zurich 1957].

Rank, O. (1919) *Psychoanalytische Beiträge zur Mythenforschung*, Leipzig.

Rank, O. (1929) *The Trauma of Birth*, London [repr. Dover Books, Mineola NY 1993; *Das Trauma der Geburt und seine Bedeutung für die Psychoanalyse*, Leipzig 1924].

Rank, O. (1932) *Modern Education: A Critique of Its Fundamental Ideas*, New York.

Rank, O. (1991) *The Incest Theme in Literature and Legend*, tr. G. C. Richter, Baltimore [*Das Inzest-Motiv in Dichtung und Sage*, Leipzig 1912].

Rank, O. (2004) *The Myth of the Birth of the Hero*, tr. G. C. Richter, E. J. Lieberman, Baltimore [*Der Mythus von der Geburt des Helden: Versuch einer psychologischen Mythendeutung*[2], Leipzig, Vienna 1922]

Rank, O. and H. Sachs (1916) 'The Investigation of Myths and Legends', in *The Significance of Psychoanalysis for the Mental Sciences*, New York, ch. 2.

Redfield, J. (1991) 'The Politics of Immortality', in P. Borgeaud (ed.), *Orphisme et Orphée: en l'honneur de Jean Rudhardt*, Geneva, 103–17.

Redford, D. B. (1992) *Egypt, Canaan and Israel in Ancient Times*, Princeton.

Reeder, E. D. (ed.) (1995) *Pandora: Women in Classical Greece*, Princeton.

Rees, A. and B. Rees (1961) *Celtic Heritage*, London.

Reid, J. D. (1993) *The Oxford Guide to Cassical Mythology in the Arts, 1300–1990s*, 2 vols, Oxford.

Reik, T. (1948) *Listening with the Third Ear: The Inner Experience of a Psychoanalyst*, New York.

Reik, T. (1957) *Myth and Guilt: The Crime and Punishment of Mankind*, New York.

Renan, E. (1992) 'Qu'est-ce qu'une nation', in *Qu'est-ce qu'une nation et autres essais politique*, ed. J. Roman, Paris, ch. 1) [Lecture given at the Sorbonne 11 March 1882].

Rhodes, P. (2003) 'Nothing to Do with Democracy: Athenian Drama and the Polis', *JHS* 123, 104–19.

Ricciardelli, G. (2000) *Inni orfici*, Milan.

Richards, R. J. (2008) *The Tragic Sense of Life: Ernst Haeckel and the Struggle over Evolutionary Thought*, Chicago, London.

Richardson, N. J. (1974) *The Homeric Hymn to Demeter*, Oxford.

Richir, M. (1998) *La Naissance des dieux*,[2] Paris [1995[1]].

Richter, D. S. (2001) 'Plutarch on Isis and Osiris: Text, Cult, and Cultural Appropriation', *TAPhA* 131, 191–216.

Ridgway, B. S. (1965) 'The East Pediment of the Siphnian Treasury: A Reinterpretation', *AJA* 69, 1–5.

Ridgway, B. S. (2000) 'The Sperlonga Sculptures: The Current State of Research' in de Grummond and Ridgway (eds) 2000: 78–91.

Riedweg, C. (1993) *Jüdisch-hellenistische Imitation eines orphischen Hieros Logos: Beobachtungen zu OF 245) und 247 (sog. Testament des Orpheus)*, Tübingen.

Riedweg, C. (1998) 'Initiation – Tod – Unterwelt: Beobachtungen zur Kommunikationssituation und narrativen Technik der orphisch-bakchischen Goldblättchen', in F. Graf (ed.), *Ansichten griechischer Rituale: Geburtstags-Symposium für Walter Burkert*, Stuttgart, Leipzig, 359–98.

Riedweg, C. (2002) 'Poésie orphique et rituel initiatique. Eléments d'un "Discours sacré" dans les lamelles d'or', *RHR* 219, 459–81.

Riedweg, C. (2003) *Pythagoras*, Munich.

Riedweg, C. (2010) 'Initiation – Death – Underworld: Narrative and Ritual in the Gold Leaves', in R. Edmonds (ed.) *The Orphic Gold Tablets and Greek Religion: Further Along the Path*, Cambridge, New York.

Robert, C. (1897–1919) *Die antiken Sarkophagreliefs* 3 Einzelmythen, 3 parts, Berlin.

Robert, C. (1920–6) *Die Griechische Heldensage*, 4 vols, Berlin.

Roberts, M. (1989) 'The Use of Myth in Latin Epithalamia from Statius to Venantius Fortunatus', *TAPhA* 119, 321–48.

Robertson, D. S. (1940) 'The Food of Achilles', *CR* 54, 177–80.

Robertson Smith, W. (1889) *Lectures on the Religion of the Semites*[1], Edinburgh.

Robinson, A. (2002) *The Life and Work of Jane Ellen Harrison*, Oxford.

Robinson, D. M. (1933) *Excavations at Olynthus* 5 Mosaics, Vases, and Lamps of Olynthus Found in 1928 and 1931, Johns Hopkins University Studies in Archaeology 18, Baltimore, London.

Rogge, S. (1995) *Die antiken Sarkophagreliefs*, 9.1 Die Attischen Sarkophage, 1 Achill und Hippolytos, Berlin.

Rohde, E. (1925) *Psyche: The Cult of Souls and Belief in Immortality among the Greeks*, London [tr. from: *Psyche. Seelencult und Unsterblichkeitsglaube der Griechen*[8], Tübingen, 1921].

Róheim, G. (1992) *Fire in the Dragon, and Other Psychoanalytic Essays on Folklore*, ed. A. Dundes, Princeton.

Róheim, G. (2005) *Animism, Magic, and the Divine King*, New York [repr. London 1930[1]].

Roller, L. (1999) *In Search of God the Mother: The Cult of Anatolian Cybele*, Berkeley.

Romm, J. S. (1992) *The Edges of the Earth in Ancient Thought: Geography, Exploration, and Fiction*, Princeton.

Rosa, F. (1997) 'À Frazer ce qui est de Frazer: vers une réinterprétation de l'intellectualisme du *Golden Bough*', *Archives européennes de sociologie* (*European Journal of Sociology*) 38, 301–10.

Rose, C. B. (2008) 'Separating Fact from Fiction in the Aiolian Migration', *Hesperia* 77, 399–430.

Rose, L. (1998) *The Freudian Calling: Early Viennese Psychoanalysis and the Pursuit of Cultural Science*, Detroit.

Rose, P. W. (1992) *Songs of the Gods, Children of Earth: Ideology and Literary Form in Ancient Greece*, Ithaca NY.

Rosen, R. M. (1997) 'Homer and Hesiod', in Morris and Powell (eds) 1997: 463–88.

Rowe, C. (1999) 'Myth, History and Dialectic in Plato's *Republic* and *Timaeus-Critias*', in Buxton (ed.) 1999: 263–78.

Rowe, C. (2010) 'On Grey-Haired Babies: Plato, Hesiod and Visions of the (Past and) Future', in Haubold and Boys-Stones (eds) 2010: 298–316.

Rudnytsky, P. (1987) *Freud and Oedipus*, New York, Oxford.

Russell, D. A. and D. Konstan (eds) (2005) *Heraclitus: Homeric Problems*, Atlanta.

Russo, J. (1997) 'The Formula', in Morris and Powell (eds) 1997: 238–60.

Rutherford, I. (2001a) *Pindar's Paeans: A Reading of the Fragments with a Survey of the Genre*, Oxford.

Rutherford, I. (2001b) 'The Song of the Sea (ŠA A.AB.BA SÌR)', in G. Wilhelm (ed.), *Akten des IV: Internationales Kongresses für Hethitologie: Würzburg, 4.–8. Oktober 1999*, Studien zu den Boğazköy-Texten 45, Wiesbaden, 598–609.

Rutherford, I. (2003) 'Pilgrimage in Greco-Roman Egypt: New Perspectives on Graffiti from the Memnonion at Abydos' in R. Matthews, C. Roemer (eds) *Ancient Perspectives on Egypt*, London, 171–90.

Şahin, S. (ed.) (1999) *Die Inschriften von Perge*, Bonn.

Saïd, S. (1993) *Approches de la mythologie grecque*[1], Paris [2008[2], revised].

Saïd, S. (1998) 'Tragedy and politics', in D. Boedeker, K. A. Raaflaub (eds) *Democracy, Empire, and the Arts in Fifth-Century Athens*, Cambridge MA, London, 275–95.

Sakellariou, M. B. (1958) *La Migration grecque en Ionie*, Athens.

Sandbach, F. H. (1967) *Plutarchi Moralia* 7, Leipzig.

Sandbach, F. H. (1977) *The Comic Theatre of Greece and Rome*, London.

Sasson, J. M. (ed.) (1995) *Civilizations of the Ancient Near East*, New York.

Sauneron, S. (1960) 'La Différenciation des langages d'après la tradition égyptienne', *BIAO* 60, 31–41.

Sauneron, S. (1961) 'La Légende des sept propos de Methyer du temple d'Esna', *Bulletin de la Société Française d'Égyptologie* 32, 43–51.

Sauneron, S. (1962) *Esna* 5 'Les Fêtes religieuses d'Esna aux derniers siècles du paganisme', Cairo.

Saussure, F. de (1915) *Cours de linguistique générale*, Geneva [*Course in General Linguistics*, tr. W. Baskin with Introduction by J. Culler, London 1974].

Sauzeau, P. (2010) 'Les Rites de passage et la théorie de la quatrième fonction', in Abry, Létoublon, and Hameau (eds) 2010: ch. 22.

Sauzeau, P. (n.d.) online 'Dumézil in Greece: from Frazer to Vernant. A Study in Comparative Mythology and the Anthropology of Ancient Greece', tr. S. Zerner, http://recherche.univ-montp3.fr/cercam/IMG/pdf/Dumezil_in_Greece.pdf (accessed 22 June 2010).

Sauzeau, P and A. Sauzeau (2004) 'La Quatrième fonction: pour un élargissement du modèle dumézilien', *Europe* 904–5 Mythe et mythologie dans l'Antiquité gréco-romaine, 231–53.

Schechner, R. (1999) 'Oedipus Clintonius', *The Drama Review* 43 (1999) 5–7.

Scheer, T.S. (1993) *Mythische Vorväter: Zur Bedeutung griechischer Heroenmythen im Selbstverständnis kleinasiatischer Städte*, Münchener Arbeiten zur Alten Geschichte 7, Munich.

Scheer, T.S. (2003) 'The Past in a Hellenistic Present: Myth and Local Tradition', in Erskine (ed.) 2003: 216–31.

Scheffer, C. (2001) 'Gods on Athenian Vases: Their Function in the Archaic and Classical Period', in C. Scheffer (ed.) *Ceramics in Context: Proceedings of the Internordic Colloquium on Ancient Pottery held at Stockholm 13–15 June 1997*, Stockholm, 127–37.

Schefold, K. (1952) *Pompejanische Malerei: Sinn und Ideengeschichte*, Basel.

Schefold, K. (1962) *Vergessenes Pompeji*, Bern, Munich.

Schefold, K. (1992) *Gods and Heroes in Late Archaic Greek Art*, Cambridge.

Schein, S. L. (1984) *The Mortal Hero: An Introduction to Homer's Iliad*, Berkeley.

Schein, S. L. (ed.) (1996) *Reading the Odyssey: Selected Essays*, Princeton.

Schein, S. L. (2002) 'Mythological Allusion in the *Odyssey*' in F. Montanari (ed.), *Omero tremila anni dopo*, Rome, 84–101.

Scheliha, R. von (1943) *Patroklos*, Basel.

Scherer, M. R. (1963) *The Legends of Troy in Art and Literature*, London.

Schiller, F. (1981) *On the Naive and Sentimental in Literature*, tr. H. Watanabe-O'Kelly, Manchester [*Über naïve und sentimentalische Dichtung*, 1795–6].

Schisling, F. (1793) *Die Hauptgötter der Fabel in Kupfern, mit ihrer Geschichte und ursprünglicher Bedeutung*, Vienna.

Schlerath, B. (1995–6) 'Georges Dumézil und die Rekonstruktion der indogermanischen Kultur', *Kratylos* 40 (1995) 1–48; 41 (1996) 1–67.

Schlesier, R. (1994) *Kulte, Mythen und Gelehrte: Anthropologie der Antike seit 1800*, Frankfurt.

Schmidt, B. B. (1994) *Israel's Beneficent Dead: Ancestor Cult and Necromancy in Ancient Israelite religion and Tradition*, Forschungen zum alten Testament 11, Tübingen.

Schmidt, M. (1969) *Der Basler Medeasarkophage*, Tübingen.

Schmitz, C. (2001) '"Denn auch Niobe …": die Bedeutung der Niobe-Erzählung in Achills Rede (Ω 599–620)', *Hermes* 129, 145–57.

Schofield, M. (2007) 'The Noble Lie', in Ferrari (ed.) 2007: 138–64.

Schofield, M. (2009) '*Fraternité, inégalité, la parole de Dieu*: Plato's Authoritarian Myth of Political Legitimation', in Partenie (ed.) 2009: 101–15.

Schott, S. (1973) 'Thoth als Verfasser heiliger Schriften', *ZÄS* 99, 20–25.

Scodel, R. (2002) *Listening to Homer*, Ann Arbor.

Scott, S. (2000) *Art and Society in Fourth-Century Britain: Villa Mosaics in Context*, Oxford.

Scully, S. (1990) *Homer and the Sacred City*, Ithaca NY.

Seaford, R. (1980) 'Black Zeus in Sophocles' *Inachus*', *CQ* 30, 23–9.

Seaford, R. (1994) *Reciprocity and Ritual: Homer and Tragedy in the Developing City-State*, Oxford.

Seaford, R. (2000) 'The Social Function of Attic Tragedy: A Response to Jasper Griffin', *CQ* 50, 30–44.

Searle, J. R. (1979) *Expression and Meaning: Studies in the Theory of Speech Acts*, Cambridge.

Segal, C. (1978) '"The Myth Was Saved": Reflections on Homer and the Mythology of Plato's *Republic*', *Hermes* 106, 315–36.

Segal, C. (1981) *Tragedy and Civilization: An Interpretation of Sophocles*, Cambridge MA.

Segal, C. (1986a) *Interpreting Greek Tragedy: Myth, Poetry, Text*, Ithaca NY, London.

Segal, C. (1986b) *Pindar's Mythmaking: The Fourth Pythian Ode*, Princeton.

Segal, C. (1986c) 'Naming, Truth, and Creation in the Poetics of Pindar', *Diacritics* 16, 65–83.

Segal, C. (1993) *Euripides and the Poetics of Sorrow*, Durham NC, London.

Segal, C. (1994) *Singers, Heroes and Gods in the Odyssey*, Ithaca NY.

Segal, C. (1995) *Sophocles' Tragic World: Divinity, Nature, Society*, Cambridge MA.

Segal, E. (ed.) (1983) *Oxford Readings in Greek Tragedy*, Oxford.

Selden, D. (1998) 'Alibis', *ClAnt* 17, 289–411.

Sellers, S. (2001) *Myth and Fairy Tale in Contemporary Women's Fiction*, Basingstoke.

Sergent, B. (1999–2004) *Celtes et Grecs*, 2 vols, Paris.

Sergent, B. (2008) *Athéna et la grande déesse indienne*, Paris.

Servadei, C. (2005) *La figura di Theseus nella cramica Attica: iconografia e iconologia del mito nell' Atene Arcaica e Classica*, Bologna.

Severyns, A. (1928) Le Cycle épique dans l'école d'Aristarque, Liège.

Sfyroeras, P. (1993) 'Pindar's *Olympian* 7 and the Panathenaic Festival', *AJPh* 114, 1–26.

Shanzer, D. (1986) *A Philosophical and Literary Commentary on Martianus Capella's De nuptiis Philologiae et Mercurii Book 1*, Berkeley.

Shapiro, H. A. (1989) *Art and Cult under the Tyrants in Athens*, Mainz.

Shapiro, H. A. (1994) *Myth into Art: Poet and Painter in Classical Greece*, London, New York.

Shapiro, H. A. (ed.) (2007) *The Cambridge Companion to Archaic Greece*, Cambridge 2007.

Sharpe, L. (1991) *Schiller: Drama, Thought and Politics*, Cambridge.

Shedid, A. G. (1994) *Die Felsgräber von Beni Hassan in Mittelägypten*, Mainz.

Shipley, G. (2000) *The Greek World after Alexander. 323–30 BC*, London.

Sichtermann, H. (1992) *Die antiken Sarkophagreliefs*, 12 Die mythologischen Sarkophage, 2 Apollon bis Grazien, Berlin.

Silk, M. S. (ed.) (1996) *Tragedy and the Tragic: Greek Theatre and Beyond*, Oxford.

Simon, E. (1994) 'Salmoneus', *LIMC* 7.1, 653–5.

Simon, R. (1961) *Nicolas Fréret, académicien*, Geneva.

Simpson, W. K. (ed.) (2003) *The Literature of Ancient Egypt*, New Haven.

Sinn, F. (1987) *Stadrömische Marmorurnen*, Mainz.

Slater, P. E. (1968) *The Glory of Hera: Greek Mythology and the Greek Family*, Boston.

Slater, W. J. (1979) 'Pindar's Myths: Two Pragmatic Explanations', in Bowersock, Burkert, and Putnam (eds) 1979: 63–70.

Slatkin, L. (1991) *The Power of Thetis: Allusion and Interpretation in the Iliad*, Berkeley.

Small, J. P. (2003) *The Parallel Worlds of Art and Text in Classical Antiquity*, Cambridge.

Smith, R. S. and S. M. Trzaskoma (eds) (2007) *Apollodorus'* Library *and Hyginus'* Fabulae. *Two Handbooks of Greek Mythology*, Indianapolis.

Snaith, N. H. (1965) 'The Sea of Reeds: the Red Sea', *VT* 15, 395–8.

Snodgrass, A. (1998) *Homer and the Artists: Text and Picture in Early Greek Art*, Cambridge.

Snowden, F. (1970) *Blacks in Antiquity: Ethiopians in the Greco-Roman Experience*, Cambridge MA.

Snowden, F. (1981) 'Aithiopes', *LIMC* 1.1, 413–19.

Snowden, F. (1996) 'Bernal's "Blacks" and the Afrocentrists', in Lefkowitz and Maclean Rogers (eds) 1996: 112–28.

Soden, W. von (1984) 'Reflektierte und konstruierte Mythen in Babylonien und Assyrien', in *Studia Orientalia memoriae Jussi Aro dedicata*, Studia Orientalia 55, Helsinki.

Sourvinou-Inwood, C. (1978) 'Persephone and Aphrodite at Locri. A Model for Personality Definitions in Greek Religion', *JHS* 98, 203–21 [repr. in C. Sourvinou-Inwood *'Reading' Greek Culture: Texts and Images, Rituals and Myths*, Oxford 1991, 147–88].

Sourvinou-Inwood, C. (1989) 'Assumptions and the Creation of Meaning: Reading Sophocles' *Antigone*', *JHS* 109, 134–48.

Sourvinou-Inwood, C. (1997) 'Medea at a Shifting Distance: Images and Euripidean Tragedy', in Clauss and Johnston (eds) 1997: 254–96.

Sourvinou-Inwood, C. (2005) *Hylas, the Nymphs, Dionysos and Others: Myth, Ritual, Ethnicity: Martin P. Nilsson Lecture on Greek Religion, delivered 1997 at the Swedish Institute at Athens*, Stockholm.

Sowa, C. A. (1984) *Traditional Themes and the Homeric Hymn*, Chicago.

Spencer, D. J. (2002) *The Roman Alexander: Reading a Cultural Myth*, Exeter.

Squire, M. (2007) 'The Motto in the Grotto: Inscribing Illustration and Illustrating Inscription at Sperlonga', in Newby and Leader-Newby (eds) 2007: 102–27.

Stalley, R. F. (2009) 'Myth and Eschatology in the *Laws*', in Partenie (ed.) 2009: 187–205.

Stanford, W. B. (ed.) (1965) *The Odyssey of Homer: Edited with General and Grammatical Introduction, Commentary and Indexes*[2], 2 vols, London.

Stanford, W. B. (1968) *The Ulysses Theme*[2], Ann Arbor, Oxford.

Starobinski, J. (1989) *Le Remède dans le mal: critique et légitimation de l'artifice à l âge des lumières*, Paris.

Stavrakopoulou, F. (2010) *Land of our Fathers*, London.

Stavru, A. (2005) 'Otto, Walter F.', in L. Jones (ed.) *Encyclopedia of Religion* 10[2], Detroit, 6932–5.

Stehle, E. (1997) *Performance and Gender in Ancient Greece: Nondramatic Poetry in Its Setting*, Princeton.

Steiner, D. (2002) 'Indecorous Dining, Indecorous Speech', *Arethusa* 35, 297–314.

Steiner, G. (2007) 'The Case of Wiluša and Ahhiyawa', *Bibliotheca Orientalis* 64, 590–612.

Stephens, S. A. (2003) *Seeing Double: Intercultural Poetics in Ptolemaic Alexandria*, Berkeley.

Stephens, S. A. and J. J. Winkler (eds) (1995) *Ancient Greek Novels: the Fragments: Introduction, Text*, Princeton.

Stern, J. (1996) *Palaephatus* Περὶ Ἀπίστων: *On Unbelievable Tales*, Wauconda.

Sternberg-El Hotabi, H. (1983) 'Die Geburt des göttlichen Kindes als mythisches Motiv in den Texten von Esna', *Göttinger Miszellen* 61, 31–48.

Sternberg-El Hotabi, H. (1985) *Mythische Motive und Mythenbildung in den Ägyptischen Tempeln und Papyri der griechisch-römischen Zeit*, Wiesbaden.

Stevens, B. (2006–7) 'Aeolism: Latin as a Dialect of Greek', *CJ* 102, 115–44.

Stewart, A. (1977) 'To Entertain an Emperor: Sperlonga, Laocoon and Tiberius at the Dinner-Table', *JRS* 67, 76–90.

Stewart, A. (2000) 'The Phantom of a Rhodian School of Sculpture', in de Grummond and Ridgway (eds) 2000: 92–110.

Stewart, J. A. (1905) *The Myths of Plato*, London 1905 [1960[2]].

Stichling, G. T. (1863) *Ludwig Preller: Eine Gedächtnisrede in der Freimaurerloge Amalia zu Weimar gehalten*, Weimar.

Stocking, G. W. (1995) *After Tylor*, Madison

Stocking, G. W. (2001) *Delimiting Anthropology*, Madison.

Strasburger, G. (1998) 'Die Fahrt des Odysseus zu den Toten im Vergleich mit älteren Jenseitsfahrten', *A&A* 44, 1–29.

Strocka, V. M. (1984) 'Sepulkral Allegorien auf dokimeischen Sarkophage', in Andreae (ed.) 1984a: 197–241.

Strong, E. and N. Jolliffe (1924) 'The Stuccoes of the Underground Basilica near the Porta Maggiore', *JHS* 44, 65–111.

Sutcliffe, S. (2003) *Children of the New Age: A History of Spiritual Practices*, London, New York.

Taplin, O. (1986) 'Homer's Use of Achilles' Earlier Campaigns in the *Iliad*', in J. Boardman, J. Vaphopoulou-Richardson (eds), *Chios*, Oxford, 15–19.

Taplin, O. (2007) *Pots and Plays: Interactions between Tragedy and Greek Vase-painting in the Fourth Century BC*, Los Angeles.

Taylor, C. C. W. (1991) *Plato: Protagoras*[2], Oxford.

Thesaurus Linguae Graecae, www.tlg.uci.edu (accessed 4 August 2010).

Thissen, H. J. (1999) 'Homerischer Einfluss im Inaros-Petubastis-Zyklus?' *Studien zur Altägytischen Kultur* 27, 369–87.

Thomas, R. (1989) *Oral Tradition & Written Record in Classical Athens*, Cambridge.

Thompson, M. L. (1960) 'Programmatic Painting in Pompeii: The Meaningful Combination of Mythological Pictures in Roman Decoration'. PhD thesis, NYU.

Thompson, M. L. (1960–1) 'The Monumental and Literary Evidence for Programmatic Painting in Antiquity', *Marsyas* 9, 36–77.

Toynbee, J. M. C. (1971) *Death and Burial in the Roman World*, London.

Traunecker, C. (2001) *The Gods of Egypt*, Ithaca NY.

Travis, R. (1999) *Allegory and the Tragic Chorus in Sophocles' Oedipus at Colonus*, Lanham MD.

Tromp, N. J. (1969) *Primitive Conceptions of Death and the Netherworld in the Old Testament*, Biblica et Orientalia 21, Rome.

Tsevat, M. (1974) 'Sun Mountains at Ugarit', *Journal of Northwest Semitic Languages* 3, 71–5.

Tsukimoto, A. (1985) *Untersuchungen zur Totenpflege (kispum) im Alten Mesopotamien*, Alter Orient und Altes Testament 216, Neukirchen-Vluyn.

Turcan, R. (1978) 'Les Sarcophages romains et le problème du symbolisme funéraire', *ANRW* 16.2, 1700–35.

Turcan, R. (1996) *The Cults of the Roman Empire*, tr. A. Nevill [*Les Cultes orientaux dans le monde Romain*, Paris 1992].

Turner, F. M. (1981) *The Greek Heritage in Victorian Britain*, New Haven, London.

Turner, F. M. (1997) 'The Homeric Question', in Morris and Powell (eds) 1997: 123–45.

Trzaskoma, S. M., R. Scott Smith, and S. Brunet (2004) *Anthology of Classical Myth: Primary Sources in Translation*, Indianapolis, Cambridge.

Tybjerg, T. (1993) 'Wilhelm Mannhardt – A Pioneer in the Study of Rituals', in T. Ahlbäck (ed.) *The problem of Ritual*, Stockholm, 27–37.

Ulf, C. (ed.) (2004) *Der neue Streit um Troia*[2], Munich [2003[1]].

Unte, W. and H. Rohlfing (1997) *Quellen für eine Biographie Karl Otfried Müllers*, Hildesheim.

Usener, H. (1899) *Die Sinthflutsagen*, Bonn.

Usener, H. (1907) *Vorträge und Aufsätze*, Leipzig, Berlin.

Usener, H. (1913) *Kleine Schriften* 4, Leipzig.

Vandier, J. (1962) *Le Papyrus Jumilhac*, Paris.

Van Dijk, J. (1995) 'Myth and Mythmaking in Ancient Egypt', in J. Sasson (ed.) *Civilizations of the Ancient Near East* 3, New York, 1697–1710.

van Gennep, A. (1960) *The Rites of Passage*, tr. M. B. Vizedom and G. L. Caffee, London [*Les Rites de passage*, Paris 1909].

van Gessel, B. H. L. (1998–2001) *Onomasticon of the Hittite Pantheon*, 3 vols, Handbuch der Orientalistik 1.33.1–3, vols 1–2: Leiden, New York, Cologne, 1998; vol. 3: Leiden, Boston, Cologne, 2001.

Van Noorden, H. (2010) '"Hesiod's Races and Your Own": Socrates' "Hesiodic" Project', in Haubold and Boys-Stones (eds) 2010: 176–99.

Van Nortwick, T. (2008) *Imagining Men: Ideals of Masculinity in Ancient Greek Culture*, Westport CT.

van Rossum-Steenbeek, M. (1997) *Greek Readers' Digests? Studies on a Selection of Subliterary Papyri*, Leiden.

Vansina, J. (1965) *Oral Tradition: A Study in Historical Methodology*, tr. H. M. Wright, London [*De la tradition orale: essai de méthode historique*, Tervuren 1961].

Vansina, J. (1985) *Oral Tradition as History*, Madison.

van't Wout, P. E. (2006) 'Amphiaraos as Alkman: Compositional Strategy and Mythological Innovation in Pindar's *Pythian* 8.39–60', *Mnemosyne* 59, 1–18.

Vasunia, P. (2001) *The Gift of the Nile: Hellenizing Egypt from Aeschylus to Alexander*, Berkeley, Los Angeles.

Ventris, M. and J. Chadwick (1956) *Documents in Mycenaean Greek*, Cambridge.

Verbrugghe, G. P. and J. Wickersham (1996) *Berossos and Manetho, Introduced and Translated: Native Traditions in Ancient Mesopotamia and Egypt*, Ann Arbor.

Vermaseren, M. J. (1977) *Cybele and Attis: the Myth and the Cult*, tr. A. M. H. Lemmers, London.

Vernant, J.-P. (1965) *Mythe et pensée chez les Grecs*, 2 vols, Paris.

Vernant, J.-P. (1974) *Mythe et société en Grèce ancienne*, Paris.

Vernant, J.-P. (1983) *Myth and Thought among the Greeks*, tr. H. Piat, London [tr. of Vernant 1965].

Vernant, J.-P. (1988) 'Oedipus without the Complex', in Vernant and Vidal-Naquet 1988, ch. 4.

Vernant, J.-P. (1991) *Mortals and Immortals: Collected Essays*, ed. F.I. Zeitlin, Princeton.

Vernant, J.-P. and P. Vidal-Naquet (1988) *Myth and Tragedy in Ancient Greece*, tr. J. Lloyd, Cambridge MA.

Vernant, J.-P. and P. Vidal-Naquet (1992) *La Grèce ancienne* 3 'Rites de passage et transgressions', Paris.

Verra, V. (1966) *Mito, revelazione e filosofia in J. G. Herder e nel suo tempo*, Milan.

Versnel, H. S. (1990) *Inconsistencies in Greek and Roman Religion* 1 'Ter Unus. Isis, Dionysos, Hermes: three studies in henotheism', Leiden.

Versnel, H. S. (1993) *Inconsistencies in Greek and Roman Religion* 2 'Transition and reversal in myth and ritual', Leiden.

Veyne, P. (1988) *Did the Greeks Believe in their Myths?: An Essay on the Constitutive Imagination*, tr. P. Wissing, Chicago [*Les Grecs ont-ils cru à leurs mythes?* Paris 1983].

Vian, F. (1987) *Les Argonautiques orphiques*, Paris.

Vidal-Naquet, P. (1981a) *Le Chasseur noir: formes de pensée et formes de société dans le monde grec*, Paris.

Vidal-Naquet, P. (1981b) 'Athens and Atlantis: Structure and Meaning of a Platonic Myth', tr. R.L. Gordon, in Gordon (ed.) 1981, 201–14 [repr. in Vidal-Naquet 1986, 263–84; tr. with additions and corrections of 'Athènes et l'Atlantide', *REG* 78 (1964), 420–44].

Vidal-Naquet, P. (1986a) *The Black Hunter: Forms of Thought and Forms of Society in the Greek World*, tr. A. Szegedy-Maszak, Baltimore [tr. of Vidal-Naquet 1981a].

Vidal-Naquet, P. (1986b) 'The Black Hunter and the Origin of the Athenian *Ephebeia*', in Vidal-Naquet 1986a: ch. 5 (and other collections) [first version: (French) *Annales ESC* 23 (1968) 947–64; (English) *PCPS* 194 (1968) 49–64].

Vidal-Naquet, P. (1992) 'Le *Philoctète* de Sophocle et l'éphébie', in Vernant and Vidal-Naquet 1992: ch. 6 (and other collections) ['Sophocles' *Philoctetes* and the Ephebeia', in Vernant and Vidal-Naquet 1988: ch. 7; first version: *Annales ESC* 26 (1971) 623–38].

Vidal-Naquet, P. (2007) *The Atlantis Story: A Short History of Plato's Myth*, tr. J. Lloyd, Exeter.

Vielle, C. (1996) *Le Mytho-cycle héroïque dans l'aire indo-européenne*, Louvain-la-neuve.

Visser, E. (1997) *Homers Katalog der Schiffe*, Stuttgart, Leipzig.

Vöhler, M. and B. Seidensticker (eds) (2005) *Mythenkorrekturen: zu einer paradoxalen Form der Mythenrezeption*, Berlin, New York.

Von Hendy, A. (2002) *The Modern Construction of Myth*, Bloomington.

Walcot, P. (1962) 'Hesiod and the Instructions of 'Onchsheshonqy', *JNES* 21, 215–19.

Walcot, P. (1966) *Hesiod and the Near East*, Cardiff.

Walcot, P. (1976) *Greek Drama in its Theatrical and Social Context*, Cardiff.

Wallis Budge, E. A. (1904) *The Gods of the Egyptians, or Studies in Egyptian Mythology* 1, London.

Walton, J. M. (2006) *Found in Translation: Greek Drama in English*, Cambridge.

Warrior, V. (2006) *Roman Religion*, Cambridge.

Wasserman, N. (2001) Review of West 1997, *SCI* 20, 261–7.

Waterfield, R. (ed. and tr.) (2000) *The First Philosophers: The Presocratics and Sophists*, Oxford World's Classics, Oxford.

Watkins, C. (1995) *How to Kill a Dragon: Aspects of Indo-European Poetics*, Oxford, New York.

Watson, W. G. E. (2008) 'A New Proposal for Ugaritic *bt hptt*', *Studi Epigrafici e Linguistici* 24, 39–43.

Webb, R. (2006) 'Rhetorical and Theatrical Fictions in Chorikios of Gaza', in Johnson 2006: 107–24.

Weiler, I. (1974) *Der Agon im Mythos: zur Einstellung der Griechen zum Wettkampf*, Impulse der Forschung 16, Darmstadt.

Weis, A. (2000) 'Odysseus at Sperlonga: Hellenistic Hero or Roman Heroic Foil', in de Grummond and Ridgway (eds) 2000: 111–65.

Weitzmann, K. (1947) *Illustrations in Roll and Codex: A Study of the Origin and Method of Text Illustration*, Princeton.

Weitzmann, K. (1952) *Greek Mythology in Byzantine Art*, Princeton.

Weitzmann, K. (1960) 'The Survival of Mythological Representations in Early Christian and Byzantine Art and their Impact on Christian Iconography', *DOP* 14, 44–69.

Wessels, A. (2003) *Ursprungszauber: zur Rezeption von Hermann Useners Lehre von der religiösen Begriffsbildung*, Berlin, New York.

West, E. B. (2009) 'Married Hero/Single Princess: Homer's Nausicaa and the Indic Citriṅgadā', *JIES* 37, 214–24.

West, M. L. (1965) 'The Dictaean Hymn to the Kouros', *JHS* 85, 149–59.

West, M. L. (1966) *Hesiod: Theogony*, edited with prolegomena and commentary, Oxford.

West, M. L. (1971) *Early Greek Philosophy and the Orient*, Oxford.

West, M. L. (1978) *Hesiod: Works and Days*, edited with prolegomena and commentary, Oxford.

West, M. L. (1983a) *The Orphic Poems*, Oxford.

West, M. L. (1983b) 'The Hesiodic Catalogue: Xouthids and Aiolids', *ZPE* 53, 27–30.

West, M. L. (1985) *The Hesiodic Catalogue of Women: Its Nature, Structure, and Origins*, Oxford.

West, M. L. (1988) 'The Rise of the Greek Epic', *JHS* 108, 151–72.

West, M. L. (1995) 'The Date of the Iliad', *MH* 52, 203–19.

West, M. L. (1997) *The East Face of Helicon: West Asiatic Elements in Greek Poetry and Myth*, Oxford.

West, M. L. (2002) '"Eumelos": A Corinthian Epic Cycle?' *JHS* 122, 109–33.

West, M. L. (2004) 'Geschichte und Vorgeschichte: Die Sage von Troia', *ST* 14, xiii–xx.

West, M. L. (2007) *Indo-European Poetry and Myth*, Oxford.

West, S. (1969) 'The Greek Version of the Legend of Tefnut', *JEA* 55, 161–83.

West, S. (1984) 'Io and the Dark Stranger (Sophocles, *Inachus* F 269a)', *CQ* 34, 292–302.

Westerink, L. G. (1977) *The Greek Commentaries on Plato's Phaedo*, 2 Damascius, Amsterdam.

Westervelt, H. (2009) 'Herakles at Olympia: The Sculptural Program of the Temple of Zeus', in P. Schultz and R. von den Hoff (eds), *Structure, Image, Ornament: Architectural Sculpture in the Greek World*, Oxford, Oakville CT, 133–52.

Whitbread, L. G. (1971) *Fulgentius the Mythographer*, Columbus.

Whitmarsh, T. (2001) *Greek Literature and the Roman Empire: The Politics of Imitation*, Oxford.

Whittaker, G. (2004), 'Word Formation in Euphratic', in J. Clackson and B. A. Olsen (eds), *Indo-European Word Formation*, Copenhagen, 381–423.

Widmer, G. (2002) 'Pharaoh Maâ-Rê, Pharaoh Amenemhet and Sesostris: Three Figures from Egypt's Past as Seen in Sources of the Graeco-Roman Period', in K. Ryholt (ed.) *Acts of the Seventh International Conference of Demotic Studies, Copenhagen 23–27 August 1999*, Copenhagen, 377–90.

Wilamowitz, U., von (1916) *Die Ilias und Homer*, Berlin.

Wilkinson, R. H. (1991) 'New Kingdom Astronomical Paintings and Methods of Finding and Extending Direction', *JARCE* 28, 149–54.

Willcock, M. M. (1964) 'Mythological Paradeigma in the *Iliad*', *CQ* 14, 141–54 [repr. in Cairns (ed.) 2001: 435–55].

Willcock, M. M. (1977) '*Ad Hoc* Invention in the *Iliad*', *HSPh* 81, 41–53.

Willcock, M. M. (1997) 'Neoanalysis', in Morris and Powell (eds) 1997: 174–89.

Willers, D. (1992) 'Dionysos und Christus – ein archäologisches Zeugnis zur 'Konfessionsangehörigkeit' des Nonnos', *MH* 49, 141–51.

Williams, D. J. R. (2005) 'Furtwängler and the Pioneer Painters and Potters' in V. M. Strocka (ed.), *Meisterwerke: Internationales Symposion anlässlich des 150 Geburtstages von Adolf Furtwängler*, Munich.

Williamson, G. S. (2004) *The Longing for Myth in Germany: Religion and Aesthetic Culture from Romanticism to Nietzsche*, Chicago, London.

Wilson, N. G. (1975) *Saint Basil on Greek Literature*, London.

Winkes, R. (ed.) (1985) *The Age of Augustus*, Louvain-la-Neuve.

Winkler, J. and F. I. Zeitlin (eds) (1990) *Nothing to Do with Dionysos? Athenian Drama and Its Social Context*, Princeton.

Wise, J. (1998) *Dionysus Writes: the Invention of Theatre in Ancient Greece*, Ithaca.

Wiseman, T. P. (1995) *Remus: A Roman Myth*, Cambridge.

Wiseman, T. P. (1998) *Roman Drama and Roman History*, Exeter.

Wiseman, T. P. (2001) 'Reading Carandini', *Journal of Roman Studies* 91, 182–93.

Wiseman, T. P. (2004) *The Myths of Rome*, Exeter.

Witzel, M. (2001) 'Comparison and Reconstruction: Language and Mythology', *Mother Tongue* 6, 45–62 [extract at http://www.fas.harvard.edu/~witzel/Comp_Myth.pdf].

Wolff, E. (2009) *Fulgence, Virgile dévoilé*, Villeneuve d'Ascq.

Wood, S. (2004) review of Zanker and Ewald 2004, in *BMCR* 2004.11.22. (http://ccat.sas.upenn.edu/bmcr/2004/2004-11-22.html, accessed 8 November 10).

Woodard, R. (2006) *Indo-European Sacred Space*, Urbana.

Woodard, R. (2007) 'Hesiod and Greek Myth', in Woodard (ed.) 2007: 83–165.

Woodard, R. (ed.) (2007) *The Cambridge Companion to Greek Mythology*, Cambridge.

Woodford, S. (1982) 'Ajax and Achilles Playing a Game on an Olpe in Oxford', *JHS* 102, 171–85.

Woodford, S. (1986) *An Introduction to Greek Art*, London.

Woodford, S. (1993) *The Trojan War in Ancient Art*, London, Ithaca NY.

Woodford, S. (2003) *Images of Myths in Classical Antiquity*, Cambridge.

Worthington, I. (2004) *Alexander the Great: Man and God*, London.

Worthington, I. (ed.) (2007a) *A Companion to Greek Rhetoric*, Malden MA, Oxford, Chichester.

Worthington, I. (ed.) (2007b) *Brill's New Jacoby*. www.brillonline.nl. (accessed 4 August 2010).

Wrede, H. (1981) *Consecratio in Formam Deorum: Vergöttlichte Privatpersonen in der römischen Kaiserzeit*, Mainz.

Wyatt, N. (1996) *Myths of Power*, Ugaritische-Biblische Literatur 13, Münster.

Wyatt, N. (2001) *Space and Time in the Religious Life of the Ancient Near East* (*BS* 85), Sheffield.

Wyatt, N. (2002) *Religious Texts from Ugarit: The Words of Ilimilku and His Colleagues*, Biblical Seminar 53² [1998¹], Sheffield.

Wyatt, N. (2005a) *'There's Such Divinity Doth Hedge a King': Selected Essays of Nicolas Wyatt on Royal Ideology in Ugaritic and Old Testament Literature*, Society for Old Testament Studies Monographs, London.

Wyatt, N. (2005b) *The Mythic Mind: Essays on Cosmology in Ugaritic and Old Testament Literature*, London.

Wyatt, N. (2007a) *Word of Tree and Whisper of Stone, and Other Papers on Ugaritian Thought*, Gorgias Ugaritic Series 1, Piscataway NJ.

Wyatt, N. (2007b) 'A la recherche des Rephaïm perdus', in Michaud (ed.) 2007: 579–613 [repr. in *The Archaeology of Myth: Papers on Old Testament Tradition*, London 2010].

Wyatt, N. (2009) 'The Concept and Purpose of Hell: Its Nature and Development in West Semitic Thought', *Numen* 56, 161–84.

Wyatt, N. (2010) 'Royal Religion in Ancient Israel', in F. Stavrakopoulou and J. Barton (eds), *Religious Diversity in Ancient Israel and Judah*, London, 61–81.

Wyatt, N. (forthcoming) 'A Garden for the Living – Cultic and Ideological Aspects of Paradise', in A. Scafi (ed.), *The Cosmography of Paradise*, Warburg Colloquia, London.

Yates, V. (2004) 'The Titanic Origin of Humans. The Melian Nymphs and Zagreus', *GRBS* 44, 183–98.

Yavetz, Z. (1976) 'Why Rome?' *AJPh* 97, 276–96.

Young, D. C. (1964) 'Pindaric Criticism', *Minnesota Review* 4, 584–641.

Young, D. C. (1971) *Pindar, Isthmian 7: Myth and Exempla*, Leiden.

Young, D. C. (1993) '"Something Like the Gods": A Pindaric Theme and the Myth of *Nemean* 10', *GRBS* 34, 123–32.

Young, M. W. (2004) *Malinowski: Odyssey of an Anthropologist, 1884–1920*, New Haven, London.

Yoyotte, J. (1980–1) 'Héra d'Héliopolis et le sacrifice humain', *Annuaire de l'École Pratique des Hautes Études, Section Sciences Religieuses* 89, 31–102.

Yunis, H. (1988) *A New Creed: Fundamental Religious Beliefs in the Athenian Polis and Euripidean Drama*, Hypomnemata 91, Göttingen.

Yunis, H. (ed.) (2003) *Written Texts and the Rise of Literate Culture in Ancient Greece*, Cambridge.

Zaccaria, V. (ed.) (1998) *G. Boccaccio: Genealogie deorum gentilium*, 2 vols [*Tutti le opere* vols 7–8, parts 1 and 2], Milan.

Zajko, V. (2007) 'Women and Greek Myth', in Woodard (ed.) 2007: 387–406.

Zajko, V. and M. Leonard (eds) (2006) *Laughing with Medusa: Classical Myth and Feminist Thought*, Oxford.

Zanker, G. (1987) *Realism in Alexandrian Poetry: A Literature and its Audience*, London.

Zanker, G. (1989) 'Current Trends in the Study of Hellenic Myth in Early Third-Century. Alexandrian Poetry: The Case of Theocritus', *A&A* 35, 83–103.

Zanker, P. (1979) 'Zur Function und Bedeutung griechischer Skulptur in der Römerzeit', in H. Flashar (ed.) 1979 *Le Classicisme à Rome aux 1ers siècles avant et après J.-C.*, Fondation Hardt Entretiens sur l'Antiquité Classique 25, Geneva, 283–314.

Zanker, P. (1988) *The Power of Images in the Age of Augustus*, Ann Arbor.

Zanker, P. and B. C. Ewald (2004) *Mit Mythen leben: die Bilderwelt der römischen Sarkophage*, Munich.

Zarker, J. W. (1965) 'King Eetion and Thebe as Symbols in the *Iliad*', *CJ* 61, 110–14.

Zeitlin, F. I. (1965) 'The Motif of Corrupted Sacrifice in Aeschylus' *Oresteia*', *TAPhA* 96, 462–508.

Zeitlin, F. I. (1990) 'Thebes: Theater of Self and Society in Athenian Drama', in Winkler and Zeitlin (eds) 1990: 130–67.

Zeitlin, F. I. (1992) 'The Politics of Eros in the Danaid Trilogy of Aeschylus', in R. Hexter and D. Selden (eds) *Innovations of Antiquity*, London, 203–52 [repr. in *Playing the Other: Gender and Society in Classical Greek Literature*, Chicago 1996, 23–71].

Zeitlin, F. I. (1995) 'The Economics of Hesiod's Pandora', in Reeder (ed.) 1995: 49–56.

Zeitlin, F. I. (1996) 'Signifying Difference: the Case of Hesiod's Pandora', in *Playing the Other: Gender and Society in Classical Greek Literature*, Chicago, 53–86.

Zoja, L. (1998) 'Analysis and Tragedy', in A. Casement (ed.) *Post-Jungians Today: Key Papers in Contemporary Analytical Psychology*, London, ch. 2.

Index of Texts Discussed

This index is divided into three parts: Greek and Roman; Oriental and Egyptian; and Biblical. Discussion of particular (numbered) passages is indicated by a colon separating the textual reference (in **bold text**) from the page numbers on which the text is discussed.

Greek and Roman

A Companion to Greek Mythology, First Edition. Edited by Ken Dowden and Niall Livingstone.
© 2014 John Wiley & Sons Ltd. Published 2014 by John Wiley & Sons Ltd.

Oriental and Egyptian

Biblical Texts

Index of Names

In this index, please be aware that generally we have adopted Greek orthography for Greek words (see pp. xix–xx and look, for example, for Klytaimestra not Clytaemnestra) and have sought to be as punctilious as amateurs can be with Sanskrit transliteration and that of near eastern languages (for instance, Gilgameš not Gilgamesh).

A Companion to Greek Mythology, First Edition. Edited by Ken Dowden and Niall Livingstone.
© 2014 John Wiley & Sons Ltd. Published 2014 by John Wiley & Sons Ltd.

Index of Names

Index of Subjects

Please note that in this index cross-references may point to one of the other indexes.

actors 143
advice 53
aegis 421
aetiology 111–12, 119–20, 188, 233,
    244, 252–5, 257–8, 296, 363, 366–7,
    379, 465, 492, 528, 535
Afro-centrism 459
afterlife 311–13; *see also* Underworld
agnus castus 513
agoge: Spartan 495
agon, tragic 152
allegory 16–17, 85, 87, 90, 132–3,
    201, 206, 288–291, 293, 296, 302,
    319–21, 324, 326–7, 330–1, 333,
    335, 380, 530–3
allusion 27
ambrosia 39
ancestors: invoked as example 199
Ancient History: disciplinary origins
    of 249
animals 52; gods disguised as 117
anthropology 3, 18, 257, 343, 488,
    517–18, 520–1, 536
anthropomorphism 131, 228, 323
anthropopoietics 518, 521
ants: men made from 69, 71
apologists 321–4

apples: golden 63, 69
archaeology 243–4, 246, 249, 259,
    261–2, 434, 488
archaic age 50, 53
archetypes 18–20, 480–2, 484
art: European 17; Greek 4, 12, 266;
    Roman 15, 265–79
art galleries: ancient 275, 278
astronomy 260, 291, 297
atthidographers 466
Augustan ideology 254–5, 258, 293
autochthony 59, 71, 153, 181,
    183–4, 466
autopsy (seeing things for oneself) 417
avatar 350

barbarians (*barbaroi*) 12, 110, 113,
    134, 145, 152, 163, 181, 200, 220
baths 268–70
bats 453
bears 489–90, 496, 498; *see also*
    Arkteia
belief in myth 4–5
Beyond *see* Underworld
Bible: allegorical interpretation of 292
binary oppositions 508, 513–15
biography of gods 37

A Companion to Greek Mythology, First Edition. Edited by Ken Dowden and Niall Livingstone.
© 2014 John Wiley & Sons Ltd. Published 2014 by John Wiley & Sons Ltd.

myth: ages of (*cont'd*)
conservatism/ traditionalism in   55,
115, 117, 122, 143, 149, 248;
criticism/correction of   57, 111–16,
122, 182, 244; definition   3,
109–10, 125, 181, 183, 189, 245,
257, 507, 539; distancing effect
of   152; feminist critique of   445–6,
450, 454–5; feminist reappropriation
of   444; historicized or
rationalized   58–60, 63, 65, 185–6,
201, 206, 244, 246, 248, 250–4,
260–1, 464; instruction, moral or
ethical   110, 112–13, 122, 181–3,
187–9, 191, 244, 288, 296, 415;
interpretation   49, 56–7, 59, 66,
122, 201, 246, 260–1, 287–8, 292,
413–23, 443–58, 471–85: defies
interpretation   247; invention/
originality in   54–6, 111–13,
115–18, 141, 143, 149–50, 153–4,
179–93, 206, 248, 415, 447, 497;
makes connections across time and
space   111–12, 120, 152, 257–8;
makes past events 'present'   111,
258; national, or nation-forming   50,
70, 119, 121, 249, 254; personal, or
familial, in Rome   254, 256, 261;
persuasiveness of   188; praise   114,
118, 122, 255–6 (*see also* praise);
psychological functions of   473, 482;
reinterpretation of   285;
ritual   111–12, 118–19, 252, 285,
454 (*see also* initiation); Roman   71,
243–63: *Aeneid* as articulation
of   255, 257; synthesis of   50;
systematic   3–4; systems of   50, 52,
55; theological   191; Trojan War as
end of   51–2, 425; true or
false?   47, 112–16, 122, 181, 187,
190–1, 198, 244; unorthodox
versions of   149, 416; used as
propaganda   62, 71, 116–17, 200,
245, 258, 293; *see also under*
aetiology, allegory, foundation myths,

history, ideology, initiation, local
nature of myth, ludic, metaphor,
nature, polysemy, praise
Myth of the Races *see* Hesiod, *Works &
Days*
mythemes   508
mythocritique   18–19
mythographers: mythography   47–50,
55, 57–8, 60–2, 64–6, 70–2
mythography   27, 232; organizing
principles of   50–1, 58, 61, 66, 70;
precondition for tragedy   58
mythologems   482, 496
mythological knowledge in Jungian
thought   480
mythos: meanings of   112–13

naïvety   247–50
narratology of myth   508–11, 515, 518
nature: myth and   38, 534
Near Eastern borrowing   29, 48–9, 54,
351–2, 377, 380–1, 386–7, 540
necromancy   398–400
nektar   39
night attack   348, 352
nomos (law/ custom)   121–2, 514
nostos (homeward journey of
heroes)   48, 70, 145, 291, 425;
metaphorical return to spiritual
realm   289
novels: ancient: allegorical interpretation
of   290; Roman   295
nymphs   49, 251, 296–7, 454–5,
457, 498

oaths   287, 432
ocean   52; *see also* Okeanos
olive trees   69, 112, 121
opera   17
optimates: in Roman politics   245
oracles   68, 71, 111, 120, 196, 200,
206, 252, 299, 419–20, 431, 465,
477, 489
oral history   195
oral poetry   53, 428